D0596261

Footprint Handbook
Sri Lanka
DAVID STOTT & VICTORIA McCULLOCH

This is
Sri Lanka

Sri Lanka has shaken off the trauma of its decades-long ethnic conflict, pulled up the shutters on its tourism industry and is ready, once again, to stake its claim to being South Asia's most idyllic and easy-going travel destination.

Many travellers are lured here by images of palm-fringed beaches, leopards stalking through lush jungle, or sari-clad tea pickers weaving their way through contours of deep green tea bushes. Yet the source of Sri Lanka's irresistible charm lies deeper, in the way it interweaves modernity with agelessness, human creativity with wild beauty.

While cranes tower over Colombo's new Dubai-lite Port City and Google helium balloons beam down internet from the stratosphere, this remains an island deeply enmeshed in its traditions. Commuters murmur prayers as they flash past roadside temples, technology tycoons leave air-conditioned offices to make barefoot climbs to holy peaks, white-robed pilgrims gather in their thousands each full moon, and, in the far north, Tamil painters swarm over temples left abandoned for years, restoring colour and glory to the Hindu pantheon on towering *gopurams*.

That Sri Lanka's diverse ethnic groups have clung fiercely to their traditions is not surprising in the wake of centuries of invasion by foreign powers. The island's early settlers migrated from India and established a Buddhist tradition that survives here as a potent 2500-year-old symbol of national identity. In establishing this identity, monks and kings of old hewed their temples, monasteries and palaces from the living rock. The forest-wreathed hill of Mihintale, the painted cave temples of Dambulla, the rocktop fortress of Sigiriya and the serene carvings of Polonnaruwa are all evidence that the most sublime Sri Lankan artistry is not imposed upon the landscape but interwoven with it.

What's more, this intoxicating mix of cultures, landscapes and histories is so easy to access, even in only a brief visit. When Marco Polo described Sri Lanka as "the finest island of its size in the world", he sold it short.

David Stott

Victoria McCulloch

Best of
Sri Lanka

❶ Galle Face Green, Colombo

Whether it's sundowners at the Galle Face Hotel or mingling with the masses out on the Green, sunset from this iconic promenade is an essential Colombo experience. Make time to see the atmospheric Gangaramaya Temple and the beautifully restored Dutch Hospital – chock full of shops and restaurants. Page 50.

❷ Wilpattu National Park

While jeeps all but climb over each other for a leopard sighting at Sri Lanka's more famous parks, Wilpattu's gently stunning landscape of tangled jungle and forest-rimmed ponds provides a more solitary experience of wild Sri Lanka. Leopard and elephant sightings are harder won here – and all the more satisfying for it. Page 92.

❸ Sinharaja Reserve

Sri Lanka's only surviving rainforest, Sinharaja's canopy harbours an incredible variety of birds, butterflies and reptiles. With dense vegetation, waterfalls and eco-lodges, it's a great place to find peace. Page 109.

❹ Galle Fort

The rambling lanes of Galle Fort are an enchanting place to wander. Check into a lovingly restored printer's workshop or grain store, explore the old buildings revamped as restaurants and boutiques, and walk the ramparts of the fort at sunset. Page 139.

❺ South coast

Sri Lanka's magnificent southern coastline is home to five of the world's seven species of sea turtle. Take time out from sunbathing or surfing to spot them at Kosgoda or Rekawa Beach. Pages 126 and 168.

❻ Kandy

Explore the rich Buddhist history of Kandy at the incredible Temple of the Tooth, but also make a circuit of the smaller temples clustered to the west of the city – Gadaladeniya, Lankatilaka Mahaviharaya and Embekke Devale. Pages 200 and 218.

❼ Ella

With rolling tea plantations to explore, the Ravana falls to visit and the beautiful trek to Little Adam's Peak to complete, you can work up a thirst wandering around Ella. Luckily, you'll never be far from a decent cup of tea. Many guesthouses have stunning views, especially at sunrise. Page 245.

❽ Anuradhapura and Mihintale

The towering brick *dagobas* of Sri Lanka's greatest ancient capital loom large over a landscape studded with treasures still to be excavated. To the east, Mihintale's giant white *dagoba* shines out from a jungle-swathed hill, marking the birthplace of Sri Lankan Buddhism. Pages 270 and 280.

⑨ Sigiriya

Fifth-century playboy-king Kasyapa had an eye for the dramatic. From the ramparts of his citadel atop Sigiriya's startling rock island you can look out over a landscape of utter beauty: pyramid mountains rise from a verdant forest plain, dotted with hundreds of shimmering ponds. Page 286.

⑩ Trincomalee and its beaches

From the dazzling clifftop temple of Konesvaram, your eye drifts north over some of Sri Lanka's finest beaches: Uppuveli, which retains the languid tourist charm that Bali lost years ago, and Nilaveli beyond, with its miles of empty sand. Pages 315 and 321.

⑪ Arugam Bay

This is one of the best surf spots in Asia. Beginners and old hands alike flock to Arugam Bay from April to October to sample the waves. Don't miss a beautiful morning trip to Kudimbigala Hermitage. Pages 334 and 343.

⑫ Jaffna and its islands

As exiles return to Jaffna after decades of war, Tamil Sri Lanka's cultural capital and its trippy landscape of god-bedecked temple towers, pancake-flat islands and arrow-straight causeways miraging into the salt haze is opening up to a slow trickle of visitors. Page 350.

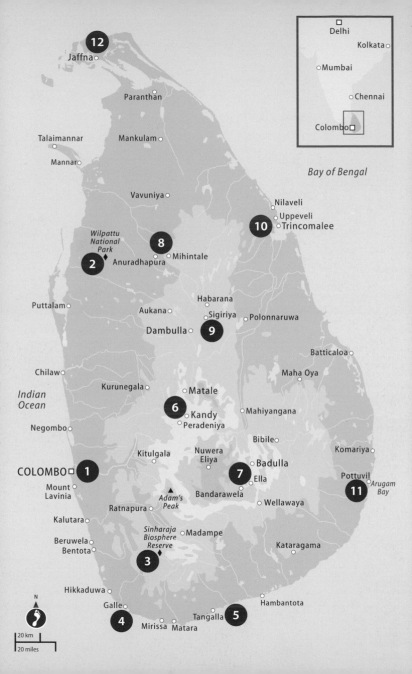

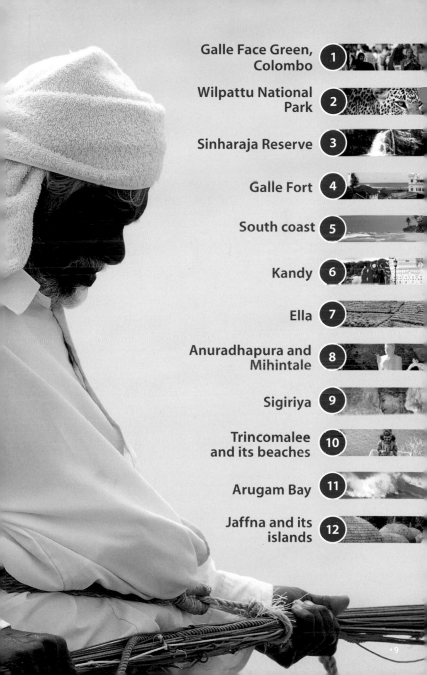

Route planner

Many visitors plan their entire trip around the beach. If this is your main reason for coming to Sri Lanka, prepare to be spoilt for choice. However, most of Sri Lanka's greatest treasures lie away from the coast in the Cultural Triangle, where you'll find extraordinary testaments to the power of human creativity. Kandy makes a good jumping off-point for exploring the Buddhist treasures to the north and the tea country to the south and east, so many travellers head directly here to plan their next move. Even if you are staying at a beach hotel on the southwest or south coast it is easy to get up to Kandy and make that a base for further exploration. Choosing a route obviously depends on your interests, the time of year and to a certain extent your mode of travel. Hiring a car allows you the greatest flexibility.

One week

a whistle-stop tour of the Cultural Triangle or the southern highlights

If you only have a week, you'd better get your skates on. A typical itinerary would head straight to **Kandy**, either on the scenic railway or by car. Kandy, in lush verdant hills studded with spice farms and temples, forms the southern tip of the Cultural Triangle, an area that is replete with cultural, religious and architectural treasures; the other two points of the triangle are the monumental ancient capital of **Anuradhapura** and the medieval city of **Polonnaruwa**. On day two, after a whirlwind tour of Kandy's Temple of the Tooth and surrounds, travel north via **Dambulla** to spend the night at **Sigiriya**. Climb the rock to the surreal royal citadel decorated with world-famous frescoes first thing the next morning; if you've energy to spare, head east to see the exquisite stone carvings at **Polonnaruwa** in the afternoon. Start at dawn on day four for a morning safari at **Minneriya National Park**, renowned for its large elephant gatherings, then head northwest to **Mihintale**, birthplace of Sri Lankan Buddhism, whose vast white *dagoba* beams out across the plains

Right: Puja festival, Kandy
Opposite page: Navam Maha
Perahera, Colombo

from a dramatic hilltop perch. Spend day five exploring the ancient ruins at Anuradhapura. From here you can return to Colombo via a day on one of the west coast beaches around **Negombo**. This trip could also be done in reverse, starting in **Negombo** and then heading northeast.

An alternative one-week trip by car might head south along the coast to **Galle**. Spend day two exploring the streets and ramparts of the Fort, then head for one of the south's beautiful beaches. The coast between **Unawatuna** and Weligama is easily accessible and has plenty of reasonably priced accommodation. Picture-perfect, laidback **Mirissa** is also increasingly popular. On day four, continue to Tissamaharama for a safari at **Yala National Park**, home to the highest density of leopards in the country, perhaps with a side trip to the temple town of **Kataragama**. From there it is a picturesque drive into the highlands, where you could explore the fading colonial grandeur of **Nuwara Eliya**, before returning to Colombo via Kandy.

Two weeks
the 'classic' tour

Two weeks gives you time for a 'classic' tour of Sri Lanka. Spend a day in **Colombo**, before heading northeast to spend four or five days exploring the **Cultural Triangle**. As well as Anuradhapura, Mihintale, Sigiriya and Polonnaruwa (see above), visit the towering Buddha statue at **Aukana** and the cave paintings at **Dambulla**. For a break from the sightseeing, go elephant spotting in **Minneriya** or **Kaudulla national parks**, or take a side trip to the east coast for the beaches north of **Trincomalee.** Then loop south to **Kandy** via **Dambulla** or **Mahiyangana**. Spend a day and a night

Top: Unawatuna
Above: Gangaramaya temple, Colombo
Opposite page: Minneriya National Park

in Kandy before touring the **Central Highlands**. The mountains provide a refreshing break, with spectacular waterfalls and some great walking trails through tea gardens around **Nuwara Eliya**, and to the pilgrimage destination of Adam's Peak. To the east, the 'gaps' at **Ella** and **Haputale** provide spectacular views. From the highlands you could head south to a trio of national parks: Yala is the most popular (see above), but there is also **Uda Walawe**, famous for its herds of elephants, and Bundala, which has coastal lagoons that are rich in birdlife. Finish by flopping on a south coast beach for a couple of days. Alternatively, from Haputale return to Colombo via **Sinharaja Reserve**, the country's last significant stretch of pristine rainforest, and make a stop in the gem capital of **Ratnapura**.

Three weeks and more
in-depth exploration and hidden treats

Three weeks or longer gives you a chance to explore the above sites in greater depth and to get off the beaten track. You could easily spend a week visiting the beaches and villages of the south coast, or a few days trekking in the hill country. Venture beyond the central area to explore **Northwestern Province**, where you'll find less popular ancient sites, such as Yapahuwa, and uncrowded national parks, such as **Wilpattu**, for good sightings and beautiful scenery. The beaches and wild country of the east are increasingly a magnet for travellers: visit the beguiling resorts of **Uppuvell** and **Nilaveli** or hip and happening **Arugam Bay** to the south. Sri Lanka's far north is now more accessible than at any point since the early 1980s, with rail and road links fully open and almost all military checkpoints removed. The flat, dry landscapes of **Mannar Island** and the **Jaffna peninsula** can't compete with the scenic delights further south, but they do offer their own surreal and esoteric charm, and if you venture into this region you can expect a real (and potentially confronting) insight into Sri Lankan Tamil culture, religion and resilience. And, when you've had enough of exploring, make the most of Sri Lanka's reputation as a centre for **Ayurvedic treatments** by checking into one of the country's specialist resorts.

Best
sacred
summits

Adam's Peak

At the top of Sri Lanka's holiest mountain, Sri Pada ('holy foot'), is a giant footprint believed variously to belong to Lord Buddha, Shiva and Adam, and therefore sacred to Buddhists, Hindus and Muslims alike. Join the pilgrims setting out in the early hours to reach the peak in time to see the rising sun cast a perfect conical shadow across the mist below. Page 237.

Dambulla Rock

Brave the persistent lotus sellers and mendicant monkeys who line the path up Dambulla Rock to the five cave temples that are among Sri Lanka's most staggering artistic achievements. The crowning glory is the 50-m-long Rajamaha Viharaya, encircled by dozens of gilded Buddhas, with intricate and dazzling murals covering every inch of the walls and ceiling. Page 259.

Left: Adam's Peak
Above: Dambulla

Opposite page
Top: Mihintale
Middle: Swami Rock
Bottom left: Pidurangala
Bottom right: Ritigala

Mihintale

Mihintale's great white *dagoba* commands the eye for miles around. The climb to the top leads up ceremonial stairways, past jungle-draped *dagobas* and tumble-down monastic cells to the cave where Mahinda received King Devanampiya Tissa and Sri Lankan Buddhism was born. From the granite lookout of Aradhana Gala there's a staggering view over mountains and plains to the city of Anuradhapura. Page 280.

Pidurangala

Hunched in the shadow of Sigiriya, this remarkable granite outcrop shelters the remains of a monastery, established after King Kasyapa took over the monks' caves at the Lion Rock. From the Buddhist temple at the base, paths climb past richly decorated cave temples, stone-walled cells and a brick reclining Buddha. The view from the summit, over Sigiriya and endless mountain ranges, is extraordinary. Page 290.

Ritigala

The jungle-clad mountain range of Ritigala forms the highest point between Sri Lanka's highlands and the mountains of southern India. Its ruined forest monastery was home to a fiercely ascetic order of monks. Ritigala's cool wet microclimate is rich in medicinal plants, supposedly deposited here (as the *Ramayana* tells it) by the monkey god Hanuman. Page 293.

Swami Rock

In a staggering clifftop setting off Trincomalee, the temple of Koneswaram boasts one of Sri Lanka's most enviable locations, overlooking glittering blue sea. Inside, coconuts crack and pilgrims file around colourful bas-relief sculptures of the 'demon king', Ravana. Page 319.

Temple of the Tooth, Kandy

When to go

Climate

The island lies just north of the equator, so temperatures remain almost constant throughout the year. However, rainfall varies widely. Sri Lanka is affected by two main

> **Tip...**
> In general, the best time to visit Sri Lanka is between the two main rainy seasons.

monsoon seasons. The **southwest monsoon** (June-October) brings heavy rain to the south, so the best time to visit this area is from late October to early March, after the monsoon has finished. The **northeast monsoon** occurs from October to January; despite the rain, this can be a good time to visit, as the countryside becomes lush with tropical vegetation. The north and east are dry but hot from June to October. The Central Highlands are much cooler throughout the year, but are very wet during both the southwest monsoon and the northeast monsoon. See also Background, page 397.

Festivals

Sri Lanka has four official religions, all of which observe special days, so the country has a remarkable number of festivals and probably more public holidays (29) than anywhere else in the world. In mid-April, the **Sinhala** and **Tamil New Year** celebrations are colourful and feature traditional games. In May and June the **Wesak** and **Poson** *poya* (full moon) days are marked with religious pageants. **Esala Perahera** (around the July/August full moon) is the most striking of all, a 10-day celebration featuring drummers, dancers, decorated elephants, torch-bearers and whip-crackers. Kandy has the most impressive parade, though major festivals are also held in Colombo, Kataragama and at other important temples. All full moon (*poya*) days are public holidays (see box, page 19), as are Saturdays and Sundays; there are also several secular holidays. Most religious festivals (Buddhist, Muslim and Hindu) are determined by the lunar calendar and therefore change from year to year. Check www.srilanka.travel/srilankan_public_holidays for exact dates.

January

Duruthu Poya Sri Lankan Buddhists commemorate the Buddha's first visit to the island. There is a large festival and parade at the **Kelaniya Temple** near Colombo.

Tamil Thai Pongal On 14th, observed by Hindus, celebrating the first grains of the rice harvest.

Navam Poya In late-January/early February, this is celebrated at Colombo's grandest *perahera* at Gangaramaya Temple, with caparisoned elephants, dancing, drummers and processions.

February

National (Independence) Day Celebrated on the 4th, involves processions, dances, parades.

Maha Sivarathri Marks the night when Shiva danced his celestial dance of destruction (*Tandava*), celebrated in late February/early March with feasting and fairs at Shiva temples, preceded by a night of devotional readings and hymn singing.

March/April

Medin Poya.

Easter Good Friday with Passion plays in Negombo and other coastal areas, in particular on Duwa Island.

Bak Poya.

Sinhala and **Tamil New Year Day** The 13th and 14th are marked with celebrations (originally harvest thanksgiving) and the closure of many shops/restaurants. Many Colombo residents decamp to the highlands, see box, page 233.

May

May Day 1 May.

Wesak Poya One of the most important *poya* in the calendar, celebrating the key events in the Buddha's life: his birth, Enlightenment and death. Clay oil-lamps are lit across the island and there are also folk theatre performances. Wayside stalls offer food and drink free to passers-by. There are special celebrations at Kandy, Anuradhapura and Kelaniya (Colombo).

National Heroes' Day This is held on the 22nd of the month but is not a public holiday.

June

Poson Poya Marks Mahinda's arrival in Sri Lanka as the first Buddhist missionary; Mihintale and Anuradhapura hold special celebrations.

Bank Holiday 30 June.

July/August

Esala Poya The most important Sri Lankan festival takes place for 10 days in Kandy, with grand processions of elephants, dancers, etc, honouring the Sacred Tooth of the Buddha. Also celebrated at Dewi Nuwara (Dondra) and Bellanwila Raja Maha Vihare in southern Colombo, among other places.

September

Binara Poya A *perahera* is held in Badulla.

October/November

Wap Poya.

Deepavali Festival of Lights, celebrated by Hindus with fireworks, commemorating Rama's return after his

FESTIVALS
Full moon

Buddhists consider the full moon as sacred and auspicious. In Sri Lanka the monthly occurrence is known as *poya* and is marked by a public holiday. Buddhists visit temples with offerings of flowers to worship and remind themselves of the precepts. Certain temples hold special celebrations in connection with a particular full moon, eg Esala at Kandy. Accommodation may be difficult to find and public transport is crowded during these festivals. No alcohol is sold (you can however order your drinks at your hotel the day before) and all places of entertainment are closed.

14-year exile in the forest, when citizens lit his way with earthen oil lamps.
Il Poya.

December
Unduwap Poya Marks the arrival of Emperor Asoka's daughter, Sanghamitta, with a sapling of the Bodhi Tree from India. Special celebrations at Anuradhapura, Bentota and Colombo.
Christmas Day Bank holiday on 25th.
New Year's Eve Special bank holiday on 31st.

Muslim holy days

These are fixed according to the lunar calendar. According to the Gregorian calendar, they tend to fall 11 days earlier each year, dependent on the sighting of the new moon.

Ramadan Start of the month of fasting when all Muslims (except young children, the very elderly, the sick, pregnant women and travellers) must abstain from food and drink from sunrise to sunset.
Id ul Fitr The three-day festival that marks the end of Ramadan.
Id-ul-Zuha/Bakr-Id Muslims commemorate Ibrahim's sacrifice of his son according to God's commandment. This is the main time of pilgrimage to Mecca (the Hajj). It is marked by the sacrifice of a goat, feasting and alms giving.
Muharram When the killing of the Prophet's grandson Hussain is commemorated by Shi'a Muslims. Decorated *tazias* (replicas of the martyr's tomb) are carried in procession by devout wailing followers who beat their chests to express their grief. Shi'as fast for the 10 days.

What to do

Ayurveda See box, page 30.

With the renewed interest in alternative forms of therapy in the West, Ayurvedic healing in Sri Lanka has become a serious subject for research and scientists have begun exploring the island's wealth of wild plants. There has been a regeneration of special Ayurvedic herbal cure centres, which are increasingly attracting foreign visitors. Day treatment centres can be found around Kandy and in many tourist towns, and most large hotels now have massage centres offering Ayurvedic treatments of variable quality. Ayurveda's ultimate experience is *Panchkarma*, a full factory reset for the body; a number of specialist Ayurvedic resorts around the country offer it, especially along the west coast. **Ayurveda Pavilions** in Negombo (see page 83) and **Siddhalepa Ayurveda Health Resort** in Kalutara (see page 119) are two of the most highly regarded resorts, while more basic accommodation is offered with treatment at the Ayurvedic hospitals in Mount Lavinia: **Mount Clinic of Oriental Medicine** (41 Hotel Road, Mount Lavinia, T011-272 3464) and **Siddhalepa Ayurveda Hospital** (106 Templer's Road, Mount Lavinia, T011-272 2524, www.siddhalepa.com).

Birdwatching

Sri Lanka is an ornithologist's paradise with 233 resident species, of which 26 (mainly in the Wet Zone) are endemic. Together with almost 200 migrant species recorded, the sheer numbers make birdwatching highly rewarding.

Sinharaja Forest Reserve, the **Peak Wilderness Sanctuary** and the **Ruhuna-Yala National Park** are particularly recommended, as they offer diverse habitats, while the reservoirs and coastal lagoons to the southeast (especially **Bundala**) attract a large variety of water birds. Local specialist tour operators are listed on page 72.

Buddhism See page 381.

The ancient Buddhist centres hold great attraction for visitors and certainly for those interested in the living religion. Sri Lanka provides rewarding opportunities to discover more about the practice of Theravada (Hinayana) Buddhism and meditation. Several centres offer courses on Buddhism in English (and occasionally in French and German). Visit the **Buddhist Cultural Centre** (see page 70) and www.buddhanet.net, for a list of addresses and websites of retreats which accept foreigners for teaching and meditation.

ON THE ROAD
One-day wonders

In a football-fixated world, the Sri Lankan passion for the gentler charms of cricket can seem both strange and refreshing. When the national team plays, everyone watches; the economy suffers as attendance at work drops dramatically, with fans clustering around their radios and TVs without a care for anything else. Cricket is played on any spare patch of grass going. The fact that the players may not have a bat or ball doesn't stop them: a plank and a piece of fruit will do.

The Test team is one of the main focuses of national identity, and its players are national icons, who become stars, politicians and sure-fire revenue-earners in the advertising world. Adoring schoolboys who speak no other word of English can reel off the names and batting averages of every international cricketer around the world.

Cricket's origins in Sri Lanka are, of course, colonial, but it wasn't until 1981 that the national team achieved Test status. Though they proved themselves far from minnows, it was almost 20 years until 'senior' nations such as England finally agreed to play them in a full series. In the meantime, they transformed themselves with flair into kings of the one-day international, the game's shorter form, surprising everyone but themselves when they blasted their way to victory in the 1996 World Cup. The key to their success lay in the attacking batting of the openers, particularly Sanath Jayasuriya, who abandoned traditional caution at the start of an innings and smashed the opposition bowlers from the off, setting unassailable targets. Their success revolutionized the game as all teams adopted these tactics, transforming the one-day game forever.

Serious cricket starts at school in Sri Lanka, and though the game can be a great national unifier, there is an undeniable bias towards privilege. Public school cricket garners enormous media coverage, and its young players are idolized like their senior counterparts – perhaps at its most bizarre in the *Sunday Observer*'s 'Most Popular Schoolboy Cricketer of the Year' competition. Until recently, progress to the Test team was virtually impossible without money, but the national team's variable showing prompted the game's administrators to spread cricket to the regions, setting up clinics, seminars and tournaments in the outstations to encourage talented youngsters from less wealthy backgrounds. A role model for many, as well as a political bridge, was the extraordinarily gifted Muttiah 'Murali' Muralitharan (retired in 2010), one of the few Indian Tamils to play for Sri Lanka. He won Test matches almost single-handed with his sometimes unplayable off-spin bowling. See www.srilankacricket.lk for further information.

Cricket

Many visitors come to Sri Lanka to support their touring cricket teams, and even if test cricket no longer attracts the crowds of old, the vibrant buzz at a T20 or one-day International match is unforgettable. Casual cricket fans should try to catch a game in Galle, whose oval ground overlooking the sea is one of the most magnificently sited sport stadiums in the world.

In the UK, **Gulliver Sports Travel**, T01684-878806, www.gulliverstravel.co.uk, is the official tour operator to the England Cricket Board; in Australia contact **Australian Sports Tours**, T1-800-026 668, www.astsports.com.au.

ON THE ROAD
Clear waters

Corals, invertebrates and dazzling fish – blue surgeon, comical parrot, butterfly, lion, large and small angels, snappers, groupers, barracudas and jackfish – all enjoy Sri Lanka's warm coastal waters, yet the island has yet to become renowned as a diving destination. Much of the coastline, particularly in the southwest, was adversely affected by 'bleaching' in 1998 but was not seriously damaged by the tsunami in 2004, and most reefs are now recovering well.

To find the clearest waters, take a boat away from the coast; further out to sea visibility of up to 25 m is possible, especially in the morning. A wealth of marine life can be seen at popular sites such as Negombo and Hikkaduwa. The south coast is even better, with wrecks in the bays at Galle and Weligama. From April to June, Dondra to Tangalla are fine in calm seas, while the more adventurous should enquire about the Great and Little Basses off Kirinda, made famous by Arthur C Clarke, before setting sail. Some of Sri Lanka's most spectacular sites are on the east coast, where the wreck of *HMS Hermes*, a Second World War aircraft carrier, lies in good condition buried deep off Passekudah Bay, near Batticaloa (see page 321). It is worth noting that there is only one decompression chamber in Sri Lanka, at the Trincomalee naval base.

Cycling See also page 408.

An increasing number of tour operators, both within Sri Lanka and abroad, run mountain-bike tours of the island. A series of way-marked **National Cycling Trails** have been developed in four diverse regions of the country. The coastal route runs for 240 km along the southwest coast from Wadduwa (near Kalutara) to Koggala; the 150-km Ancient Cities trail runs through the Dry Zone via several World Heritage Sites; the Sabaragamuwa route, runs east from Ratnagiri through lush jungle country around Sinharaja rainforest; and the spectacular 300-km Hill Country route runs through tea plantations and is best suited to mountain bikes. Each trail is divided into sections of 20-30 km (approximately two hours of easy-going cycling).

Diving and snorkelling

Dive centres on the west, south and east coasts have equipment for rent and some offer a full range of PADI courses. Diving is best avoided during the monsoons. The best time in the southwest is the winter (November to March), when the sea is relatively calm and clear. The far south and the east coast are better from April to September (July is best on the east coast); see also Swimming, below. Specialist companies will advise you on good reefs, and the website **www.divesrilanka.com** is a useful resource.

Several popular beach areas offer good **snorkelling** at reefs within walking distance of shore, notably **Hikkaduwa**, **Unawatuna**, **Mirissa** and **Polhena** (near Matara), while the clear waters of **Pigeon Island**, a short boat ride from Nilaveli near Trincomalee, are also once again accessible.

Golf

A legacy from the British period, there are some excellently maintained courses in **Colombo**, **Nuwara Eliya** and on the banks of the **Victoria Reservoir** east of Kandy.

Hiking

There is little organized trekking in Sri Lanka, but the varied countryside is richly rewarding to explore, especially in the hill country, where **Nuwara Eliya**, **Ella** and **Haputale** are particularly good bases for walkers. Existing paths include ancient pilgrim routes and colonial-era bridal pathways. Moderately fit walkers should not miss climbing the sacred mountain of **Adam's Peak**, especially during pilgrimage season (December to May), while **Horton Plains** offers crisp mountain air and stunning views at World's End with the option of camping. The **Knuckles Range** (Dumbara Hills) also has some worthwhile treks.

National parks and reserves

www.dwlc.lk; see also page 333.

Sri Lanka is home to a wide range of native species, and wildlife safaris offer the chance to see elephant, spotted deer, buffalo, wild pig, jackal, sambar and, with time and luck, leopard and sloth bear. Around 24% of Sri Lanka's land area is covered by forest, large tracts of which are protected by the government. The Forestry Department runs the island's forest reserves (such as the **Knuckles Range**) and biosphere reserves (notably **Sinharaja**), while the national parks, sanctuaries and nature reserves, which offer the best chance of wildlife-spotting, belong to the Department of Wildlife Conservation. Most of Sri Lanka's national parks are in the Dry Zone areas of the north and east, the most frequently visited by tourists being wildlife-rich **Yala National Park**; **Uda Walawe**, famous for its elephants; and **Minneriya** to the north. Closed for many years owing to the civil war, the island's largest reserve, **Wilpattu**, offers beautiful scenery with fewer crowds than the southern parks. A series of new national parks opened in the far north in 2015, notably **Delft Island** off Jaffna, and **Chundikulam** on the eastern coast of Elephant Pass.

All national parks are open daily 0630-1830. Entrance fees for most are US$15 for foreigners and US$7 for children under 12, plus fees for a compulsory tracker, taxes and service charge. These hidden charges can add up and make a visit quite expensive, although the money is ploughed back into wildlife conservation (theoretically at least). Most people choose to visit the parks on a day trip, but bungalows and campsites are available, and can be booked in advance at www.dwc.gov.lk.

Surfing and watersports

The **surf** at **Arugam Bay** on the east coast is regarded as some of the best in Asia, though only from April to October. **Hikkaduwa** is the main centre during the winter (Novemver to March), sometimes attracting international tournaments, while **Midigama** and **Mirissa** are smaller and quieter. Surfing equipment can be bought or hired and cheap accommodation aimed at long-stay surfers is available.

On the windy northwest coast, **windsurfing**, **parasailing**, **waterskiing**, and, above all, **kitesurfing**, are the main watersports. **Negombo**, **Bentota** and the **Kalpitiya Peninsula** are the most popular spots.

Swimming

The warm waters along Sri Lanka's palm-fringed coast are dotted with beach resorts ideal for **swimming**.

However, bear in mind the effects of wind and climate at different times of year: December to March is the only suitable time to swim on the west coast, while in the south swimming is usually fine from November to April, and the east coast is good for a month either side of its July to September peak season. Avoid swimming outside these months, when the southwest monsoon batters the coast and there are a number of

Shopping tips

Local craft skills are still practised widely across the country. Pottery, coir fibre, carpentry, handloom weaving and metalwork all receive government assistance. Some of the crafts are concentrated in just a few villages. The 'city of arts', Kalapura, has over 70 families of craftsmen making superb brass, wood, silver and gold items. Some specialize in fine carvings, inlays and damascene. Oil lamps are especially popular.

What to buy

Of Indonesian origin but Sri Lankan design, good-quality **batiks**, from wall hangings to *lungis* (sarongs), are widely available. **Handloom** weaving has seen a major revival in recent years, and there is also a wide range of handwoven cotton and silk textiles in vibrant colours and textures. Galle is famous for its **pillow lace** and **crochet**, introduced by the Portuguese.

Ratnapura is Sri Lanka's **gem** capital, but gems are sold throughout the country. Sapphires, rubies, cat's eye, amethyst, topaz, moonstone and zircon are a few of the locally mined stones available. **Silverware** is a specialism in Kandy, with jewellery, tea sets, trays, candle stands and ornaments available. Inlay work is a further specialization. Fine **gold** and silver chain work is done in the Pettah area of Colombo. Note that gem stones, gold jewellery and silver items are best bought in reputable shops.

Mask-making is a popular craft in the southwest of the island, especially around Ambalangoda, and is based on traditional **masks** used in dance dramas. Good-quality masks in a range of sizes can also be picked up in the craft outlets in Colombo. See box, page 71. Musical instruments, especially **drums** are another popular gift; Matara is a good place to pick them up.

Some tea and spice gardens welcome visitors and have retail outlets for their produce. (Matale is especially noted for its spices.) **Tea** is sometimes presented in attractive wooden or woven packages, and accessories such as teapots can make good gifts.

Coir and **palm leaf** are made into mats, rugs, baskets and bags, while **reed, cane** and **rattan** are fashioned into attractive household goods, including mats, chairs, lampshades, bags and purses. **Lacquerware** is another craft centred on the Kandy region. The quality of **leather** goods especially bags, is often fairly high.

drownings each year. Particular care should be taken of rip currents; check the situation locally. Many large hotels have excellent swimming pools and will usually accept non-residents for a small fee, or even for free.

Whitewater rafting and canoeing

Kelani River, which falls through a rocky gorge just above Kitulgala, is the most popular area for rafting and canoeing, offering grade IV-V rapids. There are several operators in Colombo and Kitulgala. Operators also offer two-day trips on the Kalu Ganga. Gentle rafting is possible on the **Walawe River** in Uda Walawe, while the **Mahaweli Ganga**, Sri Lanka's longest river, offers more challenging opportunities.

Where to buy
Craft department stores in the larger cities offer a range under one roof – **Lakpahana, Lanka Hands, Craft Link, Viskam Nivasa** are some you will come across. There are government **Laksala** shops in many towns, where prices are fixed. Private upmarket shops and top hotel arcades offer better quality, choice and service but at a price. Vibrant and colourful local bazaars (markets) are often a great experience but you must be prepared to bargain. **Mlesna** is a government-run chain of tea shops, where good-quality tea can be bought.

Bargaining
In some private shops and markets bargaining is normal and expected. It is best to get an idea of prices being asked by different stalls for items you are interested in before taking the plunge. Some shopkeepers will happily quote twice the actual price to a foreigner showing interest, so you might well start by halving the asking price. On the other hand, it would be inappropriate to do the same in an established shop with price-tags, though a plea for the 'best price' or a 'special discount' might reap results even here. Remain good humoured throughout.

Tips and warnings
Taxi (and three-wheeler) drivers often receive commission when they take you to shops. If you arrive at a shop with a tout you may well end up paying absurdly high prices to cover the commission he earns. The quality of goods in a shop that needs to encourage touts may be questionable too. Try to select and enter a shop on your own and be aware that a tout may follow you in and pretend to the shopkeeper that he has brought you.

Batik 'factories', mask and handicrafts 'workshops', spice 'gardens', gem 'museums' across the island attract travellers with the promise of a 'free' and insightful visit or demonstration; the main purpose of most is to get you into their shop where you may feel under pressure to buy something.

Note that the export of certain items, such as antiquities, ivory, furs and skins, is controlled or banned, so it is essential to get a certificate of legitimate sale and permission for export.

Improve your travel photography

Taking pictures is a highlight for many travellers, yet too often the results turn out to be disappointing. Steve Davey, author of Footprint's *Travel Photography*, sets out his top rules for coming home with pictures you can be proud of.

Before you go

Don't waste precious travelling time and do your research before you leave. Find out what festivals or events might be happening or which day the weekly market takes place, and search online image sites such as Flickr to see whether places are best shot at the beginning or end of the day, and what vantage points you should consider.

Get up early

The quality of the light will be better in the few hours after sunrise and again before sunset – especially in the tropics when the sun will be harsh and unforgiving in the middle of the day. Sometimes seeing the sunrise is a part of the whole travel experience: sleep in and you will miss more than just photographs.

Stop and think

Don't just click away without any thought. Pause for a few seconds before raising the camera and ask yourself what you are trying to show with your photograph. Think about what things you need to include in the frame to convey this meaning. Be prepared to move around your subject to get the best angle. Knowing the point of your picture is the first step to making sure that the person looking at the picture will know it too.

Compose your picture

Avoid simply dumping your subject in the centre of the frame every time you take a picture. If you compose with it to one side, then your picture can look more balanced. This will also allow you to show a significant background and make the picture more meaningful. A good rule of thumb is to place your subject or any significant detail a third of the way into the frame; facing into the frame not out of it.

This rule also works for landscapes. Compose with the horizon two-thirds of the way up the frame if the foreground is the most interesting part of the picture; one-third of the way up if the sky is more striking.

Don't get hung up with this so-called Rule of Thirds, though. Exaggerate it by pushing your subject out to the edge of the frame if it makes a more interesting picture; or if the sky is dull in a landscape, try cropping with the horizon near the very top of the frame.

Fill the frame

If you are going to focus on a detail or even a person's face in a close-up portrait, then be bold and make sure that you fill the frame. This is often a case of physically getting in close. You can use a telephoto setting on a zoom lens but this can lead to pictures looking quite flat; moving in close is a lot more fun!

Interact with people

If you want to shoot evocative portraits then it is vital to approach people and seek permission in some way, even if it is just by smiling at someone. Spend a little time with them and they are likely to relax and look less stiff and formal. Action portraits where people are doing something, or environmental portraits, where they are set against a significant background, are a good way to achieve relaxed portraits. Interacting is a good way to find out more about people and their lives, creating memories as well as photographs.

Focus carefully

Your camera can focus quicker than you, but it doesn't know which part of the picture you want to be in focus. If your camera is using the centre focus sensor then move the camera so it is over the subject and half press the button, then, holding it down, recompose the picture. This will lock the focus. Take the now correctly focused picture when you are ready.

Another technique for accurate focusing is to move the active sensor over your subject. Some cameras with touch-sensitive screens allow you to do this by simply clicking on the subject.

Leave light in the sky

Most good night photography is actually taken at dusk when there is some light and colour left in the sky; any lit portions of the picture will balance with the sky and any ambient lighting. There is only a very small window when this will happen, so get into position early, be prepared and keep shooting and reviewing the results. You can take pictures after this time, but avoid shots of tall towers in an inky black sky; crop in close on lit areas to fill the frame.

Bring it home safely

Digital images are inherently ephemeral: they can be deleted or corrupted in a heartbeat. The good news though is they can be copied just as easily. Wherever you travel, you should have a backup strategy. Cloud backups are popular, but make sure that you will have access to fast enough Wi-Fi. If you use RAW format, then you will need some sort of physical back-up. If you don't travel with a laptop or tablet, then you can buy a backup drive that will copy directly from memory cards.

Recently updated and available in both digital and print formats, Footprint's Travel Photography by Steve Davey covers everything you need to know about travelling with a camera, including simple post-processing. More information is available at www.footprinttravelguides.com

Where to stay

jungle lodges and beachside retreats

Sri Lanka's accommodation scene is developing in leaps and bounds, with a wide choice of places to stay for every budget. At the top end, Colombo has a fast-growing selection of very exclusive 'boutique' hotels, and, away from the capital, you can book into some exceptional one-off retreats: the Geoffrey Bawa-designed **Heritance Kandalama**; elegant plantation bungalows; eco-lodges buried in dense jungle where you sleep in open-sided treehouses, or secluded beach villas with private pools. Below this level, you can stay safely and relatively cheaply in most major tourist areas, where you'll find a choice of quality hotels offering a full range of facilities. At the lower end of the scale, there is an ever-growing range of family-run guesthouses in tourist areas offering bed and breakfast (and other meals by arrangement). See www.neverbeen.org for some good choices.

In the high season (December to March for much of the island) demand can be extremely high. It is therefore best to reserve rooms well in advance if you are making your own arrangements, and to arrive reasonably early in the day. Prices are highly inflated in Kandy during the **Esala Perahera** festival and in Nuwara Eliya during the April holiday season. Long weekends (when a public holiday or *poya* day falls on a Thursday, Friday, Monday or Tuesday) also attract a substantial increase in room rates in Nuwara Eliya. Many hotels charge the highest room rate over Christmas and New Year (between mid-December to mid-January). Large reductions are made by hotels in all categories out of season

Price codes

Where to stay	Restaurants
$$$$ US$150 and over	$$$ over US$12
$$$ US$66-150	$$ US$7-12
$$ US$30-65	$ under US$7
$ under US$30	

Price of a double room in high season, including taxes.

Price for a two-course meal for one person, excluding drinks or service charge.

in most resorts; always ask if a discount is available. During the monsoon rooms may feel damp and have a musty smell.

Online bookings
Sri Lankan hoteliers have fallen hard for Booking.com. Many places, particularly small hotels, have completely outsourced their reservation process to the internet giant and barely bother to quote room rates anymore, much less maintain their own websites. It's always worth checking the price on Booking,com and, if you can plan ahead, keep checking back for flash sales. However, don't assume the online price is the best you'll get; call the hotel to check if they can beat it.

International class hotels
Concentrated mainly in the capital, around Kandy and, to a lesser degree, in tourist-heavy areas such as the south coast and Cultural Triangle, these have the full range of four- or five-star facilities, with service standards comparable with the West. Alongside international brands including **Hilton** and **Taj**, the Sri Lankan-owned **Cinnamon** chain of hotels are of a dependably high standard.

Boutique hotels and villas
One of the fastest growing sectors of the market, these can be very special, offering a high degree of luxury, superb and very personal service, and a sense of privacy and exclusiveness that may be lacking in resort-style hotels. Often they are innovatively designed with environmental sensitivity in mind. Some sumptuous villas can also be rented by the day or week – see www.villasinsrilanka.com.

Colonial-era hotels
The colonial period has left a legacy of atmospheric colonial-era hotels, notably in Colombo, Kandy and Nuwara Eliya. Some were purpose built, others converted from former governors' residences and other colonial buildings. A number have been carefully modernized without losing their period charm. Some very good deals are available.

Resort hotels
Catering mainly to the package holiday market, most larger tourist hotels on beaches and near important sites fall into this category. Some are luxurious with a good range of facilities; others, notably in some west coast resorts, are rather tired and dated. Food served here tends to be of the 'all-you-can-eat' buffet variety. It pays to make bookings through tour operators, which offer large discounts on most resort-style hotels.

ON THE ROAD
Ayurvedic healing

Ayurveda (the science of life/health) is the ancient Hindu system of medicine – a naturalistic system depending on diagnosis of the body's 'humours' (wind, mucus, gall and sometimes blood) to achieve a balance. In the early form, gods and demons were associated with cures and ailments; treatment was carried out by using herbs, minerals, formic acid (from ant hills) and water, and hence was limited in scope. Ayurveda classified substances and chemicals compounds in the theory of *panchabhutas* (five 'elements'). It also noted the action of food and drugs on the human body. Ayurvedic massage using aromatic and medicinal oils to tone up the nervous system has been practised for centuries.

This ancient system, which developed in India over centuries before the Buddha's birth, was written down as a *samhita* by Charaka. It probably flourished in Sri Lanka up to the 19th century when it was overshadowed by the Western system of allopathic medicine.

In addition to the use of herbs as cures, many are used daily in the Sri Lankan kitchen (chilli, coriander, cumin, fennel, garlic, ginger), some of which will be familiar in the West, and have for centuries been used as beauty preparations.

Ayurvedic resorts
Mainly on the west coast, these are very popular with tourists from mainland Europe, offering a degree of luxury combined with ready- or tailor-made programmes of Ayurvedic treatment. The authenticity of the treatments on offer tends to vary. See also page 20.

Plantation bungalows
Some attractive rubber and tea plantation bungalows in the hill country can be rented out by small or large groups and provide an interesting alternative place to stay. A caretaker/cook is often provided. There is no centralized booking agency, but see individual entries in the text, speak to the tourist board or contact Red Dot Tours ① *www.reddottours.com*.

Guesthouses
Guesthouses are the staple of budget travellers and are in plentiful supply in most tourist haunts. Some are effectively small hotels, usually at the upper end of the price bracket; others are simpler and more basic affairs. At their best, usually when family-owned, they can be friendly, homely, provide superb home cooking, and be rich sources of local information.

In addition, some private homes in Colombo, Kandy and some beach areas also offer informal homestays, which can be very good value. Neverbeen ① *6 Kothalawala Gardens, Colombo 4, T076-678 6655, www.neverbeen.org*, is an excellent Sri Lankan variant of **AirBnb**, offering access to a network of homestays all over the island, with accommodation from plush to very basic. Note that away from the main tourist areas, especially in the Tamil-speaking north and east, hosts tend to speak only rudimentary English.

Hostels
Sri Lanka's burgeoning backpacker scene is focused heavily on Colombo, a welcome development in a city that has always struggled to provide good budget accommodation. Several hostels have opened along Galle Road and in Mount Lavinia, and with clean dorms and secure access, these offer the best deal for solo travellers in the city. Most also have private doubles at prices similar to a low-end hotel, and many provide optional breakfast and free Wi-Fi.

Rest houses
These government-run relics from the dawn of Sri Lankan tourism are often wonderfully atmospheric – many are in converted colonial houses – and typically occupy the best location in town. However, compared to privately run hotels, many are run-down and overpriced with hit-and-miss service. Nevertheless, in some cases, the rest house is still the best (or only) option in town. **Ceylon Hotels Corporation (CHC)** ⓘ *T011 752 9529, www.chcresthouses.com*, is responsible for management of several of the old government rest houses across the island; a select few have been polished up and are marketed through www.chcresorts.com. It's best to book through Central Reservations as occasionally an individual rest house may not honour a direct booking. Prices charged on arrival may vary from what is quoted on the phone or from the CHC's 'official' typed list showing the tariff, which only a few managers acknowledge exists. Rice and curry lunches at rest houses are often good, though slightly more expensive than similar fare elsewhere.

National park accommodation
Most of Sri Lanka's parks offer some sort of accommodation, ranging from comfortable bungalows to crammed dormitories. National park bungalows can get expensive when you factor in accommodation costs (higher for foreign tourists than for Sri Lankans), national park fees and assorted service charges, but they offer a uniquely close contact with Sri Lankan nature. If the bungalow is within the park boundaries then you will have to pay park entrance fees for two days for an overnight stay. Camping is also possible in many national parks. The Department of Wildlife and Conservation has an online booking system which appears to have cut out many of the frustrations of arranging a room: you

can check availability, book (for a maximum of three consecutive nights) and pay at dwc.lankagate.gov.lk.

Circuit bungalows
Designed mainly for government workers, these may be the only option in areas well off the beaten track. They should be booked through the government offices in Colombo. Contact details are given under individual entries.

Railway Retiring Rooms
Railway Retiring Rooms offer cheap and basic accommodation at major railway stations. Though generally pretty poorly maintained, some are open to travellers without rail tickets, and they can be a useful fall-back if you get stuck – or have a desperately early train to catch. Stations with rooms include: Anuradhapura, Batticaloa, Galle, Kandy, Mihintale, Polonnaruwa and Trincomalee.

Food
& drink

Although it shares some similarities with Indian cooking, Sri Lankan cuisine is distinct from its neighbour. At its heart lies the Island's enviable variety and bountiful supply of native vegetables, fruits and spices, which Sri Lanka's history of trade and colonization have developed into the remarkable range of dishes available today. Even before the arrival of the Europeans, the Indians, Arabs, Malays and Moors had all left their mark. The Portuguese brought chilli from South America, perhaps the most significant change to food across the East, while the Dutch and even the British also bequeathed a number of popular dishes. Sampling authentic Sri Lankan fare is a highlight of any trip.

Cuisine

Rice and curry is Sri Lanka's main dish, but the term 'curry' conceals an enormous variety of subtle flavours. Coriander, mustard seeds, cumin, fenugreek, peppercorns, cinnamon, cloves and cardamoms are just some of the spices that, roasted and blended, give a Sri Lankan curry its richness; most cooks also add Maldive fish, or dried sprats. *Rampe* (screw-pine leaf) and tamarind pulp are also distinctive ingredients. The whole is then usually cooked in coconut milk.

Sri Lankan food is renowned for its fieriness, and **chilli** is the most noticeable ingredient in some curries. While most tourist restaurants, aware of the sensitivity of some Western palates, normally tone down its use, real home cooking will usually involve liberal quantities. If a dish is still too hot, a spoonful of rice or curd, or a sip of beer or milk (not water) will usually tone down its effects.

A typical Sri Lankan meal comprises a large portion of rice, with a 'main curry' – for Buddhists usually fish, although chicken, beef and mutton are also often available – and several pulse and vegetable and (sometimes) salad dishes. *Dhal* is invariably one of these. Vegetable curries may be made from jackfruit, okra, breadfruit, beans, bananas, banana flowers or pumpkin, amongst others. Deliciously salty poppadums are also usually served, and the offering is completed by numerous side dishes: spicy pickles, sweet and sour chutneys and *sambols* made of ground coconut (*pol sambol*) or onion mixed with Maldive fish, red chilli and lime juice (*seeni sambol*). *Mallung,* a milder dish prepared with grated coconut, shredded leaves, red onions and lime, is an alternative to try. *Kiri hodhi* is a mild 'white' curry prepared with coconut milk.

Rice-based alternatives to rice and curry include the Dutch-inspired *lamprais:* this is rice boiled in meat stock with curry, accompanied by dry meat and vegetable curries, fried meat and fish or meat balls (*frikkadels*), then parcelled in banana leaf and baked. The ubiquitous *biriyani* is a Moorish dish of rice cooked in stock with pieces of chopped spiced meat, garnished with sliced egg.

The **rice** generally served is usually plain white boiled rice but it is worth searching out the healthier red rice. There are some tasty alternatives. '**String hoppers**', a steamed nest of thin rice flour noodles served with thin curries, are eaten at breakfast but are often available at any time. '**Hoppers**' (*appam*), a breakfast speciality, are small cupped pancakes made from fermented rice flour, coconut milk and yeast. Crispy on the edges (like French crêpes), thick at the centre, they are often prepared with an egg broken into the middle of the pan ('egg hoppers'). *Pittu* is a crumbly mixture of flour and grated coconut steamed in a cylindrical bamboo mould, usually served with coconut milk and *sambol*.

As befits a tropical island, Sri Lanka's **fish** and **seafood** are excellent. The succulent white seerfish, tuna and mullet, usually grilled and served with chips and salad, are widely available along the coast, while crab, lobster and prawns (often jumbo prawns) are magnificent and reasonably priced. Cuttlefish is very versatile and prepared a number of ways. Meat varies in quality; though it is cheap and usually better than you get in India.

Unsurprisingly, **Indian** food is also popular, particularly dishes from the south. Cheap, filling traditional *thali* meals (a curated selection of vegetarian curries with rice, chapatti and a sweet dish, traditionally served on a banana leaf) are most widely available in Hindu-dominated areas of Colombo, the north and along the east coast. Here too you'll find *dosai*, crispy pancakes made from rice and lentil-flour batter, often served with a spiced potato filling, and *vadai*, crispy savoury doughnuts made of fried lentil flour and spices.

Sri Lanka has a spectacular variety of superb tropical **fruit**, and this is reflected in the variety of juices on offer. Available throughout the year are pineapple, papaya (excellent with lime) and banana, of which there are dozens of varieties (red bananas are said to be the best). The extraordinarily rich jack (*jak*) fruit is also available all year. Seasonal fruit include the lusciously sweet mango (for which Jaffna is especially famous), the purplish mangosteen (July to September), wood-apple, avocado, the spiky foul-smelling durian and hairy red rambutan from July to October. In addition to ordinary green coconuts, Sri Lanka has its own variety – the golden king coconut (*thambili*), whose milk is particularly sweet and nutritious.

Breakfast

The tendency amongst most smaller hotels and guesthouses is to serve a 'Western breakfast' comprising fruit and white bread with some jam. It is well worth ordering a Sri Lankan alternative the night before. This could comprise hoppers, string hoppers (for both, see above), *kiribath* (see below) or, best of all, the delicious *rotti* (roti), a flat circular unleavened bread cooked on a griddle.

Lunch

Lunch is the main meal of the day for many Sri Lankans. Rice and curry is the standard, often served in larger hotels as a buffet. The better rest houses are a good option for sampling a variety of authentic curries (usually Rs 400-500). A cheaper and quicker alternative is to pick up a '**lunch packet**', available from local restaurants and street vendors. This takeaway option usually comprises a portion of rice, a meat, fish or vegetable curry, plus *dhal*, all wrapped up in a paper parcel. Usually costing Rs 100-150, this is a cheap and filling meal. A lighter alternative still is a plate of **short eats**: a selection of meat and vegetable rolls, 'cutlets' (deep-fried in bread crumbs), *rotis* and *wadais*, a Tamil speciality of deep-fried savoury lentil doughnut rings, sometimes served in yoghurt (*thair vadai*). You will normally be given a full plate and charged for however many you eat.

Dinner

Sri Lankans tend to eat late but light; be aware that outside Colombo and the major tourist centres, the offering in guesthouses and restaurants may be limited unless you order in advance. It may not be possible to get rice and curry, but Chinese food, such as fried rice, and devilled dishes are nearly always available. In larger hotels, dinner is usually the main meal of the day, often with enormous all-you- can-eat buffets.

Desserts

Sri Lankans tend to have a sweet tooth. Rice forms the basis of many Sri Lankan sweet dishes, palm treacle (*kitul*) being used as the main traditional sweetener. This is also served on curd as a delicious dessert (*kiri peni*) and boiled and set into *jaggery*. *Kavun* is an oil cake, made with rice flour and treacle and deep-fried until golden brown. Malay influence is evident in the popular *watalappam*, a steamed pudding made with coconut milk, eggs and *jaggery*, rather reminiscent of crème caramel. *Kiribath*, rice boiled in milk, is something of a national dish, often served at weddings and birthdays. It can be eaten with *jaggery* or as a breakfast dish with *seeni sambol*. Sri Lankan ice cream varies in quality; the best is made by soft drinks company Elephant House. Jaffna is also famous for its 'cream houses'.

Eating out

Eating out in Sri Lanka is remarkably cheap. Most restaurants serve a choice of Indian, Chinese and continental dishes. Sadly, it is not so easy to get good Sri Lankan food in most resort hotels, which tend to concentrate on Western dishes. The upmarket hotels in Colombo, however, serve first-class buffets at lunch and dinnertime, and there are an increasing number of excellent Sri Lankan restaurants in the city. Upcountry, home cooking in family-owned guesthouses is often unbeatable. It is essential to order well in advance as Sri Lankan curries take a long time to prepare. This is one of the reasons for the universal popularity of Chinese and 'devilled' dishes available throughout the island, which can be knocked together in a few minutes.

Vegetarian food is much less common in Sri Lanka than in India and, in places, can be difficult to get. Check out www.lankarestaurants.com and www.tasty.lk for reviews of restaurants, including food and ambience.

Tip...
Sri Lankans usually eat with their hands, mixing rice and curry together with the right thumb and forefingers. As a foreigner, however, you will always be supplied with a fork.

Drinks

In addition to fruit juices and coconut juice (see above), **mineral water** is available everywhere, though it is relatively expensive. There is also a huge variety of bottled **soft drinks**, including international brands. Local favourites include ginger beer, cream soda, lemonade and Necto. These are perfectly safe, but always check the seal. Elephant House is the main soft drinks manufacturer, and all their products are palatable. One potent soft drink is **Peyawa**, a ginger beer made with pepper and coriander for added kick.

The island's **coffee** harvest failed in 1869, and it would seem that Sri Lankans have never quite forgiven it, such are the crimes committed in the name of the drink. Colombo's upmarket hotels do however serve decent coffee, and there are a couple of new Western-style coffee bars opening up. As befits one of the world's great producers, **tea** is, of course, a much better option, although the highest quality varieties are generally exported.

Drinking **alcohol** in Sri Lanka is a no-nonsense male preserve. Bars, except in Colombo and tourist areas, tend to be spit-and-sawdust affairs. **Beer** is strong (5%+), popular and served in large 660 ml bottles. **Lion**, **Carlsberg** and **Three Coins** are the three main brands, each producing a Pilsner style lager

Tip...
Do not add ice to drinks as the water from which it is made may not be pure.

slightly thin to Western tastes but quite palatable. **Three Coins** make some good specialist beers: their 8% **Sando stout** is smooth and chocolatey, and **Riva** is a more than passable wheat beer. The locally brewed **arrack**, distilled from palm toddy, is the most popular spirit and a cheaper option than beer. Superior brands include **Old Arrack**, **Double distilled**, the matured **VSOA** and **seven-year-old** arrack. The frothy, cloudy cider-like **toddy** is the other national drink, produced from the fermented sap of coconut, *kitul* (palm treacle) or palmyra palms. It is available from very basic toddy 'taverns', usually makeshift shacks that spring up in toddy-producing areas. Alcohol is not sold on *poya* days (see Festivals and events, above). Note that hotels and restaurants will serve foreign tourists expensive, imported spirits and beers unless told otherwise.

Menu reader

Basic vocabulary

English	Sinhalese	Tamil
bread	pān	rotti/pān
(too much) chilli	miris wadi	kāram
drink	bima	kudi
egg	biththara	muttai
fish	malu	min
fruit	palathuru	palam
food	kama	unavu
jaggery	hakuru	sini/vellam
juice	isma	sāru
meat	mus	iraichchi
oil	thel	ennai
pepper	gammiris	milagu
pulses (beans, lentils)	parippu	thāniyam
rice	buth	arisi
salt	lunu	uppu
spices	kulubadu	milagu
vegetables	elawalu	kai kari vagaigal
water	wathura	thanneer

Fruit and nuts

banana	keselkan	valaippalam
cashew	cadju	muruthivi
coconut	pol	thengali
green coconut	kurumba	pachcha niramulla thengai
mango	(jak) kos ambul	mangai
papaya	dodam	pappa palam
pineapple	annasi	annasi

Vegetables

aubergine	vambatu	kathirikai
beans (green)	bonchi	avarai
cabbage	gowa	muttaikosu
gourd (green)	pathola	pudalankai
okra	bandakka	vendikkai
onion	luunu	venkayam
pepper	miris	kāram
prawns	isso	irāl
potato	ala	uruka kilangu
spinach	niwithi	pasali
tomato	thakkali	thakkali

Meat, fish and seafood

chicken	kukulmas	koli
crab	kakuluvo	nandu
pork	ōroomas	pantri

Ordering a meal in a restaurant: Sinhalese

Please show the menu	menu eka penwanna
sugar/milk/ice	sini/kiri/ice
A bottle of mineral water please	drink botalayak genna

Order a meal in a restaurant: Tamil

Please show the menu	thayavu seithu thinpandangal patti tharavum
sugar/milk/ice	sini/pál/ice
A bottle of mineral water please	oru pothal soda panam tharavum

Sri Lankan specialities

amblulthial sour fish curry

kaha buth kaha rice (yellow, cooked in coconut milk with spices and saffron/turmeric colouring) kiri rice is similar but white and unspiced, served with treacle, chilli or pickle

biththara rotti rotti mixed with eggs

buriyani rice cooked in meat stock and pieces of spiced meat sometimes garnished with boiled egg slices

hoppers (appa) cupped pancakes made of fermented rice flour, coconut milk, yeast, eaten with savoury (or sweet) curry

lamprais rice cooked in stock parcelled in a banana leaf with dry meat and vegetable curries, fried meat and fish balls and baked gently

mallung boiled, shredded vegetables cooked with spice and coconut

pittu rice flour and grated coconut steamed in bamboo moulds, eaten with coconut milk and curry

polos pahi pieces of young jackfruit (tree lamb) replaces meat in this dry curry

rotty or rotti flat, circular, unleavened bread cooked on a griddle

sambol hot and spicy accompaniment usually made with onions, grated coconut, pepper (and sometimes dried fish)

sathai spicy meat pieces baked on skewers (sometimes sweet and sour)

'short eats' a selection of meat and vegetable snacks (in pastry or crumbled and fried) charged as eaten.

string hoppers (indiappa) flat circles of steamed rice flour noodles eaten usually at breakfast with thin curry

thosai or **dosai** large crisp pancake made with rice and lentil-flour batter

vadai deep-fried savoury lentil doughnut rings

Sweets (rasakavilis)

curd rich, creamy, buffalo-milk yoghurt served with treacle or jaggery

gulab jamun dark, fried spongy balls of milk curd and flour soaked in syrup

halwal aluva fudge-like, made with milk, nuts and fruit

kadju kordial fudge squares made with cashew nuts and jaggery

kaludodol dark, mil-based, semi solid sweet mixed with jaggery, cashew and spices (a moorish delicacy)

rasgulla syrup-filled white spongy balls of milk-curd and flour

thalaguli balls formed after pounding roasted sesame seeds with jaggery

wattalappam set 'custard' of coconut, milk, eggs and cashew, flavoured with spices and jaggery

Colombo

Colombo is a sprawling city and has many diverse neighbourhoods. Although its origins pre-date the arrival of the Portuguese, culturally and architecturally it appears a modern city, with few established tourist sights.

Close to the enormous harbour, the banking centre of Fort houses some architectural reminders of the city's colonial origins. To the east are the narrow lanes of the Pettah district, with its colourful bazaars. Often choked with traffic and invariably chaotic, these old neighbourhoods can be challenging for the first-time visitor. Increasingly, however, the heart of modern Colombo lies to the south, where leafy avenues and elegant villas provide a more relaxing introduction to this dynamic city. Further south still, the pleasant beach resort of Mount Lavinia is only a 30-minute train ride away from the centre and is a laid-back alternative base for visitors.

As Sri Lanka's commercial capital and its only conurbation, Colombo has been a target for Tamil separatists in the recent past, with occasional curfews and a high military presence. Today, however, buoyed by a positive political climate, the barriers are down and Colombo is able to breathe again. Investment is flowing in and this characterful city is beginning to buzz with a new-found energy.

Best for
Architecture ▪ Art ▪ Food ▪ Shopping

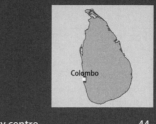

Colombo

Footprint
picks

★ Old Dutch Hospital, page 48
The beautifully restored Dutch Hospital is now home to some acclaimed restaurants, shops and a spa.

★ The Pettah, page 48
Bustling markets sell everything from gold to Ayurvedic medicines.

★ Galle Face Hotel, page 50
Sunsets at the iconic Galle Face Hotel are a quintessential Colombo experience.

★ Gangaramaya Temple, page 51
This large, atmospheric Buddhist temple has a beautiful Bo tree where people make offerings.

★ Vihara Mahadevi Park, page 53
Relax in this urban green space with a botanical garden and the city's major museums nearby.

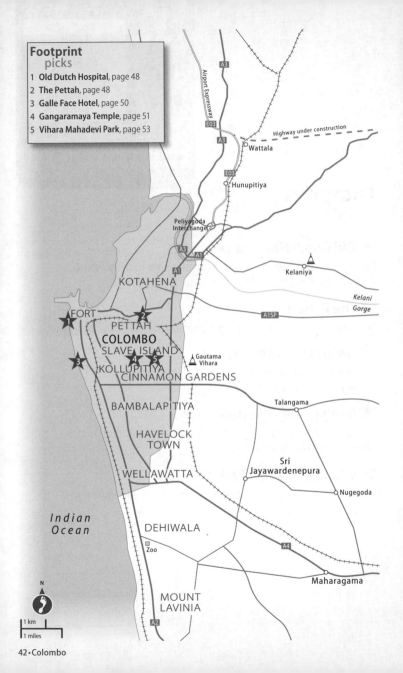

Footprint
picks

1 **Old Dutch Hospital**, page 48
2 **The Pettah**, page 48
3 **Galle Face Hotel**, page 50
4 **Gangaramaya Temple**, page 51
5 **Vihara Mahadevi Park**, page 53

Airport Expressway

A3

A3

Highway under construction

E03

A3

Wattala

E03

Hunupitiya

Peliyagoda
Interchange

A3

A1

A1

KOTAHENA

Kelaniya

Kelani
Gorge

A1SP

FORT

PETTAH

COLOMBO

SLAVE ISLAND

Gautama
Vihara

KOLLUPITIYA

CINNAMON GARDENS

Talangama

BAMBALAPITIYA

HAVELOCK
TOWN

Sri
Jayawardenepura

WELLAWATTA

Nugegoda

Indian
Ocean

DEHIWALA

A4

Zoo

Maharagama

N

MOUNT
LAVINIA

A2

1 km
1 miles

Essential Colombo

Finding your feet

Colombo (population 680,000) lies on the coast in the southwest of the island. Almost all international visitors arrive by air at **Bandaranaike International Airport** at Katunayake, about 30 km north of the city and 6 km from Negombo (see page 403). Domestic air passengers arrive at **Ratmalana Airport** to the south of the city. For details of transport from the airports to the city, see Transport, page 72.

Getting around

Although the city is quite spread out, it is fairly simple to get your bearings. If you venture beyond Fort you will need transport to explore. Short hops by three-wheeler should cost no more than Rs 150 – you will need to bargain. Radio cabs are a reliable alternative and quite affordable if you can share one. Some streets in Fort, around the president's house and major banks, are blocked or have strict security checks so it is often impossible for transport to take the most obvious route. The **Colombo City Tour** (www.colombocitytour.com, Saturday and Sunday only, US$30, children US$22 for seven hours) is easily recognizable by its red double decker buses, but currently this isn't a hop-on hop-off service so isn't ideal for most visitors. There are more interesting walking tours available (see What to do, page 72).

Orientation

The main coastal road, Galle Road, which leads to Galle and beyond, is the spine of the city. Officially the city's centre, and the area from which all suburbs radiate, is **Fort**,

Fact...

Sri Lanka's administrative capital was moved to Sri Jayawardenepura Kotte, 11 km southeast of Fort, in 1982.

Best Sri Lankan cuisine

Authentic spice at **Rangiri**, page 64
Traditional fare at **Green Cabin**, page 65
Northern flavours at **Palmyrah**, page 65
Devilled seafood at **Beach Wadiya**, page 66
Organic street food at the **Good Market**, page 69

containing the harbour, the president's house and banks, plus, to the south, some of the most exclusive hotels. East is the busy bazaar of the **Pettah**, where the main train and bus stations are located; beyond, to the northeast, is **Kotahena**. South of Fort is **Galle Face Green**, a popular place for a stroll, and **Kollupitiya**, a wealthy shopping area with many excellent restaurants. Inland, and separated from Fort and the Pettah by Beira Lake, is **Slave Island** and the busy thoroughfare of Union Place. South of here (inland from Kollupitiya) is leafy **Cinnamon Gardens**, the most exclusive area of Colombo, with the city's biggest park, main museums and some attractive guesthouses; many visitors choose to stay here. To the east is **Borella**. Back on the coast, Galle Road continues south to **Bambalapitiya** (another shopping area but progressively less exclusive), **Havelock Town** and the Tamil area of **Wellawatta** and **Dehiwala** (not strictly speaking part of Colombo). **Mount Lavinia** in the far south is a traditional bolt-hole from the city for both locals and tourists, see page 55.

Time required

Most people give Colombo short shrift, but it's worth at least a day – possibly best at the end of your trip – to explore the museums and the Pettah, sample a couple of restaurants, and take advantage of the country's best book and gift shopping.

Weather

See chart, page 44.

Sights

Colombo is a modern city with plenty of buzz but few 'must-see' sights. Its historical centre is the colonial Fort area, which combined with a visit to the hectic bazaar and Dutch period legacy of the Pettah area to its east, can make for an interesting walking tour. Most of the remaining sights are spread out in the southern suburbs, where the attractive wide boulevards of Cinnamon Gardens, the city's most exclusive district, are a highlight. Here you can visit the city's principal park and museums, small galleries and perhaps even more enticingly, sample some of the fare that is fast making Colombo one of the culinary capitals of Asia.

City centre *Colour map 3, A1.*

from the bustling markets of Fort to the wide boulevards of Cinnamon Gardens

Fort

Lying immediately south of the harbour, the compact fort area, historically Colombo's commercial centre, is a curious blend of old and new, where modern tower blocks rub shoulders with reminders of the city's colonial

> **Tip...**
> If you are going to spend any time here, it pays to become familiar with the city's postcodes (see box, page 46).

past. Although the area still contains many fine British colonial buildings, many of these are boarded up, and little remains from either the Portuguese or Dutch periods. The last traces of the fort itself were destroyed in the 19th century.

Fort was a separatist target during the war, because it is the location of the president's residence and the principal banks. Security in this area remains high, with road blocks still

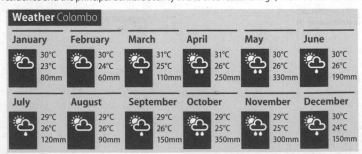

Weather Colombo					
January	**February**	**March**	**April**	**May**	**June**
30°C 23°C 80mm	30°C 24°C 60mm	31°C 25°C 110mm	31°C 26°C 250mm	30°C 26°C 330mm	30°C 26°C 190mm
July	**August**	**September**	**October**	**November**	**December**
29°C 26°C 120mm	29°C 26°C 90mm	29°C 26°C 150mm	29°C 25°C 350mm	29°C 25°C 300mm	30°C 24°C 150mm

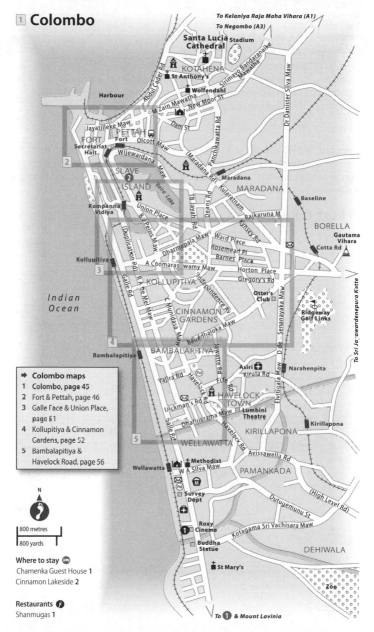

1 Colombo

To Kelaniya Raja Maha Vihara (A1)
To Negombo (A3)

Santa Lucia Cathedral
Stadium
KOTAHENA
St Anthony's
Sirimavo Bandaranaike Mawatha
Wolfendahl
New Moor St
Dam St
Dr Danister Silva Maw

Harbour

Jayatilleke Maw
PETTAH
FORT
Fort
Olcott Maw
Secretariat Halt
Wijewardana Maw
Maradana
MARADANA
Baseline

SLAVE ISLAND
Union Place
Rajakaruna M
BORELLA
Kompañña Vidiya
Ward Place
Gautama Vihara
Kollupitiya
Dharmapala Maw
Rosemead Pl
Barnes Place
Cotta Rd
A Coomaraswamy Maw
Horton Place
KOLLUPITIYA
Gregory's Rd
Otter's Club
CINNAMON GARDENS
Ridgeway Golf Links
To Sri Jayawardenepura Kotte

Indian Ocean

Bambalapitiya
BAMBALAPITIYA
Asiri
Kirula Rd
Narahenpita
Vajira Rd
Havelock Rd
Fife
HAVELOCK TOWN
Lumbini Theatre
Kirillapona
Dickman's Rd
Dharmarama Maw
Havelock Rd
KIRILLAPONA
Galle Rd
WELLAWATTA
Avissawella Rd
PAMANKADA
Wellawatta
Methodist
W A Silva Maw
Durugemunu St
(High Level Rd)
Survey Dept
Roxy Cinema
Kotagama Sri Vachisara Maw
DEHIWALA
Buddha Statue
St Mary's
Zoo
To Mount Lavinia

N

800 metres
800 yards

→ Colombo maps
1 Colombo, page 45
2 Fort & Pettah, page 46
3 Galle Face & Union Place, page 51
4 Kollupitiya & Cinnamon Gardens, page 52
5 Bambalapitiya & Havelock Road, page 56

Where to stay
Chamenka Guest House 1
Cinnamon Lakeside 2

Restaurants
Shanmugas 1

Colombo Sights•45

Postcode lottery

Colombo's citizens define themselves and their city by its postcodes. Aside from recognizing the snob value of having an office in Colombo 1 or a residence in Colombo 7 (and being suitably impressed), having a grasp of the most important postcodes will help you find your way around.

in force, and the harbour and much of the northwest section remain off-limits. As a result, Fort can be an eerily quiet place outside office hours. In fact, many offices have moved out of Fort altogether, leaving it a rather empty shell, though it is still interesting to explore the accessible areas by foot.

2 Fort & Pettah

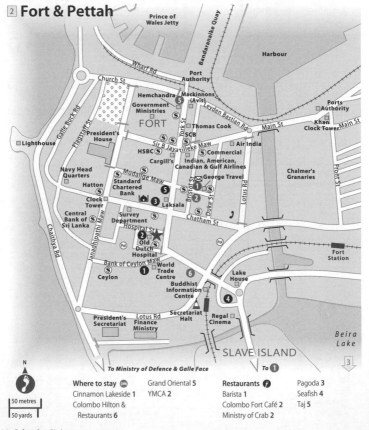

Where to stay 🛌
Cinnamon Lakeside 1
Colombo Hilton &
  Restaurants 6

Grand Oriental 5
YMCA 2

Restaurants 🍴
Barista 1
Colombo Fort Café 2
Ministry of Crab 2

Pagoda 3
Seafish 4
Taj 5

Colombo 1	Fort	Colombo 9	Dermatagoda
Colombo 2	Slave Island	Colombo 10	Maradana
Colombo 3	Kollupitiya	Colombo 11	Pettah
Colombo 4	Bambalapitiya	Colombo 12	Hultsdorf
Colombo 5	Havelock Town	Colombo 13	Kotahena
Colombo 6	Wellawatta	Colombo 14	Grandpass
Colombo 7	Cinnamon Gardens	Colombo 15	Mutwal
Colombo 8	Borella		

The **Grand Oriental Hotel** is a good place to start a tour. Formerly the first port of call for all travellers arriving by steamship, it was once the finest hotel in Colombo. It used to be said that if you waited long enough in its hall, you would meet everyone worth meeting in the world. It is rather faded now, but you can get fascinating views of the harbour area from the hotel's third-floor restaurant. From here, **York Street**, Fort's main shopping area, runs due south, passing the brick-built colonial-era department stores of **Cargill's** and **Miller's**, and the government emporium **Laksala**.

To the east on Bristol Street is the central YMCA, next to the Moors Islamic Cultural Home. Across Duke Street is the Young Men's Buddhist Association. The shrine houses a noted modern image of the Buddha.

Sir Baron Jayatilleke Mawatha, once the main banking street, stretches west of York Street. Nearly all the buildings are in red brick. At the western end of Chatham Street to the south, past the Dutch period Fort mosque, is the **Lighthouse Clocktower**, now replaced as a lighthouse by the new tower on Chaithya Road. A modern clocktower (with Big Ben chimes) takes its place. The northern end of Janadhipathi Mawatha, which includes the **president's house** (*Janadhipathi Mandiraya*), is normally closed to the public.

Heading south along Janadhipathi Mawatha, a quite different, more vibrant Fort comes into view. The 1960s **Ceylon Continental Hotel** has magnificent views along the coast to Mount Lavinia, while on Bank of Ceylon Mawatha is Fort's modern day commercial hub: the twin steel and glass towers of the 39-floor **World Trade**

Bars & clubs 🍸
Ex-Servicemen's Institute 1

Barrier —

ON THE ROAD

Colombo harbour

Given Sri Lanka's historical reliance on trade, its harbours, of which Colombo is the most important, are a nerve centre of the economy. Colombo's success lay in its strategic position on the Indian Ocean sea route between Europe, the Far East and Australasia, almost equidistant between the Red Sea and the Straits of Malacca. Development did not begin until the late 19th century – the small promontory offered little protection for larger ships, so in 1875 the British started work on a series of breakwaters which were to provide an effective harbour all year round. By 1912, when the dockyard and fourth breakwater were completed, Colombo was considered one of the top seven harbours in the world.

Currently handling almost 4000 ships a year, today Colombo is at the forefront of plans to make Sri Lanka the shipping hub of South Asia. Having developed its container terminals in recent years and refurbished its passenger terminal in anticipation of establishing ferry links with India and the Maldives, the Sri Lankan Ports Authority is planning a new container terminal, the South Port, with 12 new berths and a new breakwater. The intention is to attract mega container vessels and double capacity within 20 years.

The best views of the harbour are offered at the Harbour Restaurant at the Grand Oriental Hotel.

Centre (1991), Sri Lanka's tallest building, along with some other high-rise offices. Close to the World Trade Centre is the beautifully restored ★ **Old Dutch Hospital**, believed to be the oldest building in Fort, dating back to the 1680s. Characterized by large teak beams, it has two airy courtyards and five wings that now house a collection of restaurants and shops – a great pit stop on your walking tour. Every effort has been made to maintain the character of the building. To the south, opposite the Galadari Hotel, the colonial **Old Parliament House** is now used as the president's secretariat.

★ The Pettah

To the north and east of Fort Station is a busy market area with stalls lining Olcott Mawatha and Bodhiraja Mawatha, making pedestrian movement slow and tedious at times. The central area of the Pettah, with many wholesale outlets, bounded by these two roads as well as Main Street and Front Street, is frantic, dirty and noisy, the cries of the traders mingling with the endless traffic horns. It is fascinating and enervating in equal measure. Specialist streets house craftsmen and traders such as goldsmiths (Sea Street), fruit and vegetable dealers (the end of Main Street) and Ayurvedic herbs and medicines (Gabo's Lane). Arabs, Portuguese, Dutch and British once traded in the market area to the north. Today, most of the traders are Tamil or Muslim, as evidenced by the many *kovils* and mosques. Halfway along Main Street, on the left-hand side after 2nd Cross Street, is the **Jami-ul-Alfar Mosque** with its interesting white-and-red brick.

Also in the Pettah are three modest Hindu temples, of little architectural interest, but giving an insight into Hindu building style and worship. Perhaps the most striking is that of **Sri Ponnambula Vanesvara** at 38 Sri Ramanathan Road. The *gopuram* (gateway) has

BACKGROUND
Colombo

Sheltered from the southwest monsoon by a barely perceptible promontory jutting out into the sea, Colombo's bay was an important site for Muslim traders long before the colonial period. Its name derives from 'Kotomtota', or port to the kingdom of Kotte, which was founded in 1369, close to present-day Sri Jayawardenepura Kotte (see page 58).

However, despite its long history, Colombo is essentially a colonial city. Soon after arrival in Sri Lanka, the Portuguese set up a fortified trading post in modern-day Fort, captured in 1656 by the Dutch. The canals constructed to link up the coastal lagoons are a lasting legacy, as well as the churches and mansions of the Pettah, Kotahena and Hultsdorf. Colombo's rise to pre-eminence began in earnest in the 19th century with the establishment of British power. When the British took control of Kandy and encouraged the development of commercial estates, the island's economic centre of gravity moved north, thereby lessening the importance of Galle as the major port. Colombo became the banking and commercial hub and benefited from its focal position on the rapidly expanding transport system within the island. From 1832 the British encouraged the development of a road network which radiated out from Colombo. In the late 19th century this was augmented by an expanding rail network. Since independence Colombo has retained its dominant position.

typical sculptures of gods from the Hindu pantheon. A Shiva lingam is in the innermost shrine, with a Nandi bull in front and a dancing Shiva (*Nataraja*) to one side.

Dutch Period Museum ⓘ *Prince St, T011-244 8466. Tue-Sat 0900-1700, Rs 500, children Rs 300, camera Rs 250.* Located about 100 m northeast of Fort Railway Station at the southwestern edge of the Pettah, the museum was originally the residence of the Dutch governor, Thomas van Rhee (1692-1697). It was sold to the VOC (Vereenigde Oostindische Compagnie or Dutch East India Company) before becoming the Colombo seminary in 1696. Then, in 1796, it was handed over to the British, who turned it into a military hospital and later a post office. It has now been restored and offers a fascinating insight into the Dutch period. The museum surrounds a garden courtyard and has various rooms dedicated to different aspects of Dutch life including some interesting old tombstones. Upstairs, several rooms display Dutch period furniture.

Kotahena

At the eastern end of Main Street, Mohamed Zain Mawatha (once Central Road) goes east from a large roundabout into **Kotahena**. A left turn off Mohamed Zain Mawatha immediately after the roundabout leads to a right fork, Ratnajothi Saravana Mawatha (formerly Wolfendahl Street). At the end (about 500 m) is the **Wolfendahl Church**. Built in 1749 on the site of an earlier Portuguese church, it is prominently placed on a hill, where its massive cruciform shape stands out, commanding a view over the harbour. Its Doric façade is solid and heavy, and inside there are many tombstones and memorial tablets to Dutch officials. It is the most interesting surviving Dutch monument in Sri Lanka.

BACKGROUND
Slave Island

The high-rise hotels and offices that occupy the peninsula in Beira Lake that faces Fort show no trace of its earlier use as 'Slave Island'. 'Island' was a misnomer, but slaves played a very real part in the colonial history of Colombo.

During the Dutch period this tongue of open land was known as Kaffir Veldt. The Kaffirs – Africans from the East Coast around Mozambique – were brought to Sri Lanka for the first time by the Portuguese from Goa in 1630. When the Dutch ousted the Portuguese they made use of the slave labour force to build the fort in Colombo, when there may have been 4000 of them. Their numbers grew, but after an unsuccessful insurrection in the 18th century the Dutch authorities decided to insist that all slave labour must be identifiably accommodated. The Kaffir Veldt was the nearest open space on which special shanty houses could be built, and a nightly roll call would be held to ensure that every slave was there.

By 1807, the number of slaves had fallen to 700, though the British did not abolish slavery in Sri Lanka until 1845, and the name Slave Island has persisted until the present day.

Some 200 m to the south in New Moor Street is the **Grand Mosque**, a modern building in the style, as one critic put it, of a "modern international airport covered in metallic paint".

About 1 km to its northeast is **Santa Lucia**, the Roman Catholic cathedral, in some people's eyes the most remarkable church building in Sri Lanka. It is a huge grey structure with a classical façade and a large forecourt, begun in 1876, and completed in 1910. Inside are the tombs of three French bishops but little else of interest. The Pope conducted a service here during his visit in 1994. **Christ Church**, the Anglican cathedral back towards the harbour, is a kilometre northwest of here and is the main church in a diocese that dates from 1845.

Galle Face, Union Place and Beira Lake

Heading south from Fort past the **Ceylon Continental Hotel** and Old Parliament, you reach **Galle Face Green**, to the south of the mouth of the canal feeding Beira Lake. Originally laid out

Tip...
Be on your guard for pickpockets and touts, especially at night when the whole area comes alive.

in 1859, the area has been redeveloped and is green once more, making it a pleasant place to wander and relax; it's very popular with Sri Lankans. There are lots of food stalls and hawkers selling knick-knacks, kites and children's toys. **Speaker's Corner** is at its southwestern corner opposite the historic ★ Galle Face Hotel (see page 60).

Cross Galle Road and then the canal to reach **Slave Island** (see box, above). On Kew Street, near the **Nippon Hotel**, city tours often visit the **Sri Shiva Subharamaniya Kovil**, with its enormous colourful *gopuram*.

Beira Lake Along Sir James Pieris Mawatha to the south is the pea-green **Beira Lake**, where the endangered spot-billed pelican can be seen. A pavement leads some of the way around the lake, and there's an important commercial zone at its northern end, along Navam Mawatha, with some restaurants and bars. It is possible to hire out a **swan pedalo** ⓘ *Rs 100, children Rs 50 for 30 mins*, for a trip around a section of the lake. On the eastern side, jetties lead to two tiny islands: one is a park; the other has the tranquil **Seema Malakaya Temple**, designed for meditation by Geoffrey Bawa, with various Buddha statues. The island temple is administered by the Gangaramaya Temple (see below).

★**Gangaramaya Temple** ⓘ *61 Sri Jinarathana, Rs 600 for a joint ticket for both Gangaramaya and Seema Malakaya temples.* Located to the east of the lake, this atmospheric temple from 1885 has an interesting selection of rare curios, including an impressive set of gold Buddhas and some intricate carved ivory on show. There is a sacred bodhi tree, many large Buddha statues and a welcoming atmosphere. You might also see the temple elephant shackled up in the grounds. The temple comes alive during the Navam Perahera in January.

③ Galle Face & Union Place

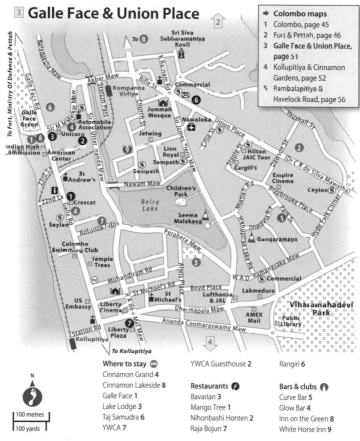

→ Colombo maps
1 Colombo, page 45
2 Fort & Pettah, page 46
3 Galle Face & Union Place, page 51
4 Kollupitiya & Cinnamon Gardens, page 52
5 Bambalapitiya & Havelock Road, page 56

Where to stay
Cinnamon Grand **4**
Cinnamon Lakeside **8**
Galle Face **1**
Lake Lodge **3**
Taj Samudra **6**
YWCA **7**

YWCA Guesthouse **2**

Restaurants
Bavarian **3**
Mango Tree **1**
Nihonbashi Honten **2**
Raja Bojun **7**

Rangiri **6**

Bars & clubs
Curve Bar **5**
Glow Bar **4**
Inn on the Green **8**
White Horse Inn **9**

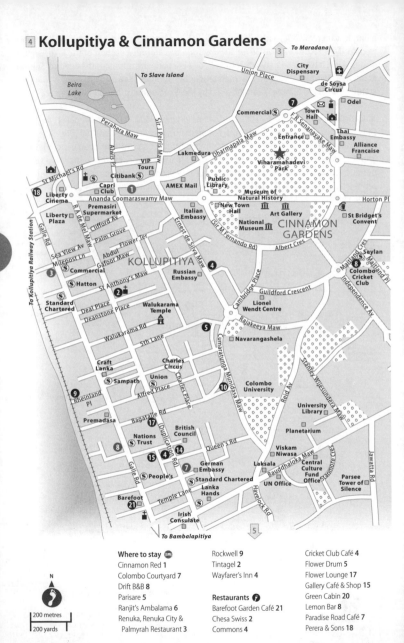

4 Kollupitiya & Cinnamon Gardens

Where to stay 🏨
Cinnamon Red 1
Colombo Courtyard 7
Drift B&B 8
Parisare 5
Ranjit's Ambalama 6
Renuka, Renuka City &
  Palmyrah Restaurant 3
Rockwell 9
Tintagel 2
Wayfarer's Inn 4

Restaurants 🍴
Barefoot Garden Café 21
Chesa Swiss 2
Commons 4
Cricket Club Café 4
Flower Drum 5
Flower Lounge 17
Gallery Café & Shop 15
Green Cabin 20
Lemon Bar 8
Paradise Road Café 7
Perera & Sons 18

Map labels

Colombo General Hospital

Norris Canal

Gnanartha Pradeepaya

Kynsey Rd

St Luke's Church

Cross Rd

Ward Place (CWW K Maw)

Seylan

wegian Embassy

Laundromat **2** **4** French Embassy **5**

Commercial

Rosmead Place

Malaysian Embassy

Carthy

Wijerama Mawatha

South African High Commission

Barnes Pl

YMBA

BORELLA

dish ssy Czech & Slovak Embassy

German Cultural Institute

Australian Embassy

Swiss Embassy

Gregory's Rd

Kynsey Rd

Japanese Embassy

National Cricket Ground

Gregory's Av

SSC

British High Commission

All Ceylon Buddhist Congress & Bookshop

ependence morial Hall

Kelaniya Rajamah a Vihara

Baudhaloka Maw

Otter's Aquatic Club

Aukana Buddha Replica

Anglican Cathedral

"e Gautama Vihoa, Sri Jayawardenepura Kotte

Elvitigala Maw

Bandaranaike Memorial International Conference Hall & Museum

Dutch Embassy CR & FC Ground

Kumaratunga Rd

Sarana Rd

Torrington Av

Thimbirigasyaya Rd

Kollupitiya, Cinnamon Gardens and the museums

On block inland from, and parallel with, Galle Road, R A de Mel Mawatha (formerly Duplication Road), runs all the way south through Kollupitiya and Bambalapitiya. These areas have some of Colombo's best shopping, with upmarket boutiques, notably **Barefoot**, see page 70. Wealthy locals also flock to the numerous excellent restaurants.

East of Kollupitiya station, Ananda Coomaraswamy Mawatha leads to the most prestigious residential area of Colombo, **Cinnamon Gardens** (widely referred to by its postcode, Colombo 7), where cinnamon trees used to grow during colonial times. Broad roads and shaded avenues make it a very attractive area, more reminiscent of Singapore than South Asia, though an increasing number of offices and government buildings have moved here in recent years from Fort. The white cupola of the impressive **Town Hall** stands out on Kannangara Mawatha. It was completed in 1927. Nearby, at the De Soysa Circus roundabout, is an equally interesting red-brick building, the **Victoria Memorial Rooms**, built in 1903.

In **Borella**, the suburb east of Cinnamon Gardens, the modest shrine room of the **Gautama (Gotami) Vihara** contains impressive modern murals depicting the life of the Buddha by the Sri Lankan artist George Keyt, painted in 1939-1940.

★ **Vihara Mahadevi Park** ① *Approach from the northeast, opposite the Town Hall, daily 0600-1800.* The centrepiece of Cinnamon Gardens, with the museums and art gallery to its south, is this attractive park, re-named after the mother of King Dutthagamenu. Early morning is an excellent time to visit. In the southwest is a **botanical garden** with a range of tropical trees, including a Bo tree, plus ebony, mahogany, *sal* and lemon eucalyptus, which attract a wide variety of birds. There is also an enormous profusion of climbing and parasitic plants as well as rare orchids. The park is particularly colourful in the spring. You may catch sight of elephants being bathed in the water tank to the southwest.

A series of rectangular lakes to the east of the park leads to a golden statue of the seated Buddha.

Colombo National Museum ⓘ *8 Marcus Fernando Mawatha (Albert Crescent), T011-269 4768, daily 0900-1800 (last entry 1700), closed public holidays. Note that some sections were closed for restoration work in early 2016 (Prehistory, Anuradhapura, Coins & currency, Arms & armory). Rs 500, children Rs 300, cameras Rs 250, video cameras Rs 2000.* The museum's imposing façade is fronted by a statue of Sir William Gregory, governor 1872-1877. Opened in 1877, it has a good collection of paintings, sculptures, furniture, porcelain and Kandyan regalia, all very well labelled and organized, making a visit here an excellent introduction to a tour of Sri Lanka. Exhibits include an outstanding collection of 10th- to 12th-century bronzes from Polonnaruwa and the lion throne of King Nissankamalla, which has become the symbol of Sri Lanka. The library houses an extremely rich archaeological and artistic collection of over 4000 *ola* (palm manuscripts). There are interesting details and curiosities too: the origin of *kolam* dancing, for example, is traced back to the pregnancy craving of the Queen of the legendary King Maha Samnatha. The ground floor displays Buddhist and Hindu sculptures, including a striking 1500-year-old stone statue of the Buddha from Toluvila. 'Demon dance' masks line the stairs to the first floor. One visitor noted: "These are more 'satire' than 'demon' in nature, with lots of characters of court officials, soldiers and 'outsiders' such as Muslims. Some were very elaborate and capable of moving their eyes, etc. It is interesting to see how these evolved as different fashions swept the court." The first floor has superb scale reproductions of the wall paintings at Sigiriya and Polonnaruwa. Other exhibits include ancient jewellery and carvings in ivory and wood.

Natural History Museum ⓘ *Entered via the National Museum or from A Coomeraswamy Mawatha, T011-269 4767, daily 0900-1800 (last entry 1700), closed public holidays. Rs 300, children Rs 150, cameras Rs 250, video cameras Rs 2000.* A Victorian-style array of ageing stuffed animals and lizards are preserved in formaldehyde, although the scope is quite impressive. The 'applied botany' section introduces visitors to Sri Lanka's rubber, timber, coconut (note the 13 different types) and tea industries, while there is also a collection of fossils found in Sri Lanka dating back to the Pleistocene Age.

> **Tip...**
> The National Art Gallery, next door to the Natural History Museum, is a one-room collection by Sri Lankan artists and is somewhat disappointing.

Lionel Wendt Centre ⓘ *19 Guildford Cres, Mon-Fri 0900-1245 and 1400-1700, Sat-Sun 1000-1200 and 1400-1700.* This registered charity fosters the arts in Sri Lanka. Local artists are supported with temporary exhibitions, while there is a permanent exhibition of Wendt's pictures. Plays and dance recitals are also performed here.

Bandaranaike Museum ① *Bauddhaloka Mawatha, Tue-Sun 0900-1600, closed* poya *holidays*. A well-presented museum is housed inside the massive and imposing Bandaranaike Memorial International Conference Hall (BMICH), built by the Chinese government. As well as commemorating the life and times of the assassinated prime minister with some interesting letters, diaries and personal effects on display, it offers a useful insight into Sri Lanka's steps into post-colonial nationhood. Opposite the BMICH is a replica statue of the Aukana Buddha.

South of the centre

shopping malls, Buddhist temples and beachside suburbs

Bambalapitiya and Havelock Town

South of Kollupitiya, Bambalapitiya extends south along Galle Road. This is a busy shopping area with two popular indoor malls at Majestic City and Liberty Plaza and some enticing eateries but few interesting sights. That said, the **Vajirarama Temple**, whose missionary monks have taken Buddhism to the west, is worth a look. To the east, **Havelock Road,** another traffic-filled thoroughfare lined with some more excellent restaurants, stretches south to Havelock Town. The **Isipathanaramaya Temple**, just north of Havelock Park, is famous for its beautiful frescoes.

Wellawatta and Dehiwala

South of Bambalapitiya, Wellawatta is the last busy suburb within the city limits. Home to many of Colombo's Tamils (and sometimes called 'Little Jaffna' as a result), it has a bustling charm far removed from the pretensions of wealthier suburbs further north.

Near the bazaar of Dehiwala, the **Subbodaramaya Temple** is a Buddhist complex with a shrine room dating from 1795. The temple has the usual *dagoba*, a Bo-tree and also a 'Seven-Week House' which illustrates the weeks following the Buddha's Enlightenment. There are several Buddha statues and some well-preserved wall paintings and woodcarvings, but the most arresting figure is the supremely serene 4.5-m reclining Buddha with eyes set in blue sapphires.

Dehiwala Zoo ① *A Dharmapala Mawatha (Allan Av), 10 km southeast of the centre, T011-271 2752, daily 0830-1800, Rs 2000, children Rs 1000, Rs 250, video camera Rs 2000. Getting there: train or buses 100 or 155 to Dehiwala Junction and walk the last km or bus 118 direct.* The 22 ha of undulating grounds are beautifully laid out with shrubs, flowering trees and plants, orchids, lakes and fountains. There are more than 3000 animals from all around the world, including big cats, crocodiles, bears and so on, although the zoo is particularly noted for its collection of birds, with a large walk-in aviary for Sri Lankan species. The aquarium has over 500 species of fish. Sea-lions perform at 1600, and a troupe of trained elephants, around 1715. By Asian standards, the animals are well housed, though some, such as the big cats, have insufficient space. A new 15-ha site is planned near the Pinnawela Elephant Orphanage (see page 199). Note that the zoo is often very crowded during holidays and at weekends.

Mount Lavinia *12 km south of Fort. Many travellers choose to explore the city from here.*
The former fishing village of Mount Lavinia is a pleasant place to stay for those put off by the noise and congestion of the city, although the drive along the busy Galle Road

scarcely marks Mount Lavinia apart from the rest of Colombo. Many visitors come seeking to recapture the atmosphere of 19th-century British Colombo at the famous **Mount Lavinia Hotel**, founded on a headland here in 1806 by the British governor, Sir Thomas Maitland. Some believe Mount Lavinia takes its name from a corruption of the Sinhalese '*Lihinia Kanda*' (Gull Rock), but another theory suggests the area is named

5 Bambalapitiya & Havelock Road

Colombo maps
1 Colombo, page 45
2 Fort & Pettah, page 46
3 Galle Face & Union Place, page 51
4 Kollupitiya & Cinnamon Gardens, page 52
5 Bambalapitiya & Havelock Road, page 56

Where to stay
Casa Colombo 1
Havelock Place Bungalow 5
Janaki 4
Ottery Tourist Inn 2
Relax-On 3

Westeern 6

Restaurants
Beach Wadiya 1
Chinese Dragon 11
Curry Bowl & Perera 13

Hotel de Majestic 12
Kinjou 16
Majesty City International
Food Hall 2
Mathura Madras
Woodlands 4

Bars & clubs
Frangipani 6

Mount Lavinia

after Lovina, an exotic and beautiful dancer of mixed Portuguese and Sinhalese race, who was the governor's secret lover. It is said that Maitland established the hotel as a place for himself and Lovinia to meet, and that for seven years she trysted secretly with him by creeping through a tunnel connecting her garden to Maitland's wine cellar! Later, the Mount Lavinia Hotel became Governor Edward Barnes' weekend retreat. He had the bungalow significantly extended in the 1820s ('Governor's Wing'), but was forced to sell it as the government in England disapproved of his expenditure and his luxurious lifestyle.

Mount Lavinia is famous for its 'golden mile' of beach, from which the high-rise buildings of central Colombo are easily visible. The attractive colonial villas and lovely scent of frangipani and bougainvillea, however, mask a slightly seedier side. Theft is more common here than elsewhere, so if you're visiting the beach do not take anything valuable with you, and beware walking around at night after the restaurants have closed.

The beach itself is cleanest south of **Mount Lavinia Hotel**, where it is 'private' for the use of the hotel residents only, although non-residents can pay for access as well as use of the pool. North of the hotel, it gets rather narrow and has a noticeable amount of litter especially at weekends and holidays. There are a number of bars/restaurants here, mostly run by the hotels immediately behind them.

Hotels close to the beach are also close to the railway line, with trains passing at regular intervals from early morning to late at night, invariably using their horns to alert pedestrians on the track. Take care when crossing the railway en route to the beach.

Kelaniya

13 km northeast of Fort. Getting there: Biyagama bus from Bastion Mawatha every 30 mins, journey time 20-30 mins.

Northeast of the city, across the Kelaniya River, is the **Raja Maha Vihara**, the most visited Buddhist temple in Sri Lanka after the Temple of the Tooth in Kandy. In the 13th century Kelaniya was an impressive city, but its chief attraction for Buddhists is the legendary visit of the Buddha to the site. The *Mahavansa* recorded that the original stupa enshrined a gem-studded throne on which the Buddha sat when he visited Sri Lanka. Ultimately destroyed by the Portuguese, the present *dagoba* is in the shape of a 'heap of paddy'. The first city on the site was believed to have been built by King Yatala Tissa. According to legend this was destroyed by a flood from the sea which was a punishment given to the king for mistreating the Buddhist *sangha*. He tried to placate the sea by setting his daughter afloat on a golden boat. Having drifted ashore in the south of the island, she married King Kavan Tissa and became the mother of one of Sri Lanka's great heroes, King Dutthagamenu. The city is subsequently believed to have been destroyed by Tamil invasions and was only re-built in the 13th century by King Vijayabahu.

The present temple, which dates from the late 19th century, is set amongst attractive frangipani trees and has an impressive bell tower. There is a famous image of the reclining Buddha, but there are also many images of Hindu deities. Each January, **Duruthu Perahera** draws thousands of pilgrims from all over the island.

Sri Jayawardenepura Kotte

11 km southeast of Colombo (30-min drive from Fort). Buses and 3-wheelers available.

Although Colombo still retains its importance as the commercial capital of Sri Lanka, most government offices have relocated to this new artificially planned capital, built in the shadow of the modern city. The decision to put the new parliament building here was influenced by Kotte's historical and almost sacred significance as the ancient capital of Sri Lanka. Alakeswara built a large fortress here in the 13th century and defeated the Tamil leader Chakravarthi. Parakramabahu VI (ruled 1412-1467) transformed the fortress into a prosperous city, building a magnificent three-storey temple to hold the Tooth relic, which he had placed within several bejewelled gold caskets. However, subsequent weak rulers left the city relatively defenceless, and it fell easy prey to the Portuguese. They destroyed the city, so that there are no traces of its former glory left apart from some panels from the old temple, which can be seen in the National Museum (see above).

The impressive **Parliament Building** itself was designed by the renowned modern Sri Lankan architect Geoffrey Bawa. It stands in the middle of a lake surrounded by parkland but is not open to the public.

The **Gramodaya Folk Arts Centre** has craftsmen working with brass, silver, leather, coir to produce jewellery, pottery, natural silk, lace and reed baskets. There is a craft shop and a restaurant serving Sri Lankan specialities. Ask the tourist office for details.

Tourist information

Travel Lanka is a free monthly tourist guide available at larger tourist offices and in major hotels. It has some useful information and listings for Colombo and the main tourist areas, though much is out of date. If the copy on display in the tourist office is months out of date, ask for the more recent edition; it's usually tucked away in a cupboard. *Time Out Sri Lanka* is available free around the city (Barefoot is a good place to pick it up). A useful online resource for tourists is yamu.lk with current happenings, restaurant reviews and more.

Sri Lanka Tourist Board
80 Galle Rd, Col 3, T011-242 6900, www.srilanka. travel. Mon-Fri 0830-1615, Sat 0830-1230.
Free literature in English (and some in German, French, Italian, Swedish and Japanese), though not much information on transport. Guides can be arranged here. Note that Cultural Triangle tickets are not sold here, and are best bought at the sites themselves. There is also an information counter at Bandaranaike Airport.

Railway Tourist Office
Fort Station, Col 11, T011-244 0048.
Friendly advice to anyone planning a rail journey. Staff will suggest an itinerary, book train tickets and hotels, and arrange a car with driver. It is better to visit in person than on the phone. Some visitors may find the sales techniques a little pushy. Special steam train excursions are offered on the *Viceroy Special* (usually groups of 30 are required for a 2-day 1-night trip to Kandy).

Where to stay

There are some very high-quality hotels, mainly in Fort, Galle Face and Cinnamon Gardens, with luxurious rooms, 1st-class service, several restaurants, pool(s), bars, nightclub, etc. Good-quality mid-range accommodation is rather thin on the ground and decent budget options are almost non-existent. Booking in advance is recommended. Many hotels and guesthouses offer airport transfers, but there are also hotels close to the airport itself (see page 63).

Fort area and the Pettah
There are several $ hotels around Fort Railway Station though they are very basic.

$$$$ Colombo Hilton
2 Sir Chittampalam A Gardiner Mawatha, Col 2, T011-249 2492, www3.hilton.com.
387 rooms, best views in the city, all facilities including 6 restaurants, 4 bars, pool, Wi-Fi,

leisure centre. There is another Hilton hotel, the **Colombo Residence** (200 Union Pl, T011-534 4644), which is smaller and popular with families.

$$$ Grand Oriental
2 York St, Col 1, T011-232 0320, www.grandoriental.com.
Iconic and charmingly faded colonial-era hotel built to accommodate travellers arriving by sea. (It was once advertized as "the largest and best equipped hotel in the East.") Fascinating view of the docks from **Harbour Room** restaurant (no photos), good food, nightclub, friendly staff, good location.

Galle Face, Union Place and Beira Lake

$$$$-$$$ Cinnamon Grand
77 Galle Rd, Col 3, T011-243 7437, www.cinnamonhotels.com.
Popular hotel with over 500 rooms and suites in 2 wings, 8 restaurants, and direct access to Crescat Mall. Beautiful open spaces, all facilities, good pool. Also check out **Cinnamon Lakeside**.

$$$$-$$$ Galle Face Hotel
2 Galle Rd, Col 3, T011-254 0101, www.gallefacehotel.com.
Originally built in 1864 and re-designed by Geoffrey Bawa, this is probably the most atmospheric place to stay in Colombo. Room price varies and there are 2 wings, Regency and Classic. Avoid rooms overlooking Galle Rd, as these can be very noisy. Carefully maintained colonial atmosphere, with beautiful furniture. Friendly staff, "superb service", 30-m saltwater pool overlooking the Indian Ocean; the **Verandah** bar is the best in Colombo for a sunset drink. Very competent travel desk.

$$$$-$$$ Taj Samudra
25 Galle Face Centre Rd, Col 3, T011-244 6622, www.tajhotels.com.

Well situated overlooking Galle Face Green and the ocean, pleasant seating areas in the lobby, attractive gardens behind. Comfortable rooms; some with good views but opt for those that have been refurbished. Excellent food, nightclub, pool. There is another **Taj Hotel** by the airport.

$$$-$$ Lake Lodge
20 Alwis Terr, Col 3, T011-232 6443, www.taruhotels.com.
Boutique hotel offering 12 stylish a/c rooms in serene courtyard setting. Quiet, good food, rooftop terrace with lake views, Wi-Fi. Highly recommended.

$$ YWCA Guesthouse
393 Colvin R de Silva, Mw, T011-232 4181, www.ywcacolombo.com.
Beautiful old building dating back to 1913 with 9 spacious rooms and large verandas. Lovely heritage property. Recommended.

$ YWCA
7 Rotunda Garden, T011-232 3498, natywca@sltnet.lk.
The best are the large double rooms with balcony, but cheaper accommodation with shared bathroom is also available (Rs 550). Clean, very central, breakfast included in the price. Has an old-fashioned, institutional feel but good value. Couples accepted but no single men.

Kollupitiya, Cinnamon Gardens and Borella

$$$$ Colombo Courtyard
32 Alfred House Ave, Col 3, T011-464 5333, www.colombocourtyard.com.
Certified as a carbon-neutral hotel, this innovatively designed hotel has an eye on upcycling and sustainability. There are spacious rooms and beautiful art throughout; the **Cloud Café and Bar** are highly recommended.

$$$$ Tintagel
65 Rosemead Pl, Col 7, T460 2122,
www.tintagelcolombo.com.
This 10-room boutique hotel from the
owners of the **Paradise Road** franchise
(see Shopping, page 70), used to be the
home of the Bandaranaike family, a political
dynasty in Sri Lanka. SWRD Bandaranaike
was shot here in 1959. The suites are as
stylishly decorated as one would expect,
and each is individual. There is a restaurant
and bar, although the government has
not yet granted an alcohol licence (guests
can BYO), pool and free 3-wheeler to other
Paradise Road properties. Staff are excellent.
Highly recommended.

$$$ Cinnamon Red
59 Ananda Comaraswamy Mawatha, Col 3,
T011-214 5145
Exceptional budget offering from Cinnamon
chain with rooms from around US$80.
Stylish, contemporary feel right in the
heart of things. Recommended.

$$$ Renuka & Renuka City
328 Galle Rd, T011-257 3598,
www.renukahotel.com.
Twin hotels with 81 comfortable a/c rooms
aimed mainly at business travellers, with TV,
fridge and IDD phone. Small pool a short
walk away. Basement **Palmyrah** restaurant
recommended for Sri Lankan curries (see
Restaurants, page 65). Good location.

$$$-$$ Rockwell
14 Cross Rd, off Ward Pl, Borella, T071-273
9394, www.rockwellcolombo.com.
Smart property with good-sized rooms
and modern facilities, including gym and
a roof garden. Just outside the prestigious
Colombo 7 postcode.

$$ Parisare
97/1 Rosmead Pl, Col 7 (no sign, next to
UNHCR, ring on arrival), T011-269 4749,
sunsep@visualnet.lk.

Well-designed and beautiful house,
3 extremely good-value fan rooms, all with
attached bath, needs a bit of TLC. Great
central location and family-run feel.

$$ Wayfarer's Inn
77 Rosmead Pl, Col 7, T011-269 3936,
wayfarer@slt.lk.
Fan and a/c rooms with TV, tea-making
facilities and fridge, and studio with
kitchen facilities. Restaurant, garden,
table tennis, not as homely as other
guesthouses though.

$$-$ Drift Bed & Breakfast
646 Galle Rd, T011-250 5336,
driftbnb@gmail.com.
A bit of a gem in the heart of the city. Smart
rooms as well as dorm, good breakfasts and
friendly staff. Funky artwork throughout and
great central location – dangerously close to
the fantastic Barefoot café.

$$-$ Ranjit's Ambalama
53/19 Torrington Av, T011-250 2403,
www.ranjitsambalama.com.
7 rooms, some with shared bathroom and
6 with the option of a/c, in house with
pleasant terrace for breakfasts. Ask about
the owner's attractive 4-room bungalow
on edge of the city.

Bambalapitiya and Havelock Town

$$$$ Casa Colombo
231 Galle Rd, Col 4, T452 0130,
www.casacolombo.com.
Boutique hotel offering 12 spacious suites
in a 200-year-old mansion, ranging in size
and layout, and each individually decorated.
Stylish mix of old and new: colonial touches,
designer furniture, flatscreen TVs, free Wi-Fi,
etc. Attentive service, pool, spa, dining areas
and bar.

$$$ Havelock Place Bungalow
6/8 Havelock Pl, Col 5, T011-258 5191,
www.havelockbungalow.com.

Stylishly designed modern guesthouse.
3 suites and 4 standard rooms, simple,
beautiful individual furnishings, restaurant,
gardens, pool and jacuzzi. Homely and quiet.

$$$-$$ Janaki
43 Fife Rd, Col 5, T011-250 2169,
www.hoteljanakicolombo.com.
50 reasonable a/c rooms with TV and
balcony, pool and restaurant.

$$-$ Hotel Relax-on
28 Melbourne Av, Col 4, T011-255 4295,
info@relaxon.com.
Decent-sized rooms in good location, a/c
available. There is a restaurant on site too.

$$-$ Ottery Tourist Inn
29 Melbourne Av (off Galle Rd), Col 4, T011-
258 3727, www.ottery touristinn.com.
8 large rooms, some with balcony, in a colonial
building. Run-down but quiet location.

Wellawatta and Dehiwala

$$$ Sapphire
371 Galle Rd, Col 6, T011-236 3306,
www.hotelsapphirelk.com.
Ugly building but 40 comfortable a/c rooms,
attached bath, good rooftop Chinese
restaurant, pool.

$$-$ Chamenka Guest House
44 Pallidora Rd, Dehiwala, T077-905 5635,
www.chamenkaguesthouse.com.
Family-run guesthouse offering 4 rooms
with shared bathroom. Welcoming place.

Mount Lavinia
Note that some of the accommodation in
Mount Lavinia is very close to the railway
line, and although trains do not run all night
the early commuter services may disturb
light sleepers.

$$$$-$$$ Mount Lavinia
100 Hotel Rd, T011-271 1711, www.
mountlaviniahotel.com.

Renovated and extended former governors'
weekend retreat located on a small but
prominent headland retaining a rich
colonial atmosphere. 275 rooms and suites,
many with sea views. There is a range of
restaurants, terrace bar (good for sunset
drinks), nightclub (see Bars and clubs),
shopping arcade, sports (including tennis
and gym), elephant rides (Sun 1000-1400),
impressive terrace pool, peaceful private
beach (cleaner than public beach to the
north). Recommended.

$$$-$$ Mount Lodge Boutique Hotel
59 A Hotel Rd, T011-773 3313,
www.nisalaarana.com.
Chic rooms with artwork and plentiful
plants inside and throughout their beautiful
gardens – a stylish oasis in Mount Lavinia.
Management also run a stylish villa in coastal
Beonta, too. Recommended.

$$ Haus Chandra & Carrington Villa
37 Beach Rd, T011-527 3672,
www.plantation grouphotels.com.
27 small a/c and fan rooms, plus 4 suites
and 1 excellent **$$$** villa for 6 people.
Restaurant on the rooftop plus cheaper
food at **Boat Haus Café** on the beach.
Small but deep pool, chauffeur-driven
Rolls Royce available for hire. Ask about
excellent sister hotels in Kitulgala.

$$ Rivi Ras
50/2 De Saram Rd, T011-271 7731,
rivirasph@eureka.lk.
Rooms and suites, fan slightly cheaper, in
2-storey villas with verandas set in attractive
garden, excellent **La Langousterie** seafood
restaurant on beach.

$$ Tropic Inn
30 College Av, T011-273 8653,
www.tropicinn.com.
16 a/c rooms with hot water, sizes
vary so check first, breakfast included,
helpful management. Internet available.

$ Blue Seas Guest House
9/6 De Saram Rd, T011-271 6298.
Good clean rooms with a/c or fan (including breakfast), some with balconies, in family-run guesthouse. Quiet location, very friendly and helpful.

$ Colombo Beach Hostel
30 de Saram Rd, T777 871 393,
www.colombobeachhostel.com.
Excellent value double rooms in crisp beach colours – blue and white. There are good dorm rooms too at US$10 and a nice roof garden. Recommended.

$ Ivory Inn
21 De Saram Rd, T011-271 5006.
Reasonable fan and a/c rooms with balcony, attractive garden.

North and east of the city: close to the airport
Those arriving late or departing early may prefer to stay close to the international airport at Katunayake (30 km north of Colombo), where there is a Ramada as well as the options listed below. Another alternative is to stay at Negombo, some 6 km north of the airport, where the accommodation choice is much wider, see page 79.

$$$$ Wallawwa
Minuwangoda Rd, Kotugoda, T011-228 1050,
www.wallawwa.com.
Beautiful boutique property with 17 spacious suites and rooms. Lovely courtyard and swimming pool, reclining chairs on the veranda. Recommended.

$$$ Tamarind Tree
1 Andiambalama Estate, Yatiyana,
Minuwangoda (4 km from airport),
T0845-154 0490.
20 a/c rooms, 30 self-catering apartments, all a bit tired, and attractive gardens and good pool. Service can be iffy.

$$-$ Full Moon Garden Hotel
754 Colombo Rd, Katunayake, T011-226 0222,
www.avenragardenhotel.com.
30 a/c rooms that aren't up to much but close to the airport. Wi-Fi, restaurant, pool, friendly staff.

Restaurants

Colombo is fast garnering a reputation as a culinary capital within Asia. As well as Sri Lankan and Indian fare, many other types of Asian cuisine are available: Thai, Japanese, Korean and even Mongolian restaurants are popping up all over the place to add to the ubiquitous Chinese offering.

Some of the best speciality restaurants are to be found in the upper category hotels, which also serve good Western food. Their eat-all-you-want buffets are particularly recommended at lunchtime, where you have the added benefit of sitting in cool comfort during the hottest part of the day. American/European-style venues are also becoming increasingly popular, particularly the 'Irish' pub.

For those on a tighter budget, lunch packets (available from street stalls all over the city) are a good idea. These normally comprise rice plus a meat, fish or vegetable curry and cost Rs 100-150.

Fort area and the Pettah
There are lots of cheap 'rice and curry' places in Fort, the Pettah and along Galle Rd ($).

$$$ Colombo Fort Cafe
Old Dutch Hospital, T011-223 4946,
www.colombofortcafe.com.
Mediterranean tastes, Spanish tapas and Middle Eastern favourites at this lovely café in the beautifully restored Old Dutch Hospital. Great place to stop for a coffee too.

$$$ Harbour Room
Grand Oriental (see Where to stay, page 60).
Serves unexceptional food, but the views over the harbour are spectacular.

$$$ Il Ponte/Curry Leaf
Colombo Hilton (see Where to stay, page 59).
For 1st-class Italian and Sri Lankan cuisine.

$$$ Ministry of Crab
Old Dutch Hospital, T011-234 2722, www.ministryofcrab.com
Bookings are essential at this amazing restaurant: imagine all the things you can do with a crab and then some. Great location in the beautifully renovated Old Dutch Hospital. Highly recommended.

$$ Seafish
15 Sir CA Gardiner Mawatha, just behind Regal Cinema, Col 2, T011-232 6915.
Excellent fish at reasonable prices, hoppers with curry (evenings).

$ Pagoda
Chatham St, Col 1.
Offers good-value Chinese plus Sri Lankan and Western.

$ Shakthi
YMCA, 39 Bristol St (see Where to stay).
Very cheap authentic Sri Lankan food, self-service.

$ Taj
54 York St, T011-242 2812.
Popular with local office workers at lunchtime, cheap rice and curry, *kotthu rotty*, short eats, a/c upstairs.

Galle Face, Union Place and Beira Lake
City dwellers take in the sea air on Galle Face Green while tucking into food from the street vendors.

$$$ Golden Dragon
Taj Samudra (see Where to stay, page 60).
Daily 1900-2330.
Excellent Chinese.

$$$ Nihonbashi Honten
11 Galle Face Terr, Col 3, T011-232 3847.
Daily 1200-1430, 1800-2230.
The best Japanese food in Colombo. There are set menus and fusion dishes, as well as sushi and sashimi. The menu is provided on an iPad. Highly recommended.

$$$ Sea Spray
Galle Face Hotel (see Where to stay, page 50).
Good seafood and Western dishes in one of the city's most atmospheric locations.

$$ 7 Degrees North
Cinnamon Lakeside (see Where to stay, page 60).
Tapas and cocktails overlooking the lake, or Mediterranean cuisine by the pool. Live music at weekends, good atmosphere.

$$ Chutneys
Cinnamon Grand (see Where to stay, page 60).
Excellent South Indian food, with the dishes on the menu separated into regions. Helpful and friendly staff.

$$ Raja Bojun
Liberty Arcade, Col 3, T471 6171.
Daily 1200-2300.
Excellent Sri Lankan buffet overlooking the ocean. Huge variety, reasonably priced.

$ Crescat Food Court
Crescat shopping mall (next to Cinnamon Grand).
Not the most authentic surroundings (self-service in Western-style shopping mall basement) but a good way to sample a wide range of Asian cuisines, notably the great South Indian food at Mango Tree. Wi-Fi available.

$ Rangiri
67 Union Pl, Col 2.
Eye-watering but tasty Sri Lankan curry plus full range of *sambols*. Friendly and popular with locals.

Kollupitiya, Cinnamon Gardens and Borella

$$$ Chesa Swiss
3 Deal Pl, off RA de Mel Mawatha, Col 3, T011-257 3433. Daily 1900-2300, closed poya days.
Excellent Swiss food, though at a price.

$$$ Gallery Café
2 Alfred House Rd, Col 3, T011-258 2162, www.paradiseroad.lk. Daily 1000-2400.
The quintessential Colombo experience – stylish restaurant, inspiring artwork and delicious food. Once the office of famed Sri Lankan architect Geoffrey Bawa; his old work table is still there. Exclusive setting with unbeatable ambience, minimalist chic decor, good fusion food, fabulous desserts and cakes, excellent wine list. Book in advance.

$$$ Lemon Bar
41 Maitland Cres, Col 7, T011-268 2122. Daily 1700-2400.
A rooftop restaurant with great atmosphere, serving interesting and tasty international cuisine. **Silk** nightclub is downstairs, see page 68.

$$$-$$ Cricket Club Café
34 Queen's Rd (near British Council), Col 3, 1011-250 1384. Daily 1100-2300.
International range of dishes, many named after famous cricketers (such as Murali's Mulligatawny or Gatting's Garlic Prawns), served in a cricket-lover's heaven, though it shows other sports on TV too. Local and touring teams usually visit. Good bar popular with expats. Food is pub fare at restaurant prices.

$$$-$$ Palmyrah
Hotel Renuka (see Where to stay, page 61). Daily 0700-1430, 1900-2200.
Widely praised for its Sri Lankan food and Jaffna specialties, it also serves Western and South Indian dishes. Attentive service, popular, try the hoppers. Recommended.

$$ Barefoot Garden Café
706 Galle Rd, Col 3, T011-255 3075. Daily 1000-1900.
Wonderfully chic terrace café serving delicious lunches, quiches, sandwiches and cakes in frangipani gardens. It has a fantastic gallery and extensive homewares, textiles and bookshop (see Shopping). Most Sun there is live jazz.

$$ Flower Drum
26 Thurstan Rd, Col 3, T011-257 4811, www.flowerdrum.net.
Excellent Chinese, extensive choice, quiet atmosphere, reasonable prices. They have another branch, **Flower Lounge**, on Bagatelle Rd in Col 3.

$$ Green Cabin
453 Galle Rd, Col 3, T011-258 8811. Daily 1000-2300.
Good-value authentic Sri Lankan food (curry and string hoppers) in pleasant surroundings. Lunchtime buffet, cakes and snacks for sale in the front area. Devilled dishes are particularly good. Recommended by every ex-pat you meet.

$$ Sakura
14 Rheinland Pl, Col 3, T011-257 3877. Daily 1130-1400, 1730-2400.
Good food in what was Colombo's 1st Japanese restaurant, reasonably priced.

$ Raffles
35 Bagatalle Rd, Col 03, T011-576 7814, www.rafflescolombo.com.
Good range of Western and Sri Lankan food in tasteful surroundings. Staff are attentive and professional. Lunch buffet available.

Cafés

The Commons
39A Ernest de Silva Mawatha, T011-269 4435. Sun-Thu 1000-2200, Fri-Sat 1100-2400.
Flavoured coffees (excellent frappuccinos), juices and snacks (bagels, burgers, wraps, etc).

Paradise Road Café
213 Dharmapala Mawatha, Col 7,
T011-268 6043. Daily 1000-1900.
Beautiful old colonial mansion open daytime
for light meals and drinks. Serves great
coffee, good fishcakes and a hearty burger,
as well as indulgent cakes.

Perera & Sons
24 Deal Pl, Col 3, T011-232 3295.
Cakes, snacks, breads, mainly takeaway
but some tables. Other branches around
the city: 2 Dharmapala Mawatha; off
Pieris Maw, Col 2, and on Havelock Rd.

Bambalapitiya and Havelock Town

$$ Chinese Dragon
11 Milagiriya Av, Col 4, T011-250 3637.
Daily 1100-1500, 1800-2300.
Long-established local favourite, outside
barbecues as well. There are also branches
in the Fort and Mount Lavinia.

$$ International Food Hall
Majestic City (basement), Bambalapitiya,
Col 4.
Great place to try out a range of
different cuisines.

$$ Kinjou
33 Amarasekera Mawatha (off Havelock
Rd), Col 5, T011-258 9477. Daily 1145-1430,
1830-2300.
Good Szechuan cooking in vibey restaurant
with a bit of Chinese kitsch.

$ Hotel de Majestic
17 Galle Rd, Col 4 (opposite Majestic City),
T011-720 3200.
String hoppers and superb Pakistani and
Singaporean curries.

$ Mathura Madras Woodlands
185 Havelock Rd, Col 5, T011-258 2909.
Daily 1100-2300.
A/c, choice of good North and South Indian
cuisine, good value lunch-time buffets.

Wellawatta and Dehiwala

$$$ Beach Wadiya
2 Station Av, Col 6, T011-258 8568 (see map,
page 56). Daily 1200-2300.
Very popular beachside seafood restaurant,
well-stocked bar, rustic surroundings, good
food but small portions and service can be
slow. Book in advance.

$$$ Shanmugas
53/3 Ramakrishna Rd, Col 6, near Roxy
Cinema, T011-236 1384. Daily 1100-2200.
Excellent South Indian vegetarian
restaurant boasting 15 varieties of *dosai*,
plus some North Indian specialities, civilized
atmosphere, close to beach. Great buffet
on Sun and *poya* days. Recommended:
considered by many as the best veggie
spot in town.

$ Curry Bowl
1 Ratnekore Rd, Dehiwala, T011-257 5157.
Daily 1000-2200.
Incredibly popular restaurant, come early
otherwise they run out of dishes. *Dosai* and
string hoppers, **Perera** bakers attached,
takeaway available.

$ Saravana Bhavan
183 Galle Rd, T011-271 8197.
Excellent South Indian chain restaurant
found across India has a home in Dehiwala –
great *dosa*, Malabar *paranthas* and thalis.

Mount Lavinia
Most hotels and guesthouses in
Mount Lavinia have a restaurant, though
many serve fairly bland food. Breakfast
is often included. For a change, head for
the beach shacks which are open all day.
Seafood is, naturally enough, the speciality.
Restaurants on the beach tend to be quite
expensive, but the views at sunset are
magnificent. Live music at weekends.

$$$ La Rambla
69 Hotel Rd, T011-272 5403.
Tastefully decorated restaurant serving
good-quality seafood and Mediterranean
cuisine, desserts are a bit disappointing.

$$$ Lavinia Breeze
*43/7 De Alwis Av, off De Saram Rd,
T077-321 5951, www.laviniabreeze.lk.*
Raised covered eating area and candlelit
tables in the sand in the evening with live
music at weekends. Seafood and international
dishes, platters are especially good.

$$$ Seafood Cove
*Mount Lavina Hotel (see Where to stay,
page 62).*
Excellent seafood in great beachside
position. Recommended.

$$ La Langousterie
Rivi Ras (see Where to stay, page 62).
This is one of the best places for seafood
in Colombo.

$$ La Voile Blanche
3/10 Beach Rd, T011-456 1111.
Unsurprisingly specializes in seafood
but has extensive menu with Asian and
Western choices. Beachfront, with chilled
atmosphere. Good cocktail list and range
of spirits.

$$ Loon Tao
*3/12 College Av, T011-272 2723,
www.loontao.com.*
Chinese restaurant serving predominantly
seafood, but meat and tofu dishes also
available. Extensive menu, upmarket beach
hut feel.

$ The Angler
71 Hotel Rd, T011-271 6626.
Family-run, also 4 rooms and apartment
to let. Good Sri Lankan, Chinese and
Western dishes.

Bars and clubs

Once confined to the big hotels, new
bars are now opening up around the city
all the time. Since drinking alcohol in Sri
Lanka remains a predominantly male
preserve, some of the older places may
feel a little unwelcoming for women, but
the newer, plusher bars have a broader
appeal. Almost all $$$$ and $$$ hotels
have pleasant, if expensive, bars. The
nightclub scene is largely restricted
to top-category hotels; most impose
a hefty cover charge on non-residents
at weekends (although 'ladies' may get
in free) and charge a lot for drinks. Some
have early evening 'Happy Hours', though
few get going much before midnight;
some stay open until 0300 or later.

Fort area and the Pettah
Bars

Echelon Pub
*Colombo Hilton (see Where to stay, page 59).
Open 1100-0230.*
Smarter than most and popular with expats
at the weekends.

Sky Lounge
*Kingsbury, 48 Janadhipata Mawatha, Col 1,
T011-242 1221.*
Great views from this chic bar. You can try
their signature Kingsbury cocktail – vodka,
Cointreau, fresh strawberries and lime.

Clubs
Most nightclubs are in hotels. Music varies
depending on the night and with it, the
clientele. Pick an animal: you can try the at
the **Colombo Hilton** or the at the **Grand
Oriental**. Alternatively, try at the **Galadari**

> **Tip...**
> On *poya* days alcohol is not generally
> available until midnight.

Hotel (64 Lotus Rd, Col 1; closed Mon), which has good resident DJs and is highly rated.

Galle Face, Union Place and Beira Lake
Bars

Curve Bar
Park Street Mews, T011-230 0133.
In the newly renovated Park Street Mews, this is a popular bar serving up cocktails and tapas.

Glow Bar
3rd floor, AA Building, 42 Sir MM Markar Mawatha, Col 3.
Cocktails, fusion food and eclectic mix of music. Popular with the under 30s, happy hour is 1800-1900.

Inn on the Green
Galle Rd, Col 3, T011-223 9440.
Daily 1600-2400.
Styled as an English pub. Serves draught bitter and a variety of imported lagers as well as expensive English crisps.

Verandah
Galle Face Hotel (see Where to stay).
A sunset drink overlooking the sea at this atmospheric bar is an unmissable Colombo experience.

Clubs

Amuseum
Taj Samudra (see Where to stay, page 60).
This stylish club at the Taj is currently the place to be seen and to flash your cash.

Kollupitiya, Cinnamon Gardens and Borella
Bars

Cricket Club Café
34 Queen's Rd, Col 3 (see Restaurants, page 65).
Serves draught Carlsberg and Guinness by the pint, plus a good selection of wines. Good atmosphere.

Cloud Café
Colombo Courtyard (see Where to stay).
In early 2016, this was the hippest bar in Colombo. True mixology, live music as well as DJs and a great view.

Cloud Red
Cinnamon Red (see Where to stay).
Great views from the 26th-floor bar – atmospheric.

Gallery Café Bar
2 Alfred House Rd, Col 3 (see Restaurants, page 65).
A very chic open-air courtyard bar, with good cocktails and a range of wines.

Clubs
Silk
41 Maitland Cres, Col 7.
Popular and stylish bar and club in the same building as **Lemon** (see Restaurants, page 65).

Bambalapitiya

On14 Rooftop Bar
OZO Colombo Hotel, 36-38 Clifford Pl, Col 4, T011-255 5570.
Great sea views and a wide range of drinks.

Mount Lavinia
Almost all restaurants serve alcohol.

Bars

Mount Lavinia Hotel
See Where to stay, page 62.
The terrace bar offers probably the best setting for an end-of-day drink (although the beach bars are a cheaper option to enjoy the sunset).

Lion Pub
Corner of Galle and Beach Rds, T011-276 1961.
You enter through a big lion's mouth. The reasonably priced food is nothing special, but the sunken beer garden is

popular with tourists and locals and has a good atmosphere.

Clubs

The Hut
Mount Lavinia Hotel (see Where to stay, page 62). Closed Mon and Tue.
A local, friendly crowd. Ideal for those who want a retro night out. There is live music at the weekends and reggae and techno nights.

Entertainment

Casinos

All casinos are open until the small hours and some are 24-hr; those mentioned below are just a small selection.
Bally's, *14 Dharmapala Maw, Col 3*. Upmarket casino open 24 hrs.
MGM Grand Club, *772 Gulle Rd, Bambalapitiya, Col 4, T011-250 2268*. Offers banco, blackjack, roulette, baccarat, has VIP 'foreigners only' lounge.
Ritz Club, *5 Galle Face Terr, Col 3 (behind Ramada)*.

Cinemas

There are a number of cinemas in Colombo: the **Liberty** (35 Dharmapala Mawatha, Col 3) and the **Majestic (**Level 4, Majestic City, Col 4) are your best bet for English-language recent releases. Alternatively, films are also shown at **Alliance Française** (11 Bomes Pl, Col 7, T011-269 4162, www.alliancefr.lk) on Fri; at the **American Center** (44 Galle Rd, Col 3, T011-233 2725) on Tue from 1800; and at the **British Council** (49 Alfred House Gardens, Col 3, T011-258 1171, www.britishcouncil.org/srilanka).

Cultural shows

Some top hotels put on regular folk dance performances (also Western floor shows/ live music for dancing); open to non-residents. The more expensive hotels also often provide live music over dinner, especially at weekends.

Theatres

Lionel Wendt Centre, *www.lionelwendt.org (see page 54). Box office daily 1000-1200, 1400-1700.* Stages both Western and local productions, and occasional classical music concerts.
Lumbini Hall, *Havelock Town*. Specializes in Sinhalese theatre.

Festivals

Jan Duruthu Perahera. Kelaniya Temple hosts a 2-day festival with caparisoned elephants, acrobats and floats.
Feb Navam Maha Perahera, Gangaramaya Temple celebrates the full-moon with processions around Beira Lake-Viharam ahadevi Park area. A large number of elephants, torch-bearers, drummers, dancers, acrobats, stilt walkers and pilgrims take part.

Shopping

Most shops are open 1000-1900 on weekdays and 0845-1500 on Sat, though tourist shops will be open for longer and sometimes on Sun. You can shop with confidence at government-run shops, although it is interesting to wander in the bazaars and look for good bargains. Shops in Fort tend to be more expensive than equally good quality items in Kollupitiya. Boutiques in the Pettah are worth a visit too. The top hotels have shopping arcades selling quality goods but prices are often higher than elsewhere.

Markets

Artists gather on Nelum Pokuna Mawatha, Col 7, daily to sell their creations. There's also a Sun bazaar on Main St in the Pettah and on Olcott St in Fort. The **Good Market** (www.goodmarket.lk), held every Sat at the Old Racecourse in Cinnamon Gardens, is a farmer's market with lots of organic treats, local eats, great coffee and a buzzy atmosphere.

Bookshops

Colombo has plenty of good bookshops, especially along Galle Rd in Kollupitiya.
Barefoot, *704 Galle Rd, Col 3, T011-258 9305, www.barefootceylon.com.* Has an excellent selection, with good range of Sri Lankan authors and books on design, photography and architecture, as well as cards and postcards. Don't miss the selection of old BOAC (British Overseas Airways Corporation) and other Sri Lanka/Ceylon advertising cards.
Buddhist Cultural Centre, *125 Anderson Rd, Nedimala, Dehiwala, T011-272 6234, bcc@sri. lanka.net. Daily 0830-1730 including poya and public holidays.*
Lakehouse, *100 Sir CA Gardiner Mawatha, Col 2, booklhb@sltnet.lk.* Branch upstairs at Liberty Plaza. Very good range.
MD Gunasena, *217 Olcott Mawatha, Col 11, T011-232 3981, www.mdgunasena.com.* The largest bookshop in Sri Lanka, with branches around Colombo and the island.

Clothes

Textiles represent Sri Lanka's biggest industry, and clothes made here are exported to major brand names around the world. Very cheap clothes can be found in the Pettah, though don't buy off street stalls. See also Barefoot (above) and Odel (below).
Cotton Collection, *40 Ernest de Silva Mawatha, Col 7, www.cottoncollection.lk.* Similar to **Odel** (see below), clothes for men, women and children.
French Corner, *24 Hyde Park Corner, Col 2.*

Department stores and shopping malls

Crescat, *Galle Rd, Col 3 (next to Cinnamon Grand).* A small but upmarket shopping mall, brighter than the others. Internet café, Dilmah Tea, Mlesna, and branch of **Vijitha Yapa** bookshop. Food court (see Restaurants, page 64) and supermarket in the basement.
Liberty Plaza, *Dharmapala Mawatha, Col 3.* Ageing mall.

Majestic City, *Galle Rd, Col 4.* The largest mall, it has a branch of **Odel** (see below), as well as a cinema (see page 69) and a food court (see Restaurants, page 66).
Odel, *5 Alexandra Pl, Lipton Circus, Col 7, T011-268 2712.* Stylish department store with a good range of clothes and accessories, books and homewares. There is a good food court too. The warehouse branch at Dickman's Rd, Col 5 is worth a visit, as it stocks different things.
Old Racecourse, *Unity Plaza, opposite Majestic City.* Branch of **Vijitha Yapa** bookshop, and there is a **Perera & Sons** in the basement (see Restaurants, page 66).

Gemstones, silver and gold

These should only be bought at reputable shops; it is probably best to avoid the private jewellers in Sea St, the Pettah.
Sri Lanka Gem & Jewellery Exchange, *World Trade Centre, East Tower.* A government institution with 34 wholesalers and retailers. The **Gem Testing Laboratory**, 5th floor, will test gems for foreigners (Rs 150 per stone).

Gifts and homewares

Lifestyle shops are becoming increasingly popular with Colombo's wealthy elite, and some high-quality gifts can be picked up amongst them.
Barefoot, *704 Galle Rd, Col 3, T011-258 9305, www.barefootceylon.com.* Funky homewares and textiles in the signature bright colours. Barefoot is really a one-stop shop for good clothes, textiles, great handcrafted toys, books, teas and good souvenirs that you will want to keep for yourself. There is an excellent café and gallery on-site too. Highly recommended.
Kalaya, *116 Havelock Rd.* Modern designer homestore, with some goods imported from India.
Paradise Road, *213 Dharmapala Mawatha, Col 7, also Gallery Shop at Gallery Café (1000-2230).* Stylish homewares collection

with kitchen accessories, candles, beautiful leather diaries, address books, etc, and well-made sarongs. For larger pieces, including furniture visit **Paradise Road Design Ware House** (61/3 Ward Pl, Col 7, T011-269 1056). Recommended.

Handloom and handicrafts

The government outlets offer good quality, reasonable prices and the added bonus of not having to haggle. Here you can pick up masks, batiks, brasswork, silverwork, etc. Government outlets include: **Laksala** (60 York St, Col 1, www.laksala.lk), which carries a wide range; **Lakmedura** (113 Dharmapala Mawatha, Col 7, daily until 1900); **Lanka Hands** (135 Bauddhaloka Mawatha, Col 4, daily 0930-1830); **Lakpahana** (21 Rajakeeya Mawatha, Col 7, www.lakpahana.com). Try also **Barefoot** (see above) and **Prasanna Batiks** (35 Main St, Col 11).

Supermarkets

Cargill's, *40 York St, Col 1; 407 Galle Rd, Col 3* (24-hr branch with pharmacy); *21 Staples St, Col 2; and at Majestic City.*
Keells, *at Crescat and Liberty Plaza.*

Tea

The supermarkets listed above all stock a wide selection of tea.
Dilmah, *www.dilmahtea.com.* At Crescat and Odel shopping malls and the airport.
Mlesna Tea Centre, *44 Ward Place, Col 7, T011-269 6348, www.mlesnateas.com.* Excellent range of teas, pots, etc. Several branches across town at the Hilton, Crescat, Liberty Plaza, Majestic City and at the airport.
Sri Lanka Tea Board, *574 Galle Rd, Col 3.*

What to do

Cricket

Colombo has several cricket stadiums. The Sri Lankan Cricket Board is based at the **Sinhalese Sports Club Ground (SSC)**

(Maitland Pl, Col 7, T011-269 5362), where Test matches and One-Day Internationals are played. Come here for tickets.
Also on Maitland Place, Col 7, are the **Colombo Cricket Club**, which has a very attractive colonial-style pavilion, and the neighbouring **Nondescript's Cricket Club (NCC)**. **R Premadasa Stadium** (Khettarama, Col 10), is a large stadium for Tests and One-Day Internationals (sometimes day/night), and is where the 2011 World Cup matches were played.

Diving

Though diving is possible off Colombo, most of the dive schools operate from coastal resorts, notably Hikkaduwa.
Colombo Divers, *Mount Lavinia, on beach, near Golden Mile, T077-736 7776, www.colombodivers.com.* Dives for US$65: 2 reef, 1 wreck and 1 reef, or 2 wreck. The wrecks nearby are a tug and a cargo ship, 30 mins by boat to site. SSI and PADI courses available. Other water sports include kayaking, water skiing and jetskis. Also operates from Negombo (see page 85).
Lanka Sportreizen, *29-b BS de S Jayasinghe Mawatha, Dehiwala, T011-258 2450, www.lsr-srilanka.com.* Organizes diving, as well as nature and wildlife holidays.

Football

Sugathadasa Stadium, *A de Silva Mawatha, Col 13.* For international matches.

Golf

Royal Colombo Golf Club, *Ridgeway Golf Links, Col 8, T011-269 5431, www.rcgcsl.com.* Offers temporary membership and has a dress code.

Rowing

Colombo Rowing Club, *51 Sir CA Gardiner Mawatha, Col 2 (opposite Lake House Bookshop), T011-243 3758.* Offers temporary membership.

Swimming

Many hotels allow non-residents to use their pool on a daily basis for a fee.

Colombo Swimming Club, *148 Galle Rd, Col 3 (opposite Temple Trees, the President's Residence), T011-242 1645, www.colombo swimmingclub.org.* Popular expats' hangout with pool, tennis, gym, bar, restaurant, initial membership Rs 100,000 (of which Rs 60,000 is refundable), temporary membership is available for Rs 1750 per week; you must be recommended by an existing member.

Tennis and squash

At the **Cinnamon Grand**, **Taj Samudra** and **Cinnamon Lakeside** hotels. Also at **Gymkhana Club** (31 Maitland Cres, Col 7, T011-269 1025), and **Sri Lanka Squash Federation** (T077-768 1168).

Tours and tour operators

Most tour operators offer half- or full-day city tours by car, typically visiting Kelaniya, Fort and the Pettah, the National Museum and usually the Buddhist and Hindu temples. All tour operators will offer car hire and island tours. Some (eg **Aitken Spence**, **Jetwing**) run a number of luxury hotels on the southwest coast and elsewhere. Prices include their hotel and breakfast (if you choose your own hotel, a large reservation fee may be added). It is also possible to arrange trips to the national parks from Colombo.

Action Lanka, *Koswatte, T011-450 3448, www.actionlanka.com.* Recommended for adventure activities such as whitewater rafting, mountain biking, canoeing and diving.

Aitken Spence, *305 Vauxhall St, Col 2, T011-230 8308, www.aitkenspencetravels.com.* One of Sri Lanka's largest operators, with some of Sri Lanka's finest hotels, full range of services, excellent if expensive tours.

A Baur, *5 Upper Chatham St, Col 1, T011-473 2600, www.abaurs.com.* Tours, including birdwatching.

Colombo City Walks, *T077-301 7091, www. colombocitywalk.blogspot.in.* Get to the heart of the city on an urban and architectural safari around the Fort and Pettah areas. The night walk is quite magical.

Jetwing, *46/26 Navam Mawatha, Col 2, T011-234 5700, www.jetwingtravels.com.* Highly recommended for personalized service, good car and driver/guide, excellent network of hotels.

Jetwing Eco Tours, *T011-238 1201, www.jet wingeco.com.* Excellent nature and wildlife tours, personal service.

Leopard Safaris, *45 Ambagahawatta, Colombo Rd, Katunayake, T077-731 4004, www.leopardsafaris.com.* Excellent tented safaris in Yala, Uda Walawe, Wilpattu and the Knuckles.

Lion Royal Tourisme, *45 Braybrook St, Col 2, T011-471 5996, www.lionroyaltourisme.com.* Personal service, reliable fleet of drivers and generous discounts on a wide range of hotels.

Quickshaw's, *3 Kalinga Pl, Col 5, T011-258 3133, www.quickshaws.com.* Includes special tours for birders, divers, cricketers, authors and honeymooners.

Shanti Travel, *138/2-3 Kynsey Rd, Col 8, T011-465 4500, www.shantitravel.com.* Predominantly for the French market but staff speak excellent English. Personal service, reliable.

Walkers Tours, *130 Glennie St, Col 2, T011-230 6306, www.walkerstours.com.* Expensive but recommended for excellent service.

Transport

Air

The **airport** at Ratmalana (T011-262 3030), just south of Mount Lavinia (500 m off Galle Rd), is used for domestic flights. It remains primarily a military airport; security is high and there are few facilities. Domestic airlines include **FITS AIR**, www.fitsair.com; also check out the **Sri Lankan Airlines** air taxi service. Airlines provide a free bus to and from the city.

Bandaranaike (Colombo) International Airport, T011-245 2911, www.airport.lk, is at Katunayake, about 6 km south of Negombo and 30 km north of Colombo. The website has good information for all arrivals and departures. The tourist information counter will give advice, brochures, maps and the useful monthly *Travel Lanka* magazine. For further information on facilities and arrivals, see page 403. A free shuttle runs from outside Arrivals to a bus stop for regular buses to Colombo's Bastian Mawatha Stand in the Pettah. There are also pre-paid taxis (Rs 1900 depending on which part of town you're heading to) and more expensive a/c taxis (from Rs 2100), which can be arranged from the taxi service counter. A breakdown of fares is available at www.airport.lk/getting-around/taxi-rates.php and includes prices to reach other destinations such as **Kandy** and **Hikkaduwa**. Taxis are also available from the travel agent counters. It is possible to rent a car at the airport, though rates tend to be steep and it usually pays to shop around in Colombo. Suburban commuter trains leave from Katunayake train station, about 1 km from the airport, north to **Negombo** (15 mins) and south to Colombo (1¼ hrs). Trains are currently infrequent, but there are plans for a 15-min shuttle service.

Boat

The passenger ferry services between Colombo Harbour and **Tuticorin**, India, have been cancelled indefinitely.

Bus

Local Colombo has an extensive network of public and private buses competing on

Tip...
Local buses have white signs, while long-distance have yellow.

Tip...
Beware of pickpockets and avoid hotel touts at bus and railway stations. See page 421 for more information.

popular routes. Although the system can get very crowded, it is not difficult to use since the destinations are usually displayed in English. Useful services are those that run from Fort Railway Station down the Galle Rd (including Nos 100, 101, 102, 106, 133) to Colombo's southern suburbs and Mount Lavinia, where many visitors choose to stay. No 138 goes from Fort past the Town Hall and the National Museum (Glass House stop, across the road); No 187 between Fort and the International airport.

Long distance Government buses (**Ceylon Transport Board** or CTB, T011-258 1120) and private buses run to Colombo from virtually every significant town in Sri Lanka. There are 3 bus stands, all close to each other, 1 km east of Fort station in the Pettah. All 3 are quite chaotic, choking with fumes, with services usually operating on a 'depart when full' basis.

CTB/Central, Olcott Mawatha, southeast corner of the Pettah (right from Fort station, and across the road), T011-232 8081. CTB buses, which are the cheapest, oldest and slowest, offer services to almost all island-wide destinations. Left luggage here is sometimes full.

Bastion Mawatha, to the east of Manning Market, T011-242 1731. The buses are privately run, with the cost and journey time depending on whether you get an ancient bone-shaker ('normal' bus), 'semi-luxury', 'luxury' (with a/c), or the wanton sensuousness of a 'super-luxury' coaster. It serves most destinations to the east, southeast and south, including **Kandy** (luxury bus 3½ hrs), **Nuwara Eliya** (6 hrs), **Hikkaduwa** (2½ hrs), **Galle** (3 hrs), **Matara** (5 hrs), **Tangalla** (6 hrs), **Hambantota** (6½ hrs) and **Kataragama** (7½-8 hrs).

Saunders Place, just to the north of the CTB bus station, which also offers private a/c coasters and bone-shakers to destinations to the north and northeast, including **Ampara** (9 hrs), **Anuradhapura** (5-6 hrs), **Badulla** (7½ hrs), **Bandarawela** (7½ hrs), **Batticaloa** (7½ hrs), **Chilaw** (2 hrs), **Dambulla** (4 hrs), **Kurunegala** (2½ hrs), **Negombo** (1½ hrs), **Polonnaruwa** (5-6 hrs), **Puttalam** (3 hrs), **Trincomalee** (7 hrs), and **Vavuniya** (6 hrs).

Private and public buses to **Jaffna** leave from Wellawatta (12-14 hrs).

Car/motorbike hire

For general information on car hire, charges and self-drive versus being driven, see page 407. Most hotels and travel agents can arrange car hire (with or without driver). For car and driver, **Lion Royal Tourisme**, **Walkers Tours** and **Quickshaws** all have a good reputation (see What to do, above). For self-drive, **Avis** (www.avis.com) and **Hertz** (Level 1, 130 Nawala Rd, T011-236 9333, www.hertz.com) are recommended.

Mal-Key, 58 Pamankada Rd, Kirulapana, Col 6, T011-250 2008, www.malkey.lk. A good local company, with a comprehensive website that gives a breakdown of costs and types of car. Self-drive from Rs 2900 per day (weekly rates are better); chauffeur rates from Rs 4250 per day to Rs 9000 for a luxury car for 100 km per day, plus Rs 750 for driver's subsistence.

Carsons Car Rental has small range of street motorbikes, T011-437 7366. For a wider range, venture up to Negombo for **Yellow Fleet**, T077-776 5919.

Taxi

Metered taxis have yellow tops and red-on-white number plates. Make certain that the driver has understood where you wish to go and fix a rate for long-distance travel.

Radio cabs are very convenient and reliable (see page 408); **GNTC**, T011-268 8688, gntc@isplanka.lk, also has a branch at the airport, T011-225 1688, recommended but pricey; **Kangaroo Cabs**, T011-258 8588 is recommended.

Three-wheeler

3-wheelers are quick but you need to bargain hard (minimum usually Rs 50 per km), unless you find a metered one. Trips around Fort will cost Rs 150; Fort to Cinnamon Gardens, Rs 300. Fort to Mount Lavinia will cost upwards of Rs 500, the exact fee depending upon your negotiating skills (see page 409).

Train

Nearly all of Sri Lanka's railway lines originate in Fort Railway Station at the southwestern corner of the Pettah (Colombo 11), which is within walking distance of the major hotels in Fort. Enquiries (express and commuter trains), T011-243 4215. Berths reservations, T011-243 2908. For foreign travellers, the **Railway Tourist Office**, Fort Station, T011-243 5838, can be useful (see page 59). Left luggage ('Cloak Room') is just past the Intercity Reservation Office, Rs 56 per locker per day but is often full.

Local Suburban services run regularly between Fort and Mount Lavinia (and beyond), approximately every 30 mins (less frequently at weekends and holidays) between 0436 and 2135, though they can get packed at rush hour. They take 30 mins to Mount Lavinia, with stops at Secretariat, Kompanna, Kollupitiya, Bambalapitiya, Wellawatta and Dehiwala. Timings of the next train are chalked up on a blackboard;

Tip...
If you are considering any train travel in Sri Lanka, your first port should be www.seat61.com, an independent website with valuable advice on services and insight into the island's rail network.

buy your ticket from counter No 13. If heading south beyond Mount Lavinia, it is quicker to change at Moratuwa than retrace your steps to Fort.

Long distance The main station is Fort, though many trains originate in Maradana. There are trains to most places of interest on 4 separate lines, with regular services to/from Kandy, main tourist areas in the highlands, Anuradhapura, west and south coast beach resorts and Trincomalee on the east coast. For many train services you have to show up on the day to purchase your ticket. The **Intercity Reservation Office** is open 0630-1430, and this is where tickets to Kandy can be arranged. The white board in the office outlines which trains and classes are full. You can only reserve seats on the privately run **Expo Rail** and **Rajdhani** services (www.exporail.lk and www.rajdhani.lk) which are more costly. There are special a/c **Hitachi** trains for day tours to Kandy and Hikkaduwa. Occasional tours are arranged on vintage steam trains; details from the Railway Tourist Office.

Intercity trains to **Kandy** leave Fort at 0700 and 1535 (1st class, including observation car, Rs 500; 2nd class, reservation also required, Rs 280; 3rd class Rs 180; 2½ hrs). Return tickets are valid for 10 days, but the return date must be booked in advance. Normal trains to **Kandy** are cheaper and leave at 1035, 1240 (to **Hatton**), 1745; they go via **Gampaha** (for **Heneratogoda**) and **Rambukkana** (for **Pinnawela**).

Trains to **Badulla** depart at 0555, 0930, 2000 (mail train); they also go through Kandy and stop close to **Nuwara Eliya**. The 0945 (Udarata Menike) is express (9 hrs) with observation car (1st class Rs 1750 Rajdhani);

the 2000 has 1st-class sleeping berths (Rs 12550), and 2nd- (Rs 600) and 3rd-class (Rs 400) sleeperettes. Normal trains take 10-11 hrs (2nd class Rs 600, 3rd class Rs 400). All trains call at **Hatton** (for **Adam's Peak**, 4½-5½ hrs), **Nanu Oya** (for **Nuwara Eliya**, 6-7 hrs), **Ohiya** (for **Horton Plains**, 7-8 hrs), **Haputale** (8½-9½ hrs), **Bandarawela** (9-10 hrs) and **Ella** (9½-10½ hrs).

On the Northern line to **Anuradhapura** (4 hrs) and **Vavuniya** (for **Jaffna**), an intercity train leaves Fort daily at 0545, 1150 and 2040 (sleeper), 1st class a/c with reservation Rs 1500, 2nd class Rs 800. Normal trains to **Vavuniya** at 1345 (4½-5 hrs to **Anuradhapura**), via **Kurunegala** (2 hrs).

Polonnaruwa is on the Trincomalee line. For **Polonnaruwa**, 0715 (intercity), 1915 (intercity). Alternatively you can take trains towards Jaffna and change at Galoya (there's a useful map on www.seat61.com). The train continues to **Trincomalee**, Rs700/370/205 or for the sleeper service Rs 1250/600/450.

Trains run every 1-2 hrs from 0520 to 2020 on the Puttalam line to **Negombo** (1½ hrs), via **Katunayake** (for the **airport**), a few continuing to **Chilaw** and **Puttalam** (4 hrs).

Trains south to **Galle** and **Matara** (3 hrs/4 hrs), no reservation or 1st class, leave Fort at 0655, 0835, 1030, 1425, 1540, 1640 (not Sat/Sun), 1720, 1750 (terminates at Galle Sat/Sun) and 1845 terminating at Galle. Most call at **Kalutara**, **Aluthgama**, **Ambalangoda** and **Hikkaduwa**, and continue to **Matara** (3½-4 hrs), with stops at **Talpe** and **Weligama** and in some cases other south coast beach resorts. Full fare all the way to Matara is Rs 230/130.

Tip...
Don't miss the Colombo to Kandy observation car – a beautiful train ride that you can book in advance (see above).

West & northwest

Other than a day or two spent on the beach at Negombo, one of the most developed and least prepossessing resorts on the west coast, most travellers tend to pass straight through this region, heading straight for the more spectacular sights of the Cultural Triangle or the cooler climes of Kandy.

Yet this region possesses its own proud history, with a reasonable claim to be the cradle of Sri Lankan civilization. It was here that Prince Vijaya, the founder of the Sinhalese race, first landed in AD 543. It boasts no fewer than four ancient capitals, founded in a game of medieval cat-and-mouse to hide the sacred Tooth Relic from foreign invaders.

The area is also where the Wet Zone meets the Dry Zone. Around the densely populated northern suburbs of Colombo, closely packed coconut groves contribute to the lush, evergreen landscape. The scenery becomes increasingly barren as you travel north. Beyond Wilpattu National Park, Sri Lanka's largest protected area, lie the arid lands of the Wanni. From west to east the landscape also undergoes a transformation, wide shallow coastal lagoons giving way to the forest-clad highlands.

Best for
Ayurveda ▪ Beaches ▪ Kitesurfing ▪ Wildlife

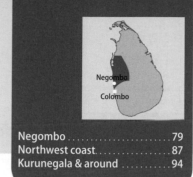

Footprint
picks

★ Negombo, page 79

This busy beach city near the airport offers a relaxed alternative
to Colombo.

★ Kalpitiya Peninsula, page 89

The windswept beaches and lagoons here are perfect for kitesurfing
and dolphin watching.

★ Wilpattu National Park, page 92

Closed for years, Wilpattu's beautiful jungle-fringed ponds are the
scene for exciting safaris to see leopard, elephant and sloth bear.

★ Yapahuwa, page 98

Climb the superb ornamental stairway that wraps around this ruined
rock fortress for stunning mountain views.

Wilpattu
National Park

Anuradhapura

Park Entrance

Nuwara
Wewa

A20

A13

Kalpitiya
Karaitivu

Nochchiyagama

Talawa

A28

Kala Oya

Kala Oya

Eppawala

Puttalam
Lagoon

Tambuttegama

Talawila

A12

Mahagalkadawala

Alankuda

Kalpitiya
Peninsula

Puttalam

Sasserawa

Palavi

A10

Yapahuwa

Medagalla

Mundel
Lake

Daladagama

Maho

Polpitigama

Andigama

A28

Udappuwa

Kiriyankalli

Nikaweratiya

Battulu-Oya

Panduwasnuwara

Padeniya

Ganewatta

Arankele

A6

A10

Hettipola

Wariyapola

Ridigama

Chilaw

Munneswaram

Ibbagandwa

Madampe

Kuliyapitiya

Kurunegala

Dandagamuwa

Dambokka

Marawila

A3

Naramala

Galketigedara

Mawatagama

A10

Dambadeniya

Pannala

Giriulla

Polgahawela

Waikkal

Dankotuwa

Maha Oya

Mirigama

Alawwa

Pinnawela

Kegalla

N

Diwulapitiya

Warakapola

A1

Negombo

10 km

10 miles

Negombo

★ Owing to its proximity to the international airport, 6 km away, Negombo (population 140,000) is the principal resort north of Colombo. It has a wide range of accommodation, including some excellent small hotels, and if you don't fancy tangling with Colombo on your first night in Sri Lanka, this makes for a relaxed and convenient place to begin or end a holiday.

The grubby beach can't compare to the white-sand wonders of the south and east coasts, but there's plenty of local colour in the shape of ad-hoc fish markets, and you'll find numerous operators willing to take you diving or kitesurfing. The town, although a little scruffy and seedy in places, has a picturesque lagoon with good birdlife and a few interesting reminders of the Portuguese and Dutch periods.

Essential Negombo

Finding your feet

Negombo town lies 37 km north of Colombo and 6 km west of the international airport. It is easily accessible from the airport by taxi, three-wheeler or bus in about 20 minutes. Hotels can often arrange a transfer on request. To get to Negombo from Colombo, take the No 240 bus (every 15-20 minutes) from Saunders Place bus stand in the Pettah, which takes about an hour; the train from Fort Station also takes about an hour.

Getting around

The main tourist area is 2-4 km north of the town itself. You can walk most of the way along the beach (which gets progressively more inviting), or take a three-wheeler (Rs 150), or the Kochchikade bus (No 905) from the bus station. Frequent buses run along the main beach road from the bus and railway stations in Negombo town. Bicycles and motorbikes can be hired to explore the area. Three-wheelers offer Negombo town tours.

When to go

Swimming and watersports are only safe from November to April, outside the southwestern monsoon period. Easter is celebrated with Passion plays, particularly on Easter Saturday on Duwa Island. In July the Fishermen's festival at St Mary's Church is a major regional celebration.

Tip...

There are a number of fish markets in Negombo: one is near the bridge on Duwa Island across the lagoon; there is another beyond the fort.

Sights   Colour map 2, C1.

churches, canals and canoes

Negombo town

The town lies at the mouth of a saltwater lagoon. The Portuguese originally built a fort on the northern headland guarding the lagoon in about 1600. Since the area was rich in spices, particularly much-prized cinnamon, it changed hands several times before the Portuguese were finally ousted by the Dutch in 1644. The Dutch built a much stronger fort here, but this was largely destroyed by the British who pulled much of it down to build a jail. Today, only the gatehouse to the east (dated 1678), with its rather crooked clock tower survives. The place is still used as a prison, and the District Court is tucked away in a corner of the grounds.

A more enduring monument is the **canal system**, originally explored in the 15th century, which was improved and expanded by the Dutch (see box, page 82). Today you can see the canal if you follow St Joseph Road into Custom House Road and around the headland. It skirts the lagoon where mainly fishing boats are moored (witness to Negombo's thriving fishing industry). The junction of the canal is just past the bridge crossing the lagoon. It is also possible to cycle stretches of the canal south and north of Negombo.

St Mary's Church dominates the town. It is one of many churches in the area that bears witness to the success of the Portuguese's drive to convert the local population to Roman Catholicism (see box, page 82). Work began in 1874 and was only completed in 1922. There are a number of alabaster statues of saints and of the Easter story as well as a colourfully painted ceiling. Also worth seeing is the church on Duwa Island (reached via the road bridge across the mouth of the lagoon), which is famous for its Easter procession (see page 85). An early morning fish market is also held here.

There are three **Hindu temples** on Sea Street. The largest, Sri Muthu Mari Amman, has a colourful *gopuram* in the inner courtyard.

Negombo harbour

Although there is much evidence of a motorized fleet in the harbour, you can still see fishermen using catamarans and ancient outrigger canoes to bring up their catch onto the beach every day. The outrigger canoes, known as *oruva* here, are not made from

Negombo Beach

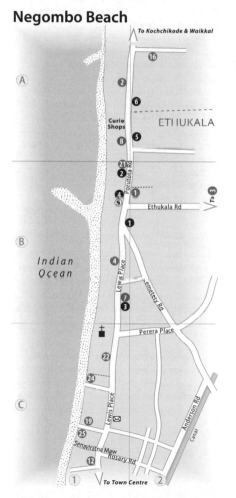

N

200 metres
300 yards

Where to stay
Ayurveda Pavilions 1 *B2*
Blue 2 *A1*
Cinnamon Guesthouse 3 *B2*
Hotel J 4 *B1*
Icebear Guesthouse 12 *C1*
Paradise Holiday
  Village 16 *A2*
Sea Drift 19 *C1*
Sea Sands 21 *B1*
Silver Sands 22 *C1*
Star Beach 24 *C1*
Sunset Beach 25 *C1*

Restaurants
Coconut Primitive 1 *B1*
Dolce Vita 2 *B1*
Edwin's 3 *B1*
King Coconut 4 *B1*
Lords 5 *A2*
Sherryland 6 *A2*

Bars & clubs
Player's Pub 7 *B1*
Rodeo Pub 8 *A1*

Catholicism and canals

The region north of Colombo was the area of Sri Lanka most affected by Portuguese colonialism. The Portuguese resolve to convert the local population to Catholicism is apparent in the high proportion of Roman Catholics, especially among the fishermen in Negombo District, and by the number of Catholic churches in the villages that line the coastal road. Nearly a quarter of the population immediately inland from Negombo is Christian, increasing in the north to almost 40%. The prevalence of names like Fernando and Perera is another clue to the success of Portuguese colonialism in this region.

Dutch influence is also evident in the now disused canal system that was built around Negombo on which flat-bottomed 'padda' boats travelled the 120 km between Colombo and Puttalam. The Dutch recognized the canals' usefulness in transporting spices – cinnamon, cloves, pepper, cardamoms – and precious gems from the interior and along the coast to the port for loading on to ocean-going trade ships.

As the Rev James Cordimer wrote in 1807 "the top of the canal (near Colombo) is constantly crowded with large flat-bottomed boats, which come down from Negombo with dried fish and roes, shrimps, firewood, and other articles. These boats are covered with thatched roofs in the form of huts".

The Dutch built canals extensively, not just around Colombo but also around Galle in the south, but these were relatively minor works compared to the 1000 km of irrigation canals already dug by the Sinhalese by the 12th century. The boats on these canals were often pulled by two men in harness.

Today the canal banks are largely the preserve of people strolling along the waterway. You can hire bikes at several points, including Negombo, and ride along a section of the banks.

hollowed-out tree trunks but rather from planks that are sewn together and caulked to produce a fairly wide canoe with an exceptionally flat bottom. Look out for them as some are often beached in front of the hotels. You can usually see the fleet early in the morning returning to harbour, each canoe under a three-piece sail. Their catch includes seer, skipjack, herring, mullet, pomfret, amberjack, and sometimes sharks. Prawns and lobster are caught in the lagoon.

Negombo lagoon

Fishermen offer boat trips on the lagoon. **Muthurajawela marsh** at the southern end is an estuarine wetland which harbours the saltwater crocodile, which can grow up to 9 m in length, as well as many species of birds such as the pied kingfisher. More information and boat tours (with wildlife guide) can be obtained from the **Visitor Centre** ⓘ *Walikatiya, T074-830150, Tue-Sun 0700-1800*. Tours are also arranged by hotels, guesthouses and tour operators in Negombo, see page 86.

Tourist information

Tourist police
Ethukala, T031-227 5555.

Where to stay

Most people choose to stay in the beach area north of Negombo town. Hotels are spread out over almost 2 km, mostly on Lewis Place and further north on Porutota Rd in Ethukala. Some hotels don't allow Sri Lankans accompanying tourists to stay, partly because the area has a somewhat dubious reputation. Most larger hotels offer watersports. There is currently a lot of building work going on in Negombo, so new hotels and restaurants are likely to be open by the time you read this.

Negombo beach

$$$$ Ayurveda Pavillons (Jetwing)
Porutota Rd, T031-487 0764,
www.jetwinghotels.com.
12 beautifully furnished villas set in tropical gardens. Each villa has a delightful front garden with frangipani tree, open-air bath, massage table and DVD player. Very ecologically sound. Great attention to detail and outstanding personal service. There is a sumptuous restaurant on-site which caters for your body type (*dosha*) during your treatment, but there are some treats on the menu too. Treatment packages from 3 days to 30 days. Recommended.

$$$$ Blue (Jetwing)
Porutota Rd, T031-229 9003,
www.jetwinghotels.com.
Large beachfront property with great pool. 103 large rooms, 6 suites and 3 family rooms, not all with good views. Typical resort hotel, with all amenities and excellent service,

entertainment and watersports such as kitesurfing. There is another Jetwing Beach property close by.

$$$ Paradise Holiday Village
154/9 Palangathurai Rd, T031-227 4588,
www.paradiseholidayvillage.com.
32 rooms and 17 apartments with kitchenette and living area built around central courtyard. Restaurant, pool, pleasant gardens.

$$$-$$ Cinnamon Guesthouse
978 Chilaw Rd, Daluwakotuwa,
5 km north of Negombo, T077-933 2032,
www.cinnamon-guesthouse.com.
Friendly guesthouse a short walk from the beach with spacious rooms, great home-cooked food and good vibes.

$$ Hotel J
331/1 Lewis Pl, T031-223 2999, www.hotelj.lk.
Great budget offering from the Jetwing chain – good-size rooms in vibey complex with beach views and small pool. Recommended.

$$ Icebear Guesthouse
103-2 Lewis Pl, T031-223 3862,
www.icebearhotel.com.
Attractively furnished rooms in bungalows and 'villas' at a well-kept Swiss-owned guesthouse. Pleasant garden with wonderful secluded feel, personal attention, good home cooking (book in advance for evening meal – lots of Swiss dishes), the morning muesli is amazing, free Wi-Fi and bicycles. Highly recommended.

$$ Sunset Beach
5 Carron Pl, T031-222 2350,
www.hotelsunsetbeach.com.
42 small a/c rooms in 3-storey block on the beach, upper floors more spacious, clean, light and airy, pool, useful local information. Can organize fishing trips.

$$-$ Silver Sands
229 Lewis Pl, T031-222 2880,
www.silversandsnegombo.com.
Great-value beachside property with
15 large, well-kept, clean fan and a/c rooms,
cheaper downstairs, best with large sea-
facing balconies, good restaurant, helpful
owner, reliable taxi service, best value in
this class, popular so book ahead.

$$-$ Star Beach
83/3 Lewis Pl, T031-222 2606,
www.starbeachhotelnegombo.com.
Clean rooms, downstairs are cheap but
gloomy, most upstairs have balcony,
private or shared, and some rooms
have sea view. Restaurant looks out
onto the beach. Friendly.

$ Sea Drift
2A Carron Pl, T031-223 5534,
www.seadriftnegombo.com.
Fan rooms in family guesthouse (one of
the originals in Negombo), kitchen facilities
available, friendly. Deservedly popular so
book ahead.

$ Sea Sands
7 Porutota Rd, T031-227 9154,
www.seasandsnegombo.weebly.com.
11 simple fan rooms with attached bath and
shared balcony, friendly, reasonable. **Dolce
Vita** at back, see Restaurants.

Towards the airport
See also page 63 for airport hotels.

$ Srilal Fernando
67 Parakrama Rd, Kurana, T031-222 2481.
5 rooms set around a courtyard, with very
clean bath and fan in spacious family home,
excellent food, good value, German spoken.

Restaurants

Negombo town

$$ Icebear Century Café
25 Main St, T031-223 8097.
Owned by the same people as the **Icebear
Guesthouse** (see Where to stay, page 83),
this café offers great fair trade coffee, tea,
cake and sandwiches in an airy space in the
town centre.

Negombo beach

$$$-$$ Edwin's
204 Lewis Pl, T031-223 9164.
Excellent Sri Lankan meals: try the delicious
devilled prawns or traditional rice and curry.
Generous portions, attentive host.

$$$-$$ Lord's
80B Portutota Rd, T077-723 4721,
www.lordsrestaurant.net.
Chic eatery with catfish in small pools in the
courtyard. British meals such as shepherd's
pie if you're feeling homesick but also Asian
fusion. Delicious cocktails and extensive
mocktail menu for non-drinkers. There is
also an art gallery.

$$ Coconut Primitive
108 Lewis Pl, on Browns Beach Junction,
T071-489 0553.
Although on the street, this place has
a good vibe and serves up immense
portions of crab and fish curry as well
as international dishes like schnitzel.
Recommended.

$$-$ Dolce Vita
27 Poruthota Rd, T077-743 6318.
Good coffee shop with relaxed vibe and
outdoor seating. They also serve up good
cakes and Western dishes. A good place to
watch the kitesurfers. Recommended.

$$-$ King Coconut
11 Porutota Rd, T031-227 8043.
Right on the beach, fantastic range of curry dishes and simple Western fare – try the delicious crab curry. Recommended.

$$-$ Sherryland
Set back from Porutota Rd in a garden.
Attentive service, good range of food, lively bar serving a selection of cocktails, good value. Set menu and Lion lager Rs 430-900.

Bars and clubs

Most hotels have at least 1 bar, or serve alcohol in their restaurant. Some of the larger hotels have nightclubs (open 2130, dress 'smart but casual'). There are also an increasing number of Western-style bars.

Players Pub has 2 billiard tables. It is popular with Brits and boasts that it stays open longer than anywhere else in Negombo (until 0130 or when the last person leaves!) **Rodeo Pub** is also very popular.

Festivals

Mar/Apr Easter holds a special place in this strongly Catholic area. There are numerous passion plays usually held on Easter Sat, the most famous of which is held at the church on Duwa Island and involves the whole community. Station yourself on Sea St (1 km south of Lewis Pl) if short of time. Young girls in spotless white dresses are carried shoulder high by 4 men between the churches. This takes place in the afternoon but preparations take most of the day.

Shopping

The curio stalls near the large hotels are handy for getting last-minute presents. Quality varies considerably and they are not nearly as good as when you buy direct upcountry. Visit them all before deciding

and then bargain hard. There are tailors all along Porutota Rd.

What to do

Many hotels offer Ayurvedic massage and treatments.

Boat trips
Trips on the lagoon and canal can be arranged directly with the fishermen on the beach; alternatively hotels and guesthouses can organize trips. Prices vary depending on who you go with, how long the trip is and what is involved.

Diving and snorkelling
The area is very rich in marine life. The nearest reef is 3 km off the beach hotel area with corals within 10-20 m, though the quality of this inner reef is poor. There are much better reefs further out, teeming with marine life including barracuda (even rare giant barracuda), blue-ringed angels and unusual starfish. Fishermen offer boat trips for snorkelling. Only dive with a PADI-qualified outfit.
Colombo Divers, *Jetwing Blue Hotel, 1077-366 8679, www.colombodivers.com.* PADI and SSI dive centre, 2 standard dives with equipment US$75. Offers Open Water, advanced and speciality courses.
Sri Lanka Diving Tours, *T077-764 8459, www.srilanka-divingtours.com.* PADI dive centre offering 2 dives for US$75. German and English spoken. Also arranges diving in Trincomalee and trips to the wreck of *HMS Hermes* (see page 321).

Fishing
Major hotels offer deep-sea fishing and 'leisure fishing'.

Swimming
It is dangerous to swim in the sea, particularly during the southwest monsoon May-Oct. Most of the larger hotels allow non-residents to use their pools (Rs 400-1500).

Tour operators

In addition to hotel travel desks, independent travel agents include: **Airwing Tours**, *68 Colombo Rd, T031-223 6620, www.airwingtours.com.* Offers several 'eco' tours for birdwatchers, photographers, trekkers, etc. Also has an office at the airport. **Lucky Tours**, *146 Lewis Pl, T077-762 4370.* Good English-speaking guide, Lakshman Bolonghe, who can arrange half-day birdwatching tours.

Watersports

Windsurfing can be arranged through **Jetwing Blue** (see Where to stay). Hire is US$20 per hr but if combined with a lesson is US$25 per hr.
The Pearl, *13 Porutota Rd, T031-492 7744, www.pearl-negombo.com.* Pioneers of Sri Lanka's fast-growing kitesurfing scene, this reliable German outfit offer beginner courses and kite rental.

Transport

To the airport

Frequent buses (No 240 to Colombo) stop close to the airport from early morning to late evening but can be crowded. Taxis cost Rs 1000 from Ethukala hotels. Expect to pay a little more at night. Most hotels/guesthouses can arrange taxis for you. 3-wheelers charge Rs 800.

Bicycle hire

Available from many hotels/guesthouses; about Rs 250 per day. Check out **Icebear** for reliable wheels. The flat roads make a short trip out of Negombo attractive.

Bus

Long-distance services depart from the huge new bus stand, T071-358 8481. There are regular services to **Colombo**, both intercity express (1-1½ hrs) and the cheaper, slower **CTB** buses. There are frequent buses to **Kandy** (No 1), which leave early morning or mid-late afternoon. Also to **Kurunegala** (No 34) and **Chilaw** (No 907).

Car/motorbike hire

Car hire is mostly through hotels; inspect vehicles carefully and expect to pay about US$200-270 per week with driver. For motorbike hire expect to pay from Rs 2000 per day. Yellow Fleet are a great company that hire out motorbikes and also offer tours (www.srilankamotorbikerours.com).

Three-wheeler

Drivers cruise the main beach road from Lewis Pl to Ethukala. From Lewis Pl to the bus or railway stations expect to pay around Rs 150, and up to Rs 200 from the hotels in Ethukala. Beware of touts.

Train

Commuter trains go to **Colombo Fort** via **Katunayake** (for the airport) 10 times a day; departures are frequent morning and evening, but there's a long gap between trains in the afternoon. Avoid this train during rush hour and especially Mon morning, when it gets very crowded. 6 trains a day run north to **Chilaw**, 2 continuing as far as **Puttalam** (3 hrs).

Northwest
coast

North of Negombo, you cross from the West to Northwest
Province, traditionally known as Wayamba Province.
It is an area of fishing hamlets and seemingly endless
groves of coconut palms, while inland is a rich agricultural
patchwork of paddy fields and plantations. The 'carpeting'
of the coastal road to Puttalam in 2002 made this the
quickest route from Colombo to Anuradhapura, and
many pass through without stopping. However, there are
some worthwhile attractions: secluded beaches, ancient
Hindu temples, a 'forgotten' peninsula, not to mention
Sri Lanka's largest national park.

North of Negombo *Colour map 2, C1.*

beaches, temples and firewalking festivals

Waikkal and Mariwala beaches

There are two main beach areas which lack the bustle (and hassle) of Negombo but are
still within easy reach of the airport. **Waikkal**, 12 km north of Negombo, is attractively
sited on a meandering river but is quite remote so you are dependent on transport to get
anywhere. It is, however, the site of one of the island's most impressive eco-resorts, which
organizes a wide array of nature-based activities.

A further 11 km north is **Marawila**, which has a large Roman Catholic church, curious
Italianate houses and a reputation for producing good-quality batiks. There are a growing
number of resort-style hotels here, though the area has never really taken off on the
scale of resorts further south. The beach is good in places but sometimes gives way to
breakwaters constructed of large rocks.

Up the coast to Puttalam *Colour map 2, B1/C1.*

Beyond Marawila, and after crossing the estuary, the road runs between the lagoon and
the railway through **Madampe**, which is known for its Coconut Research Institute and for
Taniwella Devale, a colourful harvest festival held in August in which the whole farming
community participates.

Chilaw, 75 km north of Colombo, is a small town with a large fish market and a big Roman Catholic church. Its shady claim to fame is as a smuggling centre. There is little in town to warrant a stop, but **Munneswaram**, 2 km east, is worth a detour for its Hindu temple complex of three shrines; Fridays are the busiest day. The 1500-year-old inner sanctum of the main Shiva temple has Tamil inscriptions and is an important pilgrimage centre. In August there is a month-long festival, which includes firewalking.

A left turn 26 km north of Chilaw at Battulu Oya leads to the prawn-fishing Tamil village of **Udappuwa** on the Kalpitiya Peninsula. As at Munneswaram, there is a festival with firewalking in July/August at its seaside three-temple shrine complex. Experiments in 1935-1936 showed that the coals were heated to about 500°C.

Marshes and lagoons lie between the road and the sea for much of the route north, which crosses a series of minor rivers and a few major ones such as the Battulu Oya.

The largely Muslim and Catholic town of **Puttalam**, 131 km north of Colombo, is a centre for prawn farming, dried fish and coconut plantations. It used to be famous for its ancient pearl fishery but is now better known for its donkeys and is thus a target of many Sinhalese jokes. The A12 continues northeast from Puttalam to Anuradhapura.

Listings North of Negombo

Where to stay

Many of the hotels have restaurants serving reasonable food.

Waikkal and Marawila

$$$$ Club Palm Bay
Thalawila Wella, Thoduwawa, near Marawila, T032-225 5831, www.clubpalmbay.com.
104 well-furnished a/c chalets, plus 2 suites, in an attractive setting surrounded on 3 sides by a lagoon. Sports including fishing and boating, 9-hole golf course, health centre, huge pool. Good beach close by.

$$$$ Ranweli Holiday Village
Waikkal, T031-227 7359, www.ranweli.com.
Sea- and river-view bungalows in award-winning eco-friendly resort located on a 9-ha mangrove peninsula between the river and the sea. Activities on offer include boat trips, birdwatching, guided nature walks, yoga and fishing. Well-designed and furnished rooms, with plants in the bathrooms. Peaceful atmosphere, "a naturalist's paradise".

$$$ Olenka Sunside Beach
Moderawella, near Marawila, T031-225 2172, www.olenkahotel.lk.
38 comfortable a/c rooms and 4 suites with balcony/terrace around a small pool.

$$ Ging Oya Lodge
Kammala North, Waikkal, T031-227 7822, www.gingoya.com.
The stand-out deal on this stretch of coast, Ging Oya is a lovely rustic retreat of cool and clean cabins, run by welcoming Belgian couple Leo and Myrjam. There's a good pool, excellent food and kayaks for paddling to the beach.

$$ Sanmali Beach
Beach Rd, Marawila, T031-225 4766, www.sanmali.com.
20 a/c rooms with balcony in an old-fashioned, gently decaying mini-resort on the beach. Small pool, restaurant.

Up the coast to Puttalam

$$$$ The Mudhouse
Pahaladuwelweva, Anamaduwa,
T077-301 6191, www.themudhouse.lk.
For those who want to get back to nature,
look no further. Huts made from natural,
local materials are scattered around the
jungle, some are even in the trees. Lanterns
and candles in the evenings (no electric
lights) and outdoor showers (no hot water).
Prices are all-inclusive, a lot of the fruit
and veg comes from The Mudhouse's
organic garden. Due to its remote location
a member of staff can meet visitors in the
nearest town, pick-ups can be arranged
from anywhere in Sri Lanka, or your driver
can ring for detailed directions.

$$-$ Rest House
Wadia Rd, Chilaw, across the lagoon close to
the beach, T032-222 2299.
16 a/c and fan rooms, some with balcony
overlooking sea. Close to the beach.

$$-$ Senatilaka Guest Inn
81/a Kurunegala Rd, Puttalam, T032-226 5403.
10 a/c and fan rooms with attached hot
bath, some with balcony, a/c and TV, open-
air terrace, restaurant, good value.

Transport

Bus Frequent buses go along the coast
between **Colombo** and **Puttalam** (3 hrs),
some stopping at **Negombo** (1 hr) and
Chilaw (2 hrs). There are also services inland
from Puttalam to **Anuradhapura** and
Kurunegala (both 2 hrs).

Train Regular trains run from Colombo
Fort station to **Chilaw**, via **Negombo** and
Madampe, 3 of which continue to **Puttalam**
at the end of the line. Note that the line can
flood after heavy rain.

★ Kalpitiya Peninsula *Colour map 2, A1/B1.*
windswept beaches for kitesurfing and dolphin watching

Easily accessible by causeway from the main road, this narrow, sandy spit of land on
the seaward side of the Puttalam Lagoon boasts a distinctive, almost otherworldly
landscape. The waters of Dutch Bay saw many naval skirmishes during the war, but
Kalpitiya's beaches and rich marine wildlife have now begun to attract a steady
flow of tourists. Many of them are kitesurfers, who come here for the reliably
powerful breeze that fetches in from the Indian Ocean, and who are prepared to
divert their eyes from the often scruffy beaches and silty water.

Kalpitiya's position at the head of Puttalam's lagoon made it an important port for Arab
traders from the seventh century, and the peninsula remains predominantly Muslim to
this day. Later, the Portuguese and the Dutch recognized its strategic use and the Dutch
built a fort here in order to strangle King Rajasingha's trade with India. Today it is famous
for its dried fish and prawn farming. Its sandy soil has also made its farmers some of Sri
Lanka's richest. Despite its proximity to the sea, the land overlies an abundant supply of
fresh, rather than brackish, water. Simple wells have been constructed for irrigation, and
crops including tobacco, shallots, chilli and even potatoes grow abundantly.
    In recent years the Kalpitiya Peninsula has emerged as an excellent place to see dolphins
and even whales between December and mid-April. Tours are run from a number of the

hotels (see Where to stay, below). Twitchers will also enjoy the abundance of birdlife here. The Sri Lankan government has outlandish plans to capitalize on Kalpitiya's long coastline by developing it into a Hikkaduwa of the north, with thousands of hotel rooms, theme parks and a domestic airport on the slate. To them, we can only say "good luck".

Alankuda

Near the foot of the peninsula, Alankuda is one of the peninsula's main beaches. Backed by a line of wind turbines and featuring views of the Norochcholai coal power station, it's hardly a tropical paradise, but there are some good resorts towards the northern end.

Talawila *Colour map 2, B1.*

Further up the peninsula, 22 km from Puttalam, Talawila has a wide beach and an important shrine at **St Anne's Church**. There are two accounts of its history. In one, a shipwrecked Portuguese sailor brought the image of St Anne to shore, placed it under a banyan tree and vowed to build a church here if his business prospered. In the other, a vision of St Anne appeared and left gold coins for the construction of a chapel. The present-day church, set in extensive tree-lined grounds, was built in 1843 and has fine satinwood pillars. (Remove shoes before you enter; photography is not allowed.) There are two major festivals in Talawila in March and June, featuring huge processions, healing and a rural fair. These draw up to 50,000 people, with some pilgrims arriving by boat.

Kalpitiya *Colour map 2, A1.*

The bustling, predominantly Muslim village of Kalpitiya, 19 km beyond Talawila, marks the end of the road. The small **Dutch fort**, built in 1676 on the site of a Portuguese stockade and Jesuit chapel, is one of the best preserved in Sri Lanka. It has a VOC gate (1760), an original wooden

> **Tip...**
> Photography is prohibited on the naval base.

door and, inside, the remains of the barracks, commander's house, chapel and prison. The fort is currently occupied by the navy, and you will need to ask permission from the sentry to enter; you may be asked to leave your ID at the entrance. A naval officer will accompany you around the ramparts, and you may be shown a number of rusting Indian trawlers, impounded for fishing in Sri Lankan waters. Two tunnels lead from the fort to St Peter's Kirk and a school, though these were blocked up during the war.

In contrast, the impressively gabled **St Peter's Kirk** nearby has lost many of its original features, although a heavy stone font remains and there are some well-preserved 17th- and 18th-century Dutch gravestones inside. The church's columns and semi-circular porch date from a 19th-century renovation. Outside, there is a small, weathered cemetery.

Listings Kalpitiya Peninsula

Where to stay

The resorts on Alankuda beach tend to be small and relaxed affairs, but they do charge handsomely for the privilege of staying. Cheaper digs are concentrated on Kalpitiya beach.

$$$$ Palagama Beach
12 Palmyra Rd, Alankuda, T077-781 8970, www.palagamabeach.com.
For rustic luxury, check into this collection of cabanas and villas, modelled on fishing shacks. There is a more luxurious villa

option, or a house with kitchen and living area. Restaurant, infinity pool, spa, dolphin-watching trips, watersports and trips to Wilpattu.

$$$$ Udekki
Alankuda Beach, T077-744 6135, www.udekki.com.
Owned by blues guitarist Glen Terry and his wife, Carolyn, this beautiful retreat offers a variety of cool, minimalist suites and loft rooms. There's a great pool with hot tub, and superb meals.

$$$-$$ Dolphin View Eco Lodge
Off Km 40 post, Kalpitiya Rd, 2 km towards the sea, Sethawadiya, T011-281 9457, www.dolphinviewecolodge.com.
Being swiftly rebuilt at the time of writing after a fire in 2015, this rustic and friendly camp offers simple, good-value thatched bungalows (shared and en suite) and has a great lagoon-facing location that's popular with kitesurfers. Lessons and kite hire are available, and they run dolphin-watching trips and jungle walks. The restaurant serves good seafood and vegetarian options.

$ Dolphin Village
Ilanthadiya, Norochcholai (south of Alunkudu), T077-247 0819, www.dolphin-village.com.
If you can put up with the power plant views, this friendly, family-run guesthouse is one of the cheapest beachside options in Kalpitiya. There are 3 basic rooms and 2 larger en suite rooms. Good home-cooked food, and the owner can arrange boat trips with local fishermen.

$ Taniya
Kalpitiya, T076-629 9750, www.taniyahotel.com.
14 a/c and fan rooms, as well as 2 cabanas. Restaurant, fishing trips and dolphin watching.

Restaurants

Kalpitiya doesn't have much in the way of a food scene, so most visitors stick to their hotel or guesthouse.

$ Kite House
Odai Karai Rd, Kappalady, near Talawila.
Chilled-out little beach shack serving good salads and veggie burgers, juices and milkshakes. Great palm-fringed views of the sunset over the Indian Ocean.

What to do

Dolphin and whale watching
Most resorts organize dolphin- and whale-watching trips. See Where to stay, above.

Kitesurfing
Kalpitiya Peninsula is a magnet for kitesurfers, and many resorts hire out gear. The main summer season runs May-Oct, with reliable 18-20 knot winds, and there's less frenetic activity Dec-Mar. **Dolphin View Eco Lodge** (see above) has a good kite school with European instructors.
KiteKuda, *www.srilankakiteschool.com*. Lessons for beginners (€45/US$51 for 2 hrs or €50/US$57 for a private lesson), and more advanced kiters (€135/US$153 for 4 hrs). Accommodation also available in 4 bungalows.

Transport

Bus Buses run along the main road between **Puttalam** and **Kalpitiya**.

thrilling leopard sightings amid beautiful scenery

In March 2010 a clamour of excitement greeted the reopening of Wilpattu National Park, Sri Lanka's largest, oldest and – before the war – most popular wildlife sanctuary. The 131,693 ha park is an important historical and archaeological site, as well as home to healthy populations of large mammals. Still relatively quiet compared to Yala, it's also one of Sri Lanka's most beautiful wild areas, boasting a rich variety of scenery from dense vine-draped jungle to wide sandy ponds.

The war years put Wilpattu well and truly off limits. Its tangled jungle provided a convenient hiding place for the LTTE, and, at the peak of the war, there were army checkpoints every 100 m along the main road through the park. The park was closed in 1985, immediately after an attack on its wardens and officers by a group of LTTE cadres. Except for a three-year period from 2003, it remained closed until 2011. In 2015 the park's protected status came under threat from road-building schemes and Qatari interests, which are illegally clearing land to build settlements.

Landscape and wildlife

Wilpattu has a unique topographical landscape of gently undulating terrain dominated by *villus*, natural sand-rimmed water basins, which fill up with rain and to which animals come to drink. These are among the best places to see leopards. Certain sections have a distinctive rich, red, loamy soil, and there are also areas of dense forest. The western part of the park is reminiscent of Yala (see page 184). Offshore, Dutch and Portugal bays may still support populations of dugong. A further protected area, the Wilpattu Sanctuary, lies to the north within Northern Province.

Essential Wilpattu National Park

Finding your feet

The park office, information centre and entrance are at Hunuwilagama, 7 km from the Wilpattu Junction turn-off at Maragahawewa on the A12.

Getting around

Speed is restricted to 25 mph. It is not possible to visit the park independently. You can take a private vehicle (4WD essential), but you will have to pick up a tracker at the entrance station. There are only a limited number of these, and their sole job is to show you around and point out the animals (often with little explanation). The simple lodges

along the road leading to the main entrance gate offer safaris, but, again, these can be disappointing, as the drivers are not trained naturalists, and their English is generally limited. For a more in-depth experience you'll need to stay at one of the high-end camps on the fringe of the park, the best of which is indisputably **Leopard Safaris**, run by leopard-tracking legend Noel Rodrigo (see Where to stay).

Park information

The park is open daily 0600-1830. Admission fees for foreign tourists are US$15 per adult (US$8 child) per visit, or US$25 (US$12) for two entries on the same day.

Wilpattu's wildlife suffered badly at the hands of landmines and poachers, but the park is now recovering well. Leopard sightings are frequent, along with sloth bear, elephant, water buffalo, crocodile, spotted deer, and many smaller mammals. There's also a large and healthy population of birds, including hundreds of hornbills, and resident and migratory waterfowl.

> **Fact...**
> The *Mahavansa* records that Prince Vijaya landed at Kudrimalai, southwest of the park, in AD 543. He married Kuveni, the local jungle princess, and founded the Sinhalese race.

In contrast to other parks in Sri Lanka (such as Yala, or elephant-rich Minneriya), wildlife here does not simply present itself: you have to work for your sightings. This fact makes the sight of a lone bull elephant up to its shoulders in a lotus pond, or a trio of leopards peering out of grey branches, all the more satisfying.

Listings Wilpattu National Park

Where to stay

Basing yourself near the park rather than in Anuradhapura, say, gives you a better chance of being at the park gates for opening time at 0600. There are several simple lodges along the road leading to the main entrance gate, all offering food and safaris. There are also high-end camps on the fringe of the park. Bungalows within the park itself can be booked online at dwc. lankagate.gov.lk (book well in advance).

$$$$ Leopard Safaris
T071-331 4004, www.leopardsafaris.com.
Noel Rodrigo's safari camp is, without challenge, the best wildlife destination we've ever visited in Sri Lanka. Lantern-lit mud paths lead through a patch of lush riverine jungle to a series of sturdy bug-proof tents, with comfy beds and outdoor showers. Fishing cats and civets wander through, joining the resident giant water monitors and kingfishers. Sumptuous meals emerge from the camp kitchen, along with generous post-safari sundowners. Camp manager Pila and his team of highly-trained naturalists provide the best safaris in Wilpattu – they're committed wildlife experts and go out of their way not only to get a coveted leopard sighting, but to explain the park's ecology and history. This is an old-fashioned safari in the best sense – wilderness alloyed with just enough luxury. Unsurpassed.

$$$-$$ Aanawila Bungalow
1 km from the park, T077-771 8045, aanawila@hotmail.com.
This rustic bungalow just outside the park has 2 spartan rooms with outdoor showers, and mattresses on the open sided upstairs deck where it's cooler. Meals served outside.

$ Thimbiriwewa Eco Resort
Wilpattu Rd, Thimbiriwewa, bookings via www.booking.com.
Good clean a/c rooms set around a small garden, in a peaceful spot off the highway. Good meals and campfire barbecues, and a nearby pond that attracts birds and small animals.

Transport

Bus Buses ply the **Puttalam–Anuradhapura** road; ask to be let out at Wilpattu Junction.

Kurunegala
& around

As the chosen location for four medieval Sinhalese kingdoms, the inland heart of Northwestern Province contains some important archaeological ruins, the highlight of which, Yapahuwa, rivals the rock fortress at Sigiriya. They can be visited either as a detour en route to Anuradhapura or Dambulla, or they can make a rewarding day trip from the provincial capital of Kurunegala.

Kurunegala   *Colour map 2, C3.*

a good base for exploration, set among scenic granite outcrops

Kurunegala, 93 km northeast of Colombo, is an important crossroads town astride the routes from the capital to Anuradhapura and from Kandy to Puttalam. The town is the capital of Northwest Province and is the best base for visiting the deserted royal and religious ruins in the surrounding countryside.

Sights
The town (population 28,500) enjoys a pleasant location overlooked by huge rocky outcrops, some of which have been given names of the animals they resemble: Elephant Rock, Tortoise Rock, etc. According to a legend, these 'animals' were magically turned into stone when they threatened the city's water supply during a drought. Situated at the foot of the 325-m black rock, **Etagala**, there are excellent views across the lake from the temple, where there is an enormous **Buddha statue**.

Kurunegala was the royal capital for only half a century, during the reigns of Parakramabahu III (ruled 1287-1293), Bhuvanekabahu II (1293-1302) and Parakramabahu IV (ruled 1302-1326). Parakramabahu III brought the Tooth Relic here from Yapahuwa (see box, page 201). Little remains of the Tooth Relic temple today, save a few stone steps and part of a doorway. Elsewhere in the town, you can drive up to **Elephant Rock** for wonderful views, or take a trip around the attractive lake.

Where to stay

$$$ Kandyan Reach
344-350 Kandy Rd (1 km southeast
of the centre), T037-222 4218,
www.kandyanreach.com.
Large a/c rooms with hot water, balcony
and TV. Restaurant and good (if rather
shallow) pool.

$$$ Littlemore Estate Bungalow
Pellandeniya, T072-231 9443,
www.facebook.com/littlemoreestate.
3 cool and spacious rooms in a beautifully
restored bungalow set on a working

coconut plantation. Large pool, great food,
fast Wi-Fi and wonderful grounds to explore.

$$ Diya Dahara
7 North Lake Rd, T037-222 3452,
diyadahara@sltnet.lk.
7 a/c rooms (some larger than others),
No 3 has a large balcony. Best located
restaurant in town overlooking the lake,
good buffet lunch.

$$ Situ Medura
21 Mihindu Mawatha, T037-222 2335.
2 slightly gloomy a/c rooms in large
traditional mansion once belonging
to local aristocrat. Popular restaurant.

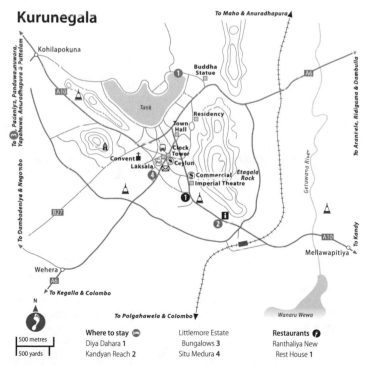

Kurunegala

Where to stay
Diya Dahara **1**
Kandyan Reach **2**

Littlemore Estate
Bungalows **3**
Situ Medura **4**

Restaurants
Ranthaliya New
Rest House **1**

Restaurants

Many of the hotels have restaurants serving reasonable food.

$$ Ranthaliya Rest House
South Lake Rd (1 km from centre), T037-222 2298.
Good rice-and-curry restaurant with views over the lake. There are a few grubby a/c rooms if you're stuck for somewhere to stay.

Transport

Bus Frequent buses to **Colombo** (2-2½ hrs depending on route); to **Negombo** (2 hrs); **Dambulla** (2 hrs); **Anuradhapura** (3 hrs); **Kandy** (1½ hrs).

Train The station is 1.5 km southeast of the town centre. Kurunegala is on the Northern line to **Anuradhapura** and **Jaffna**. More than 10 trains a day go to **Colombo Fort** (2 hrs); 8 daily to **Anuradhapura** (3 hrs), 3 continuing to Jaffna (6 hrs).One nightly train goes to **Trincomalee**, 2340, 6 hrs.

Around Kurunegala

abandoned royal capitals and Buddhist temples

Arankele *Colour map 2, B3.*
24 km north of Kurunegala. Getting there: travel 14 km along the A6 towards Dambulla, then turn left at Ibbagamuwa towards Moragollagama for 10 km. The hermitage is hard to reach by public transport.

Up a forested hillside north of Kurunegala is this sixth-century **cave** hermitage. Ancient Brahmi inscriptions have been found in some caves. Excavations have revealed meditation halls, stone-faced double platform structures and ambulatories for the *Tapovana* (forest-dwelling) sect of austere Buddhist hermits here. Typically, the platforms were aligned east–west, with the entrance porch to the east, and would be bridged by a large monolith. The smaller of the double-platform structures here was probably divided into nine 'cells' or monks' dwellings, the roof being supported on columns.

Ridigama *Colour map 2, C4.*
18 km northeast of Kurunegala. Getting there: travel northeast on the A6 through Ibbagamuwa (11.5 km), then take the first right onto the B409. At 7 km, turn right at the junction onto the B264; after 9 km you reach Ridigama. Turn left at the main junction, then right at the clock tower and follow the dirt track for 200 m. Turn left onto the sealed road, then turn right at the T-junction. Follow the road past the lake and go uphill for 1.5 km to the vihara.

The 'Silver Temple' marks the place where silver ore was discovered in the second century BC, during the reign of Dutthagamenu (Dutugemunu). It is an ancient Buddhist temple site with rock cave hermitages and an image house with Kandyan paintings. Among the finds, which mostly date from the 18th century, are Buddha statues (seated and reclining), a door frame beautifully carved and inlaid with ivory, and a curious altar with Dutch (Delft) tiles with Biblical figures gifted by a Dutch consul. There is an attractive artificial lake at the foot of the hills. Ridigama is only 18 km from Kurunegala, but the journey there is tricky.

Dambadeniya *Colour map 2, C2.*

30 km southwest of Kurunegala. Getting there: the site is just off the Negombo road, which is served by regular buses. If coming from Colombo, turn off at Ambepussa.

Dambadeniya became prominent in the mid-13th century when it became the capital under Parakramabahu II (ruled 1236-1270), who also moved the Tooth Relic here for safe-keeping. Legend states that it was the site of a monumental battle with the Indian King Kalinga, during which 24,000 men were successfully repelled and the Tooth kept safe, though shortly afterwards the relic was moved to the more secure site of Yapahuwa (see page 98).

Little remains of the ancient rock palace buildings, though six ponds where the courts used to bathe are still there. The 272-step climb to the top is nevertheless worth it for the panoramic views of the surrounding rocks and across to the ocean on a clear day. The two-storey temple (originally three) about 400 m south, which has Buddha images, is identified as the Vijayasundaramaya. It has some interesting wall paintings dating from the 18th century, when it was restored. It was used to exhibit the Tooth Relic, which was normally housed in another temple near the palace.

Panduwasnuwara *Colour map 2, C2.*

27 km northwest of Kurunegala. Getting there: follow the A10 towards Puttalam for around 17 km, then turn left at Wariyapola towards Chilaw. The site is 1 km from the main road. Buses run between Chilaw and Kurunegala.

The oldest of the royal capitals in the district, Panduwasnuwara was used by King Parakramabahu I as a stepping stone to his great citadel at Polonnaruwa (see page 297), although legend states that Panduwasdeva, Sri Lanka's second king, also had his capital here in the fifth century BC. A forested mound has been identified as his predecessor King Vijaya's tomb.

The archaeological remains at the sprawling, partly excavated 20-ha site date to the 12th century AD. There is an impressive ancient wall stretching for more than 1 km around the citadel with a moat in which crocodiles may have acted as an extra deterrent. Inside are the remains of a palace (once three storey), audience hall and storehouses as well as a monastic complex and several bathing pools. A guide may show you around, though you can clamber at will around the ruins.

Nearby, a small **Tooth temple,** reminiscent of the Tooth temple at Kandy has been restored, while back on the main road at the turn-off to the site is a small museum containing finds from local excavations, such as coins, images and jewellery.

Yapahuwa is a huge rock fortress, suggestive of Sigiriya, which stands on a very pleasant shaded site. Bhuvanekabahu I (ruled 1272-1284) moved his capital here from Dambadeniya (see page 97), seeing the need for stronger fortification against Tamil invaders, and built a palace and a temple where the Tooth and the Alms Bowl relics were housed for 11 years.

After it was abandoned, this fortress capital of the Sinhalese kings was inhabited by Buddhist monks and religious ascetics. The relics were carried away from the temple here to South India by the Pandyas and then recovered in 1288 by Parakramabahu III (ruled 1287-1293), who temporarily placed them in safety at Polonnaruwa, before moving the Tooth Relic to Kurunegala (see page 94).

Kurunegala to Yapahuwa

Yapahuwa lies off the route north from Kurunegala to Anuradhapura. To reach the site, follow the A10 past the turn-off to Panduwasnuwara to **Padeniya**. Here there is a *vihara* with 28 carved pillars, an elaborately carved door and an ancient clay image house and library. From Padeniya, take the A28 north towards Anuradhapura. Yapahuwa lies 6 km east of the main road, close to the pleasant town of **Maho**.

The site

47 km north of Kurunegala (69 km south of Anuradhapura), near Maho. Daily 0600-1800. Rs 1000, plus tip for the guide.

A vast granite rock, rising 100 m from the surrounding plain, is encircled by a 1-km-long path rising to the top. The fort palace, built of stone, is surrounded by two moats and ramparts, and there are signs of other ancient means of defence. The impressive ornamental stairway, with some fine lions and guardstones, is still well preserved and somewhat reminiscent of Far Eastern art. The steps are fairly steep so can be tiring to climb. The ruins at the head of the remarkable flight of granite steps are unique and the views over the palms towards the highlands are not to be missed.

The temple (restored in 1886) illustrates South Indian artistic influence in the fine carvings on its pillars, doorway and windows, which show dancers, musicians and animals. One of the window frames is now exhibited in the Colombo National Museum (see page 54). To the northeast, outside the fortification, are the remains of another temple, which was thought at one time to have housed the Tooth Relic; it has some sculptures visible. There is a small, fairly modern museum on site.

Where to stay

$$$ Yapahuwa Paradise Resort
Kingdom Rd, off Maho–
Moragollagama Rd, T037-397 5055,
www.hotelyapahuwaparadise.com.
Bright rooms with private balconies and a/c.
Pleasant gardens, restaurant and pool.

Transport

Yapahuwa is 5 km east of **Maho**, which
is easily accessible by bus or train. Take a
3-wheeler from Maho to the site.

Bus Buses to Maho, every 2 hrs from
Kurunegala and hourly from **Anuradhapura**.

Train Maho is on the Colombo–Vavuniya
line, with several trains daily from
Kurunegala, journey time 1 hr. From
Anuradhapura, journey time 2 hrs.

Southern
Sri Lanka

blissful beaches and wonderful wildlife

When people describe Sri Lanka as a tropical paradise, you can bet they're talking about the island's idyllic south. Here, magnificent bays, beaches and rocky headlands line the coast, while hills clad in lush jungle rise just inland.

The southwest region, from Colombo to Galle, is the most densely populated, both with industry and with Western sun-seekers who pack into resorts such as Beruwela, Bentota and Hikkaduwa. It's easy enough to escape the hordes, however, by venturing inland to explore tranquil rivers, lagoons and lush forests in Sri Lanka's Wet Zone. Here you'll find Ratnapura, the centre of the island's gem-producing region, and Sinharaja Biosphere Reserve, a World Heritage Site.

Historic Galle, the province's unrivalled capital, is rich with colonial heritage. The outstandingly beautiful 80-km stretch of road between here and Tangalla is one of the most scenic routes in the country. Though no longer a secret, there are fewer package hotels and good beachlife at laid-back Mirissa and Tangalla.

Further east, you'll find Sri Lanka's greatest national parks, in particular Yala and Uda Walawe, where there are magnificent opportunities for spotting wildlife, as well as some of the island's most sacred pilgrimage sites.

Best for
Beaches ▪ Heritage ▪ Wildlife

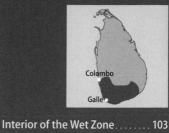

Footprint
picks

★ **Sinharaja Biosphere Reserve**, page 109

The stunning rainforest canopy is packed full of wildlife and also shelters some special eco accommodation.

★ **Galle**, page 139

The heart of Galle is the lovingly restored fort, which has beautiful heritage buildings, delicious food and chic places to stay.

★ **East of Weligama**, page 154

Come to this stretch of coast for a traditional snapshot of the stilt fishermen – or to catch a wave at this hot surf spot.

★ **Mirissa**, page 158

Get up close to whales and enjoy some lazy beachlife.

★ **Mulgirigala**, page 168

Gain an insight into Buddhist life through the exquisite paintings and temples on this imposing rocky outcrop.

★ **Yala National Park**, page 184

Glimpse leopards, langur monkeys, elephants and countless birds in the dense jungle.

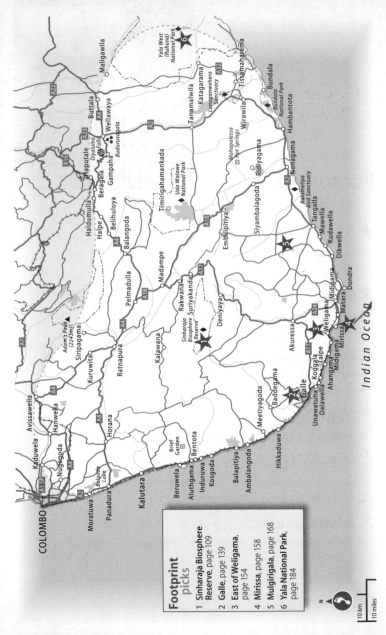

Footprint picks

1 **Sinharaja Biosphere Reserve**, page 109
2 **Galle**, page 139
3 **East of Weligama**, page 154
4 **Mirissa**, page 158
5 **Mulgirigala**, page 168
6 **Yala National Park**, page 184

Indian Ocean

N

10 km
10 miles

Interior of the
Wet Zone

Stretching inland away from Colombo and the west coast beaches towards the Central Highland ridge, Sabaragamuwa Province, with its luxuriantly verdant, gently hilly landscape, is one of Sri Lanka's most beautiful regions. Beyond the gem capital of Ratnapura lies the wonderful UNESCO-protected Sinharaja rainforest, while scattered around the region are some remarkable, if rarely visited, prehistoric cave sites.

Towards Ratnapura
Buddhist temples, interesting caves and pretty villages

The most frequently used route inland to Ratnapura heads east from Colombo along the congested A4 through Nugegoda, though a more attractive route follows the B1 along the south bank of the Kelaniya River.

Colombo to Hanwella

The B1 passes through picturesque **Kaduwela**, 16 km from Colombo, where there is a large Buddhist temple and the irrigation tank of Mulleriyawa, where you can watch a constant succession of varied river traffic from the beautifully positioned rest house. The B1 converges with the A4 near Hanwella (33 km), where the traffic begins to clear. **Hanwella** is built on the site of a Portuguese fort and is noted as the place where the last king of Kandy, Sri Vikrama Rajasinha, was defeated.

Avissawella

Avissawella (57 km), the ancient capital of the Sitawaka kings and now the centre of the rubber industry, is in beautiful wooded surroundings. The ruins of the royal palace of Rajasinha, a Buddhist king who converted to Hinduism, can still be seen. He was responsible for starting work on the unfinished **Berendi Kovil**, which still has some fine stonework despite the Portuguese attack. It climate that has been likened to a Turkish bath. Even February, the driest month, normally has nearly 100 mm of rain, while May, the wettest, has nearly 500 mm At Avissawella, the A4 turns south towards Ratnapura, while the A7 leads off east through Kitulgala (see page 240), Hatton and ultimately to Nuwara Eliya.

Essential Wet Zone

Finding your feet

Ratnapura is the main urban centre in this area. It is located 100 km east of Colombo via the A4 or the A8. To the south lies the rainforest of the Sinharaja Biosphere Reserve. To the northeast are the Central Highlands.

Getting around

There are buses from Ratnapura to all major towns in the south.

When to go

The climate around Ratnapura has been likened to a Turkish bath. Even January and February, the driest months, normally have over 100 mm of rain, while May, the wettest, has nearly 500 mm.

Time required

Allow half a day for Ratnapura (or more if you want to visit a gemstone mine). To explore Sinharaja properly takes at least a full day, ideally two or more.

Weather Ratnapura

January	February	March	April	May	June
33°C	34°C	34°C	34°C	32°C	31°C
22°C	22°C	23°C	23°C	24°C	24°C
111mm	137mm	212mm	339mm	476mm	412mm

July	August	September	October	November	December
31°C	31°C	31°C	31°C	32°C	32°C
24°C	23°C	23°C	23°C	23°C	22°C
293mm	304mm	421mm	437mm	371mm	235mm

Avissawella to Ratnapura

The road to Ratnapura periodically crosses rivers that come tumbling down from the southwest highlands. It passes through Pusella and crosses the Kuruwita River, running through a landscape that was the site of some of Sri Lanka's earliest settlements. It is also a gem-bearing area. At **Batadombalena Cave**, near Kuruwita, fragmentary human skeletal remains have been found, as well as those of several large mammal skeletons, including elephants and cattle, dating back at least 28,000 years, or possibly very much earlier. To reach the caves take the road towards Eratne, turn right after 2 km and follow it to the end (2 km). A path reaches the cave in 5 km.

A8 to Ratnapura

An alternative route from Colombo to Ratnapura follows the coastal road south to **Panadura** (see page 117), turning inland along the A8 through **Horana**, where there is a rest house built in the remains of an ancient Buddhist monastery. On the opposite side of the road is a large Buddhist temple with a particularly noteworthy bronze candlestick, over 2 m tall. Heading east from here there are some good views of Adam's Peak.

Where to stay

Kaduwela and Hanwella

$$ Rest House (CHC)
On the Kelaniya River, Hanwella, T011-250 3497, www.chcresthouses.com.

8 fan and a/c rooms with a beautiful view along the river. Edward VII (then Prince of Wales) planted a jack tree in the garden here in 1875.

Ratnapura   *Colour map 3, B3.*

clty of gems: sapphires, rubies and tourmalines galore

Ratnapura (population 109,000) is one of Sri Lanka's wettest towns, meaning that the surrounding vegetation is correspondingly luxuriant. The city has a beautiful setting on the banks of the Kalu Ganga, with views of rubber plantations and paddies. When fine, its views of Adam's Peak are also unmatched.

Ratnapura is aptly named the 'City of Gems' because of the gemstones that are washed down the riverbed here (see box, page 107). The gravel beds also contain evidence of some of Sri Lanka's earliest cultures and now-extinct wildlife. Discoveries of animal bones and a variety of stone tools have made it clear that this area was probably one of the first sites of human occupation in Sri Lanka.

Tip...
The old fort above the clock tower offers good views as does the big Buddha statue, built by a wealthy young gem merchant, on a hill behind the rest house.

Gem mining and trading

Although people seem to trade gems all over town, certain areas specialize in uncut and unpolished stones, polished stones, cut stones, while other streets will only deal in star sapphires or cat's eyes. From 0700 to 1000 the area around the clock tower is a fascinating place to visit. Here you can watch hundreds of people buying and selling gems.

Private museums in Ratnapura tend to be primarily retail outlets for gems but at the same time demonstrate the craft of gem polishing. The **Gem Bureau and Museum** ⓘ *Pothgul Vihara Rd, Getangama (2 km south), daily 0900-1700*, has gems from different parts of Sri Lanka, and an art gallery. The **Gem Bank Gemmological Museum** ⓘ *6 Ehelepola Mawatha, Batugedera, 2 km along A4 towards Pelmadulla, T045-222 2724, daily 0900-1700*, has an interesting private collection of gems and precious minerals and mining-related exhibits including a model of a pit. Don't miss the museum's rare elephant pearl.

Tip...
If you do buy a gem in Ratnapura, it is worth checking its authenticity at the **State Gem Corporation** (in the fort, daily 0800-1630). If the gem merchant is genuine, he should not mind if you check its authenticity before the transaction.

There are around 200 working **gem mines**, in the Ratnapura area. The mines are around 30 m deep, each with a series of interconnecting tunnels. Travel agents can organize visits (a tip is expected), or you can take a three-wheeler to Warallupa Road, where there are several working mines. At each mine there is a shack housing a generator, where you will be shown the mining process. Miners will demonstrate washing and sifting the stones, and it may also be possible to walk inside some mines – ask locally.

Other sights

Ratnapura National Museum ⓘ *Ehelapola Walauwa, Colombo Rd, T045-222 2451, Sat-Wed 0900-1700, Rs 45, children Rs 25.* The museum has a small dated exhibition of prehistoric fossil skeletons of elephants, hippos and rhinoceros found in gem pits, plus stuffed animals and snakes in jars. There is also a section on the arts and culture of the province with musical instruments, masks, jewellery, textiles and flags.

Maha Saman Dewale Located some 4 km west of town, this is the richest Buddhist temple in Sri Lanka. Dedicated to the guardian god of Adam's Peak, it is thought to date from the 13th century, but was rebuilt by Parakramabahu IV in the 15th century before being damaged by the Portuguese soldiers. The temple, which has been restored, has an ornamental doorway and fine wall paintings inside. Interesting features include

Ratnapura

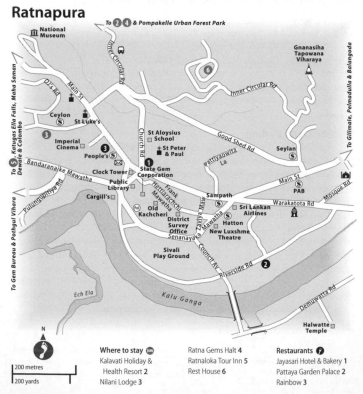

Where to stay 🏨
Kalavati Holiday &
Health Resort 2
Nilani Lodge 3

Ratna Gems Halt 4
Ratnaloka Tour Inn 5
Rest House 6

Restaurants 🍴
Jayasari Hotel & Bakery 1
Pattaya Garden Palace 2
Rainbow 3

ON THE ROAD
A gem of a place

Sri Lanka is among the top five gem-bearing nations of the world. Washed out from the ancient rocks of the highlands, the gems are found in pockets of alluvial gravel known as *illama*, usually a metre or two below the surface. Ratnapura (the 'City of Gems') is still the heart of the industry, though new pits are being explored in other parts of the island.

The quality of Ratnapura's gems is legendary. In the seventh century Hiuen Tsang claimed that there was a ruby on the spire of the temple at Anuradhapura whose magnificence illuminated the sky. Marco Polo (1293) described the flawless ruby as "a span long and quite as thick as a man's arm"! Today, sapphires are much more important. In 2010 the engagement ring of the future Duchess of Cambridge, Kate Middleton, featured a Sri Lankan sapphire, resulting in a sharp increase in demand for the stone.

Traditional gem-mining makes use of only the simplest technology. Pits are dug in the gravel and then divided in two: one half is used for extracting water while the gravel is dug out from the other half. When, after two or three days, a large enough pile of gravel has been excavated, it is systematically washed in a stream, sifting the gems and heavy minerals from the lighter material. The work is done in teams, everyone getting a share of the value of any gems found. The dressing, cutting and polishing is carried out largely in Ratnapura itself, using methods and materials that are still largely local. Hand-operated lathes, and polishing paste made from the ash of burnt paddy straw have been used for generations.

A number of precious stones are found nearby including sapphire, ruby, topaz, amethyst, cat's eye, alexandrite, aquamarine, tourmaline, garnet and zircon. Genuine stones are common. Valuable stones are by definition rarer. Advice given to travellers at the beginning of the century still holds true: "As regards buying stones, it is a risky business unless the passenger has expert knowledge or advice. It is absolute folly to buy stones from itinerant vendors. It is far better to go to one of the large Colombo jewellers and take the chance of paying more and obtaining a genuine stone."

the remains of a Portuguese fort. On the temple wall is a Portuguese soldier sculpted in stone while a slab bearing their coat of arms was also found here. There is a major **Perahera** procession during the July-August full moon, when decorated boats sail along the Kalu Ganga.

Pompakelle Urban Forest Park ⓘ *Daily 0800-1700.* A short walk northeast of town is the surprisingly large 15 ha park, where signposted trails lead you through the forest – a welcome change of pace from Main Street. Close to the entrance is a large, now defunct, natural swimming pool enclosed originally by the British as a reservoir for the town. The water is muddy and polluted and swimming is prohibited, though a clean-up is planned. In the mean time, head instead to the attractive **Katugas Ella Falls**, 2 km north from the centre, where you can swim in the river. Avoid visiting on Sundays, though, when it can get busy.

Ratnapura to Adam's Peak

Ratnapura is surrounded by rubber and tea estates in a lush and beautiful setting, and gives better views of Adam's Peak than almost anywhere else on the island. Driving up to **Gilimale** from the bridge gives you a chance to see the massive curtain wall of the Central Highlands to the north. The surrounding forests are rich in flowers, one of the most notable being the **vesak orchid**, which takes its name from the month of Vesak in which it flowers.

Ratnapura is the base for a steep and strenuous route to **Adam's Peak** starting at Siripagama, 15 km away. Buses leave Ratnapura for Siripagama regularly until 1900. Some pilgrims walk the whole 25 km from Ratnapura to Adam's Peak during the winter months. The climb takes about seven hours, though the construction of new steps may shorten the time. It begins at **Malwala** (8 km) on the Kalu Ganga to **Palabadelle** (11 km, 375 m), then follows a very steep path to **Heramitipana** (13 km, 1100 m), and to the summit (5 km, 2260 m). See page 237 for the shorter and more frequently used route.

> **Tip...**
> There are impressive caves at Kosgalla, 8 km from Ratnapura and at Eratna/ Batatota, 19 km away.

Listings Ratnapura map p106

Where to stay

$$ Ratnaloka Tour Inn
Kosgala, Kahangama (6 km from town), T045-222 2455, www.ratnaloka.com.
53 a/c rooms, deluxe are carpeted and have TV, bathtub and private balcony (views across to lotus pond and tea estates). All comfortable, good restaurant, long pool.

$$-$ Kalavati Holiday and Health Resort
Polhengoda Village, Outer Circular Rd, 1.6 km from bus stand, T045-222 2465.
18 rooms, some with a/c, no hot water, restaurant, house decorated with collector's items: antiques cabinets, palm leaf manuscripts, statues, betel cutters, etc. Beautiful tropical garden, some interesting tours (Dec to May only), natural therapy 'healing arts' practised here including oil baths and massage, herbal treatments.

$$-$ Rest House
Rest House (Inner Circle) Rd, on a hill 1 km from centre, T045-222 2299, udarest@sltnet.lk.
11 large, simple rooms (best upstairs) though no hot water, food good value, peaceful, delightful site and outstanding views from atmospheric veranda.

$ Nilani Lodge
21 Dharmapala Mawatha, T045-594 6409, www.nilani-lodge-ratnapura.com.
9 a/c and fan rooms with balcony and hot water in large, modern, white apartment-style building. Restaurant and gem museum and shop on site, tours to mines and cutters. Basically a gem shop with beds.

$ Ratna Gems Halt
153/5 Outer Circular Rd (short climb), T045-222 3745, www.ratnapura-online.com.
Spotless, excellent value rooms, all with bath, in family house. Upstairs rooms with shared veranda overlooking paddy fields and mines, smaller, darker box-like rooms downstairs. Good meals available. Small gem centre (no pressure to buy) where you can watch stones being dressed, cut and polished. Also runs a 5-day gem polishing and cutting courses; contact in advance.

Restaurants

There are plenty of good bakeries near the bus station and around Ratnapura town.

$$ Jayasiri Hotel & Bakery
198 Main St. Daily 1030-2130.
Sri Lankan rice and curry downstairs, Chinese on 1st floor, bustling with activity, friendly staff, full of local colour.

$$ Pattaya Garden Palace
14 Senanayake Mawatha, T045-222 3029.
Modern a/c restaurant with a wide choice of Chinese and Thai dishes.

$$ Rainbow
163 Main St.
Good for rice and curry meals, large airy room looking onto part of the gem traders' street market.

$$ Rest House
See Where to stay, above.
A good spot for lunch (rice and curry with reasonably priced drinks) and dinner.

Transport

Bus There are regular services to **Colombo** (2½-3 hrs), **Kalawana** for **Sinharaja** (2 hrs) and **Balangoda** (1 hr). 2 CTB buses a day to **Haputale** (4 hrs) via **Belihuloya** (2 hrs), 1 going on to **Badulla**. Several buses to **Kandy** (4 hrs), via **Avissawella** and **Kegalla**; and 3 buses a day via **Embilipitiya** to **Hambantota** and **Matara** (1 hr). For **Galle**, take an a/c bus along the A8 to Panadura and change to a Colombo–Galle bus there.

★ Sinharaja Biosphere Reserve *Colour map 3, B3/4.*

Sri Lanka's only rainforest and eco-tourist haven

Sinharaja is the last significant stretch of rainforest on the island to remain largely undisturbed; as such, it has enormous national importance. It is home to a remarkable array of endemic species. In 1989 it was recognized by UNESCO as an international Biosphere Reserve and became a World Heritage Site.

'Sinharaja' means 'Lion King' and is believed to have been the final refuge of the now extinct Sri Lankan lion. Although it is managed by the Forestry Department with less than maximum efficiency, Sinharaja's ecotourism potential is now beginning to be recognized, with some good accommodation opening up in the area. The wildlife may be harder to see here than at some of the big national parks, but just being in the thick of the rainforest can be an exhilarating experience.

The reserve
Lying in the southwest lowland Wet Zone, the reserve's rolling hills with ridges and valleys between 200-1300 m stretch 21 km from east to west, though north to south it only measures 3.7 km, bounded by the Kalu Ganga in the north and the Gin Ganga in the south. It spans the districts of Ratnapura, Kalutara, Galle and Matara. Vegetation consists of tropical wet evergreen forest and tropical lowland forest, with lofty, very straight dominant trees a distinctive feature. The forest's trees, ferns and epiphytes are largely endemic. There are two entrances: at Kudawa, 17 km southeast of Kalawana, and at Mederipitiya, 12 km north of Deniyaya (see page 110).

Essential Sinharaja Biosphere Reserve

Finding your feet

There are three entrances to the reserve. Most people enter at the main gate at Kudawa, at the northwestern edge of the reserve, where there are basic bungalows and dormitories run by the **Forest Department** (reservations in advance on T011-286 6631). Alternatively, you can approach the eastern end of the reserve from Rakwana through Morning Side, south of Rakwana, though the road may be impassable in the wet season. From the south coast the closest entrance is at Mederipitiya, 12 km from Deniyaya, on the Galle–Ratnapura road, which has the best selection of places to stay. Note that the standard walk from the southern entrance leads partly along a road with frequent motorbike traffic. It's a good idea to arrange your trip in advance with a genuine naturalist guide (see below).

Getting around

There are several walking trails for exploring the forest on foot with a guide.

Best eco-accommodation

Boulder Garden, Sinharaja, page 112
Rainforest Ecolodge, Sinharaja, page 112
Eco Village & Study Centre, Dodanduwa, page 136
Gagabees Yala, page 181
The Saraii, Tissamaharama, page 182

Bring water, food, binoculars, rainwear and a lighter or salt to get rid of leeches (see box, page 415).

When to go

The best times are December to early April and August and September, when rainfall tends to be lighter. The shaded forest, with an average temperature of 23.6°C, is fairly cool throughout the day, though afternoons are usually wet – come prepared.

Park information

An entry ticket (Rs 575, children Rs 290), plus (compulsory) guide ticket must be purchased before entry. The guide fee varies according to the length of the trail (from Rs 500 per party); they will probably expect an additional tip. There are about 30 guides, all local villagers, and, although very knowledgeable, they don't always speak English. A video camera costs Rs 500. The reserve is open 0600-1800 though guides rarely arrive before 0700-0730. If you wish to make an early start, make arrangements the previous day. Facilities and information at the park offices (Kudawa and Mederipitiya) are limited, and leaflets may not be available, so it is worth calling in at the **Forestry Department** (82 Rajamalwatta Road, Battaramulla (Colombo outskirts), T011-286 6626), for further information.

BACKGROUND
Sinharaja Biosphere Reserve

The first records on Sinharaja date back to Portuguese time when detailed lists on not only names but also agricultural produce were collected for taxation purposes. Having been mapped first by the Dutch, the forest was made Crown Property by the British in 1840. Naturalist George Henry Thwaites undertook the first surveys in the 1850s, recording many plants found in Sinharaja, and in May 1875, 2430 ha of the 'Sinharaja Mukalana' were recognized as reserved forest. Through the 20th century, numerous studies assessed the area's suitability as a source of wood, but owing to its inaccessibility the reserve remained untouched until 1968, when the government sanctioned selective logging. From 1971 to 1977, about 1400 ha of forest was selectively logged, but pressure from conservation groups brought about a complete ban in 1978 when the area was designated a Man and Biosphere Reserve. In 1988 it was declared a National Heritage Area, and it became a World Heritage Site in 1989.

Despite this, the forest remains an important source of income for inhabitants of the 22 villages surrounding the reserve. The sap from the kitul palm produces a fermented toddy and a treacle produced by heating it which in turn makes the dry brown sugar, jaggery. Rattan is collected to make baskets and mats, and also leaves and wood for construction and fuel. There is also some illicit gem-mining in some eastern areas of the reserve.

Wildlife

Sinharaja's importance lies not just in its pristine nature, but also in the high degree of endemism of its species. For example, 95% of the endemic birds of Sri Lanka and more than half of its mammals and butterflies have been recorded here. That said, animals can be hard to see in the dense forest, so don't expect game spotting on the level of Yala National Park. The purple-faced leaf monkey is the most commonly seen mammal; others include giant squirrel, dusky squirrel and sambar. The leopard population is estimated to be around 15 (very seldom seen) and there are no elephants. Birdlife, as ever, is the most rewarding to observe. Rare endemics include red-faced malkoha, Sri Lanka blue magpie, the white-headed starling and even the green-billed coucal, with plenty of others, including orange minivets, orioles and babblers. An interesting and colourful spectacle is the presence of mixed flocks, sometimes comprising up to 80 species. The most commonly seen reptile is the green garden lizard, while snakes include the endemic green pit viper and the hump-nosed viper. There are several endemic amphibian species, including the torrent toad, wrinkled frog and Sri Lankan reed frog.

Trails

There are three main **nature trails** from Kudawa. Guide leaflets are sometimes available.

Waturawa Trail (4.7 km; about three hours of gentle walking) The path starts 250 m from the camp and leads through the forest up to the visitors' centre. From here, most guides will take you to the giant newada tree, some 43 m high. There are 14 observation posts, which are marked on the guide leaflet, and two good places for spotting birds and watching monkeys. This trail is a good introduction to the rainforest.

Moulawella Trail (7.5 km; about seven hours) This is a fairly strenuous trek. It takes you through primary forest up to Moulawella Peak (760 m) from where you can see Adam's Peak and look over the forest canopy. The walk gives you a chance to see fascinating leaf-shaped frogs, lizards, tropical fish, snakes, crabs and a 300-year-old vine.

Sinhagala Trail (14 km; a full day) The trail leads through the heart of the rainforest to the 742-m 'Lion Rock' from where you can look out over the unbroken tree canopy of an undisturbed forest and see the various hill ranges. One visitor described it as "twice as good as Moulawella."

Listings Sinharaja Biosphere Reserve

Where to stay

There is accommodation at the Kudawa entrance, in Kudawa itself and at Kalawana, 17 km away. If entering through the Mederipitiya entrance, the nearest accommodation is at Deniyaya, 12 km away.

$$$$ Boulder Garden
Sinharaja Rd, Kalawana (Kudawa entrance), T045-225 5812, www.bouldergarden.com.
Genuinely creative 'eco' concept: a sort of prehistoric luxury resort upmarket hermitage, with 8 smart but simple rooms plus 2 'suites' built into a complex of 28 caves. Fully inclusive rates include a trip to Sinharaja and also a 3-hr walk along a cave route within the grounds.

$$$$ Rainforest EcoLodge
Deniyaya, T041-340 5666, www.rainforest-ecolodge.org.
Perched above the forest canopy with stunning views of surrounding tea plantations and a symphony of bird song. Each chalet has its own private deck made from recycled railway sleepers. The theme at this award-winning eco resort is reduce, reuse and recycle in order to minimize its impact on the surroundings. Recommended.

$$$$ Rainforest Edge
Balawatukanda, Waddagala, T045-225 5912, www.rainforestedge.com.
Popular oasis in the heart of the rainforest. You can find tranquillity in the spacious grounds. Beautiful infinity pool, large rooms with open showers and fantastic Sri Lankan cuisine.

$$ Blue Magpie Lodge
Close to Kudawa entrance, T011-243 1872, bluemagpielodge@gmail.com.
Deservedly popular with 12 simple rooms with hot water. Restaurant, walking trails, perfect for birdwatchers.

$$ Rainforest Lodge
Temple Rd, Deniyaya (Mederipitiya entrance), T041-492 0444, www. rainforestlodge-srilanka.de.
Family-run lodge set amidst tea plantations, offering 5 clean rooms and good food. Ayurvedic treatments are also possible.

$ Martin's Simple Lodge
200 m from park entrance, 3.5 km by jeep from Kudawa village, 2 km shortcut on foot, T045-568 1864.
Knowledgeable and highly respected former park ranger. Magnificent forest views, 7 clean and predictably 'simple' rooms.

$ Rest House
Deniyaya (Mederipitiya entrance),
T041-227 3600.
Fine position and very large, simple but clean rooms. Popular lunch spot.

$ Sinharaja Rest
Temple Rd, Deniyaya (Mederipitiya entrance),
T077-7312 0201.
/ basic fan rooms, run by Bandula and Palitha Ratnayake, very knowledgeable and enthusiastic guides. Recommended trips to Sinharaja, good food.

What to do

Tours
Bandula and Palitha Ratnayaka, who run **Sinharaja Rest** in Deniyaya (see Where to stay, above) are long-established, experienced guides with excellent English.

Tours range from 4 hrs to all day. The full-day walk takes you to Lion Rock where you can look out over the forest canopy. Walks can vary according to fitness.

Transport

Bus Buses from **Colombo**, 1 direct a day to Kalawana (4 hrs), otherwise change in Ratnapura (2 hrs). 4 buses from **Kalawana** to Kudawa (45 mins). Walkers can ask locally for the short cut from Weddagala or use the 4-km track.

At **Deniyaya** the bus stand has buses to Colombo (6½ hrs), **Ratnapura** (4½ hrs) and **Embilipitiya** (3½ hrs). For **Galle**, change at **Akuressa** (2½ hrs).

Occasional buses also run to the **Mederipitiya** entrance (45 mins), though it is easier to take your own transport.

Ratnapura to the highlands

rolling hills, tea plantations and ancient caves

Pelmadulla and around
The A4 between Ratnapura and Pelmadulla (18 km) continues across the fertile and gem-bearing low country, while the hills on either side come closer and closer to the road. **Pelmadulla** is a major road junction: the A18 goes southeast from here to Madampe, while the A4 runs east and then northeast, curving round the southern flank of the Central Highland massif towards Haputale, passing through superb lush scenery all the way. This is the heart of the rubber-producing area, with many rubber estates. Adam's Peak and the Maskeliya Range rise magnificently to the north, although during the southwest monsoon they are almost permanently covered in cloud.

Balangoda and around *Colour map 3, B4.*
Balangoda is one of an increasing number of towns overlooked by an enormous cement Buddha. The town itself has little of interest; most visitors use it as a base for excursions into the Peak Wilderness Sanctuary and to visit the nearby prehistoric cave sites.

Kuragala Cave, with the Jailani Muslim shrine nearby, can be reached by following a path uphill from Taniantenna on the Kaltota Road. It is 25 km along the Kaltota Road. In August Muslims congregate here for a large festival. **Budugala Cave Temple**, 25 km away, is across a deep gully from the shrine. Take the road to Uggalkaltota, to the east, which follows the downward sloping ridge (buses go most of the way).

From Balangoda, after passing Rajawaka on the Kaltota Road, a track leads 4 km down to the south to **Diyainna Cave**, near the village of the same name, which was inhabited between 8000 and 2500 BC. If you continue along the track southeast towards Uda

Walawe Reservoir, you will reach **Handagiriya** on the river bank. It is claimed that the old Buddhist stupa once held the Tooth Relic. This is close to **Bellan Bendi Pelessa**, the plain where large finds of prehistoric skeletons has confirmed it as an open-air site once used by *Homo sapiens belangodensis*.

Belihuloya to Haputale *Colour map 3, B5.*

A small settlement on the Ratnapura–Badulla road, Belihuloya is best known as a picturesque rest point set among tea estates on the banks of a gushing river. There is a track from here leading up to World's End on the Horton Plains (see page 236), though from this side it is a four-hour uphill walk. Heading northeast for 16 km, you reach the **Non Pareil Tea Estate**, where another dirt track also winds 24 km up to World's End.

Passing through **Halpe** (6 km), the road continues for a further 7 km to a turn off for the **Bambarakanda Falls**, which at 237 m (in three stages) are Sri Lanka's highest and are impressive after the rains; they are reached by a sealed road, 5 km off the A4. Just beyond the turn off is the settlement of Kalupahana. **Haldumulla**, nearby, has excellent views across to the sea. It is possible to visit an organic tea garden here, the **Bio Tea Project**, run by **Stassen Exports Ltd**. Their centre is signposted 3 km off the road.

Further east from Kalpahana is **Beragala**, and then a further steep climb of 10 km is Haputale. For details of Haputale, Ella and Badulla, see Uva Province, page 242.

Listings Ratnapura to the highlands

Where to stay

$$$ Landa Holiday Houses
Badulla Rd, Belihuloya, T045-228 0288, www.landaholidays.com.
4 cottages and 1 treehouse, Dutch designed and built by the stream in a jungle setting. Meals on request.

$$ Rest House (CHC)
Near the bridge, Belihuloya, T045-228 0156, www.chcresthouses.com.
14 a/c and fan rooms (best in a newer extension) by an attractive though very noisy stream. Rooms a little shabby and could be cleaner. Restaurant on pleasant covered terrace.

$$-$ River Garden Resort
Badulla Rd, Ratnapura side of the bridge, Belihuloya, T077-277 4775, www.rivergardenresort.com.

Great position, with attractive thatched huts on the hillside in extensive gardens. Rooms have fan, attached hot bath. Camping also available. Wide variety of sports offered include canoeing and mountain-biking, a 'natural pool' for bathing in the river (though take care). Good food.

Transport

Bus Buses run from Ratnapura east to **Balangoda** (1 hr) and **Belihuloya** (2 hrs), with 3 services running on to **Haputale** (4 hrs). From Pelmadulla and Balangoda there are hourly services west to **Colombo** (3-4 hrs). For the south coast, buses run from Pelmadulla to **Tangalla** via **Embilitipiya** (2 hrs).

After Pelmadulla the A18 runs southeast through Kahawatta Ford. After 10 km, at Madampe, the A17 branches off towards Galle and Matara. On the way south you pass through various towns and villages, of which Rakwana is the largest.

Rakwana

The chief village of a tea-growing district, Rakwana has a large Tamil and Muslim population and a beautiful setting. There are many flowering trees in season and wild orchids, notably the large flowered *Dendrobium maccarthaie*. The main entrance to the Sinharaja Biosphere Reserve is accessible on the road west out of town at **Kudawa** (see page 111), via Pothupitiya and Weddagala. Alternatively, you can continue south to Deniyaya (see below) for the Mederipitiya entrance to the reserve.

Rakwana to the coast

The road south of Rakwana is very scenic, with fabulous views north to the mountains and valleys of the Peak Wilderness Sanctuary, numerous fine waterfalls and some grand, if rickety, old iron bridges. Tea and rubber plantations cover the landscape and *pinus* trees often line the road. Crossing the Bulutota Pass there are ten hair-pin bends, marked by white markers, after which you pass just to the east of **Gongala Peak** (1358 m) at the easternmost edge of the Wet Zone.

From **Panilkande**, the road continues west to **Deniyaya**, one of the centres of low-altitude tea production and a main gateway to Sinharaja (see page 110). Just south of **Akuressa** the road forks, the A24 turning left to Matara down the valley of the Nilwala Ganga, and passing from one of the wettest areas of Sri Lanka to one of the driest in under 20 km. The right fork continues as the A17 to Galle, remaining in typically Wet Zone vegetation and cultivation throughout.

Southwest
coast

Beyond Colombo's urban sprawl lie the golden beaches that serve Sri Lanka's package tourism industry. To some, the coast's wealth of quality accommodation, beach restaurants and bars makes for a perfect indulgent holiday; to others it has been spoilt by over-development. Yet, away from the resorts, traditional life continues. Fishermen still bring in their catch at numerous points along the coast and the coconut palms that line the shore provide an alternative livelihood for many.

South to Kalutara

batiks, baskets, beaches and Buddhist shrines

The large number of coconut palms along the coast road marks this as the centre of the arrack industry. The island's best quality mangosteen (introduced from Malaya in the early 19th century) and rubber are also economically important. The main tourist resort is the long beach between Wadduwa and Kalutara.

Essential Southwest coast

Getting around

The road and railway line hug the ocean as they go south making for an enjoyable journey and providing easy access to the beach resorts.

When to go

The sea is rough during the monsoons; the weather is best between December and April.

Best relaxing retreats

Barberyn Reef, page 122
Nisala Arana, page 123
Secret Garden Villa, page 151
Thambapanni Retreat, page 152
Galapita Rocks, page 189
Living Heritage Koslanda, page 191

ON THE ROAD
Sap tappers

Palm toddy is a universal favourite for Sri Lankans, as is the stronger distilled arrack, both of which are found throughout the island. They (as well as sweet palm juice, treacle or jaggery) are produced from the sap which is collected in earthen pots that you'll notice hanging at the base of the long green fronds at the crown of the palms which have been set aside for 'tapping'.

The sap flows when the apex of an unopened flower bunch is 'tapped' by slicing it off and tapping it with a stick to make the cells burst and the juice to flow. This usually starts in about three weeks of the first cut. From then on successive flower buds are tapped so that sap collecting can continue for half a year. Fruit production, of course, stops during this period, but tapping seems to result in an improved crop of nuts where the yield had previously been poor.

The sap is extracted from the crown of the palms by the *duravas* (toddy tappers). The skilful tapper usually ties a circle of rope around his ankles and shins up the tall smooth trunk two or three times a day to empty the sap pot into one he has tied around his waist. An agile man collecting from a group of palms will often get from tree to tree by using pairs of coconut fibre ropes tied from one tree top to the next, which saves the tapper time and energy wasted in climbing down and up again.

Moratuwa

Moratuwa, 23 km south of Colombo, has a large Catholic population, and some fine churches. The town is also noted for its furniture-making; you will see craftsmen by the side of the road carving wood into a wide variety of intricate designs. There is plenty of accommodation in Moratuwa, mainly by **Bolgoda Lake**, which is popular for local weddings and as a weekend escape from Colombo. Here you can fish for barramundi or take boat trips out to the lake's islands.

Panadura

Panadura, to the south of a wide estuary, has many fine colonial mansions. From here, the A8 road leads east to Ratnapura and beyond, hugging the southern edge of the highlands (see page 104). The town is known for producing some of the highest quality **batik** in Sri Lanka. It is well worth the small diversion to the workshop and showroom of **Bandula Fernando** ① *289/5 Noel Mendis Rd, just off the A2, T034-223 3369*, one of the foremost batik designers in Sri Lanka. Fernando combines traditional and modern styles to produce some exceptionally vibrant and original batik designs. He is also credited with evolving mosaic art in batik, acknowledged as a uniquely individual style of batik. The designs on offer are quite different from those seen elsewhere on the island and are sold at fair prices considering the detail and excellence.

Kalutara *Colour map 3, B2.*

Kalutara, 42 km from Colombo, is a busy district capital with a population of 38,000. It has a huge stretch of fine sand which it shares with **Wadduwa** to the north, home to the area's top resorts. Kalutara itself divides into **Mahawaskaduwa** (Kalutara North), where the beach is more scenic, and **Katukurunda** (Kalutara South).

To guard the spice trade the Portuguese built a fort on the site of a Buddhist temple here. The Dutch took it over and a British agent converted it into his residence. The site, by the bridge across the Kalu Ganga, now again has a modern Buddhist shrine, the **Gangatilaka Vihara**, with a sacred Bo tree outside. It is worth stopping to visit the hollow *dagoba* (actually a *dagoba* within a *dagoba*), as others on the island contain relics and are not accessible. Most remarkable are the extraordinary acoustics, which can be quite disorienting. There are 75 paintings inside, illustrating events from the Buddha's life.

> **Tip...**
> Kalutara is renowned for basket-weaving. Leaves of the wild date are dyed red, orange, green and black, and woven into hats, mats and baskets.

Turn left immediately after the *vihara* along the Kalutara–Palatota road to reach **Richmond Castle** ⓘ *2 km inland via a track off the Palatota road, daily 0900-1630, Rs 100.* A fine country house in a 17-ha fruit garden estate, it is now used as an education centre for underprivileged local children. Built in 1896, it originally belonged to landowner-turned-philanthropist NDA Silva Wijayasinghe, the local Padikara Mudah (village leader), and was used during the British period as a circuit bungalow for officials. Note the audience hall, with intricately carved pillars and beams (two shiploads of teak were brought from Burma for its construction) and a spiral staircase leading to a gallery. Another room shows some fascinating photographs from the time.

Listings South to Kalutara

Where to stay

Moratuwa

$$ Ranmal Holiday Resort
346/5 Galle Rd, Gorakana, T038-229 8921, www.ranmalholidayresort.com.
25 large, fairly comfortable a/c rooms and 2 bungalows. Pool, plus option to sleep in a houseboat (Rs 50,000), which sounds better than it is. Shabby overall but in a good position on the lake. Boat trips (either picnics or for overnight stay) offered to nearby islands and Kalutara.

Kalutara

$$$$ Blue Water
Thalpitiya, Wadduwa, T034-223 5067, www.bluewatersrilanka.com.
Excellent rooms in a luxurious hotel with top facilities amidst palm groves, designed by Geoffrey Bawa. Spacious public areas, understated decor, ethnic feel (copied but not exceeded by other hotels along the coast), spa and large pool with resident monitor lizard.

$$$$ Privilege Ayurveda Beach Resort
260 Samanthura Rd, Molligoda, Wadduwa, T038-229 5367, www.privilegeayurvedaresort.com.
24 luxurious, well-furnished suites, with TV, some with jacuzzi. On-site jewellery shop with imaginative designs. Half board only (7-course dinner). Self-consciously 'boutiquey'.

$$$$ Royal Palms Beach
De Abrew Rd, Kalutara North, T034-867 8540, www.tangerinehotels.com.
124 superb fully equipped rooms plus suites, private balcony or patio with sea or garden views, disco and pub, sports facilities shared with sister hotel, **Tangerine Beach Hotel**, huge pool (you can almost swim around the hotel).

$$$ Hibiscus Beach
Mahawaskaduwa, T034-508 2222,
www.hibiscusbeachhotel.com.
50 large rooms and villas with jacuzzis.
Lounge bar overlooks colourful hibiscus
garden, pool, sports, good beach.

$$$ Kani Lanka Resort & Spa
St Sebastian's Rd, Katukurunda,
T034-428 0801, www.kanilanka.com.
105 comfortable a/c rooms and suites, some
with private balcony and tub, in a good
location sandwiched between sea and
lagoon. Floating restaurant, pool, mini-golf,
watersports on lagoon, Ayurvedic health
centre, traditional-style spa, cultural shows.

$$$ Mermaid Hotel & Club
Mahawaskaduwa, T034-720 0478,
www.mermaidhotelnclub.com.
72 a/c rooms, split-level restaurant, bars,
sports, excursions, mainly tour groups,
beautiful location in coconut plantation,
attractive lawn runs down to beach.

Ayurvedic resort

Siddhalepa Ayurveda Health Resort
861 Samanthara Rd, Wadduwa, T034-
229 6967, www.ayurvedaresort.com.
Siddhalepa is one of the most famous
names in Sri Lankan Ayurvedic therapy,

with a 200-year history. The resort is less
'authentic' than other new creations as it
accepts non-Ayurveda guests and possesses
a bar. There are 50 rooms, including 6 suites,
in beautiful gardens full of Ayurveda plants.
Suites are themed – 2 'caves', 2 made from
clay and 2 Chandra Vasa, traditional Sri
Lankan *kabok* and stone with furniture
of magobe wood (recommended). Other
rooms resemble a Dutch fort with mini
canal system outside (kids can paddle
around on a boat). Packages range from
1-4 weeks including consultation and all
treatments for non-Ayurveda guests.

Restaurants

Kalutara
Besides the hotel restaurants (see above),
there are numerous cheaper places to eat
(and buy souvenirs) along the roads leading
from Galle Rd to the hotels.

Transport

Kalutara
Bus Buses between **Colombo** and **Galle**
stop here.

Train Trains stop here on the **Colombo–
Matara** line, with 5-6 intercity trains per day.

Beruwela, Aluthgama and Bentota

a line-up of luxurious resorts

The coast at this point becomes more developed, with half a dozen villages
indistinguishably joined together by hotel resorts. At the north end is Beruwela
and its adjoining settlements, which has several large hotels popular primarily
with Germans. Aluthgama, a little further south, is protected from the sea by a
spit of land and has some characterful smaller guesthouses and restaurants in a
more peaceful riverside setting. South of the Bentota Bridge, which spans one
of Sri Lanka's largest rivers, are Bentota and Walauwa, where there are some
sumptuous and very expensive places to stay.

Beruwela *Colour map 3, B2.*
Beruwela is located 58 km from Colombo and has a permanent population of 34,000. Its
name is derived from the Sinhalese word *Baeruala* ('the place where the sail is lowered'),

a reference to the fact that the first Arab Muslim settlers are believed to have landed here in around the eighth century. **Kitchimalai Mosque**, on a headland 3 km north along the beach from the main hotel area, is worth seeing. It is a major pilgrimage centre at the end of **Ramadan** since it contains the shrine of a 10th-century Muslim saint; guides may tell you that it is the oldest mosque in Sri Lanka, but this is unlikely to be true.

Looking east from the mosque, **Beruwela harbour** is an interesting place to watch the fishermen unload their catch. The harbour has over 600 boats, many of which are quite sizeable since the fishermen spend up to two months at sea. The fish market is busy in the early morning; you may well see fresh shark or tuna changing hands even before the sun is up. You can also hire a boat to the lighthouse, which is raised on a small island offshore and offers an excellent view of the coastline from the top.

To the south, Beruwela merges into the adjoining settlements of Moragalla and Kaluwamodara. Fishermen offer to ferry holidaymakers across the narrow estuary to Bentota (see page opposite).

Beruwela

Aluthgama *Colour map 3, B2.*

Aluthgama, the principal town here, is situated on the north side of the Bentota River, 60 km south of Colombo. To the west a sand spit separates the river from the sea and provides excellent conditions for windsurfing and sailing. The town has a busy fish market and is famous for its oysters.

Brief Garden ① *Kalawila, T077-350 9290, daily 0800-1700, Rs 1250.* Before heading to the beach, make a detour inland to this splendid garden created between 1929 and 1989 by the late Bevis Bawa, a landscape architect, writer, sculptor, bon vivant and brother to Geoffrey. Taking its name from a court brief, the 2-ha garden lies in an undulating landscape of paddies and scattered villages on a hillside. It was created as a series of wonderfully composed views, designed in different moods, with cool, shady paths and many mature specimen trees. There are many references to European- and Japanese-style gardens, with shade-loving

> **Tip...**
> Beruwela beach is notorious for its 'beach boys', who crowd around the beach entrances to the hotels.

Where to stay
Bavarian Guest House **1**
Belfry Guest House **3**
Eden Resort & Spa **5**
Lanka Princess **2**
Panorama **7**
Riverina **8**
Ypsylon Guest House & Dive Centre **12**

1 km
1 mile

Aluthgama & Bentota

1 km
1 miles

Where to stay 🛌
Ayubowan **4**
Bentota Beach **2**
Club Bentota **12**
Ganga Garden **3**
Hemadan **7**
Nisala Arana **5**

Paradise Road The Villa **18**
Saman Villas **9**
Sun and Moon **8**
Susantha & Palm
  Restaurant **15**
Terrena **1**
Vivanta by Taj **17**
Wunderbar Beach Club **6**

Restaurants 🍴
Anushka River Inn **3**
Diya Sisila **1**
Singharaja **4**

anthurium and alocasia plants common throughout. Bawa's house, though, is the highlight. Its eclectic private collection of paintings, sculptures, photographs (note Edward VIII and Lord Olivier, both of whom stayed here) and furniture (many colonial antiques) provide an added incentive to visit. Some of the paintings were composed by Australian artist Donald Friend, who came for a week and stayed for six years. Bawa himself appears in a number of forms, both in the house and garden, at one point representing Bacchus, holding a birdbath shaped as a giant clam shell. In his outside bathroom he appears again as a water-spouting gargoyle with wild hair and blue marble eyes. From Aluthgama, take the road inland to Matugama, and then Dhargatown (8 km). From here, a 2-km rough track (right at the first fork and left at the second) takes you to the gardens.

Bentota and south Colour map 3, B2.

Bentota Bridge marks the border between the Western and Southern Provinces. The 40-ha Bentota **National Holiday Resort** is built entirely for foreign tourists, with shops, a bank and a post office. A full range of sports is available and the area is also gaining a reputation for providing first-class Ayurvedic healing centres, with many more under construction.

South of Bentota, along Galle Road towards Induruwa, the area feels less of a tourist ghetto, and the natural beauty of the coastline returns. Here are some of the most sumptuous places to stay on the entire island. Unofficial 'guides' offer nearby river and lagoon trips and visits to temples, coir factories and woodcarvers: they are very overpriced.

Tourist information

The **tourist police** can be found at Galle Rd, Moragalla, opposite **Neptune Hotel**, T034-227 6049 in Beruwela; at Galle Rd, in Aluthgama, and in the tourist complex by **Bentota Beach Hotel**, T034-227 6049, in Bentota.

Where to stay

Beruwela

All the hotels listed in this section are actually in Moragalla, with some of the more upmarket hotels further south at Kaluwamodara.

$$$$ Eden Resort & Spa
Kaluwamodara, T034-227 6075, www.edenresortandspa.com.
Large-scale but welcoming resort with 158 rooms, suites and penthouses, grand entrance, large pool, spa, full entertainment and sports facilities. Friendly staff.

$$$$-$$$ Riverina
Kaluwamodara, T034-227 6044, www.riverinahotel.com.
192 a/c rooms, full facilities including tennis, watersports, good indoor games room, 3 restaurants, Ayurvedic centre, well organized.

$$ Bavarian Guest House
92 Barberyn Rd, T034-227 6129, www.bavarianguesthouse.com.
7 large modern a/c and fan rooms around attractive courtyard with pool, hot water bath, restaurant, bar. German and English spoken.

$$ Belfry Guest House
13/4 Galle Rd, T558 1138, www.belfryguesthousesrilanka.com.
5 a/c and fan rooms with terrace or balcony, some overlooking the pool and others with a sea view. Restaurant. Helpful and friendly staff.

$$ Ypsylon Guest House
T034-227 6132, ypsylon@slt.lk.
25 a/c and fan rooms, hot water, breakfast included, pool, German-run diving school (see What to do, page 125).

$ Panorama
Maradana Rd, T034-227 7091, www.hotelpanoramalk.com.
10 simple, clean fan rooms in small guest-house, restaurant, good value for the area.

Ayurvedic resorts

Barberyn Reef
Moragalla, T034-227 6036, www.barberynresorts.com.
Opened in 1982 as the 1st Ayurvedic centre in Sri Lanka. Beautiful resort with range of rooms, some with a/c and some split-level with a living area. Extensive and recommended Ayurvedic health centre, safe swimming enclosed by a reef.

Lanka Princess
Kaluwamodara, T034-227 6711, www.lankaprincess.com.
German-managed hotel offering 110 a/c sea-facing rooms and suites. Wide range of Ayurvedic treatments, plus yoga, tai chi and pool.

Muthumuni
T034-227 7048, www.muthumuniresort.com.
German-run resort in very peaceful setting on the lagoon (own boat service to meditation temple). 1- to 2-week Ayurvedic packages. Also has an Ayurvedic beach resort.

Aluthgama

Many of the hotels referred to as being in Bentota are to the north of the Bentota Bridge and so are actually in Aluthgama.

$$$$-$$$ Club Bentota 'Island Paradise'
T034-227 5167, www.clubbentota.com.
146 bungalows, suites and rooms with
ocean or river views on small spit of land
accessible by shuttle boat from the main
road, all the watersports under the sun.

$$ Ganga Garden
126/27 Galle Rd, T034-227 1770,
www.ganga-garden.com.
Lovely property with well-furnished, a/c and
fan rooms, in attractive setting overlooking
the river. Restaurant, watersports and fishing.

$$ Hemadan
25 Riverside Rd (on the river bank),
T034-227 5320, www.hemadan.dk.
10 good clean a/c and fan rooms with hot
baths, some with balcony, though bigger
without. Danish-owned, quiet. Restaurant,
watersports, free boat shuttle to beach.

$$-$ Terrena
Riverside Rd, closest guesthouse to the
bridge, T034 420 9015.
6 small but clean and attractive a/c
and fan rooms with hot water, Austrian-
owned, pleasant terrace and garden.
Good restaurant.

$ Sun and Moon
104/8 Galle Rd, T034-494 3454,
www.sunandmoonsrilanka.com.
Good location on the river with
spacious rooms.

Bentota and south

$$$$ Nisala Arana
326/1 Circular Rd, Kammana, T077-773 3313,
www.nisalaarana.com.
Beautiful boutique property that was
former village Ayurvedic doctor's house –
the garden is full of medicinal plants and
trees. Choose from the Doctor's House or
the tree-top Mango suites. Lovely pool
and delicious food from around the globe.
Recommended.

$$$$ Paradise Road – The Villa
138/18-22 Galle Rd (1.5 km south
of Bentota), T034-227 5311,
www.paradiseroadhotels.com.
A former residence of Geoffrey Bawa,
exquisite rooms in a large villa dating from
1880, each individually designed, decorated
and furnished with antique furniture. Superb
bathrooms (open-air bath), beautiful shaded
garden, understated pool. Sublime.

$$$$ Saman Villas
Aturuwella, on a rocky headland 5 km south,
T034-227 5435, www.samanvilla.com.
27 magnificent suites with sea views set
on a spectacular rocky headland. All have
attractive furnishings, and 'astonishing'
open-air baths with rain shower. Superb
pool high above the sea which seems to
merge with the ocean, panoramic views and
access to long beaches either side. Good
spa. Expensive but worth every rupee.

$$$$ Vivanta by Taj
T034-555 5555, www.vivantabytaj.com.
162 large a/c rooms (higher floors best)
in magnificent top-class hotel in a superb
location on a headland. All rooms have
sea-facing balcony or terrace, good food,
fantastic pool.

$$$$-$$$ Bentota Beach
South of Bentota Bridge, T034-227 5176,
www.cinnamonhotels.com.
133 comfortable a/c rooms and suites built
on the site of a Dutch fort. Luxurious layout
in extensive gardens, good beach, full
facilities including pool and Ayurvedic spa,
location of **Club Inter Sport**.

$$$-$$ Wunderbar Beach Club
Robolgoda, T034-227 5908,
www.hotel-wunderbar.com.
14 a/c rooms, some with sea views,
and 1 private bungalow. There is a
good restaurant, lots of watersports
and a turtle project.

$$$-$ Ayubowan
171 Galle Rd, Bentota South, T034-227 5913,
www.ayubowan.ch.
Bright, spacious and spotless bungalows
with attractive furniture in pleasant gardens,
as well as a suite and a cheap backpacker
room. Restaurant has wide selection of
food, including pizza. Swiss-owned.

$$-$ Susantha Garden
Resort Rd, Pitaramba, next to Bentota
railway station (5 mins from beach,
across from the rail track), T034-227 5324,
www.hotelsusanthagarden.com.
Rewind to 1971 and this property was a
traditional batik factory. Now, you will find
18 spotless good-sized rooms with bath in
pleasant chalets, with one suite. Bar, good
restaurant, lovely swimming pool and
Ayurvedic centre.

Ayurvedic resorts

Aida Ayurveda Resort
12a Managala Mawatha, Bentota, T034-
227 1137, www.aidaayurveda.com.
Spacious courtyards with good local
furniture in great setting on Bentota River.
40 comfortable rooms with TV, small
balcony. 1-day Ayurveda packages available
for non-residents, including consultation,
massage or herbal bath/sauna.

Ayurveda Walauwa
Galle Rd, Warahena, T034-275 3378,
www.ayurvedawalauwabentota.com.
20 a/c rooms in treatment centre, 2-week
stays are advised for best effect.

Dalmanuta Gardens
Meegama Rd, Warapitiya, T077-343 4434,
www.dalmanuta.com.
9 bungalows in pleasant gardens near the
river. Good food, the full-board Ayurveda
rate includes all meals, doctor's consultation,
daily massages, yoga, etc. Half-day Ayurveda
packages also available. Very welcoming to
non-Ayurvedic guests as well.

Restaurants

Beruwela
There are places to eat along the roads
leading off Galle Rd. For further options
see Where to stay, page 122.

Aluthgama
There are numerous restaurants around
Bentota Bridge and on the narrow lanes
leading down to the hotels.

$$ Anushka River Inn
97 Riverside Rd, T034-227 5377, www.
anushka-river-inn.com. Daily 1100-1500
and 1900-2300.
Restaurant has fine views and serves good
seafood and rice and curry, as well as a
variety of other Western and Asian dishes.
Also has 8 guest rooms (**$$**).

$ Singharaja Bakery and Restaurant
120 Galle Rd, Kaluwamodara.
A good, clean establishment providing
excellent Sri Lankan food, including short
eats, hoppers and curries. Popular as a
roadside halt but worth visiting for a cheap
and authentic alternative to hotel food.

Bentota

$$$ Diya Sisila
T077-740 2138.
Not by the sea, but a popular place
for excellent seafood with tables in
a pleasant garden. The owner will
pick guests up if requested. BYO,
and be sure to book in advance.

$$ Susantha's
See Where to stay, above.
Serves simple Sri Lankan and
continental dishes.

Shopping

There are branches of the excellent
Mlesna Tea Centre and **Laksala**

government handicrafts emporium along Galle Rd in Beruwela, with prices more reasonable than the hotel shops. There is also a branch of **Laksala** in the shopping arcade by **Bentota Beach Hotel**.

What to do

Beruwela
Diving is best Dec-Mar.
Ypsylon Dive Centre, *Ypsylon Guest House (see Where to stay), T034-227 6132, www. ypsylon-sri-lanka.de.* German-run dive centre, SSI- and PADI-registered. 2 dives for €55 (US$62), Open Water course €300 (US$339), Advanced €250 (US$283). Also offers wreck dives.

Bentota
A range of activities is possible on the lagoon or the open sea.
Club Inter Sport, *within the grounds of Bentota Beach hotel, see Where to stay, page 123*. Watersports include windsurfing, water skiing (lessons possible) and banana boat. Also tennis, squash, archery, badminton. Sport passes available for discounted activities on 2 day (weekend) or weekly basis.
Confifi Marina, *T034-224 2766 or T227 6039 at Club Palm Garden, www.lsr-srilanka.com.* Diving, sailing, canoeing, windsurfing, snorkelling and deep-sea fishing.
Surf Bentota, *T034-227 5126, www.ceylonhotels.lk.* Diving and other watersports offered.

Transport

Aluthgama is the main transport hub for Beruwela to the north and Bentota to the south.

Beruwela
Bus Buses stop here on the route between **Colombo** and **Galle**.

Train Beruwela is on the main **Colombo–Matara** line, though only the slower trains (1¾ hrs) stop here. Best option is to take one of the express trains to/from **Aluthgama** (see below).

Aluthgama
Bus Buses running between **Colombo** and **Galle** stop here.

Train Aluthgama is a stop on the main **Colombo–Matara** line and can be reached by express trains from **Colombo** (5-6 a day) in around 1½ hrs.

Bentota
Air Sri Lankan Airlines, T011-777 1979, www.srilankan.com, has started operating an air taxi between **Bentota** and **Colombo**.

Bus Buses passing through Bentota are often full; it's better to go to Aluthgama and take a bus that originates there.

Train Bentota's tiny station is on the main **Colombo–Matara** line but only the 'slow' trains stop here so it is better to travel on an express train to/from Aluthgama (see above).

The busy town of Ambalangoda, 85 km from Colombo, is an important commercial and fish trading centre with some local colour and a fine sweep of sandy beach to its north; some visitors opt to stay here over its more touristy resort neighbours along the coast. Many of the beaches to the north are important turtle-nesting sites, and there are several turtle hatcheries in the area.

Induruwa *Colour map 3, B2.*

Induruwa, 68 km from Colombo, has a pleasant stretch of beach that is being developed with new hotels and guesthouses.

Visitors are welcome at the **Indurawa Turtle Conservation Project** ① *Galle Rd, T077-669 0168, Rs 500; donations appreciated.* Formerly part of the Victor Hasselblad Project, the hatchery has been running for about 20 years, buying eggs from local fishermen at a higher price than they would normally get if sold for food. The eggs are buried as soon as possible in batches of 50. After hatching, the baby turtles are placed in holding tanks for two to three days before being released into the sea in the evening under supervision. Depending on the time of year (best November to April), you can see the hatchlings of up to five species – green, olive ridley, hawksbill, leatherback and loggerhead – at any one time. An example of each species is also held in separate tanks for research purposes.

Kosgoda *Colour map 3, B2.*

Seventy-three kilometres south of Colombo, Kosgoda's 4-km stretch of beach has the highest density of turtle nesting in the country. In August 2003, the **Turtle Conservation Project (TCP)** launched a programme with the financial assistance of the UNDP to protect 1 km of the beach with the assistance of former poachers retrained as 'nest-protectors' and tour guides. The **Kosgoda Sea Turtle Conservation Project** ① *Galle Rd, T091-226 4567, www.kosgodaseaturtle.org, most days 0900-1700, Rs 500*, welcomes visitors and volunteers to learn more about turtles and visit the hatchery. Contact them in advance if you want to take part in an evening turtle watch.

Madu Ganga wetland *Colour map 3, C2.*

A few kilometres north of Ambalangoda, the estuary of the Madu Ganga is a major **wetlands** area, famous for its 64 islands. The marshes and scrubland are home to more than 300 varieties of plant, including 95 families of mangrove, supporting 17 species of birds and a wide variety of amphibians and reptiles; water monitors are common. Tours are offered, which usually include a visit to the 150-year-old **Koth Duwa temple** and an island where you can watch cinnamon being cut and prepared, though bear in mind that the finished oil, bark and powder for sale is overpriced. River safari operators leave from either side of the bridge, near the small town of Balapitiya (81 km from Colombo). A 1½-hour trip, visiting two islands, costs around Rs 12,000 for a six-person boat.

Ambalangoda *Colour map 3, C2.*

The town (population 20,100) is chiefly famous as the home of **devil dancing** and **mask making**, which many families have carried out for generations. It may be possible to watch a performance of *kolama* (folk theatre); ask at the museum or School of Dancing

ON THE ROAD
Turtles in Sri Lanka

Five of the world's seven species of turtle, the green, leatherback, olive ridley, loggerhead and the hawksbill, all come ashore to nest on the beaches of Sri Lanka. All are listed by the World Conservation Union (IUCN) as either threatened or endangered. Despite the measures taken by the government, marine turtles are extensively exploited in Sri Lanka for their eggs and meat. In addition, turtle-nesting beaches (rookeries) are being disturbed by tourism-related development, and feeding habitats, such as coral reefs, are being destroyed by pollution, especially polythene bags, and unsustainable harvesting. Around 13,000 turtles each year are caught, not always accidentally, in fishing gear, while the illegal 'tortoise shell trade' continues to encourage hunting of the highly endangered hawksbill turtle's carapace.

Tourism has proved a double-edged sword in the fight to save the turtles. Since the early 1980s, the government has encouraged the setting up of tourist-friendly turtle hatcheries along the coast, from Induruwa in the west to Yala in the southeast, though the Wildlife Department acknowledges that these sometimes do more harm than good. In 1998, the Kosgoda Sea Turtle Conservation Project, www.kosgodaseaturtle.org, was set up dedicated to pursuing sustainable marine turtle conservation strategies through education, research and community participation. It currently runs tourism projects at Rekawa, Kalpitiya and Kosgoda, and education schemes for school children.

(see below). Ambalangoda is also renowned for cinnamon cultivation and production; ask your hotel or guesthouse about visiting a plantation and factory. The colourful fish market is worth a look early in the morning.

Ariyapala Mask Museums ① *426 Patabendimulla, T091-225 8373, daily 0830-1730.* There are actually two mask museums, located opposite each other and run by the rival sons of the late mask-carver. The smaller one houses the museum proper, while the other is primarily a workshop and showroom. Some of the exhibits tracing the tradition of mask dancing are interesting and informative. The *naga raksha* mask from the Raksha Kolama (Devil Dance) has a fearsome face with bulging eyes that roll around, a bloodthirsty tongue hanging from a mouth lined with fang-like teeth, all topped by a set of cobra hoods (see box, page 128). You can watch the craftsmen at work, carving traditional masks from the light *kaduru* wood. The carvings on sale in the showroom are not of the best quality and are quite expensive. It is better to take your time to visit some of the smaller workshops around town on foot and compare prices and quality.

Around Ambalangoda

At **Karandeniya**, 11 km inland from Ambalangoda, along the Elpitiya Road, 208 steps lead up to the **Galabuddha Temple**, which has a 33-m supine Buddha; a sign proudly proclaims it to be the biggest in South Asia. The murals are worthy of note. At **Meetiyagoda**, 16 km inland, there is a moonstone quarry. The semi-precious stone, which often has a bluish milky tinge, is polished and set in silver or gold jewellery. The road sign claims that it's the 'only natural moonstone quarry in the world'.

ON THE ROAD

Masked dances

The **Devil Dance** evolved from the rural people's need to appease malevolent forces in nature and seek blessing from good spirits when there was an evil spirit to be exorcized, such as a sickness to be cured. It takes the form of a ritual dance, full of high drama, with a sorcerer 'priest' and an altar. As evening approaches, the circular arena in the open air is lit by torches, and masked dancers appear to the beating of drums and chanting. During the exorcism ritual, which lasts all night, the 'priest' casts the evil spirit out of the sick. There are 18 demons associated with afflictions for which different fearsome *sanni* masks are worn. There is an element of awe and grotesqueness about the whole ritual, which has a serious purpose. The dances are, therefore, not on offer as 'performances'.

The **Kolam Dance** has its origins in folk theatre. The story tells of a queen, who, while expecting a child, had a deep craving to see a masked dance. This was satisfied by the Carpenter of the Gods, Visvakarma, who invented the dances. They tell stories and again make full use of a wonderful variety of masks (often giant in size) representing imaginary characters from folk tales, Buddhist *jatakas*, gods and devils, as well as well-known members of the royal court and more mundane figures from day-to-day life. Animals (lions, bears) too, feature as playful characters. This form of folk dance resembles the more serious Devil Dance in some ways – it is again performed during the night and in a similar circular, torch-lit, open-air 'stage' (originally *kolam* was performed for several nights during New Year festivities). In spite of a serious or moral undertone, a sprinkling of cartoon characters is introduced to provide comic relief. The clever play on words can only be really appreciated by a Sinhalese speaker.

Listings Induruwa to Ambalangoda

Where to stay

Induruwa

$$$ Royal Beach Resort
Galle Rd, Galaboda, T034-227 4351,
www.royalbeach.asia.
British-owned, light and spacious if slightly tacky (map of Sri Lanka in the pond), gleaming hotel in colonial style. Attractive a/c rooms with TV, tubs and veranda with great views of the ocean, clean stretch of beach.

$$$-$$ Induruwa Beach Resort
Galle Rd, T034-227 5445, www.induruwa
beachresort.com.

84 a/c rooms and 6 suites, private balconies with sea view, pool with jacuzzi, full facilities, on good section of beach but large 4-storey block with uninspired architecture, mainly package groups, good value.

$ Long Beach Cottage
Galle Rd (next to Royal Beach Resort),
T077-661 2613, www.longbeachcottage
indurawa.com.
Deservedly popular, pretty house with 5 clean, sea-facing rooms with fan, local dishes and seafood to order, pleasant mangrove-shaded garden with direct access to a fine beach, free pick-up from Aluthgama station, friendly Sri Lankan/German owners.

Kosgoda

$$$$ Heritance Ahungalla (Aitken Spence)
Ahungalla, 6 km south of Kosgoda, T091-555 5000, www.heritancehotels.com/ahungalla.
152 a/c rooms, including 9 suites, excellent food, full sports and entertainment facilities. Imaginative landscaping merges ponds into swimming pool into sea: you can virtually swim up to reception (pool open to non-residents who stay for a meal). Lovely beach, well-run hotel.

$$$$ La Maison Nil Manel
162/4 Wathuregama, Ahungalla, T091-226 4331, www.nilmanel.info.
Small French/Sri Lankan-owned hotel offering 6 a/c rooms (1 suite), tastefully decorated. Pool, excellent food, relaxing atmosphere.

$$$ Kosgoda Beach Resort
Between the sea and lagoon, T091-226 4000, www.kosgodabeachresort.lk.
Attractive building with 42 comfortable and attractive a/c rooms, including 12 suites, open-air tubs, large garden, lovely pool, boating, restaurant. Recommended.

Ayurvedic resorts

Lotus Villa
162/19 Wathuregama, south of Ahungalla, T091-226 4082, www.lotus-villa.com.
14 rooms in exclusive Ayurvedic herbal curative treatment centre, most with sea views. Prices include transfers, all meals, consultations and treatment.

Ambalangoda

$$-$ Shangrela Beach Resort
38 Sea Beach Rd, T091-225 8342, www.shangrela.de.
25 clean, comfortable fan and a/c rooms, hot water. Large garden, organizes boat trips. Flats are also available for rent on a weekly basis.

$ Sumudu Tourist Guest House
418 Main St, Patabendimulla, T091-225 8832.
Pretty house with 6 fan and a/c rooms, good home-cooking, pleasant atmosphere, good value.

Entertainment

Ambalangoda
Bandu Wijesooriya School of Dancing,
417 Patabendimulla, T091-225 894. Mon-Sat.
Traditional dancing shows take place about once a month. A typical show will include a *kolam* dance, followed by several ritual dances, a village folk dance, and end up with some short Indian dances. Courses in dance, drumming and mask-carving are also available.

Shopping

Ambalangoda
Traditional masks worn for dancing, using vegetable colours instead of the brighter chemical paints, are available on the northern edge of the town. Prices vary considerably, with traditional masks being more expensive. Antique shops often sell newly crafted items which have been 'aged'. It is illegal to export any article which is more than 50 years old without a government permit.

Transport

Ambalangoda
Bus Regular buses run to **Colombo** and to **Hikkaduwa**, 13 km south.

Train 5 to 6 express trains a day run along the coast from **Colombo Fort** to Ambalangoda (2 hrs), and on to **Hikkaduwa** (15 mins).

If you are looking for some peace and quiet and a beach to yourself, then you might wish to avoid Hikkaduwa. A victim of its own success, the island's original surfers' hangout is now its most popular resort, with mass tourism bringing pollution and overcrowding, as well a reputation for unsavoury activities and beach boys. Natural forces are also chipping away at Hikkaduwa's charm. The beach here is gradually disappearing as the sea noticeably encroaches inland year by year.

That said, the resort still has some appeal. The coastal stretch has a vast number of high-quality hotels and guesthouses of all price ranges. The food, especially seafood, is often excellent and, with so much competition, reasonably priced. And the opportunities for watersports – swimming, snorkelling, scuba diving (as long as you don't expect living coral) and especially surfing – are probably unrivalled on the island.

Beaches
There are four parts to what is known collectively as 'Hikkaduwa'. At the northern end is **Hikkaduwa** proper, the original settlement. The beach tends to be somewhat narrower here and less appealing. Further south is **Wewala**, where the beach is a wider and more attractive. Along with **Narigama,** this is the main 'centre' with numerous beach bars and restaurants, and the cheapest accommodation. At the southern end is **Thirangama**, which is less frantic, but has good surfing waves and a wider beach. A major disadvantage though is the very busy main road which runs close to the beach.

Hikkaduwa National Park
Hikkaduwa's '**coral sanctuary**' is a shallow protected reef close to the **Coral Gardens Hotel**. Once teeming with life, it was badly affected by 'bleaching' in early 1998, when sea temperatures rose causing the coral to reject the algae on which coral life feeds. Recovery has been slow. The reef and fish population have also been degraded

Essential Hikkaduwa

Finding your feet

Hikkaduwa is 101 km from Colombo. The bus station is in the centre of Hikkaduwa town. All accommodation lies to the south. The train station is about 200 m north of the bus station. Express trains and private buses are best for those travelling from or via Colombo.

Getting around

Galle Road runs the length of the town, so watch out for speeding buses and bear in mind the street noise when choosing a room. The situation may improve when the Colombo–Matara highway opens in the future and takes the bulk of the through traffic away. It is possible to walk uninterrupted along much of the beach. Three-wheelers can be stopped along the Galle Road (bus drivers are less obliging), but you will need to negotiate the price; expect to pay Rs 150-200 from the bus stand to Wewela or Narigama. Cycles and motorbikes can be hired.

by tourism. Unregulated use of visitor boats, dynamite fishing and the dumping of garbage from beachside hotels have all contributed to the denigration of the habitat, prompting the Department of Wildlife to upgrade the area to National Park status in 2002. However, it is still possible to see reef fish, which are fed by fishermen to provide an attraction for visitors. Glass-bottomed boats can be hired from a number of places just north of the Chaaya Tranz. Some travellers find there are too many boats chasing too few viewing spots; turtles are disturbed unnecessarily, and the glass is not as clear as you might hope. Since the reef is shallow and close to shore, it is easy and less damaging to swim and snorkel to it.

Dive sites
Despite the reduced diversity and population of coral and fish, Hikkaduwa is a good base for **scuba diving,** and local operators run trips to up to 20 sites along the coast. Most rewarding close to Hikkaduwa are the rock formations, especially the deep **Kirala Gala** (21 m to 38 m), 10 minutes offshore, where there is also a wide range of pristine coral with groupers, barracuda and batfish. A number of wrecks, some in fairly shallow water, can also be visited, such as the *Earl of Shaftesbury*, though the wreck-diving is better in the bays further south at Galle or Weligama. Visibility varies from 8 m to 25 m, depending on the time of day (morning is better), and is at its best around the full moon period. See What to do, page 137

Surf spots
Hikkaduwa is Sri Lanka's **surf centre** from December to April, and has hosted numerous international competitions. It is particularly good for beginners as the waves are comparatively gentle, most breaking on the reefs rather than the beach. The focus is around the main break, known as the 'A-Frame' because of its distinctive apex, in Wewala, though this can be crowded in peak months. **Narigama** and **Thiragama** further south are usually quieter, though you will also need more experience to surf there.

Around Hikkaduwa
Alut Vihara (Totagama Rajamahavihara) at Telwatta, 2 km north of Hikkaduwa, dates from the early 19th century. It is the only temple to Anangaya on the island, where lovers make offerings to him. The carvings between the fine *makara* (dragon) arches leading to the sanctuary hide a cupid with his bow and flower-tipped arrows. The murals too are particularly impressive. Rarely visited by travellers, it is worth a trip and also makes a very pleasant bicycle ride.

Seenigama Temple, 6 km north, is on an island just offshore. The Devil's Temple here has enormous importance for local fishermen, who believe he will protect

Hikkaduwa area

To Baddegama (11km)
To Colombo, Telwatte Vihara & Ambalangoda
Gonapinuwala
HIKKADUWA
B12
WEWALA
NARIGAMA
THIRANGAMA
A7
PUTUWATHA
Indian
Ocean
Polgasduwa
N
DODANDUWA
Lagoon
To Galle

1 km
1 mile

Where to stay
Eco Village 1

Hikkaduwa & Wewala beach

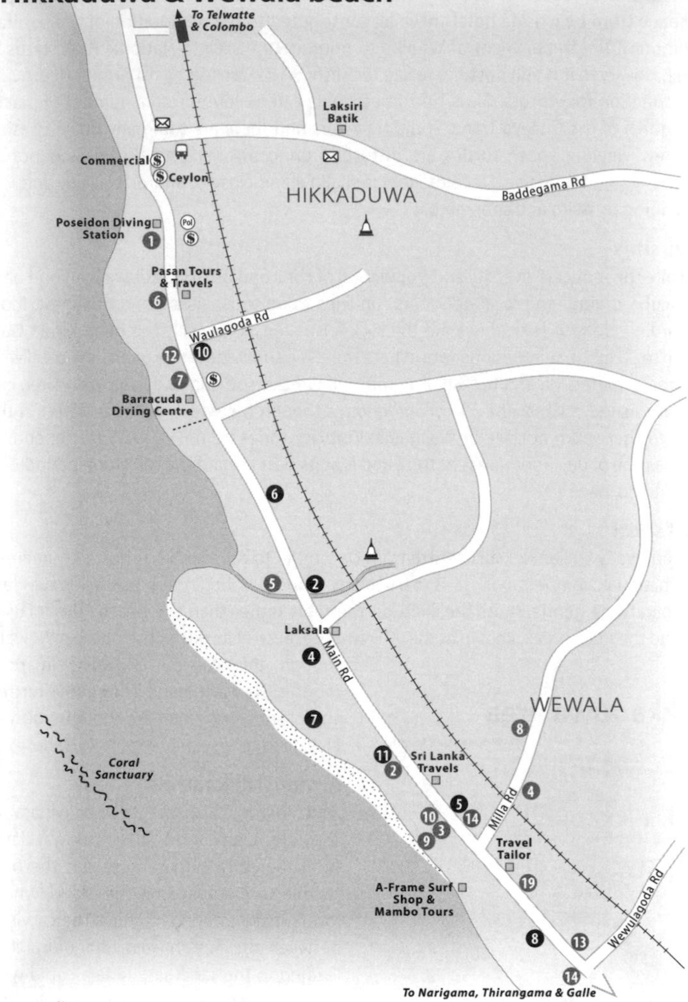

To Telwatte
& Colombo

Laksiri
Batik

Commercial ⓢ
ⓢ Ceylon

HIKKADUWA

Baddegama Rd

Poseidon Diving
Station ☐
❶

Pol
ⓢ

Pasan Tours
& Travels
❻

Waulagoda Rd

⓬ ❿
❼
ⓢ

Barracuda ☐
Diving Centre

❻

❺ ❷

Laksala ☐

❹

WEWALA

❼

Main Rd

❽

Sri Lanka
Travels
⓫
❷

Coral
Sanctuary

❺ ⓮
❿ ❸
❾

Milla Rd

Travel
Tailor

⓳

A-Frame Surf ☐
Shop &
Mambo Tours

❽ ⓭

Wewulagoda Rd

⓮

To Narigama, Thirangama & Galle

N

200 metres

200 yards

Where to stay 🛏
Blue Ocean Villa **3**
Citrus **2**

Coral Reef Beach **6**
Coral Rock **7**
Coral Sands **1**
El-Dorado **8**
Hikka Tranz **5**
Mama's Coral Beach **12**
Mandala Beach **9**
Moon Beam **14**
Surf Villa **4**

Tandem Guest House **19**
Time N Tide **10**

Restaurants 🍴
Cool Spot **2**
Curry Bowl **4**
JLH **7**
Red Lobster **10**
Refresh **11**

Sam's Bar **5**
Sea View **6**
The Coffee Shop **8**

Bars & clubs 🍸
Roger's Garage **14**
Vibration **13**

both their lives and wealth. You will need the services of a fisherman to get to the island. At another more easily accessible roadside temple, a few kilometres north on Galle Road, Sri Lankan travellers pay their respects, bringing most traffic to a temporary halt.

Kumarakanda Rajamahavihara ① *4 km south of Hikkaduwa at Dodanduwa, just before Km 103 post, donations expected*, has some murals and statues, though it is on the tourist trail so expect a dancing monkey and 'school pen' collectors. The temple is reached by a long, steep and narrow flight of stone steps. The beach opposite has a very small private **Turtle Research Centre** ① *Rs 500*, which works to protect this endangered species. You can see eggs and different stages of development.

Picturesque **Ratgama Lake** has abundant bird life and a large population of water monitors. There are three islands in the lagoon, one of which is **Polgasduwa**, where there is a forest hermitage founded by a German monk. Touts offer trips from the beach. Once you are there you can explore the lagoon by paddleboat.

Baddegama, 11 km inland along the B153, is within easy reach of Hikkaduwa by bicycle or motorbike. The road is picturesque, cutting its way through coconut and banana groves, followed by several small plantations – rubber, tea and spices. About half way the road passes the **Nigro Dharama Mahavihara** (stupa) in Gonapinuwala. On a hill above the river In the grounds of Christ Church Girls College is the first Anglican church in Sri Lanka, built in 1818 and consecrated by Bishop Heber of Calcutta in 1825. Note the ironwood pillars.

Narigama & Thirangama

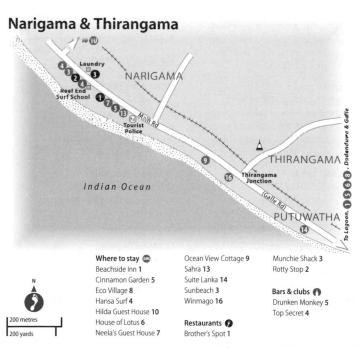

Where to stay 🛏
Beachside Inn **1**
Cinnamon Garden **5**
Eco Village **8**
Hansa Surf **4**
Hilda Guest House **10**
House of Lotus **6**
Neela's Guest House **7**

Ocean View Cottage **9**
Sahra **13**
Suite Lanka **14**
Sunbeach **3**
Winmago **16**

Restaurants 🍴
Brother's Spot **1**

Munchie Shack **3**
Rotty Stop **2**

Bars & clubs 🍸
Drunken Monkey **5**
Top Secret **4**

200 metres
200 yards

N

Tourist information

Tourist police
Police Station, Galle Rd, T060 200 9790.

Where to stay

There are innumerable hotels lining the beach here, often with very little to distinguish between them. Places away from the beach tend to be cheaper than beachfront properties with similar facilities. Many prices drop by up to 50% out of season (May-Oct). Whatever season you visit, it is worth bargaining.

Hikkaduwa

$$$$-$$$ Hikka Tranz
T091-227 4000, www.cinnamonhotels.com.
Large attractive property in great location with all mod cons, good pool and spacious gardens. There are plenty of watersports to tempt you off your sunlounger.

$$$ Citrus
Formerly Amaya Reef, 400 Galle Rd,
T091-438 3244, www.citrusleisure.com.
Hard to miss from the outside, 50 a/c rooms with balcony or terrace facing the sea. Pool, restaurant and diving available.

$$$ Coral Sands
326 Galle Rd, T091-227 7513,
www.coralsandshotel.com.
75 clean and airy a/c rooms with balcony, not all sea-facing and some newer than others, restaurant, bar, pools, diving school, friendly, reasonable value.

$$ Birdlake Villa
Maragahahena, Pathan, T077-501 9171.
Attractive villa with good size rooms and beautiful views of the lagoon – great for birdspotting.

$$ Sophie House
Galle Rd, T077 710 8266.
Stylish bed and breakfast with lovely rooftop, comfortable rooms, 1 studio with kitchenette. Deservedly popular.

$$-$ Coral Reef Beach Hotel
336 Galle Rd (Km 99 post), T091-227 7197,
www.coralreefbeachhotel.com.
27 a/c and fan rooms with sea view, although a bit spartan, bar, pool table, restaurant, **Blue Deep Diving Center**.

$$-$ Mama's Coral Beach
338 Galle Rd, T091-227 5488,
www.mamascoralbeach.com.
A/c and fan rooms with balcony, though it's a narrow property so not many have views. Highly rated seafood restaurant, the first in Hikkaduwa (see Restaurants, below).

Wewala

$$$ Mandala Beach
141/1 Galle Rd, T076-682 1075,
www.mandalabeach.lk.
Bathe with a view – outside bathtubs at this smart boutique hotel. Great location and beach vistas from large patio doors and verandas. Good restaurant on-site too.

$$ Blue Ocean Villa
420 Galle Rd, T091-227 7566,
www.blueoceaweb@blogspot.com.
8 large clean rooms, upstairs better, restaurant, hot water, good choice.

$$ Moon Beam
1/548 Galle Rd, T091-545 0657,
hotelmoonbeam@hotmail.com.
20 clean rooms, better on upper floors with sea views, good restaurant.

$$ Time N Tide Beach Resort
412/E Galle Rd, T077-706 6814,
www.time-n-tide.com.
17 rooms with a/c and hot water, Wi-Fi
available. Restaurant serving wood-fired
pizza, good sea views (although you're so
near that the surf can be almost too noisy).

$$-$ Surf Villa
Milla Rd, T077-760 4620.
Down a side road but not far from the
beach, this gem is hidden amongst a lush
tropical garden. Rooms have fan or a/c and
the bathrooms are enormous with bathtub
and showers. Very clean and friendly,
popular with surfers. Recommended.

$ El-Dorado
*Milla Rd, 200 m inland from Galle Rd, T091-
454 5590, www.eldoradohikkaduwa.com.*
6 a/c and fan rooms in small family-run
guesthouse, use of kitchen, very clean, very
peaceful setting away from busy road (but
still only 10 mins from the beach), good
value, good choice.

$ Tandem Guest House
465 Galle Rd, T091-493 3942,
www.lankaland.com.
Not on the beach but offering 9 clean
and light rooms with seating area outside.
Good value.

Narigama and Thirangama

$$$$-$$$ Suite Lanka
T091-227 7136, www.suite-lanka.com.
6 beautifully furnished standard rooms,
deluxe rooms and suites. Private verandas,
pool, 2 bars (1 on beach), very quiet and
intimate, delicious seafood.

$$ Cinnamon Garden Hotel
*T091-227 7081, www.cinnamon-
hikkaduwa.co.uk.*
10 a/c and fan rooms in bungalows. Pretty
beachfront garden, good restaurant.

$$ Ocean View Cottage
T091-227 7237, www.oceanviewcottage.net.
14 attractive, clean a/c and fan rooms
(upstairs better), 10 with sea views. Good
terrace restaurant, quiet, pleasant garden.

$$-$ Hansa Surf
T091-222 3854, www.hansasurf.com.
26 rooms ranging from dark and basic
to brighter and breezy. Shady veranda,
big-screen movies, friendly and helpful
and popular with surfers. Recommended.

$$-$ Sunbeach
T077-766 9848, www.sunbeach surf.com.
15 clean and cosy rooms, some with a/c,
plus a treehouse with great views. Wi-Fi.

$ Hilda Guest House
*Uswatta, Wawala, 300 m from Galle Rd,
T091-493 3383, www.hildaguesthouse.ch.*
4 rooms in an attractive Swiss-owned
house, 10-min walk from the beach
with a quiet garden. A pleasant escape
from the main drag.

$ Neela's Guest House
*634 Galle Rd, Narigama, T091-438 3166,
neelas_sl@hotmail.com.*
Friendly and popular guesthouse offering
fan rooms, or a/c rooms with sea views.
Recommended.

$ Winmago
794/1 Galle Rd, T091-227 7655,
www.hideawayhikkaduwa.com.
Basic rooms in an attractive building
with good views. Also known as
Hideaway Hikkaduwa.

Dodanduwa

$$$ House of Lotus
175 Galle Rd, T091-226 7246,
www.house-of-lotus.com.
A yoga retreat also offering Ayurvedic
packages, but accepts non-yoga devotees

as well. 7 a/c and fan rooms, pool. Food is mainly veggie to suit yogic lifestyle.

$$ Eco Village
Sri Saranajothi Mawatha (see map, page 131), T077-742 4088, www.ecovillagelanka.com.
On the lagoon, a former family holiday home now converted into an **Environmental Study Centre**, with a plank walkway through a mangrove swamp, and an attractive water garden. Sleep in a houseboat or stilt house; there's also a family unit.

$$-$ Beachside Inn
Galle Rd, T091-309 0073.
Guesthouse with 6 clean fan rooms (upstairs better). Hot water, pleasant garden, excellent food,

Restaurants

Wewala has the best choice, particularly for seafood. A number of *rotti* shops have sprung up, these open around 1630 and are a filling option for those on a tight budget. Crowded places may not necessarily be better; it could just be that they're mentioned in a guidebook!

Hikkaduwa

$$ Red Lobster
Waulagoda Rd.
Excellent food, good value, friendly owners.

$$-$ Cool Spot
327 Galle Rd, opposite Hikka Tranz.
Tasty curry and seafood, platters can be good value. Upstairs seating area is nicer, as it feels further from the Galle Rd traffic.

Wewala

$$$-$$ Refresh
384 Galle Rd, T091-227 7810, www. refreshsrilanka.com. Daily 0730-2230.
Classiest place in town, vast and varied menu, pizzas, jumbo prawns, enormous

mixed grill, good choice of international vegetarian options and impressive range of wines and cocktails. Great, but expensive.

$$ Curry Bowl
368 Galle Rd.
Good food and service, "delicious" garlic toast, upmarket setting.

$$ Sam's Bar
403 Galle Rd, near Blue Ocean Villa.
Tastefully decorated with dark wood, stripy cushions and long window benches. Reasonably priced food: seafood, burgers, noodles.

$$ Sea View
297 Galle Rd, T091-227 7014.
Not beachfront but a busy place serving good pizza, pasta and seafood, outdoor seating.

$$ Time n Tide Beach Resort
See Where to stay, page 135.
Only serves wood-fired pizza and pasta, but if that's what you're after you can't do better than this. Recommended.

$$-$ JLH
382 Galle Rd, T091-227 7139.
Fresh seafood, including a delicious seafood platter, and good veggie options too. Right by the water, it's a perfect place to sip cocktails.

$ The Coffee Shop
Galle Rd.
Simple but effective, homemade cake and tea or coffee. Good book exchange.

Narigama and Thirangama

$$-$ Munchie Shack
Galle Rd.
The usual choice of tourist dishes but also Australian meat and a wide range of Japanese fare.

$ Brother's Spot
Galle Rd.
5 little tables just off the road, serving Chinese, Italian and seafood dishes for lunch and dinner. A popular breakfast spot: the pancakes are superb and the bananas fresh from the owner's garden over the road.

$ Rotty Stop
Narigama.
Tasty rice and curries, excellent rottis, local clientele.

Bars and clubs

The most popular bars are **Top Secret**, **Harbour** and **Vibration**. Fri night's live drumming party at Vibration is a bit of an institution. If, however, you just want a beachfront drink there are numerous other options: pick one that grabs your fancy. Note that **Mambo's** has a bad reputation for its treatment of women and guests – be aware and stay safe in this party place.

Shopping

Hikkaduwa
There are numerous batik, handicraft, leather work, jewellery and clothing stores along the length of Galle Rd. Bargaining is expected.
Ceylon Gold Tea, *355 Galle Rd, T077-620 2615.* One of a number of tea shops on Galle Rd, this offers a wide range, and the prices are reasonable.
Raja's Jewellery, *403 Galle Rd, T091-227 7006.* Not the place for gem shopping, but stocks some interesting and modern rings and pendants in silver set with semi-precious stones.

What to do

Hikkaduwa
Ayurveda
Many places have 'Ayurveda clinics', though the treatments usually lack authenticity.

Diving
The diving season along the southwest coast is Nov-Apr. Hikkaduwa has the most dive schools on the island, though not the best local sites. There are several other dive schools in addition to those listed here. Check that they are SSI- or PADI-qualified before agreeing to a dive or course. Snorkelling equipment can be hired from shops along the main street.
Barracuda Diving Center, *356 Galle Rd, T077-985 3772, www.hikkaduwabarracuda. com.* PADI school. US$30 for 1 dive, US$50 for 2. Also offers 'discovery dive'. Very enthusiastic and informative. French and English spoken.
Poseidon Diving Station, *just north of Coral Sands Hotel, T091-227 7294, www. divingsrilanka.com.* In operation since 1973, the headquarters has an interesting selection of booty recovered by the school's Swedish founder. You can opt for numerous packages including courses including PADI and Advanced, as well as single dives and night dives. Rooms are available for divers or non-divers alike. Recommended.

Surfing
Reef End Surf School, *593 Galle Rd, Narigama, T077-704 3559, www.reefend surfschool.com.* Surf lessons from US$20 per day, or 5-days (3 hrs per day) for US$150. Board rental, surf information, and surf and accommodation packages arranged. Friendly and popular. Recommended.

Tour operators
Pasan Tours & Travels, *237/1 Galle Rd, T091-227 7898, T077-346 6706, www.*

pasantours.com. Offers tours and vehicle hire, excellent English spoken.
Rainforest Rescue International, *Organic Garden, Galle Rd, Akurala (10 mins north of Hikkaduwa), T091-223 2585, www. rainforestrescueinternational.org*. Excellent initiative set up by environmentalists in 2002, which runs eco-tours in the Galle area. These include rainforest tours and mangrove boat trips. Early morning or evening are best for viewing wildlife.

Transport

Hikkaduwa

Bus It is almost impossible to hail a bus on the Galle Rd (even from official bus shelters) so it is worth going to the bus station (at the north end of town) or taking a taxi or 3-wheeler for short journeys. Frequent buses run from the bus station to **Ambalangoda** and **Galle**. The old, slow CTB buses that travel between **Galle** and **Colombo** via Hikkaduwa can take hours. A better option is to take a private minibus to/from Colombo's Bastian Mawatha bus station, which take under 2 hrs.

Taxi and three-wheeler There are now designated spots along Galle Rd where licensed taxis and 3-wheelers wait for custom. Look for the signs, both on the vehicles and by the side of the road.

Train To **Colombo Fort**, express trains (2-2½ hrs) most stopping at **Ambalangoda**, **Aluthgama** (for Bentota and Beruwela), **Panadura** and **Moratuwa**. Slow trains north run as far as **Aluthgama**. Frequent trains to **Galle** (45 mins) every 1-2 hrs, some continuing to **Matara** (1½ hrs), via **Talpe**, **Ahangama** and **Weligama**. **Kandy** train (via Colombo) leaves at 1452 (5¾ hrs). Vavuniya train, via **Anuradhapura** (8 hrs), leaves at 1117.

Galle &
the south coast

Less package-orientated than the west coast, the spectacularly scenic bays and beaches of the south coast are a magnet for more independent sun and sea worshippers, with fewer crowds and some good-value accommodation. Unawatuna, Tangalla and, increasingly, Mirissa are the main beaches here, each with long sweeps of fine sand; while city life focuses on Matara and particularly Galle, whose colonial origins provide some historical interest. While you could pass along the south coast in under four hours, those with the time might easily spend a week here, hopping from village to village and enjoying the laid-back lifestyle.

Galle *Colour map 3, C2.*

step back in time at Galle Fort

Galle (pronounced in Sinhala as 'Gaal-le') is the most important town in the south, with a population of 97,000. Its Fort, enclosed by mighty ramparts, has some wonderful examples of colonial architecture and is a laid-back and enchanting place to explore. It was declared a UNESCO World Heritage Site in 1988.

★ Galle Fort

The Fort completely encloses the 200 or so houses of the old town. Set on a promontory, it is rather removed from the busy modern town and retains a village atmosphere, full of local gossip. You can easily spend a whole day in this area; some visitors find themselves staying far longer than they expected. Part of the appeal is being able to wander the streets, which are lined with substantial colonial buildings. Most have large rooms on the ground

Tip...
Look out for manhole covers every 20 m or so along the main streets of the Fort. These mark the location of old brick-lined sewers, built by the Dutch, which were naturally flushed twice a day by the tides.

Essential Galle

Finding your feet

Galle is 155 km from Colombo. Express trains are preferable to a crowded bus journey, provided you avoid the rush hour. Both trains and buses run frequently to/from Colombo. See also Transport, page 149.

Best secret treats

Tea at Hundunagoda Tea Estate, page 145
Idle Tours' cycle tour, page 149
Sri Serendipity's Galle Fort walking tour, page 149
Sri Yoga, near Wijaya Beach, page 157
Mulgirigala Rock Temple near Tangalla, page 168

Tip...
Beware of touts who earn commission on accommodation and shopping (gems).

Getting around

The train and bus stations are both in the new town, 10-15 minutes' walk north of the fort walls and cricket stadium. Galle Fort is so small and compact that most of the guesthouses are very easy to find. To get to the upmarket hotels outside Galle, you will need to hire a taxi or three-wheeler.

Weather Galle

January	February	March	April	May	June
31°C 23°C 103mm	31°C 23°C 86mm	32°C 24°C 117mm	32°C 25°C 242mm	31°C 26°C 296mm	30°C 26°C 207mm

July	August	September	October	November	December
29°C 26°C 165mm	29°C 26°C 155mm	30°C 25°C 214mm	29°C 24°C 340mm	30°C 23°C 302mm	30°C 23°C 177mm

floor and an arched veranda to provide shade. The arched windows of the upper floors are covered by huge old louvered wooden shutters; the lower ones have glass nowadays. Unfortunately, quite a few of these fine houses are in need of restoration. An interesting route around the old town is to walk south from the main gate, all along Church Street, then east to the lighthouse, north up Hospital Street and west along Queen Street finishing back at the post office on Church Street.

Ramparts, bastions and gates The ramparts, surrounded on three sides by the sea, are marked by a series of bastions. The two nearest to the harbour are Sun and Zwart, followed by Akersloot, Aurora and Point Utrecht bastions on the east side, then Triton, Neptune, Clippenburg, Aeolus (used by the Sri Lankan army), Star and Moon. Those on the west side are more accessible

Tip...
A walking tour around the ramparts is a must. Try to do it on a clear evening, starting at about 1630, and aim to reach the clock tower at sunset.

and stand much as they were built, although there is evidence of a signals post built in the Second World War on top of Neptune.

There are two gates in to the Fort. The more impressive is on the north side, flanked by Star bastion to the west, and by Moon and Sun bastions to the east. The ramparts here are massive, partly because they are the oldest and have been reinforced several times over the years. Just

Galle

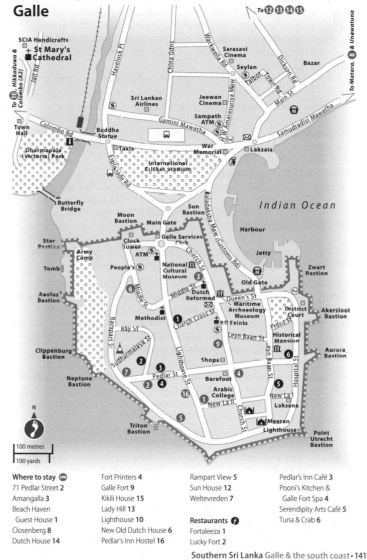

Where to stay 🛏	Fort Printers 4	Rampart View 5	Pedlar's Inn Café 3
71 Pedlar Street 2	Galle Fort 9	Sun House 12	Pooni's Kitchen &
Amangalla 3	Kikili House 15	Weltevreden 7	Galle Fort Spa 4
Beach Haven	Lady Hill 13		Serendipity Arts Café 5
Guest House 1	Lighthouse 10	Restaurants 🍴	Tuna & Crab 6
Closenberg 8	New Old Dutch House 6	Fortaleeza 1	
Dutch House 14	Pedlar's Inn Hostel 16	Lucky Fort 2	

BACKGROUND

Galle

Galle's origins as a port go back to well before the arrival of the Portuguese. Ibn Batuta, the great Moroccan traveller, visited it in 1344. The historian of Ceylon Sir Emerson Tennant claimed that Galle was the ancient city of Tarshish, which had traded not only with Persians and Egyptians but with King Solomon. The origin of the name is disputed, some associating it with the Latin *gallus* (cock), so-called because the Portugese heard the crowing of cocks here at dusk, others with the Sinhala *gala* (cattle shed) or *gal* (rock).

Lorenzo de Almeida drifted into Galle by accident in 1505. It was another 82 years before the Portuguese captured it from the Sinhala kings, and they controlled the port until the Dutch laid siege in 1640. The old Portuguese Fort, built on a promontory, was strengthened by the Dutch who remained there until the British captured Galle in 1796. The Dutch East India Company, VOC (*Vereenigde Oost Indische Campagnie*), ruled the waves during the 17th and 18th centuries with over 150 ships trading from around 30 settlements in Asia.

A P&O liner called at Galle in 1842 marking the start of a regular service to Europe. In 1859, Captain Bailey, an agent for the shipping company, built a villa in a commanding position, 3 km across the harbour. The villa, set in a tropical garden, is now the **Closenberg Hotel**, and P&O's Rising Sun emblem can still be spotted on some of the old furniture.

Galle's gradual decline in importance dates back to 1875, when reconstruction of breakwaters and the enlarged harbour made Colombo the island's major port.

inside the gate is a clock tower dating from 1883, which sometimes has a huge national flag flying from it. Southeast of the Sun bastion is the second and much older gate on Queen Street.

Under the ramparts between Aeolus and Star bastions is the tomb of a Muslim saint neatly painted in green and white, said to cover an old freshwater spring. The open space here, next to Rampart Street, is often used for unofficial games of cricket in the evenings and at weekends. Sri Sudharmalaya temple is across the street.

Church Street The **National Cultural Museum** ① *Church St (next to Amangalla hotel), T091-223 2051, Tue-Sat 0900-1700, Rs 300, children Rs 150, cameras Rs 250, video cameras Rs 2000*, is in an old colonial stone warehouse. Exhibits include a model of Galle and the fort's Dutch and Portuguese inheritance.

On the other side of the Amangalla is the **Dutch Reformed Church** (1754), which is certainly worth visiting. It was built as a result of a vow taken by the Dutch governor of Galle, Casparaus de Jong, and has a number of interesting memorials. Inside, the floor is covered by about 20 gravestones (some heavily embossed, others engraved), which originated in older graveyards which were closed in 1710 and 1804. The British moved them into this church in 1853. The organ loft has a lovely semi-circular balustrade, while the pulpit, repaired in 1996, has an enormous canopy.

Opposite the church is the old bell tower, erected in 1701; the bell, open to the elements, is hung in a belfry with a large dome on top of it. Next door is the **Maritime**

After many years languishing in apparently terminal decay, Galle Fort was declared a UNESCO World Heritage Site in 1988, and in the mid 1990s gentrification commenced. In 2002 the Indonesian luxury chain Amanresorts bought the desperately neglected 17th-century New Oriental Hotel, a former Dutch barracks and the oldest registered hotel in Sri Lanka. After substantial restoration it became the luxury Amangalla hotel (see Where to stay, page 146).

In 2004 the tsunami hit, damaging areas of the ramparts and the old town, and prompting significant donations from the Dutch government. Since then, investment from foreigners and the Dutch government has paid for the repair of the fortification walls and the restoration of over 120 buildings, including the transformation of the warehouses opposite the Dutch Reformed Church into a modern maritime museum (see below)

Many of Galle's historic houses were snapped up for renovation by foreigner investors following the abolition of the 100% foreign land tax in 2003; some have since become hotels, guesthouses, art galleries, restaurants and cafés. The international influence is noticeable and, on the positive side, has contributed to making Galle the cultural centre of the South, with its own literary festival and a successful British-owned publishing house. Tourism has resulted in new business opportunities for shopkeepers, guesthouse owners, cafés and other small businesses, with increased demand for locally produced goods. But amongst the buzz that investment has brought, some fear that Galle Fort could become a 'little Europe', culturally detached from the surrounding area and devoid of local colour. As more and more foreigners buy land and houses in the fort, prices have increased significantly, making it hard for locals, some who have been here for centuries, to resist the large sums they are offered to move. Those who wish to stay are finding it almost impossible to afford to buy property.

Archaeology Museum (see below). The old **post office**, restored by the Galle Heritage Trust in 1992, is a long low building with a shallow red-tiled roof supported by 13 columns. It is still functioning although it is very run-down inside.

Further down Church Street is **All Saints Church** (not always open). This was built in 1868 (consecrated in 1871) after much pressure from the English population, who had previously worshipped at the Dutch Reform Church. Its bell came from the Liberty ship, *Ocean Liberty*, and was gifted to the church in its centenary year by the chief officer of the Clan Shipping Company. He had acquired the bell from the *Liberty* when the ship was scrapped and also named his daughter Liberty. There is a particularly good view of the church, with its red tin roof surmounted by a cockerel and four strange little turrets, from Cross Church Street.

The old **Dutch Government House**, opposite the church, is now a hotel. Note the massive door in four sections at the Queen's Street entrance, which was built for entry on horseback.

Maritime Archaeology Museum ① *Church St, opposite the post office, T091-224 5254, daily 0900-1700, Rs 300, children Rs 100 (included in Cultural Triangle Round Ticket)*, is an enormous museum in an old Dutch warehouse replaced the National Maritime Museum. Visitors enter on one level, follow the exhibits and leave by the exit on the lower floor. An interesting film is shown first, which explains the various wrecks lying offshore, some artefacts of which are displayed in the museum. Look out for the beardman jug found at the *Avondster* wreck site in Galle harbour. Exhibits also explore how Sri Lankan dress and language (amongst other things) were influenced by visitors who came by sea to trade, and there are some interesting objects that were washed up after the tsunami. The museum currently feels a bit empty and it is disappointing that not all the objects were found nearby: some are merely examples of what would have been aboard the ships. However, there is much of interest to see.

Arab quarter At the end of Church Street lies the old Arab Quarter with a distinct Moorish atmosphere. Here you will find the **Meeran Jumma Masjid** in a tall white building that resembles a church with two square towers topped by shallow domes, but with the crescent clearly visible. Slender, tubular minarets are also topped by crescent moons. The mosque was rebuilt at the beginning of the 20th century on the site of the original from the 1750s. The Muslim Cultural Association and Arabic College, which was established in 1892, are here. The mosque is still very active; you will see many Muslims in the distinctive skullcaps hurrying to prayer at the appointed hours.

Lighthouse to Zwart Bastion Near Point Utrecht Bastion, the 20-m-high lighthouse was built by the British in 1939, nearly on top of the old magazine with its inscription 'AJ Galle den 1st Zeber 1782'. You can get good views from the top, though you will need to get permission from the lighthouse keeper (ask in the gem store next door). **Hospital Street** runs north from near the lighthouse past the Police Barracks, which were built in 1927 but fail to blend in with the older parts of the fort. The government offices on Hospital Street were once the Dutch 'factory' (warehouse). At the north end of Hospital Street is the square with the district court near the Zwart Bastion.

South of here is the **Historical Mansion Museum** ① *31-39 Leyn Bann St (well signed), T091-493 6162, Sat-Thu 0900-1800, Fri 0900-1230, 1400-1800, free,* in a restored house. A number of rooms around a small courtyard contain a potentially worthwhile collection of colonial artefacts. Several interesting and rare items are simply 'stored' here, but the real aim of the museum becomes apparent when visitors are led to the gems for sale in the adjoining shop.

New town
Galle new town was much worse hit by the 2004 tsunami, as everything inside the Fort was offered a degree of protection by the rampart walls. The **new town** is quite pleasant to wander through, and its bustle contrasts with the more measured pace of the Fort. Leave the Fort by the old gate for an easy walk along the harbour, with its rows of fishing boats neatly drawn up on the beach. Cricket fans will want to visit the rebuilt **Galle International Cricket Stadium**, just north of the fort's main gate, where there is often a match going on. You can clamber up onto the ramparts to find the spot from which Jonathan Agnew, the BBC's cricket correspondent, was forced to broadcast in February 2001 when he wasn't allowed into the ground. On the Colombo Road to the west of Victoria Park, are several gem shops. Take the road opposite them to reach **St Mary's Cathedral**, which was built in 1874 and has a very good view over the town. There is little of interest inside, though.

Around Galle
As soon as you leave the town, you are surrounded by verdant green paddy fields, untouched forests and rolling hills, ripe for exploration (see What to do, page 149). Half an hour inland from Galle is the charismatic **Hundunagoda Tea Estate**.

Hundunagoda Tea Estate ⓘ *Tittigalla; take the road towards Matara and turn inland at Koggala (30 mins by tuk-tuk), T077-771 3999.* Don't miss a trip to this beautiful tea estate in lovely grounds, famous for its Virgin White Tea. See all the processes of the tea journey from bush to cup, and take time to taste myriad varieties, including a fantastic Ceylon Oolong, or the Suicide Club, a smoky tea combined with whisky. The estate is owned by tea planter Malinga Herman Gunaratne and is often recommended as the best in Sri Lanka.

Listings Galle *map p141*

Tourist information

Ceylon Tourist Board
Victoria Park, opposite the railway station. Daily 0900-1600.

Where to stay

Beware of touts who may tell you that your guesthouse has hiked its prices or closed down, or even that the fort itself is closed –

it never shuts. If you accept a tout's recommendation, you'll be paying over the odds for their commission.

A growing number of villas in the Galle area have been bought and renovated and can be let both short and long term. **Eden Villas** (www.villasinsrilanka.com) is a British-run agency with many beautiful properties to let in the Galle area and along the coast.

28, Church Street, Galle Fort, Galle, Sri Lanka
+94 912232870 | www.galleforthotel.com

Galle
Fort
Hotel

Galle Fort

$$$$ Amangalla (formerly New Oriental Hotel)
10 Church St, T091-223 3388,
www.amanresorts.com.
17 rooms and 8 suites retain the elegance of Galle's most famous colonial hotel. Very attractive swimming pool, spa and good restaurant. Those who aren't staying can take a drink on the veranda or high tea in the lobby, and soak up some of the old world atmosphere.

$$$$ Galle Fort Hotel
28 Church St, T091-223 2870,
www.galleforthotel.com.
Restored colonial mansion with large rooms and suites, all beautifully and thoughtfully decked out. Excellent food, stylish bar and lovely small courtyard pool. Attentive and helpful staff. Recommended.

$$$$-$$$ The Fort Printers
39 Pedlar St, T091-224 7977,
www.thefortprinters.com.
Excellent conversion of a colonial mansion house with a modern twist. Stylish interiors, beautiful art and small courtyard dotted with frangipani trees around a lovely pool. Highly recommended.

$$$ 71 Pedlar Street
71 Pedlar St, T077-696 0238.
Beautiful 5 bedroom boutique guesthouse in the heart of the Fort. Another stunning renovation project with courtyard pool, eclectic artwork throughout and a relaxed vibe.

$$ New Old Dutch House
21 Middle St, T091-223 2987,
www.newolddutchhouse.lk.
6 rooms in a gleaming house with Moorish-style decor, many arches and a great spiral staircase. Internet available in the lobby.

$$-$ Beach Haven Guest House
65 Lighthouse St, T091-223 4663,
www.beachhaven-galle.com.
10 spotless rooms, some with a/c, those upstairs are better as they share a communal balcony. Very friendly family-run guesthouse, great atmosphere. Popular, so book in advance. Free Wi-Fi.

$$-$ Pedlar's Inn Hostel
62 B Lighthouse St, T091-222 7443,
www.pedlarsinn.com.
Spacious airy double rooms and good dorms around the corner from the Pedlar's Inn gallery and café. Dorms are just US$12 a night. Recommended.

$$-$ Rampart View
37 Rampart St, T091-492 8781,
www.gallefortrampartview.com.
6 sizeable, clean a/c and fan rooms with attached bath in renovated colonial house. Wonderful views from the roof. Friendly management. Free Wi-Fi. No alcohol.

$ Bourganvila Guest House
60 Pedlar St, T091-224 5738.
Good family-run place with decent-size rooms, free Wi-Fi and a friendly welcome.

New town

$$$$ Dutch House
23 Upper Dickson Rd, opposite The Sun House (see below), T091-438 0275,
www.thedutchhouse.com.
Under the same management as **The Sun House**, this former residence of a Dutch East India admiral was built in 1712 and offers 4 magnificent suites exquisitely decorated in colonial style and a magnificent treetop infinity pool. Recommended.

$$$$ The Sun House
18 Upper Dickson Rd, T091-438 0275,
www.thesunhouse.com.
5 superbly furnished rooms and 2 excellent suites, all with different themes, in a 1860s

spice merchant's house. Described as a '5-star boutique hotel', it is highly exclusive with discreet service, fine dining, pool, library. Very atmospheric.

$$$ Kikili House
Lower Dickson Rd, T091-273 4181, www.kikilihouse.com
Run by the hostess with the mostest, Hen (*kikili* in Sinhalese) and her husband Kokila, no really… This is a beautiful 4-room boutique B&B with delicious breakfasts, cute garden, an honesty bar with Moët and bags of charm. Recommended.

$$$-$$ Lady Hill
29 Upper Dickson Rd (a little further up from The Sun House), T091-224 4322, www.ladyhillsl.com.
A 19th-century mansion at the highest point of the city, with large veranda and teak ceiling. Modern extension has 15 well-furnished, if smallish, a/c rooms, with TV and balconies. **Rooftop Harbour Bar** affords spectacular views of the fort and the harbour, and some mornings as far inland as Adam's Peak. Also very good pool.

Around Galle

$$$$ Lighthouse Hotel (Jetwing)
Dadella, 4 km north of Galle, T091-222 3744, www.jetwinghotels.com.
60 superbly furnished a/c rooms, panoramic views from sea-facing terrace, 2 restaurants including excellent **Cinnamon Room** for fine dining, and 2 pools, one of which is saltwater.

$$$$ Kahanda Kanda
Angulugaha, inland from Galle, T91-494 3700, www.kahandakanda.com.
Beautiful suites with stunning views in an inland oasis surrounded by tea plantations and tropical lushness. There is a lovely infinity pool. The food is incredible with the menu changing daily. Highly recommended.

$$ Samakanda
Nakiyadeniya, Udagama Rd (20 km post), T077-042 1659, www.samakanda.org.
Travelling inland from Galle into the lush forest you are rewarded with stunning views and rolling tea plantations. At Samakanda you can stay in the pretty Tea Planter's Bungalow. There are possibilities for short walks, paddy field bike rides and cookery lessons.

Restaurants

Some of the more upmarket hotels in the fort offer excellent dining options; guesthouses are a cheaper alternative, and there are numerous cheap 'rice and curry' places around the train/bus stations,

Galle Fort

$$$ Fortaleeza
9 Church Cross St, T091-223 3415, www.fortaleeza.lk.
With seared tuna steaks and robust burgers, this chic courtyard restaurant serves up great fusion food. There are also 4 stunning rooms on-site and a beautiful luxury villa and the 'Barefoot' flat close by. Recommended.

$$$ Tuna and Crab
Dutch Hospital, T091-309 7487.
Run by the clever chaps behind Ministry of Crab and Nihorobashi in Colombo, this is a fusion restaurant serving up delicious sushi and sashimi, Japanese curries and seafood specialities, all in the beautifully restored Dutch Hospital complex.

$$ Pedlar's Inn Café
92 Pedlar St, T091-223 3415
Labyrinthine rooms in this converted property, so you can pick your nook or take a seat on the outside veranda and watch the world go by. Great range of foods from around the globe: good salads, burgers and pastas. Great coffees. Good jewellery shop too for little magpies.

$$-$ Pooni's Kitchen
63 Pedlar St, tucked behind the Galle Fort Spa.
Work up an appetite with a massage upstairs and then float down to lovely courtyard café strewn with art. On the menu, you'll find delicious salads, great sandwiches and global tastes. Recommended.

$$-$ Serendipity Arts Café
Leyn Baan St. Daily 0730-2130.
Laid-back spot with friendly staff, serving sandwiches, burgers, Sri Lankan dishes and cake. There are books and magazines to flip through (some published over the road) and excellent walking tours of the fort leave from here (see What to do, opposite).

$ Lucky Fort
7 Parawa St, off Pedlar St, T091-224 2922.
Exceptional range of seasonal curries at this family-run place tucked on a side street. Delicious veg and non-veg options, or choose their set menu which gives you 10 different tastes of Sri Lanka. Recommended.

Bars and clubs

The Galle Fort Hotel has a pleasant veranda bar, and the bar at the Rampart Hotel looks out over the ramparts. The Rooftop Harbour Bar at the Lady Hill Hotel has superlative views down across the Fort.

Festivals

Galle Literary Festival, *www.galleliterary festival.com.* Started in 2007, it usually takes place at the beginning of the year. Attracts a good range of well-known international authors, including, for example, in 2016, Amitav Ghosh, Sebastian Faulks, Meera Syal and Jeet Thayil.

Shopping

Galle is known for its lace-making, gem polishing and ebony carving. The fort is home to a number of upmarket boutiques, as well as innumerable gem shops.

Barefoot, *41 Pedlar St, T091-222 6299, barefootceylon.com.* A branch of the popular Colombo shop (see page 70), selling beautiful textiles, homewares, clothes, great range of toys and books.
Dutch Hospital, Hospital St. Beautifully restored hospital building contains a collection of shops, including several gem stores.
KK – The Collection, *36 Church St.* Stunning homewares and artefacts. Connected to the exceptional Kahanda Khana hotel (see Where to stay, above).
Laksana, *30 Hospital St.* One of a number of shops in Galle Fort selling gems and jewellery.
Natural Silk Factory, *691/1 Colombo Rd, Gintota (north of Galle), T091-223 4379. Daily 0900-1830.* Watch the silk worms, visit the showroom and shop for reasonably priced silk, with little pressure to buy.
SCIA Handicraft Centre, *Kandewatte Rd, T091-223 4304.* Workshops producing polished gems, carvings (ebony), batik, lace and leather bags, etc, employing about 50 people (approved by the State Gem Corporation and Tourist Board).
Shoba Display Gallery, *67A Pedlar St, T091-222 4351, www.shobafashion.org.* A women's cooperative, this shops sells colourful handicrafts and lace work.
Vijitha Yapa, *170 Main St.* Branch of the national bookshop chain, with a wide selection of English books.

What to do

Body and soul
Galle Fort Spa, *63 Pedlar St, www.galle fortspa.com.* Beautiful spa in a converted house offering a wide range of treatments encompassing Ayurvedic and western techniques. Great range of locally made beauty products too. Recommended.

Diving

There are a number of shipwrecks in Galle Bay but better diving is at Hikkaduwa, page 137, and Unawatuna, page 154.

Tour operators

Idle Tours, *Godawatta, Mihiripenna, T077-790 6156, www.idletours.com.* Idle Tours run accompanied tours by bike or canoe through the lush countryside around Galle. Peddle around the paddy fields and visit nearby lakes, villages and villas. You can also opt to explore the Ginganga River. Recommended. **Sri Serendipity**, *60 Leyn Baan St, T077-683 8659, www.sriserendipity.com.* Juliet Coombe and Daisy Perry run a publishing house in the Fort and offer guided excellent walking tours of the area. Tours leave from here or from the **Serendipity Arts Café**, just over the road (see Restaurants, above), usually at 1000 and again at 1600 if there's enough demand (US$20 per person for an hour's tour or US$75 for half a day). You can opt for themed walks focusing on local foods or architecture.

Transport

Bus There are regular services along the coast in both directions. Both **CTB** and

Tip...
Avoid travelling to Colombo by CTB bus on Sunday; it can be very busy with queues of over an hour before you actually get onto a bus.

private buses operate from the main bus stand. Frequent buses to **Colombo**, a/c express recommended (3 hrs). Buses east to **Unawatuna** (15 mins), **Matara** (1-1½ hrs), **Tangalla** (2-3 hrs), **Tissamaharama** (4 hrs), **Kataragama** (4½ hrs) and **Wellawaya**.

Three-wheeler Costs around Rs 500 to **Unawatuna**.

Train The station is a short walk from the bus station, the Fort and the new town. Express trains to **Colombo** (3½ hrs, 2nd class Rs 180, 3rd class Rs 100), most via **Hikkaduwa**, **Ambalangoda**, **Aluthgama**, **Kalutara** and **Panadura** at 0540, 1355, 1705, 1430. To **Kandy**, 7 hrs, Rs 320/175. Slow trains stop at other coastal destinations. To **Matara**, 1½ hrs, Rs 80/40, every 1½-2 hrs, 0500 to 2050, stopping at **Talpe**, **Koggala**, **Ahangama** and **Weligama**. Slow trains stop at **Unawatuna** (10 mins) and **Mirissa** (1¼ hrs).

Unawatuna *Colour map 3, C3.*

a popular beach and diving resort

Unawatuna, 5 km southeast of Galle, has a picturesque beach along a sheltered bay that was once considered one of the best in the world. Although rather narrow, it is more suitable for year-round swimming than say, Hikkaduwa, as the bay is enclosed by a double reef, which lessens the impact of the waves. For divers, it is a good base to explore some of the wrecks in Galle Bay, and there is some safe snorkelling a short distance from shore (though you may be disappointed by the lack of live coral).

Sadly, Unawatuna is fast becoming over-developed with poor infrastructure. (The government has even demolished several illegal structures.) The resort's popularity has also taken its toll. Beach restaurants have encroached to the point where the actual usable beach is very narrow, and the increasing number of visitors means that the beach is sometimes crowded; the western end of the bay is particularly popular with local day-trippers at weekends and public holidays. The erosion continues apace and some restaurants are now on wooden platforms in the sea. Petty theft has become a problem in recent years, as have drugs. Some parts of the beach can also be very noisy, with music blaring until the early hours. Certainly, there are quieter, more atmospheric beaches to be found further along the coast. But, during the week, if you are seeking somewhere with a beach that is safe for swimming, a wide range of clean accommodation and a variety of decent beachside restaurants, then Unawatuna is a good choice.

Unawatuna's main attraction is unquestionably its beach but it isn't the only place worth visiting. There are some lovely walks in the area.

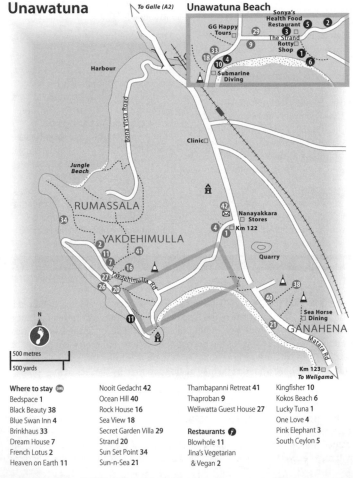

Where to stay	Nooit Gedacht **42**	Thambapanni Retreat **41**	Kingfisher **10**
Bedspace **1**	Ocean Hill **40**	Thaproban **9**	Kokos Beach **6**
Black Beauty **38**	Rock House **16**	Weliwatta Guest House **27**	Lucky Tuna **1**
Blue Swan Inn **4**	Sea View **18**		One Love **4**
Brinkhaus **33**	Secret Garden Villa **29**	**Restaurants**	Pink Elephant **3**
Dream House **7**	Strand **20**	Blowhole **11**	South Ceylon **5**
French Lotus **2**	Sun Set Point **34**	Jina's Vegetarian	
Heaven on Earth **11**	Sun-n-Sea **21**	& Vegan **2**	

Rumassala kanda (hillock)

The rocky outcrop on the coast has a large collection of unusual medicinal herbs. In the *Ramayana* epic, Hanuman, the monkey god was sent on an errand to collect a special herb to save Rama's wounded brother Lakshmana. Having failed to identify the plant, he returned with a herb-covered section of the great mountain range, dropping a part of what he was carrying here. Another part is said to have fallen in Ritigala (see page 293). This area of forest is now protected by the state to save the rare plants from being removed indiscriminately. It offers excellent views across Galle Harbour towards the Fort. On a clear day look inland to catch sight of Adam's Peak. The sea bordering Rumassala has the **Bona Vista reef** which has some of the best preserved coral in Sri Lanka. Recovery from the 1998 bleaching has been faster than elsewhere on the coast.

Jungle Beach, on the other side of the promontory, is pleasantly uncrowded and has some good snorkelling. Boat trips from some of the guesthouses run here and many three-wheelers will offer to take you. Alternatively, you can walk (around 45 minutes) from Unawatuna Beach. You might get lost but guides tend to appear as if by magic.

Listings Unawatuna *map p150*

Where to stay

Book ahead at weekends as Unawatuna is a popular getaway from the city. There are a large number of hotels and guesthouses here, catering to a range of budgets. Below are just some of the places on offer.

$$$ Dream House
T091-438 1541, www.dreamhouse-srilanka.com.
4 beautifully furnished rooms in Italian-run old colonial-style house. Wonderful bougainvillea filled garden, very Italian ambience and authentic Italian food. Very peaceful.

$$$ French Lotus
T077-152 2867, www.frenchlotus-unawatunacom.
Lovingly restored house with spacious rooms and antique decor. Lots of lovely verandas and private spaces all set within beautiful gardens. Recommended.

$$$ Thaproban
T091-438 1722, www.thambapannileisure.com.
Sister establishment to **Thambapanni Retreat**, this beachfront hotel offers great beach views and a deservedly popular restaurant.

$$$-$$ Bedspace
Egodwatta Lane, T091-225 0156, www.bedspaceuna.com.
4 stylish rooms at this funky guesthouse with beautiful garden. You can kick back in the grounds, where you'll also find an outdoor kitchen where they serve up delicious all-day breakfasts, and 3 evenings a week there are special suppers. Recommended.

$$$-$$ Nooit Gedacht
T091-222 3449, www.sriayurveda.com.
Beautiful colonial mansion (built 1735), steeped in history. Simple rooms with period furniture in the main house, or brighter and more modern ones in the new bungalows. Also full, authentic Ayurveda centre. Very peaceful and atmospheric.

$$$-$$ Secret Garden Villa
T091-224 1857, www.secretgarden unawatuna.com.
Spacious and well-decorated rooms and suites (plenty of wood) in beautiful tropical gardens, as well as more modern bungalows.

Lovely domed yoga room (see What to do, page 154). All with a friendly welcome.

$$$-$$ Thambapanni Retreat
Yakdehimulla Rd, past Dream House, T091-223 4588, www.thambapannileisure.com.
In a peaceful setting on the side of Rumassala hill, rooms on the highest level have magnificent jungle views. The best room is the one built into the side of the hill; the cheapest, standard rooms are not worth bothering with. Ayurvedic centre, inviting pool, yoga classes and reiki. Recommended.

$$ Black Beauty
Ganahena, signposted off the main rd, T091-438 4978, www.black-beauty-sri-lanka.com.
Look for the Ying Yang wooden door, which opens onto this very friendly, secluded guesthouse. Laid-back atmosphere and good value (price includes breakfast), with sparkling clean rooms with a/c and hot water. Pool, play area. Can be booked up weeks and sometimes months in advance, so call ahead. A good family choice.

$$ Sea View
Devala Rd, T091-222 4376, www.seaviewunawatuna.com.
23 spacious, clean fan and a/c rooms with large balcony in pleasant garden setting. Also a bungalow with 2 bedrooms and kitchen. One new room has an outdoor bathroom and despite being non-a/c is worth the money to shower under the stars.

$$ Sun-n-Sea
Ganahena, east end of bay, T091-228 3200, ameendeane@yahoo.co.uk.
Clean a/c and hot water rooms with covered verandas on the sea edge. Good terrace restaurant overlooking the bay with excellent view. Very friendly. As you walk in notice the piece of door on the left: Mrs Perera (the previous, charming owner) clung to this as the tsunami swept through the guesthouse in 2004.

$$ Weliwatta Guest House
T091-222 6642, www.weliwatta.com.
You get a friendly welcome at this house dating back to 1900. 5 good-sized rooms, quiet, tasty home-cooked food. Tours arranged.

$$-$ Heaven on Earth
T091-224 7775.
6 quite small rooms, simple but well furnished with private seating areas. Those upstairs have breakfast and internet included in the price.

$$-$ Strand
Yakdehimulla Rd (set back from beach), T091-222 4358, www.homestay-strand.net.
5 spacious rooms, 1 small, and 1 apartment in a 1920s colonial-style house in large grounds. The ground floor rooms are a bit dark. The 'nest room' is recommended: it's bright and has a private balcony looking out onto the garden. Friendly family, knowledgeable host, a little frayed around the edges. Encroaching disco music.

$ Brinkhaus
Welledevala Rd, T091-224 2245, www.brinkhouseunawatuna.site11.com.
Quiet and peaceful, decent rooms in shaded gardens with monkeys in the trees. Lovely family who have been here for decades and are very friendly and helpful.

$ Sun Set Point
Yakdehimulla, T091-527 3672, lalwhitehouse@aol.com.
Spacious but slightly tired rooms with veranda in impressive house on headland, with great views. Hidden away from the rest of Unawatuna.

Restaurants

There are numerous restaurants along the beach with very little to choose between them. Nearly all will serve good seafood, Chinese, Sri Lankan (full meal often only to order) and Western dishes. Almost all serve alcohol though those at the western end of the bay don't advertise it since the area close to the temple is officially 'dry'. The Rotty shop opposite **Sonja's Health Food Restaurant** is good for a light meal.

$$$-$$ Dream House
See Where to stay, page 151.
Delicious Italian food in lovely surroundings. Book in advance as the restaurant is very popular and some meals are best ordered in advance.

$$$-$$ Lucky Tuna
Attractive wooden bar and restaurant on the beach. Curry and the usual rice and noodle dishes, as well as some excellent fish. Good vibe.

$$ Blowhole
Tucked away, past Submarine Diving School, turn right by the temple.
In a great setting by the river (watch the wildlife), good place to stop on the way up to Jungle Beach or for a quiet breakfast. Simple but delicious food.

$$ Jina's Vegetarian and Vegan Restaurant
Welledevala Rd.
Run by a Buddhist practitioner, Jina's sources as much local produce as possible. Set in pleasant gardens and serving a selection of veggie and vegan food from around the globe. A little oasis.

$$ Kingfisher
Popular place serving fresh seafood and Thai dishes; arrive early if you want a seat. All the ex-pats come here for their fish suppers.

$$ Koko's Beach Restaurant
Yakdehimulla Rd.
British-run and serving up traveller favourites including exceptional fish and chips.

$$ Pink Elephant
Nightly set menus. 3 courses of interesting and inventive Western-inspired cuisine.

It may not be beachside but it's worth tearing yourself away from the sand. Recommended.

$$ Sunil's Garden Coffee Bar
Sunil Garden Guesthouse.
Tables are hidden amongst the undergrowth and there's a Wi-Fi at the back on a raised platform. The menu is limited but excellent. Food is very fresh, especially the pizzas. Homemade cake, Italian coffee, as well as tzatziki with brown toast and other snacks.

$ Hot Rock
Almost dropping into the sea (literally), this is a popular hangout serving seafood and Western dishes. Bright and colourful walls, friendly staff

Bars and clubs

The places listed in the Restaurants section generally sell beer. A couple of places have discos at weekends, starting at 2130. Sat is the big night.

Shopping

There are various shops selling provisions and tourist goods. Clothes are cheaper on Yakdehimulla Rd, but be prepared to bargain.

What to do

Cookery classes
There are a few places in Unawatuna offering cookery classes, prices range from Rs 2000 for 2 hrs to Rs 3000 for a whole day.
Sonja's Health Food Restaurant, *Unawatuna Beach Rd, T091-224 5815, T077-961 5310.* Karuna runs very popular cookery classes here that start at 1100 and end about 1530. Includes a trip to Galle to visit the market for ingredients and then pupils are taught how to make curries, sambol, etc. In the evening you eat what you've cooked and can bring a guest for free. Good value.

Diving and snorkelling

Most of the beach-side restaurants hire out snorkelling equipment, and some run their own snorkelling trips. The diving season runs Nov-Apr here. There are 5 or 6 wrecks nearby, some at a depth below 15 m, which you can visit. The best accessible wreck is the *Rangoon* in Galle Bay, though this is at a depth of 32 m. There are also some reefs and a rock dive on offer.

Sea Horse, *off Matara Rd, T077-627 7622, www.seahorsedivinglanka.com*. Run by Rohana (an experienced Dive Master), this is the smallest operation in Unawatuna. 1 dive €25 (US$28), 10 dives €220 (US$249). Contact direct for Open Water and Advanced courses €275 (US$311). Also runs great trips to Jungle Beach and short snorkelling jaunts.

Submarine Diving School, *T077-719 6753, www.divinginsrilanka.com*. €30 (US$34) (including equipment) for 1 dive. Hires out snorkelling gear for Rs 250 per hr and runs snorkelling trips. Dive courses. Check that a PADI-qualified instructor is on hand.

Unawatuna Diving Centre, *T077-224 4693, www.unawatunadiving.com*. The largest and newest dive centre, with the best equipment. Runs trips to about 15 dive sites. Contact for details of Open Water, Advanced and Refresher courses

Tour operators

Southlink Travels, *2nd floor, Selaka Building, 34 Gamini Mawatha, next to the bus station*.

Yoga and meditation

A few hotels and guesthouses offer meditation and yoga classes, the best are at **Secret Garden Villa**, which offers yoga daily at 0700, 0900 and 1700, Rs 1000.

Transport

It is very easy to miss Unawatuna when travelling by road. Look out for the Km 122 marker on the (sea) side of the road.

Bus Services between **Galle** and **Matara** will drop you on the main road on request.

Three-wheeler To **Hikkaduwa**, Rs 600, after bargaining. **Galle,** Rs 300, takes 15 mins.

Train Trains pass through Unawatuna on the **Galle–Matara** line, though only the slow trains (7 a day) stop here. 10 mins to **Galle**, 1-1¼ hrs to **Matara**. If coming from **Colombo**, take the express to Galle then change on to a Matara train. The station is to the east of the main Galle–Matara Rd, some 500 m north of the Km 122 marker (about 15-min walk to the beach). Touts and 3-wheeler drivers outside the station can be very persistent. Be sure of your destination to avoid caving in and arriving at a guesthouse of their choosing.

★ Towards Weligama   *Colour map 3, C3/4.*

stilt fishermen have given way to surfers on this beautiful stretch of coast

The road running east from Unawatuna runs close to the sea offering wonderful views and linking a series of small, attractive beaches. Although the appealing coves and well-priced hotels are no longer a secret, they still don't attract the crowds that are found at Unawatuna.

The coast between Talpe and Weligama was formerly best known for its remarkable fishermen who perched for hours on poles out in the bay. Nowadays, this is a dying tradition. The place where you are most likely to spot 'stilt' fishermen working is between Dalawella and Ahangama early in the morning or, sometimes, if they're hungry, in the evening. At other times they tend to arrive only when visitors with cameras appear, and they expect a small tip for a photograph. Further east, the stretch between Ahangama and Midigama is a renowned surfing spot, frequented by long-stay international waveriders.

Dalawella and Talpe

Dalawella is just east of Unawatuna. Though it's on the main road, it has a lovely section of beach and a natural swimming pool towards the eastern end. The fine beaches continue to picturesque **Talpe**, a short distance east, where an increasing number of upmarket hotels are beginning to open. Many of the new hotels and guesthouses here are better value than in Unawatuna itself.

Koggala and around

The coast road passes the old wartime airstrip at Koggala, which has been developed as a domestic airport; flights from Colombo land here. Koggala itself has a Free Trade Zone with some light industry. It lies to the south of an attractive, tranquil lagoon with rocky islets to the north. The lagoon is lined with mangroves and is rich in birdlife. Boat trips run to the **Ananda Spice Garden** ⓘ *T091-228 3805, for more details*, a temple and cinnamon island.

Just by the gate of the Fortress Hotel (see Where to stay), a road leads left over the railway line to the **Martin Wickramasinghe Folk Museum** ⓘ *daily 0900-1700. Rs 200 (with explanatory leaflet), children Rs 100*, which houses the respected Sri Lankan writer's personal collection: photographs, memorabilia and some history about the area. Even if you are not a fan of Wickramasinghe, the museum is still worth visiting as its glass cabinets contain some fascinating exhibits from traditional Sri Lankan life, including religious items, farming and fishing tools, and traditional games, dating from before cricket obsessed the nation. There's a colourful selection of *kolam* masks and puppets from the Ambalangoda area, and 101 different utensils for treating coconuts. The house and museum are set in an attractive garden with labelled trees, so you can swot up on your Sri Lankan flora.

Kataluva Purvarama Mahaviharaya, originally 18th century with late 19th-century additions, is 3 km from Koggala along a minor road, turning off at Kataluva (Km 132 mark); ask directions locally. The ambulatory has excellent examples of temple paintings illustrating different styles of Kandyan art. Young monks will happily point out interesting sections of the *Jataka* stories depicted on the wall friezes. Note the musicians and dancers on the south side and the European figures illustrating an interesting piece of social history. The priest is very welcoming and keen to speak with foreigners.

Ahangama to Midigama

The coast from Ahangama to Midigama is regarded as the best surfing area on the south coast, at its best between January and March. There are various breaks at Midigama. The main (or left break) is in front of **Hilten's Beach Resort** and is good for beginners and longboarders. Further east, the right break is over a shallow reef close to **Ram's Surfing Beach**. There's another break 400 m east of here which is more suitable for beginners. If you are not into surfing, this stretch of coast is probably best avoided; it is full of very cheap guesthouses, catering for surfers on long stays.

Where to stay

Dalawella and Talpe

$$$$ The Frangipani Tree
812 Matara Rd, Thalpe, T091-228 3711,
www.thefrangipanitree.com.
Owned by the same people as **The Fort**
Printers in Galle (see page 146), this
boutique hotels offers 10 suites in 4 separate
villas named after turtles. 35-m pool is at the
centre of the action; there's also excellent
food, yoga and tennis.

$$$ Sri Gemunu
Dalawella, T091-228 3202,
www.sri-gemunu.com.
20 comfortable sea-facing fan and a/c rooms
with veranda. Pleasant gardens and good
restaurant overlooking attractive beach.

$$$ Wijaya Beach
Dalawella, T091-228 3610,
www.wijayabeach,com.
Great views in a laid-back spot – stylish
rooms and large balconies above a
deservedly popular restaurant serving up
exceptional pizzas and fish suppers. You can
spot turtles from here, and the sunsets across
Frog Rock are epic. Ask about their beautiful
new inland yogashala and retreat spot a
short drive away. Highly recommended.

$$ Point de Galle
654 Matara Rd, Talpe, T077-790 1285,
www.pointdegallehotel.com.
8 airy rooms with beautiful beds and
balconies set in attractive gardens right
on the beach.

$$ Star Light
Talpe, T091-228 2216, starlight@sltnet.lk.
Attractive a/c rooms with beautiful furniture
and good attention to detail, TV, minibar and
bath tubs. Lovely open areas, great pool and
very smart restaurant.

$$-$ Shanthi Guest House
Dalawella, T091-438 0081, www.shanthi-
guesthouse.de.
A/c and fan rooms or cabanas. Rooms are
moderate size, shared balcony, facing beach.
Cabanas closer to beach set amongst a
series of ponds in attractive gardens. Stilt
fishermen on beach, and saltwater 'pool'
nearby. Excellent restaurant and pleasant,
friendly atmosphere.

Koggala and around

$$$$ The Fortress
Matara Rd, T091-438 9400, www.thefortress.lk.
Large luxury beachfront hotel hidden
behind high, imposing walls. Rooms, suites
and apartments have huge beds and are
tastefully decorated. All the facilities you'd
expect, including diving trips organized and
Ayurvedic treatments. Large swimming pool.

$$$ Kabalana Beach Hotel
Galle Rd, Kataluva, T091-228 3294,
www.kabalana.com.
Beachfront cabanas and a range of room
options on a good stretch of sand. Decor is
colonial in style, with dark wood and white
furnishings. Ayurvedic treatments and surf
lessons available. Restaurant. Popular with
surfers. Can arrange airport transfers.

$$$ Koggala Beach Hotel
Habaraduwa, T091-228 3243,
www.koggalabeachhotel.com.
102 sea-facing rooms, the superiors are
better and newer. Popular with tour groups.
Restaurants, bars, pool and lots of activities.
On a good stretch of beach.

Ahangama to Midigama

$$$-$$ Easy Beach
Ahangama (4 km east of Koggala),
T041-228 2028, www.easybeach.info.

Set in pleasant gardens, with an open, breezy feel. Rooms or cabanas (breakfast included). Surf boards for rent and trips organized.

$ Ram's Surfing Beach
Midigama, T041-225 2639.
Communal surfer's hangout with range of rooms from dirt cheap to moderate. Good food and friendly.

What to do

Dalawella and Talpe
Yoga
Sri Yoga Shala, *inland from Thalpe and Dalawella, www.sriyogashala.com.* Perfect your downward dog at this beautiful new shala with regular dance classes, as well as yoga and bodywork treatments. There is a beautiful pool and garden café, so you can make a day of it, or you can stay on site for longer retreats.

Transport

Many visitors to these beaches arrive by car or rickshaw, but it is equally feasible to reach one of the resorts by public transport.

Air Sri Lankan Airlines, T19-733 5500, www.srilankan.aero, has started operating flights between **Koggala** and **Colombo**.

Bus Local buses between Galle and Matara can be flagged down and stopped at any of these settlements.

Train Most trains between Galle and Matara stop at **Talpe**, **Ahangama** and **Weligama**, where there are 3-wheelers for onward transport. There are also local stations at **Habaraduwa**, **Kataluva**, **Midigama** and **Mirissa**.

diving, surfing and whale watching

Though Weligama town, 29 km east of Galle, is fairly unappealing, it has a picturesque location on a magnificent sheltered and sandy bay, backed by the attractive Polwatte Ganga. The bay remains safe for diving and snorkelling beyond the southwest coast's usual season and has some good surf at the eastern end of Weligama beach. A few kilometres further round the bay, Mirissa is perhaps the most attractive of the south coast resorts.

Weligama *See map, page 159.*
Weligama town (population 22,000) is a busy centre for the surrounding fishing villages. The western side is the home of the many fishermen operating out of the harbour, and there are catamarans everywhere. At the approach to the town there is a 4-m-high **statue of Kushta Raja**, sometimes known as the 'Leper King'. Various legends surround the statue, which is believed by some to be of Bodhisattva Samantabhadra. Look out for the houses decorated with *mal lali* fretwork along the road towards the centre from the statue. The area is also known for its handmade lace. Devil Dances are held in nearby villages.

Weligama is most famous however for its tiny **Taprobane Island**, walkable (at low tide) in the lovely bay. Once owned by the Frenchman, Count de Mauny, who built a

Tip...
Weligama lace is available at several outlets and workshops along the road opposite Taprobane Island.

magnificent house there, it was bought by American author Paul Bowles after de Mauny's death. After a period of neglect, it was returned in the late 1990s to its former glory and is now a luxury tourist retreat.

★ Mirissa *Colour map 3, C3.*

Of all the south coast beach resorts to have developed in recent years, Mirissa, with its beautiful wide stretch of golden sand backed by luxuriant vegetation, has received the greatest praise. For the moment the plaudits seem justified; so far, this relaxed little village, 5 km east across Weligama Bay, has been more sensitively developed than Hikkaduwa or Unawatuna, with less obvious intrusion of guesthouses and restaurants on to the beach. Mirissa is no longer a secret hideaway – its popularity increases each year, prompting concerns about over-development – but it remains one of the most idyllic places to relax along this stretch of coast.

The west end of the beach is popular with surfers. Further east, the two beaches beyond **Giragala Village** have a reef where there is some good swimming and snorkelling. Giragala (or 'Parrot') Rock is a popular place to watch the sunset. Near here is a defile, known as **Bandaramulla**, where there is a Buddhist *vihara*. Inland, you can explore the river or make forays on foot or by bike into the jungle.

In recent years Mirissa has become a centre for whale watching, and between December and April blue whales can be viewed offshore. Nearly every guesthouse and hotel now offers trips, as do three-wheeler drivers; quality varies. See page 163.

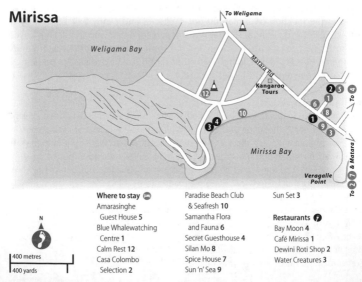

Mirissa

Where to stay
Amarasinghe
  Guest House **5**
Blue Whalewatching
  Centre **1**
Calm Rest **12**
Casa Colombo
  Selection **2**

Paradise Beach Club
  & Seafresh **10**
Samantha Flora
  and Fauna **6**
Secret Guesthouse **4**
Silan Mo **8**
Spice House **7**
Sun 'n' Sea **9**

Sun Set **3**

Restaurants
Bay Moon **4**
Café Mirissa **1**
Dewini Roti Shop **2**
Water Creatures **3**

Where to stay

Weligama
The better-value accommodation is in
Pelana, a short bus or 3-wheeler ride from
Weligama town. Marriot is opening a spa
hotel here which may change the vibe of
the area.

$$$$ Barberyn Beach Ayurveda Resort
T041-225 2994, www.barberynresorts.com.
Ayurvedic centre run by respected
Beruwela-based company. 60 attractive
a/c rooms, sea views and balconies, some
split-level with bath tub. Large Ayurveda
clinic with full list of treatments. Yoga and
meditation. Full-board only.

$$$$ Mirissa Hills
*Henwalle Rd, Henwalle, T041-225 0980,
www.mirissahills.com.*
Stunning views from this hilltop abode on a
working cinnamon estate. Choose from the
colonial bungalow or the modern hilltop
villa. There is also the world's only museum
dedicated to cinnamon.

$$$$ Taprobane Island
T091-438 0275, www.taprobaneisland.com.
Probably the most exclusive place to stay in
Sri Lanka, with bags of charm and history.
You can rent the whole island, which has
a 5-bedroom house with resident staff,
including a private chef.

$$$ The Green Rooms
*T077-111 9896, www.thegreenrooms
srilanka.com.*
A surf lodge at the eastern end of the
beach with very attractive wooden
cabanas. The whole place can be rented, or
alternatively individual rooms are available.
Many visitors stay for weeks, and there's
a family atmosphere about the place. If
you want to learn to surf there are special

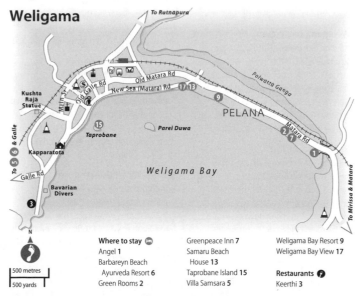

Weligama

Where to stay 🛏
Angel **1**
Barbareyn Beach
  Ayurveda Resort **6**
Green Rooms **2**

Greenpeace Inn **7**
Samaru Beach
  House **13**
Taprobane Island **15**
Villa Samsara **5**

Weligama Bay Resort **9**
Weligama Bay View **17**

Restaurants 🍴
Keerthi **3**

packages available combining tuition and accommodation. Also cookery lessons. Highly recommended.

$$$ Villa Samsara
2 km west at Kumalgama (Km 140 post), T0845-154 6218.
Beautiful colonial villa in lovely garden amongst coconut groves. 4 large, simply furnished rooms with 4 poster beds.

$$$-$$ Weligama Bay Resort
Matara Rd, Pelana, T041-225 3920, www.weligamabayresort.com.
22 a/c villas, bungalows and suites, all with sea views and contemporary furnishings. Beachfront pool, spa, and all the facilities you'd expect but a disappointing restaurant.

$$ Samaru Beach House
544 New Bypass Rd, Pelana, T041-225 1417, www.samarubeachhouse.com.
Spotless rooms, 4 a/c and 4 fan, each with own seating area. Good location on the beach, restaurant, friendly management, good value. Rents surfboards, bikes and scooters. Wi-Fi and surf lessons.

$$ Weligama Bay View
New Bypass Rd, Pelana, T091-225 1199, www.bayviewlk.com.
Along good stretch of beach, 11 large a/c and fan rooms. Reasonably clean, good restaurant. Popular with surfers. Friendly management. Surfing equipment and surfing lessons offered.

$$-$ Greenpeace Inn
New Bypass Rd, Pelana, T041-225 2957, greenpeaceinn@yahoo.com.
14 rooms close to the beach, the 2 on the top floor have the best views and the most light, but those downstairs are cheap (fan and cold water). Restaurant. Enthusiastic owner.

Mirissa
Between Nov and Apr, book ahead. Note that most of the higher-end hotels impose a minimum of half-board on their guests.

$$$$ Casa Colombo Collection
Madamawatte, Kambunrunganuwa, T011-452 0130, www.casacolombocollection.com.
Casa Colombo Collection delivers 5-star style in its spacious villas and suites. Great beachfront location, with a pool and a restaurant serving up seafood delicacies and tapas.

$$$ Paradise Beach Club
140 Gunasiri Mahime Mawatha, T041-225 1206, www.paradisemirissa.com.
Modern attractive building with 42 single- and 2-storey cabanas, both a/c and fan. Pool, smart restaurant (evening buffet), tours, located on beach, not bad value but enforced half board tends to be restrictive.

$$$ Silan Mo
Bandaramulla, T041-225 4974, hotel.silanmo@gmail.com.
Across the road from the beach. A modern building with 15 spacious rooms, all a/c and with views of the ocean. Rooftop pool. Huge balconies.

$$$ Spice House
Galle Rd, T077-351 0147
Family-run boutique guesthouse. Colonial-style building made using traditional techniques. Large 4-poster beds in stylish roms all named after spices. Good pool. Recommended.

$$$-$$ Secret Guesthouse
Babdaramulla, T077-3293 4332, www.secretguesthouse.com.
4 stylish rooms with modern 4-poster beds and billowing white fabric, plus 1 family bungalow. Lovely gardens and relaxed vibe. Delicious Sri Lankan food. Also home to the Secret Root Spa for Ayurvedic treatments. Recommended.

$$ The Sun Set
T077-734 0434, www.mirissasunset.com.
Attractive building with 13 rooms, most are spacious but the budget ones are quite small. Great seafront dining and good swimming nearby.

$$-$ Amarasinghe Guest House
5 mins inland (follow signs), T041-225 1204, chana7@sltnet.lk.
Large rooms and bungalows in a pleasant quiet garden away from the beach, Internet, cold water. Offers cookery classes. Has another property comprising 3 small, dark and basic rooms with verandas called **Blue Whalewatching Centre**, nearer to the beach. They're nothing special but a good price for Mirissa.

$$-$ Samantha Flora and Fauna
T077-635 5068.
Still close to the beach, Samantha's is a tropical garden with 5 simple rooms in a forest setting by a log bridge and lagoon. A couple of the rooms have solar-heated water and a/c.

$ Sun 'n' Sea
T077-833 9958.
Warm welcome and delicious food. This place is all about the family running it. The rooms are basic, and there's only cold water but the views and atmosphere are great.

Restaurants

Weligama
Home cooking in the privately run guesthouses is difficult to beat.

$$-$ Keerthi
After a hiatus of several years this family-run restaurant is now back. Close to the sea and peaceful, with a large whale jaw in the garden to add interest. The husband and wife team cook up a wide selection of good seafood, including mullet, snapper and sailfish, as well as the usual seerfish and cuttlefish.

Mirissa
A number of the places listed here also rent out rooms. Those on the beach display their fresh seafood nightly so diners can choose their meals. Most guesthouses have restaurants.

$$ Bay Moon
The first in Mirissa and still one of the best, with a "nice beach bar ambience, and they set a beach fire for effect."

$$ Café Mirissa
Has a limited selection of food – seafood, curry, Chinese – but a perfect position to survey the beach.

$$ Seafresh
Part of Paradise Beach Club.
The smartest place in Mirissa, offers a set menu.

$$ Water Creatures
At the far end of the beach.
Popular with surfers, serves a good range of dishes.

$ Dewmini Roti Shop
Close to Amarasinghe Guest House (see Where to stay, above), T071-516 2604, www.dewminirotishop.wordpress.com. Daily 0700-2030.
Deservedly popular. Serves tourist favourites, such as banana and honey rotti, and a whole host of delicious Sri Lankan curries. Get a sneak preview of Gayani's pumpkin curry recipe on their website.

What to do

There are plenty of fish in Weligama Bay, which makes it popular for both fishing and diving. Deep-sea angling is available here, mainly for marlin, yellowfin and sharks. Dive sites include Prinz Heinrich Patch, which offers the chance to see huge eels and rays, whilst Yala Rock has rocks, pinnacles and caves with a swim-through and lots of fish.

The whale tale

There had been efforts for over 30 years to develop whale watching in Sri Lanka but to little or no avail. Attempts were thwarted by the cost of setting up such a venture, the lack of suitable boats, and more than anything by the mistaken belief that whale watching had to take place from Trincomalee, which was periodically off-limits during the war years.

Things began to change, however, in the late nineties. In 1999 marine biologist Dr Charles Anderson suggested that whale migration between the Bay of Bengal and the Arabian Sea took blue and sperm whales close to the shores of Sri Lanka between December and April. His theory was further refined in 2005 after thousands of sightings, and he identified Dondra Head as the best viewing spot because the continental shelf is at its narrowest here.

More evidence to support the migration theory was provided by Mirissa Water Sports, a commercial venture set up after the 2004 tsunami. Simon Scarff, Sue Evans and their crew started logging sightings and by 2008 were offering trips to see the whales (see Whale and dolphin watching, opposite).

Kalpitiya (see page 89) has also recently been identified as a whale-watching hot spot, and tours are gradually starting to gain popularity there as well. It is too early to confirm Sri Lanka's position as one of the leading whale-watching destinations in the world, but it has the potential. It is hoped by many that whale watching will become as synonymous with Sri Lanka as leopard-spotting in Yala, but with that will come added problems. Already there are concerns about the number of boats operating out of Mirissa and their impact on the whales. Legislation and guidelines need to be adhered to for the safety of the whales and the watchers, but if this can be managed effectively then tourists should be able to experience seeing blue and sperm whales as well as dolphins, potentially all in one trip.

For more information on whale watching in Sri Lanka, including the history and a log of sightings, see www.jetwingeco.com/index.cfm?section=page&id=1055.

There are also numerous wrecks here and further afield: *SS Rangoon* is good but deep.

Diving and snorkelling

Bavarian Divers, *Bay Beach, Weligama, T0179-540 6573, www.bavarian-divers.de*. Highly recommended, with PADI Open Water and Advanced courses. 1 dive and check dive €30 (US$34), or €25 (US$28) per person for 2+ people. Can arrange budget accommodation for divers.

Fishing

Guesthouses in Weligama can arrange trips out on catamarans with the local fishermen. **Mirissa Water Sports**, *Mirissa, T077-359 7731, www.mirissawatersports.com*. Sport fishing, sea kayaking, dolphin and whale watching (see below) and other cruises.

Surfing

Surfboards can be rented from various places along the beach in Mirissa.

Whale and dolphin watching

Whale watching (blue and sperm whales) has taken off in a big way in Mirissa in recent years and every guesthouse, 3-wheeler driver and restaurant will offer to organize a trip for you. They vary in quality and price, so ask around: probably one of the best sources of information is other travellers. Between Dec and Apr is the best time to see whales. Trips leave around 0700 and run for about 4-5 hrs, breakfast is included.

Mirissa Water Sports, *Mirissa, T077-359 7731, www.mirissawatersports.com*. The original operator, so they know what they're doing. Whale-watching trips can be combined with any of their other activities (see above). Children half price.

Raja and the Whales, *Mirissa, T071-333 1811, www.rajaandthewhales.com*. Local family-run operator, charges Rs 6000 per person and gets consistently good reports. Boat is in good shape and crew are careful not to get too close to the whales.

Transport

Weligama

Bus Services between **Galle** and **Matara** will let you off on the New Sea (Matara) Rd, though some local buses will drop you at the bus yard on the Old Matara Rd. Buses from **Colombo,** about 4 hrs; from **Galle**, 45 mins. Local buses run from **Weligama** to **Pelana**.

Train Weligama is on the Colombo–Galle–Matara railway line, though check to make sure the train stops here if it's an express service.

Mirissa

Bus Services between **Matara** and **Galle** pass through Mirissa. From **Weligama**, a bus or 3-wheeler costs around Rs 150.

Train Slow trains from **Galle** or **Matara** stop at Mirissa, otherwise catch an express to Weligama and then take a 3-wheeler.

Matara and around   *Colour map 3, C4.*

old forts and coral beaches

Matara (pronounced locally as Maa-tre) is the South's second biggest town, with a population of 44,000. It is also an important transport hub 157 km from Colombo, with the terminus of the railway line and an enormous bus station. Locals will tell you that the city is better than Galle as it has two Dutch forts to Galle's one. Though busy and full of traffic, Matara does have a rich history, and the old town with its narrow streets and colonial buildings is a pleasant place to explore.

In the old marketplace you might still see the local wooden hackeries (oxcarts) that are sometimes used for races. Today, Ruhuna University, 3 km east, attracts students to the town. Matara is also famous for its musical instruments, especially drums, and you can pick up some good batik.

Sights

An important Dutch possession on the south coast, controlling the trade in cinnamon and elephants, Matara was well fortified. The **Main Fort**, south of the river, consists of a single rampart from which guns were fired. Its inadequacy as a defence was revealed during the Matara rebellion of 1762, when a Kandyan army managed to take the town by bombarding it with cannonballs that simply went over the wall. The Dutch retook the town the following year, and built the more successful **Star Fort** ① *generally closed, but the* *caretaker will show you around*, on the north side to defend the town against siege from the river. **Star Fort** is faced with coral. It has a moated double-wall and six points, and was designed to house ammunition, provisions and a small garrison. The gateway that shows the VOC arms and date is particularly picturesque. As in Galle, the Dutch government has recently invested money in restoring the fort, formerly a library.

Other sights in the town include a British clock tower (1883), located near the main bastion. A gleaming and impressive **mosque**, a replica of the Meeran Jumma Masjid in Galle, is located on the south side of the **Nilawala Ganga** from Star Fort. North of Star Fort, on Beach Road, is **St Mary's Church**. The date on the doorway (1769) refers to the repair work after the Matara rebellion. Close by is St Servatius College, one of Matara's two exclusive public schools, whose most famous son is Sri Lankan batting hero and former cricket captain Sanath Jayasuriya.

Though the beach at Matara is attractive, the sea is too rough for comfortable bathing for much of the year. At **Polhena**, south of the town, is a good coral beach protected by a reef which offers year-round swimming and some excellent snorkelling opportunities. There are also some good-value guesthouses, a pleasant alternative to staying in Matara town.

Matara & Polhena

Where to stay 🛏
Rest House **3**
Sunil Rest **5**
Sunny Lanka
 Guest House **6**
Surf Lanka **2**

TK Green Garden **7**

Restaurants 🍴
Chinese Dragon **2**
Galle Oriental Bakery **3**
Samanmal **6**

Where to stay

Most budget travellers choose to stay in
Polhena. The Broadway is also known as
Dharmapala Mawatha, Colombo Rd or
New Galle Rd.

$$ Rest House
*Main fort area south of bus station, T041-
222 2299, www.resthousematara.com.*
Attractive heritage-style property with large
4-poster beds. Restaurant with good Sri
Lankan breakfasts, and views of the sea.

$$-$ Surf Lanka Hotel
*Medawatta, T041-222 8190,
www.surf-lanka.com.*
11 a/c and fan rooms with balconies and sea
views (those upstairs are better), in modern
white building. Restaurant.

$ Sunil Rest
*Off Beach Rd, Polhena, T041-222 1983,
sunilrestpolhena@yahoo.com.*
Welcoming family, very friendly and helpful
guesthouse with cheap rooms. Tours
organized and bike hire available. Plentiful
food in the restaurant.

$ Sunny Lanka Guest House
Polhena Rd, Polhena, T041-222 3504.
Popular choice. Clean rooms in friendly
guesthouse, trips organized.

$ TK Green Garden
*116/1 Polhena Beach Rd, Polhena,
T041-222 2603.*
Attractive building in lovely garden setting,
popular with yoga groups. 11 good, clean
a/c and fan rooms, some with shared
veranda. Seek out the restaurant even if
you are not staying here – great food and
lovely welcome.

Restaurants

The best options are the hotels above,
but also check out Chinese Dragon and
the Galle Oriental Bakery.

Shopping

Look out for good batiks and citronella oil.

Art Batiks, *58/6 Udyana Rd, T041-222 4488,
www.sites.google.com/site/artbatiks.* Shirley
Dissanayake is a holder of the President's
Honorary Gold Medal 'Kala Booshana' in
arts. He produces top-quality batiks, only
available on site here in his workshop.
Beware of imitations.
Jez-look Batiks, *12 St Yehiya Mawatha, T041
222 2142.* Award-winning batik workshop,
wide range of clothes and hanging batiks.
Laksala, *55 Darmapala Mawatha, by the
temple, T041-222 2734.* For handicrafts.
Sri Madura, *21 Dharmapala Mawatha.*
Specializes in locally made Pahatarata Biraya
drums, which you can buy, or simply watch
craftsmen producing.

What to do

Diving and snorkelling
Ask at **TK Green Garden** for Titus, an
excellent snorkelling guide who knows the
reef like the back of his hand, having had
over 30 years' experience. The reef is good
for first-time snorkellers ("after 10 mins I felt
like Jacques Cousteau!"), and there are night
trips to see moray eels.

Transport

Bus The station is in the Main Fort area
with buses running on a 'depart when full'
basis. There are regular buses to **Colombo,
Galle, Hambantota, Kataragama,
Tangalla, Tissamaharama**, and all points

along the coast, as well as inland to **Ratnapura** and **Wellawaya** for the eastern highlands. There is also at least 1 early morning departure to **Nuwara Eliya** (8 hrs). Buses to **Mirissa** go regularly. Very irregular local buses run to the beach at **Polhena**. Alternatively, take a 3-wheeler.

Train Matara station, the terminus of this railway line, is 1 km away from town. 3-wheelers and taxis transfer passengers to the centre. To **Colombo** (4 hrs), plus slow trains as far as **Galle** (1½ hrs). **Kandy** train (8 hrs), **Vavuniya** train via **Anuradhapura** (9 hrs).

Towards Tangalla
head off the main road to find beaches, Buddha statues and a renowned blowhole

Weherahena
5 km from Matara; catch bus 349. Donation and tip for the guide requested.

Beyond Matara, a left turn leads to this modern **Buddhist sanctuary** which has a 40-m six-storey-high painted Buddha statue. Much older is the *vihara*, whose 600 m of tunnels are lined with some 20,000 friezes, some dating back to Portuguese times. **Perahera** takes place in November/December on the full moon.

Dondra
Dondra or Devinuwara is a fishing village 6 km from Matara, famous for its Vishnu temple. The original temple, one of the most revered on the island, was destroyed by the Portuguese in a brutal attack in 1588. **Devi Nuwara Devale** retains,

> **Fact...**
> The British renamed Devinuwara, which means 'City of Gods', as Dondra, because they couldn't pronounce the local name.

however, an ancient shrine possibly dating to the seventh century AD, which maybe the oldest stone-built structure on the island. The modern temple to the south has old columns and a finely carved gate. Even today the Buddhist pilgrims continuing the ancient tradition venerate Vishnu of the Hindu trinity. Some 2 km south of the town, the 50-m-high **lighthouse** (1889) on the southern promontory at Dondra Head marks the southernmost point of Sri Lanka.

Dikwella and Wewurukannala
The marvellous bays and beaches continue east to Tangalla. There are some established resort hotels at the village of **Dikwella** offering diving and watersports in the bay, while 2 km inland at Wewuurukannala is **Buduraja Mahawehera** ⓘ *Rs 100, a guide will approach.* Until an even bigger one was built in Dambulla in 2002, this was the tallest statue on the island. The statues, tableaux and Buddhist temple are in a complex which has an impressively tacky 50-m-high seated Buddha statue with a 'library' at the back. Some 635 paintings in cartoon strip form depict events from the Buddha's life covering every square centimetre of the interior. The artists are from all over the world but retain the same style throughout. There is also a garish 'Chamber of Horrors' with depictions of the punishments meted out to sinners, including some frighteningly graphic life-size models. One critic describes the site as looking 'more like an airport terminal than a temple'.

Kudawella *Colour map 3, C4.*
6 km east of Dikwella, 1.5 km off the main road. Rs 200.

The natural blowhole at Kudawella, also known as **Hummanaya** due to the 'hoo' sound that you hear, is one of the more bizarre attractions in Sri Lanka and worth the detour during the monsoon season. The water spray can rise to 25 m when the waves are strong. Take care when clambering on the rocks as they are wet and slippery in places. It is best to avoid weekends and go during school hours. The blowhole doesn't always 'perform' and is disappointing out of season, so check locally before making the trip. If travelling by bus, ask the driver to drop you off at the turn-off. The route to the blowhole is well signposted by the Elephant House.

Mawella *Colour map 3, C4.*
Mawella, 6 km west of Tangalla, has remained one of this stretch of coastline's best-kept secrets. It has a 3-km-long, very wide beach, avoids the busy main road, and offers safe swimming. It's easy to miss: turn right at the **Beach Cottage** sign.

Listings Towards Tangalla

Where to stay

$$$$ Claughton
Kemagoda (3 km east of Dikwella), T071-272 5470, www.villasinsrilanka.com.
Sumptuous Italianate villa in a magnificent setting overlooking a vast sweep of bay. 3 rooms; or hire the whole house.

$$$$-$$$ Underneath the Mango Tree
Tangalle Rd, Dickwella South, T041-203 0300, www.utmthotel.com.
Beautiful Ayurvedic resort perched on a cliff with great beach views and infinity pool. Full range of Ayurvedic packages, modern boutique rooms and villas and delicious dining using as much local produce as possible. There is also a day spa.

$$-$ Kingdom Resort
Kotteyodu, 5 km west of Dikwella (near the Km 175 post), T041-225 9364, www.kingdomsrilanka.com.
8 spotless a/c and fan rooms, some with balcony, in attractive neo-colonial house with own stretch of beach. Italian-owned, with all furnishings Italian-made. Very pleasant. Also specializing in Ayurveda.

Transport

Air Sri Lankan Airlines, T09-733 5500, www.srilankan.aero, has started operating flights between **Dickwella** and **Colombo**.

Bus Buses running between **Matara** and **Tangalla** link the main villages strung along Matara Rd. To visit the sights inland it is best to have your own transport.

Tangalla and around *Colour map 3, C5.*

beautiful beaches, Buddhas and turtles

Tangalla (pronounced Tunn-gaa-le) is an attractive fishing port, 40 km from Matara, with a palm-fringed bay. The town suffered damage during the tsunami but there are still a few distinctive colonial buildings and a picturesque *ganga*. It is a useful base for visiting the turtles at Rekawa, and the magnificent Mulgirigala Rock Temple. The surrounding bays have some of the best beaches in the southern coastal belt.

There isn't an enormous amount to see or do here except lie on the beach, but there is a **Dutch fort** standing on the slope above the bay. Built of coral with two bastions in opposite corners, it was turned into a jail after a report in 1837 declared it was in sound condition and able to safely hold up to 100 men. The exterior has now been covered over by cement.

Tangalla's beaches

Tangalla is made up of a number of settlements. **Goyambokka** and **Pallikaduwa** are on a series of bays to the south of town and have clean and secluded beaches. Goyambokka, in particular, is great for swimming. In **Tangalla town**, the cove in front has good sand and safe swimming (when the sea is not rough), so is consequently quite busy. **Medilla Beach** is lined with budget guesthouses, hotels and restaurants. The quietest location is probably **Marakolliya** to the northeast.

★ Mulgirigala

16 km north of Tangalla: take a bus to Beliatta, then change to a Wiraketiya-bound bus or alternatively jump in a 3-wheeler. Rs 500.

This monastic site situated on an isolated 210-m-high rock was occupied from the second century BC and was again used as a place of Buddhist learning in the 18th century. In 1826, George Turnour discovered the *Tika*, commentaries on the *Mahavansa*, here. This allowed the ancient texts, which chronicle the island's history from the third century BC, to be translated from the original Pali to English and Sinhala.

Although not a citadel, it is in some ways similar to Sigiriya. At the base of the rock there are monks' living quarters. The fairly steep paved path goes up in stages to the main temple and image house at the top. Along the way there are three platforms. The first platform has the twin temple, **Padum Rahat Vihara**, with two 14-m reclining Buddhas, images of Kataragama and Vishnu among others and a Bodhi tree. The wall paintings inside illustrate the *Jatakas* while the ceiling has floral decorations. The small second platform has a *vihara* with another Buddha (reclining) with two disciples. The murals show Hindu gods including Vishnu and Kataragama and the nine planets, and elsewhere, scenes from the Buddha's life. The third has four cave temples and a pond with a 12th-century inscription. The **Raja Mahavihara** with a fine door frame, has several statues and good wall paintings (though they are not as fine as at Dambulla), some partially hidden behind a cabinet which hold old *ola* manuscripts. The little cave temple, **Naga Vihara**, to the far left has a small door with a painted cobra – a cobra shielded the Buddha from rain when meditating, so is considered sacred and worthy of protection. The cave is believed to be a snake pit, so take care. The final climb is steeper. You pass a Bodhi tree believed to be one of 32 saplings of the second Bodhi tree at Anuradhapura, before reaching the summit with a renovated stupa, image house and temple.

Rekawa Beach

4 km east of Tangalla, then 3 km along Rekawa Rd from Netolpitiya Jct, www.turtlewatch rekawa.org. Turtle watch nightly at 2030, Rs 1000 (Rs 500 for children/Rs150 for Sri Lankans). Getting there: 3-wheelers from Tangalla charge around Rs 1500 including waiting time.

It is estimated that up to 75% of Sri Lanka's female green turtles nest at the 2.5-km Rekawa Beach. A 'turtle watch' takes place each night, run by a local community tourism project which employs ex-poachers as tourist guides (see box, page 127). Visitors are encouraged to observe the females laying their eggs and returning to sea. The turtles could arrive at any time (often after midnight) so be prepared for a long wait. You will first visit a small 'museum' hut, where you can read about the turtles, and then be led on to the beach by a watcher. No flash photography or torches are permitted on the beach, but you might need one to navigate the dirt track. There are no facilities.

Tangalla

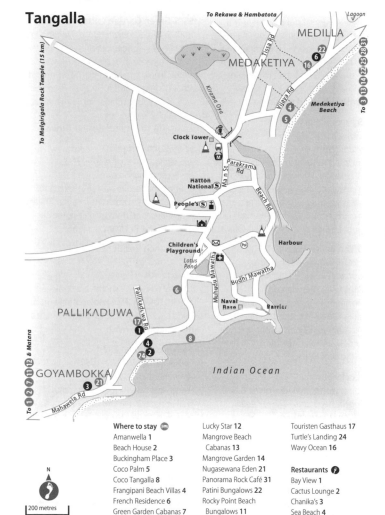

Where to stay

Amanwella 1
Beach House 2
Buckingham Place 3
Coco Palm 5
Coco Tangalla 8
Frangipani Beach Villas 4
French Residence 6
Green Garden Cabanas 7
Ibis Guesthouse 28

Lucky Star 12
Mangrove Beach
  Cabanas 13
Mangrove Garden 14
Nugasewana Eden 21
Panorama Rock Café 31
Patini Bungalows 22
Rocky Point Beach
  Bungalows 11
Sandy's 25

Touristen Gasthaus 17
Turtle's Landing 24
Wavy Ocean 16

Restaurants

Bay View 1
Cactus Lounge 2
Chanika's 3
Sea Beach 4
Starfish Beach Café 6

Where to stay

Tangalla is yet another place where 3-wheeler touts are very active. They meet travellers at the bus station and sing the praises of their friend's guesthouse. If you go with them you may find you're being charged an inflated price for your room; they will be pocketing the difference. In low season prices drop, so don't forget to bargain.

Goyambokka and around

$$$$ Amanwella
Godellawela, T047-224 1333,
www.amaresorts.com.
Luxury resort nestling in a crescent-shaped bay. 30 suites, most hidden among the trees, all with private plunge pools and terrace. Beachfront infinity pool, restaurant, contemporary design and furnishings. The public beach is good for snorkelling.

$$$$ The Beach House
Contact The Sun House in Galle for
reservations (see page 146), T091-
222 2624, www.thesunhouse.com.
An exquisitely furnished 4-bedroom house (sleeping 7) on a fine stretch of beach, extensive library, stunning pool, open-air bathrooms, and an extraordinary collage about the poet Keats.

$$$ Lucky Star
31 Tuduwewatta, at the end of the
road on the headland, T077-617 4496,
www.luckystar-srilanka.de.
7 clean fan rooms overlooking the ocean, shared balconies. German owners speak limited English but the friendly staff can translate. Nice pool, restaurant.

$$ Rocky Point Beach Bungalows
T047-224 0834, T077-497 7033,
www.srilankarockypoint.com.

Bungalows and rooms, all large, clean with private veranda, pleasant gardens in quiet location overlooking rocky promontory, good food. Friendly family-run feel.

$$-$ Green Garden Cabanas
T077-624 7628, lankatangalla@yahoo.com.
Selection of wooden cabanas and 1 of stone that would look at home in the Alps, as well as a new family cabana. All are dotted around a large garden. Excellent food and a welcoming atmosphere. Recommended.

Tangalla town and Pallikaduwa

$$$$ Coco Tangalla
365 Mahawella Rd, T081-720 1115,
www.cocotangalla.com.
6 sumptuous suites with an infinity pool at this exclusive beachside location. There is delicious food from their in-house chef, naturally seafood features highly.

$$$ French Residence
260 Matara Rd, T047-224 2231,
www.frenchresidence.fr.
10 comfortable a/c rooms, 4 with sea views, all with balcony. Nice pool rooftop terrace, good atmosphere. French management and predominantly French.

$$ Nugasewana Eden
Pallikkudawa, T047-224 0389,
www.nugasewana.com.
9 clean and tasteful rooms, 6 a/c and 3 fan, all with hot water. Free Wi-Fi, wide balconies with sea views, good showers and a restaurant. Set back from the road in a pleasant garden, justifiably popular so book in advance.

$ Touristen Gasthaus
13 Pallikaduwa Rd, T047-224 0370,
sevenvilla@live.com.
Popular with long-term guests, 2 bungalows with fan and cold water separate from

the main house, range of rooms (a/c, fan, hot water, kitchenette), plus an apartment with kitchenette ($), friendly family. No restaurant, but breakfast can be arranged on request.

$ Turtles' Landing
Next door to Cactus Lounge, T071-684 0283.
1 decent-sized room above the restaurant, with small balcony and right on the beach. Nothing special but good swimming just out the front. Long-stay discounts available.

Medilla and Medaketiya
These areas have the largest concentration of guesthouses, so it's worth trying to bargain your room price down if it's quiet.

$$ Ibis Guesthouse
T047-567 4439, www.guesthouse-ibis.de.
Spotless, attractive cabanas and rooms (hot water) in peaceful location where beach meets lagoon. Yoga, windsurfing and bikes for hire… or you can simply recline on the large veranda. Restaurant. Related to **Patini Bungalows** (see below). Friendly.

$$ Patini Bungalows
T077-540 2679, www.patinibungalows.com.
French-owned, 5 clean and attractive fan bungalows in beautiful beachside location.

$$-$ Coco Palm
Medaketiya Rd, T071-868 7280.
Chic modern-style build with boutique-style rooms and good balconies.

$$-$ Panorama Rock Café
T047-224 0458, T077-762 0092, www.panoramarockcafe.com.
Deservedly popular place with fan rooms and bungalows, some with good sea views, on lagoon. Good food (see Restaurants, page 172).

$ Frangipani Beach Villas
T077-314 8889, www.frangipani beachvilla.com.

5 large, clean fan rooms with balconies overlooking the sea. Restaurant and tours. The beach it fronts is mainly frequented by fishermen rather than sunbathers.

$ Wavy Ocean
T077-994 0750.
Cheap, simple rooms, ignore the downstairs ones. Seafood restaurant.

Marakolliya

$$$-$$ Sandy's
T077-622 5009, www.sandy cabana.com.
Chic 2-tier huts with upstairs chill-out areas with innovative design. All have great beach views. There is a good restaurant on site. The beach here is secluded. Recommended.

$$ Mangrove Garden
T077 906018, www.beachcabana.lk.
Lovely chalets with great beach vistas. Beach bar and restaurant, rock-sheltered natural pool for swimming, and a desert island feel about the place. There are also slightly cheaper cabanas and mud houses in a beautiful spot on a secluded beach, just down from Mangrove Garden. Some of these rooms have basement bathrooms accessible by a steep set of stairs so not suitable for children Restaurant offers a great selection of Sri Lankan tastes and Western dishes – try the Sri Lankan breakfast. Staff are very welcoming. Highly recommended.

Around Tangalla
Some luxury accommodation has been built at **Rekawa**, 4 km east.

$$$$ Back of Beyond Kahandamodara
15 km inland from Tangalle, Hambantota Main Rd, T077-395 1527, www.backofbeyond.lk.
Although situated inland, it is a short 15-min walk from desolate beaches. 4 beautiful villas with potential for self-catering but delicious food cooked on site too. There is

plenty of birdlife, and kayaking is available. The Back of Beyond team are committed to preserving the land. Recommended.

$$$$ Buckingham Place
Rekawa, T047-348 9447,
www.buckinghamplace.com.
British-owned luxury hotel right next to the Turtle Conservation Project (see box, page 127). 11 spacious rooms and suites with colourful splashes and modern decor, all overlooking the lagoon and most with tubs and rain showers. Excellent food, beautiful gardens, pool and almost deserted stretch of sand. Boat trips on the lagoon and bikes available for guests. Quiet and relaxing.

$$$$ Nature Lanka
Kahandamodara, Panna, close to
Back of Beyond, T077-354 8249,
www.naturelankaresort.com.
Perfect oasis for Ayurvedic healing programmes, conscious eating and massage. Lovely garden location just a short walk from beautiful beaches.

$$$ Mamboz
Gurupokuna, 20 km east of Tangalle, T077-777 7688, www.mambozbeach.com.
Remote location offering a haven of hammocks and endless beach walks. Lovely cabanas and a couple of cheaper rooms all on the beach. Owner Matthew T Gale is a Thai massage expert, so this is the place to come for advanced R&R. Rates based on half board – delicious food. Highly recommended.

$$ Golden Coconut
Rekawa, T077-992 3812, www.golden-coconut.de
Beach-side bliss, with simple 2-storey guesthouse, delicious food, Robinson Crusoe feel and endless supply of coconuts.

Restaurants

Along the beach towards the town, several restaurants and guesthouses prepare very good dishes, especially seafood. There are also some shacks on the beach offering fresh seafood and barbecues.

$$ Cactus Lounge
Pallikaduwa.
Has a good setting on the sheltered beach, fresh seafood, plus soups and snacks.

$$ Chanika's
Mahawela Rd.
An "exceptional find", serving delicious and fresh food. If you're tired of tamed down 'European' dishes, ask for Sri Lankan style. Friendly and obliging.

$$ Panorama Rock Café
See Where to stay, page 171.
Fresh seafood and fine barbecues in a beachfront location. Recommended.

$$ Turtles' Landing
See Where to stay, page 171.
Rave reviews of this shack that serves up everything from the sea.

What to do

Diving
Tangalla Diving Centre, *Tangalla Bay Hotel, Pallikaduwa, T047-627 7622, www.tangalledvingcentre.cm.* Established diving school.

Transport

Bus The station is in the town centre close to the bridge. There are regular services along the coast to **Matara** (1 hr) and **Hambantota** (1 hr), with other services continuing on to **Tissamaharama** (2 hrs) and **Kataragama** (2 hrs 45 mins). There are several morning departures for **Colombo** (5 hrs), plus some to **Wellawaya** and the hill country.

Southeast
Dry Zone

The dry southeast offers a striking contrast to the lushness of the southwestern Wet Zone. In an astonishingly short space east of Tangalla, everything changes. Open savannah and shallow wetlands take over from the dank forest and rich undergrowth, and the increasingly frequent patches of bare earth have a burnt and arid look.

From Nonagama, 25 km east of Tangalla, there are two routes through the Dry Zone. Both offer magnificent wildlife-spotting opportunities. The road inland takes you close to Uda Walawe, famous for its elephants, from where you can travel to Ratnapura, the Sinharaja rainforest, or into the highlands. Alternatively, you can continue east on the coastal road, visiting salt pans for some superb birdwatching, the remarkably varied wildlife of Yala, and the strange and wonderful pilgrimage site of Kataragama.

Towards Uda Walawe
Buddhist caves and birdlife

Kalametiya Bird Sanctuary *Colour map 3, C5.*
A short distance off the coastal road, this is ideal for watching shorebirds in the brackish lagoons and mangrove swamps, undisturbed except for a few fishermen who might pester you for money. There's a beautiful beach and lagoon, but no facilities, nor entry fees, though there is accommodation nearby. To get there, turn right off the A2 after **Hungama** at the Km 214 post and walk 2 km to the lagoon, or get off at the Km 218 post and walk 300 m. Tours can be arranged in the village of Hungama nearby.

Ridiyagama and around *Colour map 3, C5.*
Turn north off the A2 at Nonagama to reach Ridiyagama tank, which lies to the east of the A18. South of the tank, **Ridiyagama** village is well known for its fine curd and honey. Nearby are the 100 or so ancient rocky **Karambagala caves**, once occupied by Buddhist

hermits, which were discovered in the scrub land. From the A18, take the road to the right (east) at **Siyambalagoda**, cross the Walawe Ganga, and follow the track along the stream for about 5 km.

Further north, turn off the A18 at Padalangala to reach the **Madungala hermitage**. All that remains of the old monument is a square white base and some writing engraved in the rock, and a concrete *dagoba* with murals on a hilltop. However, it does afford fine views of Ridiyagama tank and Adam's Peak. A walk through the forest takes you to another *dagoba*. Nearby, in an open space north of the tank, are the **Mahapalessa hot springs**. Believed to have healing powers, the bubbling water is collected in pools for bathers.

Uda Walawe National Park   *Colour map 3, B5.*
majestic elephants, feathered friends and elusive leopards

Easily accessible from the south coast, Uda Walawe is one of the island's most popular national parks. It is best known for its elephants, large herds of which can be seen during the dry season. Birdwatching is also very rewarding. The 308-sq-km park was set up in 1972 to protect the catchment of the Uda Walawe Reservoir at the south end of the Walawe Ganga.

Essential Uda Walawe National Park

Finding your feet

The park is accessible from the A18 Nonagama–Ratnapura road. Embilipitiya, north of Nonagama, is the nearest major town. There is accommodation here and at Timbolketiya, 4 km east of the A18, which is also the location of the park office. To enter the park, you continue east along a 4-km bund across the Uda Walawe Reservoir, and take a turn after the Km 11 post.

Getting around

Only 4WD vehicles (from Rs 5000, depending on where you start) are allowed to use the dry-weather roads and jeep tracks. These can be picked up at guesthouses or at the park gate.

Park information

The park is open daily 0600-1800. Entrance is US$15, plus the usual moveable feast of extras – vehicle fee, service charges for tracker, plus a couple more administration and tax charges. Tickets can be bought at the park entrance east of the reservoir, though the main park office is in front of the **Elephant Transit Centre** in Timbolketiya.

When to go

November to April are the best months to visit, when the resident population of water birds is joined by migrants from the north.

Best nature experiences in the south

Waturawa Trail, Sinharaja Biosphere Reserve, page 111
A tour with Rainforest Rescue International, page 138
Whale watching from Mirissa, page 163
Turtle spotting at Rekawa, page 168
Elephant tracking in Uda Walawe, page 175
Safari in Yala West, page 184
Nature trail at Tree Tops Jungle Lodge, page 190

Wildlife

Along the river there is thick woodland of old teak trees, but the rest of the area is mainly open parkland traversed by streams, which makes elephant-viewing easy. The park's elephants number 400 to 450, and can be seen in herds of up to 100 or even more. They are best seen along the river and near the numerous streams and tanks. There are also healthy populations of macaque, langur, jackal and around 15 leopard; increasing numbers of sambar, spotted deer, barking deer, wild boar and water buffalo are beginning to re-establish themselves. Recent reports suggest that there are no sloth bear. Some 189 species of avifauna have been recorded, with bee-eaters, hornbills, peafowl, hawk eagles, ibis and Indian rollers frequently seen. Birds gather in large numbers around the tanks – the best spots are around Magam, Habarlu and Kiri Ibban. You may also be able to stop at the **Palugaswewa tank**, which is approached from the A18 further north, about 8 km along a dry weather track from Galpaya to the west of the reservoir. **Timbirimankada**, 3 km from Sinnukgala, at the north end of the reservoir, is also good for birdwatching. These tanks are not far from **Handagiriya village** which has a prehistoric site nearby. **Ranagala**, which can be reached in dry weather, about 7 km from Sinnukgala, is also good for birdwatching. Elephants sometimes come to the river here.

Elephant Transit Centre

Behind the main park office, Timbolketiya, 4 km east of the A18, T047-223 2147. Feeding time is every 3 hrs daily 0600-1800. Free.

Set up by the Department of Wildlife in 1995, the Elephant Transit Centre cares for abandoned calves, most of which have been injured, before returning them to the wild when they reach five years of age. Its successful reintroduction scheme, supported by the Born Free Foundation, contrasts directly with the orphanage at Pinnawela, where the animals have become too domesticated to fend for themselves. Twenty of the centre's 32 animals are 'foster parented', which costs Rs 10,000 per elephant per month (half the required sum for food and medical treatment). Although visitors are not allowed to get as close to the animals as at Pinnawela, it is worth visiting at mealtimes. The site's facilities are limited and entry at the time of writing was free.

Listings Uda Walawe National Park

Where to stay

The best accommodation is at Embilipitiya, though there is reasonable accommodation close to the park office at Timbolketiya. There are several circuit bungalows available but these need to be booked well in advance. There are also several campsites in the park. Telephone the Department of Wildlife (T047-347 5872) or the Udawalawe Travel Team (T071-832 9667), at least a month before visiting or check out www.udawalawenationalpark. com for pictures and information. The river views from the Alimandada campsite are particularly recommended.

$$$ Banyan Camp
Myalawala, 20 km northeast of park, T077-384 9878, www.banyancamp.com.
You're off the grid at this beautiful intimate camp with earth houses created from reclaimed wood, recycled doors and natural materials. Light and energy are provided by

solar power and oil lamps. You will find queen-size mattresses and spacious mosquito nets, but these are on the floor. Recommended.

$$$ Centauria
New Town, Embilipitiya, T047-223 0514, www.centauriahotel.com.
Popular lunch spot and the most comfortable place near the park, in a good location next to Chandrika tank. 51 fresh, clean and quiet rooms, mostly a/c, some with TV and balcony. Pool.

$$$ Kalu's Hideaway
Walawegama, close to the park, T077-805 0600, www.kalushideaway.com.
6 modern a/c or fan rooms, 1 top-floor suite and 2 chalets. Pool restaurant, camping also available. Cricket memorabilia scattered around the hotel, as Romesh Kaluwitharana owns it. Arranges trips to Uda Walawe.

$$ Elephant Lane
Dakunu Ela, T047-432 7601, www.elephantlane.com.lk.
A/c rooms with hot water, double-storey chalet with dorms (US$8) and shared bathrooms. The restaurant serves Sri Lankan food. A budget option.

$$ Kottawatta Village
Colombage Ara, 8 km from park, T047-223 3215.
12 rooms and well-furnished cabanas some made of mud and natural roofing, amidst pleasant gardens leading to an *oya* (lake). Friendly management, jeep tours to Uda Walawe.

$$ Niwahana
36 Ekamuthugama, T077-305 5328, www.udawalawehotelniwahana.com.
Simple rooms but with good views from balconies. The restaurant seves up local dishes with as much produce as possible coming from their organic garden.

$ Sarathchandra Tourist Guest House
Pallegama, T0470-223 0044.
Basic offering with friendly welcome. 14 clean a/c rooms and cottages, some with TV. Restaurant.

What to do

Leopard Safaris, *based near Colombo*. Offers excellent tented safaris in the national park (for contact details, see page 72).

Transport

Bus There are direct services to Embilipitiya from **Colombo**, **Ratnapura**, **Tangalla** and **Matara**. Local buses run between Embilipitiya and **Timbolketiya**.

Hambantota *Colour map 3, C6.*

fishing port and gateway to Bundala National Park

Back on the coast, Hambantota is a small fishing port, 41 km east of Tangalla, with a large Muslim population, predominantly of Malay descent. The town itself, with sand dunes immediately around it, has little to recommend it; for most visitors Hambantota is merely a base to visit the nearby lagoons and salt pans at Bundala National Park, which are excellent for birdwatching. The lagoons are visible from the road east of town.

Sights
Hambantota's square has the usual clock tower and a curious statue of a 'coolie'. There is also an interesting if neglected Catholic cemetery to explore. Hambantota was badly hit by the 2004 tsunami and damage is still visible if you walk along the beach. The new viewing

platform opposite the bus station looks a little out of place but offers good views, especially of the port and fish market down below. The small bay offers some swimming, but the beaches, where you will see outriggers, are not attractive, although the deserted eastern side is great for jogging.

Tip...
East of town, the Malala lagoon, reached by following the Malala River from the main road, is a birdwatchers' paradise, where you might also see crocodiles.

Hambantota is a centre for producing salt from evaporated sea water; you can see the salt flats of **Lanka Salt Ltd** stretching away inland. The Dutch built a stockade or 'fort' to protect both the salt pans and access to cinnamon plantations inland. Today's circular 'Dutch' fort, on a hill overlooking the bay, is a run-down British **Martello Tower** (circa 1796).

In recent years Hambantota has undergone rapid development, with the construction of an international harbour, one of the deepest in the world. The district is also home to a large convention centre, a cricket ground that was used for two of the 2011 World Cup matches and the **Mattala International Airport**, which opened in 2013 (to date it is only used for domestic and Flydubai flights).

Hambantota

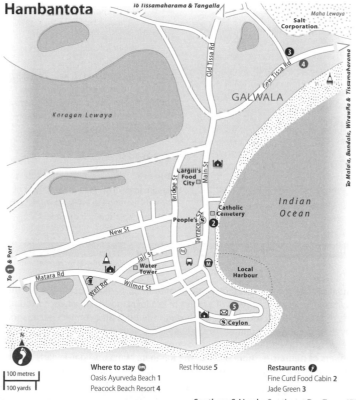

To Tissamaharama & Tangalla
Maha Lewaya
Salt Corporation
Old Tissa Rd
Lew Tissa Rd
GALWALA
Karagan Lewaya
Indian Ocean
Cargill's Food City
Main St
Bridge St
Catholic Cemetery
People's
Terrace St
New St
Jail St
Water Tower
Matara Rd
Welt Rd
Wilmot St
Local Harbour
Ceylon
To Malala, Bundala, Wirawila & Tissamaharama
To Port
N
100 metres
100 yards

Where to stay
Oasis Ayurveda Beach **1**
Peacock Beach Resort **4**

Rest House **5**

Restaurants
Fine Curd Food Cabin **2**
Jade Green **3**

Where to stay

$$$ Oasis Ayurveda Beach Hotel
Sisilasagama, 6 km west, T041-500 600,
www.oasis-ayurveda.com.
40 a/c rooms, plus 10 bright, spacious
chalets with TV and small tubs, set in large
gardens between the sea and a lagoon,
full facilities including a huge pool, good
restaurant. Recommended for Ayurvedic
treatments and programmes, mostly
German clientele.

$$$ Peacock Beach Resort
New Tissa Rd, 1 km from bus stand
at Galwala, T047-567 1000,
www.peacockbeachonline.com.
70 a/c rooms with sea views, some
with bath tubs, 2 suites. Very pleasant
gardens, pool, popular with groups.

$$ Rest House
T047-222 0299.
15 large rooms, situated in superb position
on a promontory overlooking the harbour,
terrific views. Old wing, clean and carpeted,
are better than new wing.

Restaurants

For further options see Where to stay.

$$ Jade Green
Galawala, opposite Peacock Beach Resort.
Smart, modern and Western style with
prices to match.

$ Fine Curd Food Cabin
Tissa Rd, opposite the Bus Station (beach side).
Does delicious curd and treacle and
inexpensive meals (fried rice for Rs 150).

What to do

Touts offer tours to Bundala, Yala and Uda
Walawe, but it only makes sense to make
Hambantota a base for the first of these.
Locals currently offer to take tourists to
see the new port, the new airport, the
convention centre and tsunami sites such
as the memorial. Agree a price before
setting off. Those who go in a taxi may
be able to enter the port depending on
their guide's connections.

Transport

Bus Services leave at regular intervals to
Tissamaharama (1 hr) and **Tangalla** (1 hr
20 mins). Buses go to **Weligata** every 15 mins.
Morning departures to **Colombo** (6 hrs).

Bundala National Park *Colour map 3, C6.*
salt pans and lagoons provide a haven for myriad waterfowl

Bundala is the most important wetland area in Sri Lanka outside the Northern
Province. The reserve consists of a series of shallow lagoons (*lewayas*) surrounded
by fairly dense low scrub. Tracks go through the bush and connect each lagoon,
providing great opportunities for birdwatching, with the added bonus of being
able to spot the odd elephant and basking crocodile. The salt pans attract vast
numbers of migratory shore birds to the Karagan, Maha and particularly Bundala
lewayas, which accommodate tens of thousands of birds at any one time.

Essentials Bundala National Park

Finding your feet

The entrance is 2 km south of the main road between Hambantota and Tissamaharama; turn off at Weligatta. Hambantota is closer to the park, but Tissamaharama is a more popular base as it allows visitors to access Yala National Park, too.

Getting around

Much of the park boundary is contiguous with the A2, so you do not necessarily need to go in to the park to appreciate the wildlife. To explore fully, however, you need to hire a jeep with a driver from Hambantota or Tissamaharama: about Rs 4500 for a half-day. Guides, which are mandatory, are given on rotation, and their English may not be good.

Park information

The park is open daily 0600-1800. Entrance is US$10 (children under 12 US$5), plus vehicle fee and taxes (works out about US$20 per person). There is a visitor centre at the park entrance.

Wildlife

Bundala is particularly rewarding for its winter migrants, who arrive chiefly from Eastern Europe. From September to March, you can see abundant stints, sand pipers, plovers, terns, gulls and ducks. The park's highlight, however, is its large flocks of flamingoes, which travel all the way from the Rann of Kutch in northwest India. In recent years, about 350 flamingos have made Bundala their year-round home. The migrants join the resident water birds – pelicans, herons, egrets, cormorants, stilts and storks – contributing to an extraordinarily variety.

In the scrub jungle, you may also come across elephants (though these are often difficult to see), jackals, monkeys, hares (rare; there's a Rs 1000 fine for killing one!) and, perhaps, snakes. The beaches attract olive ridley and leatherback turtles which come to nest here.

Listings Bundala National Park

Where to stay

Many visitors base themselves at Hambantota (above) or Tissamaharama.

$ Lagoon Inn
Bundala Junction, T047-248 9531.
5 fan rooms with private verandas, restaurant. In good position for visiting both Yala and Bundala.

Tip...
From the Bundala coast it is possible to see the lighthouse on the Great Basses some 40 km away to the east.

Tissamaharama, or 'Tissa', 32 km from Hambantota, is one of the oldest of the abandoned royal cities. King Dutthagamenu made it his capital before recapturing Anuradhapura, but today there is little of interest visible. Instead, the town is most notable as a base for Yala National Park, though its plentiful accommodation is also popular with Kataragama pilgrims. If you arrive by bus, touts will probably pounce on you straight away to take you on 'safari' (see box, page 183).

Sights

The ruins of the royal city were hidden in jungle for centuries and do not, in any way, compare with the better preserved Polonnaruwa or Anuradhapura. Numerous *dagobas*, including one that is 50 m high built by King Kavantissa (second

> **Tip...**
> At dawn, the view of birds roosting on large trees and then moving over Tissa Wewa tank is very beautiful.

century BC) to hold a relic, were destroyed by the invading Dravidians and then lost under the sand. These have now been restored entirely by local Buddhists. Other buildings resemble a palace and a multi-storeyed monastery on the edge of **Tissa Wewa** tank. The

Tissamaharama

Where to stay		
Chandrika **2**	Mihisara Lake View **1**	Traveller's Home **17**
Elephant Camp	Priyankara **6**	Vikum Lodge **18**
Guest House **3**	Safari **16**	
Gangabees Yala **8**	The Saraii **9**	**Restaurants**
Hibiscus Garden **4**	Sudaweli Garden	Root's Café **1**
Lakeside Tourist Inn **5**	Cabanas **7**	Sanka **2**
	Tissa **14**	

400 metres
400 yards

restored tank is thought to have been created at the end of the third century BC. It now attracts a lot of water birds.

The **Menik Wehera** and **Yatala Wehera** are east of the clock tower. The latter, dating from the second century BC, has a moonstone and an 'elephant wall'. It also houses a **museum** with a collection of low-impact but charming Buddha and Bodhisattva statues and a 2200-year-old monks' urinal. Excavations have been assisted by German archaeological groups.

Kirinda

A fishing port on the coast, 7 km south of Tissa, Kirinda has a good beach and an important Buddhist shrine on the rocks. It is historically linked to King Dutthagamenu, whose mother, having been banished by her father, landed at the village and married the local king. Kirinda is popular with scuba divers who are attracted by the reefs at Great and Little Basses off the coast, but the currents are treacherous. You can see the Great Basses lighthouse from the temple on the rock. If you walk east along the coast towards Amaduwa and Yala, there is an area of Dry Zone scrubland, contiguous to Yala itself. It is a good place for birdwatching but watch out for elephants. Buses run regularly between Tissa and Kirinda.

Wirawila to Tanamalwila

West of Tissamaharama, the A2 heads north from Wirawila, crossing the **Wirawila Wewa Bird Sanctuary** and running close to **Lunuganwehera National Park**, set up in 1995 to protect the elephant corridor between Yala and Uda Walawe. There are good views along here of the sacred Kataragama Peak. Lunuganwehera Reservoir is fed by the Kirindi Oya, which runs close to the road leading up into the highlands. You can stay in a secluded forested setting along its banks, north of Tanamalwila, the largest settlement along this stretch, see page 182. This can also be used as a base to visit Uda Walawe to the west. From here, the A2 continues north to Wellawaya, passing the Handapangala tank and Buduruvagala shrine (see page 190).

Listings Tissamaharama and around *map p180*

Where to stay

There are plenty of options, so bargain hard. Tissa is plagued by touts who get a commission for the hotel room they 'fix' and also any 'safari' you may arrange through the hotel. Some places listed here are actually in Deberawewa, about 3 km west of Tissa, where touts sometimes jump on the bus and try to persuade you that you've reached Tissa. There is also accommodation at Kirinda and at Amaduwa, close to the park gate into Yala (see below).

$$$ The Safari (CHC)
Kataragama Rd, T047-223 7201,
www.chcresorts.com

Atmospheric resort with 53 a/c rooms, some with lake views. Excellent location next to Tissa Wewa, with nice pool overlooking the tank. Restaurant and open-air bar.

$$$ Gagabees Yala
Sandagirigama, T071-620 5343,
www.gangabeesyala.com
Using 100% eco materials, this agro-eco resort boasts its own farm ensuring farm to table with zero miles on the clock. Stylish mud huts with a/c and hot water, as well as lovely private verandas overlooking the rice fields – a little bit of perfection.

$$$ Hibiscus Garden Hotel
Mahasenpura (if driving phone for directions), T047-492 5617, www.hibiscus-garden.com.
16 large, clean a/c rooms, restaurant and pool. Good value, birdwatchers will enjoy the gardens.

$$$ Kithala Resort
Kataragama Rd, T047-223 7206, www.theme-resorts.com.
26 clean a/c standard and deluxe rooms, all with private balcony overlooking paddy fields. Inviting pool, bar, good restaurant with wide wine selection, pleasant atmosphere, friendly staff.

$$$-$$ Chandrika
Kataragama Rd, T047-223 7143, www.chandrikahotel.com.
20 clean rooms a/c rooms around a courtyard, good beds, fairly modern, bar, pricey restaurant but otherwise good value, pleasant garden and pool.

$$-$ Lakeside Tourist Inn
Kataragama Rd, Akurugoda, opposite lake, T047-493 1186, www.tissalakesidehotel.com.
20 clean and comfortable a/c and fan rooms, most in new block, others mustier but with views in old wing, pleasant sitting areas overlooking the lake, lots of birdlife, good restaurant.

$$-$ Traveller's Home
195/4 Kachcheriyagama, T047-223 7958.
Clean fan rooms and a/c bungalows, friendly, good food, pleasant patio, good safaris, popular with backpackers.

$$-$ Mihisara Lake View
Deberawewa, T047-223 7322.
Basic accommodation: 6 clean, fresh a/c and fan rooms. Very friendly family home. Excellent food, order in advance.

$ Elephant Camp Guest House
Kataragama Rd, opposite The Safari, T047-223 7231, jayathunga.herath@yahoo.com.
Family-run guesthouse offering 5 clean a/c and fan rooms with individual outdoor seating areas. Excellent food, small garden, friendly hosts. Recommended.

$ Hotel Tissa
Main St, near bus stand, T047-223 7104.
8 clean a/c and fan rooms, popular bar/restaurant so can be noisy.

$ Suduweli Garden Cabanas
Down track 2 km before Kirinda from Tissa, T072-263 1059.
German/Sri Lankan-run, simple but clean rooms, plus cosy bungalows with idiosyncratic Dutch-style eaved roofs, own music system in room, friendly, good menu, jeep and cycle tours.

$ Vikum Lodge
Off Kataragama Rd down a pot-holed track, T047-223 7585.
10 cleanish rooms around attractive courtyard in quiet location. Mediocre food, find somewhere else for dinner.

Wirawila to Tanamwila

$$$$-$$$ The Saraii
Randunu Kele Watte, Wirawila, T071-307 7772, www.saraiivillage.com
Stunning eco-lodge with deluxe tree houses and stylish mud chalets – this is back to nature in style. Beautiful decor but with an eye on sustainability and a home-grown menu specializing in Sri Lankan tastes. Recommended.

$$$ Tasks Safari Camp
Kithulkotte, Kudaoya, Tanamalwila, T011-486 2225, book through www.karmasrilanka.com.
27 spacious en suite jungle tents with 'hollow log' showers, real frontier feel, hurricane lantern for light, picnics by riverside, elephants come close to drink.

ON THE ROAD
Going on safari

It seems as if every other vehicle in Tissamaharama is a jeep and you will be constantly offered a jeep safari to the national parks. Some words of advice:

1 Remember that a tracker is included in your entrance fee, so don't pay extra for a driver and separate guide.
2 Make sure that the driver will stop on request, and that they will turn the engine off for photography.
3 Ask to see the vehicle first – many are ancient and noisy, which will scare away any wildlife. It has even been known for a jeep to split into two during a safari.
4 Bring binoculars.
5 Invest in a bird-spotting guide, as birdlife is guaranteed to be rich.
6 Speak to other travellers who have already been on safari. They are often the best source of information.

Restaurants

There are a number of eating places springing up on Kataragama Rd; many hotels and guesthouses also do food, see Where to stay, above.

$$ Refresh
Akuragoda.
A branch of the excellent Hikkaduwa-based restaurant, offering a wide variety of good food. Portions are large. Very popular with tourists, overpriced and a little self-satisfied.

$$ Sanka
Kataragama Rd, T047-223 7441.
Serves OK Chinese food; safari guides and drivers hang out here.

$ Root's Café
Look for the sign off Main St.
Very cheap rice and curry; popular for a beer.

Festivals

Jun The **Poson** full moon commemorates the introduction of Buddhism with week-long festivities ending with colourful elephant processions accompanied by drummers and dancers.

What to do

Most hotels and guesthouses can arrange safaris to Yala and Bundala, although it may be cheaper to organize one independently through a driver at tout corner, opposite the **Independent Jeep Safari Association** office. There are also agencies in town, such as **Ajith Safari Jeep Tours** (418/A Debarawewa, T047-223 7557, ajithpriyantha@yahoo.com). It's worth talking to fellow travellers as well to get an idea of their experiences. Prices can vary depending on the length of safari and also the type of jeep: those with forward-facing seating are more expensive. Half-day safaris cost around Rs 4500, full-day Rs 9000, those in the morning start around 0500, so order breakfast from your accommodation. It is possible to organize a half-and-half safari visiting both Yala and Bundala; the jeep will cost the same but entry will have to be paid twice, which can be quite expensive.

Leopard Safaris, based near Colombo, offers excellent tented safaris in Yala (for contact details, see page 72).

Transport

The A32, widened and upgraded in 2003, heads northeast from Tissamaharama towards Kataragama and Buttala (see page 189).

Air At **Wirawila** there is an airbase which is being prepared for domestic commercial flights.

Bus To **Colombo** (6 hrs), via Galle, or to **Ratnapura**, via Embilipitiya. There are plenty of buses to **Kataragama**.

★ Yala West (Ruhuna) National Park Colour map 5, C5.

varied terrain supports an extraordinary range of wildlife – including leopard

---

Yala West, or Ruhuna as it alternatively known, is Sri Lanka's most popular national park. The 1260-sq-km park varies from open parkland to dense jungle on the plains. The scrubland is distinctive, with enormous rocky outcrops, or *inselbergs*. There are also several streams, small lakes and lagoons, while the ocean to the east has wide beaches and high sand dunes.

Wildlife

For many visitors, the search for the one of the park's 30 or so elusive leopards is a major attraction. Though sightings remain relatively rare, Yala's male leopards are quite

Essential Yala West (Ruhana) National Park

Finding your feet

The entrance is near Palatupana, 20 km from Tissamaharama, where there's an interesting visitor centre. Take the road from Tissa to Kirinda; the turn-off to the national park is signposed 1 km before Kirinda.

Getting around

A 4WD vehicle is required. An obligatory tracker is assigned to you, and marked tracks must be adhered to. Walking is not permitted within the park: visitors must remain in their vehicles and avoid excessive noise (eg radios or blaring music). There are no limits at present on the number of

vehicles allowed into the park on any given day, so if a leopard or elephant is spotted it can become a little chaotic with jeeps rushing to get their tourists to the best spot. As of 2015, mobile phone use is banned inside the park to prevent drivers spreading news of leopard sightings.

Park information

The park is open daily 0600-1800. Entrance is US$15 (children under 12, US$7), plus compulsory tracker fee, vehicle charge and tax (it works out about US$25 per person). If you leave the park, you will have to pay again. Entry permits, maps and leaflets are available from the visitor centre at Palatupana.

When to go

The best times for wildlife are early mornings and late afternoons between October and December.

Tip...

The Palatupana salt pans on the Tissa Road, 6 km before the park entrance, are one of the best sites in the world for watching wading birds.

Yala National Park

Yala comprises five 'blocks', of which tourists only visit Block One, the original 14,101-ha former shooting reserve, which became a protected area in 1938. This area is said to have the highest concentration of animals. Succeeding blocks, including a Strict Nature Reserve, were added, primarily in the late 1960s and early 1970s, giving the park its total area of 97,881 ha. In addition, there is a buffer zone which may in future form part of an expansion of the park. For details of the reopened Kumana National Park, reached from Pottuvil and Arugam Bay, see page 343.

There are a number of remains of ancient sites in the park, suggesting that many centuries ago the area was a part of the Ruhuna Kingdom. Thousands of Buddhist monks resided at the monastery at Situlpahuwa, now an important pilgrimage centre, while the restored Magul Mahavihara and Akasa Chetiya date to the first and second centuries BC.

bold and may be seen walking along tracks in dry sandy or rocky areas during the day. **Vepandeniya** is considered a favourite spot. Elephants are another highlight and are easily seen, especially near water sources from January to May, though the herds are not on the scale of Uda Walawe. Other animals seen throughout the park include macaque and langur monkeys, sambar, spotted deer, jackal, wild boar, buffaloes and crocodiles. Sloth bears are occasionally spotted, particularly in June, when they feed on local fruit.

The park is worth visiting for its birdlife alone. A birdwatching focused day trip, including the riverine forests of the **Menik Ganga**, may yield over 100 species during the migrating season. There are about 130 species overall, including barbets, hoopoes, malabar pied hornbills, orioles, Ceylon shamas, and paradise flycatchers, though pea and jungle fowl are the most frequently seen. The expanses of water attract eastern grey heron, painted stork, serpent-eagle and white-bellied sea-eagle, amongst many others. In addition a large number of migrant waterfowl arrive each winter to augment the resident population. You may be lucky enough to spot the rare black-necked stork near **Buttawa** on the coast.

Listings Yala West (Ruhana) National Park

Where to stay

Close to the park entrance but on the coast, Amaduwa Point is a convenient and comfortable alternative to sleeping inside the park itself, with a beautiful beach and lagoon. There are also a number of pleasant bungalows that can be rented near the entrance to the park (www. reddottours.com has a good selection). There are also park bungalows, but note that these need to be booked well in

advance; contact the Department of Wildlife (T011-288 8585). Also check out Mahoora Mobile Safaris who specialize in camps around all of the island's national parks (www.mahoora.lk).

$$$$-$$$ Back of Beyond Yala
Gurugoda, Kirinda, T077-395 1527,
www.backofbeyond.lk
Offering several eco-conscious resorts around Sri Lanka, Back of Beyond Yala takes you close to the wildlife. Beautiful

setting with attractive clay and thatch huts and delicious food in open air restaurant. Recommended.

$$$$-$$$ Yala Village
Kirinda, www.yalavillagesrilanka.com.
60 luxurious chalets with a/c and satellite TV, most situated inland and 6 with views of the ocean. Fantastic position overlooking lagoon, observation deck, large pool, fishing, cycling.

$$$ Hotel Elephant Reach
Kirinda, T077-106 5092,
www.elephantreach.com.
14 a/c standard rooms and 21 spacious chalets. Restaurant and pool set in attractive gardens. Popular with tour groups.

Kataragama *Colour map 5, C4.*

beautiful Buddhist pilgrimage site

Kataragama in Uva Province, 16 km north of Tissamaharama, is, along with Sri Pada (Adam's Peak), the most important pilgrimage site in Sri Lanka. Like Adam's Peak, it holds significance for Buddhists, Hindus and Muslims. It is most famous for its two-week Perehera in July and August, but is popular throughout the year, attracting thousands from across the island.

Kataragama is a small town, with clean, tree-lined roads where rows of stalls sell garlands and platters of fruit. The Hindu and Buddhist sanctuaries are quite separate. Buddhists visit the ancient Kirivehera *dagoba*, 500 m north of the plain white Hindu temple, but also consider the Kataragama Deviyo here sacred. Sri Lankan Muslims associate the town with the prophet Moses, who was said to have taught here and come to pray at the Khizr Takya mosque nearby.

Menik Ganga
From the bus stand or car park, a short walk takes you to the Menik Ganga. Steps lead down to the water which is quite shallow in places allowing pilgrims to take their ritual bath almost in the middle of the river. It is a very attractive area with large trees on the banks providing plenty of shade. Cross the bridge to enter the main temple complex.

Maha Devale
The wide street lined with tulip trees leads for 300 m to the Hindu Maha Devale, dedicated to Skanda (Kataragama Deviyo). The temple is itself not particularly impressive. A small gate with a large wrought-iron peacock on the reverse opens onto the rectangle, where pilgrims throw coconuts onto a stone slab to split them before making the offering. The breaking of the coconut signifies the purging of evil, so it is inauspicious if it fails to break. Trees in the rectangle are surrounded by brass railings and there are a number of places where pilgrims can light leaf-shaped candles. Here, you can see men in 'ritualistic trances': some are professionals, though, since you might see the same man, a little later, making his way to the Buddhist *dagoba*, carrying a briefcase and an umbrella.

There is often a long queue to enter the shrine (particularly on *poya* days) where platters are offered to the priests. The idea seems to be to 'hide' some money in the platter. Some say anything less than Rs 200 may be unacceptable and the gift might be refused by the deity. There is certainly evidence that the platters are 'recycled': men on bicycles can be seen returning them to the market, covered in garlands – nobody seems to mind though.

There is no image of the god Skanda in the shrine – simply his vel or lance. There are separate small shrines to others in the Hindu pantheon, including Vishnu, Ganesh and Pattini, the last also linked to the fire-walking ceremony. Nearby are the two Bodhi trees.

The largest draw is the **Esala** (July/August) full moon festival which ends with fire-walking and 'water cutting' ceremonies. Thousands of pilgrims flock to the Hindu temple for the **Kataragama Festival**. They come to perform penance for sins they have committed and some of the scenes of self-mutilation, performed in a trance, are horrific. The water-cutting ceremony, in which the waters of the Manik Ganga are 'cut' with a sword at the moment of the full moon, symbolizes the separation of pure from impure.

You may see groups of pilgrims performing the Kavadi (peacock) dance when men, women and children hold semicircular blue arches above their heads as they slowly progress towards the temple.

There is a **museum** ① *Wed-Mon, US$5, children US$2.50*, next to the Maha Devale, which houses religious objects pertaining to different faiths, including statues, moonstones and ancient inscriptions.

Kirivehera

Beyond the Hindu shrine and a meeting hall on the north side of the square, another tulip tree avenue leads to the milk-white Buddhist *dagoba*, about 500 m away. Stalls selling lotus buds, garlands and platters of fruit line the route but here there is competition with

Kataragama

Where to stay ⊜
Ceybank Rest **1**
Ceylon Tourist Board Rest House **2**

Mandara Rosen **3**
Robinson **4**
Sunil's Rest **5**

ON THE ROAD

Mind over matter

Fire-walking takes place on the eve of the great procession, the culmination of the Esala festival. A long trench is prepared and filled with hardwood logs which are burnt to cinders. The worshippers, who will have refrained from meat or fish for a week, then walk barefoot across the burning embers shouting 'Haro hara' in front of the crowds who cry in homage to the miracle. That most firewalkers emerge unhurt is a source of mystery, though many believe that the walkers are in the deepest state of self-hypnosis, in which the body can block out pain.

The origins of the tradition may hark back to the story of Sita in the epic *Ramayana*. Ravana, the King of Lanka, abducted Rama's wife Sita, an Indian princess, from the forest and carried her away to his island. After she is finally rescued by her husband, Sita proves her purity (chastity) by walking barefoot over fire and emerging unhurt. In southern Sri Lanka, devotees of Kataragama and Pattini follow her example and seek their blessing as they undergo the purification ritual.

To Western eyes, an even more shocking act of self-mutilation are the carts carrying men suspended by steel hooks attached to their skin. These grotesque parades, accompanied by great crowd noise and excitement, are designed to purge the devotee of his sins.

girls shouting out the bargains and pressing people to buy. You can often see the temple elephant shackled to the trees here, being fed a copious diet of palm leaves. The *dagoba* itself is a very peaceful place and, as usual, beautifully maintained. It is not especially large and its spire is quite squat compared with those further north.

Listings Kataragama *map p187*

Where to stay

There are many other pilgrims' guest-houses and hotels for all budgets on Sella Kataragama Rd.

$$$ Mandara Rosen
57 Detagamuwa, 2 km from Kataragama, T047-223 6030, www.mandararosen.com.
50 attractive, comfortable a/c rooms, some with bath tubs, and 2 luxurious suites. Full facilities, including pool with underwater music system.

$$-$ Robinson Hotel
Tissa Rd, Detagamuwa, T047-223 5307, www.robinson.lk.

20 a/c and fan rooms with balcony in an attractive building with pleasant garden.

$ Ceylon Tourist Board Rest House
T047-223 5227.
Simple, clean fan only rooms, or poor value a/c rooms, very cheap vegetarian restaurant, rather prison-like but friendly.

$ Ceybank Rest
T047-223 5229.
Attractive guesthouse with a/c and fan rooms. Good vegetarian meals.

$ Sunil's Rest
Tissa Rd, T047-567 7172.
10 very clean rooms with attached bath, attractive garden. Good value.

Restaurants

Note that most places, except the more upmarket hotels (these also serve alcohol), will offer vegetarian-only dishes. For further options see Where to stay, above.

$$ Nandana Hotel
40b New Town, near the clocktower.
Offers good authentic rice and curry.

Transport

Bus There are services in all directions including direct buses to **Buttala** (twice daily, 1 hr), **Nuwara Eliya**, **Galle** and **Colombo**.

North of Kataragama

wilderness area off the beaten track

Towards Buttala

The remote area north of Kataragama, fringing Yala National Park, is rarely visited by tourists, though the 35 km road to Buttala is one of the main pilgrimage routes. **Buttala** ('rice mound') was known as the rice bowl of the country and is the main centre, with plenty of opportunities for trekking, wildlife spotting, rock climbing and even rafting in the surrounding wilderness.

Maligawila and around

At **Maligawila**, southeast of Buttala, is the largest monolithic Buddha statue in Sri Lanka, regarded by some as the finest piece of all Sinhalese sculpture. Housed inside a brick *gedige*, the *Mahavansa* suggests the 10.5 m-high, 3-m-wide crystalline limestone Buddha was crafted by Prince Aggabodhi in the seventh century. The statue was originally part of a monastic complex which had a gateway, pillared hall and terraces. It was 'lost' in the jungle until 1934, before being restored fully in 1991. One kilometre away, at **Dambegoda**, is a mound where the island's largest image of Avalokitesvara Bodhisvata, who is said to give succour to the helpless, has been found and restored. There are direct buses to the site from Wellawaya and Buttala via Okkampitiya. It is also accessible from Moneragala.

Listings North of Kataragama

Where to stay

Towards Buttala

$$$$ Kumbuk River
Okkampitiya, T011-452 7781,
www.kumbukriver.com.
Award-winning eco-lodge in large grounds next to a river. Off-the-beaten-track accommodation is in the form of 3 chalets, one a 12-m-high elephant, rented out exclusively. Rates include full board. As you'd expect but might forget, there's no electricity. Minimum booking 2 nights.

$$$ Galapita Rocks
Km 31 post, Valli Amma Ara,
Kataragama Rd, Buttala, T072-
430 5417, www.galapitarocks.com.
Nature takes precedence here as stunning rooms are created around rock and tree features, and are simply adorned with antiques – many 'rooms' are open-sided with river views. Jump in the rumbling river or take off in a canoe and go panning for gems. This is a pure retreat, so chances are your mobile phone will not work. There is a beautiful yoga platform and outdoor spa.

Locally cooked food is exceptional. Whole-heartedly recommended.

$$$ Tree Tops Jungle Lodge
Illukpitiya, Weliara Rd (9 km from Buttala), T077-703 6554 www.treetopsjunglelodge.com.
A wilderness retreat set within the Yala buffer zone, so you have elephants and peacocks as neighbours. Armed with binoculars you can check out the birdlife from your veranda.

There is no electricity and delicious meals are cooked over a wood fire. Short walks possible in the local area. Recommended.

Transport

North of Kataragama
Bus To **Buttala** twice daily from **Kataragama** (1 hr) and frequently from **Wellawaya** (30 mins).

Wellawaya *Colour map 3, B6.*
crashing waterfalls, serene rice fields and tropical retreats

Wellawaya is a major transport junction with many buses leading up to the hill country from here. The A4 is the main road, skirting the southern highlands as it heads west, through Ratnapura ultimately to Colombo, and east through Buttala and Moneragala to Pottuvil for Arugam Bay. The A23 climbs north through picturesque country to Ella, while the A2 heads south towards Tanamalwila (see page 181) and the coast.

The area is known for its sugar cane fields, and it is worth a brief stop to visit a factory and have a taste of the raw sugar cane and the resulting 'honey', which is also made into jaggery. The workers are usually very happy to show the production processes to tourists, though a tip is appreciated. **Diyaluma Falls** are also within easy reach of Wellawaya (see page 253).

Buduruvagala
Rs 200. Take a Kataragama bus from Wellawaya and get off at Buduruvagala Jct (about 10 mins). It's best to go in the morning as afternoon buses are scarce.

A beautiful road leads south of town past a dammed lake to the ancient Mahayana Buddhist rock carvings of Buduruvagala. The massive rock is a short walk away from the monastery; you will be accompanied by a monk. Of the seven rock-cut figures in high relief, the 16-m-high Buddha (Buduruvagala) in the centre is the tallest of its type in Sri Lanka. Traces of the original red and yellow paint remain on the Buddha itself. Close to the right foot of the Buddha is a hole in the shape of an oil lamp flame; a mustard-smelling oil is said miraculously to flow through periodically. The Buddha is flanked by Avalokitesvara (possibly) to his right, who in turn has his consort Tara by his side and an attendant. To the Buddha's left, the figure is believed to be Maitreya who is also accompanied. The figure of Vajrayapani (or Sakra) holds a quartz implement similar to those found in Mahayana Buddhist countries such as Tibet. The quality of the carvings is more impressive close to, so it is worth removing your shoes and climbing up to the rock to view. The site itself is very peaceful and often deserted although unfortunately a pair of ugly concrete posts carrying lights have been erected in front of the carvings making photography of all seven images difficult. There is a small museum inside the meditation centre nearby.

Handapangala tank

Some 6 km south of Buduruvagala along the A2 is a left turn for the Handapangala tank, where elephants migrate from Yala for water during the summer months, a danger for villagers en route. There have been clashes between environmental groups and a local sugar factory, which has periodically attempted to drive the elephants away. In October 2002 two baby elephants were killed, prompting calls for the government to reopen a protected elephant corridor. There is a popular local bathing spot here, about 2 km off the main road, at which you can scramble up and see the elephants at a distance on the other side of the water. Alternatively, and more rewardingly, you can take a tour to see the elephants at close hand, for which you will need a boat and guide, not least since the area is dangerous if you don't know what you're doing.

Listings Wellawaya

Where to stay

$$$$ Living Heritage Koslanda
Egodawatte Estate, Naulla, Koslanda
(15 km from Wellawaya), T077-935 5785,
www.koslanda.com.
Set in expansive grounds, this stylish retreat has beautiful rooms made in a traditional style. Epic views of rolling hills from the infinity pool. Do a riverside walk to a nearby waterfall or have a cookery lesson. Whether its traditional Sri Lankan food or contemporary Western dishes, the food is amazing. Stunning.

$$-$ Rest House
Ella Rd, T055-563 7685.
5 reasonably clean but musty and overpriced rooms, plus restaurant.

Knowledgeable manager used to work for the Archaeological Department.

$ Little Rose Inn
Tissa Rd (1 km south of town), T055-567 8360/
227 4410, www.littlerosewellawaya.com.
Popular place with 9 simple clean fan rooms. Good home cooking.

Transport

Bus Wellawaya is an important bus terminus. Direct buses go to **Colombo** via **Ratnapura**, to **Tissamaharama** and to **Kataragama**. There are also a few to **Matara** via **Tangalla**. For buses east to **Pottuvil** (for Arugam Bay), change at **Monaragala**. For the hills, there are plenty of buses to **Badulla**, via **Ella**, and **Haputale**. Local buses are frequent to **Buttala** (30 mins).

Kandy & the highlands

tea, temples and trekking

Venturing inland by road or rail is a magical journey into rolling hills and verdant tea plantations. The temperature drops and the eyes are bathed with lush green as far as the eye can see. There are pretty villages, women plucking tea leaves, beautiful walks and thundering waterfalls.

Kandy, the home of the Buddha's tooth, is both the capital of and the gateway to the highlands. Protected for centuries by its mountains and forests as well as by a fierce desire to retain its independence, Kandy and its region offer rich insights into Sri Lanka's cultural traditions. Designated a World Heritage Site in 1988, the city is at the southern corner of the Cultural Triangle.

South of Kandy, the Central Highland ridge, often shrouded in cloud, reaches its apex at Mount Pidurutalagala near the former British hill resort of Nuwara Eliya. This is Sri Lanka's chief tea-growing region, and the hills are carpeted with the uniformly clipped, bright green bushes of this crucial crop. To the south lies the hauntingly bleak plateau of the Horton Plains, while to the west pilgrims flock to the sacred mountain of Adam's Peak.

To the east, Uva Province has a rich and defiant cultural history, associated in popular legend with two visits by the Buddha, and widely celebrated in the festivals at Badulla and Mahiyangana.

Best for
Scenery ▪ Tea ▪ Walks ▪ Waterfalls

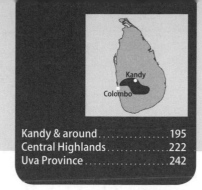

Footprint
picks

★ **Kandy**, page 200

Beautiful lakeside town with sacred Temple of the Tooth at its heart.

★ **Peradeniya**, page 216

Discover the wonderful flora of Sri Lanka in this amazing botanical garden.

★ **Heritance Tea Factory**, page 229

Award-winning conversion of an old British tea factory into an innovative hotel.

★ **Adam's Peak**, page 237

Join the pilgrims as you trek for a sunrise special at Adam's Peak.

★ **Kitulgala**, page 240

Whitewater rafting on the magnificent Kelianiya River.

★ **Ella**, page 245

Epic vistas, tea plantation strolls and dramatic waterfalls in the highlands.

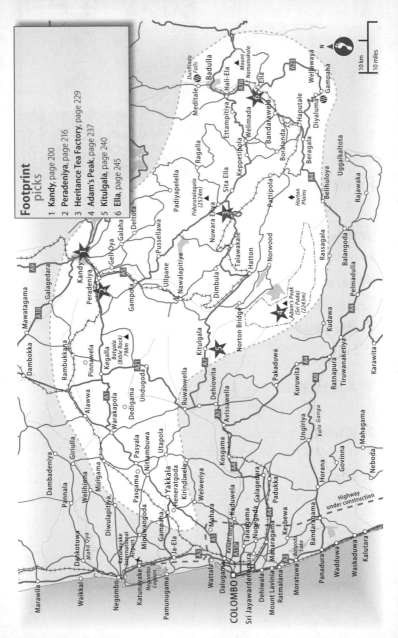

N

10 km
10 miles

Kandy
& around

Kandy, Sri Lanka's second largest city and cultural capital, serves as an important symbol of Sinhalese national identity and as the gateway to the higher hills and tea plantations of the island. Although it has a reputation as something of a tourist trap and has a problem with touts, its clear air and verdant outlook around the sacred lake make it a pleasant escape from the heat of the coast. It is a laid-back place, and many visitors base themselves here for a few days to explore the surrounding countryside, before heading into the highlands or setting off for the ancient cities to the north.

Dotted around the lush Kandyan landscape are a number of important temples which make for a good day trip from the city. Thrill-seekers could head for the misty mountains of Knuckles, while for the green-fingered the magnificent botanical gardens at Peradeniya, arguably the finest of their kind in Asia, are an undoubted highlight. South of Kandy is the world's first tea museum.

Essential Kandy and around

Finding your feet

Kandy is fairly easily accessible from all parts of the country. Some travellers head here immediately on arrival at the international airport: intercity buses leave every half an hour, taking 3½ hours. There are also direct buses from Negombo. Probably the best road in the country, the A1, runs between Colombo and Kandy. There are government buses from Colombo's Central Bus Stand in the Pettah, or private buses from Bastian Mawatha. By far the prettiest way to travel, however, is by observation car on the many trains that run from Colombo to Kandy – seats can be reserved on these trains. See also Transport, page 214.

Getting around

The bus (Goods Shed) terminus and railway station are close to each other about 1 km southwest of the centre. A three-wheeler into town will cost around Rs 100; to the guesthouses in the Sarankara Road area south of the lake will cost up to Rs 150. Air-conditioned radio cabs are very convenient, safe and reliable; telephone **New Derena Cabs**, T081-495 1951, tell them your location and allow 10 minutes. Gopallawa Mawatha, the main road into town, is horribly choked with traffic, especially at rush hour; to avoid the fumes, it's a good idea to do as the locals do and walk north along the railway line into town.

Local buses ply the routes from Kandy to Peradeniya, Pinnawela, etc. If time is very limited for sightseeing, it is possible to hire a car for the day to visit **Dambulla**, **Sigiriya** and **Polonnaruwa** (ask your hotel or guesthouse). While this is a very full day it can be very rewarding, although it is preferable to spend more time visiting this circuit. See also Transport, page 214.

When to go

Kandy has a pleasant climate throughout the year, lacking the humidity of the coast. In July, **Esala Perahera** is a truly magnificent spectacle (see box, page 212).

Time required

A day is enough to see the Temple of the Tooth and other main sights, while two days allow time to visit surrounding villages or do some short walks.

Best hidden treasures
Millennium Elephant Foundation, Pinnawela, page 199
Lankatilaka Mahaviharaya, near Kandy, page 218
Dumbara Hills, page 219
Bogoda, near Badulla, page 244
Diyaluma Falls, near Haputale, page 253

Weather Kandy

January	February	March	April	May	June
19°C 9°C 96mm	20°C 9°C 60mm	21°C 10°C 66mm	22°C 11°C 135mm	21°C 12°C 153mm	18°C 12°C 153mm

July	August	September	October	November	December
18°C 12°C 156mm	18°C 12°C 135mm	18°C 11°C 135mm	19°C 11°C 186mm	19°C 11°C 192mm	19°C 11°C 153mm

Taking 11 years to complete, the A1 trunk road from Colombo to Kandy was the first modern road to be opened in Sri Lanka in 1932, when the first mail service ran between the two cities. The route northeast, across the coastal plain, passes through lush scenery: paddy fields interspersed with coconut and areca nut palms, and endless bananas and pineapples, which are available, graded by size and price, from roadside stalls. Tour groups invariably stop to visit the baby elephants at Pinnawela, but there are some lesser known sights along this busy route which are well worth a digression. Although the road route is quicker, the train often gives better views, the last hour rattling through stunning scenery.

Sapugaskanda
Barely free of Colombo's suburbs, the road passes near the impressive temple at Kelaniya, the island's most popular (see page 58). A few kilometres further on, a right turn off the main A1 leads 3 km to a low hill topped by a small stupa. There are beautiful views from the terrace, but the temple is famous for its murals, which show the arrival of the Burmese saint Jagara Hamuduruvo in Sri Lanka.

Heneratgoda Botanical Gardens Colour map 3, A2.
Turn off the A1 just before Yakkala; the gardens are well signposted, 1 km beyond the sizeable town of Gampaha. Daily 0800-1800. Rs 800, students Rs 500. Buses from both Colombo and Negombo take approx. 1½ hrs. Most Colombo–Kandy trains stop at Gampaha, from where you can take a 3-wheeler.

These beautiful gardens are particularly famous as the nursery of Asia's first rubber trees, introduced from the Amazon Basin more than a century ago. Several of the early imports are now magnificent specimens. No 6, the first tree planted, is over 100 years old, but the most famous is No 2 because of its remarkable yield. The trees include *Hevea brasiliensis*, *Uncaria gambier*, rubber-producing lianas (*Landolphia*), and the drug *ipecacuanha*. A female of the Coco de Mer was imported from the Seychelles and bore fruit in 1915.

Bandaranaike Memorial
By the side of the road at Nittambuwa, 39 km from Colombo.

The road passes through Yakkala, and then by the former estate of Sir Solomon Dias Bandaranaike, aide de camp to the British governor at the time of the First World War. His son, Solomon Western Ridgway Dias Bandaranaike, became prime minister of independent Ceylon in 1956 but was assassinated in 1959. His widow, Sirimavo Bandaranaike, succeeded him, becoming the world's first female prime minister, and their daughter, Chandrika Kumaratunga, was elected president in 1994. The family home, where visitors such as King George V and Jawaharlal Nehru stayed, is nearby, though it is private. Solomon Dias and Sirimavo are buried together at the memorial here. A broad walkway, about 10 m wide and 100 m long and flanked by frangipanis, leads to a raised plinth with five stone pillars behind it, the whole surrounded by a coconut grove. On the other side of the road, on a small hill, is a monument to Bandaranaike Senior.

Pasyala and around *Colour map 3, A2.*

The area around Pasyala, 7 km further on, is noted for its *plumbago* (graphite) mines, betel nuts and above all, cashew nuts. This is the western edge of the Central Highlands massif. Passing through **Cadjugama** ('village of cashew nuts'), you will see women in brightly coloured traditional dress selling cashew nuts from stalls lining the road. Sadly, the cashews offered here are not always of the highest quality – they are often 'seconds'. Inspect and taste before you buy.

Warakapola, Ambepussa and around *Colour map 2, C2/3.*

The busy little village of **Warakapola**, 60 km from Colombo, is a convenient and popular stop en route to Kandy or Kurunegala and beyond. Warakapola provides an outlet for locally made cane baskets and mats in its bazaar. It is also a popular halt for those with a sweet tooth searching for sesame seed *thalagulis* which are freshly made at **Jinadisa's** shop, among others.

Ambepussa, 2 km north, is just off the road to the west, with a train station. Its rest house is claimed to be Sri Lanka's oldest, built in 1822, and is a popular lunch stop. About 1.5 km behind the rest house, near the Devagiri Vihara, is a series of caves which at one time formed a hermitage.

Near Ambepussa, a turning onto the B21 before Kegalla takes you 3 km south of the A1 to the two 12th-century *dagobas* at Dedigama, built by King Parakramabahu I, who was born here. One has 10 relic chambers. A gem-studded golden reliquary has also been found here. The nearby **museum** ⓘ *closed Tue*, is worth visiting.

Kegalla to Kandy

Kegalla is a long, straggling town in a picturesque setting. Most visitors take a detour here towards Rambukkana for the Pinnawela Elephant Orphanage (see opposite). After Kegalla, the hill scenery becomes increasingly beautiful, and the vegetation stunningly rich. About 1 km before Mawanella, a town surrounded by spice plantations, a sign points to a small monument marking the place where **Saradial** ('the local Robin Hood') lived. You then pass through **Molagoda**, a village devoted to pottery, where both sides of the road are lined with shops displaying a wide range of attractive pots. At the top of the Balana Pass is a precipice called **Sensation Point**.

At the Km 107 mark is an outdoor museum displaying the original equipment used to lay the Colombo–Kandy road, such as steamrollers and bitumen boilers. Next to the museum is a replica of the 300-year-old Bogoda Bridge (see page 244).

The railway goes through two tunnels to Peradeniya, where the road crosses the Mahaweli Ganga, Sri Lanka's longest river, and into the city.

Pinnawela *Colour map 2, C3.*
6 km north of the main Colombo–Kandy road along the B32; turn off at Udamalla if in a car.

Pinnawela is the home of one of the most popular stops on the tourist circuit, the famous elephant orphanage. There are other alternative places to meet with elephants in the area, and a number of spice gardens line the road. While most visitors are en route between Colombo and Kandy, travellers who choose to spend a night are delighted by the peace and beauty of this place with its river and jungle setting. The village becomes an oasis of calm once the tourist groups leave.

Pinnawela Elephant Orphanage ⓘ *T035-226 5284. Daily 0830-1800. Rs 2500, children Rs 1250. Video camera Rs 500 (professional Rs 1500).* This government-run elephant orphanage was set up in 1975 to rescue four orphaned baby elephants when they could no longer be looked after at Dehiwala Zoo. Now there are almost 90 elephants here, the largest group of captive elephants in the world. However, concerns have been raised about the welfare of the elephants at the orphanage. **Responsible Tourism** ⓘ *www.responsibletourism.com*, and the **Born Free Foundation** do not endorse Pinnawela. Born Free Foundation supports **Elephant Transit Centre** near Uda Walawe (see page 175).

Millennium Elephant Foundation ⓘ *Hiriwadunna, Randeniya, 3 km before the elephant orphanage, T035-226 3377, www.millenniumelephantfoundation.com. Daily 0800-1700. Rs 6000 including lunch and talk.* This registered charity, formerly Maximus Elephant Foundation, a member of WSPA, cares for elderly and disabled elephants. Although it has less of the 'aah' factor than Pinnawela, it is still worthwhile visiting. There are currently eight elephants living here, aged 21-65, but numbers fluctuate. Pooja is the youngest elephant and was born here in 1984; the others are retired working animals. The scheme also runs a mobile veterinary unit, established in 2000, which provides healthcare across the country for domesticated and wild elephants. You can help bathe and feed the elephants and also go on rides around the grounds. There is also an 'adopt an elephant' scheme: a year's adoption costs US$35 (under 16s US$25). As at the elephant orphanage, foreign volunteers can help with the project; apply direct for voluntary work placements for up to three months.

Listings Colombo to Kandy

Where to stay

Warakapola, Ambepussa and around

$$ Rest House (CHC)
Ambepussa, T035-226 7299, www.ambepussa-rest-house.srilunkahotel.net
Beautiful Dutch-style building with large teak veranda, close to a stream. 6 rooms with beautiful furniture, a/c, hot water and TV.

Pinnawela

Most places are along the Rambukkana Rd on the way to the elephant orphanage.

$$ Ralidiya
On the edge of town, T035-527 3672, www.ralidiyahotel.lakapura.com.
Catering mainly to the local wedding market, it also has 5 clean rooms with balcony and good views over the river. Restaurant.

$ Elephant View
Opposite the orphanage, T035-226 5293, eleview@sltnet.lk.
16 a/c rooms with hot water. Most rooms are in the main building from where you can see the elephants on their way to bathe; others are in the former **Pinnawela Village Hotel** on the main road.

$ Green Land Guest House
Elephant Bath Rd, T035-226 5668, www.greenlandguesthouse.com.
5 clean rooms with nets and attached bath. Upstairs is better as rooms have access to the balcony. Excellent rice and curry dinner. Recommended.

Shopping

Stop at **Pasyala** for cashew nuts, at **Warakapola** for woven goods, and at

Molagodo for pots. The roads around Pinnawela Elephant Orphanage are lined with souvenir stalls selling a wide range of trinkets, not all elephant related. Bargaining is essential. Water is very expensive.

Transport

Bus Regular buses depart from **Kandy** (Goods Shed) to **Kegalla** (1 hr). Change at Kegalla clock tower for a (regular) **Rambukkana** bus, which stops at Pinnawela (10 mins). Some Colombo–

Kandy buses will drop you at the junction for Pinnawela on the A1.

Train Most Colombo–Kandy trains stop at **Gampaha** (from here you can take a 3-wheeler to Heneratgoda). Trains run from Kandy to **Rambukkana** (a short bus or 3-wheeler ride from the orphanage) daily at 0630, 1040, 1530, 1625 and 1810 (1½ hrs). Enquire at station for return times. Trains continue to **Colombo Fort** (except the 1810), taking 2½-3 hrs.

★ Kandy *Colour map 2, C4.*

Kandy has many claims to fame: it was the last bastion of Buddhist political power against colonial forces; it is the home of the Temple of the Buddha's Tooth Relic and the site of the island's most impressive annual festival; it is also the capital of the highlands, with a population of 111,700.

Kandy's architectural monuments date mainly from a final surge of grandiose building by King Vikrama Rajasinha in the early 19th century. So extravagant were the edifices, and achieved only at enormous cost to the people of Kandy, that his nobles betrayed him to the British rather than continue enduring his excesses (see box, opposite). The result is some extraordinary buildings, none of great architectural merit, but sustaining a Kandyan style dating back to the 16th century, and rich in symbolic significance, representing the king's view of his world. The temple area, which includes the former palace, the Temple of the Tooth and its associated buildings, is a World Heritage Site and is the chief focus of interest for pilgrims and visitors to the town.

Temple of the Tooth (Dalada Maligawa)

Entrance on east side of Palace Square. Daily 0530-2000, pujas at 0530, 0930, 1830. Rs 1000 (cameras Rs 150, video cameras Rs 300). Note: the Cultural Triangle Permit does not cover the temple here. Wear a long skirt or trousers and ensure shoulders are covered, otherwise lungis (sarongs) must be worn over shorts; remove shoes and hats before entering (there's a small fee for looking after your shoes).

The temple contains Sri Lanka's most revered Buddhist relic: a tooth of the Buddha, which was brought to the city in 1542. The original temple dated from this period, but most of the present building and the Patthiruppuwa or Octagon were built in the early 19th century. The oldest part is the inner shrine built by Kirti Sri after 1765; the gilded roof over the shrine is a recent addition, however.

> **Tip...**
> Remember that the Temple of the Tooth is a genuine place of worship and not simply a site of tourist interest.

BACKGROUND
Worship of the Tooth Relic

The eyewitness account of Bella Sidney Woolf in 1914 captures something of the atmosphere when the Tooth Relic could be viewed by pilgrims.

"The relic is only shown for royal visits or, on certain occasions, to Burmese and other pilgrims. If the passenger happens to be in Kandy at such a time he should try to see the Tooth, even though it may mean many hours of waiting. It is an amazing sight. The courtyard is crammed with worshippers of all ages, bearing offerings in their hands, leaves of young coconut, scent, flowers, fruit. As the door opens, they surge up the dark and narrow stairway to the silver and ivory doors behind which lies the Tooth.

The doors are opened and a flood of hot heavy scented air pours out. The golden 'Karandua' or outer casket of the Tooth stands revealed dimly behind gilded bars. In the weird uncertain light of candles in golden candelabra the yellow-robed priests move to and fro. The Tooth is enclosed in five Karanduas and slowly and solemnly each is removed in turn; some of them are encrusted with rubies, emeralds and diamonds.

At last the great moment approaches. The last Karandua is removed – in folds of red silk lies the wondrous Relic – the centre point of the faith of millions. It is a shock to see a tooth of discoloured ivory at least three inches long – unlike any human tooth ever known. The priest sets it in a golden lotus – the Temple Korala gives a sharp cry – the tom-toms and conches and pipes blare out – the kneeling worshippers, some with tears streaming down their faces, stretch out their hands in adoration."

Tip...
It is best to visit early in the morning before it gets too busy with tourist buses and pilgrims.

Entrance The drawbridge, moat and gateway were the work of Sri Vickrama Rajasinha. There is a moonstone step leading to the archway, and a stone depicting Lakshmi against the wall facing the entrance. The main door to the temple is in the wall of the upper veranda, covered in restored frescoes depicting Buddhist conceptions of hell. The doorway is a typical *makara torana* showing mythical beasts. A second Kandyan-style door leads into the courtyard, across which is the building housing the Tooth Relic. The door has ivory inlay work, with copper and gold handles.

Shrine Room The **Udmale** (upper storey) houses the Relic. Caged behind gilded iron bars is the large outer *karandua* (casket), made of silver. Inside it are seven smaller caskets, each made of gold studded with jewels. Today the temple is controlled by a layman (the *Diyawadne*) elected by the high priests of the monasteries in Kandy and Asgiriya. The administrator holds the key to the iron cage, but there are three different keys to the caskets themselves, one held by

Fact...
The temple compound was the target of a bomb attack on 26 January 1998, which left over 20 dead and seriously damaged the temple and other buildings, including St Paul's Church (1843) to the west. Roadblocks still remain outside the temple, nearly 20 years later, although repairs were completed in 1999.

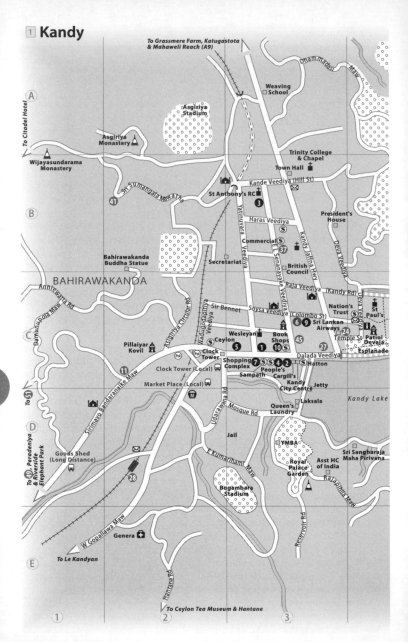

1 Kandy

To Grassmere Farm, Katugastota
& Mahaweli Reach (A9)

Dhammarasi Maw

To Citadel Hotel

Weaving School

Asgiriya Stadium

Asgiriya Monastery

Wijayasundarama Monastery

Trinity College & Chapel

Town Hall

41

Sri Sumangala Mawatha

Kande Veediya (Hill St)

St Anthony's RC

3

Haras Veediya

President's House

Deva Veediya

Bahirawakanda Buddha Statue

BAHIRAWAKANDA

Secretariat

Commercial

37

H L Senanayake Veediya

British Council

Kandy Jaffna Hwy

Anniewatta Rd

Astgiriya Circular Rd

Sir Bennet

Raja Veediya (Kandy Rd)

Nation's Trust

St Paul's

Damunupola Maw

Wadugodapitiya Veediya

Soysa Veediya (Colombo St)

6 9

Sri Lankan Airways

24

Pillaiyar Kovil

Wesleyan

Ceylon

Book Shops

45

Temple St

Patini Devala

Clock Tower

5

1 10

27

Dalada Veediya

Esplanade

11

Clock Tower (Local)

Shopping Complex

7

People's Sampath

Cargill's

2

Hatton

Market Place (Local)

M

Kandy City Centre

Jetty

Srimavo Bandaranaike Maw

Udawale Rd

Queen's Laundry

Laksala

Kandy Lake

To Si

Goods Shed (Long Distance)

Mosque Rd

Jail

E Kumarihami Maw

YMBA

Asst HC of India

Sri Sangharaja Maha Pirivana

To Peradeniya & Riverside Elephant Park

28

Royal Palace Garden

Raja Pihila Maw

Reservoir Rd

Bogambara Stadium

W Gopallawa Maw

Genera

To Le Kandyan

Hantane Rd

To Ceylon Tea Museum & Hantane

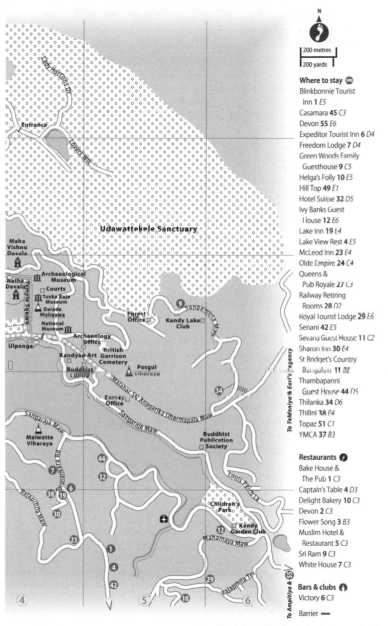

N

200 metres
200 yards

Where to stay

Blinkbonnie Tourist
   Inn **1** *E5*
Casamara **45** *C3*
Devon **55** *E6*
Expeditor Tourist Inn **6** *D4*
Freedom Lodge **7** *D4*
Green Woods Family
   Guesthouse **9** *C5*
Helga's Folly **10** *E5*
Hill Top **49** *E1*
Hotel Suisse **32** *D5*
Ivy Banks Guest
   House **12** *E6*
Lake Inn **19** *E4*
Lake View Rest **4** *E5*
McLeod Inn **23** *E4*
Olde Empire **24** *C4*
Queens &
   Pub Royale **27** *C3*
Railway Retiring
   Rooms **28** *D2*
Royal Tourist Lodge **29** *E6*
Senani **42** *E5*
Sevana Guest House **11** *C2*
Sharon Inn **30** *E4*
St Bridget's Country
   Bungalow **11** *D2*
Thambapanni
   Guest House **44** *D5*
Thilanka **34** *D6*
Thilini **38** *F4*
Topaz **51** *C1*
YMCA **37** *B3*

Restaurants

Bake House &
   The Pub **1** *C3*
Captain's Table **4** *D3*
Delight Bakery **10** *C3*
Devon **2** *C3*
Flower Song **3** *B3*
Muslim Hotel &
   Restaurant **5** *C3*
Sri Ram **9** *C3*
White House **7** *C3*

Bars & clubs

Victory **6** *C3*
Barrier ━

BACKGROUND
Kandy

Although the city of Kandy (originally Senkadagala) is commonly held to have been founded by a general named Vikramabahu in 1472, there was a settlement on the site for at least 150 years before that. On asserting his independence from the reigning monarch, Vikramabahu made Kandy his capital. He built a palace for his mother and a shrine on pillars. In 1542 the Buddha's Tooth Relic was brought to the city, stimulating a flurry of new religious building – a two-storey house for the relic itself and 86 houses for the monks. As in Anuradhapura and Polonnaruwa, the Tooth temple was built next to the palace.

Defensive fortifications were probably only started when the Portuguese began their attacks. Forced to withdraw from the town in 1594, King Vimala Dharma Suriya set half the city on fire, a tactic that was repeated by several successors in the face of expulsion by foreign armies. However, he won it back, and promptly set about building a massive wall, interspersed with huge towers. Inside, a new palace replaced the one destroyed by fire, and the city rapidly gained a reputation as a cosmopolitan centre of splendour and wealth.

As early as 1597 some Portuguese showed scepticism about the claims that the enshrined tooth was the Buddha's. In 1597 De Quezroy described the seven golden caskets in which the tooth was kept, but added that it was the tooth of a buffalo. The Portuguese were already claiming that they had captured the original, exported it to Goa and incinerated it.

By 1602 the city had probably taken the form (though not the actual buildings) which would survive to the beginning of the 19th century. The major temples were also already in place. Kandy was repeatedly attacked by the Portuguese in the early 17th century: in 1611 the city was captured and largely destroyed, and again in 1629 and 1638, when the Tooth Relic was removed for a time by the retreating King Senarat. A new earth rampart was built between the hills in the south of the city. In 1681 there is evidence of a moat being built using forced labour.

It is possible that the first incarnation of the Bogambara Lake to the southwest also dates from this time. The lake was a symbol of the cosmic ocean, but Vimala Dharma Suriya I also had a practical use for it: he is said to have kept some of his treasure sunk in the middle, guarded by crocodiles in the water. It has been suggested that there was also a symbolic link with Kubera, the mythical god of wealth, who kept his wealth at the

the administrator and one each by the high priests of Malwatte and Asgiriya, so that the caskets can only be opened when all four are present.

The **sanctuary** is opened at dawn, and ceremonies are held three times a day. These are moments when the temple comes to life with pilgrims making offerings of flowers amidst clouds of incense and the beating of drums. The casket is displayed for only a part of the day, and the Relic itself has, for many years, only been displayed to the most important of visitors. You can join pilgrims to see the casket but may well have to overcome pushing and jostling by those desperate to see the holy object. There is a separate enclosure in front of the Relic, which wealthy Sri Lankans pay to enter.

bottom of the cosmic ocean. Crocodiles are often shown on the *makara toranas* (gateways) of temples.

A new Temple of the Tooth was built by Vimala Dharma Suriya II between 1687 1707, on the old site. Three storeys high, it contained a reliquary of gold encrusted with jewels. Between 1707 and 1739 Narendra Sinha undertook new building in the city, renovating the Temple of the Tooth and enclosing the Natha Devala and the sacred Bodhi tree. He established the validity of his royal line by importing princesses from Madurai, and set aside a separate street for them in the town.

King Kirti Sri (1747-1782) added a temple to Vishnu northwest of the palace, but at the same time asserted his support for Buddhism, twice bringing monks from Thailand to re-validate the Sinhalese order of monks. The Dutch, who captured the city in 1765, destroyed the palace and the Temple of the Tooth and seriously damaged many other buildings.

Kirti Sri started re-building, more opulently than ever, but it was the last king of Kandy, Sri Vikrama Rajasinha (1798-1815), who gave Kandy many of its present buildings. More interested in palaces and parks than temples, he set about demonstrating his kingly power with an exhibition of massive building works. Once again he had to start almost from scratch, following the burning of the city in 1803 to prevent its desecration by the British. Between 1809 and 1812 there was massive re-building. The palace was fully renovated and a new octagonal structure was added, the Patthiruppuwa. Two years later the royal complex was surrounded by a moat and a single massive stone gateway replaced the earlier entrances. In the west, Sri Vikrama Rajasinha built new shops and houses, at the same time building more houses in the east for his Tamil relatives.

But by far the greatest work was the construction of the Bogambara Lake. Previously the low-lying marshy land in front of the palace had been drained for paddy fields. Between 1810 and 1812 up to 3000 men were forced to work on building the dam at the west end of the low ground, creating an artificial lake given the cosmically symbolic name of the Ocean of Milk. A pleasure house was built in the middle, connected by drawbridge to the palace. By now the city had taken virtually its present form.

Rajasinha's rule had been so tyrannical however, violating religious laws and committing brutal murders, that the terrorized Kandyan aristocracy allied themselves with the British invaders, who garnered support for a war against the king by promising to protect the people and their property. The final fall of Kandy to the British in 1815 signalled the end of independence for the whole island.

Other temple buildings
Alut Maligawa and Temple Museum ⓘ *T081-223 4226, Rs 500, 0800-1900.* The hall behind the sanctuary has a number of golden Buddha statues from Thailand and modern paintings depicting the Buddha's life and the arrival of Buddhism on the island. Upstairs, and accessed from the rear, is the museum, which contains bronze busts of the Kandyan kings and displays some of their garments, as well as photocopies of documents detailing some of the history of the temple. There is also a gallery of photographs showing the extent of the damage to the temple in the 1998 bomb.

North of the temple The **Audience Hall** was rebuilt in the Kandyan style as a wooden pillared hall (1784). The historic document ending the Kandyan kingdom was signed here, when the territory was handed over to the British. There is excellent carving on the pillars.

Tip...
North of the temple are the Law Courts, where you can watch lawyers in black gowns and white wigs going about their business in open-sided halls.

Just beyond is the **Tusker Raja Museum**, housing the stuffed body of the much-venerated elephant Raja, who carried the Tooth Relic casket in the Esala Perahera for many years. Raja was offered to the temple by a pious Buddhist family when he was very young and was 85 when he died in 1988. The museum is more easily visited before entering the temple.

Archaeological Museum
Temple Sq. Wed-Mon 0800-1700. Free.

Some good sculptures in wood and stone are housed in what remains of the old king's palace. The museum includes some architectural pieces, notably columns and capitals from the Kandyan kingdom, but the three dusty rooms are somewhat disappointing.

Kandy National Museum
Queen's Palace, east of the temple, T081-222 3867. Sun-Thu 0800-1700. Rs 500, children Rs 300, camera Rs 250.

The collection traces a vivid history of the development and culture of the Kandyan Kingdom. It features jewels, armaments, ritual objects, sculptures, metalwork, ivory, costumes, games, medical instruments, old maps – an enormous range of everyday and exceptional objects. There is much memorabilia, and the attendants will attempt to explain it all, sometimes pointing out the obvious in expectation of a tip.

British Garrison Cemetery
To the right of the Kandy National Museum is a sign pointing the way to the British Garrison Cemetery, a short walk up the hill. The cemetery was opened in 1822 and was used until burials were all but banned in the 1870s. The cemetery was restored in the 1990s and is now a tranquil place to escape the bustle of Kandy town. The caretaker is very helpful and will show you around, pointing out the most interesting graves, such as the last recorded death of a European in Sri Lanka from a wild elephant.

Bogambara (Kandy) Lake
Constructed by forced labour for Sri Vikrama Rajasinha, the last king of Kandy (see Background, page 204), the man-made lake lies south of the temple compound and dominates views of the city. There is a scenic 4-km path around the lake, and boat tours run from the jetty on the western side. On the north shore, **Ulpenge** was the bathing place of former queens and is now a police station. Further along to the east is the **Buddhist Publications Society**, which has information on courses about Buddhism and meditation (see page 213). The **Royal Palace Park** (Wace Park) ① *0830-1630, Rs 200*, is approached from the lake's southwest corner.

Malwatte and Asigiriya viharas

The 18th-century **Malwatte Vihara**, on the south side of the lake, where the important annual ordination of monks takes place in June, is decorated with ornate wood and metal work. Occasionally, a friendly monk shows visitors around the monastery and the small museum. This and the **Asigiriya Vihara** (northwest of town) are particularly important monasteries because of the senior position of their incumbents. The latter, which stands on a hill, has good wood carving and an impressive collection of old palm leaf manuscripts. There is a large recumbent Buddha statue and the mound of the old Royal Burial Ground nearby.

Udawattekele Sanctuary

Follow Kande Veediya northeast from the centre to reach the entrance gate to the sanctuary. Rs 687.

Once the 'forbidden forest' of the kings of Kandy, this is now the city's lung. Previously reserved for the use of the court, the British cleared vast areas soon after arrival, though declared it a 'reserved' area in 1856. The sanctuary now covers 104 ha and contains several endemic species of flora and fauna, with over 150 species of birds (including Layard's parakeet, Sri Lankan hanging parrot, barbets, bulbuls, bee eaters and kingfishers), monkeys, squirrels and porcupines. There are also a number of meditation centres here. Lady Horton's Drive takes you into the tropical rainforest and offers good views of the Mahaweli River further east.

Some interesting legends are attached to the forest. Look out for the trail with stone steps leading down to a cove, the Chittu Vishudi. This is where King Vickramabahu was said to have hidden when his palace was under siege. The pond is the original bathing place of the court. Gold coins are rumoured to be concealed beneath its murky waters, guarded by a serpent with glowing red eyes, which surfaces once a year.

Trinity College

Trinity College, which is approached from DS Senanayake Veediya, has a chapel with some beautiful paintings which makes a quiet diversion from the busy part of town. It is also worth exploring the school's archives.

Listings Kandy *map p202*

Tourist information

Hotel and guesthouse owners are usually the best source of information.

Tourist Information Centre
Headman's Lodge, 3 Deva Veediya (Temple St), opposite entrance to Temple of the Tooth, T081-222 2661. Mon-Fri 0900-1645. There's also a very helpful tourist information office in the city centre that can provide a free map of Kandy and information on buses, trains, sights, etc. See also www.kandycity.org.

Where to stay

Accommodation prices rise considerably during the festival. In low season, try bargaining for a good price. It is best to reserve your accommodation before arriving here.

Saranankara Rd and Rajapihilla Mawatha, a 10- to 20-min walk southeast of the lake, are popular and have a good range of reasonably priced accommodation. This area offers a good balance: it's far enough

ON THE ROAD
Accommodation touts

Beware of accommodation touts in Kandy. Some board trains approaching the town; others besiege newcomers at the bus and rail stations. They can be very persistent, will try to put you off going to certain hotels/guesthouses and then direct you to one where they can get a large commission, often demanding up to 20% of everything you spend (room, food and tours). Insist that you have a confirmed reservation. Don't tell them which hotel you will be staying at, and ignore stories that your hotel/guesthouse has closed or is no good. Some touts will follow you, if you are on foot, and pretend they have taken you to your hotel – make it clear to your host that you chose the hotel of your own accord. Many guesthouse owners refuse to pay touts: these are the ones that the touts will tell you are closed or no good. Some touts will accost you in town pretending to work for your hotel, as a chef or porter, say, claiming you have met them earlier. Ask them which hotel they work for and this should get rid of them. They will often be very friendly and want to take you to a bar; if you do go drinking with them you will find yourself saddled with an inflated tab on which they get a percentage.

out of the centre to be peaceful but not so far as to make taxi fares prohibitive. Some of the guesthouses here have fine views over the lake.

$$$$ Helga's Folly
70 Frederick E de Silva Mawatha, T081-447 4314, www.helgasfolly.com.
40 individually decorated rooms in this eccentrically designed 'anti-hotel' full of character and quirkiness, described as "the Salvador Dali of hotels". It has to be seen to be believed. Set in quiet wooded hills, with a stylish restaurant, small pool (not well maintained). Far from town but recommended for imagination and romance.

$$$ Senani
167/1 Rajapihilla Mawatha, T081-223 5118, www.senanihotels.com.
Clean, spacious a/c rooms, helpful staff and good food. Quite expensive.

$$$ Suisse
30 Sangaraja Mawatha, T081-223 3024, www.hotelsuisse.lk.

100 a/c rooms in a colonial-style hotel (1920s) that was Lord Mountbatten's wartime HQ. The best rooms have a balcony on the lakeside. Limited views of lake but friendly and helpful staff, restaurant, good pool (non-residents, Rs 250), tennis, snooker, herbal clinic, shopping arcade. Recommended.

$$$ Topaz
Anniewatte (1.6 km west of town), T081-223 2326, www.mclarenshotels.lk.
75 a/c rooms in excellent location on a high hill overlooking mountains but rather remote, balconies, good pool shared with sister hotel, **Tourmaline**. Popular with package tours.

$$$-$$ Devon
51 Ampitiya Rd, T081-223 5164, www.devonsrilanka.com.
27 rooms, TV, minibar, a/c, some with tubs, 24-hr coffee shop and renowned Devon chain food.

$$$-$$ Hill Top (Aitken Spence)
200/21 Bahirawakanda Peradeniya Rd, 2 km from centre, T081-222 4162, www.aitkenspencehotels.com.

73 a/c rooms in attractively designed hotel, comfortable and striking rooms (poolside are the best), beautiful restaurant, large pool.

$$$-$$ Queens (CHC)
45 Dalada Veediya, T081-223 3026, www.queenshotel.lk.
Full of colonial character (established 1844). 54 smallish but comfortable rooms, half a/c, but fan rooms have balcony and are better value, avoid noisy front rooms. Restaurant, good bar, super pool, "hard to beat for slightly decaying colonial charm".

$$$-$$ Thilanka
3 Sangamitta Mawatha, T081-447 5200, www.thilankahotel.com.
87 well-furnished rooms and suites, private balconies with lake views, good restaurant, nice pool, and very clean. Standard fan rooms are located in the original house which began as a small guesthouse. Helpful and friendly staff.

$$ Casamara
12 Kotugodella Veediya, T081-222 4688, www.casamarahotel.com.
Convenient location in town. Unexceptional exterior but rooms have a/c and good furniture, and staff are friendly and helpful.

$$ Sharon Inn
59 Saranankara Rd, T081-220 1400, www.hotelsharoninn.com.
Friendly welcome at this family-run guesthouse. Deservedly popular, with 11 spotless rooms with balcony and Wi-Fi. Great home-cooked food on the balcony.

$$-$ Lake View Rest
71 A Rajapihilla Mawatha, T081-223 9421.
Comfortable rooms in good location. Friendly welcome.

$$-$ Royal Tourist Lodge
93 Rajapihilla Mawatha, T081-222 2534, www.royaltouristlodge.hotels.officelive.com.

2 very large well-furnished rooms with own patio into garden, and 1 room without patio, in spacious family guesthouse. Clean and friendly, quiet.

$$-$ St Bridget's Country Bungalow
125 Sri Sumangala Mawatha, Asgiriya (west of town), T081-221 5806, www.stbridgets-kandy.com.
Pleasant rooms, peaceful surroundings, spacious garden, good food.

$$-$ Sevana City Hotel
84 Peradeniya Rd, T081-567 4443, www.sevanakandy.com.
15 clean rooms in family-run guesthouse, good food, friendly, excellent value. More expensive rooms have a/c.

$ Blinkbonnie Tourist Inn
69 Rajapihilla Mawatha, T081-594 6409, blinkbonnie@yahoo.com.
Clean a/c and fan rooms, some with private balcony, good views. Terrace restaurant with Wi-Fi, free pick-up from station.

$ Expeditor Tourist Inn
41 Saranankara Rd, T081-223 8316, www.expeditorkandy.com.
Comfortable rooms some with private balcony, 1st floor with good views, friendly Wildlife tours, see page 214. Consistently good reports. There is a self-contained flat on the top floor (Rs 3000).

$ Freedom Lodge
30 Saranankara Rd T081-222 3506.
Friendly welcome at this family run guesthouse, stylish decor, helpful owners can also arrange tours (both of the city and Sri Lanka at large), good food. Recommended.

$ Green Woods
34a Sangamitta Mawatha, T081-223 2970.
Quiet and rural location on edge of Udawattekele Sanctuary and short walk to the temple. Friendly family serving up good home-cooked food.

$ McLeod Inn
65a Rajapihilla Mawatha, T081-222 2832, mcleod@sltnet.lk.
10 clean and pleasant rooms with hot water in the mornings and evenings, the 2 rooms with views are more expensive. The restaurant has the best view of any in this area (open to non-residents with advance warning). Very friendly and helpful. Popular so book in advance. Recommended.

$ Olde Empire Hotel
21 Deva Veediya, T081-222 4284.
Atmospheric but basic accommodation with 15 rooms (those with shared bathroom are cheaper) in rambling 150-year-old colonial building. Lovely veranda overlooking temple and lake, excellent location close to Dalada Maligawa. Spruced-up new restaurant downstairs.

$ Thambapanni Guest House
28 Sangaraja Mawatha (next to Hotel Suisse), T081-222 3234.
8 simple, large, moderately clean rooms, plus bar-cum-restaurant.

$ YMCA
160a Kotugodale Veediya, T081-222 3529.
11 rooms, common bath. Cheap dormitory accommodation. Visitors are also permitted to sleep in the sports hall during the **Perahera** – together with hundreds of mosquitoes.

North of Kandy

$$$$-$$$ Hunas Falls
Elkaduwa, 27 km north of Kandy (1-hr drive on rough road), T081-247 0041, www.hunasfallskandy.com.
31 comfortable a/c rooms (2 suites, Scottish or Japanese styles), hot tubs, pool, boating, fishing, tennis, golf, games room for youngsters, many activities on offer, beautifully located in a tea garden by a waterfall with excellent walks, visits to tea estate, factory, farm (you can milk the cows) and spice gardens. Excellent base for birdwatching.

$$$$-$$$ Mahaweli Reach
35 PBA Weerakoon Mawatha, on river by Katugastota Bridge, 5 km north, T081-447 2727, www.mahaweli.com.
112 large, well-furnished a/c rooms and 4 suites (**$$$$**) in a striking building overlooking river. Tubs, TV, balconies with excellent river views, superb food (including good buffet choice), very attentive service, Kandy's biggest and best pool, Ayurvedic health centre, extensive sports facilities. Recommended.

Restaurants

The top hotels in town are good but can be expensive. Sri Lankan rice and curry is cheap but usually only available at lunchtime. There are lots of excellent bakeries in town, many of which serve lunch packets too. Beware of touts trying to take you to restaurants where they get a kick-back.

$$ Captain's Table
Upstairs from Devon (see below). Daily 1100-1500, 1800-2200.
Part of the Devon group, serves Indian and Chinese food. No alcohol. Large screen TV, live music at weekends.

$$ Flower Song
137 Kotugodalle Veediya (1st floor), T081-222 9191, www.flowerdrum.net. Daily 1100-2230.
Excellent Chinese, good portions. A/c.

$$-$ Devon
11 Dalada Veediya, T081-222 4537. Daily 0730-2000.
The main restaurant has Sri Lankan rice and curry, Western dishes and Chinese. There is an excellent self-service area (open 1100-1900) for very cheap Sri Lankan/Chinese/ seafood lunch and a fabulous bakery shop.

Very popular with locals and tourists, waiters are miserable but the food is worth the scowls. There are other branches around town.

$$-$ Old Empire Hotel
See Where to stay.
Perfect place for a temple pitstop, this is a restaurant suited to Western tastes. Renovated in 2014, the ground floor of the Empire now has kitsch decor, beautiful old Sri Lankan travel posters and lots of charm.

$$-$ Sri Ram
87 Colombo St, T081-567 7287.
Daily 1030-2100.
Excellent South Indian cuisines, 1st-class service, attractive decor, immaculate. No alcohol. Offers thali and biriyani dishes daily 1100-1500, and also sells lunch packets outside (Rs 150).

$ White House
21 Dalada Veediya, T081-223 2765.
With its white interior and glass display cases, this place has a modern, Western feel to it. There are fresh juices and good cakes, plus filling Chinese food. Rice and curry is served 1100-1400. The a/c draws in a number of tourists but this place is popular with the locals too.

Bars and clubs

Most upper-range hotels have bars.

There are traditional bars at **The Olde Empire** (see Where to stay) and the **Pub Royale** (next to Queens Hotel), both with a good atmosphere. The latter has the usual beers plus Three Coins' excellent Sando stout. **Victory** (Colombo St), is a popular locals bar and has cheap rooms upstairs, but solo female travellers may not feel entirely comfortable here. **The Pub** (36 Dalada Veediya, above the Bake House, T081-223 4868) is a popular tourist pub with a/c, serving uninspired Western food, Lion and Carlsberg on draught, plus a good selection of spirits. There is a pleasant veranda overlooking the street, although the traffic noise can be a bit much during busy periods. Good atmosphere.

Entertainment

There are performances of Kandyan dancing in several parts of the town, most starting at 1730 and lasting 1 hr. Tickets Rs 500 (touts sell tickets around the lake; be sure to pay only the printed price). Many visitors are disappointed by the shows, which are heavily geared towards the tourist market. The dances include snippets of several dances and the occasional fire-walking, and thus lack authenticity. They include:

Kandyan Art Association, *72 Sangaraja Mawath.* Some visitors have complained that shows are "stale and routine".
Kandy Lake Club Dance Ensemble, *7 Sangamitta Mawatha (off Malabar St), T081-222 3505.* Performs dances of Sri Lanka.
YMBA Hall, *Royal Palace Garden.* Kandyan and low country dancing, good value.

Festivals

Jul/Aug Esala Perahera lasts for 10 days (see box, page 212).

Shopping

There is a **Fashion Bug** on Dalada Veediya, as well as a **Cargill's** supermarket (good for water, snacks and toiletries) and the a/c **Kandy City Centre shopping mall** (with a couple of bookshops, a juice bar and a tourist information desk). The **market** near the clocktower can yield good bargains but these will rely heavily on your negotiating skills. The **municipal market**, west of the lake, is worth visiting even if you are not planning to bargain for superb Sri Lankan fruit and spices.

Esala Perahera

Esala Perahera (procession), Sri Lanka's greatest festival, is of special significance. It is held in the lunar month of Esala (named after the *Cassia fistula* which blossoms at this time) in which the Buddha was conceived and in which he left his father's home. It has also long been associated with rituals to ensure renewed fertility for the year ahead. The last Kandyan kings turned the Perahera into a mechanism for reinforcing their own power, trying to identify themselves with the gods who needed to be appeased. By focusing on the Tooth Relic, the Tamil kings hoped to establish their own authority and their divine legitimacy within the Buddhist community. The Sri Lankan historian Seneviratne has suggested that fear both of the king and of divine retribution encouraged nobles and peasants alike to come to the Perahera, and witnessing the scale of the spectacle reinforced their loyalty. In 1922, DH Lawrence described his experience as "wonderful – midnight – huge elephants, great flares of coconut torches, princes... tom-toms and savage music and devil dances... black eyes... of the dancers".

Today the festival is a magnificent 10-day spectacle of elephants, drummers, dancers, chieftains, acrobats, whip-crackers, torch bearers and tens of thousands of pilgrims in procession. Buddhists are drawn to the temple by the power of the Tooth Relic rather than by that of the King's authority. The power of the Relic certainly long preceded that of the Kandyan dynasty. Fa Hien described the annual festival in Anuradhapura in AD 399, which even then was a lavish procession in which roads were vividly decorated, elephants covered in jewels and flowers, and models of figures such as Bodhisattvas were paraded. When the tooth was moved to Kandy, the Perahera moved with it.

Following the Tree Planting Ceremony (Kap), the first five days, Kumbal Perahera, are celebrated within the grounds of the four *devalas* (temples) – Natha, Vishnu, Skanda and Pattini. The next five days are Randoli Perahera. Torch light processions set off from the temples, and the Tooth Relic Casket is carried by the Maligawa Tusker accompanied by magnificently robed temple custodians. Every night the procession grows, moving from the Temple of the Tooth, along Dalada Veediya and DS Senanayake Mawatha to the Adahanamaluwa, where the relic casket is left in the keeping of the temple trustees. The separate temple processions return to their temples, coming out in the early morning for the water cutting ceremony. Originally, the temple guardians went to the lake with golden water pots to empty water collected the previous year. They would then be refilled and taken back to the temple for the following year, symbolizing the fertility protected by the gods. On the 11th day, a daylight procession accompanied the return of the Relic to the Temple. The Day Perahera continues, but today the Tooth Relic itself is no longer taken out.

You don't necessarily need to buy tickets to watch the processions since you can get good views by standing along the street. A good vantage point is opposite or near to the Queens Hotel as much of that area is slightly better lit (the Presidential vantage point is somewhere nearby) allowing for slightly better photography.

Arts and crafts

Try the craftshops on Dalada Veediya near the Temple of the Tooth. There are also several antique shops, many along the lake and on Peradeniya Rd. Check out the curio shops on south Bandaranaike Mawatha, just past the railway station towards the botanical gardens.

Kandyan Art Association, *72 Sangaraja Mawatha*. Government sales outlet where you can watch weavers and craftsmen working on wood, silver, copper and brass, and buy lacquer-ware and batik.

Kandyan Handicrafts Centre, *10/4 Kotugodale Veediya*. Good metalwork.

Laksala, *near Lake Jetty*. Government sales outlet.

Waruna Antiques, *761 Peradeniya Rd, www.warunaantiques.com*. A stunning collection, from large pieces of furniture and sculpture, to textiles and jewellery. Recommended.

Batiks, silks and textiles

Shops along Colombo St sell material.

Fresco, *901 Peradeniya Rd*. For good batiks.

Selyn Handloom, *No 7 1/1 Temple Rd*. Fair trade handloom products – exceptional quality. Recommended.

Senani Silk House, *next to Senani Restaurant*. Has a good range of quality silks.

Books

Mark Bookshop, *151/1 Dalada Veediya*. Has a good selection of books on local history.

Vijitha Yapa Bookshop, *Kotugodella Veediya. Mon-Fri 0800-1730, Sat 0800-1630*. Wide range of books and magazines.

Tea

There are various tea outlets at the **Ceylon Tea Museum** in Hantane (see page 220).

Mlesna, *15 Dalada Veediya, T081-222 8626*. A fine selection of teas and chinaware. A very pleasant place to shop. There's another branch in the Kandy City Centre shopping mall.

What to do

Ayurvedic massage

Wedagedara, *76b Deveni Rajasingha Mawatha, T081-222 6790, www.ayurveda wedagedara.com*. Authentic treatments, 1-hr head, body massage and steam bath, resident Ayurveda doctor.

Buddhist institutes and cultural centres

Alliance Française, *642 Peradeniya Rd, T081-222 4432*. Has a library and also shows films (Mon-Sat 1100-1700).

British Council, *88/3 Kotugodella Veediya, T081-222 2410, www.britishcouncil.org/srilanka*. Has a library plus old British papers and magazines (Tue-Sat 0900-1700).

Buddhist Publication Centre, *54 Sangharaja Mawatha, T081-223 7283. Daily 0900-1630*. Good library, a bookshop and information on courses on Buddhism and meditation where serious visitors are welcome.

Dhamma Kuta Vipassana Meditation Centre, *Madhyama Palata, www.dhamma.org*. Goenka-style 10-day Vipassana meditation retreats. Check website for course dates throughout the year.

Cricket

Asgiriya Stadium, *northwest of town*. Hosts Test matches and 1-day internationals.

Pallekelle International Cricket Stadium, *east of town*. Newer. Hosted a match during the 2011 Cricket World Cup.

Swimming

Non-residents pay Rs 250 (includes use of towel) at these hotels; see Where to stay, page 208, for details.

Hotel Suisse has a large pool but during the peak season (Dec-Feb) it gets crowded. **Queens Hotel** has a pool (no chlorine), which is very clean and usually very quiet. **Mahaweli Reach** has the best pool but it is out of town. **Thilanka** pool has good views over town. **Topaz**'s uncrowded pool is worth visiting for an afternoon for the spectacular hill-top views.

Tennis

Kandy Garden Club, *Sangaraja Mawatha, T081-222 2675*. Floodlit for evening use.

Tour operators

Sri Lanka Eco Trekking, *T077-706 7314, www.srilankaecotrekking.com*. Popular outfit specializing in nature trails and the Knuckles mountain range. Variety of treks and camps available. Founder Anil Weerakoon has spent many years in the jungles researching the aboriginal Veddah people of Sri Lanka.
Sri Lanka Trekking, *c/o Expeditor Tourist Inn (see Where to stay, page 209), T081-223 8316, www.trekkingexpeditor.com*. Run by Mr Sumane Bandara Illangantilake who has 40 years' experience in leading small groups on tours of the island. Specializes in trekking and nature tours (he can recognize over 200 bird calls) as well

as rafting. Trips arranged according to experience, ranging from 'smooth' to 'adventure', lasting 4-14 days. Mr Sumane's pupil **Ravi Desappriya** specializes in trips to the Knuckles Range, T071-499 7666, www.knucklesrange.com. These can range from 1 day to 3 days/2 nights.

Whitewater rafting

There are opportunities for rafting on the Mahaweli River, starting from near the **Cinnamon Citadel**, and in the Dumbara Hills.

Transport

Bus

The **Clocktower Bus Stand** and **Market Place Bus Stand** are for buses to 'local' destinations, including Peradeniya, Katugastota and Hantane (see below). **Goods Shed Bus Stand** near the railway station is for long-distance buses. The tourist information desk in the Kandy shopping

mall (see page 211) is an excellent source of up-to-date information on bus times, where to catch them from and where to get off.

Local Buses from the Clocktower Bus Stand drop visitors near the **Gadaladeniya Temple**. There are hourly buses between Kandy and **Embekke village**, a short walk away from the *devale*. For **Nattarampota**, catch bus No 655 from the Market Bus Stand and get off at the suspension bridge across the river from the **Deqaldoruwa Cave Temple**. For **Medawala**, bus No 603 departs from the Clocktower Bus Stand near the Central Market in Kandy. For the **Ceylon Tea Museum**, take bus No 655 (Uduwela bus) from the Clocktower Bus Stand; get off at the 4th mile post about 30 mins later, alternatively take a 3-wheeler. This bus runs on to **Hindagala Temple**. Regular buses to **Peradeniya** from the Market Place Bus Station stop outside the entrance.

Long distance Frequent buses to **Colombo**, Rs 100, 3½ hrs, last bus 2200; a/c buses (intercity express) leave from Station Rd and take 2½ hrs, Rs 250, but are often congested, nerve-wracking and far less pleasant than the train. To **Anuradhapura**, every 30 mins, 4 hrs. Both CTB and private buses run approximately every 30 mins to **Nuwara Eliya**, **Dambulla** and **Badulla**. For

Polonnaruwa and **Trincomalee** (5 hrs), a/c buses leave every 2 hrs. There is 1 direct bus a day to **Sigiriya** at 0800.

Train
Tickets on the Observation Car between Kandy and **Colombo** or **Badulla** should be reserved up to 10 days in advance (window open 0530-1730). Return tickets are valid for 10 days. Intercity express to **Colombo** at 0610 and 1500 (1st class Rs 360 including observation car fare, 2nd class Rs 190, 3rd class Rs 105, 2½ hrs), plus slower trains stopping at **Rambukkana** (for **Pinnawela**, see above) at 0140, 0630, 1040, 1530 and 1625 (2nd class Rs 190, 3rd class Rs 105, 3¼ hrs). For coastal destinations south of Colombo, such as **Hikkaduwa** and **Galle**, take the 0525, which travels on to **Matara** (you cannot make reservations on this train; 2nd class Rs 360, 3rd class Rs 195, 7¼ hrs). For **Kurunegala**, **Anuradhapura** and other destinations north change at Polgahawela Train to **Badulla** (Rs 750/Rs 270/Rs 145, 7¾ hrs) leave at 0820 and 2200, via **Nanu Oya** (for **Nuwara Ellya**, Rs 300/Rs 160/Rs 90, 4 hrs), **Haputale** (5½ hrs, Rs 380, Rs 210, Rs 115), **Bandarawela** (6 hrs, Rs 420, Rs 230, Rs 125) and **Ella** (6½ hrs, Rs 440, Rs 240, Rs 130). Observation car fee Rs 50 extra. Trains to **Matale** (Rs 100, Rs 50, Rs 25, 1¼ hrs) at 0500, 0710, 1020, 1400, 1710 and 1840.

Around Kandy
botanical gardens, Buddhist temples, tea artefacts and the imposing Knuckles Range

A short distance west of Kandy, Peradeniya is famous for its magnificent botanic gardens, which have justly earned the town a place on most itineraries. Beyond is a group of 14th-century temples which display the ancient artistic skills of the islanders. The traditions continue to be practised in the crafts villages nearby. There are more temples and villages to explore to the east of town, overlooked by the richly vegetated Dumbara Hills.

★ **Peradeniya** *Colour map 2, C4.*
6 km southwest of Kandy. Daily 0730-1800. Rs 1100, students and children (under 12) Rs 550.
A useful map is handed out with the tickets.

Conceived originally in 1371 as the queen's pleasure garden, Peradeniya became the residence of a Kandyan prince between 1747 and 1782 where royal visitors were entertained. The park was converted into a 60-ha botanical garden in 1821, six years after the fall of the last Kandyan king.

There are extensive well-kept lawns, pavilions, an Orchid House with an outstanding collection, an Octagon Conservatory, fernery, banks of bamboo and numerous flower borders with cannas, hibiscus, chrysanthemums, croton and colourful bougainvillaea. The tank has water plants, including the giant water lily and papyrus reeds. You will see unusual exotic species, especially palms (palmyra, talipot, royal, cabbage), and *Ficus elastica* (latex-bearing fig or 'Indian rubber tree' with buttress roots), an amazing avenue of drunken looking pines and some magnificent old specimen trees. In all, there are about 4000 labelled species. A signboard at the entrance, with a map, features a

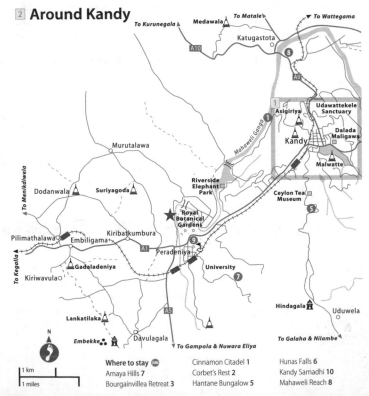

2 **Around Kandy**

Where to stay 😑
Amaya Hills **7**
Bourgainvillea Retreat **3**

Cinnamon Citadel **1**
Corbet's Rest **2**
Hantane Bungalow **5**

Hunas Falls **6**
Kandy Samadhi **10**
Mahaweli Reach **8**

numbered circuit from 1-30. The suggested route below closely follows this in reverse. It is best to keep to the paths to avoid the invisible large holes in the rough grass.

A suggested walk is to start at the **Spice Garden** (to the right of the entrance) which has many exotic spices (eg cardamom, cloves, pepper, vanilla). Follow the road to the right (east) to take in the **Orchid House**. Just off Palmyra Avenue there are Javanese Almond trees with amazing roots. The palmyra leaf was used for ancient manuscripts. The **Cabbage Palm Avenue** from South America was planted in 1905. You can then walk along the **Royal Palm Avenue** (1885) – you will notice the fruit bats in quite large colonies hanging in many of the trees. This meets the **River Drive,** which follows the course of the Mahaweli Ganga. Follow the drive to the **Suspension Bridge,** which is about halfway around the River Drive, and you can, if you wish, go back via the Royal Palm Avenue. This goes through the **Great Circle**, a large grassy central area around which are further specimens planted by a remarkably diverse list of dignitaries; alongside generations of English royalty, there are trees planted by Indira Gandhi, Yuri Gagarin, Marshal Tito, U Thant and Harold Macmillan. Between the Great Circle and the Great Lawn is the **Herbarium**. Try not to miss one of the rarest plants in the gardens – the Coco de Mer; you will find it on the path leading to George Gardner's monument, on your right as you return to the exit (or left as you enter the park). This plant has the largest and heaviest fruit (or nut) in the plant kingdom, weighing on average some 10-20 kg. Coco de Mer takes between five and eight years to mature and is surprisingly productive. It is not unusual to have over 20 nuts on one tree. They are all carefully numbered. Native Coco de Mer are only found on Praslin, an island in the Seychelles. Carry on along this path to get to the **Memorial**, a dome shaped structure. George Gardner was Superintendent of the gardens from 1844-1849. From here you overlook the lily tank which is surrounded by giant bamboo, some 40 m tall (it grows at 2-3 cm a day).

Other sights in Peradeniya Outside the gardens a bridge across the Mahaweli River takes you to the **School of Tropical Agriculture** at Gannoruwa, where research is carried out into various important spices and medicinal herbs as well as into tea, coffee, cocoa, rubber, coconuts and varieties of rice and other cash crops. The **Economic Museum** has botanical and agricultural exhibits.

Peradeniya Rest House **9**
Polwaththla Eco Village **11**
Rangala House **4**

Peradeniya is also the home of the **Sri Lanka University** (1942), built in the old Kandyan style in an impressive large park with the Mahaweli Ganga running through it. It is worth visiting the small teaching collection **museum** in the Department of Archaeology ① *call ahead, T035-238 8345 ext 518.*

West of Peradeniya *Sights further west are covered on page 197.*

Gadaladeniya Rajamaha Viharaya ① *1 km south of the main road, Rs 300.* The Buddhist temple is built on a rock in a beautiful hilltop setting. Constructed of stone and showing the influence of Indian temple architecture, it has lacquered doors, carvings and frescoes and a moonstone at the entrance to the shrine. The brick superstructure, shaped like a stupa, has an octagonal base. The inscriptions on the rock by Dharmakirti date it to 1344. The principal gilded image of the Buddha (18th century, which replaced the original destroyed by the Portuguese) is framed by elaborate *makara* decoration. Unusually, there is also a shrine to Vishnu here. Outside, there is a covered stupa and a Bodhi tree.

At **Kiriwavula village** nearby, craftsmen cast brass ornaments by the ancient lost-wax (*cire-perdu*) process. Some are for sale. To get to the village take a left turn off the A1 near Pilimathalawa. Highly recommended.

Lankatilaka Mahaviharaya ① *Hiripitiya, 4 km south of Gadaladeniya, Rs 300.* The second monument of the group sits on top of the rock Panhalgala. King Bhuvanekabahu IV (ruled 1341-1351) moved the Sinhalese capital from Kurunegala to Gampola nearby. When a monk reported the extraordinary vision of an elusive golden pot on the water of the tank here, the King saw this as a sign and had the temple built. He appears among the wall paintings.

The present two-storeyed, blue-washed brick structure was originally four storeys high. It was renovated and the tiled roof was added in 1845 after the two top storeys had fallen. You climb up a rock-cut stairway to the moonstone at the entrance and the finely carved wooden doorway flanked by guardian *gajasinghas* (elephant-lions). The inner image house, containing fine gold plated images of the Buddha, is surrounded by a *devale*. The walls and ceiling have well-preserved frescoes, some of the oldest and best examples of the Kandyan temple style. The west door has carved figures of Hindu gods (Saman, Skanda, Ganapathi and Vibhisena among others). There is a large rock inscription dating the temple to the 13th century. Craftsmen can be seen carving wood at the base of the rock.

Embekke Devale ① *1.5 km south of Lankatilaka, Rs 300.* The Hindu *devale*, dedicated to God Kataragama (Skanda), is south along a track through pleasant cultivated fields. The temple with its sanctuary, Dancing Hall and the Drummers' Hall, is famous for its carved wooden pillars (which may have once adorned the Audience Hall in Kandy), which sport vibrant figures of soldiers, wrestlers, dancers, musicians, mythical animals and birds. You can see similar stone pillars at the remains of the old Pilgrim's Rest nearby. The patterned roof tiles are attractive too. The village has craftsmen working in silver, brass and copper.

Tip...

If you have your own transport, you can combine a visit to the gardens and some temples with a visit to the Pinnawela Elephant Orphanage (see page 199). For a temple loop on foot, you could take the bus to Embekke, walk to Lankatilaka, finishing at Galadeniya, which is close to the main road.

North of the A1 If you have your own transport and wish to visit the **Suriyagoda Vihare**, turn off north from the A1 at Kiribatkumbura, signed to Murutalawa. The present 18th-century *vihara*, on a 15th-century site, has striking Kandyan wall paintings. North of Embiligama (Km 105 post), the 17th-century **Dodanwala Devale** was built by Rajasinha II. It is where the king is believed to have offered the deity his crown and sword after defeating the Portuguese. From Embiligama, to reach the textile weaving village of **Menikdiwela**, after a short distance along the Murutalawa road take the left fork for 6 km.

North of Kandy

Northwest of Kandy, across the Mahaweli Ganga, **Medawala Viharaya** is an interesting temple that marked a Buddhist revival. It was built in the 18th century where an older 14th-century temple stood. Interesting features include the small image house built in wood and wattle-and-daub, raised above the ground on stone pillars, similar to the old Kandyan grain stores. The railed balcony forms the Pradakshina Path. Inside, the marble Buddha image sits in front of a decoratively carved and painted wooden panel with representations of a Bodhi tree, protective gods, disciples and dragons. The fine Kandyan paintings on the side walls show a line of saints and disciples along the lower level and tales from the *Jatakas* along the middle (unfolding from the back of the room, to the front). Above this, the murals on the left show the weeks after the Buddha's Enlightenment, and those on the right, the 16 holiest places for Buddhists.

East of Kandy

At Nattarampota, in the beautiful Dumbara Valley, 7 km east of Kandy, you can watch traditional craftspeople at work. At **Kalapuraya Craft Village** artisans work in village homes with brass, copper, silver, wood, leather, etc. Prices are better than elsewhere but not fixed. Take a left turn down a lane off the Digana road.

Degaldoruwa Cave Temple, at Gunnepana, 3 km north of Nattarampota, has vivid wall paintings of *Jataka* stories dating from the 18th century. There is a dance academy here.

About 1.5 km along the Kalapura road from Nattarampota Junction on the Kandy–Kundasala road, the unusual incomplete 14th-century **Galmaduwa Temple** was an attempt to combine the features of Sinhalese, Indian, Islamic and Christian architectural styles.

Knuckles Forest Reserve ⓘ *Visiting hours daily 0600-1800. Rs 575, plus guide fees. Best time to visit Jan-Apr; be prepared for leeches. For tours, see page 214.* The **Dumbara Hills** northeast of Kandy incorporate peaks towering over 1500 m, thought to look like the knuckles of a fist, hence the popular name. With an annual rainfall of 2500-5000 mm, it follows that a wide variety of forest types exist here, from lowland dry patana to montane wet evergreen with their associated trees, shrubs, plants and epiphytes. These forests, in turn, harbour wildlife including leopard, sambar, barking deer, mouse deer, wild boar, giant squirrel, purple-faced langur, toque macaque and loris, as well as the otherwise rarely seen otter. More than 120 bird species recorded here include many endemic ones including the yellow-fronted barbet, dusky-blue flycatcher, Ceylon lorikeet, Ceylon grackle, yellow-eared bulbul and Layard's parakeet. Endemic amphibians and reptiles include the Kirtisinghe's rock frog and leaf-nosed lizard, which are only found here.

The importance of the range as a watershed for the Mahaweli River and the Victoria reservoir has led the government to designate the area over 1500 m as a conservation area. Soil and water conservation have become critical issues because of the way the area has been exploited so far. Cardamom cultivation, the removal of timber and fuelwood, the use of cane in basket making and the production of treacle from kitul have all been sources of concern.

South of Kandy

Ceylon Tea Museum ⓘ *3 km south of town along Hantane Rd (past the hospital), T081-380 3284, www.ceylonteamuseum.com. Tue-Sun 0830-1630 (last tickets 1530). Rs 250, students Rs 100.* Opened in December 2001, the government-backed Ceylon Tea Museum proudly claims to be the first of its kind in the world. Located in an old tea factory abandoned in 1986, it contains some impressive old machinery, polished up and laid out in manufacturing sequence, collected from various disused plantations around the highlands. The first floor holds the archive of James Taylor who set up the first tea plantation at Loolecondera in 1867, with some interesting curios such as the oldest extant packet of Ceylon Tea (still in its original packaging) and a photograph of the largest tea bush in the world, as well as a history of Thomas Lipton. The top floor has been converted into a restaurant and has a telescope for viewing the surrounding hills.

To the south, the **Hindagala Temple**, along the Galaha Road, has sixth-century rock inscriptions. The wall paintings date from different periods.

Listings Around Kandy *map p216*

Where to stay

Very pleasant accommodation is also available at the Victoria Golf Club, see What to do.

$$$$ Bourgainvillea Retreat
Victoria Golf and Country Resort, Rajawella, east of Kandy, T077-029 1896, www.bv-retreat.com.
Beautiful Tuscan-style villa on the edge of the golf course with stunning views. Chic rooms, lovely pool and delicious food. Naturally proximity to golf course takes care of some people's activities, but for others you can immerse yourself in nature, chill by the pool or go for tea and chat with local artists Raju and Radrani – highly recommended.

$$$$-$$$ Kandy Samadhi Centre
Kukul Oya Rd, east of Kandy, T077-771 0013, www.kandysamadhicentre.com.
Filled with beautiful antiques and dotted through the hills along the river, this stunning spacious resort has a beautiful

yoga space, Ayurvedic centre with in-house doctor and meditation pavilions. Each room has a unique feel – you can choose from the Shrine Room, Knuckles Pavilion, Mud House or the stunning Honeymoon Pavilion. Beautiful restaurant serves up delicious vegetarian food. Recommended.

$$$ Cinnamon Citadel
124 Srimanth Kuda, Ratwatte Mawatha, 5 km west of Kandy on Mahaweli River, T081-223 4365, www.cinnamonhotels.com.
121 large, comfortable a/c rooms (24 deluxe) with attractive door paintings, 2 restaurants, large pool, terrace gardens, popular with groups. Stunning river views.

$$$ Rangala House
92b Bobebila, Makuldeniya, 1 hr east of Kandy on a rough road, T081-240 0294, T077-600 4687, www.rangalahouse.com.
A converted tea-planter's bungalow with beautiful views from the veranda, Close to Knuckles and Corbett's Gap. Excellent

walking and birdwatching, solar-heated swimming pool. British and Sri Lankan management. Transport from Kandy available and pick-ups from the airport. Whole villa, US$290, or the 3 rooms can be booked individually, good discount when take the whole place. Excellent food. Recommend 2-night minimum stay.

$$$-$$ Hanthana House
108 Thapodarama Rd, Hanthana, T077-737 4560, www.hanthanahouse.com.
Pathi and Suba provide a sparkling welcome in their comfortable and spotless family home, set in a secluded, bird-filled valley above Kandy. Large en suite rooms come with sleek polished concrete floors. Pathi is a wonderful and obliging host with his finger on the pulse of the Sri Lankan travel scene, while Suba dishes up superb meals and offers cooking classes using produce from the garden. Highly recommended.

$$$-$$ Polwaththa Ecolodge
69/1 Wepathana, Gumagoda, east of Kandy, T072-175 1951, www.polwaththa-ecolodges.com.
Eco-conscious resort aiming to reduce their footprint and respect the nature that is their home. Lovely lake view lodges, wood cabins and mud houses – immerse yourself in nature. Water is heated by wood fires and the resort itself uses local resources and local traditions.

$$ Peradeniya Rest House
50 m east of the garden entrance, Peradeniya, 1035-238 6468.
Former residence of Captain Dawson, 10 fairly basic fan and a/c rooms, next to the noisy main road, overpriced. Better as a lunch stop.

$ Corbet's Rest
In the Knuckles Range east of Kandy, Karambaketiya, T011-286 8625 (Colombo).
5 cottages built on the hillside that blend well with their surroundings. There are dorms rooms, camping, restaurant. Popular with trekkers and birdwatchers, and there is a trekking guide on site.

$ Hantane Bungalow
Hantane Tea Estate, 6 km south, T077-157 8180 (caretaker).
4 rooms in cottage with lovely gardens, beautiful peaceful spot high above Kandy with panoramic views over Knuckles and Hatton Hills, horse riding possible. Whole cottage available for rent (**$$$**).

What to do

Golf
Victoria Golf Club, *Rajawella, 21 km east, off A26, T081-237 6376, www.golfsrilanka. com.* Excellently maintained 6879-yd, par 73 course surrounded on 3 sides by Victoria Reservoir with the Knuckles Range providing a further attraction. A round, including green fees, caddy, club and shoe hire will cost around Rs 5000 during the week, extra Rs 1000 at weekends. Some larger hotels in Kandy will provide free transfer for residents. There are also very pleasant a/c and fan chalets and bungalows available for visitors (you don't have to be golf fans), T077-784 0894. Check out the beautiful **Bourqainvillea Retreat** which is situated (see Where to stay) next to the course.

Riding
Victoria Saddle Club, *Rajawella, just before golf course, T081-237 6376*. Offers lessons (Rs 2500), pony rides for young children and accompanied trail rides for experienced riders (Rs 2000-3000). Phone in advance for information and booking.

Central
Highlands

Steep mountain passes snake up through the brooding highland landscape south of Kandy, reaching their pinnacle in the Peak Wilderness Sanctuary. To the east, the plateau of the Horton Plains represents the island's last stretch of high montane forest.

It was not until the 19th century and the coming of the British that Sri Lanka's wild and impenetrable rainforest gave way to the familiar, intensively cultivated tea plantations of today. The British legacy has lingered here, most notably in the anachronistic hill station of Nuwara Eliya, nicknamed 'Little England'. Equally distinctive is the Indian Tamil culture, which dates back to the same era when migrant plantation workers were brought in from southern India. But the area's greatest appeal lies in its cool, crisp air and the natural beauty of its scenery, carved by mountain streams and powerful waterfalls.

In 2010 UNESCO added the Central Highlands to its World Heritage list, officially recognizing the biodiversity of the Peak Wilderness Protected Area, Horton Plains National Park and the Knuckles Conservation Forest.

By either rail or road, the journey up into the Central Highlands offers some spectacular views, climbing through tea estates and passing close to some magnificent waterfalls. From Kandy you can either follow the direct route to Nuwara Eliya along the A5, or take the much longer but very scenic road over the Ginigathena pass to Hatton.

Gampola
Both the main routes into the highlands start by crossing the Mahaweli Ganga, passing through Peradeniya and then following the river valley south to the pleasant town of Gampola, a mediaeval Sinhalese capital. The Niyamgampaya *vihara,* which has some interesting stone carvings, is built on the site of the original 14th-century temple which was mostly built of brick and wood and has largely disappeared. From Gampola a road leads off towards the **Ginigathena Pass** for the alternative Adam's Peak route through the tea estates of the Hatton-Dickoya region (see page 227), but most people continue on the more direct A5. Shortly after Gampola the road crosses the river and starts the long climb of almost 1000 m up through some of the highest tea gardens in the world to Nuwara Eliya.

A5 to Nuwara Eliya
Pussellawa is a busy shopping centre and has a rest house where you can stop for a meal or a drink. The tea gardens begin just below Pussellawa. The craggy hill **Monaragala** appears to the south. Legends tell that this is where King Dutthagamenu hid in a rock while escaping from his father, who had imprisoned him.

Some 5 km later the road passes the Helbodda Oya river. By **Ramboda**, you have climbed to 1000 m. There is a fine 100-m waterfall with a twin stream on the Puna Ela, a tributary of the Mahaweli River, just off the road which can be seen from the bazaar. It may be possible to visit the **Rang Buddha Tea Estate** here.

After 54 km from Kandy the road climbs through a series of hairpins to the **Weddamulla Estate**, with great views to the west over Kothmale Reservoir. The area is covered with pine trees and ferns.

The twisty road runs alongside the 415-ha **Mackwood's Labookellie Estate** (see below) for miles along the hillside. Teams of women pluck the tea on fairly steep slopes, using plastic sacks as raincoats in wet weather. From the estate it is a short climb through more tea gardens to the narrow pass above Nuwara Eliya, and the road then drops down into the sheltered hollow in the hills now occupied by the town.

Mackwood's Labookellie Estate ⓘ *T052-223 5146, guided tours in English (and other languages) every 20 mins, free.* This is one of the island's largest tea estates. The women tea-pickers are all Tamils, descendants of the labourers who migrated from Tamil Nadu before Independence. They are keen to pose for photographs, and, as they earn very little, tipping is customary. The tea factory, an enormous corrugated iron building, welcomes visitors to drop in to the delightful tea centre and sample a free cup of tea, indulge in a piece of chocolate cake and, perhaps, buy a packet or two of tea, though there is no pressure to do so. The tour is quite informative – all stages of the process from picking, drying, oxidation and grading are shown if you go in the morning.

To Nuwara Eliya via the Ginigathena Pass

The alternative, much longer, route to Nuwara Eliya takes you within striking distance of **Adam's Peak**, running close to the railway line for much of the way. It is a full day's journey, for which the train, despite its snail-like pace, offers a relaxing alternative.

From Gampola, the B43 branches to the right towards Nawalapitiya and then joins the A7, the main Colombo–Nuwara Eliya road, at the Ginigathena Pass (38 km). There are magnificent views at the top, although they are often obscured by cloud, for the pass is in one of the wettest areas of Sri Lanka. **Ginigathena** itself is a small bazaar for the tea estates and their workers. (A right turn here takes you west on the A7 down to the

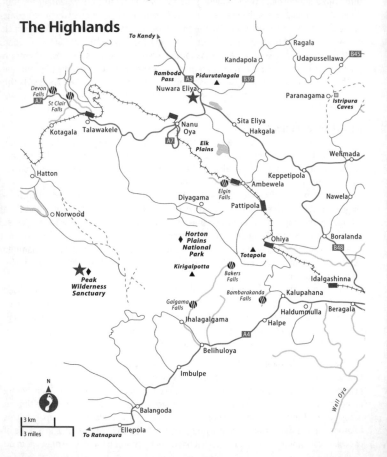

The Highlands

attractively located village of Kitulgala; see page 240). Heading southeast, the road winds up through a beautiful valley, surrounded by green, evenly picked tea bushes to **Watawala** (10 km) and past the **Carolina Falls** nearby, which are spectacular in the wet season. It then follows the Mahawelia Ganga to Hatton; the railway runs in the same direction on the opposite side of the river. The air becomes noticeably cooler, and occasionally there are views right across the plains to Colombo and the Kelaniya Valley. From Hatton it is a couple of hours' drive to **Dalhousie**, the most practical base for climbing Adam's Peak, Sri Lanka's holiest mountain (see page 237).

Beyond Hatton the A7 takes you past some spectacular waterfalls and winds through the heart of some of the finest tea-growing country in the world. For much of the way it is above 2000 m and runs through drier country in the rain shadow of hills to the southwest and northeast.

There are some magnificent views on the road towards Talawakele as it winds through the tea estates of Dimbula. Opposite the viewpoint for the 98-m **Devon Falls**, an enormous bronze tea boiler introduces you to the **St Clair Tea Centre**, a good place to stop for a brew. Beyond, you'll spy the 80-m **St Clair Falls**, dropping in three cascades down to the valley below. The road climbs as it crosses the railway line into **Talawakele**. Here, **Sri Lanka's Tea Research Institute** has played a major role in improving Sri Lanka's tea production (visits are possible if you get a permit from the Institute's office). From Talawakele, the A7 continues to **Lindula** (where a turning leads up a beautiful mountain road to Agrapatana) and Nanu Oya, before dropping towards Nuwara Eliya.

> ## **Best** places for a cuppa
> Tea tasting at Mackwood's Labookellie
> Tea Estate, page 223
> High tea at the Grand Hotel, Nuwara
> Eliya, page 230
> Tea for two in the railway carriage at the
> Tea Factory, page 231
> Afternoon tea at Tea Trails, page 239

Where to stay

A5 to Nuwara Eliya

$$$-$$ Ramboda Falls
Rock Fall Estate, 76 Nuwara Eliya Rd,
Ramboda, T052-225 9582,
www.rambodafalls.com.
20 rooms and chalets with hot bath and
excellent views, good restaurant, bar and
natural pool.

$$$-$$ Taprospa Labookellie Villa
Labookellie Tea Estate, T077-309 5516,
www.taprospa.com.

3 planters' bungalows furnished with
antiques and great views.

$$ Heritage Rest House (CHC)
Pussellawa, T081-247 8397,
www.chcresthouses.com
Colonial bungalow in an attractive
location, 3 rather dated rooms with bath.
Pleasant (though steep) terrace garden
at back with good views across the
valley compensates. Seating under large
permanent sun umbrellas covered with
the exotic 'ladies slipper' vine.

Nuwara Eliya and around   *Colour map 3, A5.*

take a trip to Little England

Nuwara Eliya (pronounced Noo-ray-lee-ya) is one of those curiosities of history – a
former British hill station. Vestiges of colonial rule are found everywhere, from the
fine golf course threading through town to the creaking grand hotels, complete
with overboiled vegetables and leaky roofs.

Visitors respond to Nuwara Eliya's fading appeal in different ways: some are delighted
by the tongue-in-cheek revelry in its colonial past; others are turned off by the town's
lack of civic pride, depressed by its English climate (nights can get very cold), or simply
confused by its archaism. For most though Nuwara Eliya represents nostalgic fun. Sri
Lanka's highest town (altitude 1990 m) remains a popular escape from the plains at long
weekends and especially during the April 'season'. It is surrounded by excellent walking
country and is a useful base for visiting Horton Plains.

Sights and walks

There are attractive walks round the small town, which has lawns, parks, an Anglican
church and the nostalgic **Hill Club**. To the south of town are the racecourse and Lake
Gregory (about 1 km from the town centre), for which boats which can be hired.
Lawns and lakeside paths are currently under construction here to make the area more
appealing to visitors.
  Nuwara Eliya is popular birdwatching country, and there are two excellent areas close
to town. **Galway's Land Bird Sanctuary** ① *daily 0600-1730, Rs 100,* covers 60 ha to the
north of Lake Gregory, while in **Victoria Park** ① *centre of town, daily 0700-1830, Rs 300,*
38 species have been identified. The park is pleasant, well kept and provides a welcome
escape from the congested New Bazaar. Take care when walking along the outside of the
park where the metal fence is in poor repair and has some sharp, rusty spikes.

Essential Nuwara Eliya

Finding your feet

Buses from Kandy, Colombo, Badulla and Hatton arrive in the centre of town at the private or CTB bus stands. There are also trains from Colombo and Kandy continuing to Badulla via Haputale. The train ride from Kandy to Nuwara Eliya is a scenic though time-consuming alternative to the bus. Booking is essential for the Observation Car, especially during busy periods; during the pilgrimage season it is often full as far as Hatton. The train station is 6 km from town at Nanu Oya, a short bus or taxi ride away (Rs 600). Avoid the touts who will offer free transport provided you go to a hotel of their choice; buses are always available and most hotels will arrange for taxis to collect you if contact them in advance. Ask to be dropped near the Town Hall if you are planning to stay in the southern part of town; most of the hotels are clustered up the hillside opposite the racecourse.

Fact...
Many Sri Lankans come to Nuwara Eliya to pick up a huge variety of vegetables at colourful roadside stalls – Sri Lanka's greengrocers.

Tip...
Never venture outside without an umbrella!

From Nuwara Eliya many travellers continue east to Badulla or Ella via Welimada, see page 243, or southeast from the Horton Plains to Haputale and Bandarawela, see page 250. Alternatively you can head west to Adam's Peak, and then return to Kandy, or back to Colombo, via Kitulgala.

Getting around

The town (population 26,000) is fairly compact, so it is easy to get around on foot but carry a torch at night to avoid holes in the pavement leading to the sewers.

When to go

The town really comes alive during the April 'season' (see box, page 233), though accommodation is very expensive and hard to find at this time. It is often cold at night, especially during January and March, when there may be frosts, though these are also the driest months.

Pidurutalagala (Mount Pedro), the island's highest peak at 2524 m, is off limits to climbers for security of the island's first TV transmitter (but see box, page 229). **Single Tree Hill**, at 2100 m, is an alternative. The path to it winds up from Haddon Hill Road, beyond **Haddon Hill Lodge** (southwest of town), towards the transmission tower, through cultivated terraces and woods. The path then follows the ridge towards the north, through Shantipura, a small village and the island's highest settlement, eventually returning close to the golf course. This walk gives excellent views across Nuwara Eliya and beyond and takes three to four hours.

Tea estates around Nuwara Eliya

Pedro Tea Estate ① *3 km southeast of town on the Boralanda rd, T052-222 2016, Rs 200*, still uses some original machinery and is less commercialized than other estates. There are some very pleasant walks through the plantations here, especially down to the tank and

Nuwara Eliya

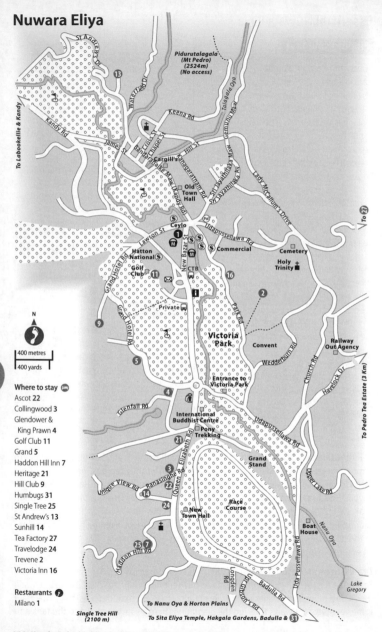

St Andrew's Dr

St Andrew's Dr

13

Pidurutalagala
(Mt Pedro)
(2524m)
(No access)

Watterfield Dr

Keena Rd

To Labookellie & Kandy

Kandy Rd

Jamek St

Bank Cross St

Badulla Chapel St

Cargill's

Hill St

Hill St

Gemunu Maw

Talagala Oya

Old Town Hall

Queen Eliza New Kandy Rd

Imperatnam Rd

Sri Jayatilaka Aw

Sri Jayatilaka Aw

Lady McCallum's Drive

To 27

27

Ceylo

Lawson St

1

M

New Bazar St

Udapussellawa Rd

S

S

Commercial

Cemetery

Holy Trinity

Hatton National

S

Golf Club

11

Bus Stand

CTB

16

2

Private

Grand Hotel Rd

Grand Hotel Rd

Park Rd

Convent

Wedderburn Rd

Church Rd

Havelock Dr

To Pedro Tea Estate (3 km)

Railway Out Agency

N

400 metres

400 yards

Victoria Park

9

5

Entrance to
Victoria Park

4

Glenfall Rd

Udapussellawa Rd

International
Buddhist Centre

Pony Trekking

21

Grand Stand

Upper Lake Rd

Unique View Rd

Ranasinghe

Queen Elizabeth Rd

3

22

14

24

New Town Hall

Race Course

Boat House

Nanu Oya

25

7

Haddon Hill Rd

Longden Rd

Johnston's Rd

Uda Pussellawa Rd

Badulla Rd

Lake Gregory

Single Tree Hill
(2100 m)

To Nanu Oya & Horton Plains

To Sita Eliya Temple, Hakgala Gardens, Badulla &

31

Where to stay

Ascot 22
Collingwood 3
Glendower &
  King Prawn 4
Golf Club 11
Grand 5
Haddon Hill Inn 7
Heritage 21
Hill Club 9
Humbugs 31
Single Tree 25
St Andrew's 13
Sunhill 14
Tea Factory 27
Travelodge 24
Trevene 2
Victoria Inn 16

Restaurants

Milano 1

BACKGROUND

An ascent of Pidurutalagala

In 1911 Hermann Hesse wrote an evocative description of his climb to the top of Pidurutalagala at the end of a journey round India and Ceylon. He wrote, "To bid India a proper and dignified farewell in peace and quiet, on one of the last days before I left I climbed alone in the coolness of a rainy morning to the highest summit in Ceylon, Pidurutalagala.

The cool green mountain valley of Nuwara Eliya was silvery in the light morning rain, typically Anglo-Indian with its corrugated roofs and its extravagantly extensive tennis courts and golf links. The Singhalese were delousing themselves in front of their huts or sitting shivering, wrapped in woollen shawls, the landscape, resembling the Black Forest, lay lifeless and shrouded.

The path began to climb upward through a little ravine, the straggling roofs disappeared, a swift brook roared below me. Narrow and steep, the way led steadily upward for a good hour. The rain gradually stopped, the cool wind subsided, and now and again the sun came out for minutes at a time.

I had climbed the shoulder of the mountain, the path now led across flat country, springy moor, and several pretty mountain rills. Here the rhododendrons grow more luxuriantly than at home, three time a man's height.

I was approaching the last ascent of the mountain, the path suddenly began to climb again, soon I found myself surrounded once more by forest, a strange, dead, enchanted forest where trunks and branches, intertwined like serpents, stared blindly at me through long thick, whitish beards of moss; a damp, bitter smell of foliage and fog hung between.

Then the forest came to an end; I stepped, warm and somewhat breathless, out onto a gray heath, like some landscape in Ossian, and saw the bare summit capped by a small pyramid close before me. A high, cold wind was blowing against me, I pulled my coat tight and slowly climbed the last hundred paces.

What I saw there was the grandest and purest impression I took away from all Ceylon. The wind had just swept clean the whole long valley of Nuwara Eliya, I saw, deep and immense, the entire high mountain system of Ceylon piled up in mighty walls, and in its midst the beautiful, ancient and holy pyramid of Adam's Peak. Beside it at an infinite depth and distance lay the flat blue sea, in between a thousand mountains, broad valleys, narrow ravines, rivers and waterfalls, in countless folds, the whole mountainous island on which ancient legend places paradise."

to Warmura Ella (ask at the tea centre). The estate can be visited on a Boralanda bus, or it is a taxi ride away; alternatively, for those feeling active, it is a very attractive walk.

The ★ **Heritance Tea Factory**, at Kandapola (30 minutes by taxi), has been innovatively converted into an award-winning hotel (see page 231) but still retains a small working unit and is well worth a visit. The original oil-driven engine, now powered by electricity, is still in place and switched on occasionally. It is a good place for lunch.

Labookellie Tea Estate is only 15 km away (see page 223).

Hakgala Botanical Gardens

10 km southeast of town, www.botanicgardens.gov.lk/hakgala. Daily 0800-1700. Rs 800, students/children Rs 400. Buses bound for Welimada or Bandarawela pass the entrance.

Established in 1861, the gardens are located within a Strict Natural Reserve and were once a Cinchona plantation. The name Hakgala or 'Jaw Rock' comes from the story in the epic *Ramayana* in which the Monkey god takes back a part of the mountainside in his jaw when asked by Rama to seek out a special herb. This delightful garden is now famous for its roses. The different sections covering the hillside include a plant house, Japanese garden, wild orchid collection, old tea trails, arboretum, fruit garden, rock garden and oaks. There are monkeys here which are quite used to visitors.

On the route to Hakgala Gardens you pass **Sita Eliya Temple**, a temple to Rama's wife which is thought to mark the spot where she was kept a prisoner by King Ravana. There are magnificent views.

Listings Nuwara Eliya *map p228*

Tourist information

Tourist information is available at www.nuwaraeliya.org.

Where to stay

Only a selection is listed here – there are more, especially on St Andrew's Dr. Some hotels are in the Raj style, well kept, with working fireplaces, good restaurants and plenty of atmosphere, and there are also a few good-value 'budget' places, mainly at the southern end of town. However, prices can rise by as much as 3 times during the Apr New Year rush, while long weekends can see prices double even if demand is low. It always pays to bargain. Usually bathrooms have hot water, though it may not always be on, and rooms have blankets provided. Avoid hotels introduced to you by touts, especially on the edge of town. Solo female travellers are advised to avoid Glenfall Inn.

Town centre

$$$$-$$$ St Andrew's (Jetwing)
10 St Andrews Dr, T052-222 3031, www.jetwinghotels.com.

52 good rooms in beautiful century-old building retaining a more homely colonial atmosphere than its rivals, good restaurant with show kitchen, attractive and pleasant garden, tubs, English-style country bar, good snooker room.

$$$ The Grand
Grand Hotel Rd, T052-867 8540, www.grand-hotel-nuwara-eliya-sri-lanka.en.ww.lk.
156 rooms in 2 wings: the Golf Wing is larger, carpeted and more comfortable than the Governor Wing. Also 2 presidential suites, 2 restaurants (1 ballroom sized, catering for package-tour buffets). Considerable colonial character in Victorian former governor's residence, efficient but can lack personal touch. Popular with tour groups. Shops, exchange and gym.

$$$ Hill Club
Up the path from The Grand, T052-222 2653.
Oozing colonial atmosphere, 39 well-furnished, comfortable rooms with fireplaces (hot water bottles in bed), including 2 **$$$** suites in 'modernized' 1930s Coffee Planter's Club, formal restaurant (jacket and tie for dinner, which can be borrowed), 2 bars (1 a 'casual bar'). Good public rooms (leaf

through the magazines in the faded leather armchairs of the library), excellent snooker room, tennis courts.

$$ Glendower
5 Grand Hotel Rd, overlooking the 2nd tee of the golf course, T052-222 2501, hotelglendower@hotmail.com.
Airy, comfortable rooms with teak floors, plus suites, stylishly decorated, attractive modern half-timbered bungalow-style hotel, pleasant lounge with good satellite TV, superb snooker table, **19th Hole Pub**, Chinese restaurant (big portions), friendly and efficient service, convenient for town.

$$ Heritage
96 Badulla Rd, opposite racecourse, T052-223 5750, www.the-heritage.srilanka.net.
Fine colonial house with 18 large, ebony furnished rooms in 2 wings (old wing better), including beautiful suite with art deco fireplace, fine sweeping staircase, restaurant, bar, open-air café outside for lunch packets. Ask for extra blankets at night.

$$ Single Tree
1/8 Haddon Hill Rd, T052-222 3009.
18 clean wood-panelled rooms, some with balcony, large beds, nice views, friendly, good tours (see Tour operators, page 234).

$$ Sunhill
18 Unique View Rd, T052-222 2878, sunhill@itmin.com.
20 good, carpeted rooms, though some a little damp, with attached hot bath. Deluxe rooms upstairs have balcony and TV.

$$ The Trevene
17 Park Rd, T052-222 2767, thetrevene@yahoo.com.
Colonial bungalow, family-run, 10 clean rooms, those at the front are larger and have fireplaces and period furniture. Internet, bike hire, good food, can arrange tours but enquire elsewhere regarding public transport.

$$-$ Golf Club
T052-222 2835, negolf@stlnet.lk.
Nuwara's best-kept accommodation secret (but only if you play a round). 11 cosy, comfortable rooms, new wing better, well-furnished, good beds, plenty of atmosphere.

$ Green Garden
16 Unique View Rd, T052-223 4166, www. hotelgreengardennuwaraeliya.com.
Family-run guesthouse with 8 carpeted rooms all with hot bath, deluxe with balcony and TV. Small restaurant serving home-cooked food.

$ Haddon Hill Inn
10 Haddon Hill Rd, T052-222 3304.
11 basic but clean and comfortable rooms, hot water, reasonable value.

Around Nuwara Eliya

$$$$ Heritance Tea Factory
Kandapola, east of Nuwara Eliya, T052-555 000, www.heritancehotels.com.
Winner of numerous awards, including a UNESCO Heritage Award, this superbly inventive conversion of an old British factory retains original features in its 57 comfortable rooms (best on top floor) including 4 suites. It is set amidst 10-ha tea plantation with magnificent views. There are 2 restaurants (eat at the 'TCK6685' restaurant – in a railway carriage), 9-hole putting green, riding, games, gym. Highly recommended for setting and originality.

$$-$ Humbugs
100 m beyond entrance to Hakgala gardens, T052-222 2709.
10 simple rooms, carpeted, hot water, balconies, quiet. Restaurant serves good snacks including strawberries and cream in season. Extensive views across the Uva basin, particularly attractive in the early morning mist. Good value.

ON THE ROAD
A superior cup

Many tea-drinkers believe that Sri Lankan tea, with its fine, rich flavour and bright, golden colour, is the best in the world. After textiles, tea remains Sri Lanka's second biggest export, and you will notice the distinctive cropped bushes all across the hill country. Although introduced by the British, the tea industry is a source of immense national pride, and recent years have seen some ingenious methods of capitalizing on the country's heritage. Near Nuwara Eliya, an old factory has been converted into a magnificent hotel, retaining its original features, while the world's first tea museum can be visited near Kandy. A visit to a working tea factory is also recommended.

Tea famously originated in China (though one legend suggests it was introduced by an Indian missionary), but it was not until 1833 that the Chinese monopoly on exporting tea was abolished and the East India Company began to grow tea in Assam in India. In Sri Lanka, the first tea bushes were planted in 1849 by James Taylor on a cleared hill slope just southeast of Kandy. It was an attempt to find a crop to replace the unfortunate diseased coffee. The experiment paid off and Sri Lanka today is the world's third biggest producer of tea, and the largest exporter, with a 20% share of global demand.

The bushes now grow from sea level to the highest slopes, though the lush 'low-grown' variety lacks the flavour, colour and aroma which characterize bushes grown above 1000 m. The slow-growing bushes at greater heights produce the best flavour and aroma when picked carefully by hand – just two leaves and bud.

The old 'orthodox' method of tea-processing produces the aromatic lighter coloured liquor of the Golden Flowery Orange Pekoe in its most superior grade. The fresh leaves are dried by fans on 'withering troughs' to reduce the moisture content and then rolled and pressed to express the juices which coat the leaves. These are then left to ferment in a controlled humid environment in order to produce the desired aroma. Finally, the leaves are dried by passing them through a heated drying chamber and then graded – the unbroken being the best quality, down to the 'fannings' and 'dust'.

The more common 'crushing, tearing, curling' (CTC) method produces tea which gives a much darker liquor. It uses machinery which was invented in Assam in 1930. The process allows the withered leaves to be given a short, light roll before engraved metal rollers distort the leaves in a fraction of a second. The whole process can take as little as 18 hours.

Despite its name and heritage, the Ceylon tea industry (as it is still called) has lost some of its dominance in the world market, cheaper producers having wrestled away traditional export markets. Britain, for example, which once absorbed 65% of total production, now only represents 3%, importing much of its lower grade tea from East Africa. Today Russia and the Middle East are the industry's biggest customers. In recent years, however, privatization and advances in production techniques have improved yields, and producers have responded to trends in the market, beginning to embrace the vogue for green, organic and flavoured teas.

ON THE ROAD
Compliments of the season

Throughout April, and particularly over Sinhalese and Tamil New Year, Nuwara Eliya is invaded by the Colombo set. A banner across the road proudly announces "Nuwara at 6128 ft: Welcome to the salubrious climate of Nuwara Eliya: cultured drivers are welcomed with affection"!

For several weeks, the normally sedate town throngs with visitors. Many come for a day at the races, beloved by all betting mad Sri Lankans, which conclude with the nine-furlong Governor's Cup. Motor racing also draws the crowds. Over 100 Formula Three cars hare around the hills at the Mahagastota Hill Climb, while the Fox Hill supercross at the nearby Diyatalawa circuit can be very exciting. Back in town, there are dances and beauty pageants, all culminating in the judging of the all-important flower show at the end of the month.

The town, of course, gets packed. Prices become inflated (tripled) and it is virtually impossible to find accommodation. Stallholders, mostly selling food and drink, pay vast amounts of money to rent a pitch alongside the main road by Victoria Park. Most hotels run all-night discos (the best is said to be at the Grand Hotel) and the crowds roam the streets for much of the night.

Restaurants

There are numerous cheap restaurants along Old and New Bazar Rds.

$$$ Hill Club
See Where to stay, page 230.
Receives mixed reviews for its food, but it's a unique dining experience: dress code after 1900 (jacket and tie though fewer constraints for women), 4-course meal served promptly at 2000 (US$17), courteous service.

$$ Grand Indian
The Grand, see Where to stay, page 230.
Excellent Indian restaurant open for lunch and dinner, serving curries, thalis and a wide selection of breads. Recommended.

$$ Milano
24 New Bazaar St, T052-222 2763.
Halal restaurant, tasty seafood, Chinese and Sri Lankan dishes, good portions, tempting wattapalam dessert, sales counter, no alcohol. Several similar restaurants nearby.

Bars and clubs

Try the Glendower, The Grand, St Andrew's and, most atmospherically, Hill Club, for old-fashioned ambience. See Where to stay, page 230.

Shopping

Cargill's (Kandy Rd) and Super K (14 New Bazaar), are both good supermarkets and sell a wide selection of tea. The **market** (west of New Bazaar St), sells warm jackets and fleeces, including some well-known brands, but bargain hard.

What to do

Boating and fishing
Boats and fishing equipment can be hired from the Lake Gregory boat house.

Golf
Nuwara Eliya is home to a beautiful and superbly maintained 5550-yard par 70 golf course, T052-222 2835. Rs 15000 for 18 holes, Rs 3000 for 1-hr practice session.

Pony-trekking
Available from large hotels (eg **St Andrew's**), and at the northwestern edge of the golf course.

Snooker
Available at the **Hill Club**, though those who play like Alex Higgins may like to note the "1 million rupees first tear" sign (presumably the 2nd one is free). 3 excellent tables at **The Grand** and at **St Andrew's**, and an antique table at **Glendower**.

Tennis
Good clay tennis courts at the **Hill Club**.

Tour operators
Most hotels and guesthouses can arrange tours to Horton Plains, the tea plantations and the waterfalls. Some also offer an Adam's Peak drop-off and return trip leaving at 2230. Prices do vary however, so it's worth asking around.
Single Tree, *see Where to stay*. Has a range of tours on offer and, at the time of writing, prices were reasonable. Can also organize treks to Single Tree Hill and the highest villages, and rafting trips to Kitulgala.

Transport

Bus To **Nanu Oya** every 30 mins. Frequent long-distance buses from both CTB and private bus stands to **Badulla** (via Hakgala, 2½ hrs); for **Haputale** and **Bandarawela**, change at Welimada. Plenty of buses to **Hatton** (intercity 1½ hrs, normal 2½ hrs) and to **Kandy** (3-4 hrs). Several a day to **Colombo** (6 hrs) including faster a/c intercity buses (5 hrs).

Train New arrivals are besieged by touts on the train and at the station who offer free transport to the hotel of their choice. You will end up paying heavily for this service in commission, so it's better to take the bus which waits for the arrival of trains, or take a taxi from the station or the main road. To **Colombo**, 0927 (6¼ hrs), 1227 (7 hrs), 2333 (7 hrs). To **Kandy** 1658 (4½ hrs). To **Badulla** (3½-4 hrs), via **Haputale** (1½-2 hrs), **Bandarawela** and **Ella** (2½-3 hrs), 0505, 0933, 1227, 1525.

Horton Plains National Park *Colour map 3, B5.*

a uniquely dramatic landscape

The island's highest (altitude 2130 m) and most isolated plateau is contiguous with the Peak Wilderness Sanctuary. Bleak and windswept, the landscape is distinctive and unlike any other on the island. It has been compared to both the Scottish highlands and the savannah of Africa.

Horton Plains' conservation importance lies in their role as the catchment area of most of the island's major rivers. Covering 3160 ha, the area was declared a national park in 1988, though had received some protection since 1873 when logging above 1500 m was prohibited. The plains are named after former British governor Sir Robert Horton.

Most people come on a day trip to see the spectacular views from the sheer 700-m drop at World's End though there is more to see within the sanctuary. In recent years, park fees have spiralled and budget travellers are increasingly choosing to forego a visit.

Flora and fauna
There is a mixture of temperate montane forest and wet patana grassland. The prominent canopy tree is the keena, its white flowers contrasting with the striking red rhododendrons

Essential Horton Plains National Park

Finding your feet

Horton Plains is accessible by car from Nuwara Eliya (32 km) and Haputale (38 km). Both journeys take around 1½ to two hours. A day trip is possible but will involve an early start (breakfast at 0600) as the plains have a reputation for bad weather after midday. Many guesthouses and hotels organize tours. By train, Haputale is the closest base for a day trip though World's End will probably have clouded over by the time you arrive. Ohiya is the nearest train station, 11 km from the entrance, from where you can take a taxi or walk. Trekkers can reach the park from Talawakale in the north on the Agrapatana–Diyagama track or from Belihuloya in the south via Nagarak, though this requires serious preparation.

Tip...

Carry food and water with you at all times.

Getting around

Horton Plains is unique amongst Sri Lanka's national parks in that walking is permitted. Keep to the footpaths, especially if misty; a number of people go missing each year.

Park information

Charges for foreigners add up to around US$15 (children under 12 US$10), an overnight pass is US$30. Fees are collected at the ticket offices at either end of the road bisecting the park. Locals and tourists have to pay just to use the road. There is a **visitor centre** at Farr Inn (daily 0600-1830), where information on the park's flora and fauna is displayed.

When to go

The best months to visit are April and August. The winter months tend to be the driest, with the best visibility, though can be very cold. The weather can be foul at any time, and it gets cold at night so come prepared. For World's End it is essential to arrive by 0930-1000, after which the area usually clouds over for the day. Avoid visiting at weekends and public holidays when it can be very noisy and busy.

---

lower down, which make the plains in some ways reminiscent of a Scottish moor. In other ways, the gently undulating grassland has an almost savannah-like feel with stunted forest on the hill tops. There is widespread concern about the condition of the forest, which appears to be slowly dying, probably due to acid rain.

The bleak and windswept area harbours many wild animals, including a few leopards though no longer any elephants. You may see sambar (*sambhur*), especially at dawn and dusk close to the entrance, and possibly toque macaques, purple-faced leaf monkeys and horned lizards. Wildlife has suffered at the hands of tourism though, with visitors' discarded plastic bags responsible for the death of large numbers of sambar. There is a rich variety of hill birds, and a number of endemics, including the dull blue flycatcher, Sri Lanka white-eye and yellow-eared bulbul, as well as a good range of butterflies. Some visitors are disappointed by how difficult it is to see the wildlife; it is possible to visit the plains and spot little more than the invasive crow. However by being attentive and patient an interesting variety of flora and fauna can be observed.

Trails

World's End Most people will take the well-trodden 4.5-km bridle path to **World's End**, returning in a loop via the scenic **Baker Falls**. The walk takes three to four hours return, depending on how many times you stop to admire the view. It is essential to visit early in the morning before the mists close in, after which only a wall of cloud is visible. You cross a small stream with lots of croaking frogs before passing across the grassland and then descending a few hundred metres through the forest. You first come to **Little (or Small) World's End** (2.5 km), a mere 260-m cliff overlooking a ravine (more a wide valley) with a tiny village 700 m below. You can look along the sheer cliff face to the big green rock which marks (Big) World's End about 1 km away. The path continues another 2 km up the escarpment to the astonishing (Big) World's End, a spectacular precipice with a 1050-m drop. On a clear day, you can apparently see the coast, but more realistic is a view of the blue-green lake of the Samanala Wewa reservoir project. Once at Big World's End, take the small path up the hill. After only a few yards, there is a split in the rock which gives an excellent view of the valley below. Return to the main path, and a track drops down to a

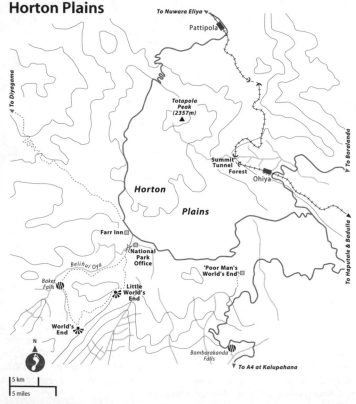

Horton Plains

To Nuwara Eliya ▼
Pattipola

To Diyagama ◄

Totapola Peak
(2357m) ▲

Summit Tunnel
Forest
Ohiya

To Boralanda ▼

Horton

Plains

Farr Inn ▢

National Park Office ▢

Belihul Oya

'Poor Man's World's End' ▢

To Haputale & Badulla ►

Baker Falls

Little World's End

World's End

N

Bambarakanda Falls

To A4 at Kalupahana ▼

5 km
5 miles

valley along which a 2-km walk leads to a small forested escarpment. A climb and then a scrambling descent (very slippery for the last few metres so take care) take you to the picturesque **Baker's Falls**. The water here is deliciously cool and refreshing, though it is said to be unsafe to swim. From Baker's Falls it is an easy 3-km walk back along the river, passing the attractive **Governor's Pool** (again prohibited to swim) on the way.

Poor Man's World's End Reached off the Ohiya–Kalupahana road, this used to be the free alternative to paying national park fees. At the time of writing, it was still accessible by several routes via the local tea plantations, but this may change. Ask locally for directions, or at guesthouses in Haputale.

Listings Horton Plains National Park

Where to stay

For all park accommodation, call the Wildlife Conservation Dept (T011-288 8585 or local 052 353 9042). Note though that park bungalows need to be booked well in advance and that visitors will have to pay for 2 days' admission to the park, as well as various add-ons to the accommodation costs. Caretakers cook the meals, but visitors must bring all provisions. It is also possible to camp in the park.

★ Adam's Peak (Sri Pada) *Colour map 3, B4.*

sacred mountain at the heart of Sri Lanka

Sacred to devotees of three of Sri Lanka's major religions, Adam's Peak (2260 m) is one of the island's most important pilgrimage sites. The giant 'footprint' on the summit is believed to be an imprint left by either the Buddha (hence 'Sri Pada', or 'Sacred Footprint') or Shiva (Sivan Adipadham) by Hindus, or Adam by Muslims. Regardless of belief, the perfectly conical-shaped mountain is worth the climb, both for the buzz and for the magnificent views, especially in the first rays of dawn.

Hatton to Dalhousie

Hatton is one of the major centres of Sri Lanka's tea industry and the base from which most pilgrims trek to the top of Adam's Peak, but the town itself is dirty and uninspiring.

It is a tortuously winding route from Hatton through Norwood up to Maskeliya at 1280 m, skirting the attractive **Castlereagh Reservoir**, an enormous HEP programme. If open it is worth stopping by the immaculately kept small stone **Anglican Church** (1878) at Warleigh in a picturesque setting overlooking the tank (give a donation). As you cross the dam, which is protected by the military, and pass through the new town of **Maskeliya** (the old one was flooded to make way for the tank), the pyramid shape of Adam's Peak begins to loom into view, looking for all the world like the Paramount Pictures logo. The air is already strikingly fresh, and the higher road is lined with tropical ferns. Stalls selling food and souvenirs for the pilgrims line the road as you descend into the makeshift settlement of **Dalhousie**. This is the best base for the climb to the summit.

Essential Adam's Peak (Sri Pada)

Finding your feet

The shorter (7 km) and more frequently used route is from the north, starting at Dalhousie (pronounced Dell-house). Much steeper, more difficult and more meritorious (for pilgrims) is the southern route from the Ratnapura side (11 km), starting from Palabadelle (see page 108). The really intrepid and fit could climb from Dalhousie and then walk down towards Ratnapura, a long but rewarding day.

When to go

The pilgrimage season runs from **Unduwap Poya** (December) to **Wesak Poya** (May), reaching its peak mid-season at **Medin Poya**. At this time, there is a constant stream of pilgrims and the top can get very crowded. The climb is still quite possible at other times of year, though you will need a torch at night as the path is not lit. It often rains in the afternoon here, especially in the off-season. Most people want to reach the summit for sunrise, for which you will need to set off around 0300. If it is wet, there will be leeches on the steps (see box, page 415); make sure you have plenty of warm clothes, as it takes a while for the sun to thaw out walkers and pilgrims alike. If climbing out of season, take a guide or climb with other people: the mountain can be dark and lonely.

> ### Tip...
> For further information, read Markus Akland's *The Sacred Footprint: A Cultural History of Adam's Peak* (Bangkok: Orchid Press, 2001).

The climb

Most people do the walk by moonlight, setting off from Dalhousie around 0300 and arriving in time to see the dawn when the sun rises behind the conical peak, casting an extraordinary shadow across the misty plains to the west. Note that it is very cold up here until well after sunrise so it is essential to take warm clothing.

It takes about three hours to reach the top (though allow an hour either way depending on your fitness). The path is clearly marked throughout, beginning fairly gently but rapidly becoming steeper, with constant steps from about halfway. The climb is completely safe, even on the steepest parts, and the route is lined with teashops and stalls if you need a break. In the company of pilgrims the trek is particularly rewarding but it can be very crowded. You may notice the first-timers with white cloth on their heads.

The summit

At the top, there are some breathtaking views across the surrounding hills, though the peak itself, only 50 m sq, is not particularly impressive. Steps lead up to the sacred footprint, on top of a 4-m rock, which is covered by a huge stone slab in which has been carved another print. Pilgrims cluster round, throwing offerings in to the 1-m hollow, before moving to the Saman shrine up another flight of stairs where thanks are given. Pilgrims then ring one of the two bells at the summit, each chime representing a successful ascent. There are three official processions a day – at dawn, midday and dusk – with music, offerings and prayers, though many people perform their own ceremonies at other times.

Where to stay

Hatton is the main centre; however there is basic accommodation available in Maskeliya and Dalhousie. Dickoya, 6 km south of Hatton on the Maskeliya Rd, has 2 estate bungalows managed by the Bank of Ceylon (www.ceybankholidayhomes.com). For accommodation at Ratnapura, see page 108.

$$$$ Ceylon Tea Trails
T011-774 5730 (Colombo), www.teatrails.com.
4 beautifully restored tea planters' bungalows are dotted through the area – the closest, Summerville, is 20 mins from Hatton, near Dickoya. Beautiful rooms and vistas and tea-inspired dining. Afternoon tea is quite the event. All rates are inclusive of gourmet food. To work it off, there are plenty of opportunities for walks and bike rides.

Hatton

$$ Lower Glencairn
T051-222 7845
5 large rooms with bath tub and hot water, no food and looking its age but good views.

$$ Upper Glencairn
T051-222 7845.
Beautiful 100-year-old bungalow in lovely gardens high on hill, good views, 5 well-furnished rooms, food available, very characterful.

$$-$ Hatton Rest House
1 km away from Hatton on Colombo Rd, T051-222 2751.
7 spartan rooms, locals' bar, run-down but good location overlooking valley.

Dalhousie

$$ Slightly Chilled Guest House
Formerly the Yellow House, near Wathsala Inn, T051-205 5502, www.slightlychilled.tv.
Popular guesthouse with large, bright rooms. Prices vary, some rooms are newer and some have balconies with views of Adam's Peak. Mountain bikes and motor bikes for hire, internet, restaurant serving good food, information on local treks and good tours. Popular so book ahead.

$$-$ River View Wathsala Inn
1 km before the bus stand in Dalhousie, T051-205 5505, www.adamspeakhotels.com.
14 rooms (most with hot bath), upstairs large and clean with balcony and good views of lake, downstairs more basic, restaurant and bar. Owners will organize pick-ups from Hatton and various trips, including whitewater rafting at Kitulgala.

$ White House
Near Wathsala Inn, T077-791 2009.
Clean, basic rooms some with hot water, in the main guesthouse. There are also basic wooden cottages in pleasant gardens. Guides and tours can be arranged. Friendly and cheap.

Restaurants

Teashops and foodstalls selling food line the approach to the mountain and the steps themselves. There's also good food at Slightly Chilled, see above.

Transport

Bus Buses run regularly to Dalhousie direct during the pilgrimage season from **Colombo**, **Kandy** and **Nuwara Eliya**. You may have to change in Hatton or Maskeliya during the off-season. Intercity buses run to Hatton from **Colombo** (4½ hrs) and normal buses from **Kandy** and **Nuwara Eliya** (each 3 hrs), with more during the pilgrimage season.

Train Trains run from **Hatton** (on the Colombo–Badulla line), with several trains a day to **Colombo** (6½ hrs), most (not all) via **Kandy** (2½ hrs), and to **Nanu Oya** (1½ hrs) and destinations further east.

★ Kitulgala *Colour map 2, A3.*

whitewater rafting on the Kelaniya River

Kitulgala is a small, peaceful village lining the main road descending gently from the highlands to Colombo. It lies on the banks of the Kelaniya River, 95 km east of Colombo, and is known as a centre for *kitul* honey production. There are some excellent places to stay in Kitulgala, so it is well worth a break on the route between the highlands and the coast. For details of the road west of Kitulgala towards Colombo, see page 103.

Sights

Aside from its beautiful setting, it has two other claims to fame which makes it well worth lingering. The first is that it provided the main location for the filming of David Lean's Oscar-winning film, *Bridge on the River Kwai*. You can wander down to the banks of the river to the site of the bridge in the film, signposted about 1 km before the Plantation Hotel (where you can pick up an interesting history of the filming), and guides will appear to show you the way. The area is surprisingly small, compared to the real bridge in Kanchanaburi, Thailand, and there is not much to see now, except for the concrete foundations of the bridge hewn into two rocks either side of the *ganga*, but for those familiar with the film the area will be recognizable. The sandbar from which the bridge was blown up has now been reclaimed by the jungle.

Some 5 km inland, near **Royal River Resort** (see Where to stay, opposite), at **Beli Lena**, are some part-excavated caves. Lying beneath a waterfall, under which you can bathe in the dry season, the caves are a wonderful place to watch butterflies and birds. Several skeletons and prehistoric tools have been found dating back 30,000 years. An old man looks after the site and will show you around (translation needed) but is so full of the dangers of the cave (vipers, cobras, even flying pigs – three once fell down the waterfall to their doom) that it's a wonder anyone survives a visit! The site is signposted off the main road. After 5 km, a track leads right at the sign for Kitulgala Tea Estate. The cave is a 1-km walk along the path from here.

Rafting

The other major reason to visit Kitulgala is that it is the base for the country's best **whitewater rafting**, which can be arranged at the local hotels or in Colombo. The rapids are grade III (grade IV during floods) and tend to start 5-6 km upriver, passing through six rapids to the 'bridge' area, where you can stop for a swim.

Where to stay

Most accommodation can arrange rafting trips.

$$$$ Royal River Resort
6 km inland, turning for Beli Lena (small sign) between Km 38 and Km 39 post, T036-527 3672, www.royal-river-resort-kitulgala-sri-lanka.en.ww.lk.
Environmentally harmonious small hotel, built around mini-HEP system from waterfall. 4 beautiful rooms, homely decor (antiques, opera posters, working fireplaces), wonderfully refreshing natural swimming pool built into rock. Wonderful secluded setting with local walks through tea and rubber plantations, good for birders. Sister hotel is the **Plantation**, see below.

$$$-$$ Kitulgala Rest House (CHC)
On riverbank before Km 37 post, T036-228 7783, www.chcresthouses.com.
19 pleasant, comfortable rooms (4 with a/c), with porches overlooking river. Restaurant and bar.

$$$-$$ Plantation Hotel
At Km 39 post, T036-471 1969, www.the-plantation-hotel-kitulgala-sri-lanka.en.ww.lk.
A fine refurbished colonial bungalow with comfortable though expensive a/c rooms with antique furniture, TV and hot water. Excellent riverside restaurants are a popular lunchtime stop for tour groups.

$$$-$$ Rafters Retreat
T036-228 7598, www.raftersretreat.com.
11 simple, but attractive wooden cabins in riverside forest setting, basic and no hot water. Restaurant overlooking the river serves good food. Runs adventure tours, trips to the caves, and is a good spot for rafting. Recommended.

What to do

Whitewater rafting trips can be arranged through the **Plantation Hotel** or **Rafters Retreat**, see above, and cost around US$30 including lunch.

Transport

Bus Buses between **Colombo** and **Hatton** or **Nuwara Eliya** pass through Kitulgala. To reach **Ratnapura** you must change in Avissawella.

Uva
Province

East of the Central Highland ridge are the picturesque hills of Uva Province, which stretches across the plains as far south as Kataragama. In contrast to the comparatively recently populated highland region, Uva is sometimes held to be the original home of the Kandyan civilization, whose people would have used the river valleys draining into the Mahaweli Ganga as a natural migration route into the hills. Protected from the Wet Zone rains by the highland massif, it has a sunny, dry climate and a relatively bare landscape. In the hills there are impressive waterfalls and some of the best views on the island.

The provincial capital, Badulla, draws Buddhist pilgrims from across the island to its festival. To the south, the triangle formed by Ella, Haputale and Welimada has an enviable climate and marvellous walking opportunities. 'Gaps' in the precipitous ridges, particularly at Ella and Haputale, afford spectacular views without the price tag of Horton Plains. A circular route from Nuwara Eliya makes for a rewarding day tour of this area, or there are plenty of attractive places to stay if you don't want to rush.

Nuwara Eliya to Badulla

From Nuwara Eliya, the A5 goes southeast across Wilson's Plains then east to Badulla. This is the island's market garden, where carrots, bean, brassicas and many other fresh vegetables are grown, much of it for export to the Middle East.

Some 10 km past the **Hakgala Botanical Gardens** (see page 230) is a superb view southeast across the hills of Bandarawela and over the baked plains of the eastern coast. The road passes through **Keppetipola**, where you can pick up information about local attractions, then drops rapidly through to **Wellmada** on the Uma Oya River. **Istripura Caves**, north of Welimada, are a pot-holer's delight. They are reached by a path from Paranagama, which is 10 km along the road north from Welimada. The maze of damp caves holds a large lake.

From Welimada, a right turn on to the B51 leads to **Bandarawela** (see page 250), past terraced fields of paddy and across occasional streams. At Hali-Ela, the A5 goes to Radulla.

Best rooms with a view
Bourgainvillea Retreat, Kandy, page 220
Tea Factory, Kandapola, page 231
98 Acres, Ella, page 247
Waterfalls Homestay, Ella, page 248
Kelburne Mountain View Cottages, Haputale, page 254

Badulla and around   *Colour map 3, A6.*

paddy fields, mountain vistas and Buddhist and Hindu temples

Badulla (population 42,000), the capital of Uva Province, is surrounded by paddy fields along the banks of the river Gallanda Oya. This area is already in the rain shadow of the hills to the west, sheltered from the southwest monsoon and much drier than Nuwara Eliya. Rubber plantations cover some of the slopes around Badulla.

Sights

Badulla has an old fort against a backdrop of mountains and a small lake. It is one of the oldest towns in Sri Lanka, though there are no traces of the earlier settlement. The Portuguese once occupied it but set the town on fire before leaving. At one time it was an extremely active social centre for planters, with a racecourse, golf, tennis and cricket clubs, long since fallen into disuse.

Veall's Park was once a small botanical garden – some impressive specimens remain, such as the huge Australian pine. Notice the little stone grey Methodist church where Major Rogers, an elephant hunter who died after being struck by lightning, is commemorated on a plaque.

Muthiyangana Vihara, attributed to Devanampiya Tissa, the first Buddhist convert on the island, is thought to have a 2000-year old ancient core. There is a small provincial museum behind. The Hindu **Kataragama Devale** was built in the 18th-century highland style in thanksgiving for King Vimaladharma's victory over the Portuguese. Note the plaster-on-wood statues and wooden pillars of the 'throne room'. There is also a revered Bo tree.

Tip...
Dunhinda Road is also known as Mahiyangana Road.

Next to the stadium, in a pleasant four-acre park are the **botanical gardens** ⓘ *Rs 100, free for under 12s*, welcome relief from the bustle of Badulla town.

Around Badulla

Dunhinda Falls ⓘ *Car park is 6 km from town; from there it's 2 km (25 mins on foot) to the falls. Rs 200. Buses from Badulla leave every 30 mins and stop about a 10-min walk from the car park.* The island's highest perennial waterfalls, **Dunhinda Falls** can be spectacular. The path to the falls is

> **Tip...**
> Numerous stalls sell cold drinks, herbs and good mangoes (in season) at the start of the walk and along it. As the falls are very popular with Sri Lankans, foreign travellers are not hassled too much.

across the road from the car park. It is quite rough and steep in places, so take care and wear suitable shoes. The valley at this point is quite narrow which can make it very hot.

Shortly after the beginning of the path you can see the lower falls (more of a cascade really), quite a long way down in the valley below. These are only about 15 m in height and much broader than the main falls. A ledge about 10 m from the top makes for a spectacular 'spurt' when the river is running high. At the main falls, the river plunges in two stages about 63 m through a 'V' in the rock which causes the misty haze (*dunhind*) that gives the falls its name. The setting is suitably spectacular, with granite cliffs on either side and a large pool at the bottom. The large, kidney-shaped observation platform has concrete tables and benches for picnics but can be very busy at times.

Bogoda ⓘ *Off the road to the north of Hali Ela, 13 km from Badulla.* Bogoda is a very peaceful place, well off the beaten track, with a small monastery and rock temple. The attractive 16th-century wooden bridge across the Gallanda Oya is built without nails (the original claimed to date from the first century). The only surviving one of its kind, it has an unusual tiled roof in the Kandyan style supported on carved pillars. The railings are painted with natural lacquer. **Raja Maha Vihara** rock temple nearby has old murals and pre-Christian inscriptions.

Listings Badulla and around

Where to stay

$$-$ Hotel Onix
69 Bandaranayaka Mawatha, north of town, T055-222 2426.
Modern complex with a/c and fan rooms, most with satellite TV. Quiet, restaurant, good value.

$$-$ Dunhinda Falls Inn
35/10 Bandaranaike Mawatha, 1.5 km from town centre, T055-222 3028.
Respectable (local Rotary club meets here) despite disconcerting one-eyed leopard in

entrance. 15 large a/c and fan rooms of very varying standards, restaurant, bar, car/cycle hire, visits to tea gardens.

$ Green Woods Holiday Inn
301 Bandarawela Rd, 2.5 km before town, T055-223 1358.
12 reasonable a/c and fan rooms with hot bath in quiet location (although can get busy with local people), good restaurant, views would be good if you could open the windows. Also has large bungalows available.

Festivals

May-Jun **Wesak** and **Poson** full moon festivals take place with drummers, dancers and elephants.
Sep **Esala Perehera** at Muthi-yangana Vihara when Veddas participate.

Transport

Bus Bus stand for private and CTB buses is about 200 m south of the **Rest House** along King St. Regular buses to **Bandarawela**; and hourly to **Colombo**.

To **Kandy** until 1400 (every 40 mins); every 30 mins to **Nuwara Eliya** until 1650; hourly to **Wellawaya**, via **Ella**; 1 bus a day in the early morning to **Pottuvil**, and early morning departure to **Galle**, via **Matara**.

Train To **Colombo** via **Demodera** (look out for the Loop!), **Ella**, **Bandarawela**, **Haputale**, **Ohiya** (for Horton Plains) on *Udarata Menike* 0545 (9¾ hrs), *Podi Menike* 0850 (11¼ hrs), or mail train 1805 (12 hrs). To **Kandy**, 0850 (8 hrs). Local trains run as far as **Ohiya** at 0715, and to **Bandarawela** at 1415.

★ Ella and around   *Colour map 3, A6.*

fabulous walks to waterfalls and tea plantations

Ella is little more than a handful of shops and guesthouses strung out along the main road, but it has an almost perfect climate and occupies a very scenic vantage point at 1043 m, with views on a fine day stretching right across to the south coast. The town is also a useful base from which to visit some local tea plantations, waterfalls and rock temples. This is excellent walking country.

Around Ella

Several **tea factories** are nearby, including the Uva Halpewatte factory off the Badulla Road. Catch a bus travelling towards Bandarawela, change at Kumbalawela Junction, on to a Badulla-bound bus. At Km 27 post, take the track on the left leading uphill, and then turn left where it forks about 2 km from main road.

Rawana Ella Cave The cave in the massive Ella Rock, can be seen from the Grand Ella Motel to the right of the Ella Gap. It is associated with the *Ramayana* story in which the demon king of Lanka, Ravana, imprisoned Rama's wife, Sita.

The cave, which is of particular interest to palaeontologists, has a small entrance, which scarcely lets light in, and then a long drop to the floor. It is filled with water from an underground stream which has hindered exploration, but excavations here have unearthed prehistoric remains of human skeletons and tools dating from 8000 to 2500 BC. The skeletons are believed to belong to *Homo sapiens balangodensis*. They are said to show evidence of a culture superior to that of the present-day Veddas (Wanniya-laeto).

To reach the caves you walk downhill beyond the **Ella Rest House** for 10 minutes until you reach the road bridge, then branch up the track to the right which climbs to a rock monastery. There are often

> **Tip...**
> A traveller writes, "The view through the Ella Gap was probably the best in the entire island. It was quite early and the isolated hills on the plain popped up like islands in the mist."

local children offering to guide you on the very steep and difficult path up to the cave, for a small fee.

Rawana Ella Falls ⓘ *6 km south of Ella on the A23 so you can get there by bus (towards Wellawaya)*. The falls can be quite dramatic and the 1½-hour walk from the Rawana Ella Cave to reach them can be enjoyable: the road isn't usually too busy and there are some fine views. From the cave, return to the main road, near the bridge, and walk downhill to

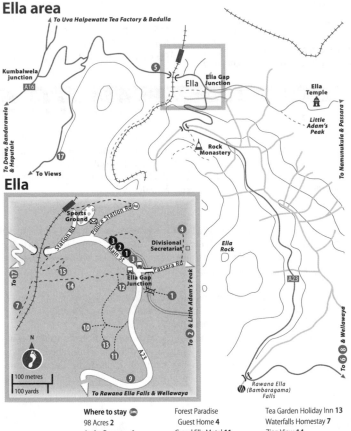

Ella area

Where to stay	Forest Paradise	Tea Garden Holiday Inn 13
98 Acres 2	Guest Home 4	Waterfalls Homestay 7
Amba Farmstay 6	Grand Ella Motel 11	Zion View 14
Ambiente 17	Highest Inn 15	
Beauty Mount	Ravana Heights 9	**Restaurants** 🍽
Tourist Inn 1	Rawana Holiday Resort 10	Café Chill 2
Ella Jungle	Rock View Guest House 12	Dream Café 1
Resort 8	Sunnyside Holiday	Rotti Cart 3
Ella Village Inn 3	Bungalow 5	

the falls. The 90-m-high Rawana Ella (or Bambaragama) Falls are to the right (west) of the road just beyond a bridge. It is possible to climb up the rocks beside the falls for quite a way, along with the monkeys who can often been seen scampering up and down. There is also a path to the right-hand side of the bathing area. Local 'guides' are always keen to show you the route though the way (up) is fairly obvious.

At the falls themselves a few enterprising vendors sell coloured stones gathered from the foot of the falls to passing tourists. A handful of small stones should not cost much more than Rs 50 but a common method of transaction is to swap the stones for a foreign coin or coins. The stone seller then waits for the next tourist, hoping to exchange the foreign coins with a native of the relevant country at the prevailing exchange rate.

Other walks around Ella There are several other walks which command magnificent views. A short walk east on the Passara Road takes you to a track, after the Km 1 post, which you follow to climb **Little Adam's Peak**. Some 10 km further east, and more

> **Tip...**
> Dowa Rock Temple can also be visited from Ella, see below.

strenuous, is the climb through tea plantations to **Namunukula**, which, at 2036 m, is one of Sri Lanka's highest mountains. You will need a guide for this walk.

Listings Ella *map p246*

Where to stay

Persistent hotel touts besiege those arriving by train. Ignore them and go to the hotel of your choice, preferably with an advance reservation. All hotels are on the Main St, unless listed, and most have hot water though check beforehand for the cheapest rooms. It's worth booking accommodation in advance, especially Jan-Apr when it can be very busy.

$$$$ 98 Acres Resort
Greenland Estate, Passara Rd, T057-205 0050, www.98acres.com.
Stunning 2-storey thatched bungalows perched on the hillside with magnificent views. Beautiful pool and landscaping, atmospheric restaurant. And the views... Recommended.

$$$ Ella Jungle Resort
12 km south of Ella on Wellawaya Rd, Karandagolla (contact Wild Holidays,

UK, +44 (0)845-527 3627), www.jungle-resort-ella-sri-lanka.en.ww.lk.
Impressive, environmentally sensitive lodge in 38 acres of forest spanning both banks of the Kirindi Oya. 10 comfortable 'rooms', comprising eco-lodges, treehouse (with own ropeway), deluxe cabanas and camping tents, plus tree-top bar/restaurant. Full array of adventure sports offered, including rock-climbing, paragliding, canoeing and abseiling, some are included in the price.

$$$ Planters Bungalow
11 km south of Ella, 10 Mild Post Uva, Karandagagolla, T055-205 5600, www.plantersbungalow.com.
The original house was built by Scottish tea planter Malcolm George, so you can opt for heritage living or a room with a view in 2 new self-catering apartments amidst the plantation. Warm welcome here.

$$$-$$ Grand Ella Motel (CHC)
*Overlooking Ella Gap, 1 km south
of railway station, T057-222 8655,
www.cncresthouses.com.*
14 large rooms, cheaper in the old wing.
Wonderful garden, with its own *Ficus
religiosa* and the best views in Ella.

$$$-$$ Zion View
*300 m from train station, T077-381 0313
www.ella-guesthouse-srilanka.com.*
Large modern build with spotless rooms
with French windows so you can lie in
bed and look at the view of Zion waterfall.
Laundry service available, excellent food
and an Ayurveda centre should be open by
the time you read this. There are also plans
for a bungalow in the future. The family are
friendly and helpful and can arrange tours
and onward travel.

$$ Ella Village Inn
*T057-222 8615/T072-465 6292,
www.ellavillageyinn.com.*
Large, modern guesthouse in very central
location. Range of clean rooms (some with
balconies), prices vary according to facilities.
Internet, free Wi-Fi available in the café,
restaurant, cookery lessons, excursions and
tourist information provided. Popular.

$$ Ravana Heights
*Opposite Km 27 post, Wellawaya Rd, T057-
222 8888, www.ravanaheights.com.*
4 classy rooms, 3 with excellent views and
outdoor seating areas. Intimate guesthouse
just outside town, personal attention, good
food. Recommended.

$$-$$ Amba Farmstay
*Ambadandegama, 30 min drive from Ella,
T057-357 5489, www.ambaestate.com.*
Unique organic farm and guesthouse
with artisanal teas, coffee plantations,
conscious foods, cosy rooms and epic
views. Recommended for getting off the
beaten track.

$$-$$ Beauty Mount Tourist Inn
*Off Main St, T057-222 8760,
www.beautymountella.com.*
Simple rooms and bungalows on a forested
hill just off Main St. Lovely gardens and great
food. Stairs are steep, so bear this in mind if
you have heavy bags.

$$-$$ Waterfalls Homestay
*T057-567 6933, www.waterfalls-
guesthouse-ella.com.*
Hidden away in the jungle with 3 bright,
clean rooms (2 have panoramic views).
Friendly, good food, lovely spot. Tricky to
find so take them up on their offer of a free
pick-up. Recommended.

$ Ambiente
*2 km up Kitalella Rd, high above the Ella town
near Kinellan Tea Plantation, T057-222 8867,
www.ambiente.lk.*
In a spectacular setting, high above the
village, 8 very clean rooms, 5 in new
block (can be noisy), most are spacious.
Magnificent views, friendly.

$ Forest Paradise Guest Home
*Passara Rd, T057-222 8797,
www.forestparadiseella.com.*
Real frontier feel on edge of pine forest.
5 clean, small rooms, with private seating
area. Friendly and can arrange activities.
Free pick-up from station. Recommended
for its setting.

$ Highest Inn
*Turn left before railway bridge, or take short
cut through tea plantation, T057-567 6933.*
Family-run guesthouse with good views all
around. 3 rooms with shared balcony, only
breakfast available. Friendly and helpful.

$ Rawana Holiday Resort
*On hill above the village, T057-222 8794,
nalankumara@yahoo.com.*
A variety of clean rooms, nice home-from-
home touches and good food. Terrace with
great views across forest, friendly. More

rooms being added at the time of writing, so view before committing.

$ Rock View Guest House
T057-222 8561.
Large rooms, newer ones are separate from the main house, and popular restaurant. Free cookery classes if you're a guest. Friendly.

$ Sunnyside Holiday Bungalow
Bandarawela Rd, T057-561 5011, www.sunnyside.go2lk.com.
Family-run guesthouse offering 3 clean rooms with attached hot bath in a bungalow surrounded by pleasant gardens. Excellent for birdwatchers. No TV, and no smoking or alcohol allowed on site. The whole bungalow can be hired (**$$**). Excellent food.

Restaurants

Many of the guesthouses listed under Where to stay offer home-cooked rice and curry, but you will need to book your meal by mid-afternoon. The set meal at Zion View is expensive but excellent; Rawana remains popular. Alternatively, a number of places on the main street serve food. Curd and treacle honey is a local speciality.

$$-$ Café Chill
Main St.
Colourful chill-out zone serving up traveller favourites from burgers and pizzas to salads and the occasional Sri Lankan treat. They offer cookery lessons here.

$$-$ Dream Café
Main St.
A perennial favourite, serving curries and a wide range of excellent Western dishes in a garden tucked down away from the road. Service is good, internet is available and the pizzas are a must-have.

$ Rotti Cart
Next door to Nescoffee. Open from 1630.
Serving delicious *rotti*, whether it be garlic or banana and honey.

Shopping

Shops on Main St near the rest houses are overpriced. Walk up the street and pay half the price for water and provisions.

What to do

Ayurveda and herbal therapies
Suwamedura, *25 Grand View, Passara Rd, T057-567 3215.* Professional establishment offering a range of treatments, including massage, steam baths and herbal saunas.

Cookery classes
A few of the guesthouses offer cookery classes (see Where to stay). **Ella Village Inn** organizes lessons for Rs 1700, which includes the ingredients and eating the meal at the end, and there are good lessons at Café Chill.

Tour operators
A number of the guesthouses can arrange tours and onward travel, if required. **Ella Village Inn**, *see Where to stay.* The owner, Suresh Rodrigo, can provide tourist information and also organizes tours such as night-caving, jungle-trekking and visits to rubber plantations and tea factories "not in any guidebook".

Transport

Bus Direct buses to **Nuwara Eliya** (2½ hrs) and **Kandy**, though more frequently if you change in Badulla. For **Colombo**, go to Kumbalawela Junction, 3 km north on the Haputale–Badulla road, where buses go every 30 mins. For the south coast, direct buses go to **Matara**. Frequent buses to **Wellawaya** for connections to Okkampitiya (for Maligawila, see page 189), and to

Bandarawela (change for Haputale, 45 mins). Buses are infrequent for **Badulla** – you may have to go to Kumbalawela Junction.

Train *Udarate Menike* departs 0643, *Podi Menike* at 0947, mail train 1907, calling at

Bandarawela (30 mins), **Haputale** (1 hr), **Ohiya** (for Horton Plains, 1¾ hrs), **Nanu Oya** (for Nuwara Eliya, 2¾ hrs), **Hatton** (for Adam's Peak, 4 hrs) and **Colombo** (8½-11 hrs). For **Kandy** (6 hrs), take the 0947 or 1907, the 1309 is a slow train. Several trains a day north to **Badulla** (1 hr).

Bandarawela *Colour map 3, A5.*

a good base for walking and Ayurveda treatments

At the centre of the Uva 'health triangle', at a height of 1230 m, many Sri Lankans regard Bandarawela's climate as the most favourable on the island. Averaging around 21ºC, it is invariably dry and sunny, although the number of vehicles passing through means the air is no longer as clean and fresh as it once was.

A centre for tea and fruit-growing, the town has a bustling market-town feel and is good for picking up supplies or visiting the ATM. Market days are Wednesday and Sunday. Though there is little in the way of sights, the town is used mainly as a good base for walks and for exploring the Uva basin. For details of Bandarawela's Ayurveda and herbal therapy centres, see What to do, opposite.

Around Bandarawela
Dowa Rock Temple, 6 km from Bandarawela, is squeezed between the road and the stream in the bottom of the valley. It is a pleasant walk if you follow the attractive valley down. The cliff face has an incomplete carving of a large standing Buddha with an exquisitely carved face, while inside the cave there are murals and first century BC inscriptions. The inner cave has a 'House of the Cobra', which is usually locked (ask a monk to let you in) and said to be still inhabited by serpents. Take a Badulla bus and ask the bus driver to let you off at the temple.

Listings Bandarawela

Where to stay

Budget options are along Welimada Rd; there are also Tea Estate Bungalows, which are worth looking at if you have your own wheels.

$$$ Orient
12 Dharmapala Mawatha, T057-222 2377, www.orienthotelsl.com.
50 large rooms and 4 suites, good views from top floor, billiard room, fitness centre,

English-style bar and beer garden. Popular with tours.

$$$-$$ Bandarawela Hotel (Aitken Spence)
14 Welimada Rd, near Cargill's supermarket, T057-222 2501, www.aitkenspencehotels.com.
Old tea planters' club (1893) full of colonial charm, 35 rather cramped rooms, including 1 suite. Period furniture, including metal bedsteads, rooms built around central courtyard (look for tortoises), good gardens,

passable restaurant, residents' bar with fireplace, good tours to Horton Plains, popular with groups but still recommended, though the noisy mosque will ensure you won't waste the day.

$ Ventnor Guest House
23 Welimada Rd, T057-572 2225.
Large, carpeted rooms, well furnished, hot water, restaurant.

Shopping

Cargill's, *opposite Bundarawela Hotel.* Branch of the supermarket chain.
Mlesna, *184a Welimada Rd, T057-2231663.* Upmarket tea shop, with a wide variety to choose from.

What to do

Ayurveda and herbal therapies
Suwamadhu, *Bindunuwewa, 3 km east, T057-222 2504. Daily 0800-2000.* Popular herbal treatment centre that produces its own creams and oils. Steam bath with 18 herbal medicines, full body massage, longer courses available.

Trekking
The **Sri Lanka Trekking Club** (www. srilanatrekkingclub.com) is based in Bandarawela. Supported by the tourist board, they offer a great range of short walks and longer treks, tuk-tuk safaris and cookery adventures around Bandarawela, Ella, Nuwara Eliya and Haputale.

Transport

Bus The main stand is to the west of town, close to the playing field. Frequent buses to **Badulla**, **Wellawaya** (via **Haputale**) and **Colombo** (from Haputale Rd). Buses to **Matara** and the south coast, or change at Wellawaya. Direct buses to **Nuwara Eliya**, or change at Welimada.

Train There are regular trains to **Colombo** all via **Kandy**.

Haputale and around   *Colour map 3, B5,*

tea factories and plantations dot the horizon

Haputale, from its ridge-top position at 1400 m, has superb views at dawn over the low country to the east. On a clear day you can see the saltpans at Hambantota to the south, and, on the horizon, is the sea. To the north, in magnificent contrast, are the hills.

A small town with a busy shopping street, Haputale is surrounded by great walks and is a good base from which to explore the area, with plenty of cheap guesthouses. The lively Sunday morning market is worth a stroll. Away from town, several tea plantations are happy to receive visitors –

Tip...
Walk down the main street from the Station Road crossing to see the road apparently disappearing over the cliff.

just stop and ask, or guesthouses can arrange transport for you. Some estates have accommodation. For more information on Haputale, see www.haputale.de.

Dambetenne Road
The Dambetenne Road east of Haputale must rate as one of the most spectacular routes on the whole island with breathtaking views across five provinces, taking in several tea

plantations and the plains. It is possible to walk the length of the road, which is not busy, or take the regular bus which ferries plantation workers the 10 km from town to the Dambetenne (Lipton) Tea Factory. Along the way you will pass a number of tea factories.

Greenfields Bio Plantations ① *3 km on Dambatenne Rd, T057-226 8102, call first for a tour*, is one of the few organic tea producers in the country. Call in advance to request a tour demonstrating the various processes involved. It's a very pleasant walk or there are hourly buses.

The more traditional **Dambetenne Tea Factory** ① *visit 0700-1200 to see the factory in full production, Rs 200 for a 30-min tour*, has the air of a philanthropic Victorian works, which indeed is what it is. Note the quote from Ruskin at the entrance, "Quality is no accident. It is the result of intelligent effort." Built in 1890 by Sir Thomas Lipton, the 20,000 sq ft factory employs 1600 workers, 90% of which are resident, and accommodates over 4000 people. Most of the tea is now exported to Europe, Japan and South Africa. There are hourly buses to Dambatenne.

Some 7 km beyond the tea factory it is a short uphill walk following a clear trail to **Lipton's Seat** from where, on a clear day, it is possible to see up to 60% of the island. This walk is highly recommended, but it's best to visit in the morning as mist tends to descend by about 1030.

West of Haputale

If you wish to return to Nuwara Eliya from Haputale, the B48 goes directly through Boralanda, Nawela and Welimada, where it rejoins the A5 to Nuwara Eliya. Alternatively, you can turn off at Boralanda and take the slower route via Ohiya and the Horton Plains.

Adisham monastery ① *3 km west of Haputale, off the B48 towards Boralanda), T057-226 8030. Visiting hours: Sat-Sun, poya days and public hols 0930-1230, 1330-1700, Rs 60. Getting there: bus 327 or 3-wheeler from Rs 600 return.* The monastery, located on a hill

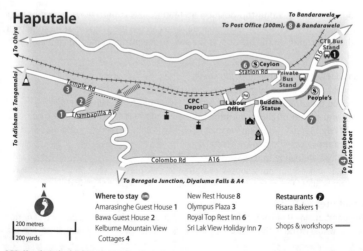

Haputale

Where to stay
Amarasinghe Guest House 1
Bawa Guest House 2
Kelburne Mountain View Cottages 4

New Rest House 8
Olympus Plaza 3
Royal Top Rest Inn 6
Sri Lak View Holiday Inn 7

Restaurants
Risara Bakers 1

Shops & workshops ——

west of town, is worth visiting at the weekend; you can walk there in about an hour or get transport from town. A quirky stone-built anachronism dating from the 1930s, it houses a Benedictine novitiate that has interesting period features. Modelled on Leeds Castle (Kent, England), it has attractive rose gardens and orchards. A few spartan rooms with cold water in an annexe are open to visitors (reserve in advance). Adjoining the monastery is the **Tangamalai Bird Sanctuary,** which is good for spotting jungle and highland species.

West from Beragala

From Haputale the A16 goes west, past the **Stassen Bio Plantation**, to Beragala (10 km), where it joins the A4, the main road to Ratnapura and Colombo. West of Beragala the A4 hugs the southern rim of the highlands passing through some of the most rugged scenery in Sri Lanka. Black rocks tower above the road towards **Belihuloya** (see page 114), and much of the route is very windy, not steep but with many blind bends.

East from Beragala

Travelling east from Beragala, there are fine views through the **Haputale Gap**, as the road leads through a marvellous area of flora – teak, rubber, pepper, cacao and coffee trees – to **Koslande**, then past the Diyaluma waterfall to **Wellawaya** (see page 190).

Diyaluma Falls ⓘ *Off the A4, 5 km beyond Koslande. Getting there: take any Wellawaya or Moneragala bus from Haputale (journey time 1¼ hrs). It is best to go in the morning as afternoon buses are scarce.* The 170-m Diyaluma Falls drop in two stages over a huge convex outcrop. They are perhaps not as spectacular as the Dunhinda Falls, mainly because the stream is much smaller, but it is quite peaceful here, and, although there are no official picnic areas, there are several large rocks to sit on. Beware of the monkeys though. You can climb up to some cool bathing pools about half way up the falls: walk about 500 m (back towards Haputale) to a minor road which winds up through rubber plantations – best to ask the way; the steady climb takes about an hour.

Tip...

If using public transport, Haputale is probably a better base than Nuwara Eliya for visiting Horton Plains National Park and World's End since you can make a round trip by train/on foot in one day. However, by the time you arrive the plains will be covered in cloud, which normally sweeps up the valleys by midday. See page 235, and Transport, page 255.

Where to stay

There is a good choice of cheap guesthouses in Haputale, most have hot water. The owners can usually advise on good walks in the area.

$$$$ Thotalagala
Dambatenne Rd, T077-241 9096/ 204 0981, www.thotalagala.com.
A niche boutique hotel that was originally a tea planter's bungalow on an estate dating from 1870. There are 7 large themed suites based on personalities such as Sir Thomas Lipton and James Taylor, who shaped the history of Ceylon Tea.

$$$ Kelburne Mountain View Cottages
2 km down Dambetenne Rd, T011-257 3382 (reservations), www. kelburnemountainview.com.
3 wonderfully furnished cottages, sleeping 4 or 6, 2 with fireplaces, at least 2 bathrooms in each, meals on order or there's a restaurant, spectacular views, unique hand-painted open-air visitors book. Superb place to unwind.

$$ Olympus Plaza Hotel
75 Welimada Rd, T057-226 8544, www.olympusplazahotel.com.
The only 'real' hotel in Haputale, this place is a little soulless but the rooms are comfortable and clean and the views are excellent. Satellite TV, internet (expensive at Rs 100 per hr), restaurant,

> **Tip...**
> There is a short cut from the railway station to Temple Road and nearby guesthouses: walk west along the tracks; climb the steps to Temple Road, then follow signposts down the steps on the other side.

bar with pool table, table tennis and a gym. Tours can be arranged.

$ Amarasinghe Guest House
Thambapillai Av, T057-226 8175, agh777@sltnet.lk.
Cosy family house with homely atmosphere and clean, comfortable rooms. Very good value, including some on 1st floor with excellent views. Good food, friendly and knowledgeable owner. Internet available. Recommended.

$ Bawa Guest House
32 Thambapillai Av, above Amarasinghe Guest House, T057-226 8260.
3 clean, bright rooms in long-running family guesthouse. Friendly owners, Mr Bawa, is a gem expert and has a small showroom. Good home-cooked vegetarian food.

$ Sri Lak View Holiday Inn
48 A Sirisena Mawatha, 200 m from bus stand, T057-226 8125, srilakv@sltnet.lk.
Clean rooms, some with views. Those in the main house are better; the new building can get quite hot. Restaurant and breakfast room with excellent views, good food, internet, friendly. Rooms overpriced.

Restaurants

The home cooking at most of the guesthouses is hard to beat; see Where to stay, above. Several provide cheap lunch packets. There's no real restaurant here, but you can buy *rottis* and snacks in food stalls and there are good groceries along the road between the rail and bus stations.

$ Risara Bakers
Near the bus station.
Serves short eats and the best samosas in Sri Lanka (spicy though). If you time it right you'll get them fresh out the fryer at the front.

Transport

Bus There are separate CTB and private bus stands with several early morning buses for **Colombo** (6 hrs), and some to **Nuwara Eliya**, but you may have to change at Welimada. Buses leave for **Bandarawela** every half an hour, while express buses run to **Badulla**. There is an early morning express bus to **Matara** (via **Hambantota** and **Tangalla**), though to get to the south coast you usually have to change at Wellawaya (every 2 hrs).

Train For **Colombo** (7½-10 hrs), *Udarate Menike* departs at 0747, *Podi Menike* at 1048, mail train at 2015, calling at **Ohiya** (for Horton Plains), **Nanu Oya** (for Nuwara Eliya), **Hatton** (for Adam's Peak). For a day trip to **Horton Plains National Park**, catch the 0747 service which reaches Ohiya in 40 mins; you can return on the 1636. For **Kandy** (5½-6 hrs), the 1048 or 2015 are best, although there is also a slow train at 1437. Faster trains north to **Badulla** (1¾ hrs), via **Bandarawela** (30 mins) and **Ella** (1 hr) at 0507, 1125, 1409 and 1734.

Ancient
Cities

The phenomenal Cultural Triangle contains five UNESCO World Heritage Sites, which between them represent the early phases of the nation's cultural development.

Anuradhapura was the capital for 1500 years, its soaring *dagobas* testament to the lofty ambitions of its kings, while an auspicious meeting at nearby Mihintale sealed the island's conversion to Buddhism. Invasions from India forced Anuradhapura's abandonment in favour of the less exposed site of Polonnaruwa, whose walls encircle the island's most rewarding archaeological complex. The unmissable highlight here is the serene rock-cut recumbent Buddha at the Gal Vihara.

But the region's most inspiring treasures lie outside the ancient capitals. Most spectacular of all is the astonishing Sigiriya rock, atop which lie the remains of a fifth-century playboy's palace. No less remarkable are the cave paintings at Dambulla, Aukana's sublime monolithic Buddha, and the jungle monastery at Ritigala.

The area's appeal extends beyond archaeology. Scramble up any of the granite domes that burst out of the forest and you'll behold a landscape of utter lushness, dotted with lakes and pockets of emerald paddy. Quiet roads make this excellent cycling country – just watch out for elephants, which migrate freely between the vast tanks at Minneriya and Kaudulla, gathering in their hundreds each dry season in one of Asia's great wildlife spectacles.

Best for
Archaeology ▪ Elephants ▪ History ▪ Landscapes

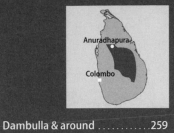

Footprint
picks

★ **Dambulla**, page 259

Intricate paintings cover every inch of this astonishing cave temple complex, perched on top of a huge granite boulder.

★ **Aukana**, page 266

Come here at dawn to see the rising sun bathe the face of Aukana's monumental, serene Buddha in golden light.

★ **Anuradhapura**, page 270

Explore the remains of Sri Lanka's greatest ancient capital, and join the throngs of pilgrims at the holy Bo tree.

★ **Sigiriya**, page 285

Scenic and artistic wonder combine in this palace fortress on the dramatic Lion Rock.

★ **Polonnaruwa**, page 297

Milky white *dagobas*, ruined temples and exquisite carved Buddhas make this the most rewarding of the ancient cities.

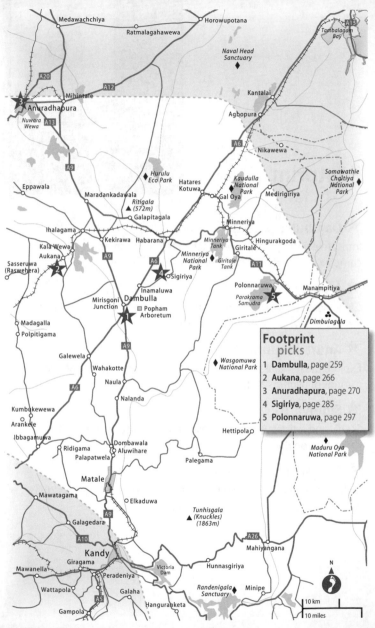

Medawachchiya
Horowupotana
Ratmalagahawewa
Tambalagam Bay
Naval Head Sanctuary
Mihintale
3 Anuradhapura
Nuwara Wewa
Kantalai
Agbopura
Nikawewa
Eppawala
Maradankadawala
Hurulu Eco Park
Somawathie Chaitiya National Park
Hatares Kotuwa
Kaudulla National Park
Gal Oya
Medirigiriya
Ritigala (572m)
Galapitagala
Minneriya
Ihalagama
Kekirawa
Habarana
Hingurakgoda
Kala Wewa
Aukana
Minneriya Tank
Giritale
2
Minneriya National Park
Giritale Tank
Sasseruwa (Raswehera)
4 Sigiriya
Polonnaruwa
5
Manampitiya
Inamaluwa
Mirisgoni Junction
1 Dambulla
Parakrama Samudra
Popham Arboretum
Dimbulagala
Madagalla
Polpitigama
Galewela
Wasgomuwa National Park
Wahakotte

Footprint picks

1 **Dambulla**, page 259
2 **Aukana**, page 266
3 **Anuradhapura**, page 270
4 **Sigiriya**, page 285
5 **Polonnaruwa**, page 297

Naula
Nalanda
Kumbukewewa
Arankele
Ibbagamuwa
Hettipola
Ridigama
Palapatwela
Dombawala
Aluwihare
Palegama
Maduru Oya National Park
Matale
Mawatagama
Elkaduwa
Galagedara
Tunhisgala (Knuckles) (1863m)
Kandy
Giragama
Mahiyangana
Mawanella
Peradeniya
Victoria Dam
Hunnasgiriya
Wattapola
Galaha
Randenigala Sanctuary
Minipe
Gampola
Hanguranketa

N

10 km
10 miles

Dambulla
& around

The richly painted cave temples at Dambulla, which lie atop a vast rocky outcrop, date to the first century BC and form one of Sri Lanka's World Heritage Sites (designated in 1991). Though the site is now privately run by wealthy monks, it is still considered to be part of the Cultural Triangle.

Nearby, you can visit the massive rock-cut Aukana Buddha and the monastery at Sasseruwa; Sigiriya rock is only 19 km away. Those coming from Kandy can visit the rock monastery at Aluwihare, near Matale, and the Nalanda *gedige* en route.

Dambulla   *Colour map 2, B4.*

stunning cave temples covered in intricate paintings

The cave temple complex at Dambulla is sited on a gigantic granite outcrop which towers more than 160 m above the surrounding land. The rock measures more than 1.5 km around its base and the summit is at 550 m above sea level.

Just to the north of the caves, Dambulla town hosts one of Sri Lanka's biggest wholesale produce markets, and makes for a convenient, if not particularly beguiling, place to base yourself if you're exploring the Cultural Triangle by public transport.

Golden Temple and Buddhist Museum
Daily 0730-2100. Free.

Once through the main entrance, most visitors head straight for the treasures on top of Dambulla's hill, bypassing the Golden Temple complex at the bottom. The kitschy Buddhist Museum squats at the feet of a giant golden Buddha and is entered through a gaudy dragon's mouth. Inside are exhibited statues gifted from around the Buddhist world, *ola* leaf manuscripts, copies of some of the cave paintings and other Buddhist objects. Its air-conditioning and piped music give it the atmosphere of a shopping mall in some surreal, Disneyfied Buddhaland.

Beside the museum, a flight of steps lead up into the Golden Temple itself. You can also climb the huge gold Buddha which is in a *dhamma chakka* pose.

Essential Dambulla

Finding your feet

Dambulla lies almost in the dead centre of the country on an important junction of the Kandy–Anuradhapura (A9) and Colombo–Trincomalee (A6) roads. After Kandy, Dambulla is often the next point of call on a tour of the Cultural Triangle.

Tip...
It can be difficult to dodge the touts and beggars who line the steps leading to the caves (not to mention the monkeys who will readily separate you from any food you carry up), and the guides as they stand in the temple doorway (Rs 500). Visit late in the afternoon for a less hassled visit.

Getting around

The town, and the sights south and northwest described in this section, can be reached by public transport, with the exception of Sasseruwa for which private transport is required. Dambulla itself is tiny. The cave temples lie 2 km south of the road junction, a short bus ride away or Rs 50-100 in a three-wheeler. Most cheaper accommodation is strung out along the main road. Buses from Kandy sometimes stop by the post office, a useful place to disembark if staying at the southern end of town.

Best accommodation
Kandalama, Dambulla, page 263
Dignity Villa, Dambulla, page 263
Dad's Holiday Home, Matale, page 266
Back of Beyond Dehigahaela, near Sigiriya, page 291
Galkadawala Forest Lodge, near Habarana, page 295

★ Dambulla cave temple
Daily 0730-1230 and 1300-1800 (last ticket 1730). Free. Carry a torch if you wish to view the cave paintings in detail. A good booklet in English and German is on sale, Rs 200.

The approach From the car park, it can be a hot and tiring climb to reach the cave temple complex about half way up the hill. There are about 600 steps altogether in a series of terraces, some longer and steeper than others. It is not too difficult to get to the top, but try to avoid the heat in the middle of the day when the sun bounces back off the scorching granite. There are panoramic views from the terrace of the surrounding jungle and tanks, and of Sigiriya.

There are five overhung cliff caves. Monastic buildings have been built in front, complete with cloisters; these in turn overlook a courtyard which is used for ceremonial purposes and has a wonderful view over the valley below. Some of the other subsidiary caves, which were occupied by monks, contain ancient inscriptions in Brahmi.

Cave I (Devaraja-Viharaya) Contains the huge lying *Parinirvana* Buddha which is 14 m long and carved out of solid rock. The unrestored frescoes behind the Arahat Ananda (a disciple) are said to be the oldest in the site, though they lack the lustre of those in other caves. 'Devaraja' refers to the Hindu god Vishnu. The deity may have been installed here in the Kandyan period though some believe it is older than the Buddha images. There is a Vishnu temple attached.

Cave II (Rajamaha-Viharaya) This much bigger cave is 7 m high; it was named after the two kings whose images are here. The principal Buddha statue facing the entrance is in the *Abhaya mudra* under a *makara torana* (or dragon arch). The cave has about 1500 paintings of the Buddha – almost as though the monks had tried to wallpaper the cave. The paintings of his life near the corner to the right are interesting: you can see his parents holding him as a baby; various pictures of him meditating (counted in weeks, eg cobra hood indicates the sixth week); some have him surrounded by demons, others with cobras, and another shows him being offered food by merchants. There are also historical scenes, including a particularly graphic representation of the battle between Dutthagamenu and Elara, illustrating the decisive moment when the defeated falls to the ground, head first from an elephant. Here, in the right-hand corner, you can see the holy pot which is never empty. Drips are collected into a bucket which sits in a wooden fenced rectangle and is used for sacred rituals by the monks.

Dambulla

Cave III (Maha Alut Viharaya) This cave is about 30 sq m and 10 m high. It was rebuilt in the 18th century and has about 60 images, some under *makara toranas*, and more paintings of thousands of the seated Buddha on the ceiling. This cave was a former storeroom and the frescoes are in the Kandyan style.

Cave IV (Pascima Viharaya or 'western' cave) The smallest cave was once the westernmost before the fifth cave was constructed. It contains about 10 images, though, unfortunately, the stupa here was damaged by thieves who came in search of Queen Somawathie's jewels. One image in particular, at the back of the cave, needed restoration. Unfortunately it is now painted in a very strong Marge Simpson yellow which jars with the rest of the cave.

Cave V (Devana Alut Viharaya) The newest cave was once used as a storeroom. The

Tip...
Large bags and shoes are not allowed into the complex but they can all be left with the shoe keepers at the top of the hill (Rs 25). Hats must also be removed, and normal temple attire should be worn (cover knees, shoulders, etc).

BACKGROUND
Dambulla

The caves were the refuge of King Valagambahu (Vattagamani Abhaya) during his 14-year exile. When he returned to the throne at Anuradhapura in the first century BC, he had a magnificent rock temple built at Dambulla. The site has been repaired and repainted several times, in the 11th, 12th and 18th centuries.

The caves have a mixture of religious and secular painting and sculpture, with frescoes dating from 15th to 18th centuries showing scenes from the Buddha's life and Sinhalese history. There are several reclining Buddhas, including a 14-m sculpture of the dying Buddha in Cave 1. Cave 2 is the largest and most impressive, containing more than 150 statues, illustrating the Mahayana influences on Buddhism at the time through introducing Hindu deities such as Vishnu and Ganesh.

The temple's monks are now housed in monasteries in the valley below, where there is also a monks' school. Thanks to large donations from Buddhists overseas (particularly from Japan) and the temple entrance fee, the monks in Dambulla drive 4WDs and enjoy many other comforts not available to others of a similar calling.

images here are built of brick and plaster and, in addition to the Buddha figures, also include the Hindu deities, Vishnu, Kataragama and Bandara (a local god).

Tip...
For further information, read A Seneviratna, *Golden rock temple of Dambulla*, (Colombo: Sri Lanka Central Cultural Fund, 1983).

Dambulla Museum
Just south of the caves and Golden Temple. Daily 0800-1600. US$2, children $1.

Don't be discouraged by the first small room, which has exhibits demonstrating how the Dambulla murals and frescoes were created. It may at first look like any local museum with bits cobbled together, but climb the stairs for a well laid-out and informative exhibition on the history of Sri Lankan painting and the development of rock and wall art. The seven rooms lead visitors from the Primitive period right through to the 20th century, via the Classical period frescoes at Sigiriya and murals from the Kandyan period. Exhibits are excellent reproductions on canvas of paintings from all over the island, bringing inaccessible frescoes and murals to people who would otherwise have little opportunity of seeing them.

Popham Arboretum
2 km east of the caves, along Kandalama Rd towards the Kandalama Hotel, T077-726 7951. Rs 1000, night entry Rs 1500.

The only arboretum in the Dry Zone was set up by Sam Popham, a former tea planter, on his retirement in 1963. Originally planning on replanting, he discovered that clearing the scrub jungle enabled the native trees to seed and the saplings to grow. He experimented by re-foresting with minimal human interference. The 'Popham method' was a success, and now over 70 tropical trees are preserved here, including ebony and satinwood. The woodland has been divided into blocks, which are cleared at different times, and visitors have access via a set of well-maintained paths; you can walk independently, or organize a guided walk with Jayantha Amarasinghe, the current custodian of the Arboretum. Birdwatching is excellent along the tracks, and in the evening you can take a guided walk to search for slender loris. Don't miss the Bawa-designed visitor centre, which was Popham's house.

Listings Dambulla *map p261*

Where to stay

$$$$ Kandalama (Aitken Spence)
Head along Kandalama Rd for 4.5 km, take right fork, 1066-555 5000, www.heritancehotels.com/kandalama.
Resort-style complex of 152 plush a/c rooms and luxury suites in 2 wings. Unique design by Geoffrey Bawa, built between a massive rock and a peaceful tank and indistinguishable from its jungle surrounds. Winner of many awards, including Asia's 1st Green Globe. Excellent cuisine and full facilities, 3 pools including one of the most spectacularly sited swimming pools in the world with crystal clear water (filtration system based on ancient Sri Lankan technology). Magnificent views across undisturbed forest, magical details, exceptional service.

$$$$-$$$ Amaya Lake
Follow Kandalama Rd for 4.5 km, take left fork, then follow lake around for 4.6 km, T066-446 1500, www.amayaresorts.com.
Variety of rooms including suites, chalets and clay eco-lodges (with TVs, DVD players and minibar) with a village theme. Good pool in large gardens, restaurant, Ayurvedic health centre. Very attractive setting on edge of lake.

$$$ Thilanka Resort and Spa
3 km south of Dambulla, follow Kandy Rd, T066-446 8001, www.thilankaresortandspa.lk.
Well-proportioned and bright rooms in villas set in pleasant grounds. Huge pool, restaurant serves average food.

$$$-$$ Gimanhala Transit
754 Anuradhapura Rd, 1 km north of Colombo Junction, T066-228 4864, www.gimanhala.com.
Comfortable, clean a/c rooms, good restaurant overlooking lovely, large and very clean pool. Bike hire, shop. Best of the town hotels, good value.

$ Chamara Guest House
121 Matale/Kandy Rd, T066-228 4488.
Simple, moderately clean rooms, with nets, fan, restaurant and pleasant communal terrace. Prices can be negotiated in low season. Relaxed, and owner is helpful and can give advice for onward travel.

$ Dignity Villa
29 Yaya Rd (off Sampath Rd behind Food City supermarket), T077-518 0902, www.thesimpletraveler.com.
A great budget option in town, with large and superbly clean a/c and fan-cooled rooms, great meals and a warm welcome from host Daniel and his family, who are only too happy to help you out with bus tickets, travel advice and tuk-tuks.

$ Oasis Tourist Welfare Centre
Down a side road opposite the caves, T077-844 2908.
Friendly and homely place, though very basic, run by German host Christiane and her husband. No food nearby, and the walk into town is a bit dodgy for lone female travellers.

Restaurants

There are cheap places to eat clustered near the bus station, and most hotels also do food. Gimanhala Transit Hotel has a good restaurant and a snack bar at the front (open at lunchtime). The Dambulla Rest House, does a lunchtime rice and curry for Rs 600, as well as lunch packets, but it's nothing to write home about and the staff are uninterested.

$ Bentota Bakehouse
Kandy–Jaffna Highway.
This local favourite serves excellent value lunchtime rice-and-curry.

Shopping

Branch of the **Buddhist Bookshop** in the Buddhist museum complex. Sells publications on Buddhism, meditation and the Rock Temple. Also may have an informative booklet for sale on the caves.

Transport

Bus
Long-distance buses, and buses to Sigiriya, use the New Bus Stand at the southern end of town. Local buses run to the site entrance, as do Kandy buses, but catching a bus from the bus station is easier than trying to flag one down on the road (although some guesthouse owners will help with this). Regular services to **Colombo** (4 hrs), **Anuradhapura**, **Kandy** and **Polonnaruwa** (about 2½ hrs each) and frequently to **Sigiriya** (30 mins).

South of Dambulla

Buddhist sites and access to the Knuckles Range

Nalanda, Aluwihare and Matale are all located along the main A9 between Dambulla and Kandy, and so can be visited en route between these towns.

Nalanda *Colour map 2, B4.*
19 km south of Dambulla (49 km north of Kandy). Free. Getting there: frequent buses between Dambulla and Kandy can drop you off near the turn-off opposite the rest house; from here a 1 km road leads east to the site.

This small reconstructed *gedige* (Buddha image house) shares some features in common with Hindu temples of southern India. Standing on the raised bund of a reservoir, it was built with stone slabs and originally dates from the seventh to the 10th centuries. Some tantric carvings have been found in the structure, which combines Hindu and Buddhist (both Mahayana and Theravada) features. Note the *Karmasutra* bas-relief. It is the only extant Sri Lankan *gedige* built in the architectural style of the seventh-century Pallava shore temples at Mamallapuram near Chennai in India. The place is very atmospheric and has comparatively few visitors, which adds to its appeal.

Aluwihare *Colour map 2, C4.*

36 km south of Dambulla (32 km north of Kandy). Rs 200 donation expected. Getting there: Buses between Matale and Dambulla stop on the main road; the caves are on the west side; you can also take a 3-wheeler.

Aluwihare has the renovated ruins of ancient shrines carved out of huge boulders. In the first and second century BC, the site was associated with King Vattagamani Abhaya (103-77 BC) and the *Mahavansa* (Buddhist chronicle of the island) was inscribed here in Pali. The original palm-leaf manuscript, prepared by 500 monks, was destroyed in the mid-19th century, and replacements are still being inscribed today.

> **Tip...**
> Aluwihare lies on a main tourist route, so you will continually be asked for donations, which can get tiresome.

Museum On payment of a Rs 200 'contribution' to the temple (for which you are given a receipt), you are guided first into the small museum, where you will be shown the technique of writing on palmyra palm. The palmyra palm strips were prepared for manuscripts by drying, boiling and drying again, and then flattened and coated with shell. A stylus was used for inscribing; this was held stationary while the leaf was moved to produce the lettering or illustration (the rounded shape of some South Asian scripts was a result of this technology). The inscribed grooves would then be rubbed with soot or powdered charcoal while colour was added with a brush. The leaves would then be stacked and sometimes strung together and sometimes 'bound' between decorative wooden 'covers'.

Caves The path up the boulders themselves is quite steep and can be slippery when wet (a newspaper cutting in the museum commemorates how the Duke of Edinburgh "nearly had a nasty fall" during the royal visit in 1956). Four of the 10 caves have ancient inscriptions. The curious 'Chamber of Horrors' has unusual frescoes vividly illustrating punishments doled out to sinners by eager demons, including spearing of the body and pouring of boiling oil into the mouth. The sculptures in another cave show torture on a 'rack' for the wrongdoer and the distress of having one's brains exposed by the skull being cut open. The impressive painted reclining Buddhas include one about 10 m long. The stupa on top of the rock, just beyond the cave temples, gives fine views of the Dry Zone plains and pine covered mountains.

Matale *Colour map 2, C4.*

The small but hustling town (population 37,000) lies 44 km south of Dambulla and just 24 km north of Kandy. It is surrounded by hills and is the base for some interesting short walks as well as some longer treks into the Knuckles Range (see page 219). The British built a fort here at the beginning of the 19th century (of which only a gate remains), and the branch railway line opened in 1880. Tour groups often stop at the Sri Muthumariamman Thevasthanam temple here.

Where to stay

$$ Dad's Holiday Home
91/9 IDH Rd, Matale, T077-998 5498,
dadsholidayhome@gmail.com.
This friendly homestay is an excellent
base for visiting Kandy, Dambulla and the
Knuckles. It's close to town, but in a quiet
spot surrounded by trees and birdsong.
The large, cool and clean rooms come with
terraces and pot plants, and Ranjan and his
wife pull out all the stops to make you feel
at home. Superb food too.

$ Nalanda Rest House
1.5 km from the gedige, Nalanda,
T066-224 6199.
Old rest house in good position close
to the *gedige*, 7 basic rooms with clean
attached bath.

Restaurants

The roadside places on the Kandy–
Dambulla Rd in Aluwihare usually serve
a limited selection of bland Westernized
food for the tour groups on the way up
from Kandy.

Shopping

As well as plantations of coffee, cocoa and
rubber, a large number of 'spice gardens' line
the road out of Matale towards Dambulla,
While some are genuine, most that are
open to visitors have very few plants and are
primarily there to sell commercially grown
spices and Ayurvedic herbal products at
extortionate prices.

Matale Heritage Centre, *The Walauwe,*
33 Aluwihare, 2 km north of Matale, T066-222
2404. This community-based enterprise, the
brainchild of the late renowned designer
Ena de Silva, is a rewarding stop for those
with a serious interest in tapestries, batiks,
furniture and brassware. Phone in advance.

Transport

Matale
Buses to/from **Kandy** run every 15 mins
or so; there are also regular buses to/from
Dambulla. Matale's railway station, in the
centre of town 100 m east of the A9, is the
terminus of a branch line from Kandy with
several slow trains daily (1½ hrs).

Towards Anuradhapura

a worthwhile detour to see an imposing ancient Buddha statue

Aukana and Sasseruwa are located just west of the A9 north of Dambulla and can
be visited en route to Anuradhapura.

★ Aukana

500 m from Aukana Junction (see Transport, below. Daily 0700-1900. Rs 500 (includes photography).

One of the island's most elegant and perfect statues, the Aukana Buddha, to the west
of the large Kala Wewa tank, has gained even greater significance to Buddhists since
the destruction of the similar (but much larger) statues at Bamiyan in Afghanistan.
(Toponymical research suggests that in ancient times Bamiyan, in the region where
Mahayana Buddhism originated, was known as Vokkana or Avakana.) Th Aukana statue is
a magnificent, undamaged 12-m-high free-standing representation of the Abhayamudra

Buddha, showing superhuman qualities, carved out of a single rock. The right hand is raised toward the right shoulder with the palm spread, signifying a lack of fear, while the position of the left draws the worshipper to Buddha for release from earthly bonds. It has been ascribed to King Dhatusena (AD 459-477) who was

Tip...
It's best to arrive first thing in the morning to see sunlight on the face of the Buddha.

responsible for the building of several tanks, including the one here. As you walk down to the base, note the small lotus flower in between the Buddha's feet. The carving is so perfectly symmetrical that when it rains the water drops from his nose down to the centre of the 10-cm flower – or at least, it did; nowadays the Buddha shelters from the elements under a large steel canopy.

Sasseruwa *Colour map 2, B3.*

13 km west of Aukana on a poor road. Rs 500. Allow 45 mins to explore – best visited early in the morning. Not accessible by public transport.

The minor road to Aukana continues to Sasseruwa (commonly spelled Raswehera) via Negampaha. This extensive complex was an ancient monastery site dating back to the second century BC, with more than 100 cave cells, remains of stupas, moonstones and inscriptions. There is a similar standing Buddha here, framed by the dark rock, though it is either unfinished or lacks the quality of workmanship found at Aukana. It was possibly carved at the same time, although some believe it to be a later copy. One legend is that the two images were carved in a competition between master and student. The master's Buddha at Aukana was completed first, so the Sasseruwa statue was abandoned. Its location, halfway up a rocky hillside, requires climbing nearly 300 steps.

Listings Towards Anuradhapura

Transport

Bus There are occasional direct buses to **Aukana** from Dambulla but it is more practical to take a bus to **Kekirawa** (45 mins), and then change to a Galnewa bus, getting off at Aukana Junction. From Anuradhapura, buses to **Kekirawa** take 1½ hrs.

Train Aukana lies on the Colombo–Batticaloa train line but trains stop more frequently at **Kala Wewa** (8 km from the site), where you can pick up a 3-wheeler for the return trip.

Anuradhapura
& Mihintale

Anuradhapura is Sri Lanka's most sacred city. Along with Mihintale, it represents the first real home of Buddhism in Sri Lanka, and thus contains some of the island's most sacred Buddhist sites. It is here that the Sri Maha Bodhi tree was planted from a cutting from the original Bo under which the Buddha received Enlightenment; to this day it draws thousands of pilgrims from around the world.

Anuradhapura's ruins and monuments are widely scattered, which makes a thorough tour exhausting and time-consuming, but for those with more than a passing interest in the island's past, it more than repays the effort.

Nearby, Mihintale, with its vast white *dagoba* glowing atop the hill, is where King Tissa received the Emperor Asoka's son Mahinda and converted to Buddhism. It makes an excellent day trip away from the bustle and noise, and can even be used as an alternative base.

Essential Anuradhapura and Mihintale

Finding your feet

Many visitors arrive from Dambulla to the southeast, along the A9/A13 (see page 259). Others come from Colombo via Kurunegala and Yapahuwa (see page 98), though the quickest route from the capital is along the A12 from Puttalam (see page 88). From Trincomalee, the route is via Horowupatana, giving you the opportunity to visit Mihintale first. Anuradhapura and Mihintale are also now accessible from the north, from Jaffna via Vavuniya (see page 347). Buses are available in all directions. By train, Anuradhapura lies on the Northern line, and all trains between Colombo and Jaffna stop here; from Kandy, change at Polgahawela. Mihintale, 11 km east of Anuradhapura, is a short bus or cycle ride east from the city.

Best sites in Anuradhapura
Ruvanwelisiya dagoba, page 270
Sri Maha Bodhi, page 271
Samadhi Buddha, page 275
Jetavanarama dagoba, page 275
Issurumuniyagala, page 276

Getting around

A three-wheeler from the train or bus station to your accommodation, assuming you are staying in the New Town, should cost around Rs 150-200. The New Town is about 2 km southeast of the ancient city; see below for the best route from the town. If you want a full day tour, consider hiring a car

Tip...
There are lots of drink stalls around Anuradhapura; the ones near the *dagobas* tend to be expensive. Souvenir sellers can be very persistent and unpleasant, so be firm.

or three-wheeler since the ruins, especially to the north, are very spread out and can be exhausting to visit under a hot sun. Many people use a bicycle (available from guesthouses) to get around, but you should be prepared to park it and walk when told to. Bear in mind, too, that unless you follow a prescribed route (and even if you do) it is easy to get lost, as there are many confusing tracks, and signposting can be poor.

Tickets

There are four ticket offices: one at the Tourist Information Counter, another at the Archaeological Museum, a third at the Jetavanarama Museum, and finally one towards the Dalada Maligawa. A single day ticket for the main sites costs US$25 (half-price for children), though the sites included are widely spread and even with a car seeing them all in a day is exhausting. It is worth getting a guide, Rs 500-800 for three to four hours.

Time required

Allow at least one full day to explore the sites in Anuradhapura. Mihintale can be visited on a day trip.

Unlike Polonnaruwa, Anuradhapura's monuments are not clustered into convenient groups, so planning an itinerary can be difficult. The order of sites below follows a figure-of-eight pattern, starting in the central area, then heading 3 km north and then east to Kuttan-Pokuna, before returning south to the Jetavanarama *dagoba*, and looping across to explore the museums and lakeside monuments south of the central area.

Approach from New Town

Anuradhapura rivals Milton Keynes for its roundabouts. If you are staying in the New Town, 2 km southeast of the ancient city, the best approach to the sites is to cycle northwest across Main Street and the railway line to Jayanthi Mawatha, where you turn right, past the two rest houses, up to **Lion Pillar**. Here you turn left on to Sri Maha Bodhi Mawatha and continue past the Tourist Information Office (where you can pick up a ticket if necessary) up to the barrier, beyond which the road leads to the **Sri Maha Bodhi**. You are not allowed to cycle past this point, and you will be asked to park your bike in the car park. Don't do this, as you will leave yourself with a long walk back from the central area to pick up your bike, though there are sometimes buses. Instead, continue past the car park for almost 1 km, heading up Nandana Mawatha (or path) towards the huge white **Ruvanwelisiya Dagoba**. Here you can park your bike (for free) close to the central area. There is a wide pedestrian walkway which leads from the *dagoba* to the Sri Maha Bodhi.

Ruvanwelisiya Dagoba

Begun by King Dutthagamenu (Dutugemunu) to house relics, this is one of the most impressive of all Sri Lanka's *dagobas*. Built with remarkable opulence, the king, who was said to have great luck, found a rich vein of silver from Ridigama to cover the expenses. Monks from as far away as Alexandria were recorded as being present at the enshrinement of the relics in 140 BC. The king however fell ill before the *dagoba*'s completion, so he asked his brother Saddhatissa to complete the work for him. Saddhatissa covered the dome with bamboo reeds and painted them with lacquer and imitation gold so that the king could witness the 'completion' of his *magnum opus* on his deathbed. Today, the dome is 80 m in diameter at its base and 53 m high. Apart from its sheer size, you will notice first the frieze on the outer wall of hundreds of life-size (and life-like) elephants, most of which are modern replacements. The *dagoba* is surrounded by the remains of sculptural pieces. You can see the remains of the columns dotted around in the grass underneath huge rain trees where monkeys play. A small passage leads to the relic chamber. At the cardinal points are four 'chapels' which were reconstructed in 1873, when renovation started. The restoration has flattened the shape of the dome, and some of the painting is of questionable style, but it remains a remarkably striking monument. Today, you may find watching the *dagoba* being 'whitewashed' an interesting spectacle (see box, opposite).

ON THE ROAD

White shrines

The ubiquitous *dagoba (Sinhalese stupa)* is one of the most striking features of the island. The domed-shaped shrines range in size from tiny village structures to the enormous monuments at Ruvanwelisiya in Anuradhapura and Mahaseya at Mihintale. They even appear in nature: the stone of the canonball tree fruit is a perfectly formed white *dagoba*.

There are of course many reasons why they stand out in a landscape: partly for their position, partly their size but mostly their colour – a dazzling white. Most are beautifully maintained and are often repainted before important Buddhist festivals.

Painting a large *dagoba is no easy job*. First, the spire is cocooned in an elaborate bamboo scaffolding, linked to the base by rickety bamboo ladders; bamboo is ideal as it can be bent to conform to the shape of the dome and its lightness makes the ladders easily moveable. A team of about five painters assembles on the ladder, while four men are deployed with ropes attached at the top and midpoints to give it some form of stability. At each stage, a painter is responsible for a section of the surface about 3 m in height at an arm's width. He starts, logically enough, by daubing the lime whitewash onto the topmost 1.5 m section; then he takes three steps down the ladder to cover the bottom 1.5 m. Once a section is completed, the bamboo structure is moved an arm's width round and the whole process starts again.

You'll notice that not all the *dagobas* have yet been restored – their red brick or plain plastered surface are dull in comparison with those that have been returned to their original condition

Brazen Palace
The site is open only on poya days.

Follow the pedestrian walkway south towards the Sri Maha Bodhi. Just before reaching the tree, you will see the many pillars of the Brazen Palace on your left. The name refers to the first monastery here and its now-disappeared roof, reputedly made of bronze. Built originally by Dutthagamenu, it was the heart of the monastic life of the city, the Maha Vihara. Described in the *Mahavansa* as having nine storeys and 1600 pillars, each just under 4 m high, laid out over an area of 70 sq m. Above, each storey was supposed to have 100 windows, with 1000 rooms overall, the building adorned with coral and precious stones. This requires imagination these days, though now a wooden first floor has been erected, aiming to recreate the monastery's top storey. Originally destroyed by Indian invasion, the monastery was rebuilt several times; much of what is visible today is the reconstruction of King Parakramabahu I in the last quarter of the 11th century, making use of the remnants of former buildings.

Sri Maha Bodhi tree
Rs 200, though this may not be demanded. Shoes must be removed on entering the terrace – there is a booth at the eastern entrance.

This is one of Sri Lanka's most sacred sites. The 'Bo' ('Bodhi') tree or Pipal (*Ficus religiosa*) was planted as a cutting from the tree in Bodhgaya in India under which the Buddha found

Anuradhapura

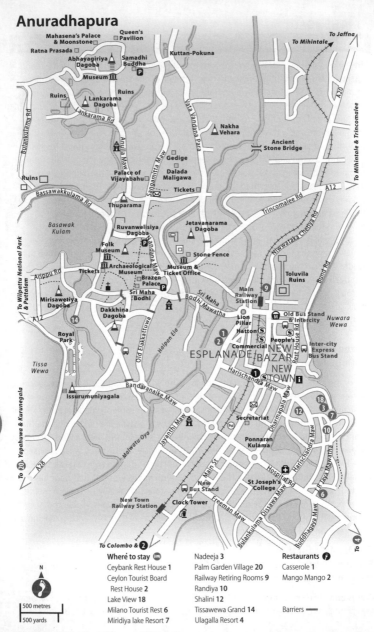

Mahasena's Palace & Moonstone
Queen's Pavilion
Ratna Prasada
Abhayagiriya Dagoba
Samadhi Buddha
Museum
Kuttan-Pokuna
To Mihintale
To Jaffna
To Mihintale & Trincomalee
A20

Ruins
Lankarama Dagoba
Lankarama Rd
Ruins
Anula Maw
Nakha Vehara
Ancient Stone Bridge

Bulankulama Rd
Ruins
Palace of Vijayabahu
Gedige
Dalada Maligawa
Tickets
A12

Bassawakkulama Rd
Thuparama
Sangamitta Maw
Vata Vandana Para

Basawak Kulam
Ruvanwelisiya Dagoba
Jetavanarama Dagoba
Folk Museum
Archaeological Museum
Stone Fence
Museum & Ticket Office
Brazen Palace
Sri Maha Bodhi
Sri Maha Bodhi Mawatha
Tickets

Niwwataraka Chatva Rd
Trincomalee Rd
Toluvila Ruins
Bund Rd

Arippu Rd
To Wilpattu National Park & Puttalam
A12
Mirisawetiya Dagoba
Dakkhina Dagoba
14
Royal Park
Tissa Wewa
Issurumuniyagala

Old Elakattuwa
Halpan Ela
Lion Pillar
Hatton
Main Railway Station
9
Old Bus Stand & Intercity
M
People's
Nuwara Wewa

Yapahuwa & Kurunegala
A8

Bandaranaike Maw
ESPLANADE
NEW BAZAR
NEW TOWN
1
2
Commercial
Inter-city Express Bus Stand

Malwatu Oya
Jayanthi Maw
Harischandra Maw
1
i
18
3
7

Secretariat
Dharmapala Maw
12
Harischandra Mawatha
10

Pol
Ponnaran Kulama
Hospital Rd
Raja Mawatha
6

Main St
St Joseph's College
Freeman Maw
Bulankulama Dissawa Maw
Buddhagaya Maw
To 4

New Bus Stand
New Town Railway Station
Clock Tower
i

To Colombo & 2

N
500 metres
500 yards

Where to stay
Ceybank Rest House 1
Ceylon Tourist Board Rest House 2
Lake View 18
Milano Tourist Rest 6
Miridiya lake Resort 7

Nadeeja 3
Palm Garden Village 20
Railway Retiring Rooms 9
Randiya 10
Shalini 12
Tissawewa Grand 14
Ulagalla Resort 4

Restaurants
Casserole 1
Mango Mango 2

Barriers ━━━

Anuradhapura

From origins as a settlement in the sixth century BC, Anuradhapura was made Sri Lanka's first capital in 377 BC by King Pandukhabhaya (437-367 BC), who started the great irrigation works on which it depended and named it after the constellation Anuradha. The first era of religious building followed the conversion of King Devanampiya Tissa (ruled 250-10 BC) to Buddhism by Mahinda at Mihintale. During his 40-year reign this included the Thuparama Dagoba, Issurumuniyagala, and the Maha Vihara with the Sri Maha Bodhi and the Brazen Palace. A branch of the Bodhi tree (see below) under which the Buddha was believed to have gained his Enlightenment was brought from Bodhgaya in India and successfully transplanted, creating one of the holiest Buddhist sites in the world.

Anuradhapura remained a capital city until the ninth century AD, when it reached its peak of power and vigour. At this time the city may have stretched for 25 km. However, successive waves of invasion from South India finally took their toll, and, after the 13th century, it almost entirely disappeared. The irrigation works on which the city had depended fell into total disuse, and its political functions were taken over first by Polonnaruwa, and then by capitals to the south.

Anuradhapura was 'rediscovered' by Ralph Backhaus around 1820. Archaeological research, excavation and restoration started in 1872 and have continued ever since. In 1988, it was designated a World Heritage Site. Construction of the New Town began in the 1950s, and it is now the most important Sinhalese city of the north. It houses the headquarters of the Sri Lanka Archaeological Survey.

Enlightenment. The cutting was brought to the island by Emperor Asoka's daughter, the Princess Sanghamitta, at some point after 236 BC. Guardians have kept uninterrupted watch over the tree ever since, making it, all tourist literature will proudly tell you, the oldest historically authenticated tree in the world. Today, in keeping with tradition, it is the army who guard the tree, while the Director of the Peradeniya Botanical Gardens tends to its health. Nowadays, you can only see the top of the Bo tree, on the highest terrace, which is supported by an elaborate metal structure and is surrounded by brass railings. There are other Bo trees around the Sri Maha Bodhi which are bedecked with colourful prayer flags, strips of cloth and coins, left by pilgrims in expectation of prayers being answered. On *poya* days, the courtyard surrounding the tree becomes a whirl of devotion, and In April a huge number of pilgrims arrive for the Snana puja, to make offerings and bathe the tree with milk. Every 12th year the ceremony is particularly auspicious.

Archaeological and Folk Museums
Wed-Mon 0800-1700, closed public hols. Rs 200 (or free with entry to Sri Maha Bodhi tree).

The **Archaeological Museum** is in the old colonial headquarters. It is an excellent small museum, with a large collection from all over the island, including some beautiful pieces of sculpture and finds from Mihintale. It is well laid out, with occasional informative labels and some fascinating exhibits. There are statues from several sites, moonstones, implements and a model of Thuparama *vatadage*. Outside in the garden are beautifully sculpted guard stones and an array of meticulously designed latrines. Separate latrine plinths were used for urinals, solid waste and bidets. Under each immaculately carved platform was a succession of pots containing sand, charcoal and limestone to purify the waste.

Nearby, the **Folk Museum** ① *Tue-Sat 0900-1700, Rs 500*, is a collection that reflects rural life in the North Central Province, with a large display of vessels used by villagers in Rajarata, and handicrafts.

Thuparama

Return to the Ruvanswelisiya *dagoba* to pick up your bike. Continuing north, turn left at the crossroads to the site's oldest *dagoba*, said to house the right collar-bone of the Buddha. Built by Devanampiya, the 19-m-high *dagoba* was originally in the shape of a 'paddy-heap' – its beautiful bell shape dates to renovation work completed in 1862. It is surrounded by concentric circles of graceful granite monolithic pillars of a *vatadage*, which was added in the seventh century, possibly originally designed to support an overarching thatched cover. It is a centre of active pilgrimage, decorated with flags and lights.

Abhayagiriya Dagoba
Left from the first crossroads, 2 km north along Anulla Mawatha to the Abhagiriya Dagoba.

First, a detour to the west takes you to the restored **Lankarama Dagoba**. Built in the first century BC it bears some similarities to the earlier Thuparama. Some columns remain of its *vatadage*.

The Abhayagiriya Dagoba was the centre of one of Anuradhapura's largest and oldest monastic complexes. It is 400 m round and was supposedly 135 m high in its original form (part of the pinnacle has disappeared). It is now about 110 m high. Built in 88 BC by Vattagamani (and later restored by Parakramabahu I in the 12th century), it has two splendid sculpted *dwarapalas* (guardians) at the threshold.

The *dagoba* and its associated monastery were built in an attempt to weaken the political hold of the Hinayana Buddhists and to give shelter to monks of the Mahayana school. It was considered an important seat of Buddhist learning; the Chinese traveller/monk Fa Hien, visiting it in the fifth century, noted that there were 5000 monks in residence. He also points out a 7-m jade Buddha, sparkling with gems, while the *dagoba* itself was said to have been built over a Buddha footprint. It is currently covered in scaffolding as restoration work is undertaken.

Abhayagiriya (Fa Hien) Museum, just south of the Abhayagiriya Dagoba, was built by the Chinese. The collection includes further examples of latrine plinths, as displayed in the Archaeological Museum. There is also an extensive display detailing the excavation of the Abhayagiriya site.

Ratna Prasada

To the west of the Abhayagiriya Dagoba are the ruins of the monastery. The area had once been the 'undesirable' outskirts of Anuradhapura where the cremation grounds were sited. In protest against the king's rule, an ascetic community of monks set up a *Tapovana* community (see box, page 283), of which this is an architectural example. This type of monastery typically had two pavilions connected by a stone bridge within a high-walled enclosure which contained a pond. The main entrance was from the east, with a porch above the entrance.

In Anuradhapura the Ratna Prasada, or 'gem palace', did not remain a peaceful haven but was the scene of bloody massacres when a rebellious group took refuge with the monks and were subsequently beheaded by the king's men.

Mahasena Palace

The nearby Mahasena Palace has a particularly fine carved stone tablet and one of the most beautifully carved **moonstones** (see page 393), though the necessary protective railing surrounding it makes photography a little tricky. Note also the flight of steps held up by miniature stone dwarfs.

Samadhi Buddha

Continue east from the Abhayagiriya Dagoba to this superb statue of the serene Buddha, probably dating from the fourth century AD. The Buddha has an expression depicting 'extinction of feeling and compassion'. Some used to think the expression changed as the sun's light moved across it, but, sadly, it has now been roofed to protect it from the weather.

Kuttan-Pokuna

A new road through the forest leads to these two ponds – recently restored eighth- and ninth-century ritual baths with steps from each side descending to the water. They were probably for the use of the monastery or for the university nearby. Though called **'twin' ponds**, one is more than 10 m longer than the other. You can see the underground water supply channel at one end of the second bath.

South to Jetavaranama Dagoba

There are two routes south from here. Sangamitta Mawatha leads back to the central area through the site of the 11th-century palace of **Vijayabahu I**. This route passes close to the original **Dalada Maligawa** where the Tooth Relic was first enshrined when it was brought to Ceylon in AD 313; only the stone columns remain. Alternatively, a 2-km cycle down Vata Vandana Para takes you straight to the vast Jetavanarama Dagoba.

Jetavanarama Dagoba

This *dagoba*, looming impressively from the plain, is said to be the highest brick built *dagoba* of its kind in the world. Started by King Mahasena (AD 275-292), its massive scale was designed in a competitive spirit to rival the orthodox Maha Vihara. The paved platform on which it stands covers more than 3 ha and it has a diameter of over 100 m. In 1860 Emerson Tennent, in his book *Ceylon*, calculated that it had enough bricks to build a 3-m-high brick wall 25 cm thick from London to Edinburgh, equal to the distance from the southern tip of Sri Lanka to Jaffna and back down the coast to Trincomalee. The *dagoba* is currently being renovated with help from UNESCO, though work periodically stops as there is a dearth of bricks.

The size of the image house here shows that an enormous Buddha image, similar to (though larger than) the one at Aukana, was once installed here facing the *dagoba*. There is a huge lotus pedestal, with large mortices for the feet of the statue. The image would have been destroyed by fire.

Jetavanarama Museum

Daily 0800-1700, closed public holidays.

This museum, well worth a visit, houses some interesting objects from the surrounding 120-ha site, including some fine guardstones and an amazingly intricate 8 mm gold chain with 14 distinguishable flowers.

Basawak Kulam tank

Continuing west across the main site towards Tissawewa, you could visit the Archaeological and Folk museums at this point (see above) en route to the **Basawak Kulam tank**, the oldest artificial lake in the city, built by King Pandukabhaya in the fourth century BC. The dried-up southern side is good for walks and birdwatching, and there are excellent sunset views from the eastern shore. Alternatively, head south from the museums to stop off for lunch or a drink at the **Nuwarawewa Rest House**. The Miraswetiya Dagoba is close by.

Mirisawetiya Dagoba

This was the first monument to be built by Dutthagemunu after his consecration, enshrining a miraculous sceptre which contained a Buddha relic. The sceptre, which had been left here by the king when he visited the tank, could not on his return be removed by any means. After a Chola invasion, the *dagoba* was completely rebuilt during the reign of King Kasyapa V in AD 930. Surrounded by the ruins of monasteries on three sides, there are some superb sculptures of *Dhyani* Buddhas in the shrines of its chapels. It is currently being renovated.

Tissawewa and Royal Park

This tank was built by King Devanampiya Tissa and was associated with the bathing rituals of newly crowned kings. You can walk/jog on the east and south sides along the raised tank *bund* and continue all round using local tracks on the west and a tarmac road on the north. The park just below the lake is very pleasant as it receives few visitors. You can wander undisturbed across large rocks among the ruined buildings and remains of bathing pools.

Issurumuniyagala Monastery

Daily 0800-1930. Rs 200. Ask for permission to take photos.

This small group of striking black rocks is one of the most attractive and peaceful places in town. It also has some outstanding sculptures. The temple, carved out of solid rock, houses a large statue of the reclining Buddha. A cleft in the rock is full of bats which are fascinating to watch. On the terraces outside is a small square pool. Don't miss the beautifully carved elephants, showing great individual character, just above the water level as if descending to it. The small **museum** is to the left of the entrance. Some of the best sculptures in Anuradhapura are now housed here, including perhaps the most famous of all – 'the lovers', which may represent Dutthagemunu's son Saliya and his girlfriend, Asokamala, for whom he forsook the throne.

Behind the temple, you can climb up steps to the top of the rock above the temple to get a good view of the countryside and tank. Here there is a footprint carved into the rock, into which money is thrown.

Nuwara Wewa

Nuwara Wewa, which lies to the east of the New Town, is the largest of Anuradhapura's artificial lakes (1000 ha). It was probably built by Gajabahu I in the second century AD.

Tourist information

Tourist office
Dharmapala Mawatha, T025-222 7106,
Mon-Fri 0900-1700, Sat 0900-1300.
Here you can pick up a local map and
planning advice.

Where to stay

Anuradhapura has a good selection of
reasonably priced hotels and guesthouses,
but is rather lacking at the top end. Except
for Ulagalla Resort and the wonderfully
atmospheric Tissawewa Grand, all are in
the New Town, 2-3 km from the ancient
sites. The main cluster is around the
junction of Harischandra Mawatha and
JR Jaya Mawatha. The guesthouses on
Freeman Mawatha are much closer to
the 'New' bus station and the 'New Town'
railway station, though even further away
from the ruins. Nearly all rent out bicycles
and can arrange guided tours.

$$$$ The Sanctuary at Tissawewa
Near the tank, T011-258 3133,
www.tissawewa.com.
Former Dutch governor's house with bags
of colonial character, wooden floorboards
and ceilings, some period furniture and
fittings, beautifully situated in secluded
parkland full of peacocks and monkeys. The
15 a/c and fan rooms are cool, spacious and
still feel fresh after a thorough renovation,
but for all the style and atmosphere, the
service leaves a bit to be desired at this price.
Restaurant, bike hire, guests can use pool at
Nuwarawewa Rest House.

$$$ Miridiya Lake Resort
Wasaladantha Mawatha, T025-222 2112,
www.miridiyahotel.lk.

39 huge, cool a/c rooms, the best of which
come with outdoor showers, some with
view over Nuwara Wewa. Restaurant, bar,
pool (non-residents pay Rs 400), pleasant
atmosphere and attractive landscaped
gardens with ponds overlooking tank ideal
for a sunset stroll.

$$$ Palm Garden Village
Km 42 post, Puttalam Rd, Pandulagama,
2.5 km from the sites, T025-222 3961,
www.palmgardenvillage.com.
40 stylish a/c rooms and 10 suites in
upmarket villas dotted around gardens
with deer. Full facilities including large pool,
Ayurvedic centre, open-sided restaurants.

$$ Randiya
Off JR Jaya Mawatha, T025-222 2868,
www.hotelrandiya.com.
Comfortable a/c rooms, standard or
deluxe, all with balcony in modern house.
Pleasant restaurant serving good food,
excellent service.

$$-$ Ceylon Tourist Board Rest House
Jayanthi Mawatha, T025-222 2188,
reservations T011-243 7059.
Set in extensive grounds, large rooms in
attractive neo-colonial building, fan or a/c,
attached bath, slightly grubby, reasonable
value though service rather slow, popular
in the pilgrimage season, restaurant with
very cheap food.

$$-$ Milano Tourist Rest
596/40, Stage One, JR Jaya Mawatha, T025-
222 2364, www.milanotouristrest.com.
Rightly one of the most popular budget
options in town, with comfortable
well-furnished rooms, fan or a/c, a
sociable restaurant and bar in the groovy
1950s-flavoured main building, and plenty
of overflow space in the annexe across
the road. Bike hire and Wi-Fi available.

The owners also manage several other hotels, but none match Milano for atmosphere and friendliness.

$$-$ Shalini
41/388 Harischandra Mawatha (opposite Water Tower Stage 1), T025-222 2425, www.hotelshalini.com.
14 large, clean, comfortable fan or a/c rooms in modern house, hot water, good food in attractive roof-top restaurant, well kept, cycle hire, free transfer from/to station, internet café.

$ Ceybank Rest House
Jayanthi Mawatha, T025-223 5520, ceybankhh@gmail.com.
Large rooms with small balconies and some family rooms, clean, mainly for local pilgrims.

$ Lake View
4C4 Harischandra Mawatha, T025-222 1593.
10 rooms, some comfortable and clean with hot water, others a bit dingy so inspect first, a/c or fan. Pleasant owner. Mihintale *dagoba* visible from here. Tours can be arranged, bikes for hire (Rs 300 per day).

$ Nadeeja
Just past Lake View, 4C6 Mihindu Mawatha, T071-830 8553, saliya.smpth@gmail.com.
A/c and fan rooms, large open communal areas on the upper floors. Good food, welcoming.

$ Railway Retiring Rooms
T025-222 2571.
10 basic rooms, not too clean but cheap and available for non-passengers. Rates are posted on a board as you enter the railway station; enquire at the counter.

Around Anuradhapura

$$$$ Ulagalla Resort
Thirapanne, 23 km from Anuradhapura, T11-567 1000 (reservations), www.ulagallaresorts.com.

It may be a distance away from Anuradhapura but this is the most luxurious hotel around. 25 tasteful a/c chalets with private plunge pools, dotted throughout the 20 ha grounds which border Ulagalla tank, Freshwater swimming pool, spa, restaurants and activities such as kayaking, horse riding and birdwatching. Electric buggies will collect guests and ferry them to the main house.

Restaurants

The north end of town lacks restaurants but has some friendly food stalls. All the guesthouses and hotels have restaurants: recommended are Milano Tourist Rest, Shalini (which has a terrace restaurant in the tree-tops serving good-value food, especially the rice and curry set menus) and Randiya.

$ Casserole
Above Family Bakers, 279 Main St, T025-222 4443.
A/c offers welcome respite from the heat, with good-value Chinese (set menus from Rs 300 upwards), but has the atmosphere of a school gym and staff are glum.

$ Mango Mango
Jayanthi Mawatha.
Clean and cool cafe serving Sri Lankan and Indian food and pastries. A good place to retreat from the heat.

$ Nelum Kole Bath Kade
AH43, 7 km north in Rambewa.
This roadside cafe couldn't get any more basic, but it's a great place to grab lunch if you're heading north to Jaffna or Mannar. Rice-curry buffets are aimed squarely at locals and are correspondingly tasty and cheap.

$ Walkers Inn

387 Harischandra Mawatha.

Ever-popular bakery, good for cheap picnic supplies, and a slightly pricey sit-down rice-and-curry restaurant tacked on to the side.

Festivals

There are several festivals during the year.
Apr **Snana Puja** is celebrated at Sri Maha Bodhi.
Jun **Poson Poya** remembers the introduction of Buddhism to Sri Lanka and is celebrated with huge processions when many pilgrims visit the area.
Jul/Aug During **Daramiti Perahera** locals bring firewood in a procession to the Bodhi tree, commemorating a time when bonfires were lit to keep away wild animals.

Transport

Bicycle hire Available from most guesthouses and hotels in the New Town (Rs 300 per day). **Mihintale** is an easy 11-km ride along a flat road.

Bus For long-distance services there are 2 bus stations. **New Bus Station**, Main St, south end of town, serves most destinations except Colombo and Kandy. Departures for **Polonnaruwa** are frequent (3 hrs); **Trincomalee** (3½ hrs); **Vavuniya** (1 hr); **Mannar** (3 hrs). Buses to **Mihintale** can be picked up on the main road (frequent, 30 mins). The **Old Bus Station**, Rest House Rd, has CTB buses to **Colombo** (hourly, 5 hrs) and **Kandy** via **Dambulla** (hourly, 4 hrs). Intercity express buses leave from diagonally opposite the Old Bus Station, to **Colombo**, **Kandy** and to **Kurunegala** and **Negombo**. There is a frequent bus service between the Old and New Bus stands.

Three-wheeler These are everywhere and will offer 3- to 4-hr trips around the ancient city. To **Mihintale** it costs about Rs 1500 for a half-day trip.

Train From the main station trains leave to **Colombo** (4-5 hrs) 8 times daily, the 0500 departure continuing to **Matara** (10 hrs). Change at **Polgahawela** for **Kandy**. For **Habarana**, **Polonnaruwa**, **Trincomalee** and other destinations east change at Maho Junction (it's more practical to reach Habarana by bus). Northbound trains leave for **Jaffna** 4 times daily (4 hrs). Note that the branch line to **Mihintale** only runs at festival time in Jul.

Tip...
Be aware that the hotels around Freeman Mawatha are closer to the New Town station (south of the main station) though intercity services do not usually stop here.

the birthplace of Sri Lankan Buddhism

Mihintale (pronounced Mihin-taalay), named as Mahinda's Hill, is revered as the place where Mahinda converted King Devanampiya Tissa to Buddhism in 243 BC, thereby enabling Buddhism to spread to the whole island.

The legend tells how King Tissa was chasing a stag during a hunting expedition. The stag reached Mihintale and fled up the hillside followed by the king until he reached a place surrounded by hills, where the animal disappeared. The frustrated king was astonished to find a gentle person who told him the Buddha's teachings. It was Mahinda, Asoka's son, who had come to preach Buddhism and was able to convert the king along with 40,000 followers.

Mihintale continues to be an important religious site and is a pleasant place to just stroll around away from the crowds that gather at more famous ancient sites. Mihintale town is little more than a junction with a few shops but comes alive with pilgrims during the June festival.

The approach

Mihintale is close to the Anuradhapura–Trincomalee road. The huge *dagoba* can be seen from miles around and is especially striking at night. Statues of six of the principal characters

1 **Mihintale**

Mihintale maps
1 Mihintale, page 280
2 Mihintale sacred centre, page 282

Where to stay
Mihintale 1

of the site mark the turn-off onto a minor road towards the hill. On the right are the ruins of a ninth-century **hospital**, which appears to have had an outer court where medicines were ground and stored, and stone tanks for oil and herbal baths. The inner court appears to have had small treatment rooms. A 10th-century stone inscription mentions the use of leeches in treatment. There is a small archaeological museum nearby (see below).

On the left at the foot of the steps, there is evidence of the quincunx *vihara* of a monastery (*arama*).

The climb

There are 1840 granite steps in total, some carved into the rock, to the top but they are very shallow and it is much less of a climb than it first looks, taking under 10 minutes from the car park to the refectory level, at a gentle pace. The width of the steps indicate the large number of pilgrims

> **Tip...**
> You can avoid about half of the steps by driving round to the upper car park, which takes you straight to the second (refectory) level.

who visited the sacred site on special occasions in the past. The climb starts gently, rising in a broad stairway of 350 steps shaded by frangipani trees to the first platform. Further steps to the right take you up to an open area with Kantaka Chetiya

The first terrace

Kantaka Chetiya is the earliest *stupa* here. Excavated in 1932-1935, it had been severely damaged. Over 130 m in circumference, today it is only about 12 m high compared with its original height of perhaps 30 m. There is some unique stonework in the four projecting frontispieces at the cardinal points, especially to the eastern and southern points. Note the marvellously detailed friezes of geese, dwarves and a variety of other animals, flanked by *stelae* with floral designs. Around the Kantaka Chetiya are 68 caves, where the first monks here resided.

Returning to the first platform, steeper steps lead to a large refectory terrace. As you climb up you can see the impressive outer cyclopean wall of the complex. As an alternative to the steps to get to the refectory level, take a faint footpath to the left between the second and third flights. This crosses an open grassy area. Walk to the end and you will see the lake, green with algae. A path to the left takes you towards the **Giribandhu Chetiya Kiri Vehara**, though it is largely ruined and grassed over on the north side. You can look down on the lower car park and the quincunx. To the right, the path approaches the refectory from the rear and you pass a massive stone trough.

The second terrace

The Refectory Immediately on the left is the **Relic House** and the rectangular **Bhojana Salava** (Monks' refectory). There is a stone aqueduct and two granite troughs, one probably used for rice, the other for gruel. The square **Chapter House** or 'Conversation Hall', with signs of 48 pillars and a 'throne' platform, is immediately to the north and is where the monks and lay members met. This has the bases of a series of evenly spaced small brick *dagobas*. At the entrance, stone slabs covered in 10th-century inscriptions on granite give detailed rules governing the sacred site.

The flat grassy terrace, which can also be approached by car from the south up the old paved road or by steps down from the Kantaka Chetiya, is dotted with trees and the outlines of three small shrines.

Sinha Pokuna (Lion Bath) To the west of the terrace, a short distance down the old road, this is about 2 m sq and 1.8 m deep and has excellent carvings of elephants, lions and warriors in the form of a frieze around the bottom of the tank. The finest, however, is the 2-m-high rampant lion whose mouth forms the spout. Water was gathered in the tank by channelling and feeding it through the small mystic gargoyle similar to the one that can be seen at Sigiriya.

The main path up the long flight of steps to the Ambasthala Dagoba starts by the 'Conversation Hall' in the square. After a five-minute climb, a path leads off to the right, round the hillside, to the Naga Pokuna, which you can visit on the way back down (see below). Continuing to climb, you pass a beautifully inscribed rock on the right-hand side listing in second-century AD script lands owned by the king.

The sacred centre
Rs 500, plus tip for shoes.

Ambasthala Dagoba At the top of the steps, you reach the ticket office, where you must leave your shoes (and hat). Straight ahead at the heart of the complex is the 'mango tree' *dagoba*, the holiest part of the site, built at the traditional meeting place of King Tissa and Asoka's son Mahinda. The monk in his office makes frequent loud-speaker announcements for donations from pilgrims; these donations have funded the erection of a large white Buddha statue on a rock overlooking the central area in 1991, up to which you can climb. The bronze Buddhas are gifts from Thailand.

Sela Cetiya A rock stupa at the site of the original mango tree has a replica of the Buddha's footprint. It is quite small and is surrounded by a gilt railing covered in prayer flags, with a scattering of pilgrims' coins.

Mahinda's cave A path leads out of the northeast corner of the compound between a small cluster of monks' houses down a rough boulder track to the cave, less than a 10-minute walk away. A stall selling local herbal and forest product remedies is sometimes set up halfway. The cave is formed out of an extraordinary boulder, hollowed out underneath to create a narrow platform at the very end of a ridge above the plain below. From the stone 'couch', known as **Mahinda's bed**, there are superb views to the north

② Mihintale sacred centre

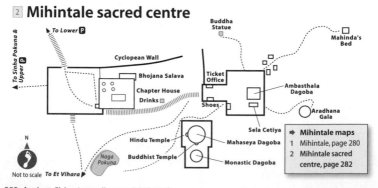

The *Pansukulika* or *Tapovana* sect of ascetic Buddhist hermits lived a simple life of deep meditation in forests and caves around the seventh to the 11th centuries. They are associated with Arankale, Mihintale and Ritigala. The monks were expected to wear ragged clothing and to immerse themselves in seeking the Truth, devoid of ritualistic forms of worship associated with Buddha images, relics and relic chambers. Such communities often won the admiration and support of kings, such as Sena I (AD 831-851).

   The sites had certain features in common. There was a porched entrance, ambulatories, a water pool for cleansing and the *padhanaghara*. Another similarity was an open terrace, possibly intended as a 'chapter house' connected to a smaller section which was usually roofed. These 'double platforms' were aligned east to west; the two raised stone-faced platforms were connected by a narrow walkway or bridge. An interesting anomaly within the austere life of the monks was the beautifully carved latrines or urinal stones they used, examples of which can be seen in the Anuradhapura Archaeological Museum (see page 273).

across the tanks and forested plains of the Dry Zone. You have to retrace your steps to the Ambasthala compound.

Aradhana Gala From the southeast corner of the compound a path with rudimentary steps cut in the bare granite rock leads to the summit of the Aradhana Gala (Meditation Rock). It is a very steep climb and, if you have no socks, very hot on the feet. A strong railing makes access quite secure. There are superb views from the top, especially across the compound to the Mahaseya Dagoba, which is at the same height.

> **Tip...**
> If you're visiting in the heat of the day, bring socks to protect your bare feet from the heat of the rock.

Mahaseya Dagoba Just beyond a small temple with a modern portrayal of Mahinda meeting King Tissa at the mango tree, a short flight of steep steps leads from the southwest corner of the compound up to the summit (310 m) with the Mahaseya Dagoba. According to legend this was built on the orders of King Tissa as a reliquary for a lock of the Buddha's hair or for relics of Mahinda. The renovated *dagoba*, which dominates the skyline, commands superb views back towards Anuradhapura to the southwest. Another monk may ask for donations here (anything above Rs 100 is recorded in a book).

   On the south side of the main *dagoba* is a smaller brick *dagoba,* while abutting it on its south side is a small Buddhist temple. To the west side is a Hindu temple with modern painted images of four Hindu deities: Ganesh, Saman, Vishnu and Kataragama.

Descent
Naga Pokuna After collecting your shoes, descend as far as the rock inscription (see above). Then take the small path which leads through cool forest to the Naga

Pokuna. This 'Snake Pond', which has a five-headed cobra carving which you can still make out, is a 40-m pool carved out of solid rock which stored water for the monastery; some believe it is where King Tissa would have bathed. At one end is a very small tank, now without water. Apparently this was where the Queen would bathe. It is a peaceful and beautiful place.

Et Vihara If you still have energy, a flight of 600 steps from the Naga Pokuna leads up to this inner temple, at the highest elevation in Mihintale. Though the small stupa is not very impressive, there are some magnificent views from here.

Other sights

After descending and exiting the main complex, head west to the Kandy Road (accessible from either car park). Close to the junction are the remains of a monastery complex with two *dagobas*, of which the **Indikatu Seya** on a raised stone square platform to the north, is the larger. It shows evidence that the monks were devotees of Mahayan Buddhism in the ninth century. South of here, inscriptions in the **Rajagiri Lena** (Royal Rock Caves) suggest that they may represent the first living quarters of Sri Lanka's earliest Buddhist monks.

Archaeology Museum This small, free museum is close to the lower car park. Displays include some terracotta dwarves, a couple of fine Ganadevi statues and a model of the middle chamber of the Mahaseya *dagoba*. There are some labels in English.

Listings Mihintale

Where to stay

$$ Hotel Mihintale (CHC)
Anuradhapura Rd, 600 m west of the crossroads, T025-226 6599.
10 a/c rooms, those upstairs far lighter, restaurant, outdoor seating.

$$ Saji – Sami Hotel
University Sq, T077-777 9774, www.sajisamihotel.com.
Stunning value in this smart new hotel, set in gardens full of birds and laden fruit trees. The rooms are clean and modern, but the self-contained villa in the grounds is really special, with an outside bath and views across the paddy fields to Mihintale. Great service from owner Ranji. Recommended.

Festivals

Jun Poson Poya is of particularly importance to Buddhists who commemorate the arrival of Buddhism on the island. Tens of thousands flock to climb to the sacred spot, chanting as they go: *Buddham saranam gachchaami. Dhammam saranam gachchaami. Sangam saranam gachchaami*, meaning 'In the Buddha I seek refuge, In Dhamma I seek refuge, In the Sangha I seek refuge'.

Transport

Bus Regular between Mihintale and **Anuradhapura**'s New Bus Station (20 mins).

Train Trains only run on the branch line to Anuradhapura during the Jun festival.

Sigiriya
& around

The bloody history of the royal fortress of Sigiriya (pronounced See-gi-ri-ya), a tale of murder and dynastic feuding, is as dramatic as its position at the summit of the vast, flat-topped 200-m-high Lion Rock, which rears starkly from the plain beneath. An exceptional natural site for a fortress, the rock dominates the surrounding countryside of the central forest and, from the top, offers views that stretch as far as the Dry Zone and south to the Central Highlands.

Deriving its name (Sinha-Giri) from the lions which were believed to occupy the caves, this impressive site is many visitors' favourite in the whole of Sri Lanka. The rewards of Sigiriya – its palace, famous frescoes and beautiful water gardens – justify the steep climb. Frequently labelled the 'Eighth Wonder of the World', it was designated a World Heritage Site in 1982.

North of Sigiriya, modest little Habarana makes a good base for visiting Kaudulla and Minneriya national parks.

Essential Sigiriya

Finding your feet

Sigiriya lies 15 km northeast of Dambulla, reached by turning off the A6 at Inamaluwa. The main bus stop is south of the rock, a 10-minute walk from the main entrance and ticket counter. (The track is signposted off the road, 1 km west from the bus stand, past the rest house.) If you arrive by car your driver will drop you at the entrance; the standard procedure is that they will meet you at a separate car park near the exit, but it's worth asking them to pick you up in the same spot, so you can visit the museum last (a good idea if you get here early in the morning). Be careful in Sigiriya at night, especially if you're a lone female.

When to go

Early morning is beautiful and very quiet until 0730, but the late afternoon light is better for the frescoes. Note that there is no access to the fresco gallery after 1700. The rock can be extremely crowded from mid-morning, and you should avoid the high sun around noon. Evenings bring out armies of mosquitoes, so take precautions and cover up. There can be long queues on public holidays. Overall, the best way to experience Sigiriya is to be at the entrance as soon as possible after the ticket counter opens at 0700 and allow at least two hours for a visit.

Visitor informaton

The ticket office at the entrance is open daily 0700-1700. Foreigners pay US$30 per person (half price for children), SAARC residents US$15. There is a road leading to the base of the rock for ease of access for disabled visitors.

★ Sigiriya   Colour map 2, B5
unmissable and unforgettable

Water gardens

Entering the site across the moat from the west, you will pass the fifth-century water gardens (restored by the Central Cultural Fund with UNESCO sponsorship) with walks, ponds and fountains that are gravity fed from the moats, just as they were 1500 years ago. The two pools in the water garden near the entrance had islands on which stood pavilions, while the shallow marble pools reflected the changing patterns of the clouds. You can see the secret changing room doors. Legend states that Kasyapa used to watch his concubines bathe here from his palace.

A straight path leads through the group of four fountain gardens with small water jets (originally fifth century), some with pretty lotuses attracting a number of water birds. Finally you reach the flower garden with colourful beds and flowering trees. To the right as you walk up to the rock is a **miniature water garden**. The whole area (including the moat and drive) is immaculate.

Base of the rock

Before reaching the steps to climb the Lion Rock, the path goes through the boulder garden, where clusters of rocks (including the **preaching rock** with 'seats') are marked with rows of notches and occasional 'gashes'. These may have been used for decorating the area with lamps during festivals. To the right are the Cobra Hood Cave and Audience Hall and Cistern rocks (see below). The ascent of the rock begins on well-maintained brick-lined stairways,

Tip...

It is advisable not to take food onto the site as it is overrun by dogs who will follow you around. Steer clear of the aggressive monkeys on the ascent.

which lead through the Elephant Gate up to the second checkpoint. As you climb it is easy to forget that the site was developed as a massive defensive fortress, with lookout points located on ledges.

Fresco gallery

From the second checkpoint, take the enclosed metal spiral staircase that winds up to the fresco gallery: it's much easier to visit the frescoes on your way up the rock than trying to fight your way back through the

Tip...
You may photograph the frescoes but a flash is not permitted. Note that there is no entry to the frescoes after 1700.

crowds on the way down. Sigiriya's frescoes, sheltered from the elements in a niche, vie with those of Ajanta in Western India, and though only 21 of the original 500 or so frescoes survive, they are remarkably well preserved.

Kasyapa gathered together the best artists of his day. In the style of Ajanta, the first drawing was done on wet plaster and then painted with red, yellow, green and black.

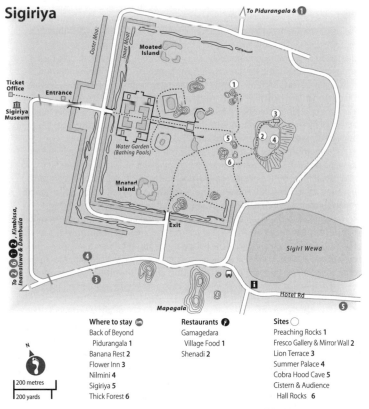

Sigiriya

To Pidurangala & 1

Outer Moat
Inner Moat

Moated Island

Ticket Office
Entrance

Sigiriya Museum

Water Garden (Bathing Pools)

Moated Island

Exit

To 2 6 1 2 Kimbissa, Inamaluwe & Dambulla

Sigiri Wewa

4

3

Mapagala

Hotel Rd

5

N

200 metres
200 yards

Where to stay 🛏
Back of Beyond
  Pidurangala 1
Banana Rest 2
Flower Inn 3
Nilmini 4
Sigiriya 5
Thick Forest 6

Restaurants 🍴
Gamagedara
  Village Food 1
Shenadi 2

Sites ○
Preaching Rocks 1
Fresco Gallery & Mirror Wall 2
Lion Terrace 3
Summer Palace 4
Cobra Hood Cave 5
Cistern & Audience
  Hall Rocks 6

BACKGROUND

Legends of Sigiriya

Inscriptions at **Pidurangala** and other evidence of early settlement in **Rama Kale** nearby suggest that this area was occupied by humans long before Kasyapa chose it for his palace fortress. But it is the legends surrounding his reign (AD 477-495) that have contributed to the romance of Sigiriya and provided inspiration for many books, plays and films.

The *Mahavansa* records that Kasyapa killed his father, King Dhatusena, by plastering him alive to a wall in order to gain the throne, after which he lived in terror that his half brother, Moggallana, who had taken refuge in India, would return to kill him. Kasyapa built a combination of pleasure palace and massive fortress on the unassailable rock at Sigiriya, but when Moggallana did come back after 18 years, Kasyapa came down from the hill to face his half brother's army on elephant back. Finding himself outnumbered and mistakenly thinking he had been abandoned by his supporters, he killed himself with his dagger.

A conflicting, if equally bloody alternative theory, propounded by historian Senarat Paranavitana, claims to have been deciphered from inscriptions by a 15th-century monk. In this version, Dhatusena is told that he can obtain imperial status by becoming a *Parvataraja*, or mountain king, ruling from a palace built on a rock summit. In the struggle for succession, Kasyapa returns from exile in India and mistakenly defeats his father's army, believing it to belong to his brother, at which Dhatusena beheads himself. Remorseful at being the cause of his father's death, Kasyapa, now king, attempts to put his father's dream into reality. In order to be accepted by overseas merchants, he proclaims himself as *Kubera*, the God of Wealth, and attempts to recreate his legendary palace on earth. He issues a gold coinage and establishes free ports, which accrue great wealth for the kingdom. In this theory Kasyapa dies in his palace after Moggallana persuades his wife to poison him.

Whatever the motives for its construction, the royal citadel was allegedly built between AD 477 and 485 and was surrounded by an impressive wall and a double moat. The construction of the royal pavilions and fortifications and the clever conservation and diversion of water, a scarce commodity in the Dry Zone, required high levels of engineering skill. Pipes, rock-cut channels and wind-powered pumps fed water into bathing pools for the palace above and enhanced the gardens below with ponds and fountains. Excavations have also revealed surface and underground drainage systems. Considering the huge effort and skill involved, it is even more extraordinary that the whole complex was constructed over a period of just seven years and effectively abandoned after 18 years.

The citadel ceased to be a palace after Moggallana's reign and was inhabited by monks till 1155, when it was abandoned. It was rediscovered by archaeologists in 1828.

The figures are 'portraits' of well-endowed *apsaras* (celestial nymphs) and attendants above clouds – offering flowers, scattering petals or bathing. (Guides are keen to point out the girl with three hands and another with three nipples.) Note the girls of African and Mongolian origin, proof of the kingdom's widespread trade at this time. Some paintings were destroyed in 1967, and others may be cordoned off because the rusty walkway is unsafe.

Mirror wall

Immediately beyond the foot of the spiral staircases the path is protected on the outer side by the 3-m-high, highly polished plaster wall, believed to have been coated with lime, egg white and wild honey. After 15 centuries it still has a reflective sheen. Visitors and pilgrims (mostly between seventh and 11th century) wrote verses in Sinhalese – yearning, libidinous 'graffiti' inspired by the painted ladies in the cliff, the natural beauty of Sigiriya's site, and Kasyapa's prowess in creating it. Some, today, find this section a little disappointing: despite the threat of a large fine or a two-year jail sentence, there is plenty of modern graffiti to obscure the originals, and it can be difficult to stop and study because of the pressure of people when the rock is busy. (Without a guide the poems remain impenetrable, but there's a good section in the museum dedicated to the Mirror Wall, and whole books devoted to the romantic poetry etched into it.)

As you continue to climb, note the massive rock, close to the Guard House, wedged with stone supports which could be knocked out to enable it to crash on the enemy far below.

Lion Terrace and final ascent

Here, the giant plaster-covered brick paws of a lion become visible. Originally, the entire head and front part of the body would have awed visitors. Though the remainder of the structure has disappeared, the size of the paws gives some clue to the height of the lion's head. The terrace marks the halfway point of the climb. The wire cage is supposed to protect people from wild bees, which nest under the metal staircase. The final stage of the ascent on the north ledge leads through the lion's paws to the top of the rock up the steep west and north sides. It is worth studying the remaining climb to the summit. You can clearly see the outline of small steps cut into the granite. The king was apparently scared of heights so these steps would have been enclosed by a 3-m-high mirror wall. Here was the lion's gate after which the place is named: *Si* (shortened form of *Sinha*, lion) *Giriya* (throat). Today, the ascent is made on 25 flights of iron steps with a small guard rail; the stairs are steep, particularly in one place where they are little more than a ladder, and can be frightening for small children.

Summer Palace

The top of the rock has a surface area of 1.5 ha and was the site of the king and queen's palace. The foundations are surprisingly small when compared with the scale of the vast rock underneath them. There was a granite throne, dancing terraces, a small pool fed by rain water, drinking water tanks, sleeping quarters for the concubines, a small flower garden and precariously positioned platforms for guards. If you walk to the sign on the west, there is a very good bird's-eye view of the water gardens below.

Cobra Hood Cave, the Audience Hall and the Cistern

Retrace your steps to the start of the Mirror Wall. Then follow the stairs that lead directly down towards the water gardens, eventually taking you left across the base of the rock. Signs pointing toward the Exit lead you past the **Cobra Hood Cave**, which is thought originally to have been a monk's cell. It has a drip ledge inscription in Brahmi script dating from the second century BC. The floor and ceiling have lime plaster; the latter is decorated with paintings and floral patterns. A headless Buddha statue is placed horizontally.

Close by, the **Cistern** and the **Audience Hall** rocks are parts of a single massive boulder which had split in half, with one section falling to the ground while another remained standing. The exposed flat surface of the horizontal section had a 'throne' at one end and came to be called the Audience Hall, while the upper part of the standing stone retained the rectangular cistern. Immediately below the audience chamber was another granite slab used as the place of execution. To the left is an ante-chamber, which was cooled by a tank of water cut into the rock above the ceiling; it too would have been covered in frescoes. Much of the construction is in brick faced with lime plaster, but there are sections built with limestone slabs which would have been carried up. The upper structures were probably wooden. Finally, you exit through the Cobra Gate – a huge, overhanging rock.

Sigiriya Museum
Daily 0830-1730 (last ticket 1700), closed 1st Mon of every month. Price included in the Sigiriya ticket.

This is the re-vamped archaeological museum. The empty, echoing building may be off-putting, but once you enter the gallery the museum comes into its own. It showcases the history of the rock from its formation to its use as a Buddhist monastery. Archaeological finds are displayed, and there is an interesting reproduction of the 'Golden Age' of Sigiriya, as well as translations of some of the graffiti from the Mirror Wall. The Fresco Gallery is of interest if you do not make it up the spiral stairs to see the originals. The museum also provides some tourist information on sights and accommodation in the area, and there are plans for a café.

Pidurangala
The prominent granite boulder visible northeast of Sigiriya is Pidurangala, home to a Buddhist temple and meditation centre and a series of **royal cave temples** ① *sunrise to sunset, Rs 500*. The climb to the top of the rock leads through the remains of an ancient monastery set in shady forest and past a stupa with a superb 10th-century reclining Buddha and an inscription dating from the first century BC. A short scramble up tumbled granite boulders leads to the top, where you emerge from a ravine to an unforgettable view of Sigiriya surrounded by jagged mountains.

Listings Sigiriya *map p287*

Tourist information

Sigiriya, by RH De Silva, Ceylon, Department of Archaeology, 1971, is recommended for further background information.

Where to stay

Accommodation in Sigiriya itself tends to be expensive or basic. There are several guesthouses and simple restaurants near the bus stop. Inamaluwa and Kimbissa, 4-6 km west of the rock, are good alternatives for mid-price accommodation. Regular buses leave from these villages to the site from early morning onwards.

$$$$ Elephant Corridor
Inamaluwa, T066-228 6950,
www.elephantcorridor.com.
80-ha site overlooking tank with stunning views of the rock. 21 suites in 5 categories (from deluxe to presidential). Each room has private plunge pool, DVD player, individual garden and lots of gadgets (eg night-vision binoculars, painting

easel). Sports facilities include stables and 3-hole golf course. Not all rooms have good views and are slightly overpriced.

$$$$ Vil Uyana (Jetwing)
Inamaluwa, T066-492 3585,
www.jetwinghotels.com.
An artificially created wetland with 25 spacious chalets, some with private plunge pools and sunken baths, in a choice of 4 habitats (marsh, paddy, forest or lake). All have private decks for wildlife viewing. Beautiful infinity pool and all the facilities you'd expect. The walk to the main building can be hard going if you're not very mobile.

$$$$-$$$ Back of Beyond Dehigahaela
T077-395 1527, backofbeyond.lk/locations.
Hidden down an unmarked track 9 km south of Sigiriya, this off-the-grid compound of secluded treehouses and timber cottages built around huge boulders offer one of the best genuine back-to-nature experiences in Sri Lanka. The location is magical, beside a jungle pool full of toe-nibbling fish, with short walks leading to burbling waterfalls and bat-filled caves. Elephants and fishing cats freely wander through the property, and bird species including hornbills, owls and kingfishers fly over the lotus pond. Comfy beds and excellent food, plus enough solar power to keep your devices charged.

$$$$-$$$ Back of Beyond Pidurangala
T077-395 1527, backofbeyond.lk/locations.
Lurking in the forest right at the foot of Pidurangala rock, the 4 huge cottage rooms here come with outdoor bathrooms. For sheer jungle atmosphere you should book the treehouse, overlooking huge boulders where langurs leap. Friendly service, great food and evening walks to search for slender loris in the trees. The young manager is a popular local character who can help arrange unusual excursions. Recommended

$$$ Kassapa Lions Rock
Digampathaha, T066-567 7440,
www.kassapalionsrock.com.
Nestled in a rural village, 31 well-appointed chalets. Certified as a bird-friendly resort.

$$$ Hotel Sigiriya
Sigiriya, T066-223 1940,
www.serendibleisure.lk.
79 well-decorated, comfortable a/c rooms, some with TV and DVD player. Large pleasant garden in attractive wooded setting. Birdwatching walks and a good freshwater pool with great view of the rock. Reasonable food, cultural shows. Internet available. Good value.

$$$ The Thick Forest
Sigiriya, T077-355 7090.
3 raised wooden chalets built amidst the forest, with views of the rock. Basic with fan and hot water. Quiet, excellent for birdwatching, good food and a good chance of seeing elephants.

$$ Banana Rest
164/A, TB Tennakone Mawatha, Kimbissa,
5 km from the site, T066-721 0016,
www.sigiriyabananarest.com.
Family-run guesthouse with 5 a/c and fan rooms with hot water. Good food, quiet surrounds with lots of birds and lizards, friendly.

$$ Grand Tourist Holiday Resort
Kimbissa, 5 km from site, T066-567 0136.
This old-fashioned, slightly faded place is neither grand nor for grand tourists, but the large, well-furnished a/c and fan rooms in Dutch-style bungalows are set in attractive gardens and the staff are friendly.

$ Flower Inn
Sigiriya, T066-567 2197.
Family-run guesthouse with 3 rooms in the main house and newer ones at the back (cold water). Good food, friendly owner.

$ Nilmini
Opposite Flower Inn, Sigiriya, T066-223 3313.
Simple rooms (shared bath cheaper) in
rather dilapidated house, good food, very
friendly, free bicycle hire. Pleasant terrace
and can arrange tours and taxis.

Restaurants

There are not many eating options in
Sigiriya, so most people eat in their
hotel or guesthouse.

$ Gamagedara Village Food
*Down the lane behind Sarath Safari,
Sigiriya, T076-522 6657.*
The simple mud hut surroundings give no
hint at the magnificent 10-course Sri Lankan
feast that awaits, cooked in front of your
eyes by the delightful Chandini. She also
does cooking classes by arrangement.

$ Shenadi
Main St, Sigiriya.
Strong contender for the pick of the main
drag eateries, with excellent rice and curry
and good noodle dishes.

Shopping

Shops in the village sell basic supplies,
snacks and postcards.
Kottegoda Batik, *Inamaluwa*. Batik.
Pethikada, *Sigiriya village*. Jagath Jayasoorya
creates wonderfully accurate reproductions
of cave paintings and temple murals. He was
one of the artists who recreated frescoes
for the Sigiriya museum. You can see him in
action and buy his superb work here.

Silk Gardens, *Inamaluwa*. Large silk
showroom, with attentive staff who can't
wait to wrap you in a sari. Low pressure.

What to do

Safaris
Several operators around the village offer
safaris to Minneriya and Kaudulla National
Parks, though it's roughly Rs 1000 cheaper
to take a bus to Habarana and find a jeep
there. It is also possible to visit the Sigiriya
Wildlife Sanctuary, which stretches from
Sigiriya to Minneriya.

Transport

Air Cinnamon Air (www.cinnamon
air.com) flies daily from Colombo's
Bandaranaike Airport to the **SLAF Sigiriya**
airfield north of Kimbissa (US$221 one-way).

Bus Despite all the tourist coaches, Sigiriya
is a backwater as far as the country's bus
network is concerned, with just 1 daily bus
to **Colombo** (4 hrs). If you're heading north
to **Habarana/Trincomalee**, you could catch
a tuk-tuk to Inamaluwa Junction (Rs 600)
and hope for a seat. For other destinations,
the most reliable route is to take a bus to
Dambulla (every 30 mins during the day)
and change. The main stop in Sigiriya is
near the rest house, close to the exit from
the site.

Car The journey by car to/from **Colombo**
takes about 4 hrs and to/from **Kandy**
about 2½ hrs.

This region is home to some of Sri Lanka's largest elephant populations. During the dry season, elephants from as far afield as Wasgamuwa National Park, Matale and Trincomalee assemble around Minneriya tank in herds of up to 300, in what must be one of Earth's weightiest wildlife spectacles.

To the northwest, meanwhile, a detour off the Anuradhapura road leads to the remote hermitage of Ritigala, buried deep within the jungle.

Habarana *Colour map 2, B5.*

Habarana is an important crossroads, with roads extending southwest to Colombo or Kandy, northwest to Anuradhapura and Jaffna, northeast to Trincomalee, and southeast to Polonnaruwa and Batticaloa. It is a good base for wildlife watching, with a large collective of eager jeep drivers ready to whisk you off to Kaudulla or Minneriya national parks (see page 294). Thanks to its accessibility, tour groups often spend a night here in the scattering of hotels and rest houses. Nearby there is an attractive **Buddhist temple** with excellent paintings. Behind the tank, next to the temple, you can climb a rock for superb views over the forest to Sigiriya.

Ritigala *Colour map 2, B4.*

8 km from Galapitagala. US$10. Getting there: You need your own vehicle to reach Ritigala. From Habarana, follow the A11 for 22 km west towards Maradankadawala, taking a right turn at Galapitagala for 5 km into the forest, then turn left along a track (suitable for a 2WD) for about 3 km where an ancient rock-cut path leads to the site.

The 148-ha archaeological site is located within a 1570-ha Strict Nature Reserve. Though it is in the Dry Zone, the Ritigala summit has a strange cool, wet micro-climate, with vegetation reminiscent of Horton Plains (see page 234). Wildlife includes elephants, sloth bear, leopard and varied bird life. The area, rich in unusual plants and herbs, is associated with the *Ramayana* story in which Hanuman dropped a section of herb-covered Himalaya here (see page 151).

The forest hermitage complex here was occupied by ascetic *Pansakulika* monks (see A simple life, page 283). The structures found here include the typical double platforms joined by stone bridges, stone columns, ambulatories, herbal baths filled by rain water, sluices and monks' cells. There are many natural caves on the mountain slopes, some quite large, in which priests would meditate. Brahmi inscriptions here date the site to the third and second centuries BC.

At the entrance to the site is a visitor centre where you can arrange a guide. As you enter, you will clamber over ruined steps leading down to the now overgrown two-acre bathing tank, the **Banda Pokuna**. Over an original stone bridge, follow a part-restored pathway laid with interlocking ashlar to the first major clearing, the monastery hospital, where you can see the remains of a stone bed, oil bath and medicine grinder. The next set of ruins is believed to be a library, now partly restored, perched atop a rock with magnificent views across to the jungle below. Beyond here, you come to the monastery, with a remarkably well-preserved urinal which would have had three clay pots beneath, of charcoal, sand and *kabok* for filtration. Here are the distinctive raised double-platforms, characteristic of Ritigala and other forest monasteries, such as Mihintale (see page 280). The platforms were probably for congregational use.

Platform 17 marks the end of the excavated territory – special permission is required from the Wildlife Department to venture further, and guides are in any case fearful of wild animals (workers have been maimed or killed in this area by elephants).

Hurulu Eco Park
Park entrance 4 km north of Habarana on the A6. US$15 plus service charge.

Hurulu Eco Park is often suggested as an alternative when it's too wet to visit Kaudulla and Minneriya. Part of Hurulu Forest Reserve, which was designated as a biosphere reserve in January 1977, it is a good place to see elephants and birds. Among the species living in the area are the turtle, Ceylon junglefowl, and small populations of leopard and the rusty-spotted cat. Facilities are limited at the moment, but there are plans to develop the park for tourists and re-open some of the walking trails.

Kaudulla National Park *Colour map 2, A5.*
Visitor centre 5 km east of Hatares Kotuwa. US$15 plus service charge, tracker, etc. Getting there: the turn-off for the park is 17 km north of Habarana at Hatares Kotuwa. Jeeps from Habarana will usually charge Rs 4500 for a 3-hr safari, leaving 1500-1600.

The national park around Kaudulla's mighty tank was established in September 2002 as another step in protecting the elephants' ancient migration routes. It completes a network of protected areas around the Polonnaruwa area, comprising Minneriya National Park, Minneriya–Giritale Nature Reserve and Wasgomuwa National Park to the south, and Flood Plains and Somawathie to the east and north.

The 6936-ha park acts mainly as a catchment for the Kaudulla tank, which dates back to the 17th century. Its most prominent feature is its large herds of elephant (up to 250), which can be seen at the tank during the dry season when water is scarce elsewhere. The vegetation, which consists of semi-mixed evergreen, grasslands and riverine forest, supports a small population of leopard and sloth bear; birdlife is excellent.

The best time to visit the park is during the dry season from August to December. Outside the dry season, elephants are easier to see from the main Habarana–Trincomalee road (on the left coming from Habarana) than in the park itself. These are their preferred feeding grounds due to the lushness of the vegetation. Jeeps in Habarana are keen to take you to this area in these months, but if you already have a vehicle there is little point getting a jeep since they feed very close to the road.

Minneriya National Park
Park entrance at Ambagaswewa, 10 km east of Habarana on the Batticaloa Rd. US$15 plus service charge, tracker, etc. Getting there: jeeps charge the same as to Kaudulla (see above).

A sanctuary since 1938, Minneriya was upgraded to national park status in 1997. King Mahasena's magnificent Minneriya tank (fourth century AD), covering 3000 ha, dominates the park. It is an important wetland, feeding around 8900 ha of paddy fields and supporting many aquatic birds, such as painted storks, spot-billed pelicans, openbill storks and grey herons. The high forest canopy also provides ideal conditions for purple-faced leaf monkey and toque monkey, while the short bushes and grasslands provide food for sambhar and chital. There are small populations of leopard and sloth bear. Mugger crocodiles and land and water monitors can also be seen.

Tip...
Keep a look out for wild elephants on the Minneriya–Giritale Road, and don't drive this route at night.

The best time to visit the park is May to October. At the end of the dry season there is little evidence of the tank, which gets covered in weeds, the vegetation on its bed becoming a vital source of food for many animals. Around September and October, an influx or local migration of elephants takes place in a spectacular wildlife event.

Giritale *Colour map 2, B5.*

Giritale also has a fine tank, which dates from the seventh century AD and occupies a site that was once a wealthy suburb of ancient Polonnaruwa. Legend has it that King Parakramabahu met his cousin and future bride here. She was the daughter of his uncle Girikandasiva, to whom he donated the tank and from whom it derives its name. There is little reason to stay here other than its position and its proximity to Minneriya (see above) and Polonnaruwa. The hotels here are more upmarket than in the ancient city itself. The road that skirts the tank south leads to **Wasgomuwa National Park** (see page 309), to which hotels also arrange trips (as well as to Minneriya and Kaudulla). As you drive out of town towards Polonnaruwa you will see a copy of the Aukana Buddha by the tank, erected in 2001. If you haven't made it to Aukana, this will give you an idea how impressive is the real thing.

Listings Habarana and the elephant lands

Where to stay

Habarana
Habarana is usually used as a base for visiting the national parks, and is a good transport hub.

$$$$-$$$ Cinnamon Lodge
T066-227 0011, www.cinnamonhotels.com.
150 tastefully decorated a/c rooms in bungalows, some deluxe with tubs and TV, and 2 suites. Excellent facilities and lush grounds, with woods, good pool, good service.

$$$$-$$$ Habarana Village
T066-227 0047, www.chaayahotels.com.
106 a/c rooms in 'rustic' cottages (deluxe have lake views), as well as 2 lodges. On the banks of the lake with extensive gardens, an excellent pool and good food. Popular with tours.

$$$ Galkadawala Forest Lodge
15 km west of Habarana, south of Palugaswewa, T077-373 2855, www.galkadawala.com
This is a real one-off: a pair of stunning rustic-modernist-steampunk lodges, designed by Colombo architect Vijitha Basnayaka and built, magpie-like, out of reclaimed bits of other buildings (windows from an old tea factory, metal decking from a decommissioned power station). Owner Maulie has created a wonderful refuge here, comfortable, luxurious and full of character, and she's a fascinating character herself. Superb meals are prepared on a traditional clay oven. A quick hop over the bund leads you to a beautiful lake, which you can explore in the lodge canoe. Highly recommended.

Giritale

The upmarket hotels in Giritale are just off the main road overlooking the tank and can make convenient bases for visiting Polonnaruwa. Other cheaper hotels are all on the Habarana–Polonnaruwa Rd.

$$$ Deer Park
T027-224 6272, wwwdeerparksrilanka.com.
Luxurious 1- and 2-storey cottages set in grounds overlooking Giritale tank, most with open-air showers. Upmarket facilities with 3 restaurants, spa, pool. Popular with tour groups.

$$$ Giritale Hotel
T027-224 6311, www.giritalehotel.com.
42 reasonable a/c rooms high above the Giritale tank. Small pool, good facilities and superb views from the restaurant and terrace. Plenty of wildlife within hotel grounds, including chital and monkeys.

$$ Lak Nilla Guest House
Polonnaruwa Rd, T077-911 5265.
A short walk or tuk-tuk ride inland from the lake, this friendly homestay offers clean, comfortable rooms, great home-cooked meals and plenty of family interaction.

$ Woodside Tour Inn
Polonnaruwa Rd, T027-224 6307.
15 large and clean fan and a/c rooms.

Restaurants

Habarana
Most groups choose to stop in Habarana, where local restaurants compete with each other to impress tourists with the number of curries they can serve at lunchtime. Prices are usually around Rs 800. Best of the bunch are:

$$ Acme Transit Hotel
1 km east of Habarana Junction, T066-227 0016.
11 curries, and the option of using a pool. Rooms available, though not well maintained.

$$ Rukmali Rest
1 km further east, T066-227 0059.
An overwhelming choice of 17 curry varieties.

Transport

Habarana
Bus Habarana Junction is a good place to pick up buses in all directions: **Dambulla** (20 mins), **Trincomalee** (2 hrs), **Polonnaruwa** (1 hr), **Batticaloa** (3 hrs), **Colombo** (5 hrs), **Anuradhapura** (1½ hrs). Note that the buses passing through Habarana are very busy, especially the long-distance to Trincomalee. Unless you're travelling very light, try and catch the earliest of the day.

Train The station is 2 km north of Habarana Junction and is on the Colombo–Batticaloa line. Trains to **Colombo**, **Trincomalee**, **Batticaloa** and **Polonnaruwa**.

Polonnaruwa
& south to Kandy

Polonnaruwa, the island's medieval capital between the 11th and 13th century, is for many visitors the most rewarding of the Ancient Cities. Flowering principally under three kings over a short period of less than 100 years, it is, in contrast to Anuradhapura, historically as well as geographically compact and so feels easier to assimilate.

Today, the ruins, built alongside the vast and beautiful Parakrama Samudra, stand witness to a lavish phase of building, culminating in the sublime Gal Vihara. In its imperial intentions and the brevity of its existence, Polonnaruwa may be compared to the great Mughal emperor Akbar's city of Fatehpur Sikri, near Agra in India.

★ Sights   *Colour map 2, B5.*

exquisite artistry and imperial design

The ruins can be split broadly into five groups. Close to the entrance and within the old walls are the Royal Citadel Group to the south and the Quadrangle to the north. The Northern Monuments, which include the magnificent Gal Vihara, are spread out for 3 km north of here. Across the main road from the main site, close to the museum and bund, is the small Rest House Group, and finally, the Southern Group is about 3 km south of the Old Town.

Unless you arrive early in the morning, then the museum is a good place to start. The entrance to the main site is 500 m from here, though you may wish to see the Rest House Group first as it is closest to the museum. Once in the main site, there is a one-way route through the sacred site that is generally quite well signed.

Archaeological Museum
Daily 0900-1800. Entry is covered by the site ticket.

This is an excellent place to start a tour of the ancient ruins, and you may wish to return afterwards. In addition to the clearly presented exhibits found on site and many

Essential Polonnaruwa

Finding your feet

The railway station and main bus stand are in Kaduruwela, 4 km east of the city, from where local buses and three-wheelers run frequently to Polonnaruwa. Arriving from Dambulla or Sigiriya, you can ask to be dropped off in Polonnaruwa Old Town, close to the main ruins; however, when leaving Polonnaruwa, you're better off boarding the bus in Kaduruwela as many long-distance services are already full by the time they pass through the Old Town. Polonnaruwa New Town is closer to the Southern Group of ruins and is where many hotels are to be found.

Getting around

The archaeological sites are too spread out to walk around under a hot sun. Even if you have a car, cycling is the most practical and fun way to explore the town (Rs 150-200 per day, available from most hotels), though take it easy as brakes are a luxury and the tracks are rough in places – you'll do well if you get round without a puncture. Tuk-tuk drivers who greet arriving buses and trains (or hang around hotels) will quote anything upwards of Rs 1800 for a half-day whizz around the main sites, on top of your entrance fee; you may get a better deal by flagging down a few different drivers. Hotels in the complex west of the Southern Group are 3 km from the Old Town, so transport is essential.

When to go

As ever, early morning or late evening is best, out of the heat. To visit many sites you will need to remove your shoes – take a pair of socks to avoid scorching your soles. Avoid visiting more remote ruins late in the day, as attacks on lone tourists have been known. You should allow at least three hours to explore; a whole day will give you a better impression of the ancient site.

Visitor information

Tickets for the Royal Citadel, Quadrangle and Gal Vihara (see below) are available from the counter at the Archaeological Museum, close to the rest house, which also acts as an information desk and sometimes sells maps of the city. Though the museum itself doesn't open till 0900, the desk is open from 0700. Tickets cost US$25; children and SAARC residents, half price. Several books on Polonnaruwa are available from the bookshop.

Polonnaruwa's substantial entry fee has fostered a black market operation among local tuk-tuk drivers. They may offer to get you into the ruins for a reduced fee – around Rs 2500, instead of the Rs 3000+ you'll pay at the ticket counter. Tempting as this may be, bear in mind that the ticket money you spend at the museum goes towards maintaining Sri Lanka's archaeological sites. And without an official ticket, you risk missing out on the sculptures of the Gal Vihara, some of the greatest ancient treasures in Sri Lanka.

Time required

You can whizz round the main sights in half a day, but it's better to stay overnight and explore in the cool of the late afternoon or early morning.

photographs, there is also a well-written commentary on Sri Lanka's ancient history. Scaled-down representations give you an idea of how the buildings would have looked during the city's prime. In the final (seventh) room, there are some extraordinarily well-preserved bronze statues.

Rest House Group

Nissankamalla (ruled 1187-1196) built his own 'New' Palace close to the water's edge in a beautiful garden setting. Today, the ruins are sadly in a poor state of repair. Just north of the rest house, beyond the sunken royal baths, are a stone 'mausoleum', the Audience Hall, and lastly the interesting Council Chamber which housed the stone lion throne that is now in the Colombo National Museum. The four rows of 12 sculpted columns have inscriptions indicating the seating order in the chamber – from the king at the head, with the princes, army chiefs and ministers, down to the record keepers on his right, while to his left were placed government administrators, and representatives of the business community. Across the water, to the northwest, the mound on the narrow strip of land which remains above flood water, has the ruins of the King Parakramabahu's Summer House, which was decorated with wall paintings.

Royal Citadel Group

Site ticket required (see Visitor information, opposite).

From the Rest House Group, a path runs along the bund, where stalls sell drinks and snacks, to the main road. Across the road is the main entrance to the walled city, for which you will need a ticket.

Vejayanta Prasada About 200 m south of the entrance (to the right as you enter) stands King Parakramabahu's Palace. It is described in the *Chronicles* as having seven storeys and 1000 rooms, but much of it was made of wood and so was destroyed by fire. The large central hall on the ground floor (31 m x 13 m) had 30 columns which supported the roof. You can see the holes for the beams in the 3-m-thick brick walls. It has porticoes on the east and west sides and a wide stairway.

Council Chamber The chamber (sometimes called Audience Hall) is immediately east of the palace. It has fine, partly octagonal, granite pillars and friezes of elephants, lions and dwarves, which follow the entire exterior of the base. Nearby, outside the palace wall, is the stepped Kumara Pokuna (Prince's Bath), restored in the 1930s. You can still see the spouts where the water is channelled through the open jaws of crocodiles.

Shiva Devale I Turning left from the entrance, you come to the Shiva Devale I, one of the many Shiva and Vishnu Hindu temples here. Built in about AD 1200, it is an example of the Dravidian Indian architectural style and shows exceptional stone carving. The brick roof no longer exists, and the fine bronze statues discovered in the ruins have been transferred to the Colombo Museum.

Quadrangle

Some 50 m further on, steps lead up to the Quadrangle, the highlight of the ruins within the ancient city wall. Though the structures here are comparatively modest in size, they

Polonnaruwa

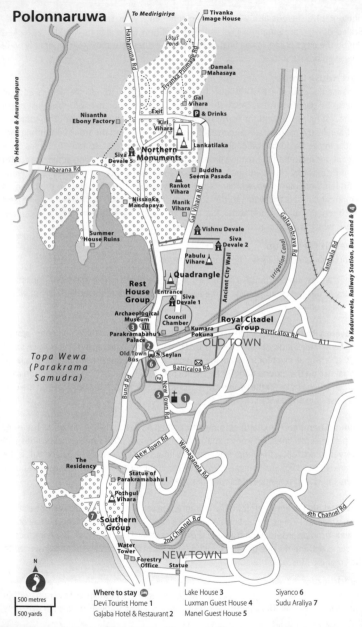

To Medirigiriya

Tivanka
Image House

Hathamuna Rd

Lotus
Pond

Tivanka Pilimage Rd

Damala
Mahasaya

To Habarana & Anuradhapura

Gal
Vihara

Exit

P & Drinks

Nisantha
Ebony Factory

Kiri
Vihara

Lankatilaka

Siva
Devale 5

**Northern
Monuments**

Habarana Rd

Buddha
Seema Pasada

Gal Vihara Rd

Rankot
Vihara

Nissanka
Mandapaya

Manik
Vihara

Gattambrava Rd

Summer
House Ruins

Vishnu Devale

Irrigation Canal

To Kaduruwela, Railway Station, Bus Stand & 4

Siva
Devale 2

Tambala Rd

Pabulu
Vihare

Ancient City Wall

**Rest
House
Group**

Quadrangle

Entrance

Siva
Devale 1

*Topa Wewa
(Parakrama
Samudra)*

Archaeological
Museum

Council
Chamber

**Royal Citadel
Group**

Parakramabahu's
Palace

Kumara
Pokuna

Batticaloa Rd

A11

Old Town
Bus

Seylan

OLD TOWN

Bund Rd

Batticaloa Rd

New Town Rd

To Habarana & Anuradhapura

**The
Residency**

Statue of
Parakramabahu I

New Town Rd

Wamaganela Rd

Pothgul
Vihara

4th Channel Rd

**Southern
Group**

Water
Tower

2nd Channel Rd

NEW TOWN

Forestry
Office

Statue

N

500 metres

500 yards

Where to stay   Lake House **3**   Siyanco **6**
Devi Tourist Home **1**   Luxman Guest House **4**   Sudu Araliya **7**
Gajaba Hotel & Restaurant **2**   Manel Guest House **5**

The Sinhalese kings of Anuradhapura in AD 369 used Polonnaruwa as a residence, but it did not rank as a capital until the eighth century. The Cholas from South India destroyed the Sinhalese Kingdom at the beginning of the 11th century, and in taking control of most of the island, they established their capital at Polonnaruwa. After defeating the Cholas, King Vijayabahu I set up his own capital in the city, and it remained a vibrant centre of Sinhalese culture under his successors, notably Parakramabahu I (1153-1186) who maintained very close ties with India, importing architects and engineers, and Nissankamalla (1187-1196).

Polonnaruwa owes much of its glory to the artistic conception of King Parakramabahu I, who planned the whole as an expression and statement of imperial power. The rectangular shaped city was enclosed by three concentric walls and was made attractive with parks and gardens. Its great artificial lake, named Parakrama Samudra (Sea of Parakrama) after its imperial designer, provided cooling breezes through the city, water for irrigation and, at the same time, defence along its entire west flank. The bund is over 14 km long and 1 m high, and the tank irrigates over 90 sq km of paddy fields. It is fed by a 40-km-long canal and a link from the Giritale tank.

After Parakramabahu, the kingdom went into terminal decline and the city was finally abandoned in 1288, after the tank embankment was breached. Fortunately, many of the remains are in an excellent state of repair though several of the residential buildings remain to be excavated. In 1982, Polonnaruwa was designated a World Heritage Site. The restoration at the site is by the UNESCO-sponsored Central Cultural Fund.

are carved in fine detail. This is still regarded as a sanctuary and shoes and hats have to be removed.

The Vatadage ('hall of the relic') To the left as you enter the Quadrangle is a circular building with a *dagoba* on concentric terraces with sculptured railings, the largest with a diameter of 18 m. A superbly planned and executed 12th-century masterpiece attributed to Nissankamalla (1187-1196), the Vatadage has modest proportions but remarkably graceful lines. It was almost certainly intended to house the Tooth Relic. There are impressive guard stones at the entrances of the second terrace and wing stones with *makaras* enclosing lion figures. The moonstone to the north entrance of the top terrace is superb. The *dagoba* at the centre has four Buddhas (some damaged) with a later stone screen.

The Hatadage The sanctuary built by Nissankamalla, with extraordinary moonstones at its entrance, is also referred to as the Temple of the Tooth, since the relic may have been placed here for a time. See the Buddha statue here framed by three solid doorways, and then look back at one of the Buddha statues in the Vatadage, again beautifully framed by the doorways.

East of the Hatadage The **Gal Pota**, or 'Book of Stone', is to the side of the path and can easily be missed. According to the inscription it weighs 25 tons and was brought over 90 km from Mihintale. It is in the form of a palm leaf measuring over 9 m by 1.2 m, over 60 cm thick in places, with Sinhalese inscriptions praising the works of the King Nissankamalla, including his conquests in India.

The **Chapter House** nearby dates from the seventh century. The ziggurat-like **Satmahal Prasada** (originally seven-storeyed) in the northeast corner, decorated with stucco figures, has lost its top level. The 9-m-sq base decreases at each level as in Cambodian *prasats*.

West of the Hatadage The **Atadage** ('house of eight relics') was the first Tooth Relic temple, constructed by Vijayabahu when he established his capital here in 1070. There are some handsome carved pillars. The ruins of the **Patimaghara**, west of here, reveal the remains of a reclining Buddha.

Nissankalata (Lotus Mandapa) To the west of the main Vatadage, this *dagoba* was built by King Nissankamalla. The small pavilion has the remains of a stone seat (from which the king listened to chanting of scriptures), steps and a stone fence imitating a latticed wooden railing with posts. The ornamental stone pillars which surround the *dagoba* are in the form of thrice-bent lotus buds on stalks, a design which has become one of Sri Lanka's emblems. A statue of a *Bodhisattva* is to its east, and the **Bo Tree shrine** lies to the south.

Polonnaruwa Quadrangle

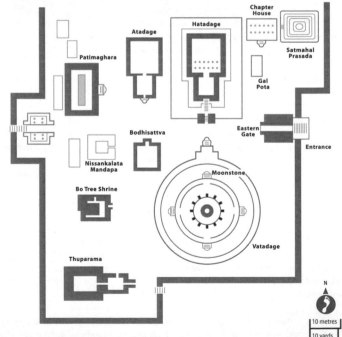

Thuparama In the south of the Quadrangle, the impressive Thuprarama is a *gedige* which was developed as a fusion of Indian and Sinhalese Buddhist architecture. This has the only surviving vaulted dome of its type and houses a number of Buddha statues. It has very thick plaster-covered brick walls with a staircase embedded in them.

Northeast of the Quadrangle

Exiting the Quadrangle by the same steps that brought you in, 500 m to the northeast are two temples which belong to different periods. If you walk past the **Pabulu Vihare**, a squat stupa, up to the north wall of the ancient city, you come to one of the earliest temples with Tamil inscriptions, **Shiva Devala II**. Built of stone by the Indian Cholas in a style they were developing in Tamil Nadu (as at Thanjavur), but using brick rather than stone, it is almost perfectly preserved.

Northern monuments

Beyond the original city wall, another group of scattered monuments stretches several kilometres further north. First, the **Alahana Parivena** (Royal Crematory Monastery) Complex, which was set aside by Parakramabahu, is worth exploring. The UNESCO restoration project is concentrated in this area. At the **Manik Vihara**, the squat cloistered stupa was restored in 1991. This originally housed precious gems. The **Rankot Vihara**, further on, is the fourth largest *dagoba* on the island with a height of 55 m. It was built by Nissankamalla in the 12th century. Note the perfection of the spire and the clarity of the statues round the drum. The tall **Buddha Seema Pasada** was the Chapter House or convocation hall where you can still make out the central throne of the chief abbot, which was surrounded by monks' cells.

Lankatilaka ('ornament of Lanka') This large *gedige* (image house) originally had five storeys. Its walls are 4 m thick and still stand 17 m high, although the roof has crumbled. The design marks a turning away from the abstract form of the *dagoba* to a much more personalized faith in the Buddha in human form. The building is essentially a shrine built to focus the attention of worshippers on the 18-m-high statue of the Buddha at the end of the nave. Though built of brick and covered in stucco, the overall design of the building shows strong Tamil influence. The exterior bas-relief sculpture, most of which is impressively well preserved, sheds light on contemporary architectural styles. To the south of the Lankatilaka is a *madipa* with carved columns.

Kiri Vihara Queen Subhadra is believed to have built the 'milk white' Kiri Vihara stupa next to it, so named because of its unspoilt white plaster work when it was first discovered. It remains the best preserved of the island's unrestored *dagobas*. The plasterwork is intact although the whitewash is only visible in place, such as around the relic box. There are excellent views from the Chapter House which has the foundations only just visible.

Gal Vihara (Cave of the Spirits of Knowledge) ⓘ *Ticket required (see page 298)*. This is rightly regarded as one of the foremost attractions of Sri Lanka and has great significance to Buddhists. It forms a part of Parakramabahu's monastery, where a Buddha seated on a pedestal under a canopy was carved out of an 8-m-high rock. On either side of the rock shrine are further vast carvings of a seated Buddha and a 14-m recumbent

Buddhas in *Parinirvana* (rather than death), indicated, in part, by the way the higher foot is shown slightly withdrawn. The grain of the rock is beautiful as is the expression. Near the head of the reclining figure, the 7-m standing image of banded granite with folded arms was once believed to be his grieving disciple Ananda but is now thought to be the Buddha himself. The foundation courses of the brick buildings which originally enclosed the sculptures are visible. Sadly, the presentation of the magnificent carved Buddhas is rather disappointing. An unattractive, protective canopy now shields the seated Buddha, which is caged in with rusty metal bars and a scratched plastic window, making clear viewing and photography impossible.

Tivanka Image House A path continues north to rejoin the road. The **Lotus Pond**, a little further along, is a small bathing pool, empty in the dry season, with five concentric circles of eight petals which form the steps down into the water. The road ends at the Tivanka Image House where the Buddha image is in the unusual 'thrice bent' posture (shoulder, waist and knee) associated with a female figure, possibly emphasizing his gentle aspect. This is the largest brick-built shrine here, now substantially renovated (though work continues). There are remarkable frescoes inside depicting scenes from the *Jatakas*, though they are not as fine as those in Sigiriya. Under the 13th-century frescoes, even earlier original paintings have been discovered. The decorations on the outside of the building are excellent with delightful carvings of dwarves on the plinth. The image house actually has a double skin, and for a small tip the guardian will unlock a door about half way inside the building. You can then walk between the outer and inner walls. The passage is lit from windows high up in the wall. It is an excellent way of seeing the corbel-building technique. The guardian may also unroll the painted copies of the frescoes, which eventually will be repainted onto the walls.

Southern Group

This group is quite separate from the rest of the ruins, though it makes sense to start here if you are staying nearby. If not, it is well worth walking or cycling down here along the bund as the view is lovely.

You will first see the giant 3.5-m-high **statue** of a bearded figure, now believed to be King Parakramabahu himself, looking away from the city he restored. In his hand is the palm leaf manuscript of the 'Book of Law' (some suggest it represents 'the burden of royalty' in the shape of a rope). Sadly, the statue is covered by an ugly canopy.

To its south is the part-restored **Pothgul Vihara**, which houses a circular *gedige* (instead of being corbelled from two sides), with four small solid *dagobas* around. The central circular room, with 5-m-thick walls, is thought to have housed a library.

Parakrama Samudra

Polonnaruwa's huge tank consists of three linked reservoirs, the northernmost and closest to town being Topa Wewa. Today it attracts numerous water birds, including cormorants and pelicans. Once you've exhausted the ruins, a few peaceful hours can be spent cycling along the bund and attractive tree-lined **canals**, perhaps catching sight of a giant water monitor. The water system is so well planned it is hard to believe it is almost 1000 years old. Some 4 km south past the Southern Group along the east bank of the tank you come to a weir, a popular spot for bathing. If you have a 4WD, you can drive down to the dam at **Angamedilla**, a beautiful spot where the tank is fed by the Amban Ganga. Here is an (unofficial) entry point for **Wasgomuwa National Park** (see page 309), though make sure you're with someone who knows the way.

Mandalagiri Vihara

Medirigiriya, 15 km from Hinguakgoda. US$5. Getting there: bus from Kaduruwela to Hingurakgoda, then bus or 3-wheeler to the site.

At Medirigiriya, 30 km north of Polonnaruwa, is a seventh- to eighth-century *vatadage* almost identical in measurement and construction to that in the ancient city's Quadrangle. The circular image house with concentric pillared terraces is located up a flight of granite steps on a hilltop site. However, it has lost its facing and, despite its atmospheric location, is less impressive than Polonnaruwa.

Listing Polonnaruwa *map p300*

Tourist information

The ticket desk at the Archaeological Museum (see page 297), close to the Rest House Group, serves as an information desk and sometimes sells maps of the city. The tourist police can be found at the junction of Habarana Rd, Batticaloa Rd and New Town Rd, T027 222 3099, near the Gal Vihara at the main site.

Where to stay

There are some good choices right in the centre, near the tank and the entrance to the ruins. For hotels near the New Town you can get a bus from either the railway station or the Old Town bus stop and then take the path signposted beyond the Statue for 1 km to the east. Many of the guesthouses have tiered pricing: the cheapest rooms are fan and cold water, then fan and hot water, and the most expensive are a/c and hot water.

$$$ Lake House
Next to Parakrama Samudra, T027-222 2299, www.ceylonhotels.lk.
The magnificent setting by the tank is the main draw here. The a/c rooms are big and modern, if a bit lacking in atmosphere,

and you might end up in the very room where Queen Elizabeth II stayed in 1954. There's also a suite **$$$**, which has a garden overlooking the tank. Service is willing, if a bit chaotic.

$$$ Sudu Araliya
Near the Southern Group, T027-222 4849, www.hotelsuduaraliya.com.
Attractive light open spaces, comfortable a/c rooms, with more under construction. TV, minibar, some rooms with tank view, bar, nice pool, herbal treatment, etc.

$$$ Siyanco
1 Canal Rd, behind Habarana Rd, T027-222 6868, www.siyancoholidayresort.com.
Excellent location, across the canal from the Archaeological Museum. 16 a/c rooms that are clean and modern, although some are on the small side. Good new pool (Rs 500 for non-guests), inviting restaurant, friendly.

$ Devi Tourist Home
Lake View Garden Rd, off New Town Rd, T027-222 3181, T077-908 1250.
Very clean and comfortable a/c and fan rooms with attached bath. Extremely welcoming family, excellent vegetarian home cooking, bike hire, free pick-up from Old Town, peaceful location. Recommended.

$$ Manel Guest House
New Town Rd, New Town, T027-222 2481,
www.manelguesthouse.com.
Rooms are large and spacious and those
in the new building at the back have
verandas and good views of paddy fields.
Fan or a/c and hot or cold water (price varies
accordingly). Service can be chaotic. Bike
hire available. Co-owner Mr Bandula and
his tuk-tuk patrol the streets and the bus
station looking for new guests; many find
him overbearing.

$ Gajaba Hotel & Restaurant
Opposite museum, near tank, T027-222 2394,
www.gajabaholidays.com.
25 basic rooms, including some with hot
water and a/c (price reflects amenities).
Good garden restaurant and cheap bike hire.
Friendly and helpful, can arrange safaris to
the national parks.

$ Luxman Guest House
33 Swarna Jayanthi Mawatha, Kaduruwela,
T077-327 0005, www.luxmanguesthouse.com.
Handy for the bus stand if a bit distant from
the ruins, this family-run guesthouse has
4 clean, bare-bones rooms and is one of the
best budget deals in town. Excellent food
and bike hire available.

Restaurants

There are several cheap eating places
along Habarana Rd. and the guesthouses
and hotels offer meals. Devi Tourist Home
offers excellent home-cooked food, but
you'll have to let them know in advance
if you want to eat there. The Lake House's
dining room is in a beautiful spot on the
water, but stick to rice and curry.

$$-$ Gajaba Restaurant
See Where to stay.
Offers good food at a reasonable price with
many guests from other hotels dining here.
There is a good selection of Sri Lankan food.

$$-$ Siyanco
See Where to stay.
Large, pleasant dining room. Wide range of
dishes, but the Sri Lankan offerings are the
best. Accommodating staff.

Transport

Bus The out-of-town bus stop is near the
railway station (see below) in **Kaduruwela**.
Local buses and 3-wheelers run between
Kaduruwela and the Old Town. When
leaving Polonnaruwa, it pays to get on
the bus in Kaduruwela in order to secure
a seat. Hourly buses to **Colombo** (6 hrs),
via **Dambulla** (1½ hrs); regular buses to
Anuradhapura (3 hrs) and **Kandy** (3 hrs),
and plenty to **Habarana** (1 hr). For **Sigiriya**,
travel to Sigiriya Junction in Inamaluwa, and
change to a CTB/private bus. Buses leave for
Batticaloa from outside the railway station.
For **Trincomalee** (4 hrs), there are few direct
buses so it may be best to travel to Habarana
Junction and change.

Train The station is in Kaduruwela, 4 km
east of the Old Town on Batticaloa Rd. To
Colombo 2 daily, 7 hrs; to **Trincomalee**,
take Colombo train and change at Gal Oya;
2 daytime trains to **Batticaloa** (2½ hrs).

Only 15 km longer than the Dambulla road, though rarely used by tourists, the route to Kandy via Mahiyangana takes you through wild and isolated country, across the vast plains irrigated by the Mahaweli Ganga Project, a monumental World Bank-funded system of dams and canals that waters 1000 sq km of Sri Lanka's Dry Zone and generates almost half of the country's electricity. The road comes close to some rarely visited archaeological sites and national parks which are worth breaking the journey for. The route also provides respite from the hordes who are drawn to the many 'star' attractions in the area.

Manampitiya

East of Polonnaruwa, the A11 follows the railway line towards the coast, leading ultimately south to Batticaloa. Road and rail converge at the impressive Manampitiya iron bridge to cross the wide Amban Ganga. After the bridge, the Mahiyangana road branches south towards the hills, with Wasgomuwa National Park accessible to the west (see page 309). Elephants are often sighted feeding close to the road here.

Dimbulagala *Colour map 2, B6.*

Dimbulagala archaeological complex is a loose series of over 100 caves carved into an imposing rock, also known as Gunner's Quoin. The caves have been in continuous use for thousands of years, first by the Veddas (see box, page 308); parts of the complex are still used as a forest hermitage. Other scattered ruins have been found from various periods between 300 BC and AD 1200. One Brahmi inscription shows that the caves were once used by Queen Sundari, the daughter-in-law of King Vijayabahu I of Polonnaruwa.

Follow the signs on the A844 for 8 km south of the A11 and you will reach first the sign for **Namal Pokuna**, where a 1-km climb brings you to a small complex with a restored *dagoba*, a *gedige* and *bodhigaraya* (wall around a Bo tree). Nearby is a lily pond (the Namal Pokuna itself) and an ancient stone bridge. The track continues uphill to a perfectly clear blue pool and a set of meditation caves. Some 4 km south of here, past the **Ahasmaligawa** ('sky palace'), a recent stupa built high on a steep rock, you come to **Pulligoda**, where there is a 12th-century cave fresco depicting five gods, four in the *anjali mudra* (palms together showing obeisance) position, seated on an embroidered scarf. They are painted using the plaster and lime method of Sigiriya, though they are nowhere near as impressive.

Maduru Oya National Park *Colour map 4, C1.*
Main entrance is 25 km south of Manampitiya. US$15.

The 58,850-ha Maduru Oya National Park lies to the east of the Mahiyangana road. It was designated a national park in 1983 to protect the catchment of the reservoirs in its neighbourhood and also to conserve the natural habitat of the large marsh-frequenting elephant which is found particularly in the Mahaweli flood plain. It is proposed to link the park with Gal Oya to the southeast via the Nilgala jungle corridor. Deer, sambar and the rare leopard and bear can be spotted and there is abundant, varied bird life.

The island's original people

There are few remaining homes for the Veddas. Living in isolated pockets (in particular in the Nilgala and Dambane jungles), normally out of sight, these aboriginal peoples can still occasionally be seen. Once hunter-gatherers, the matrilineal Veddas worshipped ancestral spirits, but most have lost their old hunting grounds and have been forced to find alternative methods of survival by adopting local Sinhalese ways, and with that many of their tribal beliefs and customs. Those in the Eastern Province, around Gal Oya, have become assimilated into the local Tamil community.

The government's resettlement schemes have been strongly resisted by some, who have remained on the forest edge carrying out subsistence farming by the *chena* ('slash and burn') method, having abandoned their customary bow and arrow. Under increasing pressure to allow some Vedda groups to return to their old settlements, the government has set aside 'reserved' areas for them and given them hunting rights.

Mahiyangana *Colour map 2, C5.*

This is a bustling town with a long history. In legend it is associated with the Buddha's first visit to Sri Lanka. **Rajamaha Dagoba**, 1.5 km south from the main Kandy road, is the site where the Buddha was supposed to have preached to the tribal people. The large *dagoba*, which was expanded by Dutthagemunu and has been restored many times, is said to enshrine a fistful of the Buddha's hair. The area is very attractive – the park with the *dagoba* in it is well kept and is overlooked by the hills on the far bank of the Mahaweli.

In the 1990s the late President Premadasa had a new temple built in Mahiyangana to resemble the famous Buddhist temple at Bodhgaya in Bihar, India. Opposite the temple, north of Kandy Road, six statues of symbolically important Sri Lankan leaders have been erected: three ancient kings (Devanampiya Tissa, Dutthagamenu and Parakramabahu); Kirti Sri, who reigned over an 18th-century Buddhist revival (see page 205); and two modern political figures (first Prime Minister DS Senanayake and his son Dudley, who oversaw the Mahaweli Ganga Project, the source of the town's importance and prosperity).

Sorabora Wewa is just on the outskirts of Mahiyangana on the road to Bibile. (You will probably have to ask someone to find the road for you.) According to legend a giant is said to have created the dam. You can see two enormous outcrops (the Sorabora Gate) through which the run off from the lake is channelled.

Vedda lands

The area to the east of Mahiyangana is one of the few areas left where Veddas, or Wanniya-laeto, the original inhabitants of Sri Lanka, are found. They live on the edge of the Maduru Oya forest (see above) and, transformed from hunter-gatherers to 'poachers' overnight by the creation of the national park, have since successfully fought for their right to hunt in some areas of the park (though bows and arrows may have been superseded by the gun).

An increasing number of tourists come this way to the meet the chief of the local Vedda village at **Dambana**, where you can witness some of their remarkable forest skills and dexterity, and buy ornaments and honey. Some visitors feel uncomfortable at invading the privacy of this fragile community, though the Veddas themselves aren't shy about earning a living from their unique culture. If you choose to visit Dambane, note that the traditional Vedda greeting (men only) is to grasp forearms.

Wasgomuwa National Park
Safaris available from park's southern entrance at Handungamuwa, 45 km north of Hasalaka (via Hettipola). Visits are best in the afternoon. Entrance US$10 per person plus service charges.

West of Mahiyangana, at Hasalaka, is the turn-off towards this remote national park, created in 1984 to conserve wildlife displaced by the Mahaweli project. The park's isolation, hemmed in on three sides by rivers, and the lack of human disturbance, have made it a rich feeding ground with a population of around 150 elephants. There is a belt of woodland on both sides of the river but otherwise the vegetation consists of grass, scrub and low bushes.

A26 to Kandy
There are three possible routes to Kandy from Mahiyangana. The first route traverses what is often referred to as Sri Lanka's most dangerous road. The other routes head south from Mahiyangana around the Randenigala Reservoir.

After Hasalaka, the A26 climbs into the hills through a series of 18 hairpin bends between 62 km and 57 km from Kandy. The relatively gentle climb and forested slopes suggest little sense of hazard, but buses often take the bends too fast for safety. There are spectacular views across the plains of the Dry Zone, now irrigated by the Mahaweli Ganga Project. Don't forget to stop near the top to look back on the glistening Mahaweli crossing the plains below. Approaching Kandy the road passes the dolomite quarries of Kajooda and the Kandy Free Trade Zone before crossing to the west bank of the Mahaweli Ganga.

Randenigala Sanctuary
Two pleasant alternatives to the A26 go through the Randenigala Sanctuary. The slightly shorter route crosses the Mahaweli Ganga at Mahiyangana and then goes due south to Weragantota immediately after crossing the river. The road climbs to the south side of the Randenigala Reservoir, then crosses the Victoria Dam (see below) to rejoin the A26 about 20 km from Kandy.

To take the second alternative, you have to take the B-road southeast out of Mahiyangana to **Pangarammana**, then join the road which also climbs to the southern edge of the **Randenigala Reservoir**. Here elephants can often be seen roaming along the shores of the lake. The irrigation development has created an area of intensive rice production and during the maha harvest (April-May) you will come across farmers winnowing and the stalks being constructed into quite large circular walls.

After passing through **Minipe** the road follows the 30-km-long Minipe Right Bank Canal, then slowly starts to rise. It crosses the river at the base of the **Randenigala Reservoir Dam**, which straddles the last gorge before the Mahaweli Ganga plunges to the plains. The crest of the dam is 485 m long and 94 m high.

The road then winds spectacularly around the southern side of the upper lake. Notice the 'contour lines' on the lakeside showing the decreasing water levels during the dry season. The road continues to climb over a small pass, where you'll see paddy fields in the valley below. Once over the pass you can see the **Victoria Dam**. There are a couple of vantage points from which you can take photographs. Towering more than 120 m high, the dam is a massive structure, even bigger than the Randenigala Dam. There is a restaurant and look-out place on the dam's north side. Not surprisingly both dams are quite heavily guarded.

Listings Polonnaruwa to Kandy

Where to stay and eat

Mahiyangana
Most of the accommodation is along Rest House Rd, 750 m west of the clock tower. (Ask the bus to drop you at the **Old Rest House** stop.) For eating the best option is at the **New Rest House** (500 m south of A26, T055-225 7304), a good place to stop for rice-and-curry. There are also small food stalls and bakeries in the bazaar.

$$ Sorabora Gedara Hotel
On the road to the lake, T055-225 7149, www.soraboravillage.com.
12 comfortable, modern a/c rooms, pool, bar and restaurant serving decent food. Wi-Fi.

$$ Tikiri Villa
Randenigala Rd, Morayaya, T055-490 1373, www.tikirivilla.com.
Across the river from town. 14 fan-cooled rooms in an appealing wood-panelled motel-style compound, surrounded by trees and with balconies overlooking paddy fields.

Wasgomuwa National Park

$$ Safari Village
10 mins from the park entrance, T011-259 1728, www.safarivillagehotels.com.
Has cabanas on the lake front. There are also jeeps available for hire.

Transport

Mahiyangana
Bus Regular buses to **Kandy** (2½-3 hrs). Also to **Colombo** (5 hrs), normal buses frequently to **Badulla** and **Bibile**; and 2-3 a day to **Batticaloa** (3-3½ hrs) and **Polonnaruwa** (3½-4 hrs). You will need to have your own transport to visit **Dimbulagala**, the **national parks** (or organize a tour via your guesthouse or hotel) and **Dambane village**. It is also best to have your own transport to visit sites en route between Mahiyangana and Kandy.

Eastern
Sri Lanka

unspoilt beaches and remote national parks

Located entirely within the Dry Zone, Sri Lanka's Eastern Province has always been one of its most sparsely populated areas. And, for many decades, it was off limits to visitors due to the war.

Though bleak reminders of the conflict still dot the landscape, the remote and beautiful beaches of the east coast are well and truly back on the map and reaping the benefits of their years of isolation: unspoiled white sands and a refreshing absence – for now – of tourist paraphernalia. The main focuses of interest are the idyllic beaches of Nilaveli and Uppuveli, just north of the magnificent natural harbour at Trincomalee, and the surfing centre of Arugam Bay, in the south of the province. In between, tiny Passekudah is forging itself a future as the east's package-holiday hotspot. All along the coast, there is great potential, largely unexploited, for whale watching, diving and snorkelling on reefs unaffected by the 'bleaching' elsewhere on the island.

Inland is some of Sri Lanka's wildest country. Traveller's who venture off the main roads will require a 4WD and plenty of patience but will be rewarded with some the island's most impressive national parks, which form an elephant corridor allowing the animals a free passage right across the region.

Best for
Adventure ■ Beaches ■ Birdwatching ■ Surfing

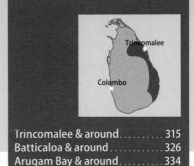

Footprint
picks

★ **Swami Rock, Trincomalee**, page 319
Cycle through raintrees and deer herds to the atmospheric clifftop temple of Konesvaram.

★ **Nilaveli and Uppuveli beaches**, page 321
Walk for miles on empty white sand in Nilaveli, or head to Uppuveli for a laid-back beach village vibe.

★ **Pigeon Island**, page 322
Snorkel among turtles, reef fish and sharks in the clear waters of this wonderful marine park.

★ **Arugam Bay**, page 334
Catch the famous right-hand break, take surfing lessons, or just lie back and enjoy this mellow backpacker bolthole.

★ **Kumana National Park**, page 343
Experience superb birdwatching and encounters with elephants in this beautiful, rarely visited reserve.

Footprint
picks

1 **Swami Rock, Trincomalee**, page 319
2 **Nilaveli and Uppuveli beaches**, page 321
3 **Pigeon Island**, page 322
4 **Arugam Bay**, page 334
5 **Kumana National Park**, page 343

Trincomalee
& around

Now easily accessible from the south once again, Trincomalee, the largest city in Eastern Province, is undergoing something of a renaissance.

Trinco's fame – and perhaps one day its fortune – lies in its magnificent natural harbour, described by Nelson as the finest in the world. Fiercely contested for centuries, it was a crucial naval base for the British during the Second World War. Today, after a recent past it would rather forget, this dusty port remains heavily militarized and scarred by war, yet the city is a uniquely balanced ethnic blend and is worth exploring, not least for its spectacular clifftop Konesvaram temple.

For most tourists Trinco serves as the gateway to the magnificent white-sand beaches at Uppuveli and Nilaveli. Resort hotels and guesthouses have been renovated and more are being built apace, and the military presence is now restricted to the odd desultory roadside checkpoint. Further afield, some important religious sites are once again accessible, although the terrible roads require a 4WD and infinite patience.

To Trincomalee from the southwest
take the A9 for speed or the A12 to get off the beaten track

There are two routes east across the Dry Zone plains to Trincomalee. The A9 via Habarana is the fastest and most frequently used route from Colombo or Kandy, but the A12 from Anuradhapura offers a more leisurely journey through lush green country in one of Sri Lanka's least populated regions.

Essential Trincomalee and around

Finding your feet

Roads into Trincomalee are now free of checkpoints and freshly paved, making travel in this region easier than ever before. There are good bus connections from Colombo and Kandy via Habarana, from Anuradhapura via Horowupatana, and from Jaffna via Vavuniya and Horowupatana. The coastal A15 is now fully open, connecting Trinco to Batticaloa without the ferry crossings that used to make this an infinitely slower, if more textured, journey. One overnight train runs from Colombo. Or if you simply can't wait to get your feet into Nilaveli sand, Cinnamon Air flies daily to Trincomalee's military airfield daily from Colombo via Sigiriya.

Getting around

The centre of Trincomalee is quite compact and is within walking distance of both the bus and train stations. Orr's Hill, 15 minutes' walk from the centre, is the main expat area, with NGO offices and a couple of fading upscale hotels. Kanniyai hot springs, the Commonwealth War Cemetery and the beaches north of Trinco can easily be visited from the city by bus or three-wheeler, with a good new coastal road running north as far as Pulmoddai. Minor roads are still in poor condition, however, and will require a 4WD. See Transport, page 320.

When to go

Trincomalee and its surrounding beaches are best visited between April and October, when the area is at its driest. Between November and March, the east is sometimes battered by strong wind and rain; the sea is unsuitable for swimming during these months.

Weather Trincomalee

January	February	March	April	May	June
27°C 25°C 170mm	28°C 25°C 70mm	30°C 26°C 40mm	32°C 27°C 50mm	33°C 27°C 60mm	33°C 27°C 20mm

July	August	September	October	November	December
32°C 27°C 50mm	33°C 26°C 100mm	32°C 26°C 100mm	30°C 26°C 220mm	28°C 25°C 350mm	27°C 25°C 350mm

A9 via Kantale Colour map 2, A5.

Beyond Habarana the A9 skirts Kaudulla National Park (see page 294). At Agbopura, the large Kantale tank become visible. There are many stalls by the side of the road selling Kantale's most famous product, deliciously creamy fresh curd in attractive clay pots. Kantale tank dates originally from the seventh century and irrigates a very intensive farming area, providing water to extensive rice fields to the southeast of the main road. The old rest house, in a scenic position by the lake, was commandeered by the army as a headquarters for many years, but has been given a thoroughly modern restoration and is now an excellent place to watch water birds. About 3 km off the main road, Kantale town has little going for it. A turn-off heads east from Kantale for the coast south of

Trincomalee. This road is the quickest land route to Seruwawila (see page 325); at Somapura it passes an approach road to **Somawathie Chaitiya National Park**, one of the four parks created as part of the Mahaweli Ganga project. There is a stupa here, set deep in jungle, said to contain another tooth from the Buddha. The stupa is also accessible from Polonnaruwa, but you'll need to hire a driver to get there.

Fact...
The restored tank bund (retaining dam) at Kantale was breached in 1987, killing hundreds.

Anuradhapura to Trincomalee

A more northerly route rambles delightfully east to Trincomalee from Anuradhapura. If you catch it at the right moment, this is one of the most beautiful drives in the north: cows graze on emerald turf beside lotus-covered tanks, pelicans perch in skeletal trees, while storks and herons in their hundreds circle above the lush forest canopy. Occasional army posts serve as reminders of Sri Lanka's various misfortunes past, while clusters of red-roofed cottages bear the name (in white roof tiles) of the development agency whose largesse paid for them.

Northeast of Mihintale, in the direction of Rambewa, is the **Mahakanadarawa tank**. An ancient stone bridge was discovered here, suggesting a road once linked Anuradhapura with the ancient harbour at Gokanna (Trincomalee). There's a great view of the white dagoba of Mihintale from the lake's eastern end. You can break the journey at the dusty crossroads town of **Horowupatana**, 42 km east of Mihintale, where an attractive road leads northwest to Vavuniya (see page 347). A more rewarding place to stop, though, is at the lake just east of the hamlet of **Morawewa**, where there's a simple cafe and excellent birdwatching. As you approach the coast, the road crosses a low range of hills.

Kanniyai ⓘ *1 km south of A12 (signposted).* About 8 km before Trincomalee is a turn-off to the hot wells at Kanniyai. This is a popular spot with locals who perform certain rites following the death of friends or family here. Hindu legend states that Vishnu appeared to Rawana here to tell him that his mother had died in order to prevent him from embarking on a foolish project. Vishnu then touched his sword to the ground and the wells burst forth. There are seven springs here, each formed into small bathing pools enclosed in tiled tubs. The tubs are not big enough to bathe in – you can only splash the water over yourself with a bucket – but the water is a perfect temperature (37-41°C) and very refreshing. The wells make an easy morning trip in a three-wheeler from Uppuveli. It is possible to combine the journey with a stop at the remains of the **Velgam Vihara**.

Listings To Trincomalee from the southwest

Where to eat

A9 via Kantale

$$ Lake Front Rest
On the lake shore, T026-326 3461.
With its breezy deck overlooking Kantale tank, this is the best place to break your journey to Trinco. Good Chinese and Sri Lankan food cooked to order and excellent juices.

Transport

A9 via Kantale
Regular buses between Habarana and Trincomalee stop in Kantale.

The main town is built on a fairly narrow piece of land between Back Bay and the Inner Harbour. While much of the harbour remains off-limits, Fort Frederick provides the main point of tourist interest. It is only possible to see sections of the magnificent bay which gives the harbour its reputation, but there are some good views from Orr's Hill. One of the town's more unusual features is its many spotted deer which can be seen grazing throughout the city, including on the beach.

Fort Frederick

Situated on a rocky headland, this is still an active army base and one of the few in Sri Lanka that you can enter unchallenged. The main reason to do so is to visit the atmospheric Koneswaram Temple, a Shaivite Hindu pilgrimage site built on the high cliffs of Swami Rock.

The fort was originally built by the Portuguese in 1623, who destroyed the original ancient Shiva temple. Entering through the gate, which dates from 1676, a noticeboard on the left gives a short history of the fort's complex vacillating fortunes: it was continually handed back and forth between the Dutch, British and French, a result of wars in Europe, until it was conclusively taken by the British in 1796. It was christened Fort Frederick after the Duke of York, son of George III, who was stationed here.

Trincomalee

Where to stay 📷
Dyke Rest **1**
Welcombe **2**

Restaurants 🍴
Annapoorani **1**
Dutch Bank Café **2**

Happy Cream House **3**

Inside, in a cordoned-off military zone, there are two cannons, a howitzer and a mortar. To the right of the path is Wellesley House, now the home of the Kachcheri. The house had a remarkable role in changing the course of European history: in 1800 the Duke of Wellington convalesced here from an illness after his South India campaign, missing his ship which subsequently went down with all hands in the Gulf of Aden. Nearby there are four British and Dutch gravestones from the early 18th century. Taking the left fork leads to a new standing Buddha, from where there are good views.

★ **Konesvaram Temple** ① *Leave your shoes at the entrance, for which a small donation will be requested.* The modern Hindu temple, one of the five most sacred Shaivite sites in Sri Lanka, stands beneath a towering blue Shiva at the furthest end of Swami

Tip...
Regular services are held at the temple; the one on Friday evening is particularly colourful.

Rock. There has been a temple on this spot since 205 BC. The original, said to have been one of the greatest buildings of its age, with four gold-plated *gopurams* and exquisite bas-relief sculpture, was torn down and hurled into the ocean by the Portuguese in 1622. Only a couple of stone pillars from the original temple have survived.

The new temple is highly decorated and painted. Inside is a lingam, believed to be one of the 69 *swayambhu* (naturally created) linga, which according to legend was brought here by Ravana, the king of Lanka. The lingam was recovered from the waters below the rock in 1956 by a team of divers, including Arthur C Clarke.

Go behind the temple to find 'Lover's Leap', apparently named after Francina van Rhede, the daughter of a Dutch official, who threw herself from the rock after her lover sailed away. The truth seems to be more prosaic than the fiction, however, for according to government archives she was alive and well when the Dutch memorial was placed here! The memorial stands on an old temple column on the rock summit, though this is now sealed off to prevent others following her example. Nearby, on a precarious ledge on the cliff side a tree has strips of coloured cloth tied to its branches, left there by devotees of the temple in the hope of having their prayers answered.

Tip...
In 2015 renovation work was underway to open up the area underneath and around the rock.

Other sights

Sadly, many of Trinco's interesting buildings, such as **Admiralty House**, the **British dockyard** and **Fort Ostenburg**, built on a hill east of Inner Bay, are not open to visitors. There is little left of the British naval days apart from vivid and graphic names on the map: Marble Bay, Sweat Bay, Yard Cove, Deadman's Cove, Powder and Sober Islands. French Pass marks the passage where the French fleet escaped.

North of the stadium and clock tower, Main Street, Central Street and North Coastal (NC) Road form a thriving shopping area where small single-storey shops and pawnbrokers, many Muslim-run, sell all sorts of goods. Just by the clock tower is a busy fish market, where you can watch tuna, rays and swordfish change hands.

Fact...
Jane Austen's younger brother, Charles, is buried in St Stephen's cemetery.

Where to stay

There's not a great choice of accommodation in Trincomalee itself, and most travellers press on to Uppuveli and Nilaveli. However, there are a couple of appealing beachside places along Dutch Bay.

$$$ Welcombe
66 Lower Rd, Orr's Hill, T026-222 3885, www.welcombehotel.com.
Trinco's original luxury hotel sits in pleasant gardens overlooking the harbour. Though the rooms (and particularly bathrooms) have seen better days, the bizarre boat-like architecture and the sense of faded glamour make this an intriguing, if not exactly luxurious, place to stay. There's a naval-themed wood-panelled bar and an inviting pool.

$$-$ Dyke Rest
228 Dyke St, T026-222 5313, www.dykerest.com.
Easily the best in a string of places along this street. Rooms off the main corridor are spacious, clean and a/c, but if you can handle the trip downstairs to the bathroom, the rustic little rooms upstairs are the pick, with wonderful views over the sweep of Dutch Bay. The beach out back is well looked after and management is obliging and efficient.

Restaurants

Most guesthouses and hotels offer food, although guests may have to give their hosts a few hrs' notice if they wish to stay in for dinner (usually rice and curry).

$$ Dutch Bank Café
88 Inner Harbour Rd, T077-269 0600.
A bit of an outlier in Trinco, this cafe occupies a trendily modernized old bank. With freezing a/c, this is a good place to come

for pizzas and Western snacks, juices and cappuccinos. It's especially good at sunset.

$ Annapoorani
415 Dockyard Rd.
Excellent, cheap, all-vegetarian canteen, good for *thosai* and *kottu*.

$ Happy Cream House
172 Central Rd.
Delicious sweets, home-made ice creams and juices.

Bars and clubs

Welcombe Hotel
See Where to stay.
A stylish place for a drink. Enjoy the view from the dining room or the veranda rather than staying cloistered in the bar.

Transport

Air Cinnamon Air flies daily from Colombo Bandaranaike Airport to the Air Force airport at China Bay, 7 km southwest of Trincomalee.

Bus CTB and private bus stations are adjacent to each other. To **Colombo** private buses (via **Habarana** and **Dambulla**) depart when full during the morning and early afternoon (5-6 hrs). **CTB** buses leave every 30 mins-1 hr (5½-7 hrs). Fairly frequent buses to **Kandy** (5 hrs). To **Habarana** hourly. To **Polonnaruwa** (4 hrs) or change in Habarana. Fairly regular buses to **Anuradhapura** (3½ hrs). 2 daily to **Batticaloa** (3 hrs) via **Valaichchenai** (for Passekudah).

Train The station is at the north end of town about 800 m northwest of the clocktower. To **Colombo Fort**, 1 daily train at 1900 (8½ hrs). Connections to **Polonnaruwa** and destinations east require an overnight stop in Habarana; better to go by bus.

★ Uppuveli *Colour map 4, A1.*

Uppuveli, 4 km north of Trinco, is one of the east coast's most beguiling beach villages, with a great range of places to stay and eat tucked away along a series of shady lanes that lead off the northbound Nilaveli Road. The beach, particularly to the north, has clean white sand and gentle waves. Uppuveli is more convenient than its neighbour for trips into town, with buses and three-wheelers running regularly, and the main road is more accessible from the beach. Tour operators here offer dive and snorkelling trips as well as excursions to the hot wells at **Kanniyai** (see page 317). Just north of Uppuveli is a huge new gilded Hindu temple on the main road. It's worth a short detour from here to the small and rarely visited beachside Hindu temple at **Salli**. (You can also get here by wading across the chest-deep creek north of the Trinco Blu resort.) If you poke around the lanes to the north of here you can find some quiet stretches of beach among the fishing boats.

Commonwealth War Cemetery *Colour map 4, A1.*

At Sampaltivu, about 5 km north of Trinco, just before the road crosses the Uppuveli creek, is the Commonwealth War Cemetery. During the Second World War, Trinco was an important naval and air force base and the harbour was the focus of Japanese air raids in April 1942. Five Blenheim bombers were shot down, and the aircraft carrier *HMS Hermes*, along with the destroyer *Vampire* and corvette *HMS Hollyhock*, were sunk off Kalkudah and Passekudah bays to the south; many graves date from this time. As the island was a leave recuperation centre, still more died as a result of their wounds.

The cemetery was damaged by bombing during Sri Lanka's civil war in the late 1980s. The damaged headstones have now been replaced and the garden is beautifully maintained in the tradition of Commonwealth War cemeteries. HRH Princess Anne visited in 1995 and planted a *margosa* tree. The cemetery has great sentimental value for many whose families were stationed at the naval base, and a visit is a sobering experience for anyone. The custodian has a register of the graves and will show the visitor some interesting documents relating to Trincomalee.

Nilaveli *Colour map 4, A1.*

Nilaveli, 16 km north of Trincomalee, is Sri Lanka's longest beach, and, before the war, was one of the island's most popular. It used to be a straight wide strip of inviting white sand stretching for miles, backed by screw pines and palmyras which provided shade. Unfortunately, the 2004 tsunami hit this area with incredible force, destroying homes and businesses, and eroding the sand. The collapse of tourism through the war years has also taken its toll, and there is still a visible military presence. However, tourists are returning, and, as their numbers rise, building and improvement work are geting underway. Expect things to change rapidly here over the next few years.

Unlike Uppuveli, Nilaveli doesn't have anything resembling a centre: it's more a series of small clusters of hotels, straggling out along a long stretch of beach. The beach's gentle waters are safe for swimming outside the period of the northeast monsoons.

★ Pigeon Island National Park
Entry fee US$10 (children US$5) plus service charges. Buy tickets from the National Park office near the Anilana hotel.

The classic excursion from Nilaveli is to hire a boat out to the narrow Pigeon Island, just a few hundred metres offshore. This uninhabited rocky islet has some sandy stretches and offers some of Sri Lanka's best snorkeling, with corals, fish, turtles and harmless reef sharks visible within a few metres of the shore. There is some good diving here, too. The island is named after blue rock pigeons which breed here; their eggs are prized by Sri Lankans. There are no facilities and little shade, so go prepared. Hotels run trips to the island while local fisherman often approach tourists direct, undercutting hotel prices. The area around the Nilaveli Beach Hotel is the best place to leave from – trips are quickest and cheapest from here.

North of Nilaveli *Colour map 1, C6.*
The good new road north of Nilaveli leads through increasingly empty country of stark and desolate beauty. White sandy beaches are backed by inland lagoons, and empty shells of buildings stand along the road. The majority of local people have yet to return.

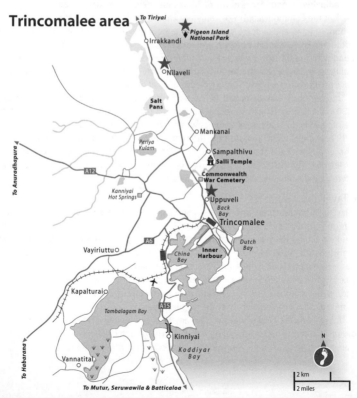

Few travellers go further north than the swish **Jungle Beach Resort** at Kuchchaveli, but it's worth pushing on at least to **Tiriyai**, 35 km north of Nilaveli, where there are the part-restored remains of an eighth-century *vatadage* with a small stupa inside and fine guardstones atop a hill, reminiscent of Medirigirya. Sri Lanka's first temple is said to have been built here during the Buddha's lifetime, enshrining a hair relic he gave to two Indian merchants as a reward, though nothing remains of this period. From the top of the hill there are fine views out to sea, 4 km away, and inland. The modern temple at the foot of the hill was destroyed by the LTTE (Liberation Tigers of Tamil Eelam), but monks returned here in May 2002 protected by a strong military presence. Elephants are often seen in this area in the evening.

Listings North of Trincomalee

Where to stay

There is currently a lot of redevelopment going on here and new places are opening all the time. Note that during high season (Apr-Oct) prices can rise significantly. In low season deals may be available, so it's worth enquiring.

Uppuveli

$$$$-$$$ Trinco Blu
Salvodaya Rd (turn off 300 m before war cemetery), T011-216 1161, www.cinnamonhotels.com.
Previously the Chaaya Blu, this bright and breezy resort offers 79 good rooms with sea views, a/c and Wi-Fi. There is a swimming pool, a dive centre, bar and 2 restaurants. Offers whale-watching trips, fishing, snorkelling and excursions to Mutur. Good location right on a curved bay.

$$$-$$ Golden Beach Cottages
24 Alles Garden, next to Trinco Blu, T026-493 1210, T077-366 2820, goldenbeachcottages@yahoo.com.
Attractively set on a quiet, clean stretch of the beach, the freshly renovated concrete-floored chalets here are big, bright and clean with shady sit-outs; try to snag one of the two directly on the beach. New owners Clare and Jo run a relaxed but efficient ship, and have built a lovely new eating area, where

they plan to launch an expat-friendly lunch and dinner menu. Good dive shop next door.

$$ Chutti's Villa (The White Villa)
Sampaltivu, 3 km north of Uppuveli, bookings via www.neverbeen.org/at/chuttis.
It's a bit of a mission to find this place, on a quiet curve of beach, but if absolute beachfront and no tourist crowds are your style, it's worth it. There's just one room – a simple but spacious and clean cottage with canopied bed and private bathroom – set in the garden of the villa, just a hop over the fence from the waves. Genial host Chutti pops in to feed you (book meals in advance – there's not much else close by) and can organize tuk-tuks into town and other essentials. Not slick by any means, but heartily recommended.

$$ Palm Beach Resort
12 Alles Garden, Nilaveli Rd, T026-222 1250.
Friendly Italian-managed guesthouse offering a/c and fan rooms. Closed during monsoon (Nov to mid-Jan) and busy the rest of the time, so book early. The breakfast offers more variety than the average guesthouse and can be enjoyed in garden restaurant. Excellent Italian food (see Restaurants) and real coffee.

$$-$ Whistle Stop Cafe
38/10 Beach Rd, Alles Garden, T071-470 5408, redlinelanka@gmail.com.

One of the best budget deals in town, with 3 simple fan-cooled rooms and private cold-water bathrooms, a 5-min walk from the beach. Friendly owner lays on great seafood and curry dinners.

Nilaveli

$$$$ Pigeon Island Beach Resort
11th Mile post, Nilaveli, T026-738 8388, www.pigeonislandresort.com.
34 a/c rooms and suites (some with sea views and balcony) in an attractive white-and wood-finished hotel. Whale and dolphin cruises, fishing and diving in season (Mar-Oct). There's a pool, a beach bar and shaded seating areas on the beach with view of Pigeon Island.

$$$ Nagena Hira Beach Villas
Next to Pigeon Island Beach Resort, T077-738 2954, www.nagenahirabeachvilla.com.
These chic modern villas are the outstanding deal on this stretch of coast. The huge, high-ceilinged rooms sport a cool minimalist look, with white walls and polished concrete fittings set off by bright organic cotton pillows and throws straight out of Barefoot Colombo. Owner Sam and the friendly staff help to organize activities and boat hire, and it's a 30-sec walk to a long stretch of empty beach.

$$$ Nilaveli Beach Hotel (NBH)
11th mile post, 4 km north of Nilaveli Village, T026-223 2295/6, www.tangerinehotels.com.
This good old Nilaveli institution has a wide range of rooms, half of which are deluxe (tubs, TVs and DVD players). Restaurant, indoor a/c bar, beach bar, pool and large tree-shaded area with hammocks. Excellent location on best part of beach. PADI diving school (Apr-Oct), trips to Pigeon Island, sport fishing, tennis and badminton.

$$$-$ White Sand Beach
9th Mile Post, Nilaveli, T026-223 2032, hotelwhitesandbeach@gmail.com.

Just over a dune from the beach, this collection of large, clean a/c rooms and fan-cooled cabanas is set around a square of lawn, and offers great off-season discounts.

$ Shahira
10th mile post (1.5 km south of NBH), Liyanage Rd, Nilaveli, 200 m from beach, T077-794 4481.
Clean, large rooms with fan around a shady garden, attached bath (cold water), restaurant and bar, friendly and good value.

North of Nilaveli

$$$$ Jungle Beach Resort
Km 27, Kuchchavekli, T026-567 1000, www.ugaescapes.com.
The most luxurious hotel on the entire east coast, with 48 huge contemporary villas carved out of mangrove forest. The best are the 4 **Jungle Villas**, which share access to a semi-private pool. Sandy tracks wind past the Ayurvedic spa to an isolated stretch of beach. Good seafood restaurant, poolside bar and many (premium-priced) activities, including snorkelling and whale watching.

Restaurants

Uppuveli
Most guesthouses and hotels offer food, though it's wise to give your hosts a few hrs' notice if you intend to eat in. Uppuveli offers a great choice of places to eat – not just the seafront hotels, but also standalone restaurants scattered in the lanes of Alles Garden.

$$ Palm Beach Resort
See Where to stay.
Home-cooked Italian food, simple but tasty. If you're craving real espresso, this is the place to come. Always full, so book ahead.

$$ Fernandos
Aqua Inn Hotel, Alles Garden.
Pleasant beachcomber bar, serves excellent and huge burgers. Slightly pricey and service can be hit and miss.

$ Rice 'n' Curry
Alles Garden, T077-740 9660.
Run by a fast-moving and friendly young crew, this open-fronted place doles out huge plates of veggie, seafood or chicken *kottu* as well as the eponymous rice and curry. You might have to line up for a table.

Nilaveli
There's not a great deal here outside resorts. The attractive poolside restaurant at **Jungle Beach Resort** is good for a splurge.

$ Cafe Nilaveli
10th Mile Post, in lane beyond Thirumalai Park hotel, near the beach, T071-663 2902.
This slightly dingy restaurant offers good Sri Lankan, Western and seafood dishes, at prices distinctly cheaper than the hotels.

Bars and clubs

Nilaveli

Nilaveli Beach Hotel
See Where to stay.
It has 2 bars, including 1 a/c with sports TV, though drinks are expensive.

Toddy Tavern
On the main road just after Shahira turn-off.

No-nonsense drinking den full of old fishermen, but toddy is cheap. Female travellers might want to give this one a miss.

What to do

A number of the hotels and guesthouses listed under Where to stay, organize diving (Nov-Mar), snorkelling, whale- and dolphin-watching trips (Dec-Apr). It is also possible to visit Pigeon Island and Mutur, and have a go at sport fishing. Fishermen also offer snorkeling trips to other spots; these have the virtue of avoiding the hefty National Park fees charged to access Pigeon Island. Ensure dive instructors are PADI or SSI certified.

Uppuveli
Sri Lanka Diving Tours, *next to Golden Beach Cottages (see Where to stay), T077-764 8459, www.srilanka-divingtours.com.* Diving and snorkelling trips and operate a glass-bottomed boat. Instructors are PADI certified.

Transport

Bus Frequent buses run to **Uppuveli** and **Nilaveli** from Trincomalee or you can take a 3-wheeler (Rs 200-300 to Uppuveli, Rs 600-800 to Nilaveli).

South of Trincomalee

minor distractions from the beach

Mutur *Colour map 4, A1.*
Sri Lanka's longest river, the Mahaweli Ganga, drains into the sea at Mutur, 12 km south of Trincomalee. Here, there is also a stone memorial under a tree to Sir Robert Knox, who was captured here by King Rajasinha II in 1660, taken upriver and imprisoned for almost 20 years. Knox's *An Historical Relation of Ceylon* was one of the inspirations for Defoe's *Robinson Crusoe*.

Seruwawila *Colour map 4, A1.*
Seruwawila Raja Maha Vihara, close to Allai tank, was originally built by King Kavantissa in the second century AD in an attempt to extend his authority to the ancient kingdom of Seru here. The small restored *dagoba* is said to enshrine the Buddha's frontal bone, around which several ancient structures remain. Nearby are two caves housing Buddha figures under the cobra hood of a Naga king.

Batticaloa
& around

Until late 2009, the Tamil town of Batticaloa, along with its two famous beaches, Passekudah and Kalkudah, was well off the tourist map. Now that it's accessible once more, curious locals and foreigners are beginning to visit this remote part of the coast and have found not a war-ravaged shell but a likeable town cautiously coming to terms with its recent troubles. Batticaloa (or 'Batti' as it is frequently called), famous for the 'singing fish' in its picturesque lagoon, has few sights, but the friendliness of its people, who are genuinely pleased that you came, can make a stop on the way through to Arugam Bay or Polonnaruwa a rewarding experience. It is a relaxed place, with bicycle the chief mode of transport.

Essential Batticaloa

Finding your feet

Buses run to Batticaloa's central bus stand from Colombo and Kandy via Habarana and Polonnaruwa, and from Badulla and the eastern hill country via Bibile (see page 330). Thanks to major work on the east coast roads, buses now run all the way to Trincomalee on the newly completed A15, and south to Pottuvil. Trains from Colombo pull into the station 1 km north of the centre, coming via Polonnaruwa and Valaichchenai (for Passekudah and Kalkudah).

Getting around

Batticaloa is small enough to walk or cycle around, but you will need your own transport or a bus or train to reach the beaches north of town.

Tip...
Though it's not really a sight, visitors won't be able to miss the new vast, blue bus stand that stands next to the river.

Fort area

The coast to the south of Batticaloa was the first landing point of the Dutch in Sri Lanka in 1602, who were welcomed by the Kandyan king to help drive out the Portuguese. They subsequently captured the Portuguese fort here in 1638, which was later rebuilt. Although overgrown and neglected, the ramparts remain intact, and it is possible to walk most of the way round them. A smattering of government agencies and NGOs are installed within the walls.

Entering from Court House Road, take a look at the tunnel, now sadly shut off and clogged up with rubbish, which ran parallel to the lagoon, formerly providing access to a jetty. At the eastern side of the fort is a VOC gate which has been widened to let in traffic, flanked by two cannons facing out to the lagoon. A small **museum** ① *daily 0900-1630*, in

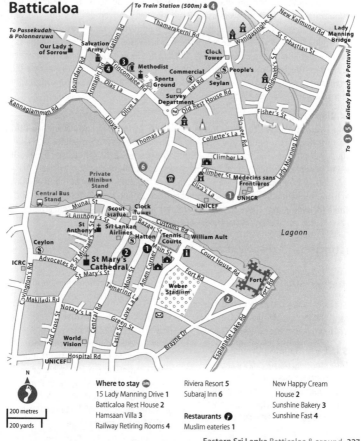

Batticaloa

N

200 metres
200 yards

Where to stay 🛏
15 Lady Manning Drive **1**
Batticaloa Rest House **2**
Hamsaan Villa **3**
Railway Retiring Rooms **4**

Riviera Resort **5**
Subaraj Inn **6**

Restaurants 🍴
Muslim eateries **1**

New Happy Cream
House **2**
Sunshine Bakery **3**
Sunshine Fast **4**

the complex holds various artefacts from the Portuguese, Dutch and British periods. This was being renovated in late 2015.

Batticaloa lagoon

At 48 sq km, this is Sri Lanka's longest navigable lagoon and is famously home to the singing fish. Numerous theories abound to the cause of this strange phenomenon, sometimes likened to a single sustained note on a guitar; one is that it is the courting call of mussels resonating against the rocks beneath. It is usually only possible to hear the fish around full moon (best between April and October), and the sound is clearest if you go out at night with a local fisherman, who will know where to find the rocks. For maximum effect, put an oar into the lagoon with the other end to your ear.

Other sights

There are some fine restored *kovils* and churches around town, as well as a couple of curious monuments: one, an unexpected statue of a boy scout by the clock tower, commemorates the 80th anniversary of Baden-Powell's movement; the other, near the fort, is a bronze statue of William Ault, a pioneer of education on the east coast.

Batticaloa's most impressive sight lies 60 m under water, 5 km offshore, and unless you are very experienced diver, you are very unlikely to see it. It is the gargantuan wreck of *HMS Hermes*, the British aircraft carrier sunk in 1942 by the Japanese. Several dive teams from Hikkaduwa explored the wreck in 2002-2003 and reported it to be in good condition. Dive trips are available. See What to do, opposite.

To Kallady beach

Taking you out of town to the south is the British-period iron **Lady Manning Bridge**, open to traffic with a pedestrian walkway alongside. It's just too small for two lanes of traffic, so crossing by vehicle can be a bruising experience. It is, however, an excellent place to watch the fishermen casting their nets. Cross the bridge and turn left to reach Batti's nearest beach at **Kallady**, 3 km from the centre of town (20 minutes by bus). Kallady beach has fine sand, though it needs a bit of a clean-up, and the sea here is rough and not suitable for swimming. There are no facilities, but you'll have it to yourself. (The beaches at Passekudah and Kalkudah, see below, are better.)

Listings Batticaloa *map p327*

Where to stay

Most places to stay can be found on the north bank of the lagoon off Trinco Rd, or 2 km out of town across the bridge in Kallady.

$$$ 15 Lady Manning Drive
15 Lady Manning Dr, T077-379 4226,
www.neverbeen.org/at/ranjans.
This wonderful old house, built by the Dutch administrators of the fort, offers 4 rooms of high-ceilinged, colonial elegance, and superb views of the lagoon from the veranda. Free Wi-Fi, excellent home-cooked meals.

$$ Batticaloa Rest House
Brayne Dr, T065-222 7882.
Since the army moved out, this place has been renovated and now offers modern clean rooms with gardens overlooking the lagoon. There is also a restaurant serving good seafood. It's in a lovely location and is one of the best value options in the town centre.

$$-$ Deep Sea Resort
New Fisheries St, Nawalady, T077-068 6860,
www.srilanka-divingtours.com/deep-sea.
Built to accommodate divers wishing to
visit the *HMS Hermes* wreck with **Sri Lanka
Diving Tours** (see below). Offers 6 spotless
a/c and fan rooms, and a good restaurant.
Visitors don't have to be divers to stay
here, but will need their own transport
to reach it independently.

$$-$ Riviera Resort
New Dutch Bar Rd, Kallady, T065-222 2165,
www.riviera-online.com.
4-ha garden in beautiful position overlooking
the bridge and lagoon, a range of clean
rooms, including a 3-room bungalow suite
and rooms with terrace near water's edge.
The restaurant serves good food.

$ Hamsaam Villa
35/1 New Dutch Bar Rd, Kallady, T065-222 8060.
3 comfortable and clean a/c rooms in this
cute, overwhelmingly blue guesthouse,
set in flower-filled gardens. Friendly family
atmosphere and delicious vegetarian meals.

$ Railway Retiring Rooms
Ask at the counter in the station.
Cheap basic fan rooms with net,
worth trying if you're desperate.

Restaurants

The Muslim eateries on Main St are a friendly
stop for lunch or a cup of tea, though
hygiene may not be high on the agenda.

$ New Happy Cream House
19 Central Rd, T065-365 5491.
Good small eats, as well as fresh juices
and ice cream.

$ Sunshine Bakery
136 Trinco Rd, T065-222 5159.
Cheap rolls and samosas, enticing cakes,
seating area at back of bakery. **Sunshine
Fast**, opposite, serves up fresh *dosai*.

Bars and clubs

Riviera Resort
See Where to stay.
A lovely place for a sunset drink.

Shopping

The market on the north side of the lagoon
is a noisy and fascinating place to pick up
clothes, fresh produce, etc. For a wider range
of goods, you might consider a visit to the
busy modern Muslim town of Kattankudi to
the south.

What to do

Sri Lanka Diving Tours, *T077-764 8459,*
www.srilanka-divingtours.com. Runs dive
trips to the *HMS Hermes* wreck as well as a
number of other wrecks in the surrounding
area. Dive leader Sashaa was the 1st woman
to dive the *Hermes*. Accommodation is
offered in Batticaloa at the **Deep Sea Resort**
(see Where to stay). Trips are available with
pick-ups from Colombo airport; contact for
prices and details.

Transport

Bus The CTB bus station and private minibus
stands are situated next to each other on
Lake Rd, on the southern edge of the lagoon.
Buses leave for **Passekudah** 6 times a day,
and **Kalmunai** every half an hour. To get to
Passekudah you can also take a Kandy bus
and get off at Valaichchenai. CTB buses run
to **Colombo** (4 daily, 9 hrs), **Trincomalee**
(4 daily, 3 hrs), **Pottuvil** (4 daily, 3½ hrs),
Badulla (2 daily, 6 hrs), **Kandy** (1 daily, 6 hrs),
and **Polonnaruwa** (1 daily, 3 hrs). Private
buses also cover the major routes.

Train 2 trains leave daily for
Colombo, at 0715 and 2015 (9 hrs),
via **Valaichchenai**, **Polonnaruwa**,
Minneriya, **Gal Oya** and **Maho**.

Passekudah and Kalkudah beaches *32 km north of Batticaloa.*

At the right time of day, you can see why Passekudah has for so long been the east coast's biggest beach honeypot. The 4-km horseshoe-shaped sweep of sand, reminiscent of Unawatuna, is still glorious, and the water that laps at it is crystal-clear, safe for swimming, shallow enough to wade out half a kilometre, and as warm as a bath.

Yet how much you actually enjoy Passekudah will very much depend on your view of mass tourism. Since the fighting stopped, there's been an official determination – verging on obsession – to catapult Passekudah back to its pre-war status as the queen of east coast beaches. A phalanx of four-star hotels have sprung up – no less than 10 of them have thrown open their extravagantly wide doors in the last five years – and it's these mostly bland red-roofed buildings, rather than swaying palm trees, that now dominate the view along the bay. For all the hype, this is hardly your Bounty Bar tropical idyll. If you're not staying in one of the beachfront hotels, there are two spots at either end of "Hotel Development Road" where you can access the sand; the southern end has a busy car park and tea stalls.

South around the headland, Kalkudah beach also has its fair share of places to stay, but is the better option if you prefer your beach time to be more solitary. The beach is less protected here, but gets the same mellow waves during the season. A recommended activity is to take a snorkelling trip from the north end of the beach; a few hundred metres offshore are good corals and large friendly tuna that happily swim up to you.

West from Batticaloa

There are two possible routes west across the scrub jungles of the Dry Zone from Batticaloa, each with the option of visiting some hot springs on the way. The quickest route heads north on the A15 through the slowly recovering town of **Valaichchenai**, near Passekudah Beach (see above). From here, Polonnaruwa is accessible within two hours via the A11, and you can stop off at Dimbulagala cave complex en route (see page 307).

Alternatively, a left turn at **Chenkaladi** heads southwest on the A5 across a vast barren plain towards Kandy via Mahiyangana, or to Badulla via Bibile. **Maha Oya** junction, 40 km on, is a good place to stop for lunch, with excellent rice and curry available at a roadside café. Two kilometres along a gravel road from Maha Oya town, you can visit some impressively hot sulphuric springs, rather unattractively pooled in concrete pots.

After passing southeast of the 687-m Kokagala hill, the road is joined by the A26 at **Padiyatalawa**. (For the route along the A26 from Mahiyangana to Kandy see page 309.) The A5 continues south through Bibile, climbing steeply to Lunugala and Tennugewatta, before heading west to **Badulla**.

Listings North and west from Batticaloa

Where to stay

Passekudah and Kalkudah
Rack rates for rooms along Passekudah beach are eye-wateringly high. Search the booking sites for a deal, or retreat to the more humble family-run guesthouses a little further inland.

$$$$ Maalu Maalu
Coconut Board Rd, Passekudah, T065-738 8388, www.theme-resorts.com/maalumaalu.

The first of Passekudah's new wave of resorts and still the only one with any kind of design flair, with its steeply pitched straw roofs. The rooms themselves don't quite carry it through, but some of them come with private plunge pools. Ayurvedic spa, pool, 2 restaurants.

$$$$ Uga Bay Resort
Coconut Board Rd, Passekudah, T065-567 1000, www.ugaescapes.com.
The most attractively landscaped of the big resorts, with large rooms done out in a corporate-contemporary-could-be-anywhere style, set in pleasant gardens. 2 pools, underground spa, efficient restaurant.

$$ Nandawanam
Passekudah Rd, Kalkudah, T065-225 7258, nandawanam@live.com
Set in pleasant green gardens off the main road, the rooms here are spacious and clean, and the in-house restaurant is one of the best places to eat in the area.

$ Vasuki
Passekudah Rd, Kalkudah, T077-376 4719, hotelvasuki@yahoo.com.
A/c rooms in 2 blocks facing a shady garden. Friendly owner, Wi-Fi, nice atmosphere. A 1st-choice good budget option.

$ New Land
283 Main St, Kalkudah, T065-568 0440.
8 simple rooms (5 a/c) in large rambling house, attached bath, cool, clean, food available.

$ Simla Inn
Passekudah Rd, Kalkudah, T077-603 1272.
Family-run guesthouse continuously open since 1981 (the last comments book lasted 19 years), but in a new spot since the tsunami. 2 simple rooms with bath, very friendly, basic. Check final bill carefully – some travellers have reported overcharging.

Restaurants

Passekudah and Kalkudah
There's not much of note outside the hotels and resorts. **Maalu Maalu** has an attractive feet-in-the-sand seafood restaurant, and **Nandawanam** does excellent rice-and-curry and spicy Sri Lankan specialities.

Transport

Passekudah and Kalkudah
Valaichchenai, on the A15 coastal highway, is the jumping off point for Passekudah and Kalkudah. Buses from **Trincomalee**, **Batticaloa** and **Polonnaruwa** stop here. A 3-wheeler to the beaches costs around Rs 300.

South of Batticaloa

Buddhist ruins and a stunning national park

The quiet but well-laid coastal road leading south toward Arugam Bay passes through alternating Hindu and Muslim fishing villages. Though the sea is rarely in sight, this is a beautiful drive rich in bird life. Rice paddies and lagoons dominate the landscape, though cultivation can be affected by frequent cyclones and flooding.

There is evidence of numerous income-generating projects, developed by Western aid agencies, and much new construction in some of the larger towns, such as **Akkaraipattu**, **Kalmunai** and **Kattankudi**, much of it in Islamic style. The Danish government is planning a harbour at **Oluvil**, with a new industrial zone which will help regenerate the local area. The places of interest to visitors, however, lie a short distance inland.

ON THE ROAD

Elephas maximus maximus

Cumbersome yet capable of remarkable grace, full of charisma yet mortally dangerous if rankled, universally revered yet critically endangered, the Asian variety of the world's largest land mammal has a complex relationship with man.

Once widespread across the country, elephants have been tamed in Sri Lanka for over 2000 years. Their massive power was harnessed by the ancient Sinhalese in wars against invaders, used to construct ancient palaces, temples and reservoirs, while some were exported as far afield as Burma and Egypt. Seemingly without paradox, they also possess a mythical and religious status: the *Jataka* tales refer to the birth of Buddha in the body of an elephant, while a caparisoned elephant carries the Buddha's Tooth in Kandy's Esala Perahera; for Hindus, they represent Lord Ganesh.

Yet despite their central place in culture and religion, Sri Lanka's wild elephants, now mainly confined to the Dry Zone, have been in crisis: their numbers have fallen from around 10,000 at the turn of the 18th century to between 3000 and 4000 in the early 2000s. The population was drastically reduced by the British, who shot them for sport and declared them an agricultural pest, and the hill country was all but cleared of herds to make way for tea plantations. After a period of recovery, aided by the establishment of protected areas, numbers since the 1960s have again declined rapidly: almost 1400 elephants were killed in the 1990s, 162 (around 5% of the population) in 2001 alone. Sri Lanka's ethnic troubles have been a contributory factor.

The problem lies, of course, in what is termed the 'human-elephant conflict'. Given the rarity of tuskers, ivory is not a major issue, but deforestation, agricultural

Ampara *Colour map 5, A5.*

The modern district headquarters of Ampara has a recent bloody history, though it is well connected and, when safe, can be a used as a base for visiting Gal Oya National Park (see below). It has accommodation, restaurants and banks. Near the **Kandavatavana tank**, on the road to Inginiyagala, is the gleaming white *dagoba* of a peace pagoda, donated by the Japanese government in 1988.

Digavapi *Colour map 5, A6.*

Donations requested (part of the complex was destroyed during the war). Getting there: from the A4, take the B607 towards Ampara and turn right at the village of Varipathanchenai.

The enormous part-restored *dagoba* here, originally 98 m high, built by King Sadhatissa in the first century BC, is one of the 16 holiest Buddhist sites in Sri Lanka. The site is said to have been visited by Buddha on his third visit. Amongst the scattered remains of this ancient complex are shrine rooms, monastic quarters, *bodhigaras* and hospitals. Three gold caskets were also found during excavations. There is a small archaeological museum nearby.

expansion and the explosion of the human population (set to double by 2035) have all deprived the elephants of their natural habitat. And, while there is a growing network of protected reserves, buffer zones and elephant corridors, in practice these areas are usually too small to accommodate these enormous animals, each of which requires 200 kg of food and 200 litres of water per day. Struggling to thrive in the protected areas, they are forced to push into adjacent agricultural lands.

Yet life is hard, too, for the farmer, who may have his entire annual staple crop destroyed in one night, or who may even have to defend his own life from a marauding bull. Various solutions have been tried for this seemingly intractable problem: in periodic elephant 'drives', the animals are immobilized and transferred to a national park, and electric fences are a common management tool. Some suggest that compensation should be introduced for crop damage (to counter the heavy fines and/or imprisonment for killing an animal). But many experts agree the real key is attempting to converge the interests of people and elephants by encouraging compatible land use, such as grazing. One way forward is for farmers to derive economic benefits from elephant products, such as manure for organic farming.

Still, there is reason for hope. By creating contiguous wildlife corridors, such as the complex of national parks that includes Minneriya and Kaudulla tanks, the Department of Wildlife Conservation (DWLC) has made good steps towards bringing entire home ranges of elephant herds under official protection. A census conducted in 2011 estimates the national population at just under 6000 – a good sign for the future of these magnificent animals.

Gal Oya National Park *Colour map 5, A5.*
Access is either on a good road southwest from Ampara to Inginiyaga, or north from the A4 at Siyambalanduwa.

This magnificent park was established to protect the catchment area of the **Senanayake Samudra**, an enormous reservoir created in 1948 by damming the Gal Oya. It remains testament to one of the most ambitious development schemes to irrigate the barren lands of the east and resettle Sinhalese from the west. Backed by sheer forested slopes, the lake is the largest in Sri Lanka and highly impressive. The park extends over 540 sq km of rolling country, most of which is covered in tall grass (*illuk* and *mana*) or dry evergreen forest which escaped being submerged. The hilly country to the west was one of the last strongholds of the Veddas (see box, page 308), and certain areas of the park still harbour medicinal herbs and plants which are believed to have been planted centuries ago. Recent reports, however, suggest there was extensive illicit logging as well as poaching during the period of the park's closure. Gal Oya is famous for its elephants and a variety of water birds which are attracted by the lake. Crocodiles and the white-bellied sea-eagle are also often seen.

At the time of writing there were few facilities for visitors, and the few tracks inside the park were overgrown and in a poor state.

Arugam Bay
& around

Even while civil war raged through the beach resorts along the coast to the north, a small but persistent body of travellers was drawn to the surfer's paradise of Arugam Bay. This laid-back little village, invitingly set between a picturesque lagoon and a magnificent sandy bay, has something of a reputation as a long-stay hippy hideaway. However, the opening up of the surrounding area should now attract a different crowd. The growing range of good-value (and sometimes quirky) accommodation here makes it an excellent base for exploring some of the wildest countryside in Sri Lanka. This feels like frontier territory: largely deserted during the civil war and rebuilt after the devastation wrought by the tsunami, it's ideal for those tired of the commercialism of the west coast.

Essential Arugam Bay

Finding your feet

There is still one daytime bus from Colombo (No 98, leaves Colombo Pettah at 0500, taking 10 hours), but the handy overnight bus direct from Colombo to Arugam Bay was suspended in 2015, so for now the most convenient option is to take a taxi. Expect to pay around US$125 one way, or try to hook up with other travellers willing to share at www.arugam.info/abay-taxi-initiative. From the Highlands, buses run from Badulla and Wellawaya, but you may need to change in Monaragala or Siyambalanduwa (see below). A few daily buses also run up and down the coast to and from Batticaloa. All buses arrive at the main bus stand in Pottuvil, about 3 km north of Arugam Bay. A few Panama-bound buses make the trip from Pottuvil across the lagoon to the Bay, or a three-wheeler costs around Rs 200.

Best surf breaks

Midigama for surfing in the winter months, page 155
Arugam Point, for arguably the best surf in the country, page 340
Baby Point, Arugam Bay, for novice surfers, page 341
Okanda for a secluded surf point in the jungle, page 342

Best eating in the east

Authentic Italian at Palm Beach, Uppuveli, page 323
Whistle Stop Cafe, Uppuveli, page 323
Seafood platter at Hideaway, Arugam Bay, page 339
Jungle Barbecue, Arugam Bay, page 340
Thai fish curry at Siam View Beach Hotel, Arugam Bay, page 340

Getting around

From the guesthouses at the southern end of Arugam Bay, three-wheeler drivers charge Rs 1500 return to Pottuvil Point, including waiting time. The roads around Arugam Bay are quiet and flat, so cycling (available from guesthouses) is a convenient way to get around the local area. For excursions further afield and to the national parks, you will need a jeep or motorbike.

When to go

Most travellers come for the surfing season from April to October, when it is dry and there are constant breezes. Off-season many guesthouses close, though the area still has its attractions: from January to March windsurfing, fishing and swimming are good, and birdwatching is most rewarding when winter migrants arrive.

To Arugam Bay from the west
jungle hideaways where wild elephants roam

There are two routes to Arugam Bay from the west. The quickest is the A4 from Wellawaya, via Buttala and Okkampitiya, where there is open-pit garnet and sapphire mining. At Kumbakkana, a turn-off leads to the ancient site at Maligawila (see page 189). The alternative, longer but more scenic route descends from the hills on the A22 from Badulla, passing Mount Namunukula and through tea country. At Hulanduwa it joins the A4, which continues to Monaragala.

Monaragala *Colour map 5, B4.*

Most people pass through the small town of Monaragala ('Peacock Rock'), backed by forested hills, in the rush for the coast. But this small district headquarters, deep within the Dry Zone, is surprisingly lush and verdant owing to its own Wet Zone micro-climate. There's little to do in Monaragala itself, but it has a laid-back appeal and is both a useful stop halfway to Arugam Bay, 71 km away, and an excellent base from which to explore the surrounding countryside, rich in wildlife and unfairly ignored by tourists.

To the north are the remains of the 12th-century palace of **Galabedda**, with a fine bathing pool reminiscent of the Kumara Pokuna in Polonnaruwa, while to the south there are some attractive walks into the cool **Geelong Hills**.

Monaragala to Arugam Bay

The road surface is good until **Siyambalanduwa**, a former major checkpoint at which all vehicles travelling west would be searched. There is a still a large police presence here but now little fuss. (The A25 here leads north to Ampara and Batticaloa; see page 326.) East of here, potholes begin to appear and the pace of life (never very fast) slows still further. Ox-pulled carts become a common mode of transport, and it is a peaceful drive along the road lined with jack, margosa and tamarind trees. The road passes through **Lahugala National Park** (see page 341), and elephants are frequently seen from the road in the afternoon.

Listings To Arugam Bay from the west

Where to stay

For some unique jungle options near Buttala (15 km west of Monagagala) see The Dry Southeast, page 189).

$$-$ Landa Villa
Wellaway Rd, Monaragala, T055-227 6725.
Friendly family-run villa close to nature. Hosts offer walking, freshwater fishing, great barbecues and delicious home-cooked food.

$ Victory Inn
65 Wellaway Rd, Monaragala, T055-227 6100.
Clean, modern a/c and fan rooms, upstairs with balcony (though not much to see), restaurant, bar.

Restaurants

For options see Where to stay. There are also some simple roadside places serving local food near the bus stand.

Transport

Bus From Monaragala, hourly buses to **Colombo**. Morning CTB buses for **Pottuvil** (Arugam Bay); 3-wheelers will run to Arugam Bay if you miss the bus, but this is dangerous as there may be elephants on the road, and it is expensive. For the highlands it is best to change at **Wellaway**, though there are infrequent direct buses to **Badulla**. Direct buses also go to **Kataragama** and **Matara**.

laid-back beachlife and breaking surf

Arugam Bay's surfing reputation is thanks to the break at Arugam Point at the southern end of the bay, regarded by many as the best in the country. From the point, the bay curves past the village of Ulla and the guesthouses in the south to another surf break at Pottuvil Point in the north. The journey to the beach here takes you across some attractive meadows teeming with wildlife. Just inland is the small town of Pottivil, south of which is Arugam Lagoon.

Around the bay

Arugam Bay's wonderful wide sweep of sandy beach is usually deserted, except at the southwest corner, where some fishing boats and thatch huts reveal the tiny fishing village of **Ulla** and the main guesthouse area. This is the safest area for swimming, which has led to a tussle between local hoteliers and fishermen. The lack of tourists, especially in the off-season, means that the beach can be dirty in some places, strewn with plastic bags and bottles. Just inland from the beach, Arugam's picturesque lagoon divides Ulla village from Pottuvil town. The bridge is an excellent vantage point for the sunset, and at night you can watch prawn fishermen throwing, gathering and emptying their nets.

Pottuvil and around

In the dusty Muslim town of Pottuvil, 3 km north of Ulla, are the ruins, half-submerged amongst the sand-dunes, of the **Mudu Maha Vihara**. A Buddha statue and two Avalokiteswara figures, dating from around the ninth or 10th century, can be found in a pillared structure, along with the boundary wall of an image house. The town has no other sights of interest, but the **lagoon**, north of town, supports a wide variety of wildlife, including crocodiles, monkeys, water snakes and plenty of birds. Partial destruction of the lagoon's mangrove forest has had a negative effect on wildlife, but re-planting schemes are afoot.

Crocodile Rock

The Crocodile Rock is 2 km south of Arugam Point, beyond **Kudakalliya Bungalow** (see Where to stay). Scramble across the dunes and ford the lagoon where it joins the sea to reach the rock, from whose summit there are magnificent views inland across the paddies and lagoon. Eagles swoop

Tip...

South of Crocodile Rock is another wonderful beach called Peanut Farm. It is the favourite of Sharon Appatu from **Hideaway** (see Where to stay, page 338).

overhead, and you can sometimes spot elephants. There is another good surf point nearby. Do be careful getting here though: currents sometimes render it impossible to cross the lagoon, and you should beware of large mugger crocodiles and the occasional elephant that attempts to climb the rock. Seek advice first.

Tourist information

The long-established hotels, Stardust and Siam View, are valuable resources with good websites: www.arugambay.com and www.arugam.com respectively. There is also a tourist information booth opposite the Siam View Beach Hotel (see Where to stay, below). The tourist police can be found next to Point View, T063-224 8022.

Where to stay

Some guesthouses close in off-season. Note that many places only have cold water bathrooms.

$$$ Kudakalliya Bungalow
2 km south of Arugam Bay, 20-min walk from Crocodile Rock, T071-273 3630, www.kudakalliya.com.
Nestled between crashing waves and a peaceful lagoon, this attractive eco-bungalow is in a secluded position with its own beach and surf point. Choice of bedroom or sleeping al fresco on the protected veranda, a cook can be provided or you can self-cater. Water from the well, solar power, veranda with magnificent views.

$$$-$$ Arugam Bay Surf Resort
T063-224 8189, www.arugambay.lk.
12 spotless rooms, bungalows and basic cabanas with good beds, satellite TV, internet. Runs tours and eco-trips on the lagoon. The restaurant serves decent food, including Mexican.

$$$-$$ Hideaway
T077-459 6670, www.hideaway arugambay.com.
Hideaway is not a secret any more. It boasts some of the most beautiful rooms in the bay, has an excellent restaurant and has a vibey café and bar on the road. The beautiful house has 5 rooms with veranda overlooking a garden, plus 9 excellent cabanas some with open-air bathrooms, beautifully decorated. Great insider knowledge on the Bay's lesser known attractions. Highly recommended.

$$$-$$ Stardust Beach Hotel
T063-224 8191, www.arugambay.com.
Danish-run, Arugam's original hotel is in a beautiful location where the beach meets the lagoon and has been for many years a traveller's oasis. There's a choice of beach cabanas with private terrace and 'luxury' rooms (upstairs, more expensive and with sea views), pleasant beach garden, excellent if pricey restaurant, cycle hire, attentive service, good source of local information.

$$ Galaxy Lounge
T063-224 8415, www.galaxysrilanka.com.
8 lovely beach cabanas (2 are on stilts and 3 have sea views), and now a block of stylish rooms. It's a friendly place with lots of space and places to chill out.

$$ Point View
Main St, T077-127 2869, www. pointviewarugambay.com.
20 a/c and fan rooms, restaurant, shaded garden area with access onto the beach.

$$ Siam View Beach Hotel
T063-224 8195, www.arugam.com.
Arugam's party centre in a Thai setting, with an excellent restaurant (see Restaurants, below). Outside is a red British phone box. Inside, the rooms are a/c with satellite TV and open onto an attractive garden. Free Wi-Fi. Surf lessons are on offer.

$$ Water Music
T077-406 1011, www.gwatermusic
arugambay.com.
Set in lovely tropical gardens and close to
the symphony of the waves, Water Music
has stylish cabanas and some 2-tiered beach
huts. Great atmosphere. Recommended.

Pottuvil & Arugam Bay

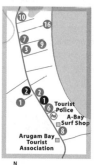

Where to stay 🛏
Arne's Place **3**
Arugam Bay Surf
  Resort **2**
Beach Hut **7**
East Surf Cabanas **4**
Galaxy Lounge **16**
Hideaway **1**
Kudakkaliya Bungalow **5**
Point View **6**
Siam View Beach **8**
Stardust Beach **10**
Water Music **9**

Restaurants 🍴
Gecko's **1**
Green Room **2**

Not to scale

$$-$ East Surf Cabanas
Deewara Niwasa, T077-982 9439,
www.eastsurfcabanas.com.
Deservedly popular with stylish but great-
value cabanas and several houses, including
the lovely **Earth House**, that sleep up to
4. Health-conscious food, with as many
organic ingredients as possible, includes
a jungle barbecue (see Restaurants).
Also cookery lessons, tuk-tuk safaris,
photography… and, of course, surf lessons.

$ Arne's Place
T077-135 8303.
Friendly atmosphere at this popular surfing
hangout. Basic cabanas, great food and
welcoming team.

$ Beach Hut
T063-224 8202.
Range of good-value accommodation
that's especially popular with long-
termers in the form of coconut-thatch
and *kadjan* cabanas (some in the trees).
Good cheap food. Recommended –
but book well in advance.

$ Paper Moon Kudils
Urani, Pottovil, T071-997 9797,
www.papermoonkudils.lk.
Beautiful bungalows close to the crashing
waves with a small pool, great restaurant
and lots of atmosphere.

Restaurants

In addition to most of the guesthouses,
there are a number of places along the
main drag serving food

$$$ Hideaway
See Where to stay.
Hideaway owner Sharon Atapattu's passion
is coming up with new recipes in her
kitchen. Taking inspiration from the sea
and the land, you can expect amazing fish
platters, delicious roast chicken and a great
spicy beef salad. Menu changes every day.

Breakfast is abundant too. No plastic policy. Highly recommended.

$$$ Jungle Barbecue
East Surf Cabanas (see Where to stay).
As a once-a-week treat, the folks at **East Surf Cabanas** take you out to their jungle farm in Panama, 15 km south of the bay. Eat under the stars and listen to nature as you enjoy fish on the grill. Swap travellers' tales around the campfire. Price includes transport.

$$$ Siam View Beach Hotel
See Where to stay.
Authentic Thai food and other international dishes including pizza. The terrace overlooking the street is a great spot for people-watching over a beer.

$$$ Stardust Beach Hotel
See Where to stay.
Great Western dishes (chefs and most ingredients imported from Denmark) served in a laid-back setting. Expensive but worth it.

$$-$ Geckos
Main St.
For the homesick, this Sri Lankan/British-owned place serves good Western meals to fill up on after a day of surfing, such as burgers, fish and chips and daily specials. Breakfast is available all day and includes a full English. Geckos tries to use local produce, home-grown veggies and herbs, free range chicken, fairtrade coffee and organic tea. Will fill up plastic water bottles with drinking water for a small fee. Also has rooms.

$$ The Green Room
Main St, on the opposite side of the road from the sea.
A characterful open-air restaurant with excellent curries and seafood dishes. Great Sri Lankan breakfasts. Recommended.

Bars and clubs

There are a number of places serving alcohol and hosting full-moon parties. Take a wander along the sand to find somewhere you like the look of. Some 'dry' eateries will allow you to bring booze but corkage is high. Mamno's is a popular party place but has a reputation for not respecting female travellers.

What to do

The guesthouses in Arugam Bay can organize watersports, trips to nearby national parks and onward travel if required. Surfing is the main activity here, but don't despair if you don't ride waves as there are a number of other activities on offer or you can just huddle in a hammock with a good book.

Birdwatching
Birdwatching is at its best Nov-Dec when the winter migrants arrive in the area. There are 225 species of birds at **Kumana National Park** (see below), while the Arugam Bay and Pottvill lagoons are also great places for twitching.

Boat trips
The **Hidayapuram Fishermen's Cooperative Society** runs 2-hr trips in outrigger canoes on Pottuvil lagoon in season, contact **Arugam Bay Surf Resort** to arrange (see Where to stay). 2-hr dolphin-watching trips in the bay are available May-Sep.

Diving
There are various opportunities for wreck diving in the bay with 5 pre-1850 ships within 5 km of each other. Diving is only possible May-Jul. Ask at **Stardust**.

Surfing
Arugam Point is regarded by many as the best surf break in the country, with a clean wall of surf allowing a ride of up to 400 m.

In season it can get crowded. In contrast, **Pottuvil Point**, at the northern end of the bay, is often deserted and is popular with more experienced surfers. Beginners and long-boarders favour **Baby Point**, towards the southern end of the beach. The season runs Mar-Oct. Equipment and lessons are widely available from guesthouses.
A-Bay Surf Shop, *T063-224 8187*. A good selection of boards for rent, as well as other surf bits and pieces.

Tour operators
For great local trips by tuk-tuk, including the great sunrise at Kudimbigala Rock (see page 342), check in with the team at **Hideaway Resort** (see Where to stay).

Transport

Bus A **Colombo**-bound **CTB** bus originating in Panama passes through Pottuvil at 0630 each morning, or a private bus leaves at around 1700. There may also be buses between Pottuvil and **Wellawaya**, though generally you have to change at Monaragala. There is a bus to **Batticaloa**, plus several buses a day to **Akkaraipattu**, where you can change. Buses occasionally run to **Panama**, or you can take a 3-wheeler. A 3-wheeler to **Okanda** takes 45 mins, Rs 2500.

Around Arugam Bay

hidden temples and wildlife galore

Magul Mahavihara
8 km west of Pottuvil along the A4.

This site was originally constructed by **King Dhatusena** in the sixth century, although an inscription plate testifies that the extensive 80-ha monastery complex (of which 20 ha have now been excavated) is a 14th century reconstruction. There is an unrestored *dagoba*, a *vatadage* with an unusual moonstone, a *bodhigara* (for enclosing a bo tree) and several pavilions. A kilometre south, a circular structure with dressed slabs of stone may be an elephant stable.

Lahugala National Park *Colour map 5, B5.*
Trips can be organized from Arugam Bay, usually leaving around 1530-1600.

This small national park west of Pottuvil covers 15 sq km and is good for watching birds and large elephant herds. Lying between Gal Oya and Yala, the park is part of the 'elephant corridor', which allows the elephant population to move freely across the southeastern part of the island.

The Lahugala, Mahawewa and Kitulana tanks here attract numerous species of water birds, while in the dry season (especially July to August) herds of 100 or more elephants are drawn to the *beru* grass that grows in the shallow tanks. The best time to watch them is in the late afternoon. The climbing perch fish is said to slither across from the Mahawewa to Kitulana tanks when the former runs dry.

South to Panama
The coastal scenery south of Arugam Bay is highly distinctive. Rising from the flat landscape are giant boulders in bizarre formations; at the foot of many are abandoned and now overgrown cave monasteries and hermitages, some dating back almost

Pada Yatra

The traditional annual Pada Yatra from Nagadipa in the Jaffna peninsula to Kataragama is one of the world's great pilgrimages, on a par with the trip to Mount Kailasa in Tibet. Though ethnic strife nearly put an end to the trek in the 1980s, the foundation of the Kataragama Devotees Trust in 1988 sparked a revival. Each Wesak Poya, a band of pilgrims, predominantly but not exclusively Hindu, set out on the perilous six-week journey down the east coast along the country's ancient tracks. Dressed as beggars (*antis*) and formed into small groups (*kuttams*), they cover 8-10 km a day, bathing in rivers, sleeping in camps and worshipping at over 70 temples en route, where they are offered alms. The final section from Pottuvil, via Okanda and Yala National Park (the only occasion on which people are allowed on foot in the park) is the most popular and dangerous. Some pilgrims get lost and even die en route; this is said to be the ultimate distinction and a sign of Kataragama's grace. The goal is the flag-hoisting ceremony at Kataragama, which marks the beginning of Esala Perahera.

2000 years. Cultivated paddy fields are interspersed with open parkland and scrub jungle, all supporting a remarkable variety of birdlife. This is wild country, largely abandoned during the war, where elephants roam freely.

The paved road ends 12 km to the south at **Panama**, the last inhabited village before Yala. Turtles can be seen in the attractive lagoon here, and crocodiles sometimes bask on its banks. A track leads to the sand dunes approaching Panama's seemingly endless beach, with its pink rocks shimmering in the distance.

Okanda and around

Brave the bumpy, unsurfaced road for another 16 km to reach Okanda, 28 km south of Arugam Bay. There is an ancient Skanda shrine here at the foot of a rocky outcrop with several associated legends. Ravana was supposed to have stopped here on his way to Konesvaram, while Skanda (Kataragama) landed here in a stone boat with consort Valli in order to fight Sooran. She is venerated by the Valli Amman *kovil* at the top of the rock. Kataragama-bound pilgrims usually stop at the shrine for the 15-day festival in July. There is also an excellent surf spot near Okanda.

Some 2 km inland, around Helawa lagoon, the large **Kudimbigala Rock** houses a forest hermitage with a part-restored stupa and drop-ledge caves from the second century BC at its base. Climbing the Sigiriya-style rock at sunrise is an amazing experience (see box, page 343).

Salute to the sun

Kudimbigala is similar to Sigiriya: a rocky outcrop that emerges from the jungle. From certain vantage points (it helps to have a guide for this), the rock looks like a reclining Buddha. Around the rock is a forest hermitage, with around 200 shrines, hermits lodgings and caves, where a small group of Buddhist monks still reside. It has a magical atmosphere.

But, as with any pilgrimage, the journey to Kudimbigala is as important as the destination. The rock is about 30 km (one hour) south of Arugam Bay; roughly one third is on a covered road, while the last two thirds are on a potholed track. Elephants roam wild and free here, so you might have to duck into the jungle cover en route. It's therefore advisable to travel with a knowledgeable rickshaw driver with good tales to tell and expert elephant navigation systems; Hideaway in Arugam Bay (see Where to stay) can offer advice and recommendations.

After the rickshaw journey, a short but steep jungle ramble will bring you to the top of Kudimbigala, where you may be rewarded with a glimpse of a Buddhist monk meditating. Making a pre-dawn pilgrimage and reaching the summit for a multi-coloured sunrise above the forest canopy is one of the highlights of the area. On the way down you can explore parts of the hermitage and then stop off at Okanda Sri Murigan Kotvil for breakfast and a swim, if the crashing waves permit.

★ **Kumana National Park** *Colour map 5, B6. For Yala West National Park, see page 184. Entrance at Okanda. US$10 plus extra charges.*

Kumana National Park (formerly Yala East National Park) reopened to the public in March 2003 after 18 years of closure owing to the war. It suffered damage in the Boxing Day tsunami in 2004 and then was closed again in 2006 when hostilities resumed in earnest. It reopened again in early 2010. As at Wilpattu (see page 92) there has been some despoliation of the park's habitats and wildlife population in the intervening years.

The focus is the wetland formed by the Kumana *villu*, fed by a channel from the **Kumbukkan-oya** when a sandbar forms at the mouth of the river in the dry season. In recent years, the tank has been unable to fill with sufficient water, thus killing off part of the mangrove, but it has now been reconstructed and is said to be filling up.

Large flocks of painted storks may be seen, while many birds can be spotted along the Kumbukkan-oya. The park still supports an elephant population, though herds are smaller, and it is evident that deer and wild boar have been poached; some arrests have recently been made.

Jaffna &
the north

explore one of Sri Lanka's most enigmatic regions

Sri Lanka's Northern Province has for centuries been the cultural heartland of the island's Tamil population. Yet, owing to its isolation from the rest of the country and its harsh, dry climate, the north was one of the least visited of the island's regions even before the vicious ethnic fighting that sealed off much of the province to the outside world for over 20 years.

Now the war has ended, a trickle of tourists is beginning to unearth the region's almost forgotten attractions. The main focus of interest is the densely populated Jaffna peninsula. Jaffna's historic centre doesn't try to hide the scars of war, but its rebuilt temples and churches are flourishing, and colourful festivals across the peninsula are once again beginning to pack in enormous crowds. Away from town are curious natural phenomena – a desert of dunes, a bottomless well and offshore islands that boast some truly deserted beaches. Further south is Mannar Island, a narrow finger of land pointing towards India, where recent evidence has uncovered the remains of a causeway almost two million years old.

Best for
Adventures ▪ Island hopping ▪ Tamil culture

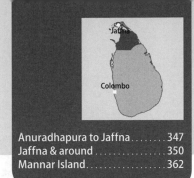

Footprint
picks

★ Nallur's chariot festival, page 353

A 10-day riot of colour, commerce and cracking coconuts, the north's biggest festival is riding a new wave as pilgrims return for the first time in decades.

★ Manalkadu Desert, page 358

Climb the shifting sand dunes of Manalkadu, where poignant tsunami graves overlook the half-buried remains of St Anthony's church.

★ Nainativu Island, page 361

Board a tiny ferry to explore spectacular Buddhist and Hindu temples.

★ Mannar Island and Adam's Bridge, page 363

Cross Mannar's dry flatlands to discover shell-strewn beaches, giant baobab trees and the drowned land bridge reaching towards India.

Palk Strait

Keerimalai · Kankesanturai · Valvedditturai · Point Pedro
Tellipalai · Valippuram
Kantarodai · Puttur
Kopai
Jaffna
Chavakachcheri
Karaitivu
Palaitivu
Analaitivu
Kayts
Velanai
Nainativu
Mandaitivu
Pungudutivu
Delft
Palaitivu
Pooneryn
Bay of Bengal
Chempiyanpattu
Pallai
Jaffna Lagoon
Chundikkulam National Park
Elephant Pass
Paranthan
Kilinochchi
A35
A32
A9

Footprint picks

1 **Nallur's chariot festival**, page 353
2 **Manalkadu Desert**, page 358
3 **Nainativu Island**, page 361
4 **Mannar Island and Adam's Bridge**, page 363

Vellankulam
Tunukkai
Mankulam
A34

Mannar Island
Adam's Bridge
Pesalai
Talaimannar
A14
Errukkilampiddu
Komputukki
Mannar
Thirukethiswaram
Mantai
Giant's Tank Sanctuary
Madhu Road Sanctuary
Madhu
A30
Vavuniya
Silavatturai
Madhu Road
Paraiyanalankulam
Madukanda
A29

Gulf of Mannar

Etakada

N

10 km
10 miles

Wilpattu National Park

A14
Medawachchiya

Rambewa

Essential Northern Province

Anuradhapura to Jaffna

there are few reasons to stop on your journey through this war-scarred region

The hot, arid Wanni region was at the heart of Sri Lanka's ethnic conflict. Even though the jungle has begun to patch over many of the scars of war, this sun-scrubbed landscape of cleared forest and still-to-be-cleared minefields, military bunkers and shelled homes remains a region to pass through rather than to linger in. Fortunately, travelling has become much easier now that almost all the military checkpoints have been removed from the renovated A9. Aside from a stop to change buses, few travellers venture beyond the highway towns of Vavuniya and the former Tiger capital of Kilinochchi.

North to Vavuniya

Heading northeast from Anuradhapura, the A20 joins the A9 at Rambewa. **Medawachchiya** is the last Sinhalese town of any size, where there is a rest house. Some 2 km north, on top of **Issin Bessa Gala rock**, is a modern temple of ancient origins, with an elephant frieze and restored *dagoba*. There are excellent views south to Anuradhapura and Mihintale. The newly resurfaced A14 leads northwest from here to Madhu Road and Mannar (see page 362).

Vavuniya *Colour map 1, C4.*

About 1½ hours north of Anuradhapura, Vavuniya has the feel of a bustling frontier town. That it once marked the start of disputed territory is evident in its strong military presence; due to its strategic crossroads position its importance and prosperity grew with the conflict. There is little to do here, but if you're killing time between buses you might visit the small **museum**, where there are some ancient Buddha statues. About 4 km east at **Madukanda** (around Rs 200 by auto) is a *vihara* on the spot where the Tooth Relic was said to have rested on its way to Anuradhapura.

ON THE ROAD

Tree of Life

Jaffna's palmyras are as much the dominant feature of the northern landscape as the southern coconut and are a cornerstone of the local economy. These tall, straight trees, which can grow up to 30 m in height, have an astonishing variety of uses. The leathery, fan-shaped leaves can be worked into mats, baskets and roof thatch, while the fruits, which grow in clusters on the stem when young, can be punctured with a finger in order to extract the juice; when mature their pulp is roasted and sun-dried. The sap is made into toddy, which is often drunk from an attractive cup (*pila*) ingeniously shaped from a frond and tied at one end. Alternatively it is distilled into arrack. The sap also makes jaggery, a more nutritious alternative to cane sugar. The seedlings can be eaten fresh or are used in cooking, while all parts of the plant may be used in local medicines.

The trees also have an important ecological role – their drought-resistant roots help retain water in the soil, paramount in this driest of regions, and the tall trunks act as natural barriers during strong winds common to the north.

Predictably, the conflict was an ecological disaster for the north's palmyras. Over 2.5 million trees were uprooted, not only for firewood and to create military bunkers, but 500 m of land either side of the region's major arteries was bulldozed in order to deter ambushes. A ban on felling palmyras has been put in place to try and aid reforestation programmes, and there are now calls for the Palmyra Development Board to do more to help this national industry, with ambitious plans in the pipeline to expand the foreign market for palmyra products.

Kilinochchi *Colour map 1, B3.*

Close to the large, modern Iranamadu tank, the dusty uninspiring town of Kilinochchi was the headquarters of the **Liberation Tigers of Tamil Eelam (LTTE)**, or the 'capital of Tamil Eelam', housing the Tigers' court complex, police headquarters and other government buildings. There has been some investment in the town and there are banks and accommodation. Some 5 km west of the A9 at Kanagapuram is a **Tamil Tiger war cemetery**, where almost 2000 cadres are interred.

Towards Jaffna *Colour map 1, A2/3.*

Connecting Jaffna peninsula to the mainland, **Elephant Pass** is so-called because elephants were once driven through its shallow waters on their way to export from Jaffna. Strategically important since the Dutch built a fort here in 1776, more blood has been spilled over possession of this narrow ribbon of land than perhaps any other part of the island. It was the site of one of the army's most humiliating defeats, when, in April 2000, groups of LTTE cadres stormed into the heavily fortified camp, forcing an abrupt capitulation from the 15,000-strong military garrison. Military presence remains palpable here, not least at the army-run **Chundikkulam National Park** ① *tuk-tuks can take you to the sanctuary from Soranpattu Jct on the A9*, at the southeastern edge of the peninsula. A rich mix of habitats (dry scrub, beaches, salt marshes and lagoons) attracts an impressive array of species, stars of which are the large winter population of flamingos. Explore northward along the coast from here to find some excellent and largely deserted beaches.

After Elephant Pass, Jaffna's distinctive palmyras become the dominant feature of the landscape (see box, opposite). The sizeable town of **Chavakachcheri** was retaken by the LTTE for several months in 2000 and reduced to rubble. After crossing numerous restored colonial bridges over the shallow lagoons, you approach the suburbs of Jaffna town.

Listings Anuradhapura to Jaffna

Where to stay and eat

The main place to stay on this route is Vavuniya, which has lots of places to sleep and eat near the bus and rail stations, though all are quite basic.

North to Vavuniya

$ Rest house (CHC)
Medawachchiya, T025-224 5699.
Comfortable, clean rooms (1 with a/c), potentially useful stopover if you're changing trains between Jaffna and Mannar.

Vavuniya

$ Prince Hotel
111 Kandy Rd.
Better for food than accommodation. Serves good short eats.

$ Vanni Inn
Gnanavairavar Kovil Lane, off 2nd Cross St, Vavuniya, T024-222 1406.
Better from outside than in, but quiet and the best of the bunch, functional a/c and fan rooms, restaurant. Very little English spoken.

Kilinochchi

$$-$ 1-9 Lodge
167 Kandy Rd, T071-234 5629.
8 rooms, 2 with attached bath, clean, nets, fan, restaurant (fried rice, noodles, devilled dishes).

$ Kanathenu Lodge
T021-222 3954.
14 rooms, some with attached bath, spartan but fairly clean, food on request.

Towards Jaffna

$$ Nature Park Holiday Resort
Chundikkulam Bird Sanctuary, T021-321 6254, www.thalsevanaresort.com/naturepark.
Basic army-run resort set in a former convalescent camp, with 4 spacious but spartan rooms, a treehouse and a comfortable and excellent value 2-room cottage.

Transport

Vavuniya

Vavuniya is the transport hub for the region.

Bus Buses leave regularly for **Colombo** (5 hrs) via **Anuradhapura** (1½ hrs), and Jaffna. There are many buses to **Omantai** (for Jaffna), but it's best to leave early. Private vans also make the journey and can be picked up along Kandy Rd. Also regular buses to **Mannar**, **Trincomalee** and **Batticaloa**.

Train Vavuniya is a main stop on the Jaffna–Anuradhapura–Colombo line, with 4 trains each way per day.

Jaffna
& around

As the centre of Sri Lankan Tamil culture and, in peaceful times, the country's second most populous city, Jaffna has been the greatest pawn and the greatest victim of the 20-year ethnic conflict of the north. Devastated by shelling, its star-shaped fort is a haunting vision of a post-apocalyptic wasteland. However, the ceasefire and the reopening of the land route to the south have brought a glimmer of hope: month by month, Jaffna's displaced citizens are returning home, and many of the town's schools, temples, churches and mosques have been rebuilt. New life vibrates through the streets surrounding the Nallur Kandaswamy Kovil, Sri Lanka's greatest Hindu temple, as Jaffna's exiles return for the first time in decades – a testament to the spirit of this proud community, as well as to its support from abroad.

With most of its heritage and 'sights' destroyed, Jaffna is hardly a place for a holiday, but those who do make the trip are often unexpectedly charmed. The city can throw up some surprises, from its lively festivals and glorious old cars to its distinctive cuisine and famous ice cream parlours. The most lasting memories, however, are of its people. Despite, or perhaps because of, the scars of battle they are amongst the warmest and most genuinely welcoming on the island.

a ruined Dutch fort and an important Hindu temple are the highlights

Historic centre

Much of Jaffna's historic centre was destroyed during the fighting, including the old town hall, post office and rest house, but rebuilding work has been swift. To see the impact of war at its starkest, walk out to the 20-ha **Dutch fort**, built on the site of an earlier Portuguese building. (It's occupied by the military, but open to the public during daylight hours.) Arguably the strongest fortification in Asia, its attractive black coralline walls, surrounded by a huge moat, remain intact, but the scene within is post-apocalyptic: mounds of tumbled masonry, bullet-ridden plaster, and fig tree roots splitting the few standing brick walls. The old Dutch Groote Kerk, pummelled in 1990 when the army camp was shelled, was destroyed by the LTTE along with all the other Dutch buildings (regarded by them as symbols of colonial oppression). Bleak as it may be, a walk through the grounds and around the walls of the fort is as visceral an insight as Jaffna has to offer into the destruction wrought by the war.

A block away to the east is the gleaming, restored Moghul-style **public library**. The original building was torched by an anti-Tamil mob in June 1981, tragically destroying almost 100,000 books and priceless *ola* leaf manuscripts. Thousands of volumes have since been donated to the library from abroad, particularly from France and India. In the

Jaffna City

Not to scale

Where to stay
Jetwing Jaffna **1**
Lux Etoiles **4**
Morgan's Guesthouse **11**
Pillaiyar Inn **2**
Theresa Inn **13**
US Guesthouse **6**

YMCA **12**

Restaurants
Cozee **3**
cream houses **1**

Green Grass Hotel & Restaurant **5**
Malayan **6**
Sri Palm Beach **2**

Essential Jaffna and around

Finding your feet

Arriving in Jaffna is infinitely easier now the railway line is open and almost all army checkpoints have been removed. Trains from Colombo and Anuradhapura pull into the railway station 3 blocks east of the city centre. (Though new and scrupulously clean, it's seriously lacking in facilities – don't arrive here expecting to buy snacks for your journey.)

The main bus stand is in Hospital Road, in the central market area – several hotels are within easy walking distance, or if you're heading for one of the guesthouses in Chundikulam, 2 km east of the centre, you can ask to be let off before the terminus.

Tip...

Don't worry about struggling with Tamil's legendarily unpronounceable names – most major towns have a user-friendly three-letter short form.

It's also possible to reach Jaffna by air from Ratmalana Airport, south of Colombo. Army-owned Helitours fly regularly to Palaly Airport (KKS) in the north of the peninsula, though ticket bookings are a bit of a hassle and there have been concerns about the safety of their aircraft. See also Transport, page 357.

Weather Jaffna

January	February	March	April	May	June
28°C 22°C 70mm	30°C 22°C 30mm	32°C 24°C 20mm	32°C 26°C 30mm	31°C 27°C 40mm	30°C 27°C 10mm

July	August	September	October	November	December
30°C 26°C 20mm	30°C 26°C 30mm	30°C 26°C 60mm	30°C 25°C 230mm	28°C 23°C 380mm	27°C 22°C 260mm

library garden is a statue of its founder, Reverend Long, who is said to have died on hearing the news of the original library's demise. Just north of the Library is Jaffna's restored **clock tower**, reopened in June 2002, with clocks donated by HRH the Prince of Wales.

Commercial centre

The busy **market area** between Stanley and Hospital roads has well and truly returned to life. It's an interesting place to wander, with the usual vegetable markets and clothes vendors but also stalls selling distinctly local products including *odiyal* chips (made from the palmyrah tree), peanut candy, high-octane cordials in bright colours and whole dried fish that flap in the wind like kites. Walk up Kankasanthurai (KKS) Road and you'll find shops selling Hindu religious paraphernalia, steel and traditional palmyra craftwork, while jewellery shops cluster along Kasturiya Road.

Getting around

The city is quite spread out, and walking around it can be tiring in the heat. There is a good local bus network, and no shortage of three-wheelers to fill in the gaps (you'll need to bargain for your fare). Cycling is an excellent way to get around the town and even across to the islands. You may be able to borrow a bike from your guesthouse. With judicious use of buses and tuk-tuks, you can do a whirlwind tour of the peninsula and a couple of islands on a day trip from Jaffna. All buses originate from Jaffna town. There are no buses along the coast, so to get from Point Pedro to Kankesanthurai, say, you'll need a tuk-tuk or taxi. Alternatively, the coastal road from Thondamanaru through Valvedditturai to Point Pedro is a pleasant cycle ride.

Kayts and Karaitivu islands are linked to the mainland by separate causeways. There are several buses a day to Karaitivu from Jaffna, either direct to Casuarina Beach, or hourly to Karainagar. A third causeway, which cuts seemingly endlessly through dazzling blue sea, joins Kayts to Punguditivu. To get from Jaffna to the outlying islands of Nainativu and Delft, take the bus which crosses Kayts island to the jetty point at Kurukkaduwan (KKD) on the southwestern corner of Pungudutivu. From here, alarmingly clapped out old ferry boats chug across to Nainativu every hour until 1630 – this may be the longest 20-minute boat journey of your life. For the 1½-hour crossing from Pungudutivu to Delft, a much sturdier-looking ferry leaves the KKD jetty at 0830 and 0930. A bus traverses Delft island, or you might hire a tuk-tuk.

When to go

March, April and May are often unbearably hot when the southwest monsoon and heatwaves from South India conspire to drive up temperatures towards 40°C. August and September can also be very hot. December and January are the coolest months. Most of the region's rain falls between October and December; other months are largely dry. The biggest festival is at Nallur in August/September (see page 356).

Time required

Jaffna town and the peninsula require a day each. Kayts and Karaitivu islands could be visited as part of day-long tour of the peninsula, but to get a good look at Nainativu and Delft islands, you'll need to allow another full day to work around boat schedules.

★ Nallur and the Kandaswamy Temple

Located 3 km northeast of the centre, the leafy suburb of Nallur was capital of the Jaffna Kingdom from the 13th to 17th centuries, and it remains the seat of Jaffna's Tamil elite. The ornate **Kandaswamy Kovil** here, dedicated to Lord Murugan, is the most important Hindu shrine in northern Sri Lanka, its golden *gopurams* and red-and-white striped walls towering over a vast rectangular courtyard.

The temple's history can be traced back to AD 948, though successive invasions of Jaffna by Sinhalese and Portuguese conquerors saw its previous incarnations razed to the ground (and in the latter case, replaced with churches). The temple on its current site dates from the 18th century, though many of the buildings you see today were built as recently as 1964. Still, the temple can be wonderfully atmospheric, especially in the evening. **Puja** takes place seven times a day; men must remove shirts before entering and photography in the inner sanctum is not allowed. Nallur temple and the streets around

BACKGROUND
Jaffna

There are few archaeological or literary clues to the early period of Jaffna's history, but the peninsula's proximity to India ensured that when Tamil settlers came to Sri Lanka 2000 years ago, Jaffna was one of their earliest homes. Ruins at Kantarodai suggest that Buddhism was once the dominant religion of the peninsula, then known as Nagadipa, or the island of the Naga people, who may have had links to Greece and Rome. The period of the Kingdom of Jaffna, often invoked by nationalists today, began in the 13th century under the Indian King Kalinga, lasting, except for a brief period of Sinhalese occupation in the 15th century, until the execution of King Sankili by the Portuguese in 1620.

Over the centuries Jaffna's Tamils built a wholly distinctive culture. Despite the unsuitability of much of the thin red soil for agriculture, Tamil cultivators developed techniques of well irrigation which capitalized on the reserves of groundwater held in the limestone, making intensive rice cultivation the basis of a successful economy. Diversity was provided by coconut and palmyra palms, tobacco and a wide range of other crops, but the Tamil population was also international in its outlook. It maintained trading links were not only with the Tamil regions across the Palk Straits but also with Southeast Asia.

The Dutch captured Jaffna from the Portuguese in 1658, losing it to the British in 1796. It was not until 1833, however, that they politically unified Tamil regions with Sinhalese for administration purposes, ending the separateness of Tamil identity.

From the mid-19th century Jaffna Tamils made the most of the educational opportunities that came from an extended period of British rule and rapidly became numerically dominant in a range of government services and jobs both inside and outside Sri Lanka. In the early 1970s, 'quota' systems were introduced for education and employment in an attempt to reduce Tamil influence, another contributory factor to the subsequent conflict (see page 373).

fill to bursting point during the annual **chariot festival**, the largest of its kind in Sri Lanka (see page 356).

Also in Nallur, the **Archaeological Museum** ① *Navalar Rd, daily 0800-1645*, contains various artefacts excavated from Kantarodai, though anti-royalists may enjoy best the portrait of Queen Victoria with a bullet-hole through her. The museum is located behind the Navalar Maddapam Hall.

Follow Temple Road west to reach **Poongani Solai (Poonkanichcholai)** ① *about 1 km west of Nallur temple, Ramalingam Rd, Mudamayadi, T021-222 2976, Rs 100*. These small pleasure gardens, impeccably kept, feature some imaginative fountains, brightly painted statues and a grotto, though the enjoyment is marred by the shackled animals on show. On some days around 1500-1600, locals come dressed up to have photos or videos taken. The gardens are 3 km northeast of town. Follow Temple Road going west and the gardens are found on the right-hand side.

ON THE ROAD
Vintage survivors

For fans of old British cars Jaffna is an unlikely Mecca. Fleets of Morris Minors, Austin Cambridges and Morris Oxfords still rattle around the town's dusty streets, preserved for posterity by Jaffna's isolation. Their lifeline came in the late 1980s when owners of newer vehicles were forced to turn them in for the war effort, leaving the sturdy old beauties as kings of the road. When the peninsula became cut off from the rest of the island by the conflict, the cars' owners were forced to find ever-more ingenious methods of keeping them on the road, hammering out spare parts in local metal shops, and, when fuel costs spiralled out of control, feeding these vintage survivors on a steady diet of kerosene with just a drop of petrol. Today, Sri Lanka does a roaring trade in exporting parts to enthusiasts worldwide. Of around 70,000 Morris Minors on the road in Britain, it is estimated that more than half are sustained by the metalworkers of Sri Lanka.

Churches and temples

The legacy of successive waves of proselytizing Christians from Europe, most notably Roman Catholics, is visible in Jaffna's many churches, some of which, like the Goan-style **St Mary's Cathedral**, 2 km east of the centre off Kandy Rd, and **St James's**, are enormous edifices. Post-war restoration has been speedy though not always of great architectural merit. The **Sri Nagaviharaya**, a short walk northeast of the bus stand, with its restored *dagoba* and 'elephant wall', is Jaffna's biggest Buddhist temple.

Listings Jaffna *map p351*

Where to stay

Accommodation in Jaffna is spread around three main areas: the city centre, handy for buses and trains; Nallur, with a small selection of quirky and upmarket places; and the expat area of Chundukuli-Old Park, 2 km east of the bus stand. Overall the standard and value of rooms is not as good as elsewhere in Sri Lanka, but as the number of visitors increases, so does the choice of places to stay. Weekends can be busy and noisy, and rates go up during the Nallur Festival.

$$$$ Jetwing Jaffna
37 Mahatma Gandhi Rd, T021-221 5571, www.jetwinghotels.com.

This brand new business hotel is the smartest option in town by miles. Smallish but smart rooms, good bathrooms and great views from the upper-floor balconies.

$$ Lux Etoiles
34 Chetty St Lane, Nallur, T021-222 3966, www.luxetoiles.com.
A/c rooms with TV (some newer than others), and a small pool. Restaurant serves excellent seafood. English and French spoken.

$$ Morgan's Guesthouse
103 Temple Rd, Nallur, T021-222 3666.
Just a few steps from Nallur temple, this eccentric little backpacker favourite has comfortable a/c rooms, and a popular garden bar. Often full.

$$ US Hotel
855 Hospital Rd, T021-222 1017,
www.ushoteljaffna.
A/c rooms with clean bathrooms and
hot water. Restaurant serves good
and reasonably priced food.

$$-$ Pillaiyar Inn
31 Manipay Rd, T021-222 2829.
Despite the haggard-looking exterior, this
oldie is still a goodie, at least if you can
get one of the renovated rooms in the
shady garden annexe. Reasonable food,
an atmospheric al fresco bar and short
walk to the bus stand make this a decent
in-town deal.

$ Theresa Inn
72A Racca Rd, T021-222 8615,
calistusjoseph89@gmail.com.
Clean rooms, 1 with balcony (often on
long-term rent to NGOs), a/c and fan, those
without hot water cheaper. Internet, TV,
friendly and helpful.

$ YMCA
*109 Kandy Rd, at the corner with Kachcheri
Rd, T021-222 2499.*
The cheapest rooms in town, with basic
but decently clean twin rooms (get one at
the back to avoid road noise) and shared
bathrooms of highly variable cleanliness.
Canteen does good cheap meals.

Restaurants

Jaffna's cream houses are legendary,
serving delicious *wadais* and other short
eats as well as ice cream. They cluster on
Hospital Rd and around Nallur, and are busy
with local families during the daytime.

$$ Cozee
*15 Sirambiyadi Ln (off Stanley Rd),
T021-222 5899.*
South Indian specialists (the cook is
from Chennai). Smart, clean. Kebabs
recommended. Also has rooms available.

$$ Green Grass Hotel and Restaurant
*33 Asservatham Ln, opposite railway station,
T021-222 2186, www.jaffnagreengrass.com.*
Seating is in a pleasant garden and menu
is wide-ranging. It's a good place to try
curry, Jaffna-style. Some meals may need
to be ordered a day in advance. Also has
($) rooms.

$$ Sri Palm Beach
205 Kasturiya Rd.
A/c restaurant and takeaway, large menu
of South Indian curries, *dosai*, noodles,
even pizzas.

$ Malayan
36-38 Grand Bazaar, near the bus station.
Excellent vegetarian food, including good
value rice and curry, all served on a banana
leaf. Cheap, cheerful and popular.

Festivals

Mar-Apr Easter is widely celebrated with
passion plays performed in churches and
at Jaffna's open-air theatre.
Jul-Aug Nallur Festival is held between
July and September and attracts millions of
devotees, reaching its zenith on the 24th day
when decorated *ratham* (chariots) are
paraded from dawn until midnight in honour
of Shiva, a swirling spectacle of incense,
cymbals and cracking coconuts. This is
the biggest Hindu festival in the north,
but there are many others – ask locally.

Shopping

Palmyra handicrafts can still be picked
up in the market area, as can arrack and
jaggery made from the palm. If you're in
the market for a sugar rush, check out the
local rosetto wine and Nelli crush (bright
green gooseberry cordial), both made by
the **Rosarian sisters** in nearby Atchuvely.

Transport

Air

Helitours (T011-311 0472, www.helitours.lk) runs the only scheduled flights to Jaffna, flying from Colombo's **Ratmalana Airport** 3 times a week (Mon, Wed and Fri) via **Trincomalee**. There have been concerns about aircraft safety. Booking tickets in advance is difficult; at time of writing the only practical way to do it is in person at a **Helitours** office. The Colombo office is at Sir Chithampalam Gardiner Mawatha, Colombo 2, T011-314 4944.

Bus

There's an excellent bus network around town, across the peninsula, and to the islands of **Kayts**, **Karaitivu** and **Pungudutivu**. Government buses pull into the bus stand on Hospital Rd; there's no ticket office as such, but you can pick up schedule information from the helpful attendants. More frequent, cramped private buses leave from outside the bus stand on Power House Rd. Long-distance buses go to **Vavuniya, Mannar, Trincomalee** and **Colombo**

Train

4 trains a day leave Jaffna's new station for **Colombo** (9 hrs) via **Anuradhapura** (4 hrs); train buffs might also fancy taking the 30-min ride north to **Kankesanthurai**, Sri Lanka's most northerly station. Facilities at Jaffna station are severely limited, and vendors on the train are few and far between – buy food and water before you arrive to avoid a hungry journey.

Jaffna peninsula

fishing boats, sand dunes and Hindu temples

An extensive road system criss-crosses the low, flat Jaffna landscape, leading through sandy scrubland where palmyras stab at the sky, alternating with intensively cultivated tobacco, banana and manioc plantations. There are few bona fide tourist sights out here, and parts of the peninsula around Palaly airport and Kankesanturai remain off limits as High Security Zones. Nevertheless, it's well worth spending a day exploring the salty fishing port of Point Pedro, set in the lee of Sri Lanka's northernmost point, and the temples and sand dunes to the west and east.

Northeast of Jaffna

At Kopai, the **LTTE war cemetery** ① *buses bound for Point Pedro pass nearby*, is a sobering experience. Over 1700 cadres are buried here in row upon row of neatly laid out graves. In the corner is a display of remains of LTTE monuments destroyed by the army on re-taking Jaffna in 1995.

At Nilavarai, the square **tidal well** ① *10 km from Jaffna town, near Puttur; take an Achchuveli bus*, is an interesting natural phenomenon. Legend states that Rama plunged his arrow into the soil here, quenching his thirst from its 'bottomless' spring. The water, fairly fresh at the surface, increases in salinity with depth, and a fissure in the limestone probably connects it directly to the sea. You can walk down to the well, though locals warn against swimming here.

Valvedditturai

Located on the coast, northeast of Jaffna, Valvedditturai (VVT) is a small fishing town with a reputation as a centre for smuggling from India and beyond. The **festival** at the large Muthumari Amman *kovil* here was resurrected in 2003 and features processions and fire-walking; it draws enormous crowds each April. The town is now most famous as the birthplace of the leader of the LTTE. After the end of the war, thousands of tourists from the south flocked to visit his childhood home 100 m west of the Amman temple, which became one of the 'must see' attractions in Jaffna. In 2010, however, it was destroyed, with some pointing the finger of blame at the army.

Point Pedro

Bustling little Point Pedro (PPD), 8 km east, is the peninsula's second largest town. A 20- to 25-km tunnel built in the 10th century is said to connect Point Pedro to Nallur. As well as several large churches, most impressive of which is the freshly restored **St Anthony's** a few blocks from the town centre, there is a fishing harbour, a beach and a lighthouse. If you're here in the evening, walk or take a rickshaw westward along the quiet seafront road to find the most northerly point in Sri Lanka. In peaceful times, a local challenge was to swim to India from here.

★ Manalkadu Desert

Off the main road leading southeast out of Point Pedro is an area of white sand dunes known as the Manalkadu Desert. Reaching 15 m high in places, the dunes are formed by sand blown onshore from South India by the monsoon winds; even if they don't quite live up to their billing as a Sri Lankan Sahara, the remains of the old **St Anthony's Church**, half-

Jaffna Peninsula & Islands

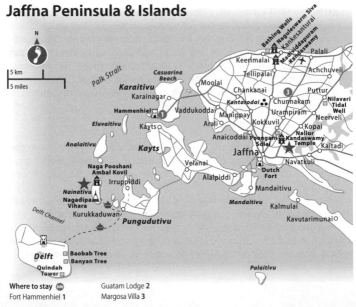

Where to stay
Fort Hammenhiel **1**

Guatam Lodge **2**
Margosa Villa **3**

submerged in the sand, are atmospheric enough in the afternoon light. From here you can walk across the dunes to a humble cemetery; most of the headstones commemorate people lost in the 2004 tsunami.

Halfway between Point Pedro and Manalkadu, **Valippuram** was once the capital of Jaffna and has a thriving temple, second in size on the peninsula only to Nallur. Vishnu was said to have appeared here as a fish. An inscription on a gold plate discovered here suggests that a *vihara* existed here during the reign of King Vasaba in the first century AD.

Kantarodai

Some 3 km west of Chunnakam Jct. Getting there: take the bus from Jaffna to Alveddi, from where you can take a 3-wheeler; if you're travelling independently, turn west off the KKS road at Chunnakam Jct for 2 km, then take another left (300 m) and turn right at the junction: the site is on the left, 600 m from here.

At Kantarodai, about halfway to Kankesanthurai (KKS), are the remains of around 30 squat Buddhist stupas, most between 2-4 m in height, crammed into a small plot. Excavations in 1918 discovered ancient Indian coins here, suggesting a 2000-year history. Some commentators have likened the stupas in form and origin to those in the upper platform at Borobudur in Indonesia. Though no theories for their existence have proved conclusive, many agree that they represent a monastic burial ground.

Kankesanturai and around

Kankesanthurai (KKS), due north of Jaffna, was the peninsula's most important port during the time of the ancient Jaffna kingdom. Now it's best known as the northern terminus of Sri Lanka's railway system, and has an army.

Just south of Kankesanturai on the Jaffna road, Tellipalai has the **Sri Durga Devasthanam**, a fine Durga temple with an enormous *gopuram*. (Buses terminate close by.) A two-week festival is held here in August with a water-cutting ceremony. The temple is especially active on Tuesdays.

West of Kankesanturai, Naguleswaram Shiva Kovil at **Keerimalai** is one of the earliest and most venerated Hindu temples in Sri Lanka. Largely destroyed in an aerial attack in 1990 and subsequently stripped of its antiquities, it remained off-limits to worshippers until 1996. Unfortunately many of the surviving older parts of the temple have been knocked down, but new buildings are close to completion, including a tall *gopuram*.

Close to the beach behind the kovil, spring water flows up through a rock fissure to form two popular **bathing wells** (one male, one female) that are pleasant for swimming. Keerimalai is associated with the visit by the Chola Princess Sangamittha in the seventh century, whose disfigured face looked like a horse's head. She was cured, legend states,

> **Tip...**
> Swimming in the sea at Keerimalai is forbidden.

by bathing in its healing waters and in gratitude constructed the **Madividdapuram Kandaswamy Kovil**, 2 km south, which has a tall *gopuram* and a festival in July/August.

Listings Jaffna peninsula *map p358*

Where to stay and eat

Jaffna is the most useful base for travelling in this area. Beyond the city, choices are limited and, to be on the safe side, you might want to take provisions with you. There are a handful of accommodation options and a couple of decent eateries in Point Pedro (open limited hours), and resort hotels in Kankesanthurai.

$$$$ Margosa Villa
Puttur Rd, Chunnakam, 10 km north of Jaffna, T021-224 0242, www.jaffna.travel/margosa.html
6 large, clean and airy rooms in a lovely colonial building, with huge bathrooms

boasting outdoor showers. Good fresh-cooked meals, friendly staff, and though it's a bit far-flung for exploring the city, it makes a good base for visiting the peninsula.

$ Gautam Lodge
1st Cross St, Point Pedro, T021-226 5870, www.neverbeen.org.
This simple guesthouse a couple of mins' walk north of the bus stand has just a handful of bare-bones rooms with cold-water bathrooms. Friendly host Mrs Pathma serves delicious meals in the family house a couple of doors up the street and can help arrange tuk-tuks for local sightseeing.

The islands
a quietly surreal landscape of causeways, ponies and colourful temples

The religious site of Nainativu (Nagadipa), sacred to both Buddhists and Hindus, is the only place in this area that receives a significant number of visitors and is increasingly thronged with day-trippers from around the country. The islands are rich in birdlife; look out for flamingos on the causeway to Kayts.

Kayts

The nearest island to Jaffna town, Kayts is regaining its pre-war status as a wealthy and sought-after area; look out for the ruins of beautiful villas lining the approach road. The road ends at a jetty for boats to Karaitivu Island to the north. Here you can see Indian fishing boats impounded for fishing in Sri Lankan waters and the well-preserved island fort of **Hammenhiel**, a long-term navy base and one-time prison that is now a luxury hotel (see Where to stay and eat).

Towards Karaitivu

This island is a short boat ride from Kayts, or a 25-km drive northeast of Jaffna. Before it crosses the causeway, the Karaitivu road passes through **Vadukoddai** on the mainland,

·Jaffna & the north Jaffna & around

where there is a large Portuguese church. Behind the church are 27 gravestones, predominantly Dutch, rescued from the Groote Kerk in Jaffna's fort. To the east at **Chankanai** are the overgrown remains of another Portuguese church, constructed of coral in 1641. Once on the island, Karaitivu's best known landmark is **Casuarina Beach**, which offers safe swimming in the calm, shallow waters. A few stalls sell drinks and snacks. The beach is named after the beefwood (*casuarina*) trees found here.

★ Nainativu

Accessed by ferry from the quiet island of **Punguditivu**, tiny Nainativu has great religious importance to both Buddhists and Hindus. For the former it is Nagadipa, the point at which the Buddha set foot on his second visit to the island, four years after the first, in order to settle a quarrel between two Naga kings over a throne, said to be enshrined here. A *vihara*, with a restored silver *dagoba* and image house, marks the spot. There is a bo tree opposite. The *vihara* is a 10-minute walk along the road leading left from the jetty where the ferry drops you off.

In a Hindu-dominated area, however, the **Naga Pooshani Ambal kovil**, a few minutes' walk further north, is the livelier temple, with a majestically colourful *gopuram*. Regular *pujas* are taken, with colourful processions, clattering drums, bells and pipes. During its 15-day festival in June, a 30-m idol of Ambal is paraded. In order to take advantage of Ambal's generosity, it is a good idea to arrive for the important *puja* at 1300, after which crowds of several hundred line up in the hall behind the temple for rice and curry, ladled on to a banana leaf. Ferries back to Pungudutivu depart from the jetty in front of the temple.

Delft

The windswept and bleak landscape of Delft, the outermost inhabited island, has been less affected by conflict and contains various reminders of the Portuguese and Dutch periods. Famous for its wild ponies, which come from a Portuguese breeding stock, it also has the remains of a coral fort, fairly tumbledown but still recognizable, behind the hospital. South of the jetty is a single baobab tree (see page 364) and, further on, a large banyan, while at the southern tip the Quindah tower is an ancient navigational landmark. Father David, head of the Delft church, may be able to help organize basic accommodation on the island, T077-644 6679.

Listings The islands

Where to stay and eat

$$$$-$$$ Fort Hammenhiel
Karaitivu island, 26 km northwest of Jaffna, T071-614 6566, bookings T011-381 8215, www.forthammenhielresort.lk.
Definitely the most left-field place to stay in the far north, this 17th-century Dutch fort and former prison sits on a tiny island 100 m off the coast of Karaitivu island. Within the high stone walls are 4 large comfortable a/c rooms shaded by a huge Bo tree; the restaurant is a boat ride away, back on the mainland. It's run by the Navy and things are a bit military – service is clipped rather than slick, hot water comes in short bursts – but for atmosphere it's hard to beat.

Mannar Island

Mannar Island is one of the driest and most barren places in the country, rarely visited except by birdwatchers, shell collectors and the occasional kitesurfer. The beaches and general scenery aren't that attractive, but Mannar does maintain a sense of intriguing isolation that makes it well worth a look. Connected to mainland Sri Lanka by a 3-km road dam and iron bridge, Mannar's historical importance lies in its proximity to India to which it was once linked by an ancient land bridge.

Towards Mannar Island

places of pilgrimage along a desolate route

Along the A14

The remote island of Mannar is accessible by road from **Medawachchiya** (86 km along the recently resurfaced A14), and via the A30 from **Vavuniya** (78 km). Both roads run through elephant country and meet at **Paraiyanalankulam**, where the A14 continues west past the turning for **Madhu Road Sanctuary** (see below) with views of **Giant's Tank**. Possibly built by King Parakramabahu I, Giant's Tank, is rich in scrub and shore birds, and though the tank is often empty, you'll see fishermen dragging their canoes through channels in the mud flats. Palmyras and umbrella thorns are increasingly visible in this barren, open landscape, interspersed with some paddy cultivation.

Essential Mannar Island

Finding your feet

The island can be reached from Medawachchiya and Vavuniya (both on the A9) and from Jaffna via the newly improved A32. A dirt road also links Mannar to Puttalam and Colombo, though it's slow and highly controversial, passing as it does through Wilpattu National Park. The re-opened railway line runs all the way out to Talaimannar Pier at the far end of the island, via Mannar town. At the time of writing Sri Lanka and India were discussing plans to build a road bridge that would eventually link Talaimannar to Rameshwaram.

Getting around

Local buses leave from Mannar town to Madhu Road church, Vavuniya, Thirukethiswaram and Talaimannar.

Madhu Road Sanctuary *Colour map 1, C2.*

Located 12 km northeast of the A14 Madhu Road Junction, the rebuilt **church** at Madhu Road is the most important Catholic pilgrimage site in Sri Lanka. Its altar houses the sacred **Our Lady of Madhu statue**, which was brought here in 1670 by 20 Catholic families fleeing persecution by the Dutch at Mantai, near Mannar. Amongst the fugitives was Helena, the daughter of a Portuguese captain, who was sanctified and founded the first church here. The Madhu statue is venerated throughout the country for its miracles, especially the cure of snakebite, and major festivals are held here throughout the year. The largest, on 15 August, attracts up to half a million visitors.

Thirukethiswaram kovil
Turn north off the A14, 5 km before the Mannar causeway. Remove shoes and shirts. There are buses from Mannar town.

A short distance inland from the Mannar causeway, the restored Saivite Thirukethiswaram *kovil* near Mantai is one of five ancient temples in Sri Lanka said to pre-date the arrival of Buddhism. Around the 1500-year-old inner sanctum are various statues of deities in scenes from stories. Apparently, after bathing in the adjacent Palavi tank, childless women bring a pot of water to pour over Shiva's lingam and drink. With most of its worshippers still refugees living in India, the temple is often deserted, except on Fridays when there is a big *puja* at 1200. At other times and in the right light, it feels pleasantly spooky. However, plans are afoot to renovate the temple; if similar enterprises elsewhere in the north are any guide, the result will be highly colourful but much less atmospheric. A 40-day festival is held here in July with a water-cutting ceremony.

★ The island *Colour map 1, B1.*
explore a history of settlement and trade that stretches back millennia

The island's distinctive character has been forged by its settlers, who first crossed Adam's Bridge from India almost two million years ago. On the mainland, Mantai was the pre-Sinhalese port of Mahatittha, which attracted traders and invaders. Arabs brought Islam, the baobab tree and the ubiquitous donkey, rare elsewhere in the country, while the Portuguese spread their influence through the Catholic church. The Dutch developed Mannar fort into one of the strongholds of the north.

Historically famous for its long-abandoned pearl banks to the south, Mannar for many years has been an impoverished and marginalized backwater. Its ferry route across to India and its railway line to the mainland were victims of the conflict, as was its road bridge, which was blown up in 1990. However, the island's enforced seclusion meant that it avoided much of the destruction inflicted elsewhere in the region, and nowadays its isolation is no longer so complete: the railway line reopened in 2015 and, at the time of writing, various plans were underway to resume ferry services from here.

Mannar town and around
It is impossible to miss Mannar's **fort**, which stands proudly on the right as you cross the mudflats to enter the town. Constructed by the Portuguese in 1560, it was taken by the Dutch in 1658 and rebuilt. The fort's ramparts and four bastions, part surrounded by a

moat, are intact, although most buildings inside have been blasted. There is an ornate Dutch stone tablet close to the main gate. A tunnel is said to connect Mannar's fort to the remains of another at Arippu, two hours south. The police occupy the fort, though permission for visits is usually granted.

The town itself is dominated by its mosques and churches. The Goan-style St Sebastian's has ornate latticework giving it a Moorish appearance.

Two kilometres east of the town centre at Pallimunai is what is Mannar's most famous **baobab tree**, claimed to be the largest tree in Asia, with a circumference of 19.5 m. A board states that it was probably planted in 1477. Other baobabs on the island have been radio carbon-dated to 1000 years old. Bus No 946 travels to Pallimunai.

West of Mannar town

The A14 continues northwest, following and, at one point, crossing the railway line through the sandy wastes and jungle scrub to Talaimannar, the westernmost point of the island. The Muslim village of **Erukkulampiddu**, 15 km northwest of Mannar (turn right at Toddaveli) along the A14, is known locally for its mat-weaving. Further on, **Pesalai** is a Catholic fishing village with one of the largest churches in Sri Lanka (rebuilt in 1999), where there is an image of Christ under a mosquito net. A Passion play is performed at Easter here using life-size dolls. Intrepid explorers with a few words of Tamil may find places to stay along the beach here.

Talaimannar and Adam's Bridge

A left-turn at **Talaimannar** takes you to South Point, close to which is the start of **Adam's Bridge**, a series of rocks, sandbanks and shallows which links Mannar to Rameswaram in India. In 2002, NASA space images revealed the crossing to be man-made because of its composition and curvature, proving that settlers arrived in Sri Lanka at least 1,750,000 years ago. This sheds light on the *Ramayana* legend in which Hanuman constructed a causeway in his attempt to rescue Sita from the demon-god Ravana. Closer relations with India have prompted talks of developing a modern bridge to Rameswaram from here, but this is likely to be years away. The tavern here serves good toddy from traditional palmyra cups. Fishermen will offer to take you for a 30- to 40-minute boat ride to the 'fourth island' of Adam's Bridge for around Rs 2000-3000. Close to here, though tricky to locate (coming back from Adam's Bridge, turn right at the dusty patch of open ground that serves as a cricket oval), is a Muslim shrine which, a legend states, is the burial place of Adam and Eve.

A kilometre north of Talaimannar town is the old pier from which, until 1984, ferry boats crossed to India. Though its timbers are gently decaying, it is possible to walk out to the end, from where you can try to catch a glimpse of India. There is an attractive but abandoned and rather forlorn lighthouse on the beach, and navy patrol boats share the water with local fishing craft; the beach buzzes with fisherfolk in the morning.

Where to stay

$$$$ Palmyrah House
T071-757 2942, T077-925 1531.
Mannar's smartest option by a comfortable margin has huge a/c rooms, pleasant gardens, a swimming pool and restaurant. Birdwatching tours with naturalist guides can be arranged.

$$-$ Adams Bridge Kitesurf
Lighthouse Rd, Urumalai, near Talaimannar, T076-659 6959, www.abkitesurf.com.
This new place run by Negombo kitesurfing pioneer Marc Pelle was just getting started in late 2015. The simple thatched cabanas, set in a grove of thorny trees with shared outdoor showers, are pitched at low-maintenance travellers, and there's good food, cold drinks, free Wi-Fi and first-class kitesurfing instruction.

$ Baobab Guest House
70 Field St, Mannar town, T023-222 2305.
Small but comfortable a/c rooms, in a quiet spot close to the centre of Mannar town.

$ Four Teess
Opposite Thoddaveli railway station, T023-323 0008, 4teessrestinn@gmail.com.

The boxy, slightly grubby fan-cooled rooms in this out-of-the-way spot come with pleasant sit-outs that somewhat make up for the basic interiors and tiny windows. The best features are the bird-filled gardens, where white-bellied sea eagles can be seen during nesting season, and the friendly manager, Lawrence, who cooks great meals (arrange dinner in advance).

Restaurants

New Kamala, opposite Mannar town bus stand, is the busiest in a line of similarly basic restaurants, serving excellent, cheap *purotta* and curries.

Weligama Bakery is good for short eats and snacks. For other options see Where to stay, above.

Transport

Bus From Mannar town buses run regularly to **Vavuniya** and to **Colombo** (7 hrs). There are also daily buses to **Anuradhapura**, **Trincomalee** and **Kalpitiya**.

Train Trains run twice daily from **Colombo** to Talaimannar pier, via Mannar town.

Background

History

Sri Lanka has a rich cultural history. In this sense it is no different from much of South Asia where religion and the migration of people are interlocked. What makes it so interesting to the traveller is its accessibility. As they look over the plains from the heights of the fortress at Sigiriya, few visitors can fail to imagine the great battle involving kings atop elephants; others will be moved as they watch the sun set over the Sun and Moon bastions at the colonial fortification in Galle.

Settlement and early history

Stone tools from the Middle Palaeolithic Age have been found in several places, evidence of settlement in Sri Lanka perhaps as much as 500,000 years ago. Recent genetic research however suggests that *Homo sapiens* may not have evolved until very much later, and spread from Africa in the last 100,000 years.

The early record of settlement in Sri Lanka is scanty. Archaeologists believe today that the first *Homo sapiens* arrived perhaps 75,000 years ago, bringing with them a life of hunting and gathering centred on open-air campsites. Evidence of their activity has been found in a variety of habitats. However, no Neolithic tools have been found, and no tools from the Copper Age, which is so well represented in peninsular India from the second millennium BC.

The picture changes with the arrival of the Iron Age, for the megalithic graves, associated with black and red pottery, suggest that Sri Lanka had direct contact with South India well before the Aryans immigrated from North India from around 500 BC. Sri Lanka's archaeological record remains comparatively sparse, with barely any evidence with which to date the development of Stone Age cultures or the later spread of domesticated animals and cultivation. At some point in the first millennium BC rice cultivation made its appearance, though whether as a result of migration from either North India or Southeast Asia remains controversial.

The earliest aboriginal settlers, of Australoid, Negrito and Mediterranean stock, have now been almost entirely absorbed in the settled populations. The earliest named culture is that of **Balangoda**, distributed across the whole island between 5000 and 500 BC. The **Veddas** are the only inhabitants today whose ancestors were in Sri Lanka before the Aryan migrations. Related to the Dravidian jungle peoples in South India, they dwelt in caves and rock shelters, and lived by hunting and gathering. They practised a cult of the dead, communicating with ancestors through reincarnated spirits. Today the Veddas have been largely absorbed into the Sinhalese community and have virtually ceased to have a separate existence. Their numbers have shrunk to just a few hundred. See the box on page 308 for further details.

Migration from India

The overwhelming majority of the present population of Sri Lanka owes its origins to successive waves of migration from two different regions of India. Most people are of Indo-Aryan origin and came from North India. The earliest migrations from North India may have taken place as early as the fifth century BC. Although these migrants brought with them a North Indian language which had its roots in the Sanskrit tradition, they were not yet Buddhists, for Buddhism did not arrive in Sri Lanka until the third century BC. It is most likely that the Sinhalese came from India's northwest, possibly Punjab or Gujarat, and it seems probable that Gujarati traders were already sailing down India's west coast by this time. The origins of Tamil settlement are unclear, but are thought to go back at least to the third century BC, when there is clear evidence of trade between Sri Lanka and South India.

Today the **Sinhalese** make up 74% of the total population. Sri Lanka's **Tamil** population comprises the long settled Tamils of the north and east (12.6%) and the migrant workers on the tea plantations in the Central Highlands (5.5%) who settled in Sri Lanka from the late 19th century onwards. At the height of the conflict, up to 750,000 Tamils had repatriated abroad, though many have since returned. The so-called **'Moors'**, Tamil speaking Muslims of Indian-Arab descent, were traders on the east coast and now number over 1.1 million (7.7%). A much smaller but highly distinct community is that of the **Burghers**, numbering about 50,000. The Dutch (mainly members of the Dutch Reformed Church) and the Portuguese intermarried with local people, and their descendants were urban and ultimately English speaking. There are similar numbers of Malays and smaller groups of Kaffirs. The Malays are Muslims who were brought by the Dutch from Java. The Kaffirs were brought by the Portuguese from Mozambique and other parts of East Africa as mercenaries.

A literate society

With the development of agriculture came the origins of a literate and complex society. Tradition associates the founding of Sri Lanka's first kingdom with Devanampiya Tissa (250-221 BC), who was converted to Buddhism by Mahinda, son of the great Indian Emperor Asoka. Myth and legend are bound up with many of the events of South Asian history, but the Sri Lankan historian KM de Silva has noted that the historical mythology of the Sinhalese "is the basis of their conception of themselves as the chosen guardians of Buddhism". The basic text through which this view of the island's history has been passed on by successive generations of Buddhist monks is the **Mahavansa** (*Great Dynasty* or *Lineage*), which de Silva suggests possibly goes back to the sixth century AD, but is probably much more recent. It is the epic history from Prince Vijaya, the legendary founder of Sri Lanka, to King Mahasena (died AD 303) and is a major source on early history and legend. It was continued in the 13th-century text by the *Culavansa*, which gives a very full account of the medieval history of the island. These works were compiled by **bhikkus** (Buddhist monks) and inevitably they have the marks of their sectarian origins.

Interpretation of Sri Lanka's early history does not depend entirely on the writings of the Buddhist monks who ultimately wrote the *Mahavansa*. The first known writings are inscriptions discovered near caves in several parts of the island. Written in the Brahmi script (which was also used in India on the great inscriptions of the Emperor Asoka to express his principles of government and to mark out the limits of his territorial power), in Sri Lanka the inscriptions are brief epigraphs, testifying to the donation of caves or rock shelters to Buddhist monks. Written in an early form of Sinhala, rather than in the Prakrit which was the language used by Asoka, they give vivid testimony to the existence of prosperous, literate agricultural societies. The alphabet and the language were common right across the country, and even from early times it is clear that wet rice cultivation using sophisticated irrigation technology was the basis of the economy. Settlement spread steadily right through to the 13th century. A notable feature of this early settlement and culture was its restriction to the Dry Zone and to altitudes below 300 m.

From the origins of this agricultural civilization in the third century BC there was a progressive economic and social evolution. The economy and the culture developed around the creation of extraordinarily sophisticated irrigation systems, using the rivers flowing from the Central Highlands across the much drier northern and eastern plains. Traditional agriculture had depended entirely on the rainfall brought by the retreating monsoon between October and December. The developing kingdoms of north Sri Lanka realized the need to control water to improve the reliability of agriculture, and a system of tank irrigation was already well advanced by the first century BC. This developed into possibly the most advanced contemporary system of hydraulic engineering in the world by the end of the fifth century AD. Many of these developments were quite small scale and today it is impossible to identify their creators. Others however were of a previously unparalleled size and are clearly identified with powerful kings, for example King Mahasena (AD 274-302) and the 15-m-high dam which impounded the Kantalai tank, covering 2000 ha and is served by a 40-km-long canal. King Dhatusena (AD 460-478) constructed the Kalawewa Lake in Anuradhapura, then by far the largest tank in Sri Lanka, to be surpassed in the late 12th century by King Parakramabahu's Parakrama Samudra ('Sea'), retained by an embankment 14 km long.

Political developments in pre-colonial Sri Lanka

Proximity to India has played a permanent part in Sri Lanka's developing history. Not only did the peoples of the island originate from the mainland, but over more than 2000 years, contact with the sub-continent has been an essential element in all Sri Lanka's political equations.

According to the *Mahavansa*, the Buddha commanded the king of the gods, Sakra, to protect Lanka as the home in which Buddhism would flourish. In recent years, much has been read into both the text and to more recent history to suggest that the Sinhalese have always been at war with the Tamils. The truth is far more complicated. The earliest settlement of the island took place in the northeast, the area now known as the Dry Zone. Until the 13th century AD this was the region of political and cultural development for Sinhalese and Tamil alike.

The political history of the island after the establishment of the first recorded kingdom was not as smooth as might be inferred from the steady expansion of settled agriculture and the spread of sophisticated irrigation technology. Before the 13th century AD three regions played a major role in the island's political life. **Rajarata** in the north-central part of the island's plains grew into one of the major core regions of developing Sinhalese culture. To its north was **Uttaradesa** ('northern country'), while in the southeast, **Rohana** (Ruhunu) developed as the third political centre.

Periodically these centres of Sinhalese power came into conflict with each other, and with Tamil kings from India. The *Mahavansa* records how the Rohana Sinhalese King Dutthagamenu defeated the Chola Tamil King Elara, who had ruled northern Sri Lanka from Anuradhapura, in 140 BC. Dutthagamenu's victory was claimed by the chroniclers as a historic assertion of Buddhism's inalienable hold on Sri Lanka. In fact it is clear that at the time this was not a Tamil-Sinhalese or Buddhist-Hindu conflict, for the armies and leadership of both sides contained Sinhalese and Tamils, Buddhists and Hindus. By that time Buddhism had already been a power in the island for two centuries, when the king Devanampiya Tissa (307-267 BC) converted to Buddhism.

Buddhism became the state religion, identified with the growth of Sinhalese culture and political power. The power of the central kingdom based at Anuradhapura was rarely unchallenged or complete. Power was decentralized, with a large measure of local autonomy. Furthermore, provincial centres periodically established their independence. Anuradhapura became one of Asia's pre-eminent cities, but from the 11th century AD, Polonnaruwa took over as capital.

Tamil involvement

Although Buddhist power was predominant in Sri Lanka from the first century BC, Sri Lankan kings often deliberately sought Tamil support in their own disputes. As a result Sri Lanka was affected by political developments in South India. The rise of the expansionist Tamil kingdoms of the Pandiyas, Pallavas and Cholas from the fifth century AD increased the scope for interaction with the mainland. In de Silva's words, "South Indian auxiliaries became in time a vitally important, if not the most powerful element in the armies of the Sinhalese rulers, and an unpredictable, turbulent group who were often a threat to political stability. They were also the nucleus of a powerful Tamil influence in the court."

It was not a one-way flow. Occasionally the Sinhalese were themselves drawn in to attack Tamil kings in India, as in the ninth century when to their enormous cost they joined with their beleaguered allies the Pandiyans and attacked the Cholas. The Chola emperor **Rajaraja I** defeated them in India and then carried the war into Sri Lanka, adding Jaffna and the northern plains, including Anuradhapura, to his empire.

The Cholas ruled from Polonnaruwa for 75 years, finally being driven out by the Rohana king **Vijayabahu I** in AD 1070. He established peace and a return to some prosperity in the north before civil war broke out and disrupted the civil administration again. Only the 33-year rule of **Parakramabahu I** (1153-1186) interrupted the decline. Some of Sri Lanka's most remarkable monuments date from his reign, including the Parakrama Samudra at Polonnaruwa. However, it was the collapse of this kingdom and its ultimate annihilation by the Tamils in the 13th century that left not only its physical imprint on the north Sri Lankan landscape, but also an indelible psychological mark on the Sri Lankan perception of neighbouring Tamil Hindus.

Sinhalese move south

Other factors, such as the spread of malaria, which occurred with the deterioration in maintenance of the irrigation system, may have led to the progressive desertion of the northern and eastern plains and the movement south of the centre of gravity of the island's population. Between the 12th and 17th centuries Sinhalese moved from the Dry Zone to the Wet Zone. This required a change in agriculture from irrigated to rain-fed crops. Trade also increased, especially in cinnamon – an activity controlled by the rising population of Muslim seafarers. A **Tamil kingdom** was set up in Jaffna for the first time, briefly coming back under Sinhalese power (under the Sinhalese king **Parakramabahu VI**, 1412-1467, based in his capital at **Kotte**), but generally remaining independent, and a frequent threat to the power of the Sinhalese kingdoms to the south. Other threats came from overseas.

As early as the 13th century, a Buddhist king from Malaya invaded Sri Lanka twice to try and capture the Tooth Relic and the Buddha's alms bowl. In the early 15th century the island was even invaded by a fleet of Chinese junks sent by the Ming emperors.

The Kandyan kingdom

Between the southern and northern kingdoms, Kandy became the capital of a new power base around 1480. Established in the Central Highlands, it became fully independent by the end of the 15th century. By the early 16th century the Sinhalese kingdom of Kotte in the south was hopelessly fragmented, giving impetus to Kandy's rise to independent power. Its remote and inaccessible position gave it added protection from the early colonial invasions. Using both force and diplomacy to capitalize on its geographical advantages, it survived as the last independent Sinhalese kingdom until 1815. It had played the game of seeking alliances with one colonial power against another with considerable success, first seeking the help of the Dutch against the Portuguese, then of the British against the Dutch. However, this policy ran out of potential allies when the British established their supremacy over all the territory surrounding the Central Highlands in 1796. By 1815 the last Kandyan king, a Tamil Hindu converted to Buddhism, was deposed by his Sinhalese chiefs, who sought an accord with the new British rulers in exchange for retaining a large measure of their own power.

Colonial power

The succession of three colonial powers – the Portuguese, Dutch and the British – finally ended independent Sinhalese and Tamil rule. Expanding Islam, evidenced in the conversion of the inhabitants of islands on the Arab trading routes such as the Maldives and the Laccadives as well as significant numbers on the southwest coast of India, had also been making its presence felt. The Portuguese arrived in Sri Lanka in 1605 and established control over some of the island's narrow coastal plains around Colombo. They were responsible for large-scale conversions to Roman Catholicism which today accounts for 90% of the island's Christians, leaving both a linguistic legacy and an imprint on the population, evidenced today in many names of Portuguese origin. During this period the rest of the island was dominated by the rulers of Sitavaka, who overpowered the Kotte kingdom in 1565 and controlled the whole of the southwest apart from Colombo. For 10 years they occupied Kandy itself, nearly evicted the Portuguese and came close to reasserting Sinhalese power in the far north.

By 1619 the Portuguese had annexed Jaffna, which thereafter was treated by the Dutch, and more importantly the British, as simply part of the island state. They were less successful in subjugating Kandy, and in 1650 the Portuguese were ousted by the Dutch. The Dutch extended their own colonial control from Negombo (40 km north of Colombo) south, right round the coast to Trincomalee, as well as the entire northern peninsula, leaving the Kandyan kingdom surrounded in the Central Highlands. Because the Portuguese and Dutch were interested in little other than the spice trade, they bent most of their efforts to producing the goods necessary for their trade. The British replaced the Dutch in 1795-1796 when British power was being consolidated in South India at the expense of the French and the Mysore Muslim raja, Tipu Sultan. Their original purpose was to secure the important Indian Ocean port of Trincomalee. Initially the British imported administrators and officials from Madras, but as BH Farmer points out, by 1802 "it was apparent that Madras-trained officials were, apart from other disabilities, quite unable to understand the language and customs of the Sinhalese, and Ceylon became a Crown Colony".

When the British came to control the whole island after 1815, they established a quite distinctive imprint on the island's society and economy. This was most obvious in the introduction of plantation agriculture. During the British period coffee took over from cinnamon, but by the beginning of the 20th century, even though coffee had largely been wiped out by disease, plantation agriculture was the dominant pillar of the cash economy. Rice production stagnated and then declined, and Sri Lanka became dependent on the export of cash crops and the import of food. In 1948 it was only producing about 35% of its rice needs.

The colonial period also saw major social changes take place. Under the Portuguese and then the Dutch the development of commercial activity in the coastal lowlands encouraged many 'low country' Sinhalese to become involved in the newly emerging economic activity. In a process which continued in the early British colonial period, the low country Sinhalese became increasingly Westernized, with the widespread adoption of an English education and the rise of an urban middle class, while the Kandyan Sinhalese retained far stronger links with traditional and rural social customs. Despite British reforms in 1833 which introduced a uniform administrative system across the whole of Ceylon, wiping out the Kandyan political system, a contrast between Kandyan and low country Sinhalese persisted into the modern period.

However, an even more significant change took place in the 19th century. British commercial interests saw the opportunities presented for the cultivation of cash crops. Cinnamon and coconuts had been planted by the Dutch and become particularly important, but after 1815 coffee production was spread to the Kandyan hills. Despite ups and downs production increased dramatically until 1875, when a catastrophic attack of a fungus disease wiped out almost the entire crop. It was replaced, particularly in the higher regions, by tea.

Labour had already begun to prove a problem on the coffee plantations, and as tea plantations spread the shortage became acute. Private labour contractors were recruited to persuade labourers to come to Ceylon from the Tamil country of South India. Between 1843-1859 over 900,000 men, women and children migrated to work as indentured labour. The cost of their transport was deducted from their wages after they arrived, and they could not leave until they had repaid their debt. Immigration on that scale created a massive change in the ethnic mix of the highlands, with a particularly significant effect on the Kandyan farmers, whose land was increasingly hemmed in by the spread of estates. The Indian Tamils however remained entirely separate from the Sinhalese, returning to South India whenever possible and sending cash remittances home.

The move to independence

Dominated by Buddhists and Sinhalese in its early stages, no one in the Independence movement at the beginning of the 20th century would have believed that British rule would end within 50 years – nor would many have wanted it to. The **Ceylon National Congress**, formed in 1919, was conservative and pragmatic, but the pressures of imminent democratic self-rule made themselves felt throughout the 1930s, as minority groups pressed to protect their position. Universal suffrage came in 1931, along with the promise of self-rule from the British government. It had the positive benefit of encouraging the development of welfare policies such as health care, nutrition and public education. However, it also had the immediate impact of encouraging a resurgence of nationalism linked with Buddhist revivalism.

Independence came with scarcely a murmur on 4 February 1948, six months after that of India and Pakistan. Ceylon's first prime minister was **Don Stephen Senanayake**. His son **Dudley Senanayake**, who followed, was identified with a pragmatic nationalism. The heart of his programme was the re-colonization of the deserted Sinhalese heartlands of the Dry Zone. It was a programme deliberately calculated to recapture the glories of the past while laying the groundwork for post-independence prosperity. In the event, its results proved far more complex than even its critics fully recognized.

Modern Sri Lanka

Sri Lanka is a parliamentary democracy with an elected president and freely contested elections. Sri Lankans enjoy a long life expectancy, a high literacy rate that belies its low per capita income, and generally an advanced health system. Over the last 50 years the island has continued to see rapid economic and social change. The plantation economy remains important though no longer as dominant as it was during the colonial period, while newer industries, including tourism, have taken on the prime role.

In the early post-independence years, Sri Lanka was regarded as a 'model colony'. The country started on a strong economic footing with a strong Sterling balance and little internal division. Within the new constitution there was a commitment to religious neutrality. Both the island's main languages, Sinhala and Tamil, had been declared national languages, and equitable access to political and administrative positions was guaranteed. However, successive governments failed to maintain commitment to either equality or economic development in the face of greater welfare spending and a rapidly growing young and literate population. The pattern of the early post-independence governments was to manipulate disaffection within the electorate in an effort to gain votes, with the effect of stirring up communal emotions between racial and religious groups. Within 10 years the seeds had been sown for the faction fighting of the last two decades which threatened to tear the country apart.

Between 1983 and 2009, Sri Lanka was involved in a bitter internal ethnic conflict, predominantly in the north and east, between the government and separatist Tamil rebels, the **Liberation Tigers of Tamil Eelam (LTTE)** or '**Tamil Tigers**'.

Post-independence and the Bandaranaikes

The origins of Sri Lanka's ethnic conflict are complex. Here, a brief sketch of significant post-war events is offered which aims to elucidate some of the immediate causes. Sri Lanka's first government was formed by the **United National Party (UNP)**, a broad union of conservative ideologies led by **DS Senanayake**, Minister of Agriculture during the last years of British rule. Senanayake saw Sri Lanka's pluralism as its strength, thwarting any divisive forces. He concentrated on economic progress, particularly in agricultural policy, including the setting up of the massive Gal Oya project in the east of the country, designed to increase rice production, as well as planting subsidies on rice. The party however was wrought by internal divisions with the first serious break occurring in 1951 when its left bloc broke away under the leadership of **SWRD Bandaranaike**, to form the **Sri Lanka Freedom Party (SLFP)**.

After Senanayake's death in a riding accident in 1952, his son Dudley succeeded him but failed to maintain the UNP's popularity when it became clear that the country faced significant economic problems. Senanayake's massive spending on welfare (up to 35% of the budget) forced him to reduce the government rice subsidy, leading to massive protests and his resignation.

Against this background, the SLFP emerged as the main opposition party. Bandaranaike, part of a wealthy Sinhalese family, had been educated – and discriminated against – at Oxford. Returning to Sri Lanka, he rejected Western values and embraced Buddhism. His election campaign of 1956 sought to provoke the nationalist passions of the Buddhist majority in order to eradicate traces of colonial rule. While this was initially targeted at Christian influence, it coincided with a greater awareness amongst Sinhalese that they had 'lost out' at independence. During the British colonial period, a disproportionate number of government and administrative positions had been given to the traditionally hardworking Tamils, who tended to be better educated than the Sinhalese and occupied a greater number of university places, a trend that continued after independence. English had been, and continued to be, the main language of administration, and since the Tamils tended to have greater mastery, Bandaranaike chose to fight the 1956 election on a platform making Sinhala the only official language. After winning the election, Bandaranaike successfully passed the **Sinhala Only Act**, which led to widespread Tamil resentment and, within two years, the first violent clashes in which hundreds, mainly Tamils, died.

Bandaranaike pursued popular but economically unfeasible nationalization policies, expanding the public sector and draining the nation's resources. By the time he was assassinated by a Buddhist monk in 1959, the country faced grave instability. The SLFP however maintained popular support, and in July 1960 his widow, **Sirimavo Bandaranaike** swept to power, becoming the world's first female prime minister. She continued her husband's socialist-style legislation, nationalizing significant sectors of the economy, including foreign-controlled industries such as petroleum, and forced a government takeover of denominational schools. This soured relations with the country's many Catholics, while her aggressive reinforcement of Sinhala as the only official language led to Tamil disobedience in the north and east, whose political activity was subsequently curtailed in a state of emergency. In 1965, Dudley Senanayake and the UNP regained power, but despite improving relations with the US (who had suspended aid in 1963) and doubling private sector investment, the economy failed to show any significant improvement, and the government was blighted by greater civil violence and states of emergency.

Rise of the LTTE

Mrs Bandaranaike returned to power in 1970 under the banner of the **United Front**, a three-party coalition, promising land reform and further nationalization, and extending diplomatic relations to countries such as the GDR, Vietnam and North Korea. The radical left mobilized at this time, and in 1971 a Sinhalese Maoist youth movement, the **Janatha Vimukthi Peramuna (JVP)** or People's Liberation Front, attempted a blitzkrieg, with fierce fighting in the North Central and Southern Provinces leaving more than 1000 dead. Ruthlessly repressed by the military, the uprising gave the government reign to force through a new constitution in May 1972, verging on the authoritarian. The military were given greater powers, while Sinhala was enshrined as the official language and the country was given a new name, Sri Lanka, invoking the ancient Sinhalese kingdoms. The constitution lacked any hint of federalism, which dismayed Tamils. Instead, it removed many minority rights, conferring greater status on Buddhism. Even more irksome to Tamils was the 'standardization' policy on university admissions, which lowered the standard required by Sinhalese to gain university places. With many Tamils disenfranchised and disillusioned, this iniquitous change in the system, combined with heavy handed treatment by the army, was the fundamental cause of the breakdown of ethnic relations in the 1970s and the radicalization of Tamil politics. The proportion of Tamils in public service had fallen from 60% in 1956 to 10% by 1970, and from 40% to 1% in the military, while the percentage of university places held by Tamils almost halved between 1970 and 1975. In 1976, the Tamil leadership (the newly formed **Tamil United Liberation Front**, or **TULF**) for the first time advocated a separate Tamil state. The LTTE at this time emerged as the most powerful of a number of underground separatist groups. They first gained notoriety in 1975 when they assassinated the Mayor of Jaffna, and from a handful of guerrilla fighters in the early years, they grew with the help of funding and military training from abroad (notably from Tamil Nadu) into a well-disciplined military unit.

During this period support for the UNP had declined but when political divisions between left and right began to split the United Front, the UNP under a new leader, **JR Jayawardene**, actively improved their image and won a convincing victory at the polls in 1977. Promising a fairer society, he radically altered the constitution the following year, replacing the Westminster-style of governance with a French-style presidential system, the democratically elected president to appoint a prime minister, with parliamentary approval. While the new constitution also included concessions to the Tamils, including giving Tamil the status of a 'national' language and abrogating the 'standardization' policy for universities, it was a case of too little too late. The country's worst rioting in 19 years had greeted the new government's inception, and in 1979 the government passed an act, condemned by international groups, to attempt to curb the rapid proliferation of Tamil terrorist groups. The possibility of an effective solution became increasingly distant when the TULF boycotted the 1982 presidential elections (which saw a confirmation of Jayawardene's presidency whose economic advances had proved popular with the Sinhalese). When TULF members were expelled from parliament for refusing to recite allegiance to the constitution, Tamil hopes of a political solution effectively ended.

Sporadic rioting continued to increase, notably over a three-month period in 1981 during which Jaffna's historic library was destroyed, but it was during 'Black July' in 1983 that the country descended into turmoil. In retaliation for an ambush of an army patrol, organized Sinhalese mobs went on the rampage, first in Colombo, where Tamil areas were devastated and hundreds were killed, and then spreading throughout the country.

More than 150,000 Tamils fled as refugees to India, many finding new homes in Europe and North America.

Civil war

Between 1983 and 1987 the LTTE waged an increasingly successful battle for control of 'Eelam' – roughly Sri Lanka's Northern and Eastern provinces. Brutal acts were perpetrated on both sides. The conflict began to assume an international dimension when the Sri Lankan government accused India of supporting the Tamil cause, and as the situation reached deadlock, Indian leader Rajiv Gandhi agreed to intervene. On 29 July 1987, Gandhi and Jayawardene signed the Indo-Lanka accord, under which the Sri Lankan government made a number of concessions to the Tamils, including some devolution of power to the provinces and a merger of the Northern and Eastern provinces. Fifty thousand troops, the **Indian Peace Keeping Force** (**IPKF**), were sent in to disarm the rebels. Most groups agreed to surrender their weapons. Within weeks, however, the LTTE announced their intention to continue the fight for Eelam, entering into a bloody battle with the Indian peacekeepers. The government pressed on with reform, holding council elections, but a return to peace was complicated when Sinhalese nationalism, opposed to concessions to the Tamils and an Indian presence on Lankan soil, rose again and the JVP, which had been quiet since the early 1970s, began to reassert itself. There followed one of the ugliest periods in Sri Lankan history. The JVP embarked on a systematic attempt to bring down the government, through strikes, sabotage, closure of schools and hospitals, assassination of politicians and the murder of hundreds of government supporters. The government, relieved of its burden in the north, responded violently. By the time the JVP insurrection was finally quashed in 1990, many thousands of suspected insurgents had been killed or 'disappeared'. The systematic abuse of human rights by the government and military at this time drew widespread condemnation from the international community.

Meanwhile, presidential elections in 1988 had been won by **Ranasinghe Premadasa**. He promptly demanded that Indian troops leave and opened up discussions with the LTTE, who agreed to a ceasefire and talks in order to speed up the Indian withdrawal. Within three months of their eventual departure in March 1990, the LTTE had resumed hostilities, 'Eelam War II', at one point murdering 600 police officers in the north whom they had promised free passage. Having been pushed back to Jaffna in 1987, they now took control of large sections of the north and east. Vendettas were also pursued. In 1991, they assassinated Rajiv Gandhi in Madras and two years later at a May Day rally, Premadasa himself. With the UNP weakened after 17 years of rule, tainted by corruption, political scandal and continued failure to solve the conflict, new president Dingiri Banda Wijetunga called elections in August 1994. Chandrika Kumaratunga, daughter of Sirimavo Bandaranaike, had by now assumed the leadership of the SLFP and led a loose coalition of parties, the **People's Alliance** (**PA**), to a narrow victory over the UNP. After appointing her mother as prime minister, she entered into negotiations with the LTTE. Once again these broke down when the LTTE's 'Black Sea Tigers' sank two naval gunboats off the coast of Trincomalee. But in launching 'Eelam War III' it soon became evident that the LTTE had themselves miscalculated. In a huge gamble, the army launched **Operation Riviresa** (Sunshine), a successful attempt to retake Jaffna in October 1995, preceded by a mass evacuation of its residents. Jaffna has remained narrowly under government control ever since.

Between 1996 and 2000, the LTTE achieved a series of military victories. Chased out of Jaffna, they regrouped in the east, assuming control of vast sections of Trincomalee and Batticaloa districts as well as the Wanni. In April 1996, they killed more than 1200 soldiers and police in retaking Mullaitivu, and successfully continued their campaign of attacking key civilian targets, including, in January 1996, a bomb at Colombo's Central Bank which killed more than 100 people. In May 1997 the army launched **Operation Sure Victory** which saw almost 30,000 troops attempt to reopen the vital northern highway to Jaffna. The Tigers resisted fiercely, retaking Kilinochchi in September 1998 and forcing the government forces to abandon its programme. By late 1999, the army had been forced back to Vavuniya, while in April 2000 it launched a massive and successful onslaught on the strategic Elephant Pass garrison, located on the isthmus between the Jaffna peninsula and the mainland. This was one of the bloodiest periods of the war, with thousands killed on both sides.

Kumaratunga herself was the target of a suicide bomber in December 1999 whilst on the campaign trail for re-election. She survived, though lost the sight of one eye, and won the election with 62% of the vote. Prior to 2000's parliamentary elections, in August the government presented parliament with a modified constitutional package with far greater autonomy for Tamil majority regions, but it failed to pass parliament. The PA was narrowly re-elected in October, but it was hardly a vote of confidence. Successive attempts to achieve a constitutional and political solution to the confrontation had met with repeated failure, and alienated not just the LTTE but much of the Sinhalese majority.

Ceasefire

With all other options exhausted, Kumaratunga accepted the Norwegian government's proposal to act as a facilitator with the LTTE, even though the LTTE refused to give up its claim to Eelam. The first meeting took place in November 2000 but it was not until the snap elections of December 2001, and the re-election of the UNP under Prime Minister **Ranil Wickremasinghe** that serious strides could be made towards peace. Wickremasinghe had been secretly negotiating with the LTTE for peace whilst in opposition. By now, all sides, as well as public opinion, were exhausted by war, the economy had slowed down, and the government faced bankruptcy. Two earth-shattering events precipitated discussions. The first was the LTTE's overrunning of the massively guarded international airport at Katunayake in July 2001. A crack unit of Tiger commandos destroyed almost half the national airline's fleet, as well as eight military planes and helicopters. It exacerbated economic ruin for the government and was the death-knell for the PA. The second was the events of 11 September 2001, which turned worldwide attention on terrorist groups, leading to the closing down of many of the LTTE's foreign sources of revenue, and greater US support for the government.

After the election of a new government in December 2001 a formal ceasefire agreement was signed in February 2002 between Prime Minister Ranil Wickremasinghe and LTTE leader Vellupillai Prabhakaran, to be monitored by the Norwegian government. This Memorandum of Understanding (MoU) successfully put a stop to hostilities and prompted several rounds of peace talks between September 2002 and March 2003, but the LTTE pulled out of the talks in April 2003 after accusing the government of failing to deliver on its promises. In late 2003, after months of tension, President Chandrika Bandaranaike Kumaratunga dissolved parliament whilst Wickremasinghe was in Washington meeting with George W Bush, and called for an election. Kumaratunga created a coalition government with the **Janatha Vimukthi Peramuna (JVP)** or People's Liberation Front, and **Mahinda Rajapakse** was appointed prime minister. The peace process stalled completely. In 2004 there was trouble within the LTTE and Colonel Karuna, commander in the east, broke away from the movement and took several thousand troops with him. He later renounced terrorism and joined the government as a member of parliament in 2008.

The tsunami

On 26 December 2004 the tsunami struck Sri Lanka, killing thousands, displacing millions and destroying homes and businesses. The economic loss was huge and the damage stood at over US$1 billion. It was hoped this tragedy would finally bring the country together, but instead there were arguments over aid distribution, reconstruction and land ownership. An aid-sharing agreement between the government and the LTTE was ratified in 2005 but the JVP pressured the Supreme Court into suspending it, believing it would establish the LTTE as the de facto government in the north.

Rajapakse comes to power

In August 2005 Lakshman Kadirgamar, Sri Lankan foreign minister, was assassinated by the LTTE at his house in Colombo. The LTTE boycotted the elections and no Tamils living in LTTE-controlled areas were allowed to vote. The reason remains unclear, however some suggest it was to encourage a return to hostilities, Ranil Wickramasinghe, who would traditionally have benefited from the Tamil vote, lost by a narrow margin to Mahinda Rajapakse. Rajapakse invited the Norwegians back and in early 2006 a statement was negotiated that included commitments to a ceasefire and further talks, and it was signed in February. By March, the fighting had begun again in earnest. In April an LTTE suicide bomber killed eight people in the main military compound in Colombo, and in retaliation the military launched air strikes on Tamil Tiger targets in the north, displacing thousands of civilians in the process. There followed months of intense fighting before the rebels were driven from the east; the country had well and truly returned to a state of undeclared civil war. Peace talks in Geneva in October failed. Once it became obvious the peace process was no more, a massive recruitment drive for the armed forces was launched. Personnel numbers almost doubled, and new weapons were purchased from countries including China, Pakistan and Russia. The army also changed tactics and started using a more guerrilla-style of warfare, sending small teams of commandos behind enemy lines.

Official ceasfire ends

After weeks of heavy fighting in 2007, the army took back the LTTE-held town of Vakarai. June saw thousands of non-resident Tamils forced from Colombo due to 'security reasons' before a court ordered an end to the expulsions, and in November SP Thamilselvan, leader of the LTTE's political wing and the Tiger's main point of contact for the outside world, was killed in an air raid.

The government pulled out of the official ceasefire in January 2008, which by this point was meaningless anyway, and concentrated on a military solution to the problem. It pledged to win the war within a year and launched a massive offensive. Bombings, assassinations, disappearances, and heavy fighting in the north continued. The LTTE offered a unilateral ceasefire but this was dismissed by the government. The army captured the LTTE administrative capital of Kilinochchi in January 2009, and failed to heed international calls for a ceasefire as they forced the LTTE back onto a narrow strip of land. Thousands of civilians were trapped in the ever-decreasing war zone as the LTTE abandoned the Jaffna peninsula and retreated to the jungle. Many were used as human shields by the Tigers; children were forced into soldiering, and others were bombed indiscriminately by the army whilst in supposed 'no-fire' zones. It is estimated that more than 40,000 civilians died in the final months of the war, and as many as 118,000 were sheltering in a 14-sq-km no-fire zone towards the end of the fighting. The UN High Commissioner for Human Rights, Navi Pillay, stated around this time that certain actions undertaken by both sides could constitute violations of humanitarian law. The LTTE again offered a ceasefire, but the government could smell victory and the request was declared a joke.

Peace and the search for truth
By May 2009 the LTTE were hemmed in, and they surrendered. Vellupillai Prabhakaran was killed, along with his family and several senior LTTE figures. Later, there were allegations that the government had ordered the execution of captured or surrendering rebels, and that some of the 250,000 Tamil refugees interned in camps after the war suffered rape and torture while they were screened for possible links with the rebels.

Having declared victory, Rajapakse called for an early election in January 2010. He won a landslide victory against former army chief General Sarath Fonseka, who led the final campaign that crushed the LTTE. Soon after the election, Fonseka was put on trial on charges of engaging in politics before leaving the army, and was also court martialled for breaching arms procurement guidelines. Found guilty, he was jailed for three years and stripped of his military rank and parliamentary seat.

Later in the year, MPs passed a constitutional amendment allowing Rajapakse to stand for unlimited terms in office. The prime minister argued this would provide Sri Lanka with much-needed stability; many critics feared the rise of a Rajapakse dictatorship.

After the war ended, the call for an independent investigation into events during the last five months of fighting became too loud to ignore. In December 2010 Tamil campaigners in the UK tried to serve a war crimes arrest warrant on Mahinda Rajapakse whilst he was visiting Britain, adding to official pressure from international sources including the United Nations.

The Sri Lankan government, irritated by continued criticism, established an internal panel of inquiry, the **Lessons Learnt and Reconciliation Commission (LLRC)**, whose report was published in December 2011. The commission found the Sri Lankan armed forces innocent of targeting civilians, while the LTTE was blamed for repeatedly violating humanitarian laws. However, the report's credibility was quickly brought into question by organizations such as Amnesty International and Human Rights Watch, who criticized it on many fronts, most heavily for its lack of independence. The commissioners were appointed by the government and many had held senior positions during the final months of fighting. The government, in return, rejected such criticism as 'flawed' or 'biased'.

A competing report was finally published by the UN in September 2015, finding evidence of war crimes on both sides and calling for a special court of international judges to try accused war criminals. Thus far Sri Lanka has been unwilling to allow international involvement beyond general advice.

The fall of Rajapaksa

The wave of victorious euphoria that swept Mahinda Rajapakse back to power in 2010 swiftly began to dissipate as the president, with increasing brazenness, busily appointed relatives to key ministries and civil service positions, and awarded lucrative contracts to his family and associates. In his final term, Mahinda and his brothers, Basil and Nirupama, between them held the ministries of Defence & Urban Development, Law & Order, Economic Development, Finance & Planning and Ports & Highways – giving them control over an estimated 50-70% of the nation's economy.

Billions of dollars were allegedly smuggled out to accounts in the Seychelles and elsewhere, while vast sums of money were funnelled into building seaport and airport facilities, and an audacious cricket stadium in the Rajapaksas' home town of Hambantota. (At the time of writing the Rajapaksa International Airport handles a grand total of two international flights per day – a handy metaphor for the waste and nepotism of the regime.)

Despite growing public distaste for the Rajapaksa dynasty, Mahinda Rajapaksa's defeat in the January 2015 election by Maithripala Sirisena, his former health minister, was widely considered a surprise. Running on a platform of stamping out and punishing official corruption and working towards reconciliation, Sirisena's victory owed much to the Tamil minority, whose concerns had been roundly ignored under Rajapaksa. In the wake of the election, several members of the Rajapaksa family fled the country to avoid prosecution. Attempts to restore Mahinda to power – this time as prime minister – in a second election in August 2015 came to nothing, but he remains a leading figure in the Sri Lankan opposition.

New beginnings

Peace has brought hope and optimism to Sri Lanka, and yet there remains a lot to be done. The east and north are still struggling to recover from the damage inflicted by the war years and also by the tsunami. People are gradually returning to their homes, but many are still displaced. The military retains control over large areas of land in the north. De-mining work also continues in a few remaining areas. The east of Sri Lanka suffered the worst floods in 50 years in early 2011, which drove thousands from their homes and ruined rice crops leading to food shortages.

Politically, Sri Lanka's dalliance with China under Rajapaksa has been reversed under Sirisena, who has built closer ties with traditional partners including India, the UK and USA. Very real concerns remain about human rights, freedom of speech, and the safety of journalists who criticize the government. Thousands of people who disappeared during and after the war remain unaccounted for, and Sirisena and his successors have much work to do to reconcile the Sinhala and Tamil populations.

Religion

The white stupas of Anuradhapura and the serene stillness of the Buddha's image captured in stone across the island testify to the interweaving of Buddhism with Sinhalese life. Yet Sri Lanka has always been a diverse society. Hinduism has been the dominant religion of Tamils in the north for over 2000 years and of many of the tea plantation workers today. Islam arrived with the Arab traders across the Indian Ocean over a thousand years ago, and the three main colonial powers – the Portuguese, Dutch and British – brought Catholicism and Protestant Christianity to the island from the 17th century onwards. In Colombo these religions all have a visible presence, and Buddhists, Christians and Muslims live peacefully side by side in many parts of the island. Statistically the population is split: Buddhists 69%; Hindus 15%; Christians 7.5%; Muslims 7.5%; others 1%.

Buddhism

In Sri Lanka Buddhism is the most widespread religion of the majority Sinhalese community. Although India was the original home of Buddhism, today it is practised largely on the margins of the sub-continent, and is widely followed in Ladakh, Nepal and Bhutan as well as Sri Lanka.

Buddha's life

Siddharta Gautama, who came to be given the title of the Buddha – the Enlightened One – was born about 563 BC in the Nepal/India foothills of the Himalaya. A prince in a warrior caste, he was married at the age of 16 and his wife had a son. When he reached the age of 29 he left home and wandered as a beggar and ascetic. After about six years he spent some time in Bodh Gaya in the modern Indian state of Bihar. Sitting under the Bo tree, meditating, he was tempted by the demon Mara, with all the desires of the world. Resisting these temptations, he received Enlightenment.

These scenes are common motifs of Buddhist art. The next landmark was the preaching of his first sermon on 'The Foundation of Righteousness' and set in motion the *Dharma Chakra* (Wheel of the Law) in the deer park at Sarnath near Benaras (Varanasi) to his first five disciples. This was followed by other sermons during his travels when he gathered more disciples. The Buddha preached Four Noble Truths: that life is painful; that suffering is caused by ignorance and desire; that beyond the suffering of life there is a state which cannot be described but which he termed nirvana; and that nirvana can be reached by following an eightfold path. The essential elements of the eightfold path are the perfection of wisdom, morality and meditation.

Ananta (his closest disciple) was a cousin. Another cousin, Devdutta, opposed the Buddha and made three attempts to have him killed but failed – a hired assassin was converted, a boulder rolled downhill split in two and finally the wild elephant sent to crush the Buddha underfoot was calmed by his sermon. By the time he died the Buddha had established a small band of monks and nuns known as the *Sangha*, and had followers across North India. The male monks were divided into *sramana* (ascetics), *bhikku* (mendicants), *upasaka* (disciples) and *sravaka* (laymen); the nuns were known as *bhikkuni*.

On the Buddha's death or *parinirvana* (Parinibbana or 'final extinction') at the age of 80, his body was cremated, and the ashes, regarded as precious relics, were divided up among the peoples to whom he had preached. Some have been discovered as far west as Peshawar, in the northwest frontier of Pakistan, and at Piprawa, close to his birthplace.

Sri Lankan Buddhism

The recent history of Sri Lanka's **Theravada** Buddhism may conceal the importance of the cultural and historical links between Sri Lanka and India in the early stages of its development. The first great stupas in Anuradhapura were built when Buddhism was still a religious force to be reckoned with in mainland India, and as some of the sculptures from Sigiriya suggest there were important contacts with Amaravati, another major centre of Buddhist art and thought, up to the 5th century AD.

The origins of Buddhism in Sri Lanka are explained in a legend which tells how King Devanampiya Tissa (died 207 BC) was converted by Mahinda, widely believed to have been Asoka's son, who was sent to Sri Lanka specifically to bring the faith to the Island's people. He established the Mahavihara monastery in Anuradhapura. Successors repeatedly struggled to preserve Sri Lankan Buddhism's distinct identity from that of neighbouring Hinduism and Tantrism. It was also constantly struggling with Mahayana Buddhism, which gained the periodic support of successive royal patrons. King Mahasena (AD 276-303) and his son Sri Meghavarna, who received the famous 'Tooth of the Buddha' when it was brought to the island from Kalinga in the fourth century AD, both advocated Mahayana forms of the faith. Even then Sri Lanka's Buddhism is not strictly orthodox, for the personal character of the Buddha is emphasized, as was the virtue of being a disciple of the Buddha. Maitreya, the 'future' Buddha, is recognized as the only Bodhisattva, and it has been a feature of Buddhism in the island for kings to identify themselves with this incarnation of the Buddha.

The Sinhalese see themselves as guardians of the original Buddhist faith. They believe that the scripture in Pali was first written down by King Vattagamani Abhaya in the first century BC. The Pali Theravada canon of scripture is referred to as *Tipitakam Tripitaka* ('three baskets'), because the palm leaf texts on which they were written were stored in baskets (*pitakas*). They are conduct (*vinaya*), consisting of 227 rules binding on monks and nuns; discourses (*sutta*), the largest and most important, divided into five groups (*niyakas*) of basic doctrine which are believed to be the actual discourses of the Buddha recording his exact words as handed down by word of mouth; and metaphysics (*abhidhamma*) which develop the ideas further both philosophically and psychologically. There are also several works that lack the full authority of the canon but are nonetheless important. Basham suggests that the main propositions of the literature are psychological rather than metaphysical. Suffering, sorrow and dissatisfaction are the nature of ordinary life, and can only be eliminated by giving up desire. In turn, desire is a result of the misplaced belief in the reality of individual existence. In its Theravada form, Hinayana Buddhism taught that there is no soul and ultimately no God. *Nirvana* was a state of rest beyond the universe, once found never lost.

The cosmology

Although the Buddha discouraged the development of cosmologies, the Hinayana Buddhists produced a cyclical view of the universe, evolving through four time periods.

Period 1 Man slowly declines until everything is destroyed except the highest heaven. The good go to this heaven, the remainder to various hells.

Period 2 A quiescent phase.

Period 3 Evolution begins again. However, 'the good *karma* of beings in the highest heaven' now begins to fail, and a lower heaven evolves, a *world of form*. During this period a great being in the higher heaven dies, and is re-born in the world of form as Brahma. Feeling lonely, he wishes that others were with him. Soon other beings from the higher heaven die and are reborn in this world. Brahma interprets these people as his own creation, and himself as The Creator.

Period 4 The first men, who initially had supernatural qualities, deteriorate and become earthbound, and the period fluctuates between advance and deterioration.

The four-period cycles continue for eternity, alternating between 'Buddha cycles' – one of which we live in today – and 'empty cycles'. It is believed that in the present cycle four Buddhas – *Krakucchanda*, *Kanakamuni*, *Kasyapa*, and *Sakyamuni* – have already taught, and one, *Maitreya*, is still to come.

In Sri Lanka the scriptures came to be attributed with almost magical powers. Close ties developed between Buddhist belief and **Sinhalese nationalism**. The Sinhalese scholar *Buddhaghosa* translated Sinhalese texts into Pali in the fifth century AD. At the beginning of the 11th century Sri Lankan missionaries were responsible for the conversion of Thailand, Burma, Cambodia and Laos to Theravada Buddhism. Subsequently, in the face of continued threats to their continued survival, Sri Lanka's Buddhist monks had to be re-ordained into the valid line of Theravada lineage by monks from Southeast Asia. Buddhist links with Thailand remain close.

Buddhist practice

By the time Buddhism was brought to Sri Lanka there was a well developed religious organization which had strong links with secular authorities. Developments in Buddhist thought and belief had made it possible for peasants and lay people to share in the religious beliefs of the faith. As it developed in Sri Lanka the main outlines of practice became clearly defined. The king and the orders of monks became interdependent; a monastic hierarchy was established; most monks were learning and teaching, rather than practising withdrawal from the world. Most important, Buddhism accepted a much wider range of goals for living than simply the release from permanent rebirth.

The most important of these were 'good rebirth', the prevention of misfortune and the increase in good fortune during the present life. These additions to original Buddhist thought led to a number of contradictions and tensions, summarized by Tambiah as: the Buddha as a unique individual, rather than a type of person (*Bodhisattva*) coming into the world periodically to help achieve release from *samsara* (rebirth), or rebirth into a better life; Buddhism as a path to salvation for all, or as a particular, nationalist religion; Buddhism as renunciation of the world and all its obligations, in contrast with playing a positive social role; and finally, whether monasteries should be run by the monks themselves, or with the support and involvement of secular authorities. These tensions are reflected in many aspects of Buddhism in Sri Lanka today, as in debates between monks who argue for political action as against withdrawal from the world.

Sects Until the 16th century Buddhism in Sri Lanka enjoyed the active support of the state. It remained longest in Kandy, but was withdrawn steadily after the British took control in 1815. The 18th-century revival of Buddhism in the Wet Zone was sponsored by the landowning village headmen, not by royalty, and castes such as the *Goyigama* and *Salagama* played a prominent role. Through the 19th century they became the dominant influence on Buddhist thought, while the remaining traditional Buddhist authority in Kandy, the *Siyam Nikaya*, suffered permanent loss of influence.

The *Siyam Nikaya*, one of the three sects of Sri Lankan Buddhism today, originated in the 18th mission of the Kandyan kings to Ayuthya in Thailand (Siam) to revalidate the Buddhist clergy. By a royal order admission to the sect's two branches was restricted to high caste Sinhalese. Today their monks are distinguished by carrying umbrellas and wearing their robe over one shoulder only. The exclusion of lower castes from this sect however bred resentment, and in 1803 a new sect, the *Amarapura Nikaya*, was established to be open to all castes, while in 1835 the third contemporary sect, the *Ramanya Nikaya*, was set up in protest at the supposedly excessive materialism of the other two. Both these sects wear robes which cover both shoulders, but while the *Amarapura* sect carry umbrellas the *Ramanya* carries a traditional shade. Sri Lankan monks wear orange robes and take the vows of celibacy and non-possession of worldly wealth, owning only the very basic necessities including two robes, begging bowl, a razor, needle and thread. They do not eat after midday and spend part of the day in study and meditation. The order of nuns which was introduced in Sri Lanka in the early days was short-lived.

This new, independent Buddhism, became active and militant. It entered into direct competition with Christians in proselytizing, and in setting up schools, special associations and social work. After Independence, political forces converged to encourage State support for Buddhism. The lay leadership pressed the government to protect Buddhists from competition with other religious groups. The Sinhalese political parties saw benefits in emphasizing the role of Buddhism in society.

Buddhist worship

The Buddha himself refuted all ideas of a personal God and of worshipping a deity, but subsequent trends in Buddhism have often found a place for popular worship. Even in the relatively orthodox Theravada Buddhism of Sri Lanka personal devotion and worship are common, focused on key elements of the faith. Temple complexes (*pansalas*) commonly have several features which can serve as foci for individual devotion. Stupas or *dagobas*, which enshrine personal relics of the Buddha, are the most prominent, but Bodhi or Bo trees and images of the Buddha also act as objects of veneration.

Sri Lankan Buddhists place particular emphasis on the sanctity of the relics of the Buddha which are believed to have been brought to the island. The two most important are the sacred Bo tree and the tooth of the Buddha. The Bo tree at Anuradhapura is believed to be a cutting from the Bo tree under which the Buddha himself achieved Enlightenment at Bodh Gaya in modern Bihar. The Emperor Asoka is recorded as having entrusted the cutting to Mahinda's sister Sanghamitta to be carried to Sri Lanka on their mission of taking Buddhism to the island. As the original Bo tree in Bodh Gaya was cut down, this is the only tree in the world believed to come directly from the original tree under which the Buddha sat, and is visited by Buddhists from all over the world. Many other Bo trees in Sri Lanka have been grown from cuttings of the Anuradhapura Bo tree.

The tooth of the Buddha, now enshrined at the Dalada Maligawa in Kandy, was not brought to Sri Lanka until the fourth century AD. The Portuguese reported that they had captured and destroyed the original tooth in their attempt to wipe out all evidence of other religious faiths, but the Sinhalese claimed to have hidden it and allowed a replica to have been stolen. Today pilgrims flock from all over the island, queuing for days on special occasions when special access is granted to the casket holding the tooth in the Dalada Maligawa.

In ordinary daily life many Buddhists will visit temples at least once a week on *poya* days, which correspond with the four quarters of the moon. Full moon day, a national holiday, is a particularly important festival day (see page 19). It is also an opportunity for the worship of non-Buddhist deities who have become a part of popular Buddhist religion. Some have their origins explicitly in Hinduism. The four Guardian Deities seen as future Buddhas, include Natha, Vishnu, Skanda and Saman. **Skanda**, described below, the Hindu god of war, is worshipped as Kataragama, and **Vishnu** is seen as the island's protector. It is not surprising, therefore, to see the Hindu deities in Buddhist temples. Other deities have come from the Mahayana branch of Buddhism, such as **Natha**, or *Maitreya*, the future Buddha. Thus in worship as in many other aspects of daily life, Sinhalese Buddhism shares much in common with Hindu belief and practice with which it has lived side by side for more than 2000 years.

A final feature of Buddhist worship which is held in common with Hindu worship is its individualism. Congregational worship is usually absent, and individuals will normally visit the temple, sometimes soliciting the help of a *bhikku* in making an offering or saying special prayers. One of the chief aims of the Buddhist is to earn merit (*punya karma*), for this is the path to achieving nirvana. Merit can be earned by selfless giving, often of donations in the temple, or by gifts to *bhikkus*, who make regular house calls early in the morning seeking alms. In addition merit can be gained by right living, and especially by propagating the faith both by speech and listening.

Caste system

Some elements of the caste system were probably present in pre-Buddhist Sri Lanka, with both the priestly caste of Brahmins and a range of low caste groups such as scavengers. Although Buddhism encouraged its followers to eradicate distinctions based on caste, the system clearly survived and became a universal feature of social structures among Buddhists and subsequently Christians, despite their beliefs which explicitly condemn such social stratification. However, the complexities and some of the harsh exclusiveness of the caste system as practised in India was modified in Sri Lanka.

Sinhalese Buddhism has no Brahmin or Kshatriya caste, although some groups claim a warrior lineage. The caste enjoying highest social status and the greatest numbers is the Goyigama, a caste of cultivators and landowners who are widely seen as roughly equivalent to the Vellala caste among Jaffna Tamils. The Bandaras and the Radalas comprise a sub-caste of the Goyigamas who for generations have formed a recognizable aristocracy. Among many other castes lower down the social hierarchy come fishermen (*Karavas*), washermen (*Hena*), and toddy tappers (*Durava*).

Some caste groups, such as the **Karava**, have achieved significant changes in their status. Ryan suggests for example that the original Karava community came from South India and converted to Buddhism and began to speak Sinhalese while retaining their fishing livelihoods. Subsequently many converted to Roman Catholicism, located as they were in the heart of the coastal region just north of modern Colombo controlled by the Portuguese. Through their conversion many Karavas received privileges reserved by the Portuguese for Christians, enabling them to climb up the social ladder. Thus today, unlike the fishing communities of Tamil Nadu who remain among the lowest castes, the Karava are now among Sri Lanka's upper caste communities.

Hinduism

Hinduism in northern Sri Lanka was brought over by successive Tamil kings and their followers. It has always been easier to define Hinduism by what it is not than by what it is. Indeed, the name Hinduism was given by foreigners to the peoples of the sub-continent who did not profess the other major faiths, such as Muslims, Christians or Buddhists. The beliefs and practices of modern Hinduism began to take shape in the centuries on either side of the birth of Christ. But while some aspects of modern Hinduism can be traced back more than 2000 years before that, other features are recent. Hinduism has undergone major changes both in belief and practice. Such changes came from outside as well as from within. As early as sixth century BC the Buddhists and Jains had tried to reform the religion of Vedism (or Brahmanism) which had been dominant in some parts of South Asia for 500 years.

Modern Hinduism

A number of ideas run like a thread through intellectual and popular Hinduism, some being shared with Buddhism. Some Hindu scholars and philosophers talk of Hinduism as one religious and cultural tradition, in which the enormous variety of belief and practice can ultimately be interpreted as interwoven in a common view of the world. Yet there is no Hindu organization, like a church, with the authority to define belief or establish official practice. Although the Vedas are still regarded as sacred by most Hindus, virtually no modern Hindu either shares the beliefs of the Vedic writers or their practices, such as sacrifice, which died out 1500 years ago. Not all Hindu groups believe in a single supreme God. In view of these characteristics, many authorities argue that it is misleading to think of Hinduism as a religion at all.

Be that as it may, the evidence of the living importance of Hinduism is visible among Hindu communities in Sri Lanka as well as in India. Hindu philosophy and practice has also touched many of those who belong to other religious traditions, particularly in terms of social institutions such as caste.

Hindu beliefs

For many Hindus there are four major human goals: material prosperity (*artha*), the satisfaction of desires (*kama*), and performing the duties laid down according to your position in life (*dharma*). Beyond those is the goal of achieving liberation from the endless cycle of rebirths into which everyone is locked (*moksha*). It is to the search for liberation that the major schools of Indian philosophy have devoted most attention. Together with *dharma*, it is basic to Hindu thought.

Dharma (dhamma to Buddhists) represents the order inherent in human life. It is essentially secular rather than religious, for it doesn't depend on any revelation or command of God but rather has 10 'embodiments': good name, truth, self-control, cleanness of mind and body, simplicity, endurance, resoluteness of character, giving and sharing, austerities and continence. In *dharmic* thinking these are inseparable from five patterns of behaviour: non-violence, an attitude of equality, peace and tranquillity, lack of aggression and cruelty, and absence of envy.

According to *karma*, every person, animal or god has a being or self which has existed without beginning. Every action, except those that are done without any consideration of the results, leaves an indelible mark on that self. This is carried forward into the next life, and the overall character of the imprint on each person's 'self' determines three features of the next life. It controls the nature of his next birth (animal, human or god) and the kind of family he will be born into if human. It determines the length of the next life. Finally, it controls the good or bad experiences that the self will experience. However, it does not imply a fatalistic belief that the nature of action in this life is unimportant. Rather, it suggests that the path followed by the individual in the present life is vital to the nature of its next life, and ultimately to the chance of gaining release from this world.

The belief in the transmigration of souls (*samsara*) in a never-ending cycle of rebirth has been Hinduism's most distinctive and important contribution to the culture of India and Sri Lanka. The earliest reference to the belief is found in one of the Upanishads, around the seventh century BC, at about the same time as the doctrine of karma made its first appearance. By the late Upanishads it was universally accepted, and in Buddhism there is never any questioning of the belief.

AL Basham pointed out that belief in transmigration must have encouraged a further distinctive doctrine, that of non-violence or non-injury – *ahimsa*. Buddhism campaigned particularly vigorously against the then-existing practice of animal sacrifice. The belief in rebirth meant that all living things and creatures of the spirit – people, devils, gods, animals, even worms – possessed the same essential soul.

Hindu philosophy

It is common now to talk of six major schools of Hindu philosophy. The best known are yoga and Vedanta. Yoga is concerned with systems of meditation that can lead ultimately to release from the cycle of rebirth. It can be traced back as a system of thought to at least the third century AD. It is just one part of the wider system known as Vedanta, literally the final parts of the Vedantic literature, the *Upanishads*. The basic texts also include the *Brahmasutra of Badrayana*, written about the first century AD, and the most important of all, the *Bhagavadgita*, which is a part of the epic the *Mahabharata*.

Hindu worship

Some Hindus believe in one all-powerful God who created all the lesser gods and the universe. The Hindu gods include many whose origins lie in the Vedic deities of the early Aryans. These were often associated with the **forces of nature**, and Hindus have always revered many natural objects. Mountain tops, trees, rocks and above all rivers, are regarded as sites of special religious significance. They all have their own guardian spirits. You can see the signs of the continuing lively belief in these gods and demons wherever you travel. Thus trees for example are often painted with vertical red and white stripes and will have a small shrine at their base. Occasionally branches of trees will have numerous pieces of thread or strips of coloured cloth tied to them – placed there by devotees with the prayer for fulfilment of a favour. Hilltops will frequently have a shrine of some kind at the highest point, dedicated to a particularly powerful god. Pilgrimage to some important Hindu shrines is often undertaken by Buddhists as well as Hindus.

For most Hindus today worship (often referred to as 'performing **puja**') is an integral part of their faith. The great majority of Hindu homes will have a shrine to one of the gods of the Hindu pantheon. Individuals and families will often visit shrines or temples, and on special occasions will travel long distances to particularly holy places such as Kataragama. Acts of devotion are often aimed at the granting of favours and the meeting of urgent needs for this life – good health, finding a suitable wife or husband, the birth of a son, prosperity and good fortune. In this respect the popular devotion of simple pilgrims of all faiths in South Asia is remarkably similar when they visit shrines, whether Hindu, Buddhist or Jain temples, the tombs of Muslim saints or even churches. Performing *puja* involves making an offering to God, and darshan – having a view of the deity. Although there are devotional movements among Hindus in which singing and praying is practised in groups, Hindu worship is generally an act performed by individuals. Thus Hindu temples may be little more than a shrine in the middle of the street, housing an image of the deity which will be tended by a priest and visited at special times when a darshan of the resident God can be obtained. When it has been consecrated, the image, if exactly made, becomes the channel for the godhead to work.

The **image** of the deity may be in one of many forms. Temples may be dedicated to Vishnu or Shiva, for example, or to any one of their other representations. The image of the deity becomes the object of worship and the centre of the temple's rituals. These often follow through the cycle of day and night, as well as yearly life cycles. The priests may wake the deity from sleep, bathe, clothe and feed it. Worshippers will be invited to share in this process by bringing offerings of clothes and food. Gifts of money will usually be made, and in some temples there is a charge levied for taking up positions in front of the deity in order to obtain a darshan at the appropriate times.

Hindu sects

Today three Gods are widely seen as all-powerful: **Brahma**, **Vishnu** and **Shiva**. Their functions and character are not readily separated. While Brahma is regarded as the ultimate source of creation, Shiva also has a creative role alongside his function as destroyer. Vishnu in contrast is seen as the preserver or protector of the universe. There are very few images and sculptures of Brahma, but Vishnu and Shiva are far more widely represented and have come to be seen as the most powerful and important. Their followers are referred to as Vaishnavite and Saivites respectively, the majority in Sri Lanka today being Saivites.

Caste

One of the defining characteristics of South Asian societies, caste has helped to shape the social life of most religious communities in South Asia. Although the word caste (meaning 'unmixed' or 'pure') was given by the Portuguese in the 15th century AD, the main features of the system emerged at the end of the Vedic period. In Sri Lanka the Tamils of Jaffna have a modified form of the caste social structure typical of neighbouring Tamil Nadu. Brahmins occupy the same priestly position that they hold in India, and have also played an important role in education. Beneath them in ritual hierarchy but occupying a dominant social and political position, until recent times at least, were the cultivating and landlord caste known as the *vellalas*. Below them in rank was a range of low and outcaste groups, filling such occupations as washermen, sweepers and barbers, such as the Pallas and Nallavas. The tea plantation workers are all regarded as low caste.

Virtually all Hindu temples in Sri Lanka were destroyed by the Portuguese and the Dutch. Those that have been rebuilt never had the resources available to compare with those in India. However, they play a prominent part in Hindu life. De Silva suggests that Arumuga Navalar's failure to argue for social reform meant that caste – and untouchability – were virtually untouched. The high caste Vellalas, a small minority of the total Hindu population, maintained their power unchallenged until after Independence. Removal of caste disabilities started in the 1950s. The civil war over the demand for a separate Tamil state, Tamil Eelam, during which the Liberation Tigers of Tamil Eelam (LTTE) took complete control of social and political life in Jaffna and the north, may have changed the whole basis of caste far more thoroughly than any programme of social reform.

Islam

Islam was brought to Sri Lanka by Arab traders. Long before the followers of the Prophet Mohammad spread the new religion of Islam, Arabs had been trading across the Indian Ocean with southwest India, the Maldives, Sri Lanka and South East Asia. When the Arab world became Muslim the newly converted Arab traders brought Islam with them, and existing communities of Arab origin adopted the new faith. However, numbers were also swelled by conversion from both Buddhists and Hindus, and by immigrant Muslims from South India who fled the Portuguese along the west coast of India. The great majority of the present Muslim population of Sri Lanka is Tamil speaking, although there are also Muslims of Malay origin. Both in Kandy and the coastal districts Muslims have generally lived side by side with Buddhists, often sharing common interests against the colonial powers. However, one of the means by which Muslims maintained their identity was to refuse to be drawn into colonial education. As a result, by the end of the 19th century the Muslims were among the least educated groups. A Muslim lawyer, Siddi Lebbe, helped to change attitudes and encourage participation by Muslims.

In 1915 there were major Sinhalese-Muslim riots, and Muslims began a period of active collaboration with the British, joining other minorities led by the Tamils in the search for security and protection of their rights against the Sinhalese. The Muslims have been particularly anxious to maintain Muslim family law, and to gain concessions on education. One of the chief of these is the teaching of Arabic in government schools to Muslim children. Until 1974 Muslims were unique among minorities in having the right to choose which of three languages – Sinhala, Tamil or English – would be their medium of instruction. Since then a new category of Muslim schools has been set up, allowing them to distance themselves from the Tamil Hindu community, whose language most of them speak.

Muslim beliefs

The beliefs of Islam (which means 'submission to God') could apparently scarcely be more different from those of Buddhism or Hinduism. Islam has a fundamental creed; 'There is no God but God; and Mohammad is the Prophet of God' (*La Illaha illa 'Ilah*

Mohammad Rasulu 'llah). One book, the Qur'an, is the supreme authority on Islamic teaching and faith. Islam preaches the belief in bodily resurrection after death, and in the reality of heaven and hell.

The idea of heaven as paradise is pre-Islamic. Alexander the Great is believed to have introduced the word paradise into Greek from Persia, where he used it to describe the walled Persian gardens that were found even three centuries before the birth of Christ. For Muslims, paradise is believed to be filled with sensuous delights and pleasures, while hell is a place of eternal terror and torture, which is the certain fate of all who deny the unity of God.

Islam has no priesthood. The authority of Imams derives from social custom, and from their authority to interpret the scriptures, rather than from a defined status within the Islamic community. Islam also prohibits any distinction on the basis of race or colour, and there is a strong antipathy to the representation of the human figure. It is often thought, inaccurately, that this ban stems from the Qur'an itself. In fact it probably has its origins in the belief of Mohammad that images were likely to be turned into idols.

Muslim sects

During the first century of its existence Islam split in two sects which were divided on political and religious grounds, the Shi'is and Sunnis. The religious basis for the division lay in the interpretation of verses in the Qur'an and of traditional sayings of Mohammad, the *Hadis*. Both sects venerate the Qur'an but have different *Hadis*. They also have different views as to Mohammad's successor.

The **Sunnis** – always the majority in South Asia – believe that Mohammad did not appoint a successor, and that Abu Bak'r, Omar and Othman were the first three caliphs (or vice-regents) after Mohammad's death. Ali, whom the Sunni's count as the fourth Caliph, is regarded as the first legitimate Caliph by the Shi'is, who consider Abu Bak'r and Omar to be usurpers. While the Sunni's believe in the principle of election of caliphs, **Shi'is** believe that although Mohammad is the last prophet there is a continuing need for intermediaries between God and man. Such intermediaries are termed Imams, and they base both their law and religious practice on the teaching of the Imams.

From the Mughal Emperors in India, who enjoyed an unparalleled degree of political power, down to the poorest fishermen in Sri Lanka, Muslims in South Asia have found different ways of adjusting to their Hindu or Buddhist environment. Some have reacted by accepting or even incorporating features of Hindu belief and practice in their own. Akbar, the most eclectic of Mughal emperors, went as far as banning activities like cow slaughter which were offensive to Hindus and celebrating Hindu festivals in court.

Muslim year

The first day of the Muslim calendar is AD 16 July 622. This was the date of the prophet's migration from Mecca to Medina, the Hijra, from which the date's name is taken (AH = Anno Hijrae). The Muslim year is divided into 12 lunar months, alternating between 29 and 30 days. The first month of the year is *Moharram*, followed by *Safar, Rabi-ul-Awwal, Rabi-ul-Sani, Jumada-ul-Awwal, Jumada-ul-Sani, Rajab, Shaban, Ramadan, Shawwal, Ziquad* and *Zilhaj*.

Christianity

Christianity was introduced by the Portuguese. Unlike India, where Christian missionary work from the late 18th century was often carried out in spite of colonial government rather than with its active support, in Sri Lanka missionary activity enjoyed various forms of state backing. One Sinhalese king, Dharmapala, was converted, endowing the church, and even some high caste families became Christian. When the Dutch evicted the Portuguese they tried to suppress Roman Catholicism, and the Dutch Reformed Church found some converts. Other Protestant denominations followed the arrival of the British, though not always with official support or encouragement. Many of the churches remained dependent on outside support. Between the two World Wars Christian influence in government was radically reduced. Denominational schools lost their protection and special status, and since the 1960s have had to come to terms with a completely different role in Sri Lanka.

Christian worship

Although Christians are encouraged to worship individually as well as together, most forms of Christian worship centre on the gathering of the church congregation for praise, prayer the preaching of God's word, which usually takes verses from the Bible as its starting point. Although Christian services may be held daily in some churches most Christian congregations in Sri Lanka meet for worship on Sunday, and services are held in Sinhala and Tamil as well as in English. They are open to all.

Thanks to the Portuguese, today Roman Catholics account for 90% of the island's Christians. The Dutch brought with them their Dutch Reformed faith and left a number of churches, and subsequently during British colonial period the Anglican Church (Church of England) also became established, and several Protestant missionary denominations including Baptist and Methodist, established small churches. The reunification of the Protestant Christian churches which has taken significant steps since 1947 has progressed faster in South Asia than in most other parts of the world.

Culture

Art and architecture

Sri Lankan architecture has many elements in common with Buddhist and Hindu Indian traditions, but the long period of relative isolation, and the determined preservation of Buddhism long after its demise in India, have contributed to some very distinctive features.

Buddhist architecture

Buddhist and Hindu architecture probably began with wooden building, for the rock carving and cave excavated temples show clear evidence of copying styles which must have been developed first in wooden buildings. The third and second century BC caves of the Buddhists were followed in the seventh and eighth centuries AD by free standing but rock-cut temples.

Stupas Stupas were the most striking feature of Buddhist architecture in India. Originally they were funeral mounds, built to house the remains of the Buddha and his disciples. The tradition of building stupas was developed by Sri Lanka's Sinhalese kings, notably in the golden age of the fourth and fifth centuries AD, and the revival during the 11th and 12th centuries. In Sri Lanka, a stupa is often referred to as 'dagoba' (from Sanskrit *dhatu* – relic, *garbha* – womb chamber) and sometimes named 'saya' (from *cetiya* – funeral mound) or 'wehera' (from *vihara* – monastery). Some of the stupas (*dagobas*) are huge structures, and even those such as the fourth century *Jetavana* at Anuradhapura, now simply a grassed-over brick mound, is impressively large.

Few of the older Buddhist monuments are in their original form, either having become ruins or been renovated. Hemispherical mounds built of brick and filled with brick and rubble, they stand on a square terrace, surmounted by three concentric platforms. In its original or its restored form, the brick mound is covered with plaster and painted white. Surrounding it on a low platform (*vahalakadas*) is the ambulatory, or circular path, reached from the cardinal directions by stone stairways. Around some of the *dagobas* there are fine sculptures on these circular paths at the head of each stairway.

The design is filled with symbolic meaning. The hemisphere is the dome of heaven, the axis of the cosmos being represented by the central finial on top, while the umbrella-like tiers are the rising heavens of the gods. Worshippers walk round the stupa on the raised platform in a clockwise direction (*pradakshina*), following the rotational movement of the celestial bodies.

Many smaller stupas were built within circular buildings. These were covered with a metal and timber roof resting on concentric rows of stone pillars. Today the roofs have disappeared, but examples such as the Vatadage at Polonnaruwa can still be seen. King Parakramabahu I also built another feature of Sri Lankan architecture at Polonnaruwa, a large rectangular hall in which was placed an image of the Buddha. Most of Sri Lanka's early secular architecture has disappeared. Made of wood, there are remnants of magnificent royal palaces at both Anuradhapura and Sigiriya.

Moonstones Sri Lanka's moonstones (not the gem) are among the world's finest artistic achievements. Polished semi-circular granite, they are carved in concentric semi-circular rings ('half-moons', about 1 m in radius) portraying various animals, flowers and birds, and normally placed at the foot of flights of steps or entrances to important buildings. There are particularly fine examples in Anuradhapura and Polonnaruwa.

The moonstones of pure Buddhist art at Anuradhapura comprise a series of rings and are often interpreted in the following way. You step over the flames of fire, through which one must pass to be purified. The next ring shows animals which represent the four stages of life: 1 Elephant – birth; 2 Horse – old age; 3 Lion – illness; 4 Bull – death and decay. These continue in an endless cycle symbolizing the continuous rebirths to which one is subject. The third row represents the twisting serpent of lust and desire, while the fourth is that of geese carrying lotus buds, representing purity. The lotus in the centre is a symbol of nirvana.

The steps have on either side beautifully carved **guard stones** with *makaras* designed to incorporate features from eight symbolically significant creatures: the foot of the lion, the crocodile's mouth and teeth, an elephant's tusk, the body of a fish, the peacock's feather, the serpent inside the mouth and the monkey's eyes.

Hindu architecture

Hindu temple building The principles of religious building were laid down in the *Sastras*, sets of rules compiled by priests. Every aspect of Hindu and Buddhist religious building is identified with conceptions of the structure of the universe. This applies as much to the process of building – the timing of which must be undertaken at astrologically propitious times – as to the formal layout of the buildings. The cardinal directions of north, south, east and west are the basic fix on which buildings are planned. The east-west axis is nearly always a fundamental building axis.

Hindu temples were nearly always built to a clear and universal design, which had built into it philosophical understandings of the universe. This cosmology, of an infinite number of universes, isolated from each other in space, proceeds by imagining various possibilities as to its nature. Its centre is seen as dominated by **Mount Meru** which keeps earth and heaven apart. The concept of separation is crucial to Hindu thought and social practice. Continents, rivers and oceans occupy concentric rings around the mountain, while the stars encircle the mountain in another plane. Humans live on the continent of **Jambudvipa**, characterized by the rose apple tree (*jambu*).

The *Sastras* show plans of this continent, organized in concentric rings and entered at the cardinal points. This type of diagram was known as a **mandala**. Such a geometric scheme could then be subdivided into almost limitless small compartments, each of which could be designated as having special properties or be devoted to a particular deity. The centre of the mandala would be the seat of the major god. Mandalas provided the ground rules for the building of stupas and temples across India, and provided the key to the symbolic meaning attached to every aspect of religious buildings.

Temple design Hindu temples developed characteristic plans and elevations. The focal point of the temple lay in its sanctuary, the home of the presiding deity, known as the womb-chamber (*garbhagriha*). A series of doorways, in large temples leading through a succession of buildings, allowed the worshipper to move towards the final encounter with the deity himself and to obtain *darshan* – a sight of the god. Both Buddhist and

BACKGROUND
Grand designs

Geoffrey Bawa (1919-2003) was Sri Lanka's best known, most prolific and most influential architect. Amongst his many projects Bawa was the creative visionary behind some of the country's most spectacular hotels, from the austerity of the 1-km- long camouflaged jungle palace of Kandalama near Dambulla, to the colonial-influenced Lighthouse at Galle. He also constructed Sri Lanka's first purpose-built tourist complex, the Bentota Beach in 1968.

Bawa's work blends traditional Sri Lankan architecture and use of materials with modern ideas of composition and space. Hallmarks include a careful balance and blurring of the boundaries between inside and outside, the creation of vistas, courtyards and walkways that offer a range of perspectives, and an acute sensitivity to setting and environment. His work builds on Sri Lanka's past, absorbing ideas from the west and east, while creating something innovative and definably Sri Lankan.

Bawa went to England in 1938, where he studied English at Cambridge and took up the law. It was not until 1957, at the age of 38, that he qualified as an architect. On his return to Ceylon, he gathered together a group of talented young artists who shared his interest in the island's forgotten architectural heritage, including batik artist Ena de Silva and designer Barbara Sansoni. The architectural practice he established set new standards in design over the next 20 years for all styles of buildings, from the residential and commercial to the religious and the educational.

Bawa's fame was sealed in 1979 when he was invited by President Jayawardene to design the new parliament building in Kotte. The result, which required the dredging of a swamp to create an artificial lake and island, itself symbolizing the great irrigation of the ancient period, was a series of terraces with copper domed roofs rising from the water, with references to monastic architecture, Kandyan temples and South Indian palace architecture, all within a Modernist framework. Other high-profile buildings include the Ruhuna University near Matara, dramatically arranged on two rocky hills overlooking the ocean.

In 1998 he suffered a massive stroke but continued to instruct his colleagues from his bed with a nod of assent or shake of the head. Official recognition came in 2001 when he was awarded the prestigious Chairman's Award for Lifetime Achievements by the Aga Khan.

Hindu worship encourages the worshipper to walk clockwise around the shrine, performing *pradakshina*.

The elevations are designed to be symbolic representations of the home of the gods, the tallest towers rising above the *garbagriha* itself, symbolizing the meeting of earth and heaven in the person of the enshrined deity. In both, the basic structure is usually richly embellished with sculpture. When first built this would usually have been plastered and painted, and often covered in gems. In contrast to the extraordinary profusion of colour and life on the outside, the interior is dark and cramped. Here is the true centre of power.

Hindu architecture on the island bears close resemblances with the Dravida styles of neighbouring Tamil Nadu. Although all the important Hindu temples in Sri Lanka were destroyed by the Portuguese, the style in which they have been re-built continues to reflect those southern Indian traditions.

Tamil Nadu has been at the heart of southern Indian religious development for 2000 years. Temple building was a comparatively late development in Hindu worship. Long before the first temple was built shrines were dotted across the land, the focus of **pilgrimage**, each with its own mythology. Even the most majestic of South Indian temples have basic features in common with these original shrines, and many of them have simply grown by a process of accretion around a shrine which may have been in that spot for centuries. The **myths** that grew around the shrines were expressed first by word of mouth. Most temples today still have versions of the stories which were held to justify their existence in the eyes of pilgrims. There are several basic features in common. David Shulman has written that the story will include 'the (usually miraculous) discovery of the site and the adventures of those important exemplars (such as gods, demons, serpents, and men) who were freed from sorrow of one kind or another by worshipping there'. The shrine which is the object of the story nearly always claims to be supreme, better than all others. Many stories illustrate these claims of superiority: for example, we are often told that the **Goddess Ganga** herself is forced to worship in a South Indian shrine in order to become free of the sins deposited by evil-doers who bathe in the river at Benares. Through all its great diversity Hindu temple architecture repeatedly expresses these beliefs, shared though not necessarily expressed, by the thousands of Sri Lankan Hindus who make visiting temples such a vital and living part of their life.

Today the most striking external features of Hindu temples in Sri Lanka are their elaborately carved towering gateways (*gopurams*). These were first introduced by the **Pandiyas** in the 10th century, who succeeded the Cholas a century later. The *gopuram* took its name from the 'cow gate' of the Vedic village, which later became the city gate and finally the monumental temple entrance. This type of tower has an oblong plan at the top which is an elongated vaulted roof with gable ends. It has sloping sides, usually 65°, so that the section at the top is about half the size of the base. Although the first two storeys are usually built solidly of stone masonry, the rest is of lighter material.

By the 15th century the Vijayanagar kings established their empire across much of South India. Their temples were built on an unprecedented scale, with huge *gopurams* studding the outside walls. None of the Sri Lankan temples were built on a scale anywhere near that of the 16th- and 17th-century Vijayanagar temples of South India. Furthermore, all Hindu temples were destroyed by the Portuguese during the period in which Vijayanagar architecture was flourishing across the Palk Straits. Thus contemporary Hindu temples in Sri Lanka, while retaining some of the elements common to Hindu temples in Tamil Nadu, are always on a much smaller scale.

Sculpture and painting

Early Sri Lankan sculpture shows close links with Indian Buddhist sculpture. The first images of the Buddha, some of which are still in Anuradhapura, are similar to second and third century AD images from Amaravati in modern Andhra Pradesh. The middle period of the fifth to 11th centuries AD contains some magnificent sculptures on rocks, but there is a range of other sculpture, notably moonstones. There are decorated bands of flower motifs, geese and a variety of animals, both Anuradhapura and Polonnaruwa having outstanding examples. While the moonstones are brilliant works in miniature, Sri Lankan sculptors also produced outstanding colossal works, such as the 13-m-high Buddha at Aukana, now dated as from the ninth century, or the 13th-century reclining Buddha at Polonnaruwa.

Sri Lanka's most famous art is its rock paintings from Sigiriya, dating from the sixth century AD. Polonnaruwa saw a later flowering of the painting tradition in the 12th and 13th centuries. The wall paintings of Dambulla are also noteworthy (although many of the original paintings were covered by later ones), but thereafter classical Sri Lankan art declined though the folk tradition of scroll painting carried on. The mid-18th century saw a new revival of painting in the Kandyan kingdom, this time based on folk art which were inspired by traditional tales instead of religious themes.

Language and literature

Sinhala

Sinhala (or Sinhalese), the language of the Sinhalese, is an Indo-European language with North Indian affinities, unlike the Dravidian language, Tamil. Brought by the North Indian migrants, possibly in the fifth century BC, the language can be traced from inscriptions dating from the second century BC onwards which show how it had developed away from the original Sanskrit. The spoken language had changed several vowel sounds and absorbed words from the indigenous races and also from Tamil. Sinhala language had acquired a distinct identity by the beginning of the first century.

Although at first glance the **script** might suggest a link with the South Indian scripts, it developed independently. The rounded form was dictated by the use of a sharp stylus to inscribe on palm-leaf which would later be filled in with 'ink' instead of the North Indian technique of writing on bark.

The early verse and later prose **literature** were religious (Buddhist) and apart from inscriptions, date from the 10th century although there is evidence of some existing 300 years earlier. Non-religious texts only gained prominence in the last century.

Tamil

Like Sinhala, Tamil is also one of South Asia's oldest languages, but belongs to the Dravidian language family. It originated on the Indian mainland, and although Sri Lankan Tamil has retained some expressions which have a 'pure', even slightly archaic touch to them, it remains essentially an identical language both in speech and writing to that found in Tamil Nadu.

The first Tamil literature dates from approximately the second century AD. At that time a poets' academy known as the **Sangam** was established in Madurai. The poetry was devoted to religious subjects. From the beginning of the Christian era a development began to take place in Tamil religious thought and writing. Krishna became transformed from a remote and heroic figure of the epics into the focus of a new and passionate devotional worship – *bhakti*. From the seventh to the 10th century there was a surge of writing new hymns of praise, sometimes referred to as 'the Tamil *Veda*'. Attention focused on the 'marvels of Krishna's birth and infancy and his heroic and amorous exploits as a youth among the cowherds and cowherdesses of Gokula'. In the ninth century Vaishnavite Brahmans produced the *Bhagavata Purana*, which, through frequent translation into all India's major languages, became the vehicle for the new worship of Krishna. Its tenth book has been called 'one of the truly great books of Hinduism'. These influences were transmitted directly into Hindu Tamil culture in Sri Lanka, which retained intimate ties with the southern Tamil region.

Land &
environment

Geography

Sri Lanka is practically on the equator so there is little difference between the length of night and day, both being about 12 hours. The sun rises around 0600 and it is completely dark by 1900.

Only 100 million years ago Sri Lanka was still attached to the great land mass of what geologists call 'Pangaea', of which South Africa, Antarctica and the Indian Peninsula were a part. Indeed, Sri Lanka is a continuation of the Indian Peninsula, from which it was separated less than 10,000 years when sea level rose to create the 10-m-deep and 35-km-wide **Palk Straits**. It is 432 km long and at its broadest 224 km wide. Its 1600 km of coastline is lined with fine sandy beaches, coral reefs and lagoons.

Climate

Sri Lanka's location, just north of the equator, places it on the main track of the two monsoons which dominate South Asia's weather systems.

Nearly three quarters of Sri Lanka lies in what is widely known as the '**Dry Zone**', comprising the northern half and the whole of the east of the country. Extensively forested and with an average annual rainfall of between 1200-1800 mm, much of the region does not seem unduly dry, but like much of southeast India, virtually all of the region's rain falls between October and January.

The '**Wet Zone**' (the mountains and the southwestern part of the country) also receives some rain during this period, although the coastal regions of the southwest are in the rain shadow of the Central Highlands, and are much drier than the northeast between November and January. The southwest corner of Sri Lanka has its main wet season from May to October, when the southwest monsoon sweeps across the Arabian Sea like a massive wall of warm moist air, often over 10,000 m thick. The higher slopes of the Central Highlands receive as much as 4000 mm during this period, while even the coastal lowlands receive over 500 mm.

Wildlife

For one small island Sri Lanka packs an enormous variety of wildlife. This is largely because in that small space there is a wide range in altitude. The Central Highlands rise to over 2500 m with damp evergreen forests, cool uplands and high rainfall. Within 100 km there are the dry coastal plain and sandy beaches. The climatic division of the island into the larger, dry, mainly northern and eastern region, and the smaller, wet, southwestern section is of importance to observers of wildlife. In the Dry Zone remnants of evergreen and deciduous forests are interspersed with cultivation, and in the east of this region the

Mahaweli Ganga

By far the largest of the 103 river basins in Sri Lanka is that of the Mahaweli Ganga, which covers nearly one fifth of the island's total area. The river itself has a winding course, rising about 50 km south of Kandy and flowing north then northeast to the sea near Trincomalee, covering a distance of 320 km. It is the only perennial river to cross the Dry Zone. Its name is a reference to the Ganga of North India, and in Sri Lanka all perennial rivers are called *ganga*, while seasonal streams are called *oya* (Sinhalese) or *aru* (Tamil). A number of the rivers have been developed both for irrigation and power, the Victoria project on the Mahaweli Ganga being one of the biggest in Asia – and one of the most controversial. It has created island's largest lake, the Victoria Reservoir.

The short rivers of Sri Lanka's Wet Zone sometimes have severe floods, and the Kelani, which ultimately reaches the sea at Colombo, has had four catastrophic floods in the last century. Others can also be turbulent during the wet season, tumbling through steamy forests and cultivated fields on their short courses to the sea.

savannah grasslands are dominated by the metre high grass, *Imperata cylindrica*, widely regarded as a scourge. The whole vegetation complex differs sharply from both the Central Highlands and the Wet Zone of the southwest. These different areas support very different species. Many species occur only in one particular zone, but there are some, often the ones associated with man, which are found throughout.

Mammals

The **Asiatic elephant** (*Elephas maximus*) has a sizeable population, some wild which can be seen in several of the national parks. The animals come down to the water in the evening, either in family groups or herds of 20 or so. The 'Marsh Elephants', an interesting, significantly larger sub-species, are found in the marshy basin of the Mahaweli River. Wild elephants increasingly come into contact with humans in the growing settlements along their traditional migration routes between the northwest and southeast of the island and so the Wildlife Conservation Department is attempting to protect migration corridors from development.

The solid looking **Asiatic wild buffalo** (*Bubalus bubalis*), with a black coat and wide-spreading curved horns, stands about 170 cm at the shoulder. When domesticated, it is known as the water buffalo.

The **leopard or panther** (*Panthera pardus*), the only big cat in Sri Lanka, is found both in the dry lowland areas and in the forested hills. Being shy and elusive, it is rarely seen. The greyish **fishing cat** (*Felis viverrina*), with dark spots and dashes with somewhat webbed feet, search for prey in marshes and on the edge of streams.

The **sloth bear** (*Melursus ursinus*), about 75 cm at the shoulder, can be seen in areas of scrub and rock. It has an unkempt shaggy coat and is the only bear of the island.

The deer on the island are widespread. The commonest, the **chital (or spotted) deer** (*Axis axis*), only about 90 cm tall, is seen in herds of 20 or so in grassy areas. The bright rufous coat spotted with white is unmistakable. The stags carry antlers with three tines. The magnificent **sambar** (*Cervus unicolor*) (150 cm tall) with its shaggy coat varying from brownish grey to almost black in older stags, is seen in wooded hillsides. The stags carry large three-tined antlers and have a mane-like thickening of the coat around the neck. The **muntjac or barking deer** (*Muntiacus muntjak*) is small and shy (60 cm at the shoulder). It is brown with darker legs with white underparts and chest. The **stag** carries a small pair of antlers. Usually found in pairs, their staccato bark is heard more often than they are seen.

The **wild pig** (*Sus scrofa*) is easily identified by its affinity to the domestic pig. It has a mainly black body sparsely covered with hair except for a thick line along the spine; the young are striped. Only the male (boar) bears tusks. Commonly seen in grass and light bush, near water, it can do great damage to crops.

The interesting **purple-faced langur** (*Presbytis senex*) is only found in Sri Lanka. A long-tailed, long-legged monkey about 125 cm in length, nearly half of it tail, it has a dark coat contrasting with an almost white head. Hair on the head grows long to form swept back whiskers, but the face itself is almost black. Usually seen in groups of a dozen or so, it lives mainly in the dense, damp mountain forests but is also found in open woodland.

Apart from animals that still live truly in the wild, others have adapted to village and town life and are often seen near temples. The most widespread of the monkeys is the **grey langur** (*Presbytis entellus*), another long-tailed monkey with a black face, hands and feet. The **tocque macaque** (*Macaca sinica*), 60 cm, is a much more solid looking animal with shorter limbs. It varies in colour from grey to brown or even reddish brown above, with much paler limbs and underparts. The pale, sometimes reddish, face has whorls of hair on the cheeks. On top of the head the hair grows flat and cap-like, from a distinct parting!

Look out for the **flying fox** (*Pteropus giganteus*) which has a wingspan of 120 cm. These are actually fruit-eating bats, found throughout, except in the driest areas. They roost in large, sometimes huge, noisy colonies in tree tops, often in the middle of towns or villages, where they look like folded umbrellas hanging from the trees. In the evening they can be seen leaving the roost with slow measured wing beats.

The **ruddy mongoose** (*Herpestes ismithii*) is usually found in scrub and open jungle. The **brown mongoose** (*Herpestes fuscus*) can also be seen in gardens and fields. The mongoose is well known as a killer of snakes, but it will also take rats, mice, chickens and bird's eggs.

Birds

Sri Lanka is also an ornithologist's paradise with over 250 resident species, mostly found in the Wet Zone, including the Sri Lanka myna, Sri Lanka whistling thrush, yellow-eared bulbul, red-faced malkoha and brown-capped babbler. The winter migrants come from distant Siberia and western Europe, the reservoirs attracting vast numbers of water birds such as stilts, sandpipers, terns and plover, as well as herons, egrets and storks. The forests attract species of warblers, thrushes, cuckoo and many others. The endemic **jungle fowl** (*Gallus lafayetti*) is Sri Lanka's national bird. It is common to see large ornaments topped by a brass jungle fowl which has an honoured place in the home on special occasions. The recently reopened **Kumana** sanctuary in the southeast, and **Bundala** (famed for flamingoes) and **Kalametiya** sanctuaries between Tissamaharama and Hambantota in the south, both with lagoons, are the principal bird sanctuaries.

Reptiles

Two species of crocodile are found in Sri Lanka. The rather docile **mugger (or marsh) crocodile** (*Crocodilus palustrus*), 3-4 m in length, lives in freshwater rivers and tanks in many parts of the island. The **estuarine (or saltwater) crocodile** (*Crocodilus porosus*) prefers the brackish waters of the larger rivers where it can grow to 7 m. Among the lizards, the large water **monitor** (*Varanus*), up to 2 m long, greyish brown with black and yellow markings, is found in a variety of habitats. They have become quite widespread and tame and can even be seen scavenging in the rubbish dumps and market places. The land monitor lacks the yellow markings.

Seashore and marine life

Among the living coral swim a bewildering variety of colourful fish. There are shoals of silvery **sardinella** and stately, colourful **angelfish** (*Pomacanthus*) often with noticeable mouths in a different colour. Butterfly fish (*Chaetodontidae*) are similar to small angelfish but their fins are rounded at the end. The **surgeon fish** (*Acanthuridae*) get their name from the sharp blades at the base of their tails. Rounded in outline, with compressed bodies and pouting lips, they are often very brightly coloured (eg 17-cm **blue surgeon**). Striped like a zebra, the **scorpion fish** (*Pteriois*) is seen among live coral, and sometimes trapped in pools of the dead reef by the retreating tide. Although it has poisonous dorsal spines it will not attack if you leave it alone.

Corals are living organisms and consist of two basic types: the typical hard coral (eg Staghorn) and the less familiar soft corals which anchor themselves to the hard coral – one form looks like the greyish pink sea anemone. The commonest shells are the **cowries** which you can find on the beach. The **ringed cowrie** (*Cypraea annulus*) has a pretty grey and pinkish white shell with a golden ring, while the **money cowrie** which was once used as currency in Africa, varies from greenish grey to pink, according to its age. The big and beautiful **tiger cowrie** (*Cypraea tigris*) (up to 8 cm), has a very shiny shell marked like a leopard. The spectacular **spider conch** (*Lambis*) and the common **murex** (*Chicoreus*) can grow 15-20 cm. **Sea urchins** (*Echinoidea*), fairly common on sandy beaches and dead coral, are extremely painful to tread on, so be sure to wear shoes when beach combing.

Of the seven species of marine turtle in the world, five return to lay their eggs on Sri Lankan beaches but all are on the endangered list. One of the rarer species is the giant **leather-back turtle** (*Dermochelys coriacea*) which grows to 2 m in length, has a ridged leathery skin on its back instead of a shell. The smaller **olive ridley turtle** (*Lepidochelys olivacea*) has the typical rows of shields along the shell. The Turtle Conservation Project is carrying out a very worthwhile programme near Tangalla on the south coast, see page 126.

Books

Current affairs and politics

Grant, T *Sri Lanka's Secrets: How the Rajapaksa Regime Gets Away With Murder (2014)* Monash University. This heartfelt, Australian-authored account of the recent plight of Sri Lanka's Tamil population pulls few punches, and paints a dark picture of corruption, violence and vindictiveness.

McGowan, W *Only man is vile: The Tragedy of Sri Lanka (1983)* Picador. An account of the background to the 1983 Tamil-Sinhalese conflict.

Subramaniam, S *This Divided Island: Stories from the Sri Lankan War (2014)* Penguin Superbly readable account of the author's journey through Sri Lanka after the war, which forensically picks apart the causes and consequences of violence.

Sundarji, PR *Sri Lanka: The New Country (2015)* Harper Collins. Interesting vignettes of post-war Sri Lanka, written by a former Der Spiegel correspondent whose sympathies seem to lie (a rarity) with the Rajapaksa regime.

Weiss, G *The Cage: The fight for Sri Lanka and the Last Days of the Tamil Tigers (2011)* Bodley Head. Written by a journalist and former UN official, looks at the last days of the war including the plight of the humanitarian aid workers and the media.

History

Deraniyagala, SU *The Prehistory of Sri Lanka (1992)* Colombo: Department of Archaeological Survey of Sri Lanka, 2 Vols. An erudite and detailed account of the current state of research into pre-historic Sri Lanka, available in Colombo and at the Anuradhapura Museum.

de Silva, KM *A History of Sri Lanka (2005)* London: OUP. Arguably the most authoritative historical account of Sri Lanka.

Knox, Robert *An Historical Relation of Ceylon (1981)* Dehiwala: Tisara Prakasayo. Fascinating 17th-century account of the experiences of a British seaman imprisoned by a Kandyan king for 20 years.

Literature

Gunesekhara, Romesh *Monkfish Moon (1998)* Penguin. Evocative collection of short stories of an island paradise haunted by violent undercurrents; *Reef (1994)*. The story of a young boy growing up in modern Sri Lanka; *Heaven's Edge (2003)* Bloomsbury. College graduate returns to a (thinly disguised) Sri Lanka to connect with his dead father's memory; and *Noontide Toll*, a collection of stories of war, the tsunami, and those who have returned to Sri Lanka looking for their roots, as seen through the eyes of a van driver.

Ondaatje, Michael Novels featuring Sri Lanka include the amusing auto- biographical, *Running in the family (1983)* Penguin, and *Anil's Ghost (2000)* Picador. Winner of the Irish Book Prize, a young forensic anthropologist returns to Sri Lanka to investigate the 'disappearances' of the late 80s, rich and evocative.

Selvadurai, Shyam *Funny Boy (1995)* Vintage. A Tamil boy comes to terms with his homosexuality and racism in 1980s Colombo. *Cinnamon Gardens (2000)* Anchor Books. A young school teacher is caught between her own and her parents' desires for her future.

Tearne, R *Mosquito (new edition 2010)* HarperPress. A love story between an English writer and a Sri Lankan woman. Sri Lanka is vividly and beautifully captured in the text.

Woolf, L *The Village in the Jungle (new edition 2005)* Eland. 1st published in 1913 and translated into both Tamil and Sinhalese, this is a classic novel of colonial Ceylon.

Practicalities

Getting there

Air

All international flights arrive at **Bandaranaike International Airport** in Katunayake, 30 km north of Colombo. International airlines flying to Sri Lanka include: **Aeroflot, Cathay Pacific, El Al, Emirates, Gulf Air, Indian Airlines, Korean Airlines, Kuwait Airways, Lufthansa, Malaysia Airlines, Oman Air, Qatar Airways, Royal Jordanian, Saudi Arabian, Singapore Airlines** and **Thai International. Sri Lankan Airlines** ① *www.srilankan.com*, the national carrier, flies to over 20 countries, and has offices all over the world. A source of great national pride, it compares favourably with the best of the Southeast Asia airlines for comfort and service.

November to March is high season with Christmas, New Year and Easter the most expensive times to visit. The lowest prices are often during May and June when it's monsoon season in the south. Check the likes of www.skyscanner.com, www.kayak.com and www.momondo.com for the best fares for your dates. However, be aware that the very cheapest fares are usually offered by agencies who have a reputation for using bait-and-switch tactics: you may book and pay for your bargain flight, only to be informed a few hours later that the date, time or price has suddenly changed. Pursuing a flight change through these operators, or worse still a refund, is notoriously expensive and futile. It can be worth paying the extra to deal directly with the airline.

A number of charter companies offer package tours, operating mainly from Central Europe (Germany, Italy, etc). These can work out cheaper than scheduled flight fares, but may have limitations. They are not available to Sri Lankan nationals and usually must include accommodation. You can also arrange a stop-over in Sri Lanka on a Round the World and other long-distance tickets.

From the UK and Ireland
Sri Lankan Airlines ① *T033-0808 0800, www.srilankan.com*, flies daily from London to Colombo, though it is usually cheaper to fly via the Middle East with one of the Gulf carriers; **Gulf Air, Emirates, Etihad, Oman Air** and **Qatar Airways** all offer reasonable connections. Another option is to go via Mumbai with **Jet Airways**.

From the USA and Canada
From the east coast, you can choose the conventional route to South Asia via London, or if you're not afraid of a 13-hour flight, go via the Gulf. From the west coast, the most convenient routes to Colombo are via Hong Kong, Singapore or Thailand using one of those countries' national carriers.

From Australasia via the Far East
There are no direct flights to Colombo from Australia or New Zealand. but **Cathay Pacific, Malaysian Airlines, Singapore Airlines** and **Thai** are the main linking airlines and offer the best deals. **Sri Lankan** also flies to the major Southeast Asian regional capitals.

Packing for Sri Lanka

Travel light. Most essentials are available in the cities; items are cheap and laundry services generally speedy. Take light cotton clothes – it is a good idea to have some very lightweight long sleeve cotton tops and trousers in pale colours for evenings, as they also give some protection against mosquitoes. It can be cool at night in the Central Highlands and some warm clothing is essential. Dress is usually informal, though one or two clubs and hotels expect guests to be formally dressed at evening meals. In Colombo short-sleeved shirts and ties are often worn for business. For travelling, loose clothes are most comfortable. Trainers or canvas shoes are good options for protecting feet against cuts and so on. Women should dress modestly. Even on the beach, very revealing swimwear attracts unnecessary attention. Remember the adage, take twice as much money and half the clothes you think you will need.

Items you might find particularly useful include: toiletries, including barrier contraceptives and tampons (available in the larger towns but you may prefer to take your own supply); personal medicines and inhalers and a copy of a prescription; international driving licence; photocopies of essential documents (flight information, passport identification and visa pages) or email yourself this information; spare passport photographs (in case you want to extend your visa); student (ISIC) card which can be used for discounts on some site entrance fees; hat and sunglasses; insect repellent; high-factor sun protection cream; Swiss army knife; torch; wet wipes and/or hand sanitizer; zip-lock bags; contact lens cleaning solutions (available in the larger towns and cities but it is best to bring your own).

Budget travellers may also want to take the following: sheet sleeping bag (for when the sheets are less than clean); earplugs; eyeshades; padlock (for room and baggage); soap; string (or washing line); towel; washbasin plug; a spork (useful for eating lunch packets with when you don't feel like plunging your filthy fingers into the rice). Mosquito mats/coils are readily available in Sri Lanka but take your own mosquito net (these are standard in all but the very cheapest hotels but many have holes or are filthy).

From South Asia

Sri Lanka is well connected to India, especially the southern cities. Between **Sri Lankan**, **Jet Airways** and **Air India** you can reach major cities including Bengaluru (Bangalore), Chennai, Delhi, Kochi, Mumbai, Thiruvananthapuram and Tiruchirappalli, while no-frills airline **Spicejet** offers a cheap hop to Madurai. **Sri Lankan** and **Maldivian** also serve Male in the Maldives.

Airport information *www.airport.lk.*

Disembarkation Cards are handed out to passengers during the inward flight. Complete parts 1 and 2 and hand them in at the immigration counter on arrival along with your passport.

Bandaranaike International Airport is, for practical purposes, Sri Lanka's only international airport (the **Rajapaksa International Airport** in Hambantota having so far proven to be a white elephant). Though modest in size it has modern facilities, including duty free shops (with a large selection of electrical goods). Major banks are represented by branches in the Arrivals hall, offering a good rate of exchange, and there are ATMs which accept most cards. You'll also find desks of all the major mobile phone operators, who offer traveller-targeted SIM packs at a price only

Tip...
Many flights arrive in Sri Lanka in the small hours. If you are going to arrive late, it is best to book a hotel or guesthouse in Negombo for the first night (and arrange in advance to be picked up from the airport) and move to Colombo or another beach resort the following day.

slightly higher than you'll pay in the city; if you plan to get connected it can be less hassle to do it here on arrival rather than through a shop. The tourist information counter has limited information but it is worth picking up copies of *Travel Lanka* and the *Sri Lanka Tourist Board Accommodation Guide*.

There is a pre-paid taxi stand and several hotel and tour company booths just after the Arrivals hall (see page 73). Outside, porters will offer (though not with any great insistence) to transport your luggage for a fee; the trolleys are free. There are several hotels and guesthouses within a few kilometres of the airport (see page 63), and a wider choice of accommodation at Negombo, 6 km away (see page 83). Taxis operate 24 hours, though public transport does not.

On departure, give yourself enough time to pass through security. Travellers are not allowed into the terminal building before their luggage has been x-rayed and their documents have been scrutinized.

Sea

At the time of writing no passenger ferries were operating between Sri Lanka and India, though the countries have been trying to resume services on the Tuticorin–Colombo route for years. With the completion of the railway line to Mannar, the much shorter crossing from Talaimannar to Rameswaram may also reopen – though this is contingent on major rebuilding works on both sides.

Cruise ships occasionally stop at Colombo, and you may be able to get a berth on a cargo or container ship from ports in the Gulf region or Southeast Asia, but it is impossible to book trips in advance. Sailors in their own vessels may be able to berth in Galle, although immigration formalities should be carried out in Colombo. Check with your nearest Sri Lankan representative in advance.

Getting around

Public transport in Sri Lanka is very cheap and, in the case of buses, island-wide. Due to overcrowding on buses, the train is a marginally more comfortable alternative, although the network is limited and there are often delays. The majority of travellers hire a car – whether self-drive or with a chauffeur – for at least part of their stay, especially if they are only here for a short time.

Air

Not many people bother taking internal flights in Sri Lanka, but if you need to cover a long distance quickly they can be worth considering.

Sri Lankan Airlines ① *T077-777 1979, www.srilankan.com*, flies an air taxi service using Cessna seaplanes. Scheduled flights to Batticaloa, Dickwella, Kandy, Koggala, Sigiriya and Trincomalee leave from a separate domestic terminal at Colombo Bandaranaike Airport, with charters available to other destinations. **Cinnamon Air** ① *T011-247 5475, www.cinnamonair.com*, runs a similar service to the same list of destinations, plus Bentota. **Helitours** ① *T011-314 4944, www.helitours.lk*, a commercial wing of the Air Force, runs scheduled flights from Colombo's Ratmalana airport to Palaly (for Jaffna) via Trincomalee. Those visitors with money to burn can charter planes or helicopters to take them to their destination.

Road

The main roads in Sri Lanka are generally well maintained but traffic often moves very slowly, especially in Colombo and its surrounds. The country has invested heavily in improving its roads, and there are now 'carpeted' roads throughout the country; work has recently been completed on roads along the east coast, to Mannar Island, and to Jaffna. In Colombo, the new airport expressway has made access to the city much more efficient, and work continues to extend the fast Colombo–Matara Expressway.

Bus

Government-run CTB buses are the cheapest, slowest and most uncomfortable of the options as they are always very crowded. Private buses follow the same routes, offer a higher degree of comfort (if you can get a seat) and cost a little more.

Private intercity buses are often air-conditioned minibuses (sometimes coaches on popular routes). They cost about double the fare of ordinary buses, but they are quicker and you are guaranteed a seat since they operate on a 'leave when full' basis. They can be quite cramped, especially if you have a lot of luggage (if your bag takes up a whole seat you will probably have to pay for it), but on the whole they are the best option for travelling quickly between the main towns. They are generally non-stop but will let you off on request en route (ask the conductor in advance), although you will still have to pay the full fare to the end destination. If

> **Tip...**
> In general it is best to board buses at the main bus stand in order to get a seat. Once out on the road it is normally standing room only.

you do want to get off en route it is best to sit near the door since the aisle is used by passengers on fold-away seats. The fare is usually displayed on the front or side window.

Car hire

Many people choose to travel by car for at least part of their trip. A car gives you much greater flexibility when touring, allowing you to visit places along the way without having to find somewhere to store your luggage, and gives you the chance to see some places which are hard to access any other way. On the downside, car travel is much the most expensive way of getting around, and it cuts out some of the interaction with local people which can be one of the most rewarding aspects of travel by public transport.

Car and driver The vast majority of visitors hire a car with a local driver, either as part of a package through an international travel agency, or on the ground with a local agency or a private driver in Sri Lanka. (You can do it through your hotel too, but most charge a very hefty mark-up.) In most large towns you can find someone willing to provide you with a car for between US$55-75 per day with unlimited kilometres; check whether the quoted rate includes driver meals and, if you're travelling for more than a day, accommodation. Most large hotels offer free driver accommodation and will provide a meal for them, but guesthouses and hotels off the beaten track often do not – in these instances you should agree in advance who will pay for the driver's accommodation.

Before setting off, you should agree some ground rules, as there are a number of potential pitfalls. First and foremost, check that the driver is content for you to pick the route and accommodation. Many hotels, restaurants and gift shops reward drivers with tasty commissions for delivering them fresh customers, and these are rarely the best options in town. In general it's best not to depend on your driver for an unbiased recommendation. It is also worth checking that the driver will stop for photographs; that his allowance will cover parking fees at sites; and, if you plan a long trip, that he is prepared to spend the time away from home. Finally, note that a driver who speaks Tamil can be a huge asset if you're travelling in the north and east, where neither English nor Sinhala will get you far.

Self drive There are several self-drive car hire firms based in Colombo including some linked to international firms. You have to be 25 to 65 years old and have an International Driving Permit (contact your local Automobile Association), which you must convert to a Sri Lankan driving permit through the Automobile Association of Sri Lanka. To get this 'recognition permit', which is issued up to the expiry date of your International Driving Permit, call at the **Automobile Association of Sri Lanka** ① *3rd floor, 40 Sir MM Markar Mawatha, Galle Face, Colombo 3, T011-242 1528, Mon-Fri 0800-1630*. It's a simple process, and costs Rs 1000. Some hire firms (eg **Avis**) will arrange this for you in advance.

Hire charges vary according to make and mileage and can be very high for luxury models. For a self-drive car from a large rental agency, expect to pay around US$60 per day for a mid-size car (Toyota Corolla or similar), up to $70 per day for a larger car. As well as the international brands, check out **Shineway** ① *T071-278 9323, www.rentalcarsrilanka.com*.

Road rules The rule of 'might is right' applies in Sri Lanka, and the standard of driving can be appalling. Many foreign visitors find the road conditions difficult, unfamiliar and sometimes dangerous. Most visitors hire a driver for a good reason: driving yourself requires you to be on constant watch for the unexpected. Many Sri Lankan drivers take seemingly unbelievable risks, notably overtaking at inopportune times when approaching a blind bend. In the absence

Tip...
Hitchhiking is rare in Sri Lanka, partly because public transport is so cheap.

of pavements, pedestrians often walk along in the middle of the road, and cattle and dogs roam at will. Never overtake a vehicle in front of you which indicates to the right. It usually means that it is unsafe for you to overtake and rarely means that they are about to turn right. Flashing headlights mean 'get out of the way, I'm not stopping'. In these circumstances it is best to give the oncoming vehicle space, since they usually approach at great speed. Roundabouts are generally a free-for-all, so take your chance cautiously. Horns are used as a matter of course, but most importantly when overtaking, to warn the driver being overtaken.

Cycling

Cycling is very worthwhile in Sri Lanka as it gives you the opportunity to see authentic village life well off the beaten track. Foreign cyclists are usually greeted with cheers, waves and smiles. It is worth taking your own bike (contact your airline well in advance), or mountain bikes can be hired from various adventure tour companies around the island. Bicycles can be transported on trains, though you will need to arrive two hours ahead at Colombo Fort station. While cycling is fun on country byways, hazardous driving means that you should avoid the major highways (especially the Colombo–Galle road) as far as possible. Cycling after dark can be dangerous because of the lack of street lighting and poor road surfaces. Take bungee cords (to strap down a backpack), spare parts and good lights from home, and take care not to leave your bike parked anywhere unattended. Repair shops are widespread and charges are nominal. Always carry plenty of water.

Local bikes tend to be heavy and often without gears but on the flat they offer a good way of exploring short distances outside towns. Many people choose to hire one to explore ancient city areas such as Polonnaruwa and Anuradhapura. Expect to pay Rs 200-300 per day for cycle hire from hotels and guesthouses, depending on the standard of hotel and condition of the bike. See also Cycling, page 22.

Motorcycling

Motorcycles are popular locally and are convenient for visiting different beaches and also for longer distance sightseeing. Repairs are usually easy to arrange and quite cheap. Motorcycle hire is possible for around €14/US$16 per day (unlimited mileage) in some beach resorts (eg Hikkaduwa, Mirissa) or in towns nearby. You will generally need to leave a deposit or your passport. Check all bikes thoroughly for safety. If you have an accident you will usually be expected to pay for the damage. Potholes and speed-breakers add to the problems of a fast rider.

Taxi

Taxis have yellow tops with red numbers on white plates, and are available in most towns. Negotiate the price for long journeys beforehand. **Radio cabs** operate in Colombo, and though they're slightly more expensive than a meter cab with higher minimum charges, they are generally very reliable, convenient, air-conditioned, and some accept credit cards. They run 24 hours from the airport, Colombo and Kandy. The car usually arrives within 10–15 minutes of phoning (give exact location). **Kangaroo Cabs** ⓘ *T011-258 8588, www.2588588.com*, offers good value and reliable airport pick-ups

In tourist resorts, taxis are often Toyota vans which can carry up to 10 people. Ask at your hotel/guesthouse for an estimate of the fare to a particular destination, but prepare to bargain to reach this. Agree on the fare before getting in.

Three-wheeler

Three-wheeled motorized tricycles, the Indian auto-rickshaws made by Bajaj, move quickly through traffic but compare poorly against taxis for price. Sri Lanka's three-wheeler drivers are always keen to procure business, and you will be beeped constantly by those looking for a passenger. An alarming 40% lack licences, and the driving is frequently of the kamikaze variety, but they are often the only option available. Three-wheelers in Colombo are metered (although plenty of drivers will swear blind their meter is out of order; you can simply wave them away and flag down the next one). Elsewhere you'll have to negotiate a price before starting – the going rate varies between around Rs 25 and Rs 50 per km. You can offer about 60% of the asking price, though it is unlikely that you will get to pay the same rate as locals.

Train

Although the network is limited, there are train services to a number of major destinations. Journeys are comparatively short and very cheap by Western standards. Train journeys are leisurely and an ideal way to see the countryside and meet the people without experiencing the downside of a congested bus journey through dusty crowded roads. You should be aware of touts on major train routes (especially Colombo to Kandy and Galle). Third-class has hard seats; second has some thin cushioning; first class is fairly comfortable. Many slow trains may have second- and third-class coaches only, with first-class only available on some express trains. The time of the next train in each direction is usually chalked onto a blackboard. There are three principal lines:

Northern Line Fully reopened in 2015, the Northern Line runs from Colombo via Anuradhapura, Vavuniya and Jaffna to Kankesanturai on the northern coast of Sri Lanka. Several important lines branch off the Northern Line. The Batticaloa line branches off at Maho Junction, travelling northeast to Gal Oya where it splits again: for Trincomalee to the north, and Batticaloa via Polonnaruwa to the east. North of Anuradhapura, the Mannar Island line branches off at Medawachchiya, with trains running all the way to Talaimannar Pier.

Main Line This most scenic railway line runs east from Colombo Fort to Kandy (with a branch line to Matale), climbing through spectacular scenery after Rambukkana. The line splits at Peradeniya, just outside Kandy: some trains continue to the terminus in the centre of Kandy, while most continue on to Badulla through the hills, stopping at Nanu Oya (for Nuwara Eliya), Hatton (for Adam's Peak), Ohiya (for the Horton Plains) and Ella. This is a wonderful way of travelling to the hill country, though it's a good idea to book well in advance (up to 10 days).

Colombo–Matara Line Running south, this line connects all the popular coastal resorts, following the coast to Galle and as far as Matara. Serving the southern suburbs of Colombo, trains on this line can be crowded in the rush hour, but it's worth riding at any time of day for a look at what must be one of the world's most scenic commutes: right along the coast, with the breaking waves almost within arm's reach.

Other useful lines include the **Puttalam Line**, which runs north from Colombo Fort to Puttalam via Katunayake (for the airport), Negombo and Chilaw, and the **Kelani Valley Line**, which goes from Maradana to Avissawella.

Intercity trains

There are air-conditioned intercity trains running to Kandy and Vavuniya (via Anuradhapura), which should be booked in advance. Kandy train also has a first-class observation car, which must be booked well in advance as it is very popular (for information on reserving these whilst in Colombo, see page 75). You will need to specify your return date at the time of booking the outward journey, as tickets are not open-ended.

There are also some special through trains, such as a weekly service from Matara all the way to Anuradhapura, and another from Matara to Kandy, both via Colombo. Extra services are put on during festivals and holidays, eg from January for four months to Hatton (for the Adam's Peak pilgrimage season); April holiday season to the hills; in May and June for full moon days to Buddhist sites such as Kandy, Anuradhapura, Mihintale; and July/August for **Kandy Perahera**.

Maps

The Survey Department's *Road Map of Sri Lanka* (scale 1:500,000), available at Survey Department branches in large towns, as well as some shops, including Odel in Colombo, is useful and generally up to date, though recent changes and upgrades to roads may not yet have made it to print. It has some street maps for larger towns. For more detail the department's four large sheet maps covering the island (scale 1:250,000) are the best on offer. These may not be available to buy for security reasons, but you can ask to consult them at the Survey Department's Map Sales Branch in Colombo. *Sri Lanka Tourist Board* branches both in Sri Lanka and abroad give out a 1:800,000 Sri Lanka itinerary map plus several city and site guides with sketch maps free, but these are not particularly clear.

There are a number of user-friendly fold-out sheet maps produced abroad. These are mainly 1:500,000 scale and show tourist sights. Some have town street maps and some tourist information. The **Reise** *Know How* map is probably the most detailed, while **Insight** and **Berndtson & Berndtson** maps are both nicely laminated; **Periplus**'s has some tourist information and clear street maps of Colombo, Kandy, Anuradhapura, Galle, Negombo, Nuwara Eliya and Polonnaruwa; **Nelles Verlag** also has some city insets.

TRAVEL TIP
Local customs

Greeting

'Ayubowan' (may you have long life) is the traditional welcome greeting among the Sinhalese, said with the hands folded upwards in front of the chest. You should respond with the same gesture. The same gesture accompanies the word 'vanakkam' among Tamils.

Conduct

Cleanliness and modesty are appreciated even in informal situations. Nudity and topless bathing are prohibited and heavy fines can be imposed. Displays of intimacy are not considered suitable in public and will probably draw unwanted attention. Women in rural areas do not normally shake hands with men as this form of contact is not traditionally acceptable between acquaintances. Use your right hand for giving, taking, eating or shaking hands as the left is considered to be unclean.

Visiting religious sites

Visitors to Buddhist and Hindu temples are welcome, though the shrines of Hindu temples are sometimes closed to non-Hindus. Visitors should be dressed decently in skirts or long trousers – shorts and swimwear are not suitable. Shoes should be left at the entrance and heads should be uncovered. In some Hindu temples, especially in the north, men will be expected to remove their shirts.

Do not attempt to shake hands with Buddhist *bhikkus* (monks). See also Photography, below. Monks are not permitted to touch money, so donations should be put in temple offering boxes. Monks renounce all material possessions and so live on offerings. Visitors may offer flowers at the feet of the Buddha.

Mosques may be closed to non-Muslims shortly before prayers. In mosques women should be covered from head to ankle.

Photography

Do not attempt to be photographed with Buddhist *bhikkus* (monks) or to pose for photos with statues of the Buddha or other deities behind you (turning your back on the deity is considered the height of disrespect). Photography is prohibited in certain sections of the sacred sites as well as in sensitive areas such as airports, dams and military areas.

Essentials A-Z

Accident and emergency

Emergencies T119/118. **Police** T011-243 3333; **Tourist Police** T011-242 1052; **Fire and ambulance** T110.

Children

Children of all ages are widely welcomed and greeted with warmth, which is often extended to those accompanying them. Many hotels and guesthouses have triple rooms, at little or no extra cost to the price of a double, or you can ask for an extra bed. The biggest hotels provide babysitting facilities.

Health

Care should be taken when travelling to remote areas where health services are primitive, since children can become seriously ill more rapidly than adults. Extra care must be taken to protect children from the strong sun by using high factor sun cream, hats, umbrellas, etc, and by avoiding being out in the hottest part of the day. Cool showers or baths help if children get too hot. Dehydration may be counteracted with plenty of drinking water (bottled, boiled furiously for 5 mins or purified with tablets). Preparations such as 'Dioralyte' may be given if the child suffers from diarrhoea. Moisturizer, zinc and castor oil (for sore bottoms due to change of diet) are worth taking. Keep children away from stray animals which may carry parasites or rabies; monkeys too can be aggressive. To help young children to take anti-malarial tablets, one suggestion is to crush them between spoons and mix with a teaspoon of dessert chocolate (for cake-making) bought in a tube. Note that wet wipes and disposable nappies are not readily available in many areas.

Food

In the big hotels there is no difficulty obtaining safe baby foods. For older children, tourist restaurants will usually have a non-spicy alternative to Sri Lankan curries. Grilled or fried fish or chicken is a good standby, often served with boiled vegetables, as are eggs. Fruit is magnificent but should be peeled first. Toast and jam or hoppers (with bananas) are usually served for breakfast. Fizzy drinks are widely available, although king coconut is a healthier and cheaper alternative. Bottled water is available everywhere.

Transport

Buses are often overcrowded and are probably worth avoiding with children. Train travel is generally better (under 12s travel half-price, under 3s free) but hiring a car hire is by far the most comfortable and flexible option; see page 407.

Customs and duty free

On arrival visitors to Sri Lanka are officially required to declare all currency, valuable equipment, jewellery and gems, even though this is rarely checked. All personal effects should be taken back on departure. Visitors are not allowed to bring in goods in commercial quantities, or prohibited/restricted goods such as dangerous drugs, weapons, explosive devices or gold. Drug trafficking or possession carries the death penalty, although this is very rarely carried out on foreigners.

In addition to completing Part II of the Immigration Landing Card, a tourist may

Tip...

If transiting through another country after leaving Sri Lanka, check beforehand that any duty free alcohol you purchase will be allowed into the country or on to your next flight; if you not you may find yourself in India or the Middle East pouring it down a sink in front of customs officials.

be asked by the Customs Officer to complete a Baggage Declaration Form.

Duty free

You are allowed 1.5 litres of spirits, 2 bottles of wine, 200 cigarettes, 50 cigars or 250 g rolling tobacco, a small quantity of perfume and 250 ml of eau de toilette. You can also import a small quantity of travel souvenirs not exceeding US$250 in value. For more information visit Sri Lanka Customs, www.customs.gov.lk.

Export restrictions

The following are not permitted to be exported from Sri Lanka: all currencies in excess of that declared on arrival; any gems, jewellery or valuable items not declared on arrival or not purchased in Sri Lanka out of declared funds; gold (crude, bullion or coins); firearms, explosives or dangerous weapons; antiques, statues, treasures, old books, etc (antiques are considered to be any article over 50 years old); animals, birds, reptiles or their parts (dead or alive); tea, rubber or coconut plants; mahogany or ebony; dangerous drugs.

Import of all the items listed above and in addition, Indian and Pakistani currency, obscene and seditious literature or pictures is prohibited.

Disabled travellers

Specific provision for the disabled traveller is practically non-existent in Sri Lanka,

and gaining access to buildings, toilets, pavements and public transport can prove frustrating. You should be prepared to pay for mid-price hotels or guesthouses, private car hire and taxis, and you are strongly advised to travel with an able-bodied companion who can scout around and arrange help; that said, it is usually easy to find people to lend a hand with lifting and carrying.

Some travel companies now specialize in exciting holidays, tailor-made for individuals depending on their level of disability. **Global Access – Disabled Travel Network Site**, www.globalaccessnews.com, is dedicated to providing information for 'disabled adventurers' and includes a number of reviews and tips from members of the public. For one disabled traveller's account of travel through Sri Lanka, see www.chairbounder.com. You might also want to read *Nothing Ventured* edited by Alison Walsh (Harper Collins), which gives personal accounts of world-wide journeys by disabled travellers, plus advice and listings.

Organizations in Sri Lanka include **Sri Lanka Federation of the Visually Handicapped (SLFVH)**, 74 Church St, Col 2, Colombo, T011-243 7758, www.slfvh.org.

Drugs

Penalties for the possession, use, or trafficking of illegal drugs in Sri Lanka are strict, and convicted offenders may expect jail sentences and heavy fines.

Embassies and consulates

For all Sri Lankan embassies abroad and all foreign embassies and consulates in Sri Lanka. see http://embassy.goabroad.com.

In Kandy, the **Assistant High Commissioner of India**, 31 Rajapihilla Mawatha, T081 222 4563, www.ahci kandy.org, Mon-Fri 0830-1030, will issue Indian visas in a day.

Gay and lesbian travellers

Homosexuality between men remains technically illegal in Sri Lanka, even in private, and may lead to a prison sentence of up to 12 years. The situation does seem to be relaxing but it's wise to be discreet to avoid the attentions of over-zealous and homophobic police officers.

Campaigning gay group **Companions on a Journey**, 46/50 Robert E Gunawardena Maw, Col 6, T011-485 1535, has a drop-in centre and arranges events.

The internet is a good source of information: www.utopia-asia.com/tipssri.htm, though prehistoric-looking by today's internet standards, is a useful community-updated site listing gay- and lesbian-friendly accommodation and tour operators. Another resource is **Equal Ground**, T011-567 9766, www.equal-ground.org, which regularly holds activities for lesbian and bisexual women. Travellers are welcome to call for information about activities in the gay community.

Health

Local populations in Sri Lanka are exposed to a range of health risks not encountered in the Western world. Many of the diseases are major problems for the local poor and destitute and, although the risk to travellers is more remote, they cannot be ignored. Obviously 5-star travel is going to carry less risk than backpacking on a budget.

Before you go

See your GP or travel clinic at least 6 weeks before departure for general advice on travel risks and vaccinations. Try phoning a specialist travel clinic if your own doctor is unfamiliar with health conditions in Colombia. Make sure you have sufficient medical travel insurance, get a dental check, know your own blood group and if you suffer a long-term condition, such as diabetes or epilepsy, obtain a Medic Alert bracelet/necklace (www.medicalert.co.uk). If you wear glasses or contact lenses, take a copy of your prescription.

Vaccinations

Confirm that your primary courses and boosters are up to date. If you need vaccinations, see your doctor well in advance of your travel. Most courses must be completed by a minimum of 4 weeks. Travel clinics may provide rapid courses of vaccination, but are likely to be more expensive.

The following vaccinations are recommended: typhoid, polio, tetanus, infectious hepatitis and diptheria. For details of malaria prevention, see page 416. The following vaccinations should also be considered: rabies, possibly BCG (since TB is still common in the region) and in some cases meningitis and diphtheria (if you're staying in the country for a long time). Yellow fever is not required in Sri Lanka but you may be asked to show a certificate if you have travelled from Africa or South America. Japanese encephalitis may be required for rural travel at certain times of the year (mainly rainy seasons). An effective oral cholera vaccine (Dukoral) is now available as 2 doses providing 3 months' protection.

Health risks

Bites and stings If you are bitten or stung by a snake, spider, scorpion or sea creature, try to identify the creature, without putting yourself in further danger. Victims of snake bite should be taken to a hospital or a doctor without delay; commercial snake bite and scorpion kits are available, but are of limited use. It is best to rely on local practice in these cases so that appropriate treatment can be given. To prevent bites, do not walk around in bare feet or sandals, wear proper shoes or

TRAVEL TIP

Leeches

When trekking in the monsoon be aware of leeches. They usually wait on the ground for a passerby and get into your boots when you are walking. Then, when they are gorged with blood, they drop off.

Don't try pulling one off as the head will be left behind and cause infection. Salt or a lighted cigarette have always been heralded as ways to remove leeches, but if neither are to hand a Dettol solution works wonders and even a hand sanitizer will encourage them to fall off. It helps to spray socks and bootlaces with an insect repellent before starting in the morning and tucking trousers into socks. If planning to do a lot of trekking it may be worth purchasing the leech socks sold in some camping stores.

boots, and walk heavily to warn the snake you are coming. Keep beds away from the walls and look inside your shoes and under the toilet seat every morning. Wear plastic shoes for swimming if venomous fish are known to be present; the symptoms of fish venom can be relieved by immersing the foot in very hot water for as long as the pain persists and by bathing the foot in citric fruit juices.

Diarrhoea This is the most common health problem for travellers. The standard advice for diarrhoea prevention is to be careful with water and ice for drinking. If you have any doubts about where the water came from then boil it or filter and treat it. There are many filter/treatment devices now available on the market. Avoid having ice in drinks unless you trust that it is from a reliable source. Food can also transmit disease. Be wary of salads (what were they washed in, who handled them), re-heated foods or food that has been left out in the sun having been cooked earlier in the day. Also be wary of unpasteurized dairy products, these can transmit a range

of diseases from brucellosis (fevers and constipation), to listeria (meningitis) and tuberculosis of the gut (constipation, fevers and weight loss).

Swimming in sea or river water that has been contaminated by sewage can also result in stomach upset; ask locally if water is safe. Diarrhoea may also be caused by a virus, bacteria (such as E-coli), protozoal (such as giardia), salmonella and cholera. It may be accompanied by vomiting or by severe abdominal pain. Any kind of diarrhoea responds well to the replacement of water and salts. Sachets of rehydration salts can be bought in most chemists and can be dissolved in boiled water. If the symptoms persist, consult a doctor.

Insects (See also Malaria, below). Mosquitoes and other insects are a nuisance and some are carriers of serious diseases. Heed all the anti-mosquito measures that you can. Try to avoid being bitten as much as possible by sleeping off the ground and using a mosquito net and some kind of insecticide. Mosquito coils release insecticide as they burn and are available in many shops, as are tablets of insecticide, which are placed on a heated mat plugged into a wall socket. In terms of mosquito repellents, remember that DEET (Di-ethyltoluamide) is the gold standard.

Tip...
There is a simple adage for avoiding contaminated food: wash it, peel it, boil it or forget it.

Apply the repellent every 4-6 hrs but more often if you are sweating heavily. If a non-DEET product is used, check who tested it. Validated products (tested at the London School of Hygiene and Tropical Medicine) include Mosiguard, Non-DEET Jungle formula and non-DEET Autan. If you want to use citronella remember that it must be applied very frequently (hourly) to be effective. If you are a target for insect bites or develop lumps quite soon after being bitten, carry an Aspivenin kit.

Chikungunya is a relatively rare mosquito-borne disease that has had outbreaks in Sri Lanka, particularly during the monsoon when flooded areas encourage the carrier mosquitoes to breed. The disease manifests within 12 days of infection and symptoms resemble a severe fever, with headaches, joint pain, arthritis and exhaustion lasting from several days to several weeks; in vulnerable sections of the population it can be fatal. Neither vaccine nor treatment are available, so rest is the best cure.

Unfortunately there is no vaccine against **dengue fever** and the mosquitoes that carry it bite during the day. You will be ill for 2-3 days, then get better for a few days and then feel ill again. It should all be over in 7-10 days.

Leishmaniasis is a parasite that is transmitted by the bite of a sandfly. You may notice a raised lump, which leads to a purplish discolouration on white skin and a possible ulcer. Sandflies do not fly very far and the greatest risk is at ground levels, so if you can avoid sleeping on the jungle floor do so; sleep under a permethrin-treated net and use insect repellent. Seek advice for any persistent skin lesion or nasal symptom. Several weeks of treatment is required under specialist supervision.

Certain **tropical flies** can lay their eggs under the skin with the unpleasant result that a maggot grows under the skin and pops up as a boil or pimple. The best way to remove these is to cover the boil with oil, Vaseline or nail varnish to stop the maggot breathing, then to squeeze it out gently the next day. **Ticks**, however, should not be treated in this way; instead they must be removed gently with a pair of tweezers, so that they do not leave their head parts in your skin causing a nasty allergic reaction. If not removed, ticks can transmit Lyme disease.

Malaria A malaria risk exists throughout the year in Sri Lanka, predominantly in the area north of Vavuniya and the northeastern coastal districts. There is a low to no risk in the rest of the country. Take specialist advice on the best anti-malarials to use: in the UK Chloroquine and Paludrine are recommended as sufficient for Sri Lanka; other countries may recommend either Malarone, Mefloquine or Doxycycline. The best prevention is to avoid been bitten as much as possible (see Insects, above).

Rabies Rabies is endemic in most districts in Sri Lanka, so avoid dogs that are behaving strangely. Rabies vaccination is worthwhile if you are spending any length of time in developing countries. If you are bitten by a domestic or wild animal, do not leave things to chance: scrub the wound with soap and water and/or disinfectant; try to determine the animal's ownership, where possible, and seek medical assistance at once. If you have already been satisfactorily vaccinated against rabies, some further doses of vaccine are all that is required. If you are not already vaccinated, then you may need anti-rabies serum (immunoglobulin) in addition. It is important to finish the course of treatment. Note that Sri Lanka suffers from shortages of immunoglobulin, so if planning to spend time in rural areas it may be worth investing in the pre-travel vaccine.

STDs Unprotected sex can spread HIV, hepatitis B and C, gonorrhea (green discharge), chlamydia (nothing to see but may cause painful urination and later female infertility), painful recurrent herpes, syphilis and warts, just to name a few. You can cut down the risk by using condoms, a femidom or avoiding sex altogether.

Sun and heat Remember that the sun in tropical areas can be fierce, so take precautions to avoid heat exhaustion and sunburn. Use high-factor sun screen and wear a hat. Prickly heat can be avoided by frequent washing and by wearing loose clothing. It is cured by allowing skin to dry off through use of powder – and by spending a few nights in an a/c hotel.

If you get sick

Contact your embassy or consulate or the tourist office for a list of recommended local doctors and dentist who speak your language. Healthcare in the region is varied, with the best facilities being available in Colombo where there are some excellent private clinics/hospitals. If you get ill, and you have the opportunity, you should also ask your medical insurer whether they are satisfied that the medical centre/hospital you have been referred to is of a suitable standard.

Medical services

Colombo There are a number of pharmacists on Galle Rd, Union Place and in the Pettah and Fort. **State Pharmaceutical** outlets are at Hospital Junction, Col 7, and on Main St, Fort. There are also pharmacies in **Keells Supermarket** (Liberty Plaza, Dharmapala Mawatha, Col 3) and **Cargill's** (Galle Rd, Col 3), open 24 hrs. If you need an English-speaking doctor, ask at your hotel or guesthouse. **General Hospital** (10 Regent St, T011-269 2222/269 1111) is the main public hospital with 24-hr A&E. Foreigners often prefer to use the more expensive private hospitals: **Asha Central** (33 Horton Pl, Col 7, T011-269 6411); **Asiri Central** (114 Norris Canal Rd, Col 10, T011-466 5544); **Durdan's** (3 Alfred Pl, Col 3, T011-541 0000); **McCarthy's** (22 Wijerama Mawatha, Col 7, T011-269 7760); **Nawaloka** (23 Sri Deshamanya HK Dharmadasa Mawatha, Col 2, T011-254 4444; 24-hr A&E).
Dambulla Medical centre, opposite Commercial Bank, T066-228 4735.
Galle General Hospital, T091-222 2261.
Kalutara General Hospital, T034-222 2261.
Kandy General Hospital, T081-222 2261.
Negombo General Hospital, Colombo Rd, T031-222 2261.

Useful websites

www.bloodcare.org.uk A Kent-based charity "dedicated to the provision of screened blood and resuscitation fluids in countries where these are not readily available". They will fly certified non-infected blood of the right type to your hospital/clinic.
www.cdc.gov US government site that gives excellent advice on travel health and details of disease outbreaks.
www.fco.gov.uk British Foreign and Commonwealth Office travel site has useful information on each country, people, climate and a list of UK embassies/consulates abroad.
www.fitfortravel.scot.nhs.uk A Z of vaccine/health advice for each country.
www.hpa.org.uk Up-to-date malaria advice guidelines for travel around the world, with information for those who are pregnant, suffering from epilepsy or planning to travel with children.
www.travelhealth.co.uk Independent travel health site with advice on vaccination, travel insurance and health risks.
www.travelscreening.co.uk A private clinic dedicated to integrated travel health. The clinic gives vaccine, travel

health advice, email and SMS text vaccine reminders and screens returned travellers for tropical diseases.

www.who.int The WHO site has links to the *WHO Blue Book* on travel advice, listing diseases in different regions of the world, vaccination schedules, yellow fever vaccination certificate requirements and malarial risks.

Insurance

Although Sri Lanka is not a crime-ridden society, accidents and delays can still occur. Full travel insurance is advised, including medical insurance and coverage for personal effects. There are a wide variety of policies to choose from, so it's best to shop around. Your local travel agent can advise on the best and most reliable deals available. Always read the small print carefully. Check that the policy covers the activities you may end up doing, such as trekking, rafting, surfing and diving. Also check exactly what your medical cover includes, eg ambulance, helicopter rescue or emergency flights back home. Also check the payment protocol. You may have to pay first before the insurance company reimburses you. **STA Travel**, www.statravel.co.uk, offers a range of good-value policies.

Internet

Internet access is now widespread across Sri Lanka, and most hotels and guesthouses offer Wi-Fi, generally for free. If you're travelling with a smartphone, it's definitely worth getting a local SIM: the process is quick and simple, coverage is almost universal and data is incredibly cheap. As of early 2016, Sri Lanka was preparing to launch Google-provided helium balloons into the stratosphere to beam down internet signals even to the most remote corners of the island.

Language

Sinhala and Tamil are the official languages, but English is widely spoken and understood in the main tourist areas though not by many in rural parts. German, French, Chinese and other languages may be spoken in hotels in the beach resorts. See page 431 for Sinhala and Tamil phrases.

Media

Newspapers and magazines

It is well worth reading the newspapers, which give a good insight into Sri Lankan attitudes. The *Daily News* and *The Island* are national daily newspapers published in English; there are several Sunday papers including the *Sunday Observer* and *Sunday Times*. Each has a website with archive section which is worth investigating. In Colombo and some other hotels a wide range of international daily and periodical newspapers and magazines is available. The *Lanka Guardian* is a respected fortnightly offering news and comment. *Lanka Monthly Digest* is aimed primarily at the business world but has some interesting articles.

Travel Lanka is a free monthly tourist guide available at larger tourist offices and in major hotels. It has some useful information and listings for Colombo and the main tourist areas, though much is out of date. If the copy on display in the tourist office is months out of date ask for the more recent edition, it's usually tucked away in a cupboard. For a more contemporary view, pick up a copy of *Leisure Times*. Also monthly, it has the latest restaurant, bar and nightclub openings, and a rundown of the month's events in Colombo. Free copies are available at the airport, big hotels, shopping complexes, and some bars and clubs.

Radio and television

Sri Lanka's national radio and television network, broadcasts in Sinhalese and English. **SLBC** operates between 0540 and 2300 on 95.6 FM in Colombo and 100.2 FM and 89.3 FM in Kandy. **BBC World Service** (1512khz/19m and 9720khz/31m from 2000 to 2130 GMT) has a large audience in both English and regional languages. Liberalization has opened the door to several private channels and an ever-growing number of private radio stations. **Yes FM** (89.5 FM), **TNL** (101.7 FM) and **Sun FM** (99.9 or 95.3 FM) broadcast Western music in English 24 hrs a day.

The 2 state TV channels are **Rupavahini**, which broadcasts 24 hrs a day, and **ITN**. Many Sri Lankans now watch satellite TV with a choice of channels, which offer good coverage of world news and also foreign feature films and 'soaps'.

Money

£1 = Rs 205, US$1= Rs 145, €1 = Rs 160 (Mar 2016)

Notes are in denominations of Rs 2000, 1000, 500, 200, 100, 50, 20, 10 and coins in general use are Rs 10, 5, 2 and 1. Visitors bringing in excess of US$10,000 into Sri Lanka should declare the amount on arrival. All Sri Lankan rupees should be re-converted upon leaving Sri Lanka. It is also illegal to bring Indian or Pakistani rupees into Sri Lanka, although this is rarely, if ever, enforced. See Customs, page 412. It is now possible to bring Sri Lankan rupees into the country but at the time of writing the limit was set at Rs 5000 and it was only available at some foreign exchange desks in the UK and had to be ordered in advance.

It is best to carry credit cards in a money belt worn under clothing. Only carry enough cash for your daily needs, keeping the rest in your money belt or in a hotel safe.

Keep plenty of small change and lower denomination notes as it can be difficult to change large notes, this is especially helpful if taking 3-wheelers or bargaining for goods.

Banks

Banks are generally open Mon-Fri 0900-1500, although some banks in Colombo have extended opening hours. Private banks (eg **Commercial Bank**, **Hatton National Bank**, **Sampath Bank**) are generally more efficient and offer a faster service than government-owned banks like **Bank of Ceylon** and **People's Bank**.

ATMs are now common throughout Sri Lanka. A small fee (less than the commission charged for changing TCs) will be charged on your bill at home and will vary depending of your bank. The majority of Sri Lankan banks now accept Visa, MasterCard and Cirrus, but check the sign for assurance. Queues at ATMs can be very long on public holidays.

Changing money

There are ATMs and several 24-hr exchange counters after you clear Customs at the airport; the counters give good rates of exchange. Larger hotels often have a money exchange counter (sometimes open 24 hrs), but offer substantially lower rates than banks. It may be useful to carry some small denomination foreign currency notes (eg £10, US$10) for emergencies.

Keep the encashment receipts you are given when exchanging money, as you may need at least 1 to re-exchange any rupees upon leaving Sri Lanka. Unspent rupees may be reconverted at a commercial bank when you leave. Changing money through unauthorized dealers is illegal.

Cost of travelling

The Sri Lankan cost of living remains well below that in the industrialized world, although is rising quite sharply. Food and public transport, especially rail and bus, remain exceptionally cheap, and accommodation, though not as cheap as in India, costs much less than in the West. The expensive hotels and restaurants are also less expensive than their counterparts in Europe, Japan or the US. Budget travellers (sharing a room) could expect to spend about Rs 2000 (about £11, €12 or US$18) each per day to cover cost of accommodation, food and travel. Those planning to stay in fairly comfortable hotels and use taxis or hired cars for travelling to sights should expect to spend at least Rs 8000 (about £45, €50 or US$70) a day. Single rooms are rarely less than about 80% of the double room price.

Many travellers are irritated by the Sri Lankan policy of 'dual pricing' for foreigners – one price for locals, another for tourists. Sites that see a lot of tourists, particularly in Kandy and the Cultural Triangle, carry entrance charges comparable to those you might expect to pay in the West, while national park fees have increased exponentially in recent years and carry a catalogue of hidden extra taxes. Many hotels have one price for Sri Lankans and expats and another for foreign tourists. In common with many other Asian countries, some shops and 3-wheeler drivers will try to overcharge foreigners – experience is the only way to combat this.

Credit cards
Major credit cards are increasingly accepted in the main centres of Sri Lanka both for shopping and for purchasing Sri Lankan rupees, but do not let the card out of your sight. Ensure that transactions are carried out in front of you and check the amounts before confirming payment. Larger hotels also accept payment by credit card. Cash can also be drawn from ATMs using credit cards but charges will be applied. Notify your bank in advance that you will be using your credit card and/or debit card whilst in Sri Lanka to avoid the card being stopped. It is also recommended that you check your statements on returning home.

Traveller's cheques (TCs)
Travellers' cheques issued by reputable companies (eg **American Express, Thomas Cook**) are accepted without difficulty and give a slightly better exchange rate than currency notes in Sri Lanka. They also offer the security of replacement if lost or stolen assuming the case is straightforward. TCs in pounds sterling, US dollars and euro are usually accepted without any problem and the process normally takes less than 15 mins in private banks and moneychangers (longer in government-owned banks). Larger hotels will normally only exchange TCs for resident guests but will offer a substantially lower rate than banks or private dealers. A 1% stamp duty is payable on all TCs transactions plus a small commission which varies from bank to bank.

Take care to keep the proof of purchase slip and a note of TCs numbers separately from the cheques. In the case of loss, you will need to get a police report and inform the issuing company.

Service charge
A service charge of 10% is applied to some accommodation, and a further 15% government tax, which is added to food and drink as well, can also apply. The more upmarket the establishment, the more chance these will be added to the total. Enquire beforehand about additional taxes, otherwise it can give you a nasty shock when you come to pay.

Opening hours

Banks Mon-Fri 0900-1500 (some 1300), some open Sat morning
Government offices Mon-Fri 0930-1700, some open Sat 0930-1300 (often alternate Sat only).
Post offices Mon-Fri 1000-1700, and Sat mornings.
Shops Mon-Fri 1000-1900 and Sat mornings with most closed on Sun. Sun street bazaars in some areas.

Poya days (full moon) are holidays when government offices, etc, will be closed. More establishments remain open in tourist areas.

Post

Postcards to most countries beyond the Middle East cost Rs 20. Try to use a franking service in a post office when sending mail, or hand in your mail at a counter. Many towns often have private agencies which offer most postal services.

For valuable items, it is best to use a **courier**, eg **DHL Parcel Service** in Colombo. It takes 2-3 working days to the UK or USA; 3-4 working days to mainland Europe.

Poste restante at the GPO in larger towns will keep your mail (letters and packages) for up to 3 months.

Safety

Restricted and protected areas

Since 2009, almost all roads have reopened in the north and east, and major towns and tourists areas are once again accessible. Some places, however, remain no-go or have limited access due to high security and, in a few remaining cases, land mines. Check www.fco.gov.uk for the latest information. Travel off road should only be undertaken after checking with locals.

Other areas with restricted access include certain archaeological sites, national parks and reserves which require permits before visiting. Refer to the relevant sections of the travelling text for details.

Confidence tricksters

Confidence tricksters and touts who aim to part you from your money are found in most major towns and tourist sites. It is best to ignore them and carry on with your own business while politely, but firmly, declining their offers of help.

Accommodation touts are common at rail and bus stations often boarding trains some distance before the destination. After engaging you in casual conversation to find out your plan, one will often find you a taxi or a 3-wheeler and try to persuade you that the hotel of your choice is closed, full or not good value. They will suggest an alternative where they will, no doubt, earn a commission (which you will end up having to pay). It is better to go to your preferred choice alone. Phone in advance to check if a place is full and make a reservation if necessary. If it is full then the hotelier/guesthouse owner will usually advise you of a suitable alternative. Occasionally, touts operate in groups to confuse you, or one may pose as the owner of the guesthouse you have in mind and tell you that it is sadly full but he is able to 'help' you by taking you to a friend's place.

Another trick is to befriend you on a train (especially on the Colombo to Galle or Kandy routes), find out your ultimate destination and 'helpfully' use their mobile to phone for a 3-wheeler in advance, telling you that none will be available at the station. Once at the other end, the 3-wheeler driver may take you on an indirect route and charge up to 10 times the correct fee. In fact, 3-wheeler drivers are nearly always waiting at major stations. It's worth checking the distance to your destination (usually given in the guidebook) and remember that the going rate for 3-wheeler hire is around Rs 25-50 per km.

Another breed of tout is on the increase especially in towns attracting tourists (Kandy, Galle). Someone may approach on the street, saying they recognize you and work at your hotel. Caught off-guard, you feel obliged to accept them as your guide for exploring the sights (and shops), and so are ripe for exploitation. Some may offer to take you to a local watering hole, where at the end of your drinking session the bill will be heavily inflated. Be polite, but firm, when refusing their offer of help.

A gem shop may try to persuade you to buy gems as a sample for a client in your home country – usually your home town (having found out which this is in casual conversation). A typical initial approach is to request that you help with translating something for the trader. The deal is that you buy the gems (maybe to the value of US$500 or US$1000) and then sell them to the client for double the price, and keep the difference. Of course, there is no client at home and you are likely to have been sold poor-quality gems or fakes. Only buy gems for yourself and be sure of what you are buying. This is a common trick in Galle and Ratnapura where various methods are employed. It is worth getting any purchase checked by the State Gem Corporation in Colombo. It is also essential to take care that credit cards are not 'run off' more than once when making a purchase.

Travel arrangements, especially for sightseeing, should only be made through reputable companies; bogus agents operate in popular seaside resorts.

Personal security

In general the threats to personal security for travellers in Sri Lanka are small. In most areas it is possible to travel without any risk of personal violence, though violent attacks, still very low by Western standards, are on the increase. Care should be taken in certain lesser visited areas of popular beach resorts such as Hikkaduwa, Negombo and Mirissa; don't walk along the beach at night after the restaurants and bars have closed.

Basic common sense needs to be used with respect to looking after valuables. Theft is not uncommon especially when travelling by train or crowded bus. It is essential to take good care of personal possessions both when you are carrying them, and when you have to leave them anywhere. You cannot regard hotel rooms as automatically safe. It is wise to use hotel safes for valuable items, though even they cannot guarantee security. It is best to keep TCs and passports with you at all times. Money belts worn under clothing are one of the safest options, although you should keep some cash easily accessible in a purse.

Police

Even after taking all reasonable precautions people do have valuables stolen. This can cause great inconvenience. You can minimize this by keeping a record of vital documents, including your passport number and TCs in a separate place from the documents themselves, with relatives or friends at home, or even email them to yourself before setting off. If you have items stolen, they should be reported to the police as soon as possible. Larger hotels will be able to help in contacting and dealing with the police.

Many tourist resorts now have an English-speaking tourist police branch. The paper work involved in reporting losses can be time-consuming and irritating, and your own documentation (eg passport and visas) will normally be demanded. Tourists should not assume that if procedures move slowly they are automatically expected to offer a bribe. If you face really serious problems, for example in connection with a driving accident, you should contact your consular office as quickly as possible.

Student travellers

Full-time students qualify for an **ISIC** (International Student Identity Card) which is issued by student travel and specialist agencies at home (eg **STA Travel**). A card allows some few travel benefits (eg reduced prices) and acts as proof of student status. Only a few sites in Sri Lanka will offer concessions, however.

Telephone

Sri Lanka country code: T+94. National operator: T1200. International operator: T101 to change to 11201. Directory enquiries: T1234, International directory enquiries T1236.

Calls within Sri Lanka STD codes are included with each number in the text. Dial the local number within the town but use the STD area code first (eg Kandy 081) when dialling from outside the town. Mobile prefixes are 071, 072, 077 and 078.

IDD (International Direct Dialling) is now straightforward in Sri Lanka with many private call offices throughout the country. Calls made from hotels usually cost a lot more (sometimes 3 times as much). They can be made cheaply from post offices though you may need to book. There are also IDD card-operated pay phones; phone cards can be bought from post offices, kiosks near the pay phones and some shops. Pay phones can, of course, be used for local calls as well.

The cheapest way to phone abroad is to use **Skype**, and this is becoming increasingly available in Sri Lanka at internet cafés and some guesthouses.

Mobile phones

Mobile phones or 'hand phones' are very popular in Sri Lanka, and networks extend across virtually every square inch of the island. Most foreign networks are able to roam within Sri Lanka – enquire at home before leaving – but if you're staying in Sri Lanka for more than a few days, consider getting a pay-as you-go SIM card. You will need to provide a copy of your passport for their records, but topping up is straightforward once everything is set up, and calls and mobile data are almost unbelievably cheap. When topping up in shops the process is completed by the shopkeeper and you are not handed a voucher; wait until the confirmation text comes through before leaving the premises. The main mobile phone providers are **Etisalat**, **Mobitel** and **Dialog**. Dialog currently has the best island coverage.

Time

GMT + 5½ hrs. Perception of time is sometimes rather vague in Sri Lanka (as in the rest of South Asia). Unpunctuality is common so you will need to be patient.

Tipping

A 10% service charge is added to room rates and meals in virtually all but the cheapest hotels and restaurants. Therefore it is not necessary to give a further tip in most instances. In many smaller guesthouses staff are not always paid a realistic wage and have to rely on a share of the service charge for their basic income.

Tour companies sometimes make recommendations for 'suitable tips' for coach drivers and guides. Some of the figures may seem modest by European standards but are very inflated if compared with normal earnings. A tip of Rs 100 per day from each member of the group can safely be regarded as generous.

Taxi drivers do not expect to be tipped but a small extra amount over the fare is welcomed.

Tour operators

If you don't wish to travel independently, you may choose to try an inclusive package holiday or let a specialist operator quote for a tailor-made tour. The lowest prices quoted by package tour companies in 2016 vary from about £1000 for a fortnight (flights, hotel and breakfast) in the low season, to £1500+ during the peak season at Christmas and the New Year. For the cheaper hotels, you pay very little extra for an additional week. Package operators include: **Monarch**, T0333-003 0700, www.monarch.co.uk, **Thomas Cook**, T01783-224 4808, www.thomascook.com, and **Virgin**, T0344-557 4321, www.virginholidays.co.uk. All allow you to book a return flight with the 1st night's accommodation, leaving you free to arrange the rest yourself.

UK and Ireland
Abercrombie & Kent, T01242-547 760, www.abercrombiekent.co.uk.
Adventures Abroad, T01142-473 400, www.adventures-abroad.com. Outward bound adventures.
Audley Travel, T01993-838 000, www.audleytravel.com. Fairs, festivals, culture, religion.
Barefoot Traveller, T020-8741 4319, www.barefoot-traveller.com. Diving specialist (with Maldives).
Cox & Kings, T020-3773 7856, www.coxandkings.co.uk. Ancient sites and tourist high spots.
Exodus Travels, T0845-287 1341, www.exodus.co.uk. Includes cycling holidays.
Experience Sri Lanka, T020-3411 1995, www.experiencetravelgroup.com. Can arrange homestays and takes in lesser-publicized sights such as Mannar.

Paradise Vacations, 1 Olympic Way, Wembley, Middlesex HA9 0NP, T020-3011 0182, www.paradisevacations.co.uk. Tailor-made holidays including honeymoon and sports packages.

Red Dot Tours, Orchard House, Folly Lane, Bramham, Leeds LS23 6RZ, T0870-231 7892, www.reddottours.com. Tailor-made tours but also an excellent accommodation booking service (good range of villas and bungalows). Professional service, knowledgeable advice. Good for local knowledge.

SpiceLand Holidays Ltd, 29 Harley St, London W1G 9QR, T020-7183 8963, www.spicelandholidays.com. Tailor-made holiday packages and other specialist travel services.

Sri Lanka Insider Tours, 107964-375 994, www.insider-tours.com. Cooperative tour organization using local transport, homestays or locally owned hotels. Recommended for insider wisdom.

Steppes Travel, 51 Castle St, Cirencester, Gloucestershire, T01285-601 7776, www.steppestravel.co.uk. Specializes in tailor-made tours.

Tikalanka Tours UK Ltd, Keldhead, Heltondale, Askham, Penrith, Cumbria CA10 2QL, T020-3137 6763, www.tikalanka.com. This boutique agency organizes superb tailor-made tours of Sri Lanka and has a happy knack of unearthing wonderful, unusual places to stay that other agents ignore. Reliable multilingual drivers and a warm welcome from Sri Lankan partner Pathi. Unreservedly recommended.

Trans Indus, T0844-879 3960, www.transindus.co.uk. Tailor-made tours in Southeast Asia, Japan, China, India and Sri Lanka.

Visit Asia, G45 Waterfront Studios, 1 Dock Rd, Docklands, London E16 1AH, T020-8617 3358, www.visitasia.co.uk. Specialist regional operator offering private, small-group and tailor-made tours.

North America
Absolute Travel, 90 Broad St, Suite 1706, New York, NY 10013, T212-627 1950, www. absolutetravel.com. Upmarket, offering including Ayurveda and adventure travel.
Adventures Abroad, T1-800-665-3998, www.adventures-abroad.com. Range of tours, small groups guaranteed.

Australia and New Zealand
Exotic Lanka Holidays, T1300 374734, www.exoticlankaholidays.com.au. Specializes in Sri Lanka, tours include birding and cricket.
Passport Travel, T+61 3 9500 0444, www. travelcentre.com.au. For cycling holidays.

Sri Lanka
See also Colombo, page 72.
Boutique Sri Lanka, T011-269 9213, www.boutiquesrilanka.com. Also offers yoga and Ayurvedic holidays.
Lion Royal Tourisme, 45 Braybrook St, Col 2, Colombo, T011-471 5996, www. lionroyaltourisme.com. Tailor-made tours with an excellent network of hotels. Also extends services to the Maldives.
Quickshaws, 3 Kalinga Pl, Col 5, Colombo, T011-230 6306, www.quickshaws.com.

Celebrating Sri Lanka's wildlife and offering alternative wedding and honeymoon destinations and writers haunts. Recommended for birders and wildlife enthusiasts.
Roads Less Travelled Sri Lanka, 216 de Saram Rd, Colombo 10, T077-748 8262, www. roadslesstravelledsrilanka.com. Bespoke tours and 1-day adventures, with an accent on wildlife and less touristy destinations.
Sri Lanka in Style, T011-239 6666, www. srilankainstyle.com. Unique insight into the island. Visit virgin white tea plantations, experience Ayurveda, plan the honeymoon of a lifetime or visit local artists.

Tourist information

Sri Lanka Tourist Board, 13 Hyde Park Gardens, London W2 2LU, T0845-880 6333, www.srilanka.travel, has some information for planning your trip. The website has details of sights, accommodation and transport. There are Sri Lanka Tourist Board offices in Colombo and a few major tourist centres, such as Kandy. They are listed in the relevant sections throughout the book.

Useful addresses
Central Cultural Fund (Cultural Triangle Office), 212/1 Bauddhaloka Mawatha, Col 7 (to the right and halfway to the back of building), T011-250 0732, www.ccf.lk. Information on archaeological and cultural

sites including Anuradhapura, Kandy, Polonnaruwa and Sigiriya.

Department of Wildlife Conservation, 382 New Kandy Rd, Malabe, on the outskirts of Colombo, T011-288 8585.

Useful websites

www.divesrilanka.com Information on dive sites, and when and where to dive.
www.lakdasun.org A site for Sri Lankans rather than foreign tourists, but hugely useful with in-depth tips about accommodation and transport.
www.srilanka.travel The official website of the Sri Lanka Tourist Board, with useful general tourist information.
www.tamilnet.com Has a fairly balanced Tamil perspective.

Blogs

There are a number of blogs written by people living in Sri Lanka and travellers passing through. Travel blogs include **www.flashpackatforty.com**; **www.ritchy feet.com**; **www.thesrilankatravelblog.com** and **srilanka.for91days.com**.
www.lankareviewed.blogspot.com Hotel reviews, places to eat and sites.
www.riceandcurry.wordpress.com A food site with Sri Lankan recipes and some restaurant reviews.

Visas and permits

For short visits to Sri Lanka, citizens of most countries can apply online for a **Short Visit Visa**; this takes the form of an **Electronic Travel Authority** (**ETA**). For full details see www.eta.gov.lk. At present the ETA costs US$35 (US$20 for SAARC citizens) and allows for a visit up to 30 days. Fill in the form, print out your confirmation, and present it with your passport at the Immigration counter on arrival.

All tourists should have a valid passport (valid for 6 months upon entry) and where

necessary have a valid visa for the country that is their next destination; check with your nearest Sri Lankan representative before travelling. It may sometimes be necessary to show proof of sufficient funds (US$30 per day) and a return or onward ticket, although this is rarely checked on arrival. Transit passengers are issued with a **Transit Visa**.

A 60-day **extension** to the Short Visit Visa is available to nationals of all countries upon paying a fee, which varies according to the reciprocal fee charged to Sri Lankans when entering your country. Apply in person during office hours, to the **Department of Immigration and Emigration**, 41 Ananda Rajakaruna Mawatha, Col 10, Colombo, T94-11-532 9000, www.immigration.gov.lk. Bring passport, flight information and passport photo. It is not necessary to wait until shortly before the expiry of your original visa. Extensions will be granted at any time within the original 30-day period.

Voltage

230-240 volts, 50 cycles AC. There may be pronounced variations in the voltage, and power cuts are common. 3-pin (round) sockets are the norm. Universal adaptors are widely available.

Women travellers

Compared with many other countries it is relatively easy and safe for women to travel around Sri Lanka, even on their own, although they may experience a lot of unwanted attention and have unsavoury remarks directed at them. Travelling with a male companion does not guarantee a quiet life, although those travelling solo may want to invent an imaginary husband and consider wearing a fake wedding ring.

Modest dress for women is always advisable: loose-fitting, non-see through clothes. Cover the shoulders, and wear skirts, dresses or shorts that are at least knee-length. Don't walk through towns in a bikini. Make a note of how the local women are dressing and act accordingly; you'll soon notice a difference between say Colombo and Trincomalee town.

It is always best to be accompanied when travelling by 3-wheeler or taxi at night. Do not get into a taxi or 3-wheeler if there are men accompanying the driver. Travelling on buses can be uncomfortable because of the number of people packed into a small space, and wandering hands are not unusual. If someone is pressing themselves against you a little too enthusiastically, jam your bag in between. If travelling alone, try and sit next to another woman; on the east coast this is expected of you, and women will pat the seat to invite you to join them. Do the same on trains, or sit with a family.

Remember that what may be considered normal, innocent friendliness in a Western context may be misinterpreted by some Sri Lankan men. It's not recommended for women to frequent the local bars; instead drink in hotel bars or restaurants.

Avoid visiting remote areas of archaeological sites, such as Polonnaruwa, late in the day (ie after the tour groups have left). Care should also be taken in certain lesser visited areas of popular beach resorts, such as Hikkaduwa, Negombo and Mirissa. As at home, do not walk around alone at night, or on deserted stretches of beach, and use your common sense.

Working in Sri Lanka

All foreigners intending to work need **work permits**. No one is allowed to stay longer than 6 months in a calendar year, or to change their visa status. The employing organization should make formal arrangements. Apply to the Sri Lankan representative in your country of origin.

UK and Ireland
The **World Service Enquiry directory**, www.wse.org.uk, lists voluntary placements overseas.
International Voluntary Service, Thorn House, 5 Rose St, Edinburgh EH2 2PR, www.ivsgb.org.
i-to-i International projects, Woodside House, 261 Low Lane, Leeds LS18 5NY, T0113-205 4620, www.i-to-i.com. Arranges for students and young people to spend part of a gap year teaching English, looking after the disabled or helping with conservation work.
Link Overseas Exchange, The Hayloft, Wards of Keithock, Near Brechin, Angus DD9 7PZ, T01356-629134, www.linkoverseas.org.uk.
Project Trust, The Hebridean Centre, Isle of Coll, Argyll PA78 6TE, T01879-230444, www.projecttrust.org.uk.
Teaching and Projects Abroad, Aldsworth Parade, Goring, Sussex BN12 4TX, T01903-708300, www.projects-abroad.co.uk.
VSO, Carlton House, 27A Carlton Dr, Putney, London SW15 2BS, www.vso.org.uk.

USA and Canada
Council for International Programs, 3500 Lorain Av, Suite 504, Cleveland, OH 44113, T216-566 1088, www.cipusa.org.
i-to-i, T800 985 4864 (see above). English-teaching placements.
Projects Abroad, 347 West 36th St, Suite 903, New York NY 10018, T1-888-839 3535, www.projects-abroad.org. Also has an office in Canada.
United Nations Volunteers, www.unv.org. Usually mature, experienced people with specific qualifications.
World University Service of Canada, T1-800-267 8699, www.wusc.ca. Runs a development project on a tea plantation.

Australia
Australian Volunteers International, 71 Argyle St, Fitzroy Victoria 3065, T3-9279 1788, www.australianvolunteers.com.

Notes

Footnotes

Language

Sinhalese useful words and phrases

Pronunciation
ah is shown ā as in car
ee is shown ī as in see
oh is shown ō as in old
These marks, to help with pronunciation, do not appear in the main text

General greetings	*Ayubowan*
Thank you/No thank you	*Es-thu-thee/mata epa*
Excuse me, sorry	*Samavenna*
Pardon	*Ah*
Yes/no	*Ou/na*
Nevermind/that's all right	*Kamak* na
Please	*Karunakara*
What is your name?	*Nama mokakda*
My name is …	Mage nama …
How are you?	*Kohamada?*
I am well thanks	*Mama hondin innava*
Not very well	*Wadiya honda ne*
Do you speak English?	*Ingirisi kathakaranawatha*

Shopping
How much is this?	*Mika kiyada?*
That will be 20 rupees	*Rupoal wissai*
Please make it a bit cheaper	*Karunakara gana adukaranna*

The hotel
What is the room charge?	*Kamarayakata gana kiyada?*
May I see the room please?	*Kamaraya karnakara penvanna?*
Is there an a/c room?	*A/c kamarayak thiyenawada?*
… a fan/mosquito net	… *fan/maduru delak*
Please clean the room	*Karnakara kamaraya suddakaranna*
This is OK	*Meka hondai*
Bill please	*Karunakara bila gaynna*

Travel
Where is the railway station?	*Dumriyapola koheda?*
When does the Colombo bus leave?	*Colombata bus eka yanne kiyatada?*
How much is it to Colombo?	*Colombota kiyada?*
Will you go for 10 rupees?	*Rupiyal dahayakata yanawada?*
Left/right	*Wama/dakuna*
Staight on	*Kelin yanna*
Nearby	*Langa*

Please wait here	Karunakara mehe enna
Please come here at 8	Karunakara mehata atata enna
Stop	Nawathinna

Time and days

right now	dang	week	sathiya
morning	ude	month	masy
afternoon	dawal	Sunday	irrida
evening	sawasa	Monday	sanduda
night	raya	Tuesday	angaharuwada
today	atha	Wednesday	badhada
tomorrow	heta	Thursday	brahaspathinda
yesterday	iye	Friday	sikurada
day	dawasa	Saturday	senasurada

Numbers

1	eka	9	namaya
2	deka	10	dahaya
3	thuna	20	wissai
4	hathara	30	thihai
5	paha	40	hathalihai
6	haya	50	panahai
7	hatha	100/200	siayai/desiyai
8	ata	1000/2000	dahai/dedahai

Basic vocabulary

Some English words are widley used such as airport, bathroon, bus, embassy, ferry, hospital, stamp, taxi, ticket, train (though often pronounced a little differently).

bank	bankuwa	open	arala
café/food stall	kamata kadyak	police station	policiya
chemist	beheth sappuwa	restaurant	kamata
clean	sudda	road	para
closed	wahala	room	kamaraya
cold	sithai	shop	kade
dirty	apirisidui	sick (ill)	asaneepai
doctor	dosthara	station	istashama
excellent	hari honthai	this	meka
ferry	bottuwa	that	araka
food/to eat	kanda/kama	water	wathura
hospital	rohala	when?	kawathatha?
hot (temperature)	rasnai	where?	koheda?
hotel	hotalaya		

Sri Lankan Tamil useful words and phrases

general greeting	*vanakkam*
Thank you/no thank you	*nandri*
Excuse me, sorry, pardon	*mannikkavum*
Yes/no	*ām/illai*
never mind/that's all right	*paruvai illai*
please	*thayavu seithu*
What is your name?	*ungaludaya peyr enna*
My name is...	*ennudaya peyr*
How are you?	*ningal eppadi irukkirirgal?*
I am well, thanks	*nan nantraga irrukkirain*
Not very well	*paruvayillai*
Do you speak English?	*ningal angilam kathappirgala*

Shopping

How much is this?	*ithan vilai enna?*
That will be 20 rupees	*athan vilai irupatha rupa*
Please make it a bit cheaper!	*thayavu seithu konjam kuraikavuam!*

The hotel

What is the room charge?	*arayin vilai enna?*
May I see the room please?	*thayavu seithu arayai parka mudiyama?*
Is there an a/c room?	*kulir sathana arai irrukkatha?*
Is there hot water?	*sudu thanir irukkuma?*
...a bathroom?	*oru kuliyal arai...?*
...a fan/mosquito net?	*katotra sathanam/kosu valai...?*
Please clean the room	*thayavu seithu arayai suththap paduthava*
This is OK	*ithuru seri*
Bill please	*bill tharavum*

Travel

Where's the railway station?	*station enge?*
When does the Galle bus leave?	*eppa Galle bus pogum?*
How much is it to Kandy?	*Kandy poga evalavu?*
Will you go to Kandy for 10 rupees?	*paththu rupavitku Kandy poga mudiyami?*
left/right	*idathu/valathu*
straight on	*naerakapogavum*
nearby	*aruqil*
Please wait here	*thayavu seithu ingu nitkavum*
Please come here at 8	*thayavu seithu ingu ettu*
stop	*nivuthu*

Time and days

right now	*ippoh*
morning	*kalai*
afternoon	*pitpagal*
evening	*malai*
night	*iravu*
today	*indru*
tomorrow/yesterday	*nalai/naetru*
day	*thinam*
week	*vaaram*
month	*maatham*

Sunday		*gnatruk kilamai*	
Monday		*thinkat kilamai*	
Tuesday		*sevai kilamai*	
Wednesday		*puthan kilamai*	
Thursday		*viyalak kilamai*	
Friday		*velli kilamai*	
Saturday		*sanik kilamai*	

Numbers

1	*ontru*	10	*pattu*
2	*erantru*	20	*erupathu*
3	*moontru*	30	*muppathu*
4	*nangu*	40	*natpathu*
5	*ainthu*	50	*ompathu*
6	*aru*	100/200	*nooru/irunooru*
7	*aelu*	1000/2000	*aiyuram/iranda*
8	*ettu*		*iuram*
9	*onpathu*		

Basic vocabulary

Some English words are widely used, often alongside Tamil equivalents, such as, airport, bank, bathroom, bus, embassy, ferry, hospital, hotel, restaurant, station, stamp, taxi, ticket, train (though often pronounced a little differently).

airport	*agaya vimana nilayam*
bank	*vungi*
bathroom	*kulikkum arai*
café/food stall	*unavu kadai*
chemist	*marunthu kadai*
clean	*sushtham*
closed	*moodu*
cold	*kulir*
dirty	*alukku*
embassy	*thootharalayam*
excellent	*miga nallathu*
ferry	*padagu*
hospital	*aspathri*
hot (temp)	*ushnamana*
hotel/restaurant	*sapathu*
juice	*saru/viduthi*
open	*thira*
road	*pathai*
room	*arai*
shop	*kadi*
sick (ill)	*viyathi*
stamp	*muththirai*
station	*nilayam*
this	*ithu*
that	*athu*
ticket	*anumati situ*
train	*rayil*
water	*thannir*
when?	*eppa?*
where?	*enge?*

Glossary

A

aarti (arati) Hindu worship with lamps

abhaya mudra Buddha posture signifying protection; forearm raised, palm facing outward fingers together

ahimsa non-harming, non-violence

ambulatory processional path

amla/amalaka circular ribbed pattern (based on a gourd) on top of a temple tower

Ananda the Buddha's chief disciple

anda lit 'egg', spherical part of the stupa

antechamber chamber in front of the sanctuary

apse semi-circular plan, as in apse of a church

arama monastery (as in Tissamaharama)

architrave horizontal beam across posts or gateways

Arjuna hero of the Mahabharata, to whom Krishna delivered the Bhagavad Gita

arrack spirit distilled from palm sap

aru river (Tamil)

Aryans literally 'noble' (Sanskrit); prehistoric peoples who settled in Persia and N India

asana a seat or throne; symbolic posture

ashlar blocks of stone

ashram hermitage or retreat

Avalokiteshwara Lord who looks down; Bodhisattva, the Compassionate

avatara 'descent'; incarnation of a divinity, usually Vishnu's incarnations

B

banamaduwa monastic pulpit

Bandaras sub-caste of the Goyigama caste, part of the Sinhalese aristocracy

bas-relief carving of low projection

basement lower part of walls, usually adorned with decorated mouldings

bazar market

beru elephant grass

Bhagavad-Gita Song of the Lord from the Mahabharata in which Krishna preaches a sermon to Arjuna

bhikku Buddhist monk

bhumi 'earth'; refers to a horizontal moulding of a *shikhara* (tower)

bhumisparasa mudra earth-witnessing Buddha posture

Bo-tree Ficus religiosa, large spreading tree associated with the Buddha; also Bodhi

Bodhisattva Enlightened One, destined to become Buddha

Brahma universal self-existing power; Creator in the Hindu Triad. Often represented in art, with four heads

Brahman (Brahmin) highest Hindu (and Jain) caste of priests

Brahmanism ancient Indian religion, precursor of modern Hinduism and Buddhism

Buddha The Enlightened One; founder of Buddhism who is worshipped as god by certain sects

bund an embankment; a causeway by a reservoir (tank)

Burghers Sri Lankans of mixed Dutch-Sinhalese descent

C

cantonment large planned military or civil area in town

capital upper part of a column or pilaster

catamaran log raft, logs (*maram*) tied (*kattu*) together (Tamil)

cave temple rock-cut shrine or monastery

chakra sacred Buddhist Wheel of Law; also Vishnu's discus

chapati unleavened Indian bread cooked on a griddle

chena shifting cultivation

chhatra, chatta honorific umbrella; a pavilion (Buddhist)

Chola early and medieval Tamil kingdom (India)

circumambulation clockwise movement around a stupa or shrine while worshipping

cloister passage usually around an open square

coir coconut fibre used for making rope and mats

copra dried sections of coconut flesh, used for oil

corbel horizontal block supporting a vertical structure or covering an opening

cornice horizontal band at the top of a wall

crore 10 million

Culavansa Historical sequel to Mahavansa, the first part dating from 13th century, later extended to 16th century

D

dagoba stupa (Sinhalese)

darshan (darshana) viewing of a deity

Dasara (dassara/dussehra/dassehra) 10-day Hindu festival (September-October)

devala temple or shrine (Buddhist or Hindu)

Devi Goddess; later, the Supreme Goddess; Siva's consort, Parvati

dhal (daal) lentil 'soup'

dharma (dhamma) Hindu and Buddhist concepts of moral and religious duty

dharmachakra wheel of 'moral' law (Buddhist)

dhyana meditation

dhyani mudra meditation posture of the Buddha, cupped hands rest in the lap

distributary river that flows away from main channel, usually in deltas

Diwali festival of lights (September-October) usually marks the end of the rainy season

Dravidian languages – Tamil, Telugu, Kannada and Malayalam; and peoples mainly from S India

Durga principal goddess of the Shakti cult; rides on a tiger, armed with weapons

dvarpala doorkeeper

E

eave overhang that shelters a porch or veranda

eri tank (Tamil)

F

finial emblem at the summit of a stupa, tower or dome; often a tier of umbrella-like motifs or a pot

frieze horizontal band of figures or decorative designs

G

gable end of an angled roof

ganga perennial river

garbhagriha literally 'womb-chamber'; a temple sanctuary

gedige arched Buddhist image house built of stone slabs and brick

gopura towered gateway in S Indian temples

Goyigama landowning and cultivating caste among Sinhalese Buddhists

H

Haj (Hajj) annual Muslim pilgrimage to Mecca (Haji, one who has performed the Haj)

hakim judge; a physician (usually Muslim)

Hanuman Monkey hero of the Ramayana; devotee of Rama; bringer of success to armies

Hari Vishnu

harmika the finial of a stupa; a pedestal where the honorific umbrella was set

Hasan the murdered eldest son of Ali, commemorated at Muharram

howdah seat on elephant's back

Hussain the second murdered son of Ali, commemorated at Muharram

I

illam lens of gem-bearing coarse river gravel

imam Muslim religious leader in a mosque

Indra King of the gods; God of rain; guardian of the East

Isvar Lord Sanskrit

J

jaggery brown sugar made from palm sap

jataka stories accounts of the previous lives of the Buddha

JVP Janatha Vimukhti Peramuna (People's Liberation Army) – violent revolutionary political movement in 1970s and 1980s

K

kadu forest (Tamil)

kalapuwa salty or brackish lagoon

Kali lit 'black'; terrifying form of the goddess Durga, wearing a necklace of skulls/heads

kalyanmandapa (Tamil) hall with columns, used for the symbolic marriage ceremony of the temple deity

kapok the silk cotton tree

kapurala officiating priest in a shrine (devala)

karandua replica of the Tooth Relic casket, dagoba-shaped

Karavas fishing caste, many converted to Roman Catholicism

karma present consequences of past lives

Kataragama the Hindu god of war; Skanda

Kartikkeya/Kartik Son of Siva, also known as Skanda or Subrahmanyam

katcheri (cutchery, Kachcheri) public office or court

khondalite crudely grained basalt

kolam masked dance drama (Sinhalese)

kovil temple (Tamil)

kitul fish-tailed sago palm, whose sap is used for jaggery

Krishna Eighth incarnation of Vishnu; the cowherd (Gopala, Govinda)

Kubera Chief yaksha; keeper of the earth's treasures, Guardian of the North

kulam tank or pond (Tamil)

L

laddu round sweet snack

lakh 100,000

Lakshmana younger brother of Rama in the Ramayana

Lakshmi Goddess of wealth and good fortune, consort of Vishnu

lattice screen of cross laths: perforated

lena cave, usually a rock-cut sanctuary

lingam (linga) Siva as the phallic emblem

Lokeshwar 'Lord of the World', Avalokiteshwara to Buddhists and of Siva to Hindus

LTTE Liberation Tigers of Tamil Eelam, or "The Tigers", force rebelling against Sri Lankan Government

lungi wrap-around loin cloth

M

maha great; in Sri Lanka, the main rice crop

Mahabodhi Great Enlightenment of Buddha

Mahadeva literally 'Great Lord'; Siva

Mahavansa literally "Great Dynasty or Chronicle", a major source on early history and legend

Mahayana The Greater Vehicle; form of Buddhism practised in East Asia, Tibet and Nepal

Mahesha (Maheshvara) Great Lord; Siva

mahout elephant driver/keeper

Maitreya the future Buddha

makara crocodile-shaped mythical creature

malai hill (Tamil)

mandapa columned hall preceding the sanctuary in a Jain or Hindu temple

mandir temple

mantra sacred chant for meditation by Hindus and Buddhists

Mara Tempter, who sent his daughters (and soldiers) to disturb the Buddha's meditation

mawatha roadway

maya illusion

Minakshi literally 'fish-eyed'; Parvati, Siva's consort

Mohammad 'the praised'; The Prophet; founder of Islam

moksha salvation, enlightenment; lit 'release'

moonstone the semi-circular stone step before a shrine; also a gem

mudra symbolic hand gesture and posture associated with the Buddha

Muharram period of mourning in remembrance of Hasan and Hussain, two murdered sons of Ali

N

Naga (nagi/nagini) Snake deity; associated with fertility and protection

Nandi a bull, Siva's vehicle and a symbol of fertility

Narayana Vishnu as the creator of life

Nataraja Siva, Lord of the cosmic dance

Natha worshipped by Mahayana Buddhists as the bodhisattva Maitreya

navagraha nine planets, represented usually on the lintel of a temple door

navaratri literally '9 nights'; name of the Dasara festival

niche wall recess containing a sculpted image or emblem,

nirvana enlightenment; (literally 'extinguished')

O

ola palm manuscripts

oriel projecting window

oya seasonal river

P

pada foot or base

paddy rice in the husk

padma lotus flower. Padmasana, lotus seat; posture of meditating figures

pagoda tall structure in several stories

Pali language of Buddhist scriptures

pankah (punkha) fan, formerly pulled by a cord

pansukulika Buddhist sect dwelling in forest hermitages

parapet wall extending above the roof

Parinirvana (parinibbana) the Buddha's state prior to nirvana, shown usually as a reclining figure

Parvati daughter of the Mountain; Siva's consort

pilimage Buddhist image house

potgul library

pradakshina patha processional passage or ambulatory

puja ritual offerings to the gods; worship (Hindu)

pujari worshipper; one who performs puja

punya karma merit earned through actions and religious devotion (Buddhist)

R

raj rule or government

raja king, ruler; prefix 'maha' means great

Rama seventh incarnation of Vishnu; hero of the Ramayana epic

Ramayana ancient Sanskrit epic

Ravana Demon king of Lanka; kidnapper of Sita

rickshaw 3-wheeled bicycle-powered (or 2-wheeled hand-powered) vehicle

Rig Veda (Rg) oldest and most sacred of the Vedas

rupee unit of currency in Sri Lanka, India, Pakistan and Nepal

S

sagar lake; reservoir

Saiva (Shaiva) the cult of Siva

sal hardwood tree of the lower mountains

sala hall

salaam greeting (Muslim); literally 'peace'

samadhi funerary memorial, like a temple but enshrining an image of the deceased; meditation state

samsara eternal transmigration of the soul

samudra sea, or large artificial lake

sangarama monastery

sangha ascetic order founded by Buddha

Saraswati wife of Brahma and goddess of knowledge; usually seated on a swan, holding a veena

Shakti Energy; female divinity often associated with Siva; also a name of the cult

shaman doctor/priest, using magic

Shankara Siva

sharia corpus of Muslim theological law

shikhara temple tower

singh (sinha) lion

Sita Rama's wife, heroine of the Ramayana epic

Siva The Destroyer among Hindu gods; often worshipped as a lingam (phallic symbol)

Sivaratri literally 'Siva's night'; festival (February-March) dedicated to Siva

Skanda the Hindu god of war

sri (shri) honorific title, often used for 'Mr'

stucco plasterwork

stupa hemispheric funerary mound; principal votive monument in a Buddhist religious complex

Subrahmanya Skanda, one of Siva's sons; Kartikkeya in South India

sudra lowest of the Hindu castes

svami (swami) holy man

svastika (swastika) auspicious Hindu/Buddhist emblem

T

tale tank (Sinhalese)

tank lake created for irrigation

Tara historically a Nepalese princess, now worshipped by Buddhists and Hindus

thali South and West Indian vegetarian meal

torana gateway with two posts linked by architraves

tottam garden (Tamil)

Trimurti Triad of Hindu divinities, Brahma, Vishnu and Siva

U

Upanishads ancient Sanskrit philosophical texts, part of the Vedas

ur village (Tamil)

V

Valmiki sage, author of the Ramayana epic

varam village (Tamil)

varna 'colour'; social division of Hindus into Brahmin, Kshatriya, Vaishya and Sudra

Varuna Guardian of the West, accompanied by Makara (see above)

vatadage literally circular relic house, protective pillar and roofed outer cover for dagoba

Veda (Vedic) oldest known religious texts; include hymns to Agni, Indra and Varuna, adopted as Hindu deities

vel Skanda's trident

Vellala Tamil Hindu farming caste

vihara Buddhist or Jain monastery with cells opening off a central court

villu small lake (Sri Lanka)

Vishnu a principal Hindu deity; creator and preserver of universal order; appears in 10 incarnations (Dashavatara)

vitarka mudra Buddhist posture of discourse, the fingers raised

W

Wesak Commemoration day of the Buddha's birth, enlightenment and death

wewa tank or lake (Sinhalese)

Y

yala summer rice crop

yoga school of philosophy concentrating on different mental and physical disciplines (yogi, a practitioner)

yoni female genital symbol, associated with the worship of the Siva Linga (phallus)

Index

Entries in bold refer to maps

FOOTPRINT

Features

About the authors

David Stott

It took David Stott a decade of travelling India before he finally rolled up his trousers and waded across to the kinder gentler waters of Sri Lanka; but it only took one Sri Lankan sunset to turn him from an avowed Indophile into a fully fledged South Asia addict. When not on the road, he lives in the Blue Mountains of Australia with his partner, Helen, and son, Benjamin.

Victoria McCulloch

Victoria McCulloch is a nomad currently calling India home. Armed with a laptop and a yoga mat, she plies her trade as a freelance journalist and Kundalini Yoga teacher. With a well-stamped passport even before the age of five, she inherited her wanderlust from her father, who was an airline pilot. She is fascinated by the Ayurvedic systems of Sri Lanka and India and has recorded two mantra albums.

Acknowledgements

David Stott

First and foremost, thanks to trailblazers Bob and Roma Bradnock, who did all the hard work over the first five editions of this book, and to Sara Chare for her work on the last edition. For on the road support, thanks to John Beswetherick at Tikalanka Tours for invaluable advice and help with logistics; Pathi and Suba in Kandy for the kind of family welcome you don't even get from your own family; and Satheesh for great company and Tamil translations. Also to Noel, Cecile and Pila; Marten and Dishan at Neverbeen; Yohan, Samanthi, Thushitha and Anand at Back of Beyond; Sam in Nilaveli and Claire and Jo in Uppuveli; Maulie for moonlit canoe rides at Galkadawala; and Kishani Gunawardene. Believe it or not, we still get letters from readers, so hearty thanks to Peter Phillips for your frequent hand-written updates from the road. Finally, on the home team, to Victoria for blazing through the highlands and south coast, to the incandescent Sophie Blacksell Jones for singlehandedly dragging this script to print, and to Helen and Ben for hanging tight.

Victoria McCulloch

For great insights not only about where to visit but what it means to live in Sri Lanka, thanks to Sharon Atapattu at Hideaway, Pi Fernandez at Bourgainvillea, Henri and Koki at Kikili House, Lars at TreeTop, Eva Priyanka Wegner at Sri Yoga and the team at Icebear. Thanks to Jaya for the epic sunrise at Kudimbigala and artists Raju and Rudrani for their twilight tea. On other shores, thanks to Alexandra Denkinger and Laura Nowell for pointing me in the right direction. And, as ever, thanks to Adam for his expert reservations of train seats – do as the locals do, throw something through the train window!

Credits

Footprint credits

Editor: Sophie Blacksell Jones
Production and layout: Emma Bryers
Maps: Kevin Feeney
Colour section: Angus Dawson

Publisher: Felicity Laughton
Patrick Dawson
Marketing: Kirsty Holmes
Sales: Diane McEntee
Advertising and content partnerships:
Debbie Wylde

Publishing information

Footprint Sri Lanka
6th edition
© Footprint Handbooks Ltd
May 2016

ISBN: 978 1 910120 67 5
CIP DATA: A catalogue record for this book
is available from the British Library

® Footprint Handbooks and the
Footprint mark are a registered
trademark of Footprint Handbooks Ltd

Published by Footprint
6 Riverside Court
Lower Bristol Road
Bath BA2 3DZ, UK
T +44 (0)1225 469141
F +44 (0)1225 469461
footprinttravelguides.com

Distributed in the USA by
National Book Network, Inc.

Printed in Spain by GraphyCems

Every effort has been made to ensure that
the facts in this guidebook are accurate.
However, travellers should still obtain advice
from consulates, airlines, etc about travel
and visa requirements before travelling.
The authors and publishers cannot
accept responsibility for any loss, injury
or inconvenience however caused.

Footprint Mini Atlas
Sri Lanka

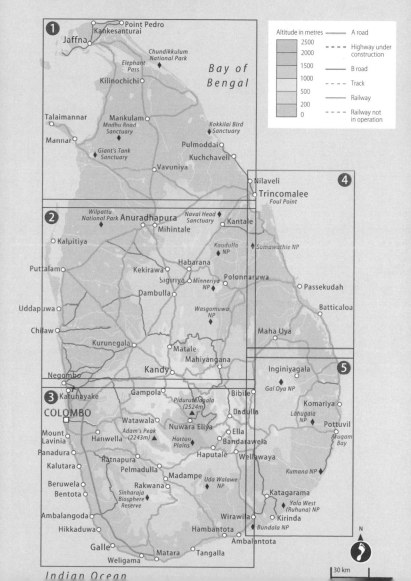

Altitude in metres
- 2500
- 2000
- 1500
- 1000
- 500
- 200
- 0

— A road
- - - Highway under construction
— B road
- - - Track
— Railway
- - - Railway not in operation

① Point Pedro
Kankesanturai
Jaffna
Chundikkulum National Park
Elephant Pass
Kilinochichi
Bay of Bengal
Talaimannar
Mankulam
Madhu Road Sanctuary
Kokkilai Bird Sanctuary
Mannar
Giant's Tank Sanctuary
Pulmoddai
Kuchchaveli
Vavuniya

④
Nilaveli
Trincomalee
Foul Point

② Wilpattu National Park
Anuradhapura
Naval Head Sanctuary
Kantale
Mihintale
Kalpitiya
Kaudulla NP
Somawathie NP
Puttalam
Kekirawa
Habarana
Polonnaruwa
Sigiriya
Minneriya NP
Dambulla
Passekudah
Uddapuwa
Wasgomuwa NP
Batticaloa
Chilaw
Kurunegala
Matale
Maha Uya
Mahiyangana
Kandy

Negombo
Katunayake
Gampola
Bibile
Inginiyagala ⑤
③ COLOMBO
Pidurutalagala (2524m)
Gal Oya NP
Watawala
Badulla
Komariya
Adam's Peak (2243m)
Nuwara Eliya
Lahugala NP
Mount Lavinia
Hanwella
Horton Plains
Ella
Pottuvil
Panadura
Bandarawela
Arugam Bay
Ratnapura
Haputale
Wellawaya
Kalutara
Pelmadulla
Madampe
Uda Walawe NP
Kumana NP
Beruwela
Rakwana
Bentota
Sinharaja Biosphere Reserve
Katagarama
Ambalangoda
Wirawila
Yala West (Ruhuna) NP
Hikkaduwa
Hambantota
Kirinda
Bundala NP
Ambalantota
Galle
Weligama
Matara
Tangalla

Indian Ocean

N

30 km

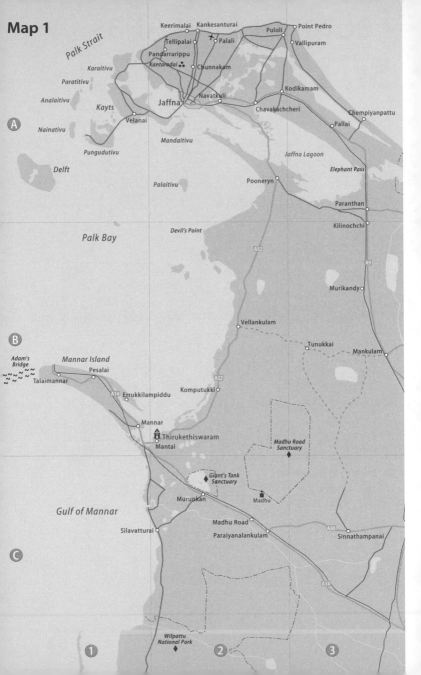

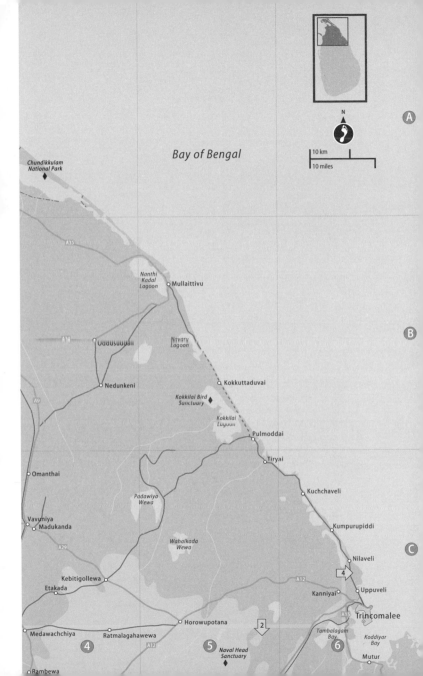

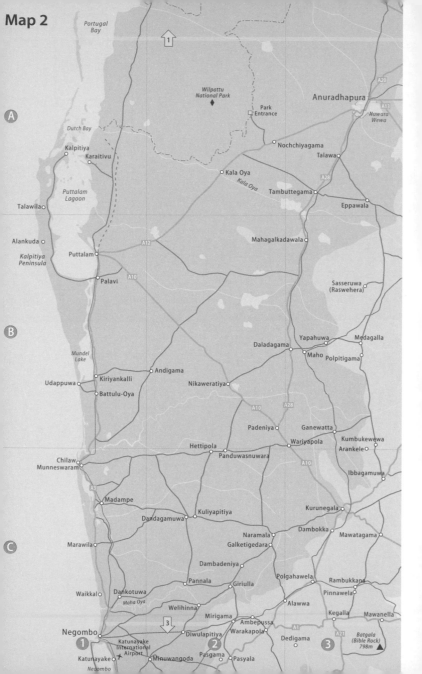

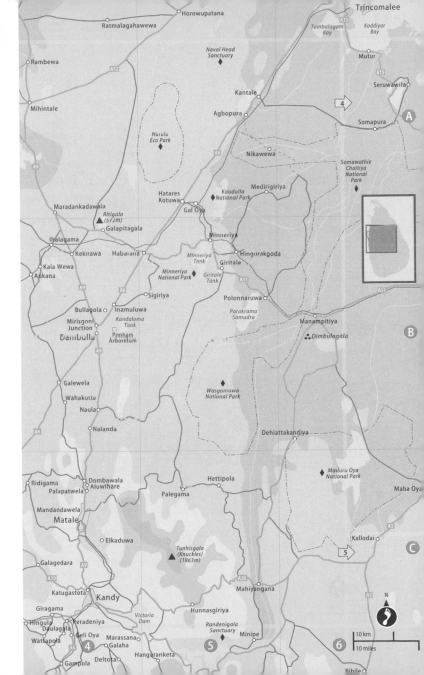

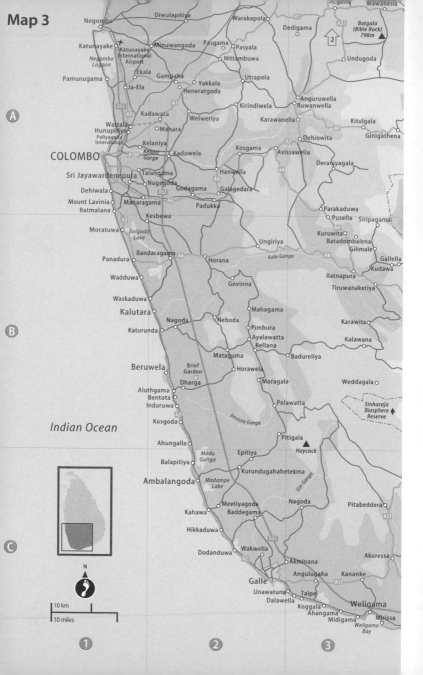

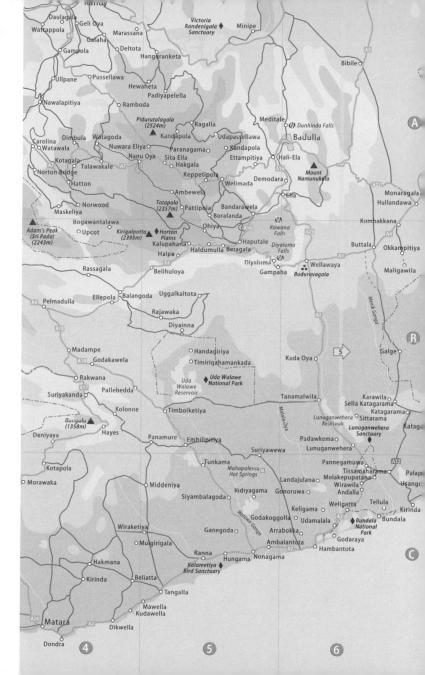

Map 4

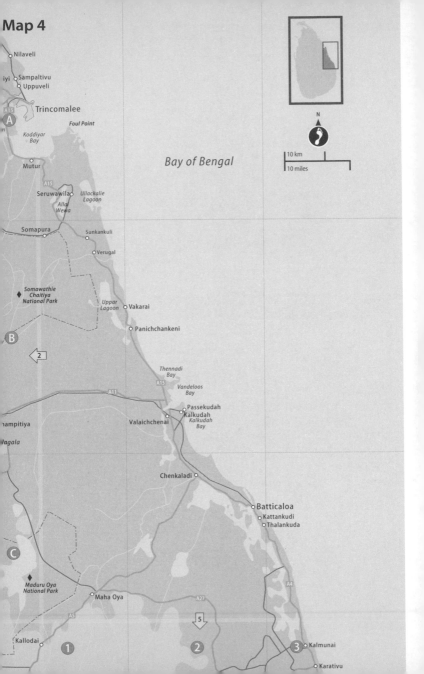

Nilaveli

Sampaltivu
Uppuveli

Trincomalee

Foul Point

*Koddiyar
Bay*

Bay of Bengal

N

10 km
10 miles

Mutur

Seruwawila

*Ullackalie
Lagoon*

*Allai
Wewa*

Somapura

Sunkankuli

Verugal

*Somawathie
Chaitiya
National Park*

*Uppar
Lagoon*

Vakarai

Panichchankeni

*Thennadi
Bay*

*Vandeloos
Bay*

Passekudah
Kalkudah

hampitiya

Valaichchenai

*Kalkudah
Bay*

Jagala

Chenkaladi

Batticaloa

Kattankudi

Thalankuda

*Maduru Oya
National Park*

Maha Oya

Kallodai

Kalmunai

Karativu

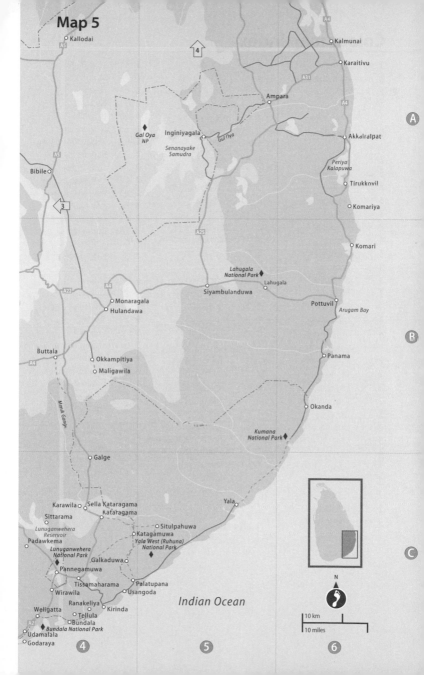

Map 5

Kallodai

Kalmunai

Karaitivu

A4

A5

A31

Ampara

A

Gal Oya
NP

Inginiyagala

Gal Oya

Senanayake
Samudra

Akkalralpat

Periya
Kalapuwa

Bibile

Tirukkovil

A5

Komariya

3

A25

Komari

Lahugala
National Park

Lahugala

A4

Siyambulanduwa

Monaragala

Pottuvil

Arugam Bay

Hulandawa

A22

B

Buttala

Panama

A4

Okkampitiya

Maligawila

Menik Ganga

Okanda

Kumana
National Park

Galge

Yala

Karawila

Sella Kataragama

Situlpahuwa

Sittarama

Kataragama

Katagamuwa

Lunuganwehera
Reservoir

Yala West (Ruhuna)
National Park

Padawkema

Lunuganwehera
National Park

Galkaduwa

C

Pannegamuwa

Tissamaharama

Palatupana

Wirawila

Usangoda

Indian Ocean

Ranakeliya

Weligatta

Kirinda

Tellula

Udamalala

Bundala National Park

Bundala

Godaraya

N

10 km

10 miles

4

5

6

Colour map index